INTRODUCTION TO LAW IN CANADA

Ontario Edition
(As of Fall 2011)
Volume 2

INTRODUCTION TO LAW
IN CANADA

Ontario Edition
Volume 2

Laurence M. Olivo
B.A., M.A., LL.B of the Ontario Bar

Captus Press

INTRODUCTION TO LAW IN CANADA, Volume 2
Laurence M. Olivo

Copyright © 1995–2011 by Laurence M. Olivo and Captus Press Inc.

ISBN 978-1-55322-266-8 (2-volume set: Volume 2)

The publisher and the editor gratefully acknowledge the authors, publishers and organizations for their permission to reproduce their work in this book. Care has been taken to trace ownership of copyright material contained in this book. The publisher will gladly take any information that will enable the rectification of any reference or credit in subsequent editions and apologizes for any errors or omissions.

Captus Press Inc.
Mail: Units 14 & 15
       1600 Steeles Avenue West
       Concord, Ontario
       Canada   L4K 4M2
Telephone: (416) 736–5537
Fax: (416) 736–5793
Email: info@captus.com
Internet: http://www.captus.com

Canada　 We acknowledge the financial support of the Government of Canada through the Canada Book Fund for our publishing activities.

0 9 8 7 6 5 4 3 2 1
Printed in Canada

Volume 2
Contents

Preface

In 1994, after a variety of experiments, I realized that if I was going to meet the needs of my college students for introductory legal materials, I was going to have to dragoon my colleagues to join me in writing the necessary text material. That effort produced our first 5-module edition. Since then, the number and variety of college programs across Canada have increased, as has the demand for a text that presents legal subject matter on a variety of topics that are informative and interesting. We have responded to this challenge over the years by constantly updating and improving modules, and adding modules on a variety of subjects, including some that are quite specialized.

This new edition continues and builds on our previous efforts. Existing modules have been updated with additional review questions, references, and websites. New ones have been added — environmental law, the law of sport, and intellectual property, are but some examples. We have also added a variety of province specific versions of some modules.

Once again, I wish to thank all of our authors, some of whom have been with us for over a decade and some of whom are joining us for the first time, for promptly getting their material to us. Getting a new edition out is always a challenge, and as always, Pauline Lai and her crew at Captus met the challenge — making order out of chaos and producing as usual, a high quality text, on time.

L.M. Olivo
Toronto, Ontario
August 2008

Consumer Law

Alan Auerbach
WILFRID LAURIER UNIVERSITY

Learning Objectives

At the conclusion of this chapter, the reader should be able to:

- define "consumer" and "consumer law"
- appreciate the history of consumer-protection legislation
- know the relevance of product standards
- differentiate among basic types of laws
- recognize consumer responsibilities
- know how to locate federal and provincial statutes
- understand the main federal ministries and statutes
- know the key federal regulations and policies on financial services
- be familiar with Ontario's consumer-related ministries and regulations
- see Quebec's new *Consumer Protection Act* as a model
- integrate and understand the best and worst features of consumer legislation that affect you
- understand insurance from a consumer's perspective
- know basic consumer aspects of motor vehicles
- know the Ontario regulations on private transfers of car ownership

TABLE OF CONTENTS

INTRODUCTION

The Meaning of "Consumer Law"

What, exactly, is **consumer law**? You know that legal practice is divided into various specialty areas such as commercial, criminal, real estate, family, and litigation law. But consumer law is not one of these branches, at least as recognized by the profession. "Consumer law" does not appear in law dictionaries; it is a lay term rather than a legal one because it's hard to define. Nonetheless, we will try.

Consumer is broadly used to mean "ordinary person", and more specifically to mean "purchaser" or "end user". The earliest use of this word in law was by Boston lawyer Louis Brandeis; when he was litigating public interest cases, he argued at an 1897 tariff hearing on behalf of what he termed "the consumer".

In the sense of "end user", most of us are consumers of hundreds of products such as toasters, televisions, and trucks. Certainly we need some form of product protection because a few of these goods are costly and complex, sometimes frustrating and fragile, and at times dangerous or even deadly.

We are also consumers of services, professions, political parties, and even business, religious, and volunteer organizations; here, it is harder to differentiate protection from intrusion. When you buy a television set, of course the law should protect you from being electrocuted by it, or from the seller's demand for more than the ticket price. But as a consumer of the programs and advertisements that you see on the set, it is less clear what level of protection should apply. As another example, maybe the law should protect vulnerable youngsters from being "brainwashed" by "cults", but sociologists have difficulty in defining such terms, and the law needs clear definitions. Similarly, if your neighbour sells you a "natural" product to cure your ills, the law may have problems differentiating among drugs, herbs, and dietary supplements, and in knowing how to treat a home-based business. A final complexity of the word "consumer" is that its common derivative word, "consumerism", has various socio-political meanings.

The Coverage of Consumer Law in This Chapter

This chapter highlights marketplace laws as they apply to lay persons (as opposed to corporations or to lawyers). It omits the laws of real estate, tort, employment, debtors/creditors, and the court system, as each of these topics is available as a chapter in the present series. Given how broadly "consumer" must be defined, other omissions had to be a judgment call. If you spend summers panning for gold and winters getting your muscles massaged, you might deem the statutes on mining, stake-claiming, and precious metals, and those on massage therapists, physiotherapists, and chiropractors all to be "consumer legislation". But space limitations require that we address the more typical consumer.

Most statutes relating to the marketplace are in the hands of Canada's 10 provinces and three territories. The provincial legislation is generally similar (with the exception of Quebec), and there is sporadic coverage of consumer issues in the territories. Despite the prominence of provincial jurisdiction, a few consumer-relevant laws are federal. (In cases where the same laws are covered by different jurisdictions, federal statutes take precedence over provincial ones, which override municipal by-laws.)

Accordingly, this chapter covers, after the introductory topics, the relevant federal legislation, that of Ontario, and of Quebec, with some reference to other provinces. After a short commentary on Canadian consumer law, the chapter ends on two topics that come under both federal and provincial regulation: insurance and motor vehicles.

The History of Consumer Law

The phrase *caveat emptor* sums up the attitude of early lawmakers to protecting the consumer. It is Latin for "let the buyer beware", meaning that purchasers buy at their own risk; the sellers or manufacturers are free of responsibility in the transaction. Until recently there were seven reasons for the absence of consumer laws:

1. Although most charges and prosecutions of violations of consumer law are made by the government agency responsible for the legislation, the law also expects that ordinary people can take legal action against merchants, manufacturers, and corporations. But in past generations, the law was not available to the average person. Back when most people were so impoverished and illiterate that legal action was impractical, there was no thought of drafting laws that would allow a consumer to sue.

2. The first consumer laws protected against defective products, but until recently, so few consumer goods were available that there was little to worry about. Even if you are young, you probably own more varied possessions than your grandparents ever did. (Yes, in past centuries the highest stratum of society did own possessions galore, but these goods were often chosen more for their artistic than their utilitarian merit.)

3. The few goods that were widely available were simple to understand and operate, and easy to adjust or repair. Prior to electricity, food might be kept cool in a cold cellar or ice box, structures that would last virtually forever; the life of today's complex refrigerator is around 15 years, and is likely to need repairs within that period. Similarly, compare a sundial with a watch, a quill pen with a data-communications system, or a bow-and-arrow or spear with an auto-loading firearm.

4. The consequences of failure used to be relatively minor. For instance, contrast the results of a defective steering system on a horse-drawn wagon with that on an automobile or aircraft. A watchdog failing to bark might have meant the loss of the family cooking pot and the next day's food; today's faulty burglar alarm could cost possessions accumulated over a lifetime. Defects in a hot water bottle would be easy to detect, and if missed would result only in a damp bed, but hidden flaws in an electric blanket could expose the sleeper to harmful electric shock or fire.

5. Personal calamities were once common; everyone was affected by losses due to accident or disease. Product failures, like the many other losses, were seen as part of life. If a newly purchased horse died, it was seen as an act of God, so when people bought the first cars and they "died", the owners tended to be fatalistic rather than litigious. But in today's climate of "entitlement to perfection", consumers are less willing to accept lapses in product durability, safety, or efficiency.

6. People have long been conditioned not to challenge authority, whether religious, educational, or professional, so this later spilled over into business and commerce. Thus, after centuries of accepting that the earth was flat because those in power said so, when you bought a pair of "Neverleak" rubbers, you were not likely to complain — despite your wet feet.

7. Finally, organized religion was a dominant influence on most of the cultures that Canadian law derives from. All major religions date from simpler times and do not dwell on material possessions. Thus, it was illegal in Canada to blaspheme long before it was against the law to store guns improperly or to sell unsafe microwave ovens.

When consumer-protection laws arrived, some of the first ones covered medicines. They were needed: back then, some "patent medicines" included opiate drops as baby soothers, alcohol as tonics, and pills containing tape worms for weight reduction. But other early product-fitness laws were intended not to protect the ordinary consumer but the businessman. For instance, we will cover Ontario's *Sale of Goods Act*,[1] which seems designed to protect the consumer. But this statute was drafted in the late 19th century to ensure that if a merchant or manufacturer bought some business equipment for a declared purpose, as a presumed expert the seller was responsible for ensuring that it was suitable.

Early consumer-protection legislation focused on products only. That's because until recently, services were even more limited than goods were. To be "in service" originally meant that you were a live-in servant, and if your employer were dissatisfied with your work you could be dismissed without warning, justification, holiday pay, or references. Thus, service inadequacy was not considered to be a problem. But today, you can get your lawn, your dog, and your image groomed by professional service providers, and increasingly legislation is designed to protect those who buy services.

This is not to say that today's legislation always reflects today's consumer problems, because laws tend to evolve much more slowly than society and technology change. Most current statutes predate, sometimes by a century, consumer issues such as credit cards, multilevel marketing plans, computers, the Internet, and telemarketers, and they catch up slowly.

Not only do laws change, but so does the interpretation of them as established by **caselaw**. Marketplace issues have undergone staggering transformations recently, so the establishment of caselaw can be more substantial than changes to statutes. For instance, prior to the globalization of industry, an item either was or was not made in Canada. However, a recent charge of misleading advertising in regard to a "Made in Canada" label was dismissed at trial when the Court found that at least 51 per cent of the labour and raw material was Canadian. This case, then, effectively redefined the meaning of "Made in Canada."

Product Standards and the Law

The word "standard" has various meanings; it's employed in government documents to mean legislative criteria, and by policy makers to mean policy criteria. It's also used to ensure that millions of things fit together, from trains on tracks to rear ends on seats. With the globalization of trade, information systems, and financial transactions, universally accepted standards are critical. For instance, the Internet exists only because of international standards that allow you to access the World Wide Web (www) from various types of computers using various browsers.

In this chapter, we are more interested in the world of trade, where "standard" refers to technical aspects that establish safety or performance criteria. It's not a new concept; the Magna Carta included a chapter on standards, and over two centuries ago the United States Constitution dealt with establishing the "standards of weights and measures".

Some products have no legally-mandated standards. Household clocks can vary in accuracy, noise, longevity, or design, and novelty clocks run backward or show a ten-hour day. Some systems have standards that are quite strict and universal but not due to any law; for instance, each of 800,000 firms in almost 100 countries use a distinctive "Universal Product Code" for each of its products — because of bar-code standardization. But every car sold in Can-

---

[1] R.S.O. 1990, c. S.1.

ada *must* conform to a hundred federal standards; dozens of them govern just the lighting system, ensuring, for instance, that all cars' rear lights are of prescribed intensity, hue, and location.

Product standards are not usually created or designed by lawmakers but by a consensus of technical experts, manufacturers, and consumer representatives. However, the standards are often required by governments through reference in legislation. For instance, it may be illegal to install electrical equipment that has not been certified by an organization recognized by the government, or for a child to ride a bicycle without wearing a helmet certified to a "voluntary" standard.

Product liability cases are often trials of product standards, insofar as makers argue that their compliance with the requisite standard shows that they acted properly. Suits are virtually never brought against the standardization organizations themselves, because they take pains to ensure that their procedures for establishing standards are comprehensive, reasonable, and fair. There are many government-recognized standardization organizations in the world; the main one in this country is the **Canadian Standards Association (CSA)**. This not-for-profit institution, founded in 1919, has offices throughout Canada and elsewhere. Its headquarters is 178 Rexdale Blvd., Etobicoke ON, M9W 1R3, 416-747-4000; its Web site is <www.csa.ca>. The second most important one, **Underwriters' Laboratories of Canada (ULC)**, is concerned only with safety and protection; its site is <www.ulc.ca>. A product that is certified by these agencies bears a stylized CSA or ULC logo; CSA claims that a billion products are so designated.

Most developed countries have their own standards organizations; for instance, the British Standards Institution (BSI) was founded in 1901, the American National Standards Institute (ANSI) in 1918, and ULC in 1894. Standards are still being developed. In 1987, the Geneva-based International Organization for Standards (ISO) published the "ISO 9000" series of standards. Applied to manufacturing, software, service, and internal corporate procedures, these standards have been adopted by the 90 countries that represent 95 per ent of the world's industrial output. The Standards Council of Canada (www.scc.ca) is a federal Crown corporation to promote standardization. Based in Ottawa and reporting to Parliament through the Minister of Industry, it accredits organizations for certification, testing, ISO registration, and standards development.

Levels of Laws

As we will be covering many consumer-related statutes of different types under various headings, the following outline of Canadian laws as they apply to consumer legislation may be helpful.

Common vs. Statutory Law

Many laws are not to be found in the statutes cited in this chapter. **Common law** is the unwritten law of the land based on reason, custom, usage, and **precedents**. Except in Quebec, Canadian common law is largely based on the ancient unwritten law of England, about which Sir Edward Coke (1552–1634) wrote that "the common law is nothing else but reason." The most familiar use of this phrase is "common-law marriage" (a marital partnership not solemnized by a formal religious or civil ceremony or recorded in the jurisdiction's archives).

Common law is contrasted with **statutory laws**, which are formalized by governments that write, label, and print them. Federal statutes are enacted by the Parliament of Canada, provincial statutes are passed by a provincial legislature, and municipal ones are in the hands of a municipal council or equivalent.

Civil vs. Criminal Law

Civil law deals with private rights. Thus, a civil legal suit is between two individuals or corporations (the plaintiff who initiates the action, and the defendant against whom the action is taken). The court hears arguments from the two, and reaches a decision based on precedent and logic.

Criminal statutes deal with violations of public rights as defined and governed by elected officials, and enshrined in the Criminal Code of Canada. The "plaintiff" is the government, the outcome is guilty or not guilty of violating a specific statute, and the penalty-range upon conviction is specified in the statute. If, after parking by a hydrant, you drove at top speed to run down your enemy, you could be charged by the municipality, the province, and the federal criminal justice system. On the parking charge you could settle out of court by paying a fine, for the speeding you might be able to as well, but for the third — attempted murder, manslaughter, or murder, depending on your aim and other factors — you would have to appear in court.

Consumer Duties and Responsibilities

"The customer is always right" was a slogan advanced by a retailer, but it does not represent reality. Buyers should recognize that most products should not be expected to serve them indefinitely; most have a finite "design life". With some items it is the responsibility of consumers to unpack, assemble, and set them up in accordance with directions. With other products, proper maintenance or servicing is their responsibility. Product abuse, whether in storage, servicing, or operating, can void warranties.

It is also the buyer's obligation to know the retailer's return policy before purchase. Many stores are so liberal, accepting goods for refund or exchange for any or no reason and after considerable time, that consumers assume all stores follow this model. In law, when you buy something it becomes your property and your payment becomes the seller's property; you can no more demand a refund than the store can tell you it changed its mind, does not want your money, and demands the product back.

Where to Find Federal and Provincial/Territorial Statutes

This ends the introductory material; we now engage the laws themselves as they relate to Canadian consumers. All the laws of the federal government, as well as of the 10 provincial ones, and those of the territories (Yukon, Northwest Territories, and Nunavut), are available on the Web at <www.ACJNet.org> (the Access to Justice Network). More specific or specialized sources are presented at the end of the sections below.

FEDERAL CONSUMER LEGISLATION

Federal law was created to help consumers in general, by prohibiting all activities that are deemed harmful to society; an example is false or misleading advertising. Whereas provincial law focuses on providing remedies for consumers hurt by unethical or unfair business activities, federal legislation is more concerned with banning certain conduct and punishing those who practise it.

Industry Canada

Industry Canada (formerly Consumer and Corporate Affairs Canada) is mandated to: provide protection from product-related hazards, establish and administer rules and guidelines for business conduct, encourage competition among businesses, enforce standards for trade in commodities, and encourage the disclosure and diffusion of technological information and ensure that information presented to consumers is accurate. Its address is 50 Victoria St., Hull, QC,

K1A 0C9; 819-997-1591/1177 for food and non-food products respectively. Its site called Consumer Connection at <www.strategis.ic.gc.ca> links to every federal statute.

Four statutes are enforced by Industry Canada:

1. The ***Consumer Packaging and Labelling Act***[2], under the Consumer Products Branch, requires that the label on dry goods indicates the product identity or generic name, the quantity if other than one, and the name and place of business for postal delivery of the "dealer" (maker, importer, distributor, or retailer).

2. The ***Textile Labelling Act***[3], which applies mainly to clothing, requires the label to show the name of the fibre and, if more than one, the percentages by weight.

3. The ***Precious Metals Marking Act***[4] governs primarily gold and silver, but also platinum and palladium. It regulates relevant claims and abbreviations or symbols such as "k" for karat. For instance, to be stamped or referred to as "sterling", the item must be 92.5 per cent silver.

4. The ***Competition Act***[5] is the most complex, and is outlined next.

The Competition Act

The *Competition Act* prohibits misleading advertising and deceptive marketing practices in promoting the supply or use of a product or service, or any business interest. The Marketing Practices Branch of the Competition Bureau administers and enforces these provisions under the authority of the Director of Investigation and Research. The Director can resolve matters through prohibition orders or undertakings, or can lay criminal charges.

The *Competition Act* is the only federal statute of general application to all forms of advertising in Canada. It sets the boundaries between what Parliament defines as acceptable business practices and those that it deems to be unlawful. This law applies to all means of making representations, including print, TV and radio ads, and audio-visual illustrations. Its provisions are worded broadly enough to include representations that are generated and distributed electronically. This new "borderless marketplace" presents legal complexities, for instance, when the buyer resides in Canada, the seller is in Colombia, the goods are shipped from Japan, and payment is cleared through a Swiss bank. However, charges were laid in Canada under this law in 1996 against a company that advertised a **multilevel marketing plan** (also called "pyramid selling") on the Internet to prospects both inside and beyond Canada.

In respect to investments and share offerings, most cases of false or misleading representations come under the purview of provincial securities statutes rather than under the *Competition Act*. But there are exceptions; in 1992 the Principal Group was fined $500,000 under this statute for making false representations in its annual report.

The *Competition Act* covers diverse consumer issues such as testimonials and product tests. However, the parts that connect with most consumers are sections 52 to 59, which are related to *misleading advertising and deceptive marketing*. Here is a plain-language outline:

---

[2] R.S.C. 1985, c. C-38.
[3] R.S.C. 1985, c. T-10.
[4] R.S.C. 1985, c. P-19.
[5] R.S.C. 1985, c. C-34; S.C. 1986, c. 26.

- All representations, in any form whatever, that are false or misleading in a material respect are prohibited.

- Any representation in the form of a statement, warranty, or guarantee of the performance, efficacy or length of life of a product, not based on an adequate and proper test, is prohibited; the onus is on the one making the claim to prove that it is based on an adequate and proper test.

- Any representation that purports to be a warranty or guarantee of a product, or a promise to replace, maintain or repair an article or part thereof, is prohibited where their form is materially misleading or where there is no reasonable prospect that the warrantee, guarantee, or promise will be carried out.

- Any materially misleading representation as to the price at which a product is ordinarily sold (in the market area, unless specified to the advertiser's own selling price) is prohibited.

- Where two or more prices are clearly shown on a product, its container, or wrapper, the product must be supplied at the lower price.

- A multilevel marketing plan that features "head hunting" fees, required purchases as a condition of entry into the plan, and inventory loading or the lack of a buy-back guarantee on reasonable commercial terms constitutes a prohibited "scheme of pyramid selling".

- An operator or participant in a multi-level marketing plan cannot make representations relating to compensation unless the representations include disclosure of compensation received by a typical participant.

- Section 57 is commonly termed the "non-availability" provision. Advertising a bargain price product (defined as an article or a service) that the advertiser does not have available for sale in reasonable quantities is prohibited — unless the advertiser establishes that the non-availability of product was due to unavoidable circumstances, or the customer was offered a "rain check" (a promise to supply the product or its equivalent at the advertised price within a reasonable period of time). The Act does not prohibit "upselling" (the promotion of items that are costlier or more profitable than those that attracted the buyer but the cheaper goods must be available in reasonable quantities); in **bait-and-switch** advertising, the offence involves the "bait" rather than the "switch": that is, the cheaper goods are not available in reasonable quantities.

- An "advertisement" includes any representation that can be generally defined as a "public notice", even when addressed to a comparatively small number of people. A purely private communication is not advertising, but a bargain price on a label is. The term "bargain" has been held to connote to the average person a "price that is less than the usual price"; whether the price is actually a bargain is irrelevant. The maximum penalty under this section is a fine of $25,000 and imprisonment of one year; fines have increased substantially in recent years.

- The supply of any product at a price higher than the price currently being advertised is prohibited (unless the price advertised was erroneous and immediately corrected, or where the seller is not engaged in the business of dealing in that product).

- Any contest that does not disclose the number and approximate value of prizes or important information related to the chances of winning, that does not select participants or distribute prizes on the basis of skill or on a random basis, or in which the distribution of prizes is unduly delayed, is prohibited.

- In the early 1990s, the publication *Guiding Principles for Environmental Labelling and Advertising* dealt with the new concern of improper "green" claims. For instance, assertions such as "mercury free", "recycled", and "biodegradable" must (in the absence of qualifiers) mean that the products are totally mercury free, recycled, or biodegradable; and declarations of degradability must be supported by recognized tests.

The Act also forbids certain mergers and monopolies that are deemed to be against the public interest. In 1999 there was an unprecedented number of merger proposals involving petroleum, the media, retailing, and especially banking. The Act also prohibits price fixing that would eliminate normal competition among businesses in the marketplace. One serious form of price-fixing is **bid rigging**. This is an agreement whereby bidders on a contract refrain from submitting bids, or where bidders agree to submit a pre-arranged price, all without making their intentions known to the potential purchaser beforehand. In 1997, four electrical contractors were prosecuted by the Attorney General of Canada and fined a total of $2.55-million; the following year, because another electrical contracting firm pleaded guilty to 10 counts of bid rigging, it was fined only $100,000. The Competition Bureau offers an educational program to assist purchasers in the detection and prevention of bid rigging.

Other examples of prohibited trade practices are (a) conspiracy between parties with the intent of lessening competition, (b) **predatory pricing** (selling at an unreasonably low price to eliminate competition), and (c) **discriminatory allowances** (discounts and rebates that are not offered to competing purchasers).

Violations committed under the Act are criminal offences for which offenders are subject to substantial fines and/or imprisonment terms; for instance, (a), above, carries a penalty of up to a $10-million fine and five years imprisonment. The Act also provides for the recovery of damages to consumers who have been misled or unfairly treated, and the consumer may initiate civil action in any court.

In 1999, five foreign firms comprising what was described as "the world bulk vitamin cartel" confessed to a conspiracy that rigged Canadian prices. They were fined a total of $88-million, the largest criminal fines ever imposed under the *Competition Act*, and the largest in Canadian history. Moreover, the then-vice-president of a sixth firm that conspired with one of the five was sentenced to nine months imprisonment; other executives are also facing jail terms at the time of this writing.

Prosecutions for competition offences are criminal prosecutions, and for this reason, the Crown must prove its case to the criminal law standard of "beyond reasonable doubt". This is a very high standard of proof and explains why there are relatively few federal prosecutions for competition and trade offences.

Under the Program of Advisory Opinions, businesses wishing to avoid coming into conflict with the Act can request an opinion on whether proposed promotions would cause an inquiry to be initiated. The Bureau also has a program by which anyone can, anonymously if wished, bring forward information concerning possible violations of the Act. Pamphlets, videos, and other information are available from: Competition Bureau, Complaints and Public Enquiries Centre, 50 Victoria St., Hull, QC, K1A 0C9, or at 1-800-348-5358. The Web site is <www.competition.ic.gc.ca, where among other information, the Annual Report of the Commissioner of Competition can be found.

Health Canada

Health Canada is an agency concerned with diverse health issues such as fitness, medical devices, and protection from disease and other hazards. It is one of the most up-to-date of the federal agencies, needing to keep up with contemporary additions to the marketplace such as genetically engineered foods, the wildly popular assortment of so-called natural or herbal dietary supplements, and domestic devices that emit various types of radiation. We will look at only two of its many sets of regulations.

The Food and Drugs Act[6]

Canada was a pioneer in grading certain common foods for quality, and in controlling the labelling of canned goods. For instance, as early as 1790, Nova Scotia required that either "prime", "second", or "third" be branded on every barrel of butter; in 1874 a national law forbade the adulteration of food and drugs.

In the early 1900s, some 60,000 brands of "patent medicines" were being sold, some of them containing stimulants, sedatives such as alcohol or cocaine, or dangerous adulterants. In 1920, the first comprehensive federal *Food and Drugs Act* was designed to insure standards of purity in foods, household chemicals, cosmetics, medicines, vitamins, and contraceptives. However, the patent medicine market continued to flourish. Following a 1977 crackdown that required manufacturers to validate their claims and justify their ingredients, all but 1,200 of these "liver pills" and "gout drops" were discontinued.

The Act protects Canadians from possible risk to health, and from fraud and deception in regard to food, drugs, and cosmetics. It outlaws the sale of foods that contain poisonous or harmful substances, and prohibits the sale of food that is unfit for human consumption, and food that has been processed under unsanitary conditions. Furthermore, it regulates the packaging and labelling of food and drugs to ensure that the contents match the label claims.

As examples, the following would violate this Act: cream cheese without a "best-before" date, packaged food with no list of ingredients, and an orange "punch" labelled as "orange juice". The maximum penalty for such violations is $5,000 and/or imprisonment for three years. In addition, government inspectors have the authority to seize a product or commodity.

The Hazardous Products Act[7]

The Hazardous Products Act outlaws dangerous products, and alerts consumers to items that require care when used. The Act divides such products into two categories. The first comprises goods that subject the public to unnecessary and unacceptable hazards. Such products might be poisonous, toxic, explosive, corrosive, or infectious, and cannot be sold in Canada. The second involves items such as household cleaners and detergents, goods that can be imported, advertised, and sold in Canada, but only under the conditions stipulated in the Act.

Financial Services

If you need funds to buy a house, you go to a bank. Where does the bank go to get *its* money? Except in their objective to make a profit for themselves and their shareholders, banks are unlike other business because they can lend money that they get from, in essence, the Government of Canada — meaning you. Conversely, suppose you win the lottery and want to become a lender by opening "The Bank of Jennifer." Sorry, you cannot compete; existing banks

---

[6] R.S.C. 1985, c. F-27.
[7] R.S.C. 1985, c. H-3.

basically have a monopoly, although this may change due to Canada's free trade treaty commitments to permit foreign banks to operate more freely in Canada.

Under the *Bank Act*, which is overseen by The Office of the Superintendent of Financial Institutions, banks have amassed huge assets, significant market control of financial services, and considerable economic power in a country with one of the most highly concentrated banking systems in the world. They have also developed political power that they use to resist attempts by consumer groups and political organizations such as the 1998 *National Liberal Caucus Task Force on the Future of the Financial Services Sector* to make them as accountable and consumer-oriented as their American and British counterparts.

The federal government deals with topics such as credit unions, bank service charges, and whether banks should be allowed to retail insurance policies at their branches. Through the Canada Deposit Insurance Corporation, it insures, consumers' bank deposits. It may also determine if banks can be sold or merged. (In 1999, the Minister of Finance rejected merger proposals by the Bank of Montreal and the Royal Bank of Canada, and by the CIBC and TD Bank, but accepted the purchase of Canada Trust by TD.)

Regulation of interest rates also falls within federal jurisdiction. Bank credit cards originated in 1968, and by 1997 there were over 50 million of them in circulation in Canada (some 30 million of which are Visa or MasterCard). Their users pay an interest rate of around 10 to 12 percentage points higher than the Bank of Canada rate. Retail credit cards are even more costly for users with an unpaid balance; most charge 28.8 per cent. The only federal law that deals with credit-card interest rates is Section 305.1 of the Criminal Code; it defines a criminal interest rate as an effective annual rate that exceeds 60 per cent on the credit advanced under an agreement. Most users are unaware that they are not credited for partial payments in terms of interest, and don't understand the complex formulas used by the credit card firms. By contrast, the U.S. *Fair Credit and Charge Card Disclosure Act* of 1988 is an example of effective disclosure provisions.

Currently, 43 per cent of retailed vehicles are leased rather than purchased. Revisions to the *Bank Act*[8] in 1980 permitted banks to lease vehicles over 21 tonnes, and 1992 legislation extended these powers to federal trust companies and life insurance firms. At the time of this writing, banks are applying for the right to lease light vehicles as well; this is being resisted by the government on the basis that banks' access to confidential client information, plus the possibility of competing with the same car-leasing small businesses to which they provide credit, creates a conflict of interest and may amount to unfair competition under the *Competition Act*.

The federal government also covers **tied selling**. This is the requirement of a consumer to buy one product as a condition of purchasing another one, as when consumers must move their RRSP to a financial institution in order to apply for a line of credit there. (This differs from **cross selling**, also termed **product bundling**, which is the offer of a lower price for a product if the consumer agrees to buy another one, as in the offering of a lower mortgage rate for moving all bank accounts to that institution.) Tied selling with respect to insurance is illegal under the *Competition Act*, the *Bank Act*, and the *Trust and Loan Companies Act*.[9]

[8] R.S.C. 1985, c. B-1.
[9] S.C. 1991, c. 45.

The Web site of the Office of the Superintendent of Financial Institutions is <www.osfi-bsif.gc.ca>. A free complaint resolution process is available through each participating bank's ombudsman (in place for all the major banks), and, if not successful, through the Canadian Banking Ombudsman, <www.bankingombudsman.com>.

This ends the sections on federal legislation and practice. Next, we look at two provinces: Ontario because of its large population and economic importance, and Quebec because it has a recently revised, comprehensive set of consumer laws.

ONTARIO

Ministry of Consumer and Commercial Relations

The Government of Ontario has more statutes, rules, and regulations than any other jurisdiction in Canada; indeed, it has more than the average country. Most of the statutes relating to consumers come under the Ministry of Consumer and Commercial Relations (**MCCR**); it oversees some 60 statutes, more than any other Canadian ministry.

MCCR's regulations affect you throughout your life: your birth and marriage are recorded according to the *Vital Statistics Act* and the *Marriage Act*; your entertainment may be governed by the *Theatres Act*, *Wine Content Act*, and *Liquor Control Act*; your activity under the *Racing Commission Act* may bring you into contact with the *Debt Collectors Act*; and you can expect to eventually be subject to the *Funeral Directors and Establishments Act* and the *Cemeteries Act*.

This massive ministry can be contacted at 1-800-268-1142, from which you can access, for instance, the gas busters hotline; the seniors line; information on loan brokers, credit, and collection agencies; fitness and modelling operations; home repairs; and you can order various brochures. Five administrative bodies were recently established to oversee motor vehicle dealers, real estate agents and brokers, travel agents and brokers, electrical safety, and technical standards and safety businesses (including fuel and elevator safety); but primarily, MCCR is organized into the following three divisions.

The Corporate Services Division deals mainly with alcohol, gaming, and racing; the Registration Division covers property registration and marriage and name-change regulations. The Business Division oversees some 20 statutes of interest to consumers. Those of particular relevance to consumers are described below, but this division is responsible also for the *Business Regulation Reform Act*, *Collection Agencies Act*, *Consumer Protection Bureau*, *Discriminatory Business Practices Act*, *Funeral Directors and Establishments Act*, *Loan Brokers Act*, *Motor Vehicle Dealers Act*, *Ontario New Home Warranties Plan*, *Prepaid Services Act*, *Real Estate and Business Brokers Act*, *Safety and Consumer Statutes Administration*, and *Travel Industry Act*.

The Business Practices Act[10]

The **Business Practices Act** (sample in Exhibit 20.1) is designed to eliminate abusive selling tactics by defining false and deceptive representations, and by prohibiting business practices such as representing that (a) goods have qualities, benefits, and characteristics that they do not possess; (b) the goods are new when they are not; (c) a service, replacement, or repair is needed when it is not; and (d) a price advantage exists when it does not.

---

[10] R.S.O. 1990, c. B.18.

Unfair Business Practices in Ontario

EXHIBIT 20.1

2. For the purposes of this Act, the following shall be deemed to be unfair practices:

(1) A false, misleading or deceptive consumer representation including, but without limiting the generality of the foregoing,

i. a representation that the goods or services have sponsorship, approval, performance characteristics, accessories, uses, ingredients, benefits or quantities they do not have,

ii. a representation that the person who is to supply the goods or services has sponsorship, approval, status, affiliation or connection the person does not have,

iii. a representation that the goods are of a particular standard, quality, grade, style or model, if they are not,

iv. a representation that the goods are new, or unused, if they are not or are reconditioned or reclaimed, provided that the reasonable use of goods to enable the seller to service, prepare, test and deliver the goods for the purpose of sale shall not be deemed to make the goods used for the purposes of this subparagraph,

v. a representation that the goods have been used to an extent that is materially different from the fact,

vi. a representation that the goods or services are available for a reason that does not exist,

vii. a representation that the goods or services have been supplied in accordance with a previous representation, if they have not,

viii. a representation that the goods or services or any part thereof are available to the consumer when the person making the representation knows or ought to know they will not be supplied,

ix. a representation that a service, part, replacement or repair is needed, if it is not,

x. a representation that a specific price advantage exists, if it does not,

xi. a representation that misrepresents the authority of a salesperson, representative, employee or agent to negotiate the final terms of the proposed transaction,

xii. a representation that the proposed transaction involves or does not involve rights, remedies or obligations if the representation is false or misleading,

xiii. a representation using exaggeration, innuendo or ambiguity as to a material fact or failing to state a material fact if such use or failure deceives or tends to deceive,

xiv. a representation that misrepresents the purpose or intent of any solicitation of or any communication with a consumer.

(2) An unconscionable consumer representation made in respect of a particular transaction and in determining whether or not a consumer representation is unconscionable there may be taken into account that the person making the representation or the person's employer or principal knows or ought to know,

i. that the consumer is not reasonably able to protect his or her interests because of physical infirmity, ignorance, illiteracy, inability to understand the language of an agreement or similar factors,

ii. that the price grossly exceeds the price at which similar goods or services are readily available to like consumers,

iii. that the consumer is unable to receive a substantial benefit from the subject-matter of the consumer representation,

iv. that there is no reasonable probability of payment of the obligation in full by the consumer,

v. that the proposed transaction is excessively one-sided in favour of someone other than the consumer,

vi. that the terms or conditions of the proposed transaction are so adverse to the consumer as to be inequitable,

vii. that he or she is making a misleading statement of opinion on which the consumer is likely to rely to his or her detriment,

viii. that he or she is subjecting the consumer to undue pressure to enter into the transaction.

(3) Such other consumer representations under paragraph 1 as are prescribed by the regulations made in accordance with section 16.

Source: *Business Practices Act*, R.S.O. 1990, s. 2.

This Act provides consumers with remedies that were unavailable to them under common law. In the case of proven misrepresentation it allows the cancellation of a contract and the total refund of payment. It allows for damages when consumers fall victim to innocent misrepresentation, and outlines available remedies.

The statute requires an element of "reliance"; if a retailer's misrepresentation of an item did not influence the decision to purchase, the Act would not apply. Otherwise, there are three avenues for relief: (a) a request to the seller to cancel the agreement if sought within six months, (b) a request to the Court to cancel it, and (c) a request for mediation by the government.

The Consumer Protection Act[11]

The **Consumer Protection Act** deals mainly with **executory contracts**, those that are to be partially or fully performed in the future. It's designed to protect vulnerable people such as live-alone seniors from aggressive and persistent door-to-door salespeople. It allows a 48-hour (two working days) "cooling off" period on such contracts with a value above $50 if the transaction takes place at a location other than the seller's place of business, and if either the payment is not made in full or if all the goods are not provided at once.

For instance, if you make a time-payment purchase of a vacuum cleaner at home, or a massage chair at a county fair, you may rescind the contract within 48 hours after receiving your copy of the bill. (At the time of this writing, if passed, the *Red Tape Reduction Act, 1999* will increase the "cooling off" period to 10 days, telephone calls excepted.) The cancellation can be registered-mail postmarked within that time, and sent to the name/address required to be shown on the contract (or delivered personally). Any deposit or trade-in must be returned; title of the trade-in does not pass to the seller until the two-day period has expired without **recission**. And you can return the partial goods at the seller's expense. (If the full goods are delivered at once, or if you sign a credit card or cheque for full payment, the 48-hour provision does not apply. You may have other remedies such as suing for misrepresentation, but persistence in the course of selling is legal.)

The Act also protects you from having to pay for, or even having to return, any unsolicited goods. Also, it prohibits a seller from repossessing goods (except as permitted by an Ontario Court judge) after you have paid two-thirds the amount owing. It requires that full disclosure be made on credit transactions, including the amount owed and the cost of borrowing expressed as an annual percentage. **Referral selling**, the rewarding of a buyer for finding other customers, is prohibited by the statute. Finally, there can be an order for immediate cessation of the use of "statements in an advertisement, circular, pamphlet or similar material" if the director "believes on reasonable and probable grounds" that a seller or lender is being false, misleading, or deceptive.

The Consumer Reporting Act[12]

What kind of information is filed on you, for whom, and why? If you apply to rent an apartment, the renter needs to know if you can afford it; if you apply for a job, the employer might need to know if you are bondable; and if you want a loan or credit card, your payment history and character could be in issue. This statute states the kind of data that a consumer reporting agency

---

[11] R.S.O. 1990, c. C.31.
[12] R.S.O. 1990, c. C.33.

can disclose to an inquirer, stipulates how it can be used, and protects consumers against outdated and inaccurate information.

One type of business covered by the *Consumer Reporting Act* is a **credit reporting agency**. It keeps records of writs and judgments that might affect your ability to pay your bills, and of your credit transactions. The records are usually filed at the nearest credit bureau. The other type is a **personal information reporting agency**. It might collect and store data on your lifestyle (character, reputation, health, mode of living) as well as your credit history. Both kinds of agency sell their information to businesses that need to know about you (not to the public); they must be registered with the MCCR, and must advise you when an inquiry is made.

After seven years there can be no listing of criminal convictions, writs, tax or fine information, and a discharged once-and-only bankruptcy. Also excluded are criminal charges that were dropped, and a notice of claim representing the intention to sue if issued over 12 months before the report date unless there is proof on file that it is still active.

The *Consumer Reporting Act* emphasizes accuracy; for instance, agencies must make a "reasonable effort" to verify any unfavourable information before listing it. You are entitled to an easily readable, plain language copy of all the information in both your credit history and personal information files. If you contest an entry and supply proof of the error upon request, the agency must either support its entry, delete it, or correct the error, and must report any corrections to certain recipients of the incorrect data. See *Credit Report Agencies* in the Yellow Pages. Otherwise, you can complain to the Registrar of Consumer Reporting Agencies.

If a business seems to downgrade your creditworthiness (denying you a benefit or increasing your fee) you can demand to receive, within 60 days, the name and address of the agency or the nature and source of the information that's being acted upon. A conviction of knowingly providing false information or contravening the Act can result in a $2,000 fine and/or a year in prison; the maximum fine for a corporation is $25,000.

The Repair and Storage Liens Act[13]

Centuries before there was much in the way of machinery to fix, common law protected innkeepers from not being paid for lodging and food provided; they could hold onto the guest's luggage or horse as security. This "holding onto" became enshrined in statutory law as a **lien**, which is the entitlement of one person to keep another's property or to put a claim on it until paid the related funds due. (The word comes from the Latin verb *ligare*, to bind, from which we also get terms such as ligature.) The law of liens on personal property, the ***Repair and Storage Liens Act (RSLA)***, protects both those who fix or store goods and their owner.[14]

Essentially, if you don't pay me on time for my agreed-upon work or storage, I can retain possession of what I repaired, improved, or stored for you until you do — through a lien on it. After three months awaiting payment and giving proper notice, I can dispose of (sell, keep, or donate) it.

What if I fix some machinery at your factory or farm, or if I let you take your van so you can earn the funds to pay my bill on it? Even without possession of the goods on which I am owed payment, I have **non-possessory lien** rights. I may obtain "a signed acknowledgement of indebtedness" (such as an invoice for the services performed) from you, and register a *Claim for*

---

[13] R.S.O. 1990, c. R.25.

[14] For the law regarding liens on land for improvements to land, see the *Construction Lien Act*, R.S.O. 1990, c. C.30.

Lien in the Personal Property Security Registration (PPSR) system, which is covered next. The RSLA could allow a sheriff to seize the article so that it could be sold to satisfy the lien.

Personal Property Security Registration (PPSR) System

The PPSR system records and reproduces data on (a) consumer and business loans where personal property is used as collateral and (b) repair and storage liens. For instance, to borrow money to buy a car, you can expect to sign a "security agreement" turning over rights to the car if you don't repay the loan.

The "financing statement" sent to the Personal Property Registration Branch is recorded in a computer file and is available for searching by lenders and buyers. Within 30 days of registering the financing statement the lender must give the borrower the registration details. The statement contains the lender's name and business address, the registration period, identification of the collateral, and the amount and maturity date of the loan. It also holds the borrower's name, address, and birth date (the latter for identification, in that there are some five million registrations in the PPSR system). The borrower should check these details for accuracy.

Unlike business loans (which can be registered in perpetuity), consumer loans are limited to a five-year registration period at a time. When repaid, the lender must register a "discharge" within 30 days or be subject to any resulting damages plus up to a $500 payment to the borrower.

Performing a Search

Searches can be performed in Toronto at 375 University Ave. Elsewhere, one of the 55 local land registry offices can inform you of the closest location. Also, it can be done by mail using an enquiry form available at any office that handles PPSR searches, or by telephone at 1-800-267-8847 (325-8847 in Toronto) with an approved credit card.

Many registrations now are of vehicles rather than the horse or luggage of a guest at an inn. But a consumer need not conduct a search when buying from a registered dealer a new car or other item, or a used car worth $15,000 or less. If a search is conducted, it can be performed against a vehicle's **VIN** (vehicle identification number), against a business (by its registered or incorporated name), or against an individual by full name and date of birth.

Other modules are available for this text that provide more detailed information on other aspects of lien rights and obligations and their extension into, for instance, construction liens, repossession in a conditional sales contract, liens for real estate taxes and utility services, the use of liens by professionals such as architects, and liens by employees against their employers for unpaid wages or benefits.

The Motor Vehicle Repair Act

Historically, MCCR received more complaints about car repairs than any other topic. Following the passage of this fairly recent statute, the percentage has dropped from top place. This act balances the protection of consumers from being "held up" for unnecessary repairs or charged for repairs not performed, and of car technicians from giving a best-guess estimate and finding, once the work has started, that further repairs are required.

This statute requires repairers to "post a sign in a conspicuous place clearly visible to prospective customers" stating, for instance, that written estimates are available, how all charges are calculated, that your replaced parts will be returned upon request, and the MCCR complaints phone number. It must also indicate whether any commissions are paid. (If you are told that many parts need replacement and you know that the mechanic receives extra payment for parts you agree to buy, you might want a second opinion.)

If you request a written estimate, it must be free (unless you are first given a written estimate for making the estimate, or if the mechanic cannot get authorization to repair and must assemble or repair the vehicle in order to move it out of the way). The estimate must be detailed, including the type of parts to be used, hourly rate, and number of hours, and cannot be exceeded by more than 10 per cent.

You cannot be charged for repairs undertaken without your authorization in writing or by telephone if the repairer records your name, phone number, date, and time of authorization (an OK by phone allows for slippage, so be careful what you say). The invoice must be detailed; among the 10 requirements are the labour itemization, the warranty, and whether replaced parts are new, used, or reconditioned. If your repaired car becomes inoperable or unsafe because of faulty work, you can, if it is the only reasonable solution, take it to a nearby garage and later demand reimbursement for the new bill from the original repairer.

The *Sale of Goods* Act

Ontario's *Sale of Goods Act*[15] says that goods must be suitable for the declared purpose for which they were bought. "Where the buyer, expressly or by implication, makes known to the seller the particular purpose for which the goods are required, ... there is an implied condition that the goods will be reasonably fit for such purpose...." (Section 15). Thus, if you buy a cell phone without comment and find that it doesn't work where you live, your only recourse is the retailer's return policy. But if you initially inform the seller that you are buying it for use in Hidden Valley, then if you find that this location is a "dead spot", the seller cannot simply maintain that it is your phone now, and that any complaints should go to the manufacturer.

This Act is administered not by MCCR but by the office of the Attorney General (416-326-2220). It is based on an English statute of 1893 that derived in turn from common law. Although revised in 1960, some of the language retains century-old obscurity, for instance, "An implied warranty ... may be annexed by the usage of trade." This 53-section Act also gives the following consumer rights:

Good Title
Each purchaser has the right to receive good title for goods purchased. This gives the new owner the option to resell the item, the full use of the merchandise, and the sole control over it.

Compliance with Description
Purchasers who do not receive the goods at the time of making the contract can demand to inspect the goods before accepting them. Those who choose not to inspect the goods must accept them at their own risk.

Merchantability
Consumers have the right to receive products that are of good quality and that can perform their purpose or task with little difficulty.

---

[15] R.S.O. 1990, c. S.1.

EXHIBIT 20.2

When Will Ontario Catch Up?

Ontario's consumer-protection laws date from simpler times when you handed over cash and the merchant gave you the goods. If they disintegrated on the way out of the store, bad luck. There were no cars to repair, no data-transmission to invade our privacy, and no junk mail, phone calls, or faxes.

Now cashiers juggle high-tech credit cards, bar-codes, and debit cards. Phone hucksters computer-dial you with dubious deals from far-off states, provinces, and countries. You can buy a computer from your TV screen, then buy a TV from your computer screen.

Consumers have also changed: they want a marketplace in which they are informed and protected. Yet, Ontario laws say little about telemarketing, negative-option schemes, refunds and exchanges, third-party warranties, cross-border mail orders, home repairs, or late delivery of pre-paid goods. Though half of all transactions in Ontario now involve services, the law still ignores most services.

Ontario's original consumer legislation hardly changed for 50 years, but starting in the 1960s, the MCCR has been adding to and patching the laws in response to consumer complaints, resulting in a maze of general and specific statutes.

A legislative review to update, consolidate, and simplify these laws occurred in 1986, sparked by MCCR chief Monte Kwinter under Liberal David Peterson. Kwinter's successors William Wrye and Greg Sorbara added further changes based on wide consultations. Before Peterson called the 1990 election, Sorbara tried to ensure that the changes would be continued by the next government; he circulated a draft for public comment, which was supportive. Enter the NDP, and Bob Rae put the MCCR in the hands of Peter Kormos (who left the overhaul on a back burner), and then replaced Kormos with Marilyn Churley.

Churley, the fifth minister to deal with this law reform, renewed the project, added sharper teeth to the measures, and named the statute **The Fair Marketplace Code.** She also replaced its legalisms with plain language, so that "Rescissions pursuant to itinerant hawkers" would become "Cancellations of deals made with in-home sellers." The Code integrates six statutes (including the *Sale of Goods Act*), plus common law, into one that basically says, "If you want to do business in Ontario, whether with goods or services, here are the ground rules that will be fair to both sides."

The Code was welcomed by sellers because it clarifies good business practices (which should reduce disputes and lawsuits), and deters fly-by-nighters from skimming the cream. It specifies not only consumer rights and remedies but responsibilities too; all parties will know where they stand. It would show the world that Ontario's a good place to do business and to be a consumer.

University of Waterloo economist Bob Kerton called it "a framework which encourages honest sellers to succeed, while deterring scam artists." Other consumer advocates said that Ontario consumers need "this clear, generic law stipulating that you can't lie, cheat, or take advantage of a consumer, because at the moment, consumers often don't know where they stand." Another asserted that the code "will make Ontario the best jurisdiction in North America for consumers."

That's not the case at the moment. Ontario has been outdistanced by Quebec and several states and western provinces, for instance, Alberta's *Fair Trades Act.* But the three ministers who have headed the MCCR since the Progressive Conservative Party assumed power in June of 1995 (David Tsubouchi, Norm Sterling, and Bob Runciman) have shelved this comprehensive change, making it the most delayed modern statute in Ontario legislative history.

Financial Services Commission of Ontario

Another government body related to consumer law is the *Financial Services Commission of Ontario*. This new organization combines the former Ontario Insurance Commission, the Pension Commission of Ontario, and the Deposit Institutions Division of the Ministry of Finance. Its phone is 800-668-0128; the Web site is <www.fsco.gov.on.ca>.

Its insurance sector, the Ontario Insurance Commission, regulates all insurers licensed to do business in Ontario (whether for auto, life, or travel), provides a dispute-resolution ombudsman (whose report is not binding on either side), and offers various brochures. Its Web site <www. ontarioinsurance.com> lists all licensed car insurers by type, gives rate information and other consumer advice, and posts a comprehensive car insurer Claims Satisfaction Survey. (General information on insurance is provided in the second-last main section below.)

Accessing Ontario Statutes

The complete texts of all Ontario statutes can be viewed at <www.gov.on.ca> and choosing Language (English or French), Look up Acts and Regulations, Full Text of Ontario's Legislation (acts and regulations), Access to the Statutes and Regulations site, and English or French. The Web postings are not considered official; for that, official copies of statutes can be ordered from the Ontario Government Bookstore (1-800-668-9938 or <www.gov.on.ca/MBS/english/publications>).

QUEBEC

We now turn to the second major province. Quebec is reviewed here because (a) the *Civil Code of Quebec* was updated recently (January 1, 1994), (b) the Code includes the *Consumer Protection Act*, a comprehensive set of regulations for consumer protection and business regulation, and (c) only Quebec law derives from the Napoleonic Code rather than English common law. The full statutes can be found in a bilingual paperback listed in the suggested readings at the end of this chapter.

In the summary below, the word "Act" will refer to the **Consumer Protection Act** [*Loi sur la protection du consommateur*]. It was drafted in French; where the English translation seems less precise, or where the French version might be helpful, the latter is shown in brackets. In the summary below, the abbreviation "M/M/A" will mean *merchant, manufacturer or advertiser* (a phrase that appears in many of the Act's 365 sections); "s" means section.

The *Consumer Protection Act*

The Act starts, unfortunately, with some hazy definitions. A "consumer" is a "natural person [*personne physique*], except a merchant who obtains goods or services for the purposes of his business." A merchant "includes any person doing business or extending credit in the course of his business." Thus, the Act's consumer protection apparently applies to all people in Quebec other than business people in the context of their work.

Section 22 says that a merchant soliciting a consumer for a "remote-parties" contract (one in which the buyer and seller are not in direct contact) cannot demand total or partial payment prior to the performance of the principal obligation. Thus, if I offer you my shopping service in which I will furnish goods not from my own stock but from other suppliers, I cannot extract your money until I deliver the main items. (If you solicited the transaction with me, I could require advance payment.)

In Chapter III on warranties, "Goods forming the object of a contract must be fit for the purposes of which goods of that kind are ordinarily used ... [and] must be durable in normal use for a reasonable length of time, having regard to their price, the terms of the contract and the conditions of their use." Where the goods "are of a nature that requires maintenance, replacement parts and repair service must be available for a reasonable time after the making of the contract" unless the merchant or manufacturer warns the consumer in writing prior to the contract that these services are not supplied. Moreover, the goods or services must conform to their description in the contract and to the statements or advertisements regarding them made by the merchant or manufacturer.

Itinerant merchants, those doing business elsewhere than "at his address", are covered where the contract exceeds $25. For instance, the contract must be fully detailed, and under section 58 the consumer has the right to cancel it within 10 days; moreover, the merchant must inform the consumer of this entitlement in writing. If the goods are not delivered within the cancellation period, no payment can change hands.

One of the largest parts of Chapter III (over 80 sections in Division III) relates to credit. As examples, the credit rate must be described in a simple and standardized format, the contract must provide for one deferred payment and permit full or partial payment prior to maturity, and the merchant must furnish the consumer a statement at least 21 days prior to the imposition of credit charges. If the consumer defaults on payment after having paid half of the debt, the merchant cannot repossess the goods except with a court order.

Division IV on automobiles (and motorcycles) provides comprehensive protection to the Quebec consumer. When a car under warranty needs towing or breakdown service, the owner does not pay, and all provisions apply equally to subsequent owners of the vehicle; coverage applies to both parts and labour. Under section 237, it is illegal to misleadingly replace a car's odometer reading or alter it.

Used cars offered for sale or long-term lease must bear a label, readable from the exterior, showing the price, full model-identifying details, the distance the vehicle has travelled, any type of commercial service it has undergone, the warranty offered, and all repairs carried out when in possession of the seller. If the label includes defects and a price estimate of repairs, the merchant is bound by that estimate. A certificate of mechanical inspection must be included, and the name and phone number of the previous owner must be provided upon request. The warranty covers between six months or 10,000 kilometres (whichever comes first) down to one month or 1,700 kilometres, depending on the class of vehicle, which is a function of age and distance driven.

Before performing any repairs, the merchant must provide a detailed written estimate that cannot be exceeded without a written waiver from the owner. There are nine items that must be included in the bill, and most replaced parts must be provided upon request. If the owner refuses to pay an amount not in accordance with the requirements, the merchant may not retain possession of the car. Moreover, the consumer entitlements must be conspicuously posted in the shop.

Under Division V, the repair of major household appliances is also subject to a written estimate that cannot be charged for without advance notice, and the bill for repairs must be complete and detailed. Repairs are warranted for three months.

Division VI requires that physical fitness studios (health clubs, or *studios de santé*) provide clients with detailed and complete contracts that cannot exceed one year. Prior to the beginning of the delivery of the services, the merchant cannot receive payment, and the client can cancel the contract. The client can also cancel within the first 10 days of the commencement of services, or during the first 10 per cent of the contract duration; any payment exceeding one-tenth of the contract amount must be returned within 10 days.

In terms of general business practices, there is considerable emphasis on being truthful; under Title II, merchants, manufacturers, and advertisers are prohibited from making any false or misleading representations to consumers. Apart from this general restriction, many specific types of such representations are specified as illegal, such as misrepresenting the quantity of goods on hand, or discrediting goods or services offered by others. This particularly applies to the sale price: section 223 stipulates that it must be indicated clearly and legibly, higher amounts cannot be charged, and any installment payments indicated cannot overshadow the total price.

To give another example, and to illustrate the plain yet specific wording in the Act, here is section 225 verbatim: No M/M/A "may, falsely, by any means whatever, (a) invoke a price reduction; (b) indicate a regular price or another reference price for goods or services; (c) let it be believed that the price of certain goods or services is advantageous." It's evident that this section was sparked by consumer complaints: "No merchant or manufacturer may refuse to perform the warranty granted by him on the pretext that the document evidencing it has not reached him or was not validated." And in case anything was left out, no M/M/A "may fail to mention an important fact in any representation made to a consumer." Thus, if a car for sale had undergone major repairs, this must be disclosed.

The distinction between businesses and consumers is becoming blurred, as non-business people are increasingly being offered commercial opportunities to operate out of their residences. It would violate the Quebec statutes to, "... when soliciting or making a contract, make false representations concerning the profitability or any other aspect of a business opportunity offered to a customer." Nor can a person be charged for goods that were not ordered.

Those who advertise must have a sufficient quantity "to meet public demand" unless the ad indicates to the contrary. Premiums (such as price rebates) cannot be emphasized more than the goods or services themselves. Ads promoting contests for gifts, prizes, or rebates must include all the terms clearly. As for multilevel or **pyramid selling** plans, no benefit can be offered for the consumer signing up other individuals.

No M/M/A can falsely indicate (a) certification, recommendation, sponsorship, approval, affiliation, or association with a third party, (b) the latter's approval, certification, or sponsorship of goods or services, or (c) a particular status or identity. Nor can a M/M/A distort the meaning of any information, opinion, or testimony, or "rely upon data or analyses falsely presented as scientific."

The holding of a permit under the Act does not entitle anyone to imply that it means competence, solvency, recognition, or approval. The holding of a permit or the furnishing of a required security cannot be mentioned in an ad. Every ad must specify that the sponsor is a merchant who must be identified, including the street address. Ads cannot urge consumers to obtain goods or services by credit.

Applications for credit must explicitly state that's what they are. Moreover, credit rates and terms, and the conditions of a long-term lease, must be stated in accordance with the Act.

Commercial advertising cannot be directed to persons under the age of 13 years, in terms of the context, nature, purpose, manner, and time and place of the ad. Nor can ads invite payment by cheques from the government of Quebec, Canada, or a municipality. If such cheques are accepted as payment, no charge can be levied for this service.

A merchant who accepts payment prior to issuing a contract must place those funds in a trust account (until the funds are repaid on demand, or a contract is made). This account must be a single one in an institution recognized under the *Deposit Insurance Act*, the president of the institution must be informed of the account, and the details must be entered in the merchant's books.

Schedule 1 prescribes the forms to be used in consumer matters. These include forms for a loan contract, an installment contract, and cancelling a contract. Another section of the Act, comprising 180 sections, deals with its application. For instance, farm and forestry loans come under a different statute, as do student loans.

The Application of the Act

In the second half of the Act, a number of "Schedules" specify the design and wording of the *forms* prescribed under the Act. For instance, section 58 mentioned above permits a contract with an itinerant merchant to be cancelled within 10 days; Schedule 1 [Annexe 1] gives the applicable forms, namely, the detailed "Statement of Consumer Cancellation Rights", and the forms to be completed by the buyer and seller. It also covers the "Form of Writings", specifying the minimum quality of the paper, and even how the reader is to be informed if the writing is continued on the back. In brief, contracts may be handwritten or printed; if typed, the font, colour, and minimum size are specified.

There are 180 clauses on how the Act is to be applied. These include definitions (e.g., a "mobile home" is "any structure intended to be used all year round as a dwelling and to be connected to public services and capable of being transported on its own frame by towing or by any other means"), and exemptions (for instance, section 22 does not apply to the subscription to a newspaper, periodical, or magazine).

The application section specifies what consumer-protection information must be included in a contract. Such required material comprises specified clauses from the Act, a recommendation that the consumer refer to other relevant clauses, and advice to consult the "Office de la protection du consommateur" (not all the material is provided in English). Contracts requiring such information include those involving itinerant merchants, credit and loans, long-term lease of goods contracts, the lease of services involving sequential performance, and those that contain a provision of forfeiture of benefit of the term. Other contracts requiring such announcements are those involving automobiles, motorcycles, and household appliances. Similar stipulations regard certain types of advertising, such as for credit and long-term lease.

A repairer of cars or motorcycles must "post up, in a conspicuous place of his establishment, a sign giving the following particulars" (the regulations outlined in the paragraph starting "The section on automobiles" above, but in French only). Moreover, the sign must be on "stiff material with a white non-glossy surface"; the minimum size and the font details are also specified. When a car odometer is replaced with one that cannot be reset, a permanent label must be affixed to the inside of the instrument panel window, near the odometer, clearly indicating the reading of the replaced odometer.

Although advertising directed to children is prohibited, the section on applications permits it in limited circumstances such as in some material (primarily magazines) directed at children. It also further restricts it; for instance, ads may not exaggerate product attributes, use superlatives, directly incite a child to buy, or portray "reprehensible social or family lifestyles". Nor can a comic strip be included (except to promote a comic book), nor can an ad suggest that a product "will develop in a child a physical, social or psychological advantage over other children his age."

You may recall that section 223 covers how prices must be indicated; the Applications sections exempts various categories of goods, such as those selling for no more than 40 cents, and those in automatic vending machines. Also excluded from coverage are categories representing a minority of those sold in a given store — if those categories are themselves posted on a clear list and the prices are clearly and legibly shown near where the articles are sold.

The Applications also covers the various permits required of merchants, and the forms they must use to apply for them or for renewals. For instance, an application to be a physical fitness studio operator must include financial records and a security deposit of $15,000.

Commentary on the Quebec Code

In terms of content, Quebec consumers now have the strongest and clearest protection in Canada. Nonetheless, two forms of promotion that could be covered more specifically are telemarketing, and improper claims made or implied by individuals on behalf of a company. Additionally, the restrictions should apply to the government itself. The Advertising Standards Canada (ASC) ruled that a $520,000 series of 1999 Quebec government ads claiming that the province received less money than Ontario in the last federal budget violated national advertising standards in that they were inaccurate and left out key information. (ASC is a voluntary organization funded by 100 media outlets, ad agencies, and corporations; its only power over advertisers is to list bad ones in its biannual report.)

The definition of "consumer" is restrictive, as it only applies to merchants. Consumer-protection laws generally exclude commercial transactions; a railway company would hardly expect government laws or offices to redress its complaint that its new locomotive was delivered scratched. Moreover, a doctor (if considered a "merchant" under the Act) should know how to choose a stethoscope, a psychologist should be able to safely buy a test. But not every "merchant" is a skilled professional or a corporation with its own purchasing agent. Presumably, a butcher would be protected while buying a car or having the house painted, but not in buying a delivery van or having the shop fumigated. So if you buy your first dough-mixer for your new, one-person pizza parlour and it is defective, the best consumer-protection statute in Canada excludes you. Whereas Ontario seems to favour the merchant over the consumer (as in the history of its *Sale of Goods Act*, which primarily created a vehicle for merchants to sue other merchants), Quebec disregards the needs of small business people in its definition of "consumer".

COMMENTARY ON CANADIAN CONSUMER LEGISLATION

Generally, Canadian consumers are reasonably well served by their provincial and federal legislation, although, as one example, Australia has more complete coverage, better provisions for consumer redress, and a much better capacity to address cross-border infractions. Here are some specific ways in which our consumer laws could be improved.

Style Weaknesses

In the past few decades, the use of "plain language" (wording that is clear to most readers) has become a feature of many types of documents such as textbooks, insurance contracts, instruction manuals, and also laws — including the new Quebec statute. It's time to refine and define this aspect with all laws that touch the ordinary person, as is the case with consumer-protection legislation. In some American states such as Florida, the law requires that any written contract must be fully understandable by 60 per cent of the population.

The use of gender-exclusive language has been increasingly considered unacceptable, a departure from the definition of a "person" as male under Canadian law in the early 20th century. When women were included and allowed to vote, most writers (who were generally male) maintained that male nouns and pronouns properly referred to both males and females; the word "man" was supposed to refer to a human being. Today we have to accept the fact that laws rely on precedent and long-established conventions in the meaning of terms. Statutes are gradually being written and revised with non-exclusionary language, but these changes are taking place slowly, and parts of the past are still with us.

Content Weaknesses

A comprehensive way of improving Canadian statutes would be to increase the consistency among the provinces and territories. For instance, as a result of Quebec's requirement that all material facts about a car must be disclosed to the potential buyer, some wrecked Quebec cars that had been written off as total losses by the insurer and then repaired were brought to Ontario for sale to unknowing buyers. Ontario's laxer legislation provided an outlet for cars that in Quebec would be sold for scrap. As other examples, a substance-abuser could have a driver's licence revoked in one province and obtain a new one in another, a bankrupt could leave creditors stranded in one province and obtain new credit in another, and a fraud artist could close down in one jurisdiction and set up in another.

Consistency would help interprovincial trade and commerce. Picture a firm with many successful branches in Ontario that wishes to open another in Manitoba. To do so, it must hire a Manitoba law firm to ensure that it would be in compliance with all of the relevant consumer and business legislation that differ in subtle ways from that of Ontario. That may be just enough to kill the expansion. Similarly, imagine an Asian firm planning to invest in many new branches throughout either England or Canada. It learns that it must learn and conform to either one set of consumer regulations or as many as 14 (federal, 10 provincial, three territorial).

Consistency could also benefit some consumers. Time was, most people were buried within a few blocks of the house in which they were born. Today, many people move a number of times during their lives and careers, often changing provinces. Nowadays you can communicate with, buy from, or sell to someone across the country more easily than the previous generation could have done just across town. In this sense the country is shrinking and thereby calling for uniformity in how business is conducted and consumers are treated.

As society and technology become more complex, and as our demands for safety and security increase, it is understandable that our lives will become increasingly rule-regulated. It's also understandable that past history and current problems differ across areas of Canada. But when a simple, common occupation and tool-of-the-trade such as a taxi and driver are subject to hundreds of regulations and statutes, including federal, provincial/territorial, and municipal/regional ones, surely consistency, currentness, and clarity should be worthy objectives for all of our legislators.

Another area for improvement is the need for currentness; most of the statutes discussed date from the 1960s and 1970s, when the marketplace was different. Legislation is needed that would invite the investigation and prosecution of "scam artists" whose targets are beyond the jurisdiction in question. Authorities in BC were recently unsuccessful when the court refused to prosecute deceptive telemarketers who were phoning Americans, because the relevant statute was worded to protect only British Columbians. We cannot expect other jurisdictions to crack down on those who prey on us if we do not reciprocate.

Finally, the Canadian consumer movement is small, fragmented, and underfunded. Most volunteer organizations have experienced recent funding cuts, and some such as the Consumers' Association of Canada have been particularly hard hit. Investing in volunteerism is practical because the members do not get paid, and legislative support for such organizations would benefit all consumers.

We conclude this chapter with coverage of two special topics that most consumers deal with uncertainly, insurance and motor vehicles. Unlike the other subjects covered, these often-troublesome areas are treated from a general consumer advisement or paralegal perspective as well as from a legal one.

INSURANCE

The principal of insurance is that you (or your parent, spouse, or employer) pay now for protection that you might be entitled to collect on later. Considering what would happen if the insurer were unwilling or unable to fulfill its contractual obligations when the time comes, you can see that the government is obligated to protect policyholders. Recently, more than 100 disabled employees of a venerable department store had been receiving disability benefits while unable to work. When Eaton's prepared a bankruptcy proposal in late 1999, it turned out that it had been "self-insuring" its long-term disability and drug plans, and almost all payments stopped without warning. If the store had bought insurance to protect its employees, the regulators and the insurance industry would have ensured that the carrier itself would never fail to protect those who depended on it.

Although the shared-risk principle of insurance is simple, the legislation and terminology are complex. A firm or individual licensed by the federal government (under the *Insurance Companies Act*) can sell insurance anywhere in Canada; an insurer licensed by a province (as by the *Insurance Act of Ontario*) can conduct business only in that province.

Theoretically, you can insure anything, from tomorrow's weather to having to cancel a prepaid trip. But the three basic types of insurance are motor vehicle, property (which together is called "general insurance"), and life. Car insurance is handled provincially (the province itself insures cars in British Columbia, Manitoba, and Saskatchewan); the others can be federally or provincially regulated, depending on the insurer's licence.

The Insurance Policy

An insurance policy is a binding contract between the insurer and the policyholder that specifies what "perils" are covered, how, and to what extent; no policy covers "everything". A consumer-friendly policy clarifies what is and is not insured in plain, unambiguous language. The onus should not be on the policyholder to ask every question in advance, but on the insurer to predict and answer it, at least generally or by examples.

For instance, most home policies exclude damage from vermin, but if a squirrel or raccoon gets trapped in your house and damages it, you would need to know if your insurer deems all creatures that cause damage to be "vermin". Similarly, a life insurance policy should state what proof of death must accompany a claim, and within what time limit. (Imagine that the death occurs in a foreign country, and that various insurers would require any or all of a local or any newspaper obituary, a certificate from a provincially licensed or any funeral director, a specific or any medical certificate of death, or a costly and time-consuming document from the provincial registrar of records.)

One common factor among motor vehicle policies is that all provinces require cars to be insured for minimum amounts for certain perils; for instance, third-party liability coverage of at least $200,000 is usual. But each jurisdiction's is unique; for instance, Alberta uses a **tort-based insurance** system whereas Ontario is **no-fault**, and you can sue for pain and suffering in some cases and not in others.

Within a province all car policies are identical, whereas non-car policies vary. That is, if 10 people in the same block have life or home policies from 10 insurers, probably no two policies would be the same. But the terms are identical in, for instance, Ontario's five million vehicle policies sold by about 150 competing firms.

As with all insurance, the **premium** relates to the risk as calculated by the insurer. Thus, the standard variables for car insurance rates are (apart from the insured's choices for optional extra coverage): where the principal driver lives, the amount driven and for what purposes, and the age and/ or driving record of the principal and other drivers. The last variable is the car's make and year as related to predicted cost of repair or replacement, likelihood of theft, and occupant injury protection; data on these variables are available from the Vehicle Information Centre of Canada, <www.vicc.com/>.

Private car insurers differ in other ways within a province, especially how much and on what basis they charge, whom they accept for a new policy and for a renewal, and the handling of claims. They also vary in billing and payment practices such as how far in advance they bill, whether they accept post-dated cheques or automatic fund withdrawal, and in the case of expiration due to non-payment, how they notify you, and how long any **grace period** is. Other differences include procedures for resolving disputes, the amount and duration of surcharges for what type of claims, and acceptance by telephone of temporary changes such as removing road coverage during periods of car storage.

Questions to Ask Insurers

All insurance tends to be complex and the language esoteric; for instance, the word "premium" has a different meaning to insurers than it does to others in other contexts. Moreover, most insurance buyers spend a few minutes deciding on coverage every few years whereas sellers ply their trade all day long, thus making for an unequal relationship.

Even though all policies within a province have the same terms, it seems that few vehicle owners have studied them. For instance, suppose you lend your Ontario-registered vehicle to a friend whose licence, unknown to either of you, had just expired. Following a collision, you would find that your car was not insured during the loan. Or, if the insurer discovers that you made inaccurate statements in your application, they could reject any claim.

Accordingly, questions that consumers might ask a private insurer are:

- If I have a full replacement coverage for property that becomes a write-off, how would you respond to my preference for a cash settlement rather than a replacement?

- If the property depreciates during my policy renewals, will you lower the premium for replacement coverage to reflect your decreased exposure?

- If I report minor damage in a telephone inquiry but decide not to file a claim, would my record be downgraded as if I had filed a claim on it?

- Will I be able to see my complete file on request?

- If I have complex questions, will I have access to your experienced experts as opposed to front-line office staffers?

- Have your terms been updated to cover modern needs such as home offices, satellite dishes, and laptop computers that are taken on trips?

- Will you make all your coverage options clear to me?

- Do you provide 24-hour claims service?

- How long after an incident do I have to make a claim?

- Assuming that your claims records differentiate between at-fault and not-at-fault claims, if you judged me to have been one per cent at fault in an incident, would you log it as an "at-fault" claim?

- Does your firm have an arbitration service for an *independent* review of disputes, such as The Co-operators and Royal have?

- If in my initial interview I answered "No" to the question "Do you deep fry?" would a claim for a fire caused by a visiting relative who left a deep fryer unattended be rejected?

- In 1999, an Ontario widow tried to collect on a life insurance policy her husband had bought to cover their $63,000 mortgage. After his sudden fatal heart attack, the insurer rejected the claim. He had indicated no intestinal illness, but his medical records showed mild colitis (which was unrelated to his death at age 45). A judge ruled that the application form was poorly worded and easily misunderstood, and that the husband had not intended to mislead. The insurer filed an appeal. How would your firm handle such a case?

In the case of agents and brokers, it might be useful to find out which insurers they represent (usually between one and eight), and how they are paid (for instance, whether some forms of optional coverage are particularly lucrative). You can also ask what services they offer, for instance, if you want help with an after-hours problem, or information on an insurer's underwriting guidelines.

The complete insurance statutes of at least five provinces (Alberta, British Columbia, New Brunswick, Ontario, and Quebec) can be accessed from <www.insurance-finance.com/canada.htm> and choosing Canadian Insurance Law Links. A comprehensive summary of provincial and territorial car policies is in the brochure "Facts" from the Insurance Bureau of Canada, 151 Yonge, Toronto M5C 2W7, or <www.ibc.ca>.

MOTOR VEHICLES

It often costs a year's income to buy a car; some are as expensive as an average house. Many owners think of the subsequent operating expenses in terms of fuel only, disregarding maintenance and repair costs. Additionally, the fixed expenses (insurance, licensing, and perhaps storage and periodic safety checks) continue throughout the ownership and can exceed the purchase price.

It's commonly believed that one's most expensive purchase is a house, with the car coming second. But real estate generally increases in value whereas cars depreciate, usually dropping half their value in three years and becoming near-worthless within a decade. Thus, over their lifetimes, many people have lost more money on their motor vehicles than on any other assets.

In addition, mechanically defective vehicles are troublesome to the owner and potentially dangerous to the public, and cosmetic imperfections that the dealer dismisses can destroy owner satisfaction. Automobiles do come with warranties, but they are not always the answer. Prior to the 1950s, most warranties lasted 30 to 90 days; today they range from one to four years. But this can be false security on modern, complex cars that are not designed to be fixed in the backyard as they once were. This is illustrated in the following composite example:

> When Ms. Buyer's new car does not start she has it towed to the dealer and later picks it up. Next day, it still won't start. After it has been in the shop for several days more, she is told the battery is bad, and as the manufacturer's warranty excludes tires and batteries she has to deal with the battery maker. A new battery is not a cure; the starter is serviced after two weeks at the dealer. The problem recurs; this time, after a month "waiting for parts" a computer chip is replaced. When it still hesitates she is accused of flooding the engine, using the wrong or dirty fuel, or leaving the lights on. When she insists that the car is defective, the dealer refers her to the manufacturer ("We only sold it to you; we did not make it"), who referred her back ("Your contract is with the dealer.") She has only paid for towing and taxis, but the car has been out of service for months, the problem persists, and when the warranty expires she will have to pay for work that she is not sure was performed competently or at all.

Those who purchase extended coverage may find that there are so many restrictions, which are always interpreted by the insurer (if it remains in business), that it is worthless. To seek redress through the court system generally requires time, expertise, funds, and the help of a mechanically adept lawyer to argue against the weight of an experienced dealer, service technician, and factory representative. The above are the reasons for the coverage of motor vehicles here. The next two sections are more on legal alternatives than entitlements.

Automobile Protection Association

The Automobile Protection Association (APA) is a Canadian non-profit association that publishes *Lemon-Aid*, which is both a quarterly magazine that is sent to members, and an annual paperback book series sold in bookstores. APA advises on vehicles, publishes information on "secret warranties" and dealer costs, lobbies for improved legislation on industry quality and sales practices, and recommends garages and products.

For instance, in early 1977, the Canadian car industry announced a plain language lease agreement designed to correct long-standing abuses. Subsequently, APA researchers posing as ordinary shoppers visited some 50 dealers. They found that meaningful disclosure of the lease details were still hard to find; for instance, "Not one Ford dealer outside Quebec accurately revealed the true cost of a two-year Red Carpet lease."

APA's head office is 292 St. Joseph Blvd. W., Montreal H2V 2N7, (514) APA-5555; the Toronto office is 2 Carlton St., M5B 1J3, (416) 204-1444; the Web site is <www.apa.ca>. Annual membership costs $52 plus tax.

CAMVAP

Lemon Laws

In the 1980s, some American states were passing **lemon laws** to protect car buyers from being stuck with a vehicle that proved to be unduly troublesome. Now, every state has such a law but there is none in Canada. Each state's law is unique, but a typical provision is that after three attempts or a total of 30 days in the shop to repair the same component or system on a non-commercial, low-mileage new car, the buyer is entitled to a refund of the purchase price. (Many states require that every "manufacturer buy-back" be so designated on the vehicle registration, so that the next buyer will be aware of serious problems.) Canadians wondering if their car would be considered a "lemon" elsewhere can review a summary of every state's definition at <www.carprices.com/insider_tips/lemon_law.html>.

To preclude lemon laws from entering Canada, the car manufacturers, in consultation with the MCCR, proposed an arbitration service for Ontario (where about half the country's cars are purchased), with a view to extending it nationally if successful. The Ontario Motor Vehicle Arbitration Plan (OMVAP) originated in 1986; in 1994 it became CAMVAP, the Canadian Motor Vehicle Arbitration Plan. Its Web site is <www.camvap.ca>.

Using CAMVAP

If your car has a defect that the dealer cannot or will not rectify, and you report this without success to the manufacturer's representative, you are entitled to invoke the plan. You will receive a list of three local arbitrators with their backgrounds and qualifications, and you choose any one to review the documentation and to schedule a hearing at which both sides present their case. The arbitrator, with the power to order full repayment of the purchase cost, is given the task of coming to a decision that is fair to both sides.

The arbitrator functions like a judge in a court of law, but there are no costs to you (the plan is funded by the car industry), and the hearings take place in a casual atmosphere in your home town; in a recent year, hearings occurred in 100 communities throughout the country, usually in a hotel room or Better Business Bureau office. Arbitrators are trained in CAMVAP issues and procedures; three-quarters are lawyers, sometimes retired. There are about 150 on call, one-third of whom are in Ontario. The plan pays $300 plus expenses and disbursements for the arbitrator's time and expertise in running the hearing and issuing a report and decision; for instance, the arbitrator can hire a technician (usually through the Canadian Automobile Association) to examine the case.

After invoking CAMVAP, you may receive an offer from the manufacturer or dealer to rectify the problem (or to compensate you) as an alternative to proceeding with a hearing. It is your option to accept this or to continue with the CAMVAP process. Once a hearing takes place, you waive the right to take further legal action if you are not satisfied with the outcome. After the repairs or replacements ordered by the arbitrator have been completed within the stipulated time but not to your satisfaction, you may request a further hearing; in one such case the follow-up result was a buy-back.

CAMVAP is universal with two exceptions. Every province and territory except Quebec is a signatory, and all Canadian manufacturers/importers participate other than BMW and its subsidiary Land Rover (and a few exotic, high-performance brands such as Aston Martin and Lamborghini). The plan covers the current model year and back four model years (the cut-off date being Sept 30) for the original and all successive owners.

In 1997, the most recent year for which full data is available at the time of this writing, of the 469 cases processed, 329 were arbitrated (over half of which were in Ontario). About 200 were decided in favour of the consumer; in 148 cases repairs were made or the consumer was reimbursed for those already paid for (averaging over $1,000 per case), 49 involved the car being bought back (with or without a price reduction, averaging over $18,000 per vehicle) or, in three cases, replaced; and 15 consumers were reimbursed for miscellaneous out-of-pocket expenses. The 659 problems involved, in order, the engine, transmission, exterior, steering/suspension, brakes, computer/electrical, interior temperature, and accessories.

Who appeared before the arbitrator? The consumer arrived alone in 182 of the hearings, accompanied by a relative in 129, with a witness in 14, and with a lawyer in four. On the other side, the manufacturer's representative attended alone in 223 cases, with a technician in 84, and accompanied by a dealer representative in 22 of the hearings.

All consumers who use the plan are surveyed for their satisfaction with various dimensions of their experience by an outside firm; the results are also posted on the Web and listed in the annual report. A major determinant of satisfaction is a speedy resolution of a usually long-standing problem; the average time to complete the arbitration was 60 days.

The plan is continually undergoing modification based on participant feedback. For instance, vehicles used for any commercial purpose were excluded, but as the distinction between business and personal use became blurred, this restriction was lifted in 1999. As another example, until 1999 all participants were bound by a confidentiality agreement, but as of October the Web site will report quarterly results by consumer complaint and arbitrator decision in terms of car year, make, and model.

CAMVAP is self-described as fast, fair, friendly, free, and final. Indeed, it is a well-run and powerful remedy serving the interests of Canadian car buyers, costing the Canadian car industry over $1-million per year. Nonetheless, there are two serious weaknesses. One is public awareness, which could be rectified if a CAMVAP brochure were placed in the glove compartment of every eligible vehicle sold by dealers. The other is what happens to vehicles that are bought back, over 250 so far. If the provincial licensing authorities agreed to note or "brand" on the registration that the vehicle was a CAMVAP-ordered buy-back, it would alert subsequent purchasers to the possibility of problems that were not fixable for the previous owner.

CAMVAP can be accessed throughout Canada at 1-800-207-0685; the Web site is <www.camvap.ca>. A consumer brochure is available in most car dealerships and in small claims and civil courts, or by mail, and contact information is provided in the owners or warranty manuals of most new cars currently sold in Canada. Services are available in French as PAVAC (Programme d'arbitrage pour les véhicules automobiles du Canada) at the same Web site. The head office is Suite 300, 595 Bay St., Toronto M5G 2C2; regional offices are Atlantic, Ontario, Manitoba, Saskatchewan, British Columbia & Yukon, and Alberta & Territories.

Buying/Selling a Used Vehicle in Ontario

Within living memory, transferring ownership of a used car was little harder than switching cat ownership; it is now more complex than buying/selling a house. The Ontario regulations are covered here because more used vehicles change ownership each year in this province than in any other (one million yearly), and because Ontario's car-transfer regulations date from the 1990s.

Legal and procedural aspects, and a few consumer pointers, are provided in this section. In it, the word "car" refers also to motorcycles, vans, and light trucks. Trucks over 3,000 kg are subject to different regulations, as are commercial dealers.

Obligations of the Seller

If you sell your car privately, you can expect to get more for it than a dealer would pay you, but less than the dealer would sell it for. If you plan to buy a replacement car, consider that by trading it in at a car dealership you would pay taxes amounting to 15 per cent only on the additional amount rather than on the total cost of the new car. But to sell it yourself, read on.

You must complete a Used Vehicle Information Package. Available for $20 from the MCCR or any of the 300 Driver and Vehicle Licence Issuing Offices, it addresses the vehicle's registration and lien record and retail sales tax. Fill out the Bill of Sale portion, and remind the buyer to take the package to a Driver and Vehicle Licence Issuing Office within six days. You also complete and sign the Application for Transfer on the back of the registration permit, and give it (but not the "plate portion") to the buyer.

If you sign any document attesting to the condition of the car, make sure there can be no question as to accuracy. Otherwise, preface your statements about the distance it has gone (odometers can be reset or replaced), accident history, mechanical condition, and so forth, with "As far as I know, ..."

Before surrendering the car, get the payment, total and secure, in hand. Also remove and keep your licence plates; otherwise, if the buyer has a collision or gets a speeding or parking ticket, you are responsible. You can attach them to another car after advising a Driver and Vehicle Licence Issuing Office of the change, or you can hand them in and apply for a refund for any full non-expired months that you had paid for.

Obligations of the Buyer

When you have found a prospective purchase, if it is claimed to come with the manufacturer's warranty still in effect, ask a dealership to verify this from the VIN and to tell you if any manufacturer recalls on this car have been performed. It is also prudent to ask the seller for a written statement that summarizes the condition and the accident and repair history of the car, and to read it carefully. As well, ask if the owner's manual and repair and service invoices are available for inspection (so you can see if it has been properly serviced) and included with the car.

The cost savings from buying a car used are such that most owners seldom ever buy a new one. But if the above tips are news to you, and if you are not savvy about cars and you do not get the help of someone who is, you are unwise to buy one from a private seller you do not know and trust. For instance, in suits for misrepresentation, breach of contract, or negligence, plaintiffs are at a disadvantage when the defendant is a private individual rather than a licensed business. But we will assume that you have come to an informed decision to make an offer to a private seller, and want to know the procedure.

Ask to see the Used Vehicle Information Package and check it for any outstanding liens registered against the car, anything untoward in the registration history (such as past ownership by Toronto Taxi or Peel Police), and whether the name and signature of the seller exactly match those on the registration. If the car has a safety certificate, check that the date is current and the VIN is accurate; if not, you can make your offer conditional on the seller providing the certificate (or you can buy it "as is"). In southern Ontario the car will also have to have a valid emission inspection certificate.

After purchase, you must register the car at a Driver and Vehicle Licence Issuing Office within six days. Bring the Used Vehicle Information Package, the Application for Transfer (the vehicle portion of the permit), your Ontario Driver's Licence or other identification, and (if you are using the existing licence plates) the plate portion of the permit. Then you pay for the new licence plates if required, and the registration fee.

You will also pay the retail sales tax, which is based on the larger of the declared purchase price or the "Canadian Red Book" wholesale value calculated at the time of the transaction. If you paid less than the Red Book figure and an accepted appraisal supports the low price, you pay tax on the higher of the declared amount paid or the appraised value; details on the procedures are available from the licensing office. No sales tax is paid when the car is gifted to a spouse, parent/step-parent, offspring, grandparent, grandchild, or in-law (son, daughter, father, mother). It is also exempt for Status Indians and most diplomats. The GST is also collected at this time.

Even if it's a gift from a relative, before you can drive the car (as opposed to storing it, using it off-road or on private property, or towing it on a public roadway), it will need a Safety Standards Certificate. This can be obtained at a licensed Motor Vehicle Inspection Station; there are over 10,000 across Ontario. The certificate, for which either you or the seller pays, is issued when a mechanical inspection indicates that the car meets the minimum safety standards required by the *Highway Traffic Act*.[16] It is valid for 36 days after the date recorded on the certificate, but it does not warrant that the car will not need repairs one day after that date. It ignores non-safety components; some, such as the engine or transmission, may be costly to fix, so you can ask to have them evaluated separately for an additional fee.

Another requirement before registering the car for use on the road system is a written declaration of insurance coverage. If convicted of giving false information, this is fraud for which you could be fined $2,500, and lose your car for three months and your driver's licence for a year. Your insurance must include third-party liability of $200,000 (throughout Canada except Quebec where it is $50,000), but prudent owners, especially if they own other property of value, pay the small extra premium to insure for $500,000 or $1-million.

The car's driver, whether or not the owner, must have at hand the insurer-supplied pink form (or a photocopy) showing that the required coverage is in force on that date; if you do not produce it when asked by a police officer you are subject to a $75 fine. An officer who believes you didn't produce it because you're not insured could repeatedly charge you if you drive off. Driving an uninsured car is a more serious offence; the fine is $5,000 to $25,000 on the first conviction and $10,000 to $50,000 on subsequent ones plus possible loss of your driver's licence. This includes producing a pink slip that is found to be invalid because, for instance, you cancelled it for a refund, or the coverage lapsed when you did not pay for a renewal (claiming you did not receive the bill will not protect you).

Having bought the car, read the owner's manual, ensure that your licence (and that of any borrower) is valid, drive carefully, and think of all the money you saved. More information about transferring ownership is available from the Ministry of Consumer and Commercial Relations at 1-800-267-8847 (325-8847 in Toronto).

CHAPTER SUMMARY

The unofficial terms "consumer" and "consumer law" refer to lay persons and the regulations that affect them in the marketplace. Most statutes could be "consumer legislation" for someone, so the introduction explains what was chosen for coverage. The history behind the lack of consumer protection until recently is explained. One basic and hidden aspect of consumer-protection law is the establishment of product standards; types and regulators are outlined. Types of laws are differentiated. The chapter focuses on rights, but also touches on responsibilities. The introduction ends with how to locate federal and provincial laws.

The next main section outlines federal consumer legislation. The prime agency is Industry Canada, which governs various aspects of marketing. Three of its statutes regulate the labelling of dry goods, textiles, and precious metals; the fourth is the *Competition Act*, which deals with deception and inac-

---

[16] R.S.O. 1990, c. H.8.

curacy in advertising as well as fair trade practices. Health Canada's *Food and Drugs Act* sets purity and labelling standards in products such as foods and medicines, and the *Hazardous Products Act* regulates potentially harmful items. *The Bank Act* regulates many aspects of the banking industry.

Ontario consumers are protected primarily by the MCCR. The *Business Practices Act* focuses on misrepresentation, and the *Consumer Protection Act* covers executory contracts. The *Consumer Reporting Act* regulates what are commonly termed credit bureaus. When someone does not pay for having goods repaired or stored, The *Repair and Storage Liens Act* establishes the rights and procedures for both sides. The *Motor Vehicle Repair Act* is a recent statute designed to protect car-owners from being overcharged by mechanics. The *Sale of Goods Act* protects you if you tell a presumably knowledgeable seller what you want an item for and it turns out to be unsuitable for that use. The Financial Services Commission regulates insurance and financial institutions.

Quebec was then examined; there the *Consumer Protection Act* is a 1994 statute designed to comprehensively protect consumers and regulate businesses. Except for the occasional weak spot, it is a set of regulations that could serve as a model for other jurisdictions.

The Commentary section made a number of minor suggestions for improvements. The main recommendation is for all equivalent jurisdictions to modify their legislation with the aim of achieving as much consistency as regional differences allow.

The section on insurance outlines the principles of this industry and the federal and provincial legislative control. It also provides some basic consumer advice and sources of further information. The following main section on motor vehicles is similar, providing general consumer information and legislative data, particularly around the private transfer of car ownership in Ontario.

GLOSSARY OF NEW TERMS AND KEY CONCEPTS

bait-and-switch	A behaviour that consists of luring a customer to a store for a bargain that the seller does not plan to honour, and switching the buyer to a more profitable item.
Bank Act	The federal statute that tightly regulates banks and bank-like institutions such as trust companies.
bid rigging	The collusion by competing firms to increase the size of the bid that will be accepted.
Business Practices Act	The Ontario statute that defines and prohibits abusive selling practices.
Canadian Standards Association (CSA)	This organization is the main developer and tester of standards for a vast range of products, from boxes to boxing gloves.
caselaw	Law made up of legal rules that have been established by past court judgments, as opposed to statute law.
caveat emptor	In Latin this phrase means "Let the buyer beware."
civil law	The law and legal procedures governing disputes between individuals or between individuals and businesses constitutes the civil law, in contrast to criminal law.
common law	The unwritten law established by custom and precedent, as opposed to statutory law; the phrase also describes the Anglo-Canadian judicial system.
Competition Act	A federal statute prohibiting misleading advertising and deceptive marketing practices.
compliance with description	The right to inspect delivered goods before accepting them and to reject them if they are not as ordered.

consumer	A common, general term referring to an average or ordinary person, as opposed to a corporation, business, or professional person.
consumer law	A phrase generally refers to regulations that affect lay people in the marketplace.
Consumer Packaging and Labelling Act	A federal statute regulating the label on dry goods.
Consumer Protection Act	A comprehensive recent set of statutes that protect consumers and regulate businesses in the Province of Quebec and is part of the *Quebec Civil Code*.
Consumer Reporting Act	An Ontario statute governing credit-reporting agencies.
credit-reporting agency	A commercial firm that collects, keeps, and sells to merchants records of writs and judgments, and credit transactions.
criminal law	The law based on the *Criminal Code of Canada*, and other federal criminal law, enforced by the government prosecuting an individual or firm. Contrast with civil law.
cross selling	Behaviour consists of discounting one product if the customer buys another.
discriminatory allowance	Behaviour consists of discounts or rebates that are offered to only certain purchasers.
executory contract	A contract in which delivery of goods, performance of a service, or payment in full, is not made at the time the contract is entered into.
Financial Services Commission of Ontario	The commission regulates financial and insurance institutions.
Food and Drugs Act	A federal statute regulating purity in and labelling of products such as foods, cosmetics, medicines, and contraceptives.
good title	Meaning what you bought is yours to control, use, or resell.
grace period	In insurance, this is a time that your coverage remains in effect (while awaiting the payment for renewal) even though the policy has expired.
Hazardous Products Act	A federal statute prohibiting or regulating products that can be harmful.
Industry Canada	The prime federal government consumer-protection agency, mainly governing marketing, including packaging and labelling, and advertising.
lemon laws	A popular term for U.S. state laws that provide recourse to owners of persistently defective cars.
lien	The right of someone to keep or to put a claim on another's property to secure an unpaid bill usually for repairs or storage.
MCCR	An abbreviation stands for the Ministry of Consumer and Commercial Relations, the largest Ontario governmental agency, the main source of consumer protection in the province.
merchantability	Products that are of good quality and that can properly serve their purpose.
multilevel marketing	*See* pyramid selling.
no-fault insurance	Insurance coverage that pays all or part of the policyholder's loss regardless of who was to blame. It reduces wrangling and litigation, although fault still determines police charges and insurance premiums.
non-possessory lien	A lien on property that the owed party does not have physical possession and control over.
personal information reporting agency	A commercial firm that collects, keeps, and sells data on individuals' lifestyles and credit history to merchants.
Precious Metals Marking Act	A federal statute regulating the claims for and symbols stamped on precious metals, primarily gold and silver.
predatory pricing	A behaviour of setting a price so low as to drive out competitors.
premium	The fee charged by insurers for coverage.

product standards	Rules or conventions that ensure the safety, quality, fit, or other aspects originally of products and increasingly of services, too.
pyramid selling	The distribution of products in which the first buyer recruits others, each of whom recruits still others, and so forth is called pyramid selling and is also termed multilevel marketing.
recission	This means cancellation.
referral selling	The behaviour of offering a benefit to a buyer for finding another customer for the seller. It is illegal in Ontario and some other provinces.
Repair and Storage Liens Act **(RSLA)**	An Ontario statute governing the rights and procedures for both sides when a bill for repairs or storage is not paid.
Sale of Goods Act	A statute derived from common law, found in many jurisdictions, generally specifying that goods must be suitable for the purpose for which you announced to the seller that you will use them.
statutory laws	Laws that are enacted, written down, and printed by some level of government, as opposed to common law that originates less formally.
Textile Labelling Act	A federal statute governing the labelling mainly of clothing.
tied selling	A scheme requiring a client to buy one product as a condition of buying another.
tort-based insurance	Insurance coverage in which the insurer of the at-fault driver pays more than the not-at-fault driver, fault possibly determined at trial.
Underwriters' Laboratories of Canada (ULC)	The main developer and verifier of product standards related to safety.
VIN	The acronym that means Vehicle Identification Number, a unique series of digits and letters on a plate attached under the front left window and elsewhere on every motor vehicle. A standardized code identifies the maker, date and plant of assembly, type of vehicle, and certain equipment. Used in registration, insurance, and usually for repair records.

REVIEW QUESTIONS

1. How would you define consumer and consumer law?

2. What products that you can see right now likely have no standards, voluntary standards, and required standards?

3. Why are there more consumer protection laws concerning your purchase of a T.V. set than there are for services offering to repair it?

4. What is meant by pyramid selling, and why should it be illegal?

5. If you wanted to offer a biodegradable product, how would you justify the use of the term?

6. How are consumers protected when buying a used car in Ontario?

7. How do banks differ from other businesses?

8. Hamilton door-to-door seller Sid E. Slikker pressures Vera E. Olde to buy a Mira-Vac for $1,000. She pays $300 in cash, is credited $400 for a trade-in on her Hoover, and promises to pay the balance the next day, whereupon Sid delivers the Mira-Vac and takes the Hoover. The moments he leaves, she changes her mind. What are their rights?

9. Give an example of how you would protect yourself under the *Sale of Goods Act* in making a purchase.

10. Why are many consumers uncertain or confused about insurance?

DISCUSSION QUESTIONS

1. Why would you not expect the phrase consumer law to appear in a dictionary of legal terms?

2. Why do many commercial buildings show outside banners stating "ISO 9000 Registered"?

3. Think of an example of how the *Competition Act* would not seem easily applicable to a consumer issue in the next generation.

4. You are a federal minister. A trade organization complains that the penalties for prohibited trade practices are unreasonably high. How would you respond?

5. If you were overhauling the regulations on interest rates, what changes would you make?

6. What aspects of the *Bank Act* would you tighten and what aspects would you loosen; why?

7. How does the consumer legislation in Quebec differ generally from that in other provinces?

8. How much might you pay for motor vehicles over your lifetime, and how does this contrast with other major expenses?

9. If the Quebec *Consumer Protection Act* were to serve as a model for other jurisdictions, what changes would you recommend?

SUGGESTED READINGS

Kenkel, Joseph H., & William S. Chalmers. *Small Claims and Simplified Procedure Litigation*, 3d ed. (Markham, Ont.: Butterworths, 1998).

Morin, Guy, & François Tôth. *Loi sur la protection du consommateur et règlement d'application. Consumer Protection Act and Regulation Respecting its Application* (Scarborough, Ont.: Carswell, 1998).

Olivo, Laurence M. *Debtor Creditor Law and Procedure* (Toronto, Ont.: Emond Montgomery Publications, 1999).

Smyth, J.E., & D.A. Soberman. *The Law and Business Administration in Canada*, 8th ed. (Toronto, Ont.: Prentice-Hall, 1998).

Stikeman, E. *Competition Act and Commentary — 2000* (Markham, Ont.: Butterworths, 1999).

Willes, John A. *Contemporary Canadian Business Law*. 4th ed. (Toronto, Ont.: McGraw-Hill Ryerson, 1994).

Zuher, Marvin A. *Ontario Small Claims Court Practice*. Annual editions (Toronto, Ont.: Carswell).

Human Rights in Ontario

Stanley Gershman
BARRISTER AND SOLICITOR

Learning Objectives

At the conclusion of this chapter, the reader should be able to:

➢ understand the history of human rights legislation and the reasons for its existence

➢ distinguish between international, federal, and provincial legislation relative to human rights

➢ comprehend the history and evolution of the *Ontario Human Rights Code*

➢ identify the grounds, social areas, and exceptions included in the Code

➢ appreciate the fluidity of human rights legislation and how it continues to evolve in response to changes in our concept of social justice

TABLE OF CONTENTS

THE HISTORY OF HUMAN RIGHTS

> Human Rights legislation ... is the skillful blending of educational and legal techniques *in the pursuit of social justice*. (Daniel Hill, former chair of the Ontario Human Rights Commission, italics added.)

The provincial and federal human rights laws and the *Canadian Charter of Rights and Freedoms* are relatively recent manifestations of a human rights revolution that can be traced through certain outstanding historical documents. The first was the proclamation of the Magna Carta ("The Great Charter") by King John of England in 1215 after the barons had rebelled against his disregard for the limits of his power. Later, in 1689, Parliament passed the Bill of Rights, confirming the rights of the people and further limiting the powers of the king. The demand by the English nobility for the sharing of political power by the monarchy was a demand for greater equality and a response to the tyranny of the monarchy. The revolution was broadened and carried forward in the American Declaration of Independence of 1776, which preceded the American Revolution; the French Declaration of the Rights of Man and Citizen of 1789, which inspired the French Revolution; and the American Bill of Rights of 1791, which was enacted as an amendment to the American Constitution. These latter proclamations were the response of peoples oppressed by the tyranny of both the monarchy and the nobility, and they were demands made by such people for greater equality. They helped provide the basis for the formation of modern democratic institutions and forms of government.

The Declaration of Independence stated that, "We hold these truths to be self-evident, that all men are created equal, that they are endowed by their Creator with certain inalienable Rights, that among these are Life, Liberty and the pursuit of Happiness — That to secure these rights, Governments are instituted among Men...." In fighting against the tyranny of the English monarchy and the English social system, the Americans wished to emphasize the equality of all men, in the sense that they wished to denounce the notion of special advantages being meted out to people on the basis of their accident of birth (i.e., the English class system and an aristocracy based on birthright). They stated that the very justification for the existence of government was the notion that it exists to promote and secure certain basic rights for all its citizens equally.[1]

Unfortunately, their concept of the equality of all men and their notion of social justice were grounded in a different social milieu and reality than what exists today. The early Americans were predominantly of white, European background, and they brought with them their prejudices towards others of different backgrounds. These "others" — such as Aboriginals and Blacks — being different, were conceived of as devoid of the same human attributes or qualities as they themselves possessed. The Americans also came from a monarchical society conceived of as a hierarchy of graded ranks and degrees. These influences persuaded the Americans to subjugate and exploit these others, and deny them the full rights of citizenship. The Americans also brought with them the accumulated prejudices of their culture towards women. These "others", then, did not, at first, appear to fit the definition of the "men" referred to in their stated ideal of equality. As a result, the members of the American power structure were not only victims but also per-

---

[1] Not only did the American Colonialists wish to create a different sort of social hierarchy, they were also concerned about the oppressive taxes and trade restrictions imposed by a British king and a British Parliament in which they had no representation. The Americans were influenced by the Lockean concept of liberty in their belief that political power could only be legitimately exercised with the consent of the governed.

petrators of oppression.[2] Nonetheless, according to one prominent American historian, by the time the American Revolution had run its course, American society had been radically and thoroughly transformed. Far from remaining monarchical, hierarchy-ridden subjects, Americans soon became the most liberal and democratic people in the world. The Revolution and its ideology were conducive to, and made possible, the anti-slavery and women's rights movements of the 19th century, as well as current egalitarian thinking. It made the interests and the prosperity of ordinary people — their "pursuit of happiness" — the goal of society and government. They substituted their own notion of a meritocracy for the European aristocracy, and they considered that a man's merit rested entirely with himself, without any regard to family, blood, or connection. But the achievement of higher office and position was not considered available to the existing poor and humble inhabitants, and was more likely to accrue to their sons, who could acquire the requisite education, skills and refinement. Black slavery became conspicuous in a way that it had not been in the older monarchical society, and many Americans began attacking it with a vehemence that had been inconceivable earlier. This change in attitude led inexorably to the Civil War and the eventual abolition of slavery in 1875 with the 13th amendment to the U.S. Constitution.[3]

Strangely, however, slavery as an institution had been abolished in England and Canada earlier than in the United States. The Kings Bench, in 1772, made its first anti-slavery decision. In 1833 Britain passed the *Abolition of Slavery Act*, and in 1838 it abolished slavery throughout the Empire. In 1793 Upper Canada prohibited slavery but did not free the existing slaves until 1819. A study was released in 2002 by Anti-Slavery International to coincide with the United Nations session on slavery, which reported that tens of millions of slaves continue to exist today in Africa, Asia, and Latin America.

Canada's founding ideal was never stated in terms of rights and equality, but was based on "peace, order, and good government". The British government was perceived relatively benignly by both the French Canadians, whose rights were guaranteed by the *Quebec Act* in 1774, and the United Empire Loyalists, who were given the right to settle in Ontario in 1791 and who felt more loyal and less rebellious towards the British government than the Americans did. Protection of individual liberty and equality was less of a priority to the Canadians of the time than it had been to the early Americans.[4]

World War II was a great catalyst for the continued evolution of human rights. It brought together groups whose differences faded before the common threat of the Axis powers (Germany, Italy and Japan). People of different nationalities, colour and ethnic and religious backgrounds fighting together against tyranny helped to break down the barriers created by such differences. The prominent role of women in maintaining industrial productivity while men were away fighting changed society's perception of their proper place. The Jewish Holocaust made obvious to the world community the need for united action to protect human rights. It led to the formation of the United Nations — the beginning of a world community — and to the proclamation and acceptance of the Universal Declaration of Human Rights. The later struggle

---

[2] Thomas Jefferson, who drafted the Declaration of Independence, apparently wished to condemn slavery (in an early draft of the Declaration) but was prevented from doing so by his fellow Virginian slaveholders. It was ironic that the United States would proclaim that all men were created equal and engage in a fight for freedom and liberty, and yet be a nation of slaveholders.

[3] Gordon S. Wood, "The War of Independence was a Social Revolution" in William Dudley, ed., *The American Revolution — Opposing Viewpoints* (San Diego, Calif.: Greenhaven Press Inc., 1992) at 264–67.

[4] Mr. Justice Mark McGuigan, "The Protection of Freedom and the Achievement of Equality in Canada" in G. Gall, ed., *Civil Liberties in Canada — Entering the 1980s*, 9th ed. (Toronto, Ont.: Butterworth's, 1982) at 225–26.

The "Persons" Case: *Edwards v. Attorney General for Canada*
[1930] A.C. 124

EXHIBIT 21.1

> ... if in the past no women had acceded to such a position, it was because custom prevented it, and customs become traditions stronger than law and remain unchallenged long after having lost their raison d'être.
>
> — The British Privy Council

Canadian women received the legislative right to vote in their own name in 1918, and by 1921 the first woman was elected to the House of Commons.[†] Despite this progress towards equality between men and women, there remained the question of whether or not women could be appointed to the Senate of Canada. The issue was brought to the forefront in 1927 when Emily Murphy, an Edmonton judge and women's rights advocate, spearheaded a group of five women who put the constitutional question, based on the *British North America Act of 1867* ("BNA"), before the Supreme Court of Canada. Ingeniously, Murphy found a little-known section of the *Supreme Court Act* that allowed five persons to petition the government to obtain a legal interpretation of a provision in the BNA.

Section 24 of the *British North America Act* stipulated that properly qualified "persons" appointed by the Governor General "had to be at least 30 years old, hold property, be worth at least four thousand dollars and reside within the province for which they were appointed". While some women would have met the qualifications regarding age, property, finances, and residency set out in the Act, the issue soon boiled down to the pivotal question of whether or not women were considered "persons" under the BNA.

In 1928 the Supreme Court of Canada ruled that women were not "persons" under the BNA. The Court based this decision on a narrow and historical interpretation of the word "persons", stating that at the time the BNA was enacted, women were unable to serve in public office at common law and, thus, the word "persons" did not apply to women. Canada could be seen to be a patriarchical society at the time, and Ms. Murphy determined that the most efficient way to resolve the issue was to have it looked at from a "purely legal" aspect: that is, does "persons", under the BNA, include women? Therefore, it was decided to put the matter before the final court of appeal for Canadians — the Judicial Committee of the Privy Council in London, England.

The Privy Council heard the appeal in the summer of 1929 and rejected the Crown argument based on the narrow, historical interpretation of the word "persons". The court indicated that the word "persons" was an ambiguous term that did not provide clarity as to the intention of section 24. Therefore, their Lordships stated in the decision rendered that "[t]he Act should be on all occasions interpreted in a large, liberal and comprehensive spirit, considering the magnitude of the subjects with which it purports to deal in very few words". (Even today the courts favour this broad approach to the interpretation of constitutional rights, and this approach has facilitated the ongoing evolution of human rights.) The Privy Council went on to say that the fact that women had been given the right to vote under the BNA grew from an interpretation of "persons" that included both men and women. In addition, their Lordships had analyzed sections of the BNA in the hopes of illuminating the meaning of "persons". The BNA included the term "male persons" in other sections, and their Lordships concluded that where such term was "expressly used it is desired to confine the matter in issue to males". In other words, the Act was clear when it was speaking to only one sex and, therefore, the more general "persons" should be read to include both men and women.

Based on this analysis, their Lordships stated that they "have come to the conclusion that the word 'persons' in section 24 includes members both of the male and female sex and that, therefore, the question propounded by the Governor-General must be answered in the affirmative and ... women are eligible to be summoned to and become members of the Senate of Canada". Prime Minister Mackenzie King appointed Canada's first woman senator in 1930.

---

† Historical background sourced from "The 'Persons' Case", National Archives of Canada; and "Defining 'Persons' Under the BNA Act", Department of Justice Canada: <http://canada.justice.gc.ca/en/justice2000/30mile.html>.

EXHIBIT 21.2	Preamble to the *Ontario Human Rights Code*

"WHEREAS recognition of the inherent dignity and the equal and inalienable rights of all members of the human family is the foundation of freedom, justice and peace in the world and is in accord with the Universal Declaration of Human Rights as proclaimed by the United Nations;

AND WHEREAS it is public policy in Ontario to recognize the dignity and worth of every person and to provide for equal rights and opportunities without discrimination that is contrary to law, and having as its aim the creation of a climate of understanding and mutual respect for the dignity and worth of each person so that each person feels a part of the community and able to contribute fully to the development and well-being of the community and the Province;

AND WHEREAS these principles have been confirmed in Ontario by a number of enactments of the Legislature and it is desirable to revise and extend the protection of human rights in Ontario;

Therefore, Her Majesty, by and with the advice and consent of the Legislative Assembly of the Province of Ontario, Enacts as follows....

---

for racial equality by the civil rights movement in the United States and the parallel movements promoting women's rights, gay rights, Aboriginal rights, children's rights, seniors' rights, language rights and the rights of the disabled have all put social justice at the top of our political and social agenda. These developments have led to an evolving concept of social justice and to the enactment and development of rights legislation.

It is the recognition of the equal worth and dignity of all men and women, of whatever race, colour, ethnicity, nationality, political or religious belief, gender, or any other characteristic that seemingly differentiates us, that underlies the equality provisions of our Charter and our human rights codes. These codes reflect a new morality and a new concept of social justice.

As with all conceptions of morality, a misunderstood, distorted, or misapplied idea of human rights can deteriorate into the dangerous absurdities and over-reactions sometimes referred to as a concern for the "politically correct".[5] Together with a disregard for due process, this mindset can lead to hearings akin to witch hunts. It is surprising how often in history an instrument created to achieve justice has, instead, been used as an instrument of oppression.[6]

---

[5] An example is the statement that a person's value is necessarily associated with a group identity rather than an individual character. It is illustrated by material distributed in a university orientation course that teaches that Blacks, not being in a dominant position in society, cannot be racist, and that white males in positions of power generally make racist decisions that consciously impact more favourably on white people than on minorities: Alan Charles Kors & Harvey Silverglate, *The Shadow University* (New York, N.Y.: The Free Press, 1998) at 220. Contrast this with Martin Luther King's famous plea for the day when a person would be judged by the content of the person's character rather than by the colour of the person's skin.

[6] A further example is provided by Ian Hunter in his *Globe and Mail* article, "What next? Anti-harassment training in the crib?" (December 29, 2006), where he refers to a decision by an administrator of the Washington County School Board who imposed a suspension on a five-year-old student in the State of Maryland for sexual harassment of a girl in his class. The boy had mischieviously pinched her bottom. Online: <http://www.iapm.ca/newsmanager/anmviewer.asp?a=511&z=13&print=yes>

THE NATURE OF HUMAN RIGHTS CODES

Human rights codes, including Ontario's, can be seen to be an effort to provide the citizens of our society, especially those identified with minority groups who have traditionally been discriminated against, with freedom from discrimination and to remove any unfair disadvantages that may have been imposed on them by the majority or by those who have exercised social and economic power. These Acts also seek to recognize and preserve the dignity and self-esteem of our citizens by protecting such persons against any harassment based on such discrimination. To that extent, our human rights legislation extends our democratic values. As we discuss later, it also paradoxically limits the freedom of others. People are restricted from interfering with equality rights, and these restrictions may interfere with such constitutionally recognized freedoms as freedom of speech, freedom of opinion, and freedom of religion, as well as certain economic freedoms, such as freedom of contract and freedom of commerce.[7]

It may seem contradictory that, in order to protect the rights of some, we must restrict the rights and freedoms of others; but our ultimate goal is not solely to protect individual rights or freedoms but, rather, to achieve social justice and a peaceful community free from oppression and abuse.

As has been stated, what is sought is equality of access and opportunity: that is, freedom from discrimination or differential treatment based on characteristics (e.g., gender, creed) that our sense of justice dictates should not be considered relevant to one's opportunity to obtain the services, goods, or advantages available in our community.[8] There are, and likely always will be, benefits, advantages, and opportunities that will accrue to some because of individual merit, personal characteristics, or good fortune. Thus, these codes do not purport to remedy all forms of differential treatment but only discrimination based on those characteristics considered to be irrelevant. Our sense of justice dictates that it is a person's character, not the person's skin colour, and the person's conduct, not the person's group identity, that should determine how we deal with that person.

There has been some criticism that the scope of human rights legislation is too narrow. It has become generally accepted that social justice requires that the distribution of wealth and income in society cannot be allowed to be determined solely by the natural distribution of abilities and talents.[9] In other words, he who has been given less in life may have to be given more by the law — the notion of distributive justice. But the degree of one's adherence to this notion depends on one's political orientation, and so is not crystallized as a human right in our Charter or our human rights codes. There is a concern that ensuring greater equality of benefits would lead to social stagnation. This type of social justice would lead to economic inefficiency. It would rob individuals of the incentive to work — to achieve results by utilizing their talents and abilities. Some say that society may even undermine the self-confidence of those at the bottom by telling them that the answer to poverty involves granting them more rights rather than any efforts they may make to improve themselves through their own hard work and self-denial. Our rights revolution

---

[7] Our later discussion of the provisions of the *Ontario Human Rights Code* will illustrate this point.

[8] It should be noted that the *Charter of Rights and Freedoms* does not appear to restrict illegal discrimination to specific grounds. The grounds are listed merely as examples of particular forms of discrimination. In effect, this allows the courts to find illegal grounds for discrimination beyond those listed in s. 15. In Ontario, any new grounds for discrimination under the *Human Rights Code* can be added only by the legislature. In these ways our human rights legislation can grow to keep pace with our evolving concept of social justice.

[9] Mr. Justice Mark MacGuigan, *supra* at 35.

and rights culture has created too much emphasis on social rights and not enough emphasis on individual responsibility and duty.

Although there is some truth in these criticisms of a broader human rights approach, ensuring equality of opportunity may require more than simply providing negative rights or protection from discrimination on what we perceive to be irrelevant grounds. It could be argued that if we value equality of opportunity for all our citizens as a measure of social justice, then perhaps we must institute positive rights that create the economic, social, and educational conditions for this to occur: certain government services, the maintenance of public institutions, some measure of income redistribution, and the definition of rights that will encompass such values. Most people cannot overcome the barriers that a lack of resources entails without a more even playing field. These measures would help accomplish the goal, stated in the preamble to the *Ontario Human Rights Code*, that each person should feel a part of the community and be able to contribute fully to its development and well-being. It would also give more citizens the opportunity to be engaged in what Thomas Jefferson proposed as their inalienable right to pursue happiness.

COMPARISON OF THE UNIVERSAL DECLARATION OF HUMAN RIGHTS, THE CHARTER AND HUMAN RIGHTS CODES

The UN Universal Declaration of Human Rights ("Universal Declaration") was, along with certain international covenants, an international statement of rights agreed to by many of the world's nations, and ultimately was a catalyst for the formulation of the human rights codes in many nations, including Canada and its provinces, as well as for the enactment of a charter of rights as part of our Constitution.[10] The Ontario *Human Rights Code*, the first such code enacted in Canada, was originally passed in 1962, and was followed by enactments by the other provinces and the federal government. The rights set out in the Universal Declaration went far beyond those subsequently set out in the Ontario Code because, in addition to equality rights and freedom from discrimination, the Universal Declaration purported to also guarantee economic and educational rights. In article 25 it declared that "everyone has the right to a standard of living adequate for the health and well being of himself and of his family, including food, clothing, receiving medical care, and necessary social services, and the right to security in the event of unemployment ..." and in article 23.3, "everyone who works has the right to a just and favourable remuneration ensuring ... an existence worthy of human dignity." In article 26, it proclaimed that everyone has the right to a free elementary education, and that higher education should be equally accessible to all on the basis of merit. Civil and political rights, as well as equality rights, were guaranteed in a subsequent *International Covenant on Civil and Political Rights* and in other covenants that the member nations agreed to. The inclusion of social and economic rights in the Universal Declaration reflected the broader interpretation of equality of opportunity described in the previous section.

The *Charter of Rights and Freedoms* ("Charter") forms part of our Constitution and applies to the actions and legislation of federal and provincial governments. The Charter protects various rights and freedoms, such as civil rights, political rights, legal rights, and equality rights, including freedom from discrimination, but does not protect economic or educational rights (other parts of the Constitution, however, do offer some protections for educational

---

[10] John Humphrey, a Canadian law professor at McGill University, played a prominent role in the drafting of the Universal Declaration and in shepherding it through the process of its adoption by the General Assembly in 1948.

rights), as such protection would appear to violate the prevailing North American political ethos. The Charter, in this sense, then, fails to fulfill all the goals of the Universal Declaration.

Human rights codes such as Ontario's ("Code") are even more limited than the Charter. The Code protects only those rights known as equality rights, or the freedom from discrimination that is found in section 15 of the Charter:

> (1) Every individual is equal before and under the law and has the right to the equal protection and equal benefit of the law without discrimination and, in particular, without discrimination based on race, national or ethnic origin, colour, religion, sex, age or mental or physical disability.

> (2) Subsection (1) does not preclude any law, program or activity that has as its object the amelioration of conditions of disadvantaged individuals or groups including those that are disadvantaged because of race, national or ethnic origin, colour, religion, sex, age, or mental or physical disability.

The Code carries over into the private sphere the constitutional restrictions imposed on government by section 15 of the Charter. The concept of human rights in Ontario's legislation also has a much more restrictive meaning than it does in the Universal Declaration because it is based on the more restrictive concept of social justice and equality of opportunity that does not extend to shared benefits or economic rights.

Neither does the Code deal directly with an individual's political and civil rights, as such rights are related to the relationship between government and the individual and so are dealt with in the Charter. The Code protects individuals against discrimination in private transactions with other individuals and private institutions or agencies.[11] The Code is not part of the Canadian Constitution but is only a statute passed by the provincial legislature. Because of the importance of its subject, however, it has been given a quasi-constitutional status by legislation[12] and by the courts[13] so that its provisions are generously and broadly interpreted and given primacy over other statutes within the same jurisdiction: that is, any provision in another Ontario statute that conflicts with a provision in the Code will be considered inoperative.

In fact, as discussed above, human rights codes can simply be looked at as the application of section 15 of the Charter — equality rights — to the private sphere. The courts have indicated that all human rights codes must be interpreted in a manner consistent with the interpretation of section 15 of the Charter.[14] And all provincial and federal human rights legislation is said to be relevant to the interpretation of any one human rights statute, regardless of mere differences in terminology, because their objectives are the same and, legally, must comply with section 15 in order to be valid.

The court will apply this notion in cases that come before it where a particular human rights code does not reflect the protections given against discrimination in the Charter. The court will strike out the Code's offensive provision.[15]

---

[11] It also protects individuals against the actions of government officials and programs that provide public services or benefits to such individuals (OHR Code, s. 47(1)): *Ontario Human Rights Commission v. Ontario Ministry of Health* (1994), 19 O.R. (3d) 387 (C.A.).

[12] In Ontario by s. 47(2) of the Code.

[13] *Winnipeg School Division No. 1 v. Craton*, [1985] 2 S.C.R. 150, 21 DLR (4th) 1.

[14] *Entrop v. Imperial Oil Ltd.* (2000), C.C.E.L. (3d) 19 (Ont. C.A.).

[15] In fact, the Supreme Court of Canada has even gone so far as to amend a provincial human rights statute to add a ground of discrimination (sexual orientation) that was absent from the statute. In the case, the employee of a college was terminated on the grounds of violating the college's policy against homosexuality. The Alberta Human

An example was the case of *Re Blainey v. Ontario Hockey Association, et al.*[16] Justine Blainey had qualified on the basis of her ability to play for a hockey team that belonged to the Ontario Hockey Association ("O.H.A."). The rules of the Association, however, prohibited females from playing on its hockey teams. Blainey then lodged a complaint with the Ontario Human Rights Commission ("O.H.R.C."), claiming the prohibition violated her right under section 1 of the Code to equal treatment with respect to services and facilities without discrimination because of sex. The O.H.R.C. dismissed her case because of section 19 of the Code (now s. 20(1)), which stated that section 1 was not infringed where participation in an athletic activity is restricted to persons of the same sex. The Ontario Court of Appeal allowed Blainey's appeal from this decision on the basis that section 19 violated section 15 of the Charter, since it was governmental legislation that denied equality of treatment based on sex. The court struck out this section of the Code so that Blainey could then re-apply under the Code without having to face section 19. The O.H.R.C. then allowed Blainey her new application, striking out the O.H.A.'s regulation as a violation of section 1 of the *Ontario Human Rights Code*.

The court pointed out, however, that section 15 equality rights are not absolute by virtue of section 1 of the Charter.[17] An enactment may deny equality of treatment based on a prohibited ground and, nonetheless, be constitutional if it is shown to be a reasonable limit on such rights that is justifiable in a free and democratic society. Section 19's allowing discrimination against females was too broad a prohibition to be justified. It was not limited to situations where it would be justified: that is, where it was necessary to promote public decency or for the physical protection of participants. Had section 19 stated these limitations, it likely would have been considered valid and enforceable and could have been applied in the Blainey case to test the enforceability of the O.H.A. regulation.[18]

The idea that human rights are not absolute is also reflected in the provisions of the human rights codes and the way they are interpreted. Part II of the Code reflects this concept, as does the reasonableness requirement in the definition of harassment in the Code and the interpretations of the Human Rights Code sections by Human Rights Boards of Inquiry.

THE HISTORY AND EVOLUTION OF HUMAN RIGHTS LAW IN ONTARIO

The courts used to consider acts of discrimination irrelevant on the basis of freedom of contract and freedom of commerce. Any person could conduct a business or execute a deal in the manner that would best advance that

---

Rights Commission refused to accept his complaint that the grounds for his dismissal were discriminatory because the Alberta Human Rights statute did not include sexual orientation as a prohibited ground of discrimination. The court found that the omission of this protection was an unjustified violation of s. 15 of the Charter, and ordered that the term "sexual orientation" be "read" into the statute as if it were part of the statute. (*Vriend v. Alberta* (1998), 156 DLR (4th) 385.)

[16] (1986), 54 O.R. (2d) 513, 26 DLR (4th) 728 (Ont. C.A.)

[17] The *Canadian Charter of Rights and Freedoms* (s. 1) guarantees the rights and freedoms set out in it subject only to such reasonable limits prescribed by law as can be demonstrably justified in a free and democratic society.

[18] The Ontario government subsequently introduced s. 20(1) of the *Ontario Human Rights Code*, which states that the right under s. 1 to equal treatment with respect to service and facilities without discrimination because of sex is not infringed where the use of the services or facilities is restricted to persons of the same sex on the ground of public decency.

person's own interests, even if that meant discriminating against others on the basis of their race or colour, so long as that person complied with any contractual obligations he or she had entered into.[19] This meant that while, in 1899, a theatre was found to be in breach of contract for refusing to seat a black couple who had purchased tickets in advance for a concert, in 1919 a theatre was able to refuse to enter into a contract to sell an orchestra seat to a black man and to offer to sell him only a balcony seat. In the 1899 example, a contract had been broken, and the fact that the couple were black was irrelevant. In the second case, the theatre's policy that prohibited the sale of orchestra seats to Blacks was considered lawful because it offended neither morality nor public order. In 1924 a court upheld the decision of a restaurant owner who refused to serve some patrons solely because of their race. A person had the freedom to decide with whom to enter into contracts. Even if public policy at the time would consider racial discrimination as offensive (which it didn't), there would be a problem prohibiting discrimination using the common law.

It is true that contracts that offended public policy (i.e., contracts that the courts considered by their terms to be prejudicial to the social or economic interest of the community) were forbidden. The difficulty is that public policy would allow the courts to strike out a term of a contract already entered into, but there was no contractual or common law concept that required a person to enter into a contract he or she did not wish to enter into in the first place. Contracts were by definition supposed to be voluntary arrangements. Human rights legislation, in effect, embodied the novel concept that persons would be required to *enter into contracts* they did not wish to enter into to provide goods or services, or, at least, they could not refuse to enter such contracts on the basis of any of the prohibited grounds.

In 1944 Ontario passed the *Racial Discrimination Act*. The Act prohibited the displaying of signs or other representations expressing racial or religious discrimination. For the first time, an Ontario legislature recognized that racial and religious discrimination was against public policy. This meant that human rights could no longer be subordinated to commercial, contractual or property rights. In 1945 Mr. Justice Mackay of the Ontario High Court, in the case *Re Drummond Wren*,[20] used the statutory recognition of this policy to strike down a property covenant that prohibited the sale of a property to "Jews or persons of objectionable nationality". The illegal covenant did not violate the actual provision of the Act, but it did violate the public policy expressed by the Act's provisions.[21]

In 1947 Saskatchewan passed a more comprehensive statute, the *Saskatchewan Bill of Rights*, which dealt with discrimination as well as political and civil liberties. The Ontario *Racial Discrimination Act* and the Saskatchewan *Bill of Rights* were both quasi-criminal in nature, so complainant victims had to resort to penal sanctions through the criminal courts to enforce the rights they had been given. There were many drawbacks. First, many victims were reluctant to take criminal action. There were also many obstacles to a successful prosecution. The victims had to substantiate their claim using the criminal burden of proof: that is, beyond a reasonable doubt, which was more onerous than the civil burden of proof. It was extremely difficult to prove that a person had not been denied access for a reason other than a discriminatory one. Criminal court judges were also reluctant to convict anyone for what they

---

[19] *Christie v. York Corporation* [1940], S.C.R. 140.
[20] (1945), O.R. 778.
[21] Ian Hunter, "Human Rights Legislation in Canada: Its Origin, Development and Interpretation" (1976) 15 U. Western Ontario. L. Rev. 21 at 25.

did not regard as a criminal act. The sanction of a fine did not really help the person discriminated against in obtaining a job or accommodation or service. Victims were discouraged from lodging complaints because of these difficulties and, often, the very existence of the anti-discriminatory legislation was not well publicized (or promoted) and, therefore, not well known.[22]

As a result, in 1951 Ontario passed the *Fair Employment Practices Act*[23] and, later, the *Fair Accommodation Practices Act*[24]. In the place of the victim having to lay an **information** to initiate a prosecution, provision was made for the filing of a complaint with the relevant government ministry. The process continued with an administrative investigation, then conciliation and possible settlement. However, the onus for bringing the matter forward was still placed on the individual victim, although the administrative machinery of the state was placed at his disposal. There were few or no ministry staff who were assigned this task on a full-time basis. As a result, few complaints were made or, if made, processed.

Finally, in 1962, Ontario enacted the *Ontario Human Rights Code*, which encompassed a broad range of human rights protections to be administered by the Ontario Human Rights Commission, which had been established a year earlier. The rationale behind the establishment of the Commission and of the procedural and substantive provisions of the Code was that the prevention of discrimination was important not only to the individual victim but also to the community as a whole. The Supreme Court of Canada pointed out in a 1986 decision that the Code's main approach is not to punish the perpetrator of discrimination but to provide relief for the victim of discrimination.[25]

THE ONTARIO HUMAN RIGHTS CODE

The 1962 version of the Code was a much simpler version of the present Code. There were only six recognized grounds of discrimination: race, creed, colour, nationality, ancestry, and place of origin. By 1980 there were 8 grounds, sex and marital status having been added. By 1990 there were 13 basic grounds, and a 14th ground was added in 1999. In the 1990s, new concepts, such as constructive discrimination, discrimination by association, harassment, and the validity of affirmative action programs were added. The continued addition of new grounds over time and the introduction of new concepts reflect the continuing evolution of our society's vision of social justice.

The Code is directed to eliminating discrimination in various social areas, yet does not define the concept of **discrimination**. A survey of early human rights decisions by Professor Ian Hunter led him to define the term as follows:

> Discrimination means treating people differently because of ... [one of the prohibited grounds] as result of which the complainant suffers adverse consequences, or a serious affront to dignity; the motive for the discriminatory treatment, ... is irrelevant, except possibly in mitigation of the penalty.[26]

The Basic Rights and Responsibilities

The *Ontario Human Rights Code* contains an introductory section (or preamble) and five parts. Part I sets out the basic rights and responsibilities, and

---

[22] See *R v. McKay* (1955), 113 CCC 56.
[23] S.O. 1951, c. 24.
[24] S.O. 1954, c. 28.
[25] *O'Malley v. Simpson-Sears Ltd.* (1986), 64 NR 161 (S.C.C.).
[26] Ian Hunter, *Human Rights Legislation in Canada* at 33–34.

consists of nine sections. These sections set out the right of every person to equal treatment with respect to what are called various "**social areas**", including services, goods and facilities (s. 1), and the occupancy of accommodation (s. 2(1)), the making of contracts (s. 3), employment (s. 5(1)), and membership in any trade union, occupational association or self-governing profession (s. 6). The protection directed against discrimination in these areas is based on 15 grounds, including the original 1962 grounds, except for nationality:

- race
- ancestry
- place of origin
- colour
- ethnic origin
- citizenship
- creed (religion)
- sex
- sexual orientation (heterosexuality or homosexuality)
- age
- marital status (single, married, divorced, separated, common law partnership)
- family status (parent, child relationship)
- disability
- the receipt of public assistance
- criminal record

Same-sex partnership status was added in 1999.[27] The right to equal accommodation now also includes discrimination against those in receipt of public assistance, which was added as a 14th prohibited ground of discrimination in 2005.[28] The right to equal treatment with regard to employment adds record of offences as a 15th prohibited ground as of 2005, but this ground is defined as meaning a provincial offence (as opposed to a criminal or federal offence) or a criminal offence in respect of which a pardon has been granted. Therefore, a criminal record can still be used as a basis for refusing employment without attracting a human rights complaint.

Part I also prohibits various forms of harassment based on the 15 grounds in accommodation (s. 2(2)) and employment (s. 5(2)). Harassment on the basis of sex in accommodation and the workplace is set out separately (s. 7(1) and (2)), and protects everyone from sexual solicitation by a person in a position to confer a benefit and from reprisal for turning down such a solicitation (s. 7(3)). Harassment is defined in Part II, section 10 as engaging in a course of vexatious comment or conduct that is known or ought reasonably to be known to be unwelcome. Boards of Inquiry have expanded the statutory definitions so that both the victim's reaction to the harassing conduct or words must be a reasonable reaction in the circumstances and, also, a reasonable respondent would be aware that the words or conduct were offensive. As stated by the Board in *Gnosh v. Douglas Inc. (No. 2)*[29] (a case involving harassment based on handicap), "[whether the comments in that case amounted to harassment] depends upon whether reasonable people similarly handicapped would find such conduct to be unwelcome, and if so, whether reasonable people in the respondent's position would know that to be the case."

---

[27] S.C. 1999, c. 6, s. 28.
[28] OHR Code, s. 2(1).
[29] 17 C.H.R.R. at D221–223

Indirect Discrimination

According to section 9, "No person shall ... do, directly or indirectly, anything that infringes a right under this part." This section prohibits **indirect discrimination** or harassment. For example, if a building manager directs her superintendent not to rent to people of a particular ethnicity, both the manager and the superintendent can be named in the human rights complaint because the manager indirectly caused the discrimination on the prohibited ground. The section can also be used to support a claim for the creation of a **poisoned environment** or indirect harassment. The complainant feels that her workplace or housing is hostile or unwelcoming to her because of insulting or degrading comments about others, similarly situated, in the context of a ground in the Code.

Constructive Discrimination

Finally, it should be noted that identical treatment is not necessarily synonymous with equal treatment and might amount to discrimination. In a B.C. case a mining company, after a complaint, made its campsite accommodations available to both male and female employees. The company, however, made no structural alterations to its bunkhouses, so female employees would have to share toilet and shower facilities with male residents. A female employee filed a complaint of sex discrimination, and the company stated that it had made its camp accommodation available to its female employees on the same terms and conditions as its male employees. The Board of Inquiry found discrimination, saying that discrimination can result from strict equality as well as inequality and that identical treatment does not necessarily mean equal treatment or the absence of discrimination.[30] The female employee would, in effect, have to endure embarrassment, and modesty would prevent her from continuing her employment. This situation is now covered by section 11(1) of the Ontario Code, which introduced the concept of constructive discrimination.

    Constructive discrimination arises when the application of a nondiscriminatory requirement, qualification, or other factor results in discrimination (s. 11(1)).[31] The requirement (qualification or other factor) does not *expressly* exclude any group. However, when the particular requirement is met, the *result* is discriminatory. The section, however, exempts the respondent in such a situation from liability where the questioned requirement is reasonable and bona fide in the circumstances,[32] or the Act specifically indicates that to discriminate because of such ground is not an infringement of a right. Imposing a height or weight restriction as a requirement for a job that would effectively exclude women would amount to a violation of this section unless the respondent could show that the requirement or policy was reasonable and bone fide in the circumstances, or that the Code declares that such requirement is not an infringement.

The BFOR (Bona Fide Occupational Requirement) Defence

Section 11(1) allows an employer to refuse to employ a member of a "discriminated" group if the refusal is based on a BFOR, but the Board of Inquiry must first be satisfied that the needs of members of that group cannot be accommodated without undue hardship to the respondent (s. 11(2)). In the B.C. mining case discussed above, if the mining company had refused to hire the female complainant on the basis that she would have to share shower and

---

[30] Ian Hunter, *ibid.* at 32, referring to *Tharp v. Lornex Mining Corporation, Report of a Board of Inquiry under the B.C. Human Rights Code* dated 1975 at 13.

[31] This is why constructive discrimination is also referred to as adverse effect discrimination.

[32] This is known as a BFOR (i.e., a bona fide occupational requirement).

change room facilities with the men, then the company could argue that in the light of common conceptions of public decency, this factor for refusing employment was reasonable and bona fide. The employer, to be successful, however, would have to show that building a separate shower and change room facility was excessively expensive and would create an undue hardship.[33]

The Balancing of Rights and Freedoms

Part II is called "Interpretation and Application" and clarifies definitions and the interpretation and application of the rights set out in Part I. Its provisions implicitly recognize that rights and freedoms are not absolute and, in any given situation, may be in conflict, requiring a balancing of such rights. This approach supports the idea that the remedying of a violation of a person's equality or group rights might conflict with another person's individual rights or freedoms or other values, and supports the Code's overriding philosophy that the proper resolution of a human rights complaint may often involve mediation or conciliation. As one Ontario Court of Appeal judge stated, "Most legislation that attempts to benefit one segment of society is [in a broad sense] discriminatory of those not the object of its beneficence."[34]

In order to understand the basis for such competing claims, we need to consider the section of the Charter in which many such claims or rights are set out. Section 2 states the following:

> Everyone has the following fundamental freedoms:
> (a) freedom of conscience and religion;
> (b) freedom of thought, belief, opinion and expression, including freedom of the press and other media of communication;
> (c) freedom of peaceful assembly; and
> (d) freedom of association.

These and other Charter rights must also be balanced against section 1 of the Charter as discussed on page 500 above. To illustrate the conflict between competing rights and values, the *National Post*, in an editorial, recently criticized a ruling of a one-woman Board of Inquiry of the Saskatchewan Human Rights Commission. The ruling dealt with a 1997 newspaper advertisement placed by the individual respondent, Mr. Owens, who is an evangelical Christian. The ad contained a drawing of two men holding hands surrounded by a circle with a slash through it. Accompanying the drawing were four passages from the Bible that support the view that homosexuality is a sin. The inquiry officer stated that this ad infringed the equivalent of the *Ontario Human Rights Code*, section 13, prohibiting a person "who publishes, displays or causes the publication or display of any ... representation" that is intended by the person to cause the infringement of a right under Part I. The officer stated the ad would "tend to expose homosexuals to hatred and ridicule." The officer said that "[t]here [was] no question that the respondent believed that he was publicly expressing his honestly held religious belief." Yet, since those beliefs could be interpreted to be "an affront to the complainants' dignity on the basis of their sexual orientation", the adjudicator ordered both respondents (Mr. Owens and the newspaper) to pay $4,500.00 to the complainants and forbade them from publishing similar messages in the future. The *National Post* editorial was concerned about the violation of the respondent's freedom of speech. The bedrock principle of free speech is that

---

[33] For an authoritative interpretation and application of this concept by the Supreme Court of Canada, see *British Columbia (Public Service Employee Relations Commission) v B.C. G.S.E.V.* (1999), 176 DLR (4th) 1.
[34] Finlayson J.A., *ibid.* at 37, *Re Blainey*.

society should not prohibit "the expression of ideas that we find offensive or disagreeable". Another author, commenting on a similar case in the same newspaper, stated that when it comes to the expression of any opinion that reflects the moral principles that Canadians have historically held, the principle of free speech tends to be cast aside in favour of the modern liberal notion that an individual has the right not to be offended by anything they see or hear. Thus, to maintain a non-offensive climate, unwelcome views are suppressed rather than debated.[35] Of course, this ruling might be said to also violate Mr. Owen's freedom of conscience and religion, or his right to act on or express his religious belief.

In another case in Ontario, the O.H.R.C. ruled in 2000 that Scott Brockie,[36] a professional printer with traditional Christian views on sexuality, could not decline job orders from a gay organization, as a violation of section 1 of the *Ontario Human Rights Code*. The Commission stated that while he was free to hold his religious beliefs and practise them in his home and in his Christian community, homosexual rights took precedence elsewhere. It appears that there is a hierarchy of values and freedoms, where certain rights and freedoms take precedence over others.

On the other hand, certain other rights and freedoms are specifically given precedence over the rights set out in Part I. For example, freedom of association is specifically protected in section 21(1), which allows for discrimination in the occupancy of residential accommodation where the owner of the premises, or his or her family, will be sharing a bathroom or kitchen facility with a prospective occupant in the house where they reside. The right to freedom of association is given further precedence in section 20(3), which allows a recreational club to discriminate in restricting access to its services and facilities, and section 24(1), which allows a person to discriminate in the hiring of an employee to look after the medical or personal needs of an ill child or aged or ill spouse or relative. Section 24(1)(a) allows a religious, philanthropic, educational, fraternal, or social institution or organization primarily engaged in serving the interests of persons identified by their race, place of origin, colour, ethnic origin, creed, sex, age, etc., to employ only persons similarly identified if the qualification is a reasonable and bona fide qualification because of the nature of the employment.

There are other values that are judicially recognized as justifiable limitations, such as biological limitations, social mores, public policy, academic freedom and economic freedom. Thus, while age is a prohibited ground of discrimination, the notion of the biological and human limitations of childhood (as well as economic rights and social mores) are recognized, since age as a prohibited ground is defined as meaning 18 years of age or more (s. 10(1)), which allows for children under 18 to be treated differently than adults and allows for limiting their freedoms and rights regarding employment as well as the other social areas. The Code also formerly recognized the biological limitations of age regarding seniors by stating in section 10 that age did not include persons 65 years of age or older so that such persons could be treated differently, and they could be "discriminated" against by, for example, imposing mandatory retirement of such persons in an employment contract. However, in 2006, section 10 was amended to omit the reference to the 65-year limitation in the age definition so that today a person 65 years of age or more cannot be discriminated against (as a general rule) by forced retirement. An

---

[35] *National Post* (June 23, 2001)

[36] *Brillinger v. Brockie* (September 29, 1999) Doc. 99-012 (Ont. Bd. of Inquiry) and (February 24, 2000) Doc. 000-003-R (Ont. Bd. of Inquiry).

employer can still refuse to employ an elderly person on the basis of age only if such disqualification can be justified as bona fide and reasonable because of the nature of the employment. Similarly, employment discrimination on the basis of sex, marital status, or record of offence (s. 24(1)(b)) is allowed if the qualification is bona fide and reasonable.

Social and economic realities may intercede to modify restrictions or exemptions. In certain circumstances, necessity may obviate the need to restrict a minor's rights. Accommodation cannot be denied to a person who is 16 or 17 years old if he or she has withdrawn from parental control (s. 4). Nor can a person under 65 years of age complain of discrimination on the basis of age where persons over 65 years of age, in recognition of their reduced earning power, are given a special advantage or preferential treatment, such as a lower rate charged for bus fares or for theatre tickets (s. 15). Similarly, section 14 allows for special programs to overcome barriers or disadvantages to traditionally disadvantaged groups recognized in the various grounds. An interesting illustration of the potential use of this section is the argument used in the *Blainey* case that if girls were allowed to play on boys' teams, then there would be nothing to stop a team in the girls' hockey league from gaining an unfair advantage by recruiting boys to play on its team. The Board of Inquiry stated that the women's league could prohibit its teams from recruiting boys. Women's hockey qualified as a special program under the auspices of section 14, to assist a disadvantaged group (women), and such a program could, therefore, be limited to such group. This limitation would not, therefore, be considered adverse discrimination.[37]

A handicapped person can be refused a job — i.e., "discriminated" against — in the area of employment on the basis of handicap where said person is incapable of performing the essential duties or requirements of such job because of such handicap (s. 17(1)); otherwise, the employer's economic right to earn a living or run the business efficiently would be seriously compromised. But the employer must be able to argue that the disability cannot be accommodated without undue hardship (s. 17(2)) so that there is a positive obligation to alleviate conditions that might constitute a barrier to a person with a particular handicap to be hired for or continue in a job so long as the burden on the employer is not excessive. This duty to accommodate handicapped persons is not restricted to employment. For example, section 17(1) by implication would also require accommodation for handicapped persons in the provision of services in the absence of undue hardship (e.g., special toilet facilities or space for wheelchair ramps to allow entrance to facilities open to the public, such as movie theatres or sports venues).

Allowing landlords to do credit checks and use income information and rental history without these practices being complained of as acts of discrimination or harassment implicitly recognizes landlords's economic right to conduct their business efficiently.

Discrimination on the basis of sex precludes depriving a woman of any services or opportunities because she is or may become pregnant (s. 10(2)). However, social mores or public policy are recognized when the use of services or facilities are restricted to persons of the same sex on the ground of public decency (s. 20(1)); or when persons under 19 years of age are denied entry to premises where liquor is served or prohibited from purchasing alcoholic beverages (s. 20(2)) or from purchasing tobacco or tobacco products (s. 20(4)); or when accommodation in a residence is restricted to persons of the same sex (s. 21(2)).

---

[37] Adverse discrimination involves giving an unfair advantage to a member of a group ordinarily discriminated against.

The definition of "harassment" in the Code as interpreted by Boards of Inquiry that is described above incorporates the use of objective or community standards as to whether the conduct in question is acceptable in the circumstances or infringes our sense of justice. The definition as interpreted invites us to judge the reasonableness of both the respondent's conduct or words and the reasonableness of the victim's response to such conduct. Without this dual reasonableness requirement, respondents could be subject to irrational or abusive complaints based solely on an alleged victim's alleged subjective response. This would make people in certain positions, such as teachers, landlords, employers, and employees extremely vulnerable if they have to deal with those who might be vengeful, paranoid, hypersensitive, ignorant, irrational, or manipulative, and those who can take advantage of the stated grounds of complaint. There is no definition of discrimination in the Code and also no statutory reasonableness requirement, but Boards of Inquiry appear to incorporate a reasonableness test where the context requires it.

Another potential defence could be the legitimate purpose defence. In the case of *Matthews v. Memorial University of Newfoundland, Faculty of Medicine*,[38] a medical student complained to the Newfoundland Human Rights Commission, alleging that he had been discriminated against and harassed by members of the Faculty of Medicine of Memorial University. The student complained because certain instructors and the dean placed evaluations and a letter in the student's academic file referring to the student's having a speech impediment (a stutter), which they stated was a serious communication problem and which, in the long run, would affect his ability to function with patients. These comments were considered to constitute harassment on the ground of disability. The comments had caused the complainant a great deal of stress and affected his ability to perform at his best capacity. The evidence showed that a majority of those doctors who had had an opportunity to come into contact with the complainant stated they had had no problem understanding him and felt that his speech impediment did not impact on his ability to function as a competent physician. Had the majority opinion been otherwise, the board implied, it would have dismissed the complaint. It stated that the fact that the subject comments were vexatious to the complainant does not necessarily mean that harassment exists. They may be excluded from the purview of the harassment section if they were legitimate comments regarding the complainant's performance as a medical student. This decision recognizes that comments that are vexatious to a complainant and that are related to a prohibited ground may nonetheless be protected from complaint because the person making these comments has a legitimate reason for doing so. The person made these comments in furtherance of a relationship with the complainant gave that person the obligation or licence to render such judgments or opinions. This approach could be used to assist teachers, employers, and other persons in mentor or supervisory positions.

Part III of the Code deals with the structure and function of the Commission. Part IV deals with how the rights given in Parts I and II are enforced.

These parts are discussed in another chapter. Part V defines certain terms, including the use of the term "person", and extends its meaning beyond that given in the *Interpretation Act* to include several types of organizations, associations, and municipalities (s. 46). It indicates that the Act binds the Crown (s. 47) and also, in section 48, sets out the type of regulations that can be made by the Lieutenant Governor in Council (i.e., the Ontario Cabinet).

---

[38] (1989) 15 C.H.R.R. D/399 (Nfld. Bd. of Inquiry).

THE FUTURE OF HUMAN RIGHTS CODES

> At the end of the twentieth century, the liberal myth that humanity is progressing to an ever more enlightened and tolerant state looks as fantastic as any of the other millennial myths we have considered.[39]

Historically, human rights has appeared to be an evolving concept driven by an expanding notion of social justice: a movement towards bringing the right to dignity and equality to an ever larger segment of an increasingly diverse society. But in a volatile and unstable world beset by burgeoning poverty, cultural and religious clashes, environmental degradation, scarcity of resources, social instability, and economic crises, can we continue to look forward to the evolutionary expansion of human rights, or is such a process in danger of being halted or even reversed?

As already discussed,[40] the expansion of human rights can lead to conflict with other rights, freedoms and values, even those deeply held by certain increasingly influential constituencies within society. A balance must be found, allowing certain rights to predominate over others. The current balance seems to favour the equality rights[41] that underlie the human rights code, where these rights conflict with certain important individual freedoms, such as religious freedom, freedom of speech and opinion, and commercial and property rights associated with free enterprise economies.

The case of *Bruker v. Marcovitz*[42] serves to illustrate the degree of intrusion of equality rights into the realm of religious freedom in the sense of the right of the members of a particular religious group to follow their religion's rules and traditions. The Supreme Court of Canada decided to uphold a trial court's decision that a wife should receive a $47,000.00 damage award, compensating her for her husband's exercising his traditional religious right to refuse his consent to a Jewish religious divorce. The husband had agreed to grant the consent as part of a settlement agreement arrived at in the course of civil divorce proceedings but delayed honouring this agreement for 15 years until the wife was almost 47, effectively destroying her opportunity to validly remarry and bear children in accordance with her Jewish religion.

The majority of the Court (in a 7–2 decision) stated that the husband's claim to the freedom to practise his religion was outweighed by the harm to the wife personally and to the public's interest in protecting fundamental values, such as equality rights, autonomous choice in marriage and divorce and the enforcement of contractual obligations. The dissenting judges pointed out that in this case the wife's civil rights were not an issue. She had been granted a civil divorce and was free to remarry civilly. It was only her religious rights that were at issue as a result of religious rules, and the Court should not intrude in the religious sphere or in religious disputes.

So the Court here interfered in the realm of religion by sanctioning the husband for following a religious rule that would have had the effect of promoting gender inequality. By doing so, it would justify the Court's interfering with the traditional faiths and practices of not only Judaism but also of Islam, Catholicism, fundamentalist Protestantism and other religions whose rules and practices might offend the Court's notions of gender or other equality rights.[43]

---

[39] Karen Armstrong, *The Battle for God* (New York, N.Y.: Ballantine Books, 2001) at 367.

[40] See "The Balancing of Rights and Freedoms" on page 505.

[41] The right of members of certain groups or segments of society that have been traditionally discriminated against to be free from discrimination and harassment.

[42] (2007) S.C.C. 54

[43] Although this was not a case brought under any human rights code, it illustrates the Court's policy bias in favour of equality rights underlying such codes.

Other illustrations where the courts have promoted equality rights over religious freedom include a decision upholding a conviction under an Ontario law requiring the use of motorcycle helmets by all persons against a Sikh who claimed an exemption from such law because his religion required him to wear a turban as a head covering *(R. v. Badesha*, [2008] O.J. No. 854), as well as the illustrations given on pages 505 and 506 in the previous section ("The Balancing of Rights and Powers").

Many scholars and commentators, however, have pointed out the growing resurgence in number and political influence of religious fundamentalism, an ideology which stands in opposition to the secularist approach of human rights advocates. The fundamentalist religious approach promotes the notion of traditional absolute values and adamantly opposes secularist concepts of democracy, separation of church and state and tolerance. Kevin Phillips in *American Theocracy* points out that according to a *Newsweek* Poll of December 2004, 55 percent of the U.S. population believes that the Bible is literally accurate and inerrant.[44] In addition, there are those in other religions that hold the same belief about their holy books such as the Hebrew Bible and the *Koran*.[45] These books all promulgate patriarchal values that run counter to the equality rights that underlie human rights legislation. Those who hold such beliefs emphasize the dominating authority of the husband and father, oppose women's equality and gay rights and are intolerant of any dissent to their beliefs. They are antinomians — i.e., they believe the laws of God should trump the laws of man and that any religious beliefs and practices other than their own are satanical.

The fundamentalist Christian credo includes a belief that each person must find personal salvation by mastering his or her own soul and coming to an acceptance of and belief in Jesus as his or saviour. Fundamentalist Christians do not hold society (or government) responsible for man's failings and so are less concerned with social change as they are with personal change — another reason for them to challenge any government effort to effect social change through regulation — i.e., human rights codes.[46]

Another problem facing the maintenance and expansion of human rights legislation is the recent effort to expand the scope of such legislation in certain jurisdictions to interfere with freedom of speech and opinion. A complaint was made to the Canadian Human Rights Commission recently regarding an article written by Mark Steyn, alleging many Muslims who are sympathetic to terrorism are migrating to Western societies and are intending to take over these societies by exploiting their religion's high birth rate. A similar complaint was made to the Alberta Human Rights Commission regarding Ezra Levant's publishing controversial cartoons depicting the Prophet Mohammed in an unflattering light. Both of these commissions are operating under the auspices of human rights legislation (unlike Ontario's *Human Rights Code*) that allows for complaints against publication of material likely to expose a person

---

[44] Kevin Phillips, *American Theocracy: The Peril and Politics of Radical Religion, Oil and Borrowed Money in the 21st Century* (New York, N.Y.: Viking, 2006) at 184.

[45] Both the United States and Canada are governed federally by neo-conservative parties who are strongly influenced by fundamentalist religionists. Between the two chambers of Congress, 186 members of the U.S. House of Representatives and 45 Senators earned high approval ratings from fundamentalist Christian advocacy groups. The U.S. President and the Secretary of State profess their allegiance to fundamentalist Christian religions. See Lewis Lapham, "The Wrath of the Lamb", *Harper's Magazine* (May 2005) at 8–9; Chris Hedges, *American Fascists: The Christian Right and the War on America* (New York, N.Y.: Free Press, 2006) at 22–23).

[46] A leading Canadian pollster, Michael Adams, finds Canadians to be about half as religious as Americans, although as many as 61% to 69% hold religious beliefs (e.g., belief in heaven and God). See *The Globe and Mail*, "My Canada doesn't include religiosity" (January 10, 2005).

or class of persons to hatred or contempt. Neither of these publications incited violence or other injustices against Muslims. Both of these complaints are being seriously entertained. This so-called hate speech legislation constitutes a serious restriction on the right to freedom of speech and opinion and should likely be considered a violation of the Canadian *Charter of Rights and Freedoms*.[47]

This attack on freedom of speech is an example of overreaching by those in charge of protecting human rights. Other examples of absurd and insidious applications of human rights concepts include the illustration in note 6 on page 496 involving a five-year-old Maryland student. In the same article, Ian Hunter also referred to a four-year-old pre-kindergarten student in Texas, who was suspended for inappropriately hugging a female teacher's aide. Such overreaching can only have the effect of bringing human rights legislation and tribunals into disrepute.

A third line of attack on human rights legislation comes from the neo-conservative ideologues who oppose government regulation or control over the private economy. As they point out, human rights laws grant privileges to those who are relatively poor and powerless over those who are relatively rich and powerful (employers, owners of businesses and landlords). After all, these laws forbid those in such positions of power from discriminating against potential or actual employees, customers, or tenants on the basis of their gender, religion, race, disability, etc. Employers, for example, must go out of their way to accommodate employees belonging to disadvantaged groups "regardless of resulting hardship for their employer".[48] Employees, on the other hand, can refuse any job offer or quit their jobs even if their reason for doing so is the employer's gender, religion, colour, creed, etc. Similar unbalanced restrictions apply to business owners vis-à-vis consumers, and landlords vis-à-vis tenants.[49]

We see how our equality rights legislation can interfere with the honoured rights, such as freedom of contract and private property rights, freedom of religion and freedom of speech. Such legislation interferes with these rights and freedoms when those who attempt to exercise such rights hold certain rigid ideologies and exercise certain practices that favour imposing dominant hierarchical relationships among religions, groups and genders. There is a conflict between them and those who emphasize the need to acknowledge and respect the equality and inherent dignity of individuals regardless of their particular group, race or gender. The future of human rights may depend on which world view will gain the ascendancy. It may depend on which world view will help our western nations and perhaps civilization itself meet the coming challenges outlined at the beginning of this topic.

---

[47] The Supreme Court of Canada in the John Ross Taylor case (*Canada (Human Rights Commission) v. Taylor* [1990] 3 S.C.R. 892) indicated that the Canadian Human Rights Commission hate speech prohibition was constitutionally acceptable on certain conditions. Jeremy Waldron refers to hate speech legislation that might protect members of minority groups against religious or racial hatred while safeguarding freedom of speech and opinion in a constitutionally acceptable manner. The United Kingdom's 2006 *Racial and Religious Hatred Act*, which prohibits such hatred, provides that it shall not be interpreted "to prohibit or restrict discussion, criticism or expression of antipathy, dislike, ridicule or insult of particular religions or the beliefs or practices of their adherents, or urging such adherents to cease practising their religion or belief system." The purpose of this language is to distinguish between hatred of persons (forbidden) and opposition to institutions and doctrines (allowed). (See "What to Do About Hate Speech", *The New York Review of Books*, 55:12 (July 17, 2008) 52). But note also s. 319 of the Canadian *Criminal Code*, which prohibits public incitement of hatred towards identifiable groups, where such incitement is likely to lead to a breach of the peace.

[48] This notion is somewhat distorted as seen in my previous discussion regarding employee accommodation (page 504, "The BFOR Defence").

[49] See Karen Selick, "There are some rights we can do without" *The Globe and Mail* (August 24, 2007).

CHAPTER SUMMARY

This chapter provides the reader with a brief history of the evolution of human rights by tracing the topic back to its early roots in both Europe and North America. The impact of World War II entailed a more mature concept of equality and social justice, as illustrated by the adoption of the Universal Declaration of Human Rights that recognized the equal worth and dignity of all men and women.

The nature of human rights codes was discussed relative to their goal of providing equal opportunity and freedom from discrimination, along with how these negative rights may interfere with other rights. The preamble to the Ontario *Human Rights Code* ("Code") was investigated, as was the ongoing addition of new grounds by the legislature that exemplify how human rights are constantly evolving.

A comparison of the Universal Declaration of Human Rights (an international covenant between nations), the *Canadian Charter of Rights and Freedom* (which forms part of our Constitution), and the human rights codes (which protect equality rights in dealings between individuals in the private sphere) was conducted. The idea that human rights are not absolute was discussed.

The history and evolution of human rights law in Ontario was examined. Early legislation was based on contract law, and later legislation comprised separate Acts that had a narrow application. These former Acts were later codified into our present Code. The quasi-criminal focus of earlier legislation was examined, along with the associated drawbacks that led to our present administrative process.

The substantive parts of the Ontario *Human Rights Code*, along with the preamble, were reviewed. The social areas and grounds were defined, and the Code's relationship to the Charter regarding conflicting rights was discussed. It was noted that discrimination and justifiable limitations in certain circumstances were permitted under the Code.

GLOSSARY OF NEW TERMS AND KEY CONCEPTS

constructive discrimination	The treatment of members of a group that is identical to treatment of members of another group that, because of the characteristics of the members of the first group, results in unequal treatment or opportunities for the members of the first group.
discrimination	Treating a person in a different manner because of one of the prohibited grounds, as a result of which the person suffers some adverse consequence or a serious affront to dignity.
indirect discrimination	Another term used to describe a poisoned environment.
information	The equivalent, in the criminal context, of a statement of claim in the civil context — the name of an originating process.
poisoned environment	Comments or conduct directed towards others that create a hostile or unwelcoming environment for a person.
social areas	Relating to the areas of services, accommodation, employment, contracts, and membership in vocational associations and trade unions, which are covered by the Code.

REVIEW QUESTIONS

1. Describe the apparent difference in the concept of the "equality of all men" for the early Americans and for our society today.

2. How did World War II act as a catalyst in the evolution of human rights?

3. What are the main goals of human rights codes?

4. (a) In what major way do the rights set out in the United Nations Universal Declaration of Human Rights differ from the rights set out in our Charter and human rights codes?

   (b) In what ways does the *Charter of Rights and Freedoms* differ from the Ontario *Human Rights Code*?

5. What is the legal effect of section 15 of the *Canadian Charter of Rights and Freedoms* on the Ontario *Human Rights Code*?

6. Why is the concept of requiring a contract to satisfy public policy by itself inadequate to protect equality rights?

7. What difficulties were presented for effective enforcement of human rights by quasi-criminal legislation, such as the former Ontario *Racial Discrimination Act*?

8. What are the various social areas for which the Ontario Human Rights Commission requires equal treatment?

9. What are the basic 14 grounds that apply to every social area?

10. What are the statutory and Board of Inquiry requirements for a finding of harassment?

11. What is indirect discrimination?

12. What is constructive discrimination?

13. What is the BFOR defence, and how is it applied in an employment situation?

14. What freedoms often come into conflict with the Code's equality rights?

15. What values often provide justifiable limitations on equality rights?

16. The *Charter of Rights and Freedoms* applies to the actions and legislation of which level(s) of government?

17. How did the courts perceive acts of discrimination in contracts or the provision of services prior to the enactment of our human rights code?

DISCUSSION QUESTIONS

1. Is Ontario's *Human Rights Code* aimed at prohibiting all forms of differential or discriminatory treatment? Can you think of a type of discriminatory treatment that would not be prohibited?

2. Is there an argument for including social and economic rights in Ontario's *Human Rights Code*? Why might it not be a good idea?

3. Why have several additional grounds and concepts been introduced in Ontario since the introduction of its human rights code in 1962?

4. Robin is handicapped and has applied for a full-time job for which she meets the required qualifications. The potential employer doesn't hire Robin and says that the reason is that Robin cannot perform all the duties required in the job. Can the employer not hire Robin for this reason?

SUGGESTED READING

Bowland, Adelyn L. *The 2008 Annotated Ontario Human Rights Code* (Toronto, Ont.: Carswell, 2007).

Gall, G. *Civil Liberties in Canada — Entering the 1980s,* 9th Edition (Toronto, Ont.: Butterworths, 1982).

Hunter, Ian. "Human Rights Legislation in Canada: Its Origin, Development and Interpretation" (1976) 15 U.W.O. L. Rev. 21.

Ignatieff, Michael. *The Rights Revolution* (Toronto, Ont.: House of Anansi Press, 2000).

Kors, Cl., & H. Silverglate. *The Shadow University* (New York: The Free Press, 1998).

Ontario Human Rights Commission, *Report of the Ontario Human Rights Commission,* 2006–2007. Available online: <http://www.ohrc.on.ca/en/resources/annualreports/ar0607?page=eng-Contents.html>.

The Resolution of Human Rights Complaints in Ontario

Janet I. Mason

BARRISTER AND SOLICITOR

Learning Objectives

At the conclusion of this chapter, the reader should be able to:

➢ understand the various roles of the Human Rights Commission and the Human Rights Tribunal of Ontario in the human rights enforcement process

➢ comprehend the steps involved in the complaint process with the Human Rights Commission

➢ distinguish between mediation and conciliation

➢ describe how a decision is made by the Human Rights Commission

➢ comprehend the procedural steps at the Tribunal

➢ understand the types of evidence that are admissible at a hearing

➢ describe the types of orders that can be imposed

➢ identify pending charges to resolution process

TABLE OF CONTENTS

THE ROLE OF THE HUMAN RIGHTS COMMISSION

The Ontario Human Rights Commission ("Commission") was the first human rights enforcement agency to operate in Canada. It came into operation in 1962 with the proclamation of the Ontario *Human Rights Code*[1] ("Code"). The Commission's function is set out in Part III of the Code, with amendments pending:

> **29.** It is the function of the Commission,
> (a) to forward the policy that the dignity and worth of every person be recognized and that equal rights and opportunities be provided without discrimination that is contrary to law;
> (b) to promote an understanding and acceptance of and compliance with this Act;
> (c) to recommend for consideration a special plan or program designed to meet the requirements of subsection 14(1), subject to the right of a person aggrieved by the implementation of the plan or program to request the Commission to reconsider its recommendation and section 37 applies with necessary modifications;
> (d) to develop and conduct programs of public information and education and undertake, direct and encourage research designed to eliminate discriminatory practices that infringe rights under this Act;
> (e) to examine and review any statute or regulation, and any program or policy made by or under a statute and make recommendations on any provision, program or policy, that in its opinion is inconsistent with the intent of this Act;
> (f) to inquire into incidents of and conditions leading or tending to lead to tension or conflict based upon identification by a prohibited ground of discrimination and take appropriate action to eliminate the source of tension or conflict;
> (g) to initiate investigations into problems based upon identification by a prohibited ground of discrimination that may arise in a community, and encourage and co-ordinate plans, programs and activities to reduce or prevent such problems;
> (h) to promote, assist and encourage public, municipal or private agencies, organizations, groups or persons to engage in programs to alleviate tensions and conflicts based upon identification by a prohibited ground of discrimination;
> (i) to enforce this Act and orders of the Tribunal;
> (j) to perform the functions assigned to it by this or any other Act.

The Commission is made up of a chair and vice-chair who are designated by the Lieutenant Governor in Council—i.e., the provincial Cabinet. The Commission must provide an annual report by June of each year to the Attorney General, detailing the affairs of the Commission for the year ended March 31st of the year in which the report is submitted. The report details, among other things, the number of cases opened and closed, the average length of time until resolution, and whether project objectives for the relevant year were met.[2]

The Commission has the power to decide whether or not a complaint is carried forward at any stage of the process. As the Commission does not deal with complainants directly (in that a party does not meet with a commissioner), it relies on the recommendations of an employee of the Commission, the human rights officer, when making a decision, but it is not bound to fol-

---

[1] R.S.O. 1990, c. H.19.
[2] See Ontario Human Rights Commission, *Annual Report 2006–2007*, online: <http://www.ohrc.on.ca/en/resources/annualreports/ar0607/pdf> (September 17, 2007).

low the recommendation submitted. The Commission may initiate a complaint itself in the case of systemic discrimination, or if it feels that it would be in the public interest to bring the complaint forward, or at the request of any person whose right under Part I of the Code has been infringed. The Commission may decide to combine complaints where the same individual is involved or where there is a question of law or fact common to several complaints. It is important to note that the Commission has discretion as to whether or not to deal with any complaint. The limits of this discretion are set out in section 34 and regard the appropriateness of the involvement of the Commission in the matter, the validity of the complaint, jurisdiction, and the time limit for filing a complaint. Following are the limits of discretion set out in section 34:

1. Matters that can be more appropriately dealt with under another Act should be dealt with under that other Act: for example, the *Labour Relations Act* (in a unionized work environment), where there is a collective agreement and grievance procedure in place. This prevents and minimizes duplication of proceedings. The Commission retains the power to investigate any human rights complaint, notwithstanding the existence of alternative procedures under another Act when it appears that it is in the public interest to ensure the discrimination is eradicated.

2. Where the Commission considers the complaint to be trivial, frivolous, vexatious or made in bad faith, the Commission may exercise its discretion not to deal with the complaint (e.g., if the complaint has no basis in law or evidence to support it).

3. Where the complaint is not within the jurisdiction of the Commission (such as a complaint against a bank or post office, which would fall under federal jurisdiction and would therefore be handled by the Canadian Human Rights Commission), the Commission cannot consider the complaint.

4. If the facts on which the complaint is based occurred more than six months prior to the complaint being filed with the Commission, the Commission has the right not to proceed with the complaint.

If appropriate, the person will be referred to the proper jurisdiction or agency by the intake officer when the Commission is contacted. The referral of an unsettled complaint to the Human Rights Tribunal of Ontario ("Tribunal" or "the HRTO") for a hearing remains at the discretion of the Commission under section 36(1).[3]

Human rights officers employed by the Commission investigate and mediate between the parties to effect settlement of the complaint and to provide recommendations to the Commission. There is also a department exclusively dedicated to investigating systemic discrimination, and another comprising policy analysts responsible for the development and application of the Code, specially trained mediators and lawyers who argue on behalf of the Commission at the Tribunal.

---

[3] Note: many complaints are handled internally in a workplace or other institutional setting where such workplace or institution has its own human rights policy and enforcement process. If the Ontario Human Rights Commission feels the matter has been, or could have been, dealt with satisfactorily, it will dismiss or refuse to pursue the complaint.

The 2006–2007 statistics published in the Commission's *Annual Report* identified that the Commission began the year with a pre-existing caseload of 2,889 cases. The Commission received 42,937 inquiries and opened 2,337 formal complaints during the reporting year — i.e., only about 5 percent of inquiries resulted in a formal complaint being filed. There were 1,978 files "completed", with the average time to completion identified as 14.6 months. The Commission exercised its section 34 discretion to dismiss in 7.1 percent of cases completed or referred to the Tribunal. A total of 58.9 percent of cases (completed or referred) were resolved by mediation or settlement in an average timeframe of 13.7 months, and 18.5 percent were withdrawn. There are 762 backlogged cases — i.e., about 25 percent of active cases — and 169 cases are over three years old. The Commission ended the year with a 7.6 percent higher active caseload (3,099 cases) over the previous reporting year.

THE ROLE OF THE HUMAN RIGHTS TRIBUNAL OF ONTARIO

The Tribunal is independent of and functions separately from the Ontario Human Rights Commission. The Tribunal's members are appointed by the Lieutenant Governor in Council, who also appoints a chair and may appoint one or more vice-chairs. The chair can assign a **panel** of one or more members to act as adjudicators at a hearing. Therefore, it is not necessary that all members be present at each hearing, allowing for less delay and increased efficiency.

The Tribunal has the authority to make rules governing its own practice and procedure relevant to the conducting of its affairs.[4] Tribunal regulations are not legislative regulations under the *Regulations Act* but are, simply, a venue through which the Tribunal can establish procedural efficiency.

The Tribunal is an administrative body that hears human rights complaints that have been referred to it by the Commission. The proceedings are quasi-judicial and similar in format to a trial. At the hearing, evidence is transcribed and witnesses swear/affirm their testimony prior to delivering it. However, there are a few differences that the reader should be aware of. In criminal proceedings, the burden of proof must be beyond a reasonable doubt. In a tribunal hearing, the burden required is, as in a civil proceeding, on the balance of probabilities. To meet the balance of probabilities, it must be shown that it is more likely than not that the respondent infringed a right of the complainant. Civil remedies, such as compensation for losses suffered by the complainant (general and/or special damages), are available. The Commission can also request remedies in the public interest to prevent future occurrences of similar conduct. The Code is remedial in nature. Its purpose is to correct policy and/or educate a respondent who has deliberately or inadvertently infringed on a person's right. Hearings are generally open to the public and media, but this is at the discretion of the chair. Tribunal decisions are published in the *Canadian Human Rights Reporter* and can be appealed to Divisional Court by any party.

---

[4] The *Statutory Powers Procoedure Act*, R.S.O. 1980, c. S.22 ("SPPA"), empowers the Tribunal to make its rules (s. 25.1), deals with procedural matters and applies to hearings. In the event of a conflict between the rules and SPPA, the SPPA governs (r. 3).

THE COMPLAINT PROCESS AT
THE HUMAN RIGHTS COMMISSION

People can contact the Commission when they believe that one of their rights under the Code has been infringed. Ideally, prior to contacting the Commission, the person should document the instances of the alleged infringement(s), including dates, times, witnesses present, and any attempts that have been made to remedy the situation by any party. The inquiry services representative will generally be the first contact at the Commission. Information provided will assist the representative in determining whether or not the Code is involved. If the situation falls under one of the categories in section 34 of the Code listed earlier in this chapter, the person may be referred to an appropriate agency (e.g., a union) if that person is under a collective agreement or to the Ontario Rental Housing Tribunal where the matter concerns an illegal rent increase, for resolution.

If the matter appears to be one where it is suitable for the Commission to assure jurisdiction and there is possible infringement under the Code, a complaint form will be forwarded to the person making the complaint. The completed form is then returned to the Commission. An infringement must be based on an enumerated ground and have occurred in one of the **social areas**[5] covered by the Code. Alternatively, the Commission may decide to bring a complaint itself if it receives multiple complaints against the same alleged offender. This may, for example, include an employer who is repeatedly not hiring people from a particular ethnic background or a landlord who won't rent units to single women.

Upon the Commission's receiving a completed complaint form that reveals what it considers a potentially valid complaint under the Code that is within its jurisdiction, the complainant may be contacted for further information and/or documents. A remedy must be included in the complaint, and Commission staff may assist the complainant in determining the best remedy available. Once the complaint has been signed by the complainant and delivered to the Commission, it is considered "filed".

The complaint is regarded as a legal document and must follow a prescribed form. The complaint process is considered a legal proceeding, and the parties are referred to as the **complainant**, who is the person alleging the infringement of a right under the Code, and the **respondent**, who is the individual alleged to have infringed a right under the Code. The Commission does not formally represent the complainant in the proceeding; it represents the public interest. There may be more than one respondent in a complaint. For example, if the infringement occurred in the workplace, respondents can include the worker who committed the infringement, the supervisor who was informed of the infringement and did not make any attempt to remedy it, and the corporation itself that did not have an effective human rights policy in place. The Commission can add parties at any time during the proceeding when it appears that an additional party has also infringed a right. Legal or agent representation is an option available to all parties in a complaint. All named parties in the complaint must be served with a copy of the complaint, and the Commission generally sends the complaint out within 30 days of its completion.

[5] The Code identifies that a person has the right to equal treatment (freedom from discrimination) in the following social areas to which the Code applies: services, goods and facilities (s. 1); occupancy of accommodation (s. 2); contracts (ss. 3, 4); employment (s. 5); and vocational associations (s. 6).

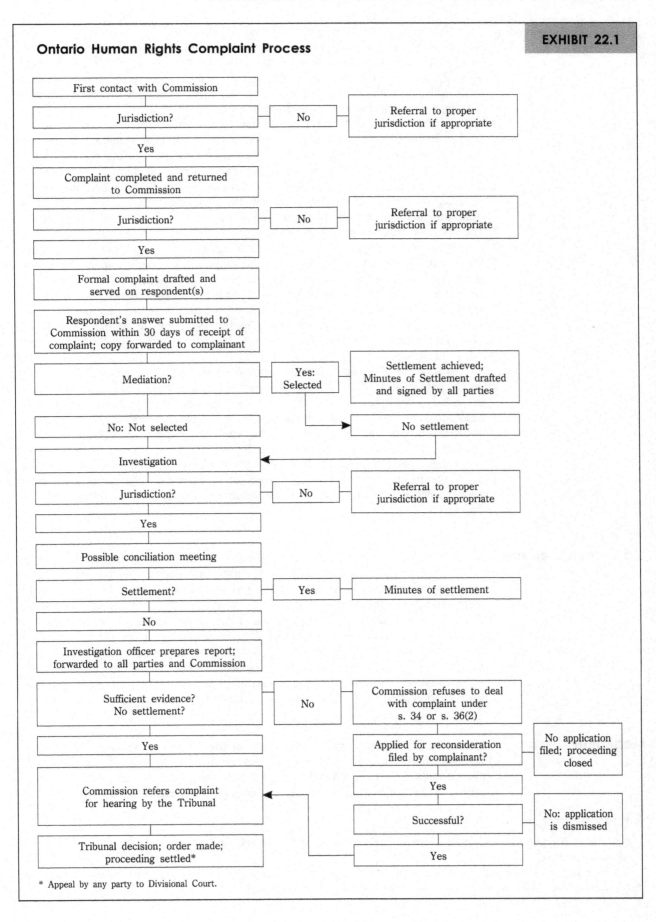

Ontario Human Rights Complaint Process

EXHIBIT 22.1

* Appeal by any party to Divisional Court.

The respondent is required to answer the complaint within 30 days from the date of the covering letter that accompanied the complaint. The answer written generally contains a rebuttal to the alleged complaint and may argue that the complaint should be dismissed pursuant to section 34. The respondent will also include any relevant documents and names of witnesses. A copy of the written answer is forwarded to the complainant.

In the event that the Commission determines that the matter is not within its jurisdiction, a written response from the Commission will be sent to the complainant. The Commission's reason(s) for not dealing with the complaint will be stated, along with the applicable part of section 34 of the Code. If the complainant disagrees with the reasons given by the Commission for refusing to handle his or her complaint, the complainant may ask the Commission for **reconsideration** of the decision under section 37 within 15 days of the date of mailing of the reasons.

A complaint may be amended after filing, but generally only if the amendment will not result in prejudice to the respondent — for example, by adding elements that contradict the complaint as originally stated. If the complaint progresses to a tribunal hearing, the Tribunal has the power to amend the grounds of a complaint if the evidence demonstrates — for example, an additional ground for the complaint arises under the Code, or it appears that the complainant has been the object of retaliatory behaviour by the respondent since filing.

Where the Tribunal amends a ground in the complaint, the respondent is given notice and will likely be allowed an adjournment to prepare for the amended ground(s). Though the Tribunal's power in this matter may seem heavy-handed, it is important to appreciate how the complaint proceeding, with its originating complaint, differs from a criminal proceeding and its related indictment. A complaint simply serves as a *general notice* to the respondent regarding the nature of the complaint, whereas an indictment is a *specific* printed or written accusation of crime made against one or more people.[6] Moreover, the Code is remedial and in compliance with the overarching goal.

Case Management

In 2006 and 2007, the Commission began two case management initiatives in an attempt to clear up the backlog of cases and reduce delay. Case assessments were conducted in May 2006, and conciliation was emphasized. Files were reviewed for completeness and missing information and documents obtained. Some files were prepared for investigation and legal assessments of complaints obtained. There were 598 files reviewed and assessed in total; 301 files were prepared for investigation and the backlog reduced by 101 files. A similar pilot project commenced in February 2007 to provide for the early assessment of complaints and to institute "fact-finding meetings" as a pre-investigation tool that also imposed a fixed mediation date.[7]

Mediation

Mediation is voluntary within the scope of the Code and, in combination with conciliation, is successful in resolving over half of the complaints filed with the Commission.[8] It is offered to the parties where the respondent's answer is received. Specially trained mediators oversee and facilitate the process but

---

[6] *Cousens v. Nurses' Assn. (Canada)* (1981), 2 C.H.R.R. D/365 (Ont. Bd. of Inquiry).

[7] *Supra* note 2 at 33.

[8] Voluntariness may be vitiated with the application of the 2007 pilot project above. If so, "mediation" is really an early "conciliation". Mediation is arguably an inherently voluntary process.

	EXHIBIT 22.2
When Does Encouraging a Settlement become Coercing a Settlement?	

In 1985, Ms. Johnson agreed to settlement of her human rights complaint, but later felt that she had been coerced by the Commission into accepting the settlement offer. In 1991 she submitted an application for judicial review of the Commission's decision not to appoint a Board of Inquiry (now the Tribunal) to hear and decide her complaint. Unfortunately for Ms. Johnson, the application was dismissed, as all members of the court agreed that too much time had elapsed since she had accepted the settlement to set aside the decision of the Commission.

However, Rosenberg J. noted in the written reasons for dismissal of the application that the Commission had, in fact, inappropriately coerced Ms. Johnson into agreeing to the settlement by stating that they would not refer the matter to the Board if she did not accept the settlement offer presented and would refuse to carry it forward. Furthermore, the Commission indicated that it would dismiss her complaint upon non-acceptance. Rosenberg J. found that the Commission did not consider whether the evidence warranted inquiry or whether inquiry was an appropriate procedure under the circumstances. The decision identified that the Commission is entitled to consider two primary matters after a failure to settle: (1) Is the procedure — e.g., referral to the Board of Inquiry — appropriate; and (2) does the evidence warrant an inquiry (i.e., does the evidence support the alleged complaint sufficiently to refer the matter for a hearing, as under section 36(1) of the Code?)

Source: *Johnson v. Hamilton (City)* (1992), 15 C.H.R.R. D/254 (Ont. Div. Ct.).

do not make any decision regarding potential outcomes. Rather, a mediation simply provides a neutral environment for discussion and resolution of the issue at hand. Mediation is not a "discovery" event where each party shares its evidence with the other, and all negotiations and statements made are confidential. Mediation allows those involved to work towards a settlement by clarifying misperceptions and checking facts to ensure that all parties are fully knowledgeable of the requirements of the Code and their proper application.

Although mediation is not technically mandatory, the Commission has a duty to endeavour to effect settlement of the complaint under s. 33(1) prior to referring the matter to the Tribunal. However, while the Commission has a duty to try to effect a settlement, as noted in Exhibit 22.2, it cannot coerce the parties into a settlement.

Settlement

When the parties reach a settlement during mediation, the mediation officer prepares Minutes of Settlement. The Minutes include the specifics agreed to by the complainant and respondent, along with releases, assurances, and any other document requiring the signature of the parties that is necessary for resolution. Settlement can also occur outside of mediation and will be similarly put in writing and signed by the parties. The Commission must approve settlements that include a term that will be implemented at a future date. The future term, for example, may relate to the design and implementation of a human rights policy. A Commission-approved settlement is the only settlement that can be enforced under s. 43.

Settlement may include requirements such as the complainant being granted housing, the reestablishment of a benefit, financial compensation, an apology, or human rights education for employees of a Corporation. A respondent does not usually admit to a human rights violation in a settlement, nor does the complainant retract an allegation. The Commission will no longer be involved in the complaint once settled, and the matter is considered closed.

Investigation

Where one or more of the parties do not wish to participate in mediation, or where no settlement is reached and s. 34 does not apply, a human rights investigation officer is assigned to investigate the complaint. This officer cannot be the same officer who was involved in mediation since the investigating officer should be a neutral party to the complaint. The officer will request evidence and information from all parties in order to establish an accurate view of the events of the complaint.

Section 33 of the Code empowers an investigation officer to enter into a place that is not a dwelling to review, examine, and obtain copies of relevant documents or things (e.g., computer files), or he/she can request that evidence be provided to them for analysis. If it is deemed necessary to enter a dwelling in order to obtain evidence or if a party refuses to disclose evidence, a search warrant can be obtained from a justice of the peace. Alternatively, the matter may be promptly referred to the Tribunal for a hearing. Parties and witnesses may be interviewed by the officer and are allowed to have a representative present should they so choose.

Effective February 2007, the investigation officer will review newly filed complaints. The officer will schedule a mediation meeting, if considered suitable, and a subsequent fact-finding meeting between the parties. If a respondent has not filed an answer to the complaint by the date of the scheduled mediation meeting, the officer will require the answer within 10 days. If the answer remains outstanding after that time, the officer may decide to cancel the fact-finding meeting and recommend that the complaint proceed directly to the Tribunal.

A letter will be sent to the parties requiring the production of certain documents, people or information prior to the fact-finding meeting. Pursuant to s. 33(6), if a respondent does not fulfill the production demand, the matter may proceed directly to the Tribunal. If a complainant does not produce what was requested, the matter may not be referred to the Tribunal.

Conciliation

Conciliation is a separate entity from mediation, and may not occur where unsuccessful mediation has taken place. It forms part of the Commission's mandate under s. 34 to effect settlement. Conciliation is usually scheduled by the investigating officer after the completion of the investigation. It would seem to be in a party's best interest to attend conciliation in order to assess the evidence gathered from investigation. There is a significant difference between mediation and conciliation: while mediation is confidential, conciliation is not. Statements made during a conciliation meeting may be introduced at a tribunal hearing via the case analysis that is prepared after investigation. Additionally, if a complainant refuses a reasonable offer of settlement at conciliation, the investigation officer will include this fact in the case analysis, which in turn may affect the Commission's decision as to whether or not to refer the matter for a hearing. Only "with prejudice" offers open for 30 days can be disclosed in the case analysis report. The parties will generally be asked to submit written settlement offers at conciliation.

At the conciliation meeting the investigation officer will present her/his findings concerning the evidence, which will indicate what the recommendation to the Commission would be in order to facilitate settlement between the parties. Remedies may also be presented and discussed. This is as close to a discovery process as the Commission gets, as there is no formal discovery in human rights proceedings at this stage.

Case Analysis

When conciliation fails to effect settlement or is not used, the investigation officer prepares a written report called a **case analysis**. The case analysis is forwarded to all parties and includes a summary of the evidence and may include a recommendation as to whether or not the matter warrants a tribunal hearing.[9] The case analysis is a thorough report that details the findings of the investigation, a summary of the evidence and conclusions regarding the complaint. Each party may make a written submission in response to the report and submit it to the Commission within 21 days from the date of mailing. This written response should bring to the attention of the Commission any evidence that the party feels has been overlooked in the analysis that should be brought to the Commission's attention. It could also raise issues not addressed in the summary. The Commission may ask the investigating officer to get clarification on an issue raised and may postpone its decision until the additional information is received.

The investigating officer does not have decision-making power regarding a referral of the matter to the Tribunal, but the commissioners do base their decision on the report submitted by the officer. The recommendation is not binding on the commissioners. The commissioners decide whether or not to send the matter to the Tribunal or discuss it under section 34 or 36(2) of the Code.

Commission jurisdiction is evaluated at virtually every step of the process. Where evidence is found that places the matter outside the jurisdiction of the Commission — e.g., it is discovered that the corporation has a union environment and collective agreement in place, but the complainant chose not to file a grievance — the Commission may refuse to deal with the matter under section 34. Reasons for the Commission refusing to deal with the complaint are in writing and sent to all parties.

Where the Commission does not effect settlement and the circumstance is appropriate and the evidence is sufficient to warrant a hearing, the Commission may refer the matter to the Tribunal under section 36. The Commission does not have to disclose the notes in its investigation file or evidence when referring the complaint to the Tribunal. The case analysis is considered sufficient.

Reconsideration

If the Commission decides to dismiss the complaint, the complainant has the right to ask the Commission to reconsider its decision under section 37 of the Code. No such right is available to the respondent. The Application for Reconsideration must be filed within 15 days of the decision's date of mailing (s. 37) with the Commission. The Application for Reconsideration must contain a concise statement of material facts supporting the complainant's position that the matter deserves reconsideration. This statement can raise a procedural or legal error, or involve new facts that have become available. Following is a list of material facts that can warrant reconsideration:

1. Where the original investigation missed relevant evidence, which may have some bearing on the Commission's original decision
2. Where changes in the factual circumstances have some bearing on the Commission's original decision
3. Where a witness recants on an earlier statement before the Commission made its original decision and/or provides new evidence, which has some bearing on the Commission's original decision
4. Where a witness who did not participate in the original investigation provides relevant and persuasive evidence in the application for reconsideration

---

[9] A disclosure letter may be completed instead of a case analysis. The phrase "case analysis" may be alternatively read as disclosure letter. Both documents disclose the substance of the case.

EXHIBIT 22.3	**Jurisdiction Issue**

On April 3, 1990, the complainant and respondent each received a letter from the Commission indicating its decision not to appoint a Board of Inquiry (now the Tribunal) regarding a complaint previously filed. The complainant's solicitor responded by sending a letter, dated April 12, 1990, requesting reconsideration and including an additional request for extra time to make a "meaningful and complete submission". The Commission acknowledged the receipt of the request for reconsideration and indicated that it had forwarded a copy of the request to the respondent. However, the respondent's solicitor did not receive any notification from the Commission until November 29, 1991, when a reconsideration request report was received. In early December the respondent replied to the letter, stating that the Commission could not allow reconsideration due to the non-compliance with section 37(1) (reconsideration must be filed within 15 days of receipt of the date of mailing of the Commission's decision), and that the application should be refused. Furthermore, it turned out that the complainant did not submit the required statement of material facts in support of reconsideration until April 1992 — a year after the original request for reconsideration.

In July 1992, the Commission informed all parties that it had granted the complainant's request for reconsideration and had requested a Board of Inquiry to settle the complaint but failed to give reasons for changing its decision. In October 1992, the parties were notified by letter that a Board of Inquiry had been appointed. The respondent appealed the appointment of the Board to the Divisional Court.

The Divisional Court judge decided the matter by stating that the decision made after reconsideration cannot stand because the Commission failed to comply with statutory requirements. Following is an outline of the list of statutory requirements that were not complied with:

i)   The Commission failed to give reasons for changing its decision, as required under section 37(3), and the judge indicated that this failure gave an appearance of unfairness to the respondent.

ii) Under section 37(1), the complainant has only 15 days from the date of mailing of the Commission's decision regarding the appointment of a Board of Inquiry in which to submit an application for reconsideration, and an extension of this time limit must be supported by written reasons that specify the "special reasons" that support the extension. The Commission had not properly given any time extension to the complainant, nor had the written statement in support of reconsideration been provided to the respondent.

iii) The complainant had failed to provide the necessary concise statement of the material facts in support of reconsideration, as required in section 37(1).

The judge went on to say that the Commission's conduct in the matter was obviously contrary to the provisions of its governing statute. As such, it was ordered that the decision of the Commission to appoint a Board of Inquiry be quashed. In addition, the Commission was ordered to pay the employer respondent its costs in the amount of $4,500.00.

Source: *Ontario (Ministry of Health) v. Ontario (Human Rights Commission)* (1993), 20 C.H.R.R. D/421, 48 C.C.E.L. 182 (Ont. Div. Ct.)

5. Where authoritative case law, or applicable legislation, has some bearing on the Commission's original decision[10]

Upon receipt of the application, the Commission notifies the respondent(s) that reconsideration has been requested. The respondent has the opportunity to make a written submission to the application within 21 days, and a reconsideration officer will be assigned to the file. The officer will then

[10] Ontario Human Rights Commission, *Internal Guide for Processing Complaints* (March 2007).

review the file and determine whether the evidence warrants a reconsideration report. The parties will have 21 days to file additional submissions concerning the officer's reconsideration report if one is completed. The decision of the Commission regarding reconsideration is sent to all parties and is final. Judicial review of the Commission's decision is available and is generally based on an alleged breach of administrative duty or a lack of jurisdiction.

THE COMPLAINT PROCESS AT THE HUMAN RIGHTS TRIBUNAL OF ONTARIO

Once the Commission makes its decision to refer the matter to the Tribunal, a conference call will be scheduled within 30 days of the referral date. Then, once referred, the role of the Commission changes: it ceases to be an investigative body and becomes a party to the proceedings and has carriage of the complaint.

The Tribunal may add a party to the proceeding at any time if it feels that a new party has infringed a right under the Code. This may include someone who knew of the infringement, or ought to have known, and had authority to penalize or prevent the conduct regarding harassment in accommodation, harassment in employment, or harassment because of sex in accommodation or the workplace. For example, if the owner of a rental building knew that the property manager was discriminating against welfare recipients by refusing to offer them accommodation and did nothing to rectify the situation, the owner may be added to the proceeding as a party.

As in civil proceedings, motions, expert witnesses, summons to witnesses, requests for costs, and adjournments are available to a party in a tribunal hearing. Appropriate documents — e.g., a notice of motion — are filed with the Registrar. As proceedings are quasi-judicial, witnesses are required to swear or affirm their testimony. The Tribunal has its own rules of procedure, available online at its website <www.hrto.ca>. The rules identify service and filing requirements among other things.

EXHIBIT 22.4

The Mission of the Human Rights Tribunal of Ontario

- ¤ The Tribunal will play its role as a pillar in the human rights system by providing expeditious and accessible processes to assist the parties to resolve complaints brought before the Tribunal, and to determine complaints where the parties are unable to resolve them.

- ¤ The Tribunal will be activist to seek a fair, just and expeditious resolution of the merits of an application.

- ¤ The Tribunal will provide and promote meaningful and effective public interest remedies in appropriate cases. The Tribunal will not bar settlements where parties freely desire to resolve their dispute.

- ¤ The Tribunal will seek to maintain the highest standards of integrity and quality of work.

- ¤ The Tribunal will strive for consistency to enhance the parties' reasonable expectations of Tribunal policy and process, but will remain responsive to differing cases and party needs, and to an evolving understanding of human rights and discrimination.

- ¤ The Tribunal will strive to promote a clear understanding of the Tribunal's work among the general public. The Tribunal will work to be responsive to the needs of its stakeholder communities.

Source: Human Rights Tribunal of Ontario website <http://www.hrto.ca/NEW/about/mandate.asp>.

A party can request mediation through the Tribunal office at any time in the process, and mediation will be explored during the initial conference call. In the event that the Commission obtains a settlement with the respondent that satisfies its public interest mandate, it will withdraw from the proceeding. If the complainant does not similarly reach settlement with the respondent, a hearing may still take place. Upon the withdrawal of the Commission, the complainant assumes carriage of the proceeding. Settlement between the complainant, the Commission and the respondent is required in order to remove the proceeding from the hearing list.

A hearing can occur even when another court proceeding regarding the same facts but requesting a different remedy is underway. The Tribunal deals only with discrimination and harassment under the Code, and a civil suit — e.g., for lost wages as a result of being wrongfully dismissed due to ethnic origin — may be launched concurrently with the complaint. There is no apparent conflict with both proceedings running concurrently, provided the human rights claim is excluded from the civil action. Current case law supports a civil action that includes a corollary human rights claim. Legal advice should be obtained to determine the best forum under the particular circumstances.

A hearing is adjudicated by a panel, which usually consists of one person. The hearing is open to the public unless the chair decides otherwise, and Tribunal decisions are published in the *Canadian Human Rights Reporter*.

Intervenors: Persons Not a Party to the Proceeding

A person who is not a party to the proceeding but who wishes to participate in the proceeding must bring a motion to the Tribunal (r. 17). The motion sets out the person's interest in the matter and the degree of participation (intervention) being sought. The request must be served, along with proof of service, to all parties. The panel may decide to limit the right of intervention to a specific part of the proceeding and may further limit it to only a written submission.

The Tribunal applies a broad approach to its interpretation of the Code and its application to the complaints before it. The public interest is as important as the private interests of the complainant and the respondent. Therefore, other groups concerned with the public interest may be able to provide input and bring a broader perspective to the proceeding before the Tribunal.

It is also important for the Tribunal to ensure that everyone who may be affected by the remedy sought is given notice of the hearing. An example of this would be a human rights complaint on the grounds of disability in the social area of employment by a unionized employee, where the issue raised or remedy sought — e.g., the workplace must institute an accommodation policy, such as a building renovation to accommodate a wheelchair — has potential impact on the rights of other bargaining members (e.g., wheelchair access for additional entrances). Although they are not a party to the complaint, the hearing would be relevant to the entire bargaining unit and the Tribunal would ensure that the union received notice of the proceeding.

There are two types of intervenors, and status is determined by the Tribunal.[11] One is a person or persons who have a right or interest that may be affected by the decision (see example above) and who may be given the opportunity to submit evidence and lead witnesses. The other is referred to as **amicus curiae**, a Latin term indicating that the person is perceived as a "friend of the court" or, in this case, the Tribunal. A designation of amicus curiae indicates that the party is likely restricted to making written submis-

---

[11] *Sinclair v. Peel Non-Profit Housing Corp. (No. 2)* (1989), 11 C.H.R.R. D/342 (Ont. Bd. of Inquiry); *Leshner v. Ontario (No. 1)* (1991), 16 C.H.R.R. D/175 (Ont. Bd. of Inquiry).

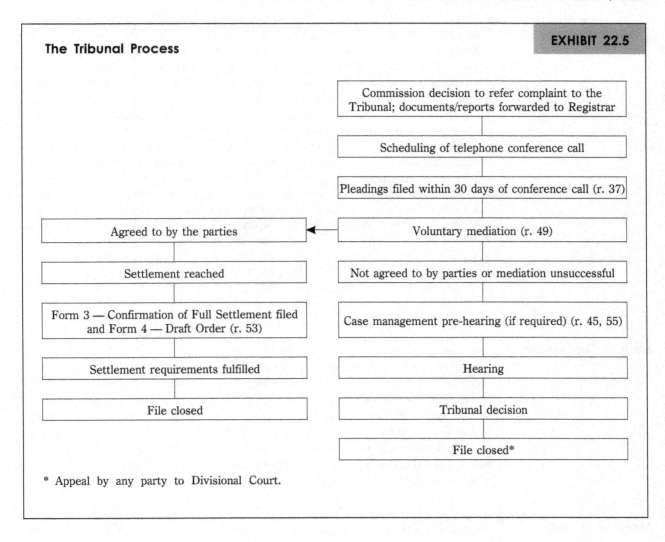

The Tribunal Process

EXHIBIT 22.5

Commission decision to refer complaint to the Tribunal; documents/reports forwarded to Registrar

Scheduling of telephone conference call

Pleadings filed within 30 days of conference call (r. 37)

Agreed to by the parties ← Voluntary mediation (r. 49)

Settlement reached / Not agreed to by parties or mediation unsuccessful

Form 3 — Confirmation of Full Settlement filed and Form 4 — Draft Order (r. 53) / Case management pre-hearing (if required) (r. 45, 55)

Settlement requirements fulfilled / Hearing

File closed / Tribunal decision

File closed*

* Appeal by any party to Divisional Court.

sions for the purpose of assisting the panel in achieving a broader understanding of the facts or associated issues connected to the complaint. For example, a disability advocacy research group may request to intervene as an amicus curiae where the complaint involves accommodation for disabled people.

The Commencement of the Hearing

The hearing commences with the scheduling of the telephone conference call between the Tribunal and all parties and/or their representative within 30 days of the date of referral. The purpose of the conference call is to schedule relevant dates — e.g., for mediation — and to identify any preliminary and procedural matters that will need to be dealt with (r. 33). If there are such matters, then a case management pre-hearing will be scheduled, along with mediation agreed to. The conference call and/or pre-hearing will also identify any additional individuals who are not already named in the complaint and who require notice of the proceeding. This may happen where the Tribunal determines that the corporation that employs the respondent should be included as a party in the complaint. The Tribunal may also determine that additional sections of the Code are applicable to the complaint; the complaint would then need to be amended to include the additional section where an alleged infringement has occurred. The panel who oversees the conference call is not necessarily the same panel who will preside over the hearing.

Pleadings

The pleadings (r. 37 to 40) include a statement of the facts, the issue(s) in dispute, the desired remedy, and a notice of motion to amend the complaint if applicable. Pleadings are served on all the other parties in the proceeding and filed, with a statement of service (Form 1), with the Tribunal within 30 days of the conference call. In the event that the Commission has been permitted to withdraw from the hearing by the panel, the complainant must file the pleadings and assumes carriage of the proceeding.

The respondent must serve and file, along with a statement of service, a written response to the pleadings within 25 days of service of the statement of the facts, etc., noted above (r. 39). The response deals with issues raised in the complaint and the statement of facts that the respondent is relying on in his or her defence. The facts of the complaint that the respondent is willing to admit are listed along with the respondent's desired remedy and representation contact information. The respondent is also obligated to identify any person who is not named in the complaint but who may be affected by the proceeding, and must provide the person's contact information. The Commission and/or the complainant have five days from the date of service of the response in which to serve and file a reply (r. 40).

Mutual Disclosure

The Commission is required to give full disclosure of the results of its investigation to all parties within 30 days of the conference call (r. 41). Disclosure includes witness statements, documents, and evidence that relates to the complaint. The complainant is required to deliver witness statements and evidence by the same deadline (r. 42), while the respondent has 25 days after service of the Commission and complainant's disclosure to provide his or her material (r. 43). A failure to disclose by a party may mean that the party cannot refer to or enter the document or physical evidence at the hearing without the permission of the panel (r. 48).

Mediation and Settlement

With the consent of the parties, the matter can be referred to a mediator at any time during the tribunal process. Mediation is confidential, and statements made during the mediation cannot be admitted at the hearing without the agreement of the parties. Mediation usually takes place before a pre-hearing conference.

Settlement can also occur at any time and must be in writing and signed by the parties. Where settlement is reached, a Confirmation of Settlement (Form 3) is filed within 45 days of the date of settlement. The Confirmation of Settlement is signed by the parties and includes a draft order (Form 4).

Pre-hearing Conference

The pre-hearing conference takes place in the majority of cases before the Tribunal. The registrar will send notice to all parties identifying the date, time, place, and purpose of the case management pre-hearing. There may be more than one conference, depending on the complexity of the proceeding. The usual practice is for all parties and their representatives to attend. The Tribunal may issue notice requiring a party's attendance when the party's absence from the meeting results, or will result, in delay or is for the purpose of avoidance. A statement is also included in the notice, informing parties that whether they attend or not, binding orders may be made.

The Tribunal has the authority to compel a party to attend the pre-hearing conference to simplify or narrow down contentious issues and to allow for a more efficient use of the time scheduled for the hearing (r. 54, 55).

Evidence

A document submitted for evidence at the hearing must be filed in the Tribunal's record and marked as an exhibit with copies given to relevant witnesses, the panel, and each party. The panel may admit without proof or evidence any fact(s) agreed to by the parties. It is significant to note that the panel has discretion, through the SPPA, to admit any evidence, including hearsay and/or circumstantial evidence, that is relevant to the complaint. The weight and measure given to hearsay and/or circumstantial evidence at a hearing will turn on the particular facts and the body of other evidence presented.

Similar Act Evidence

Similar act evidence may be allowed at the hearing,[12] particularly in cases of alleged harassment. Harassment frequently occurs without witnesses. In some cases the matter may rest on the credibility of the parties involved. If so, the Tribunal may allow similar fact evidence where a pattern of behaviour is alleged. However, similar act evidence must relate to the complaint before the Tribunal. A complainant cannot submit similar act evidence of discrimination based on creed if the complaint only alleges sexual harassment. However, similar act evidence can be relevant, for example, in a complaint where a female employee is repeatedly told jokes of a sexual nature by her manager, which the employee finds offensive and sexually suggestive. Even though there are no witnesses to the alleged harassment, if other female employees have been told similar inappropriate jokes by the same manager named in the complaint, it is the evidence of these other female employees that may be admitted by the Tribunal as similar act evidence. Moreover, proving an intent to breach the Code is unnecessary, and similar act evidence, and/or circumstantial evidence, may be sufficient to meet the burden of proof.

Notice of Constitutional Question

If a party (a) plans to raise a question regarding the constitutional validity or applicability of an Act or of a regulation or by-law made under an Act or a rule of common law, or (b) intends to claim a remedy under section 24(1) of the *Canadian Charter of Rights and Freedoms [Charter]*,[13] the party must file a Notice of Constitutional Question and serve it on all the other parties, along with the Attorney General of Canada and the Attorney General of Ontario, at least 15 days prior to the date the party plans to argue the question.[14] This notice is not a frequent occurrence at a tribunal hearing. If desired, the relevant attorney can intervene in the proceeding and make submissions to the panel regarding the question raised.

Orders

Once the hearing is concluded, the Tribunal is required to make its decision within 30 days (s. 41(5)). There are a number of remedies available, under section 41 of the Code, to the Tribunal, where discrimination or harassment is proven. As stated, the mandate of the Tribunal is to ensure that the Code is complied with, and it seeks to put complainants in the position they would otherwise have been in had the discrimination or harassment not occurred. This is accomplished through monetary and non-monetary orders or a combination of the two. An example of a non-monetary remedy could involve an employee who was denied a promotion on a discriminatory ground and the Tribunal orders a promotion equal to the one wrongly denied. That order may

---

[12] The Tribunal can admit and act on similar act evidence under SPPA, s. 15(1).

[13] Anyone whose rights or freedoms, as guaranteed by the Charter, have been infringed or denied may apply to a court of competent jurisdiction to obtain such remedy as the court considers appropriate and just in the circumstances: *Charter*, s. 24(1).

[14] Rule 70, *Ontario Board of Inquiry Rules of Practice*, 2004.

be accompanied by an order for back pay equal to the raise associated with the promotion, commencing on the date it was improperly denied (monetary damages). Section 41(1)(a) of the Code gives a broad power for orders to be made that require a respondent to perform a task — e.g., implement a human rights policy or conduct a human rights education seminar for management — that, in the Tribunal's opinion, is necessary to prevent a future breach. A letter of assurance regarding future compliance to the Code may also be required, and corporate respondents may be ordered to post the Tribunal decision in their office.[15] It is this type of non-money order that the Commission would seek in the public interest.

Monetary remedies are influenced by the particulars of each complaint, as illustrated in case law. They are used for compensating the complainant for an infringement of a right and may include compensation for losses suffered as a result of that infringement. An amount may also be ordered where a respondent is shown to have discriminated with intent, or where the harassment has been ongoing or particularly severe. A lesser amount may be ordered where the complainant has been shown to engage in retaliatory name-calling.[16] Monetary remedies available under section 41 of the Code are summarized below:

1. **General damages** are for mental anguish and/or damages for the loss of the right to be free from discrimination and breach of the Code. Mental anguish damages are capped at $10,000 (s. 41(1)(b)) and require a finding that the act(s) of the respondent was wilful (i.e., a deliberate act) or reckless (i.e., an act or practice engaged in with indifference as to its effect). Expert medical evidence is generally not required. Additional general damages may be awarded for infringing the complainant's right to be free from discrimination generally and/or for the specific breach of the Code as it relates to the complainant's injury to dignity and self-respect resulting from the act(s) of the respondent. While there is no statutory cap on this second category of general damages, some Tribunal decisions have applied the same $10,000 cap imposed on mental anguish damages.

2. **Special damages** may also be awarded — for example, in a situation where an employee has been denied a promotion on a discriminatory ground. The employer may be ordered to compensate, with interest, the employee for the difference between the employee's present salary and the salary of the higher position. Non-monetary relief may include an order entitling the complainant to the next available position.

3. **Pre-judgment interest** may apply to monetary remedies at the Tribunal's discretion.

4. **Costs** may be awarded, at the discretion of the Tribunal, to a respondent where the complaint has been shown to be trivial, frivolous, vexatious or made in bad faith by the complainant and would be paid by the Commission who initiated the claim (s. 41(4) and r. 71).

In the event that a respondent elects to disregard a Tribunal order, the respondent may be found guilty of an offence and be liable for a fine up to

---

[15] *Styres v. Paiken* (1982), 3 C.H.R.R. D/926 (Ont. Bd. of Inquiry) and *Abouchar v. Toronto (Metro School Board (No. 4)* (1999), 35 C.H.R.R. D/175 (Ont. Bd. of Inquiry).

[16] *Ahluwalia v. Metropolitan Toronto (Municipality) Commissioners of Police* (1983), 4 C.H.R.R. D/1757 (Ont. Bd. of Inquiry).

$25,000.00. It is prudent for a successful complainant to obtain a copy of the tribunal decision from the registrar and file it with the Ontario Superior Court of Justice. The filing ensures that the order can be enforced as an order of the court and post-judgment interest requested if necessary.

Appeals

Any party may appeal the decision of the Tribunal to the Divisional Court, and the appeal operates as a stay of the proceeding (s. 42(1) and r. 73). The court is free to make a decision on the appeal as it sees fit, and is not bound in any way by the decision of the Tribunal (s. 42(3)). An application for judicial review does not automatically stay the Tribunal's order (r. 74).

2007: ONTARIO'S NEW HUMAN RIGHTS REGIME

A variety of issues have plagued Ontario's human rights regime for decades, with delay being a frequently cited concern.[17] The current process can result in years passing before a complainant reaches the hearing stage. Criticism has also raised issues of the Commission and the Tribunal's independence, the conflicting role of the Commission in regard to its screening complaints while charged with promoting Code compliance and inadequate government funding. After reports from government-appointed task forces, along with consultation and discussion with various stakeholders, the legislature drafted extensive changes to Ontario's human rights regime.

On December 20, 2006, *An Act to Amend the Human Rights Code*[18] ("amendment") was **assented to** by the legislature. The amendment represents the most comprehensive changes to Ontario's human rights law since enactment in 1962. The changes address issues that include delay, education, accessibility and provision for greater transparency in the human rights process. The most significant procedural and structural changes are identified in this section.[19]

The amendment involves more than an overdue redesign of the existing system, which comprises the OHRC and HRTO. It includes the creation of an independent legal resource centre and the formation of two secretariats. As well, there will be choices for many applicants concerning the commencement of a proceeding and the provision of legal advice. A right to make oral submissions means that applicants will be guaranteed the opportunity to be heard. Remedies have been expanded and enforcement made easier.

The majority of the changes to Ontario's human rights regime came into force on June 30, 2008.[20] Transitional provisions permitted the Tribunal to make rules, appoint members, allow a complaint filed with the OHRC under the old regime to be transferred to the new regime and identify when the

---

[17] There have been many discussion papers and articles written about, and criticizing, the current regime. See, for example, The Cornish Task Force Report (1992), the La Forest Task Force (2000) and the Ontario Human Rights Commission, "Reviewing Ontario's Human Rights System", Discussion Paper (2005), online: <http://www.ohrc.on.ca/english/consultations/human-rights-review-discussion-paper.pdf> (August 29, 2007). The OHRC website provides a list of consultation and discussion documents at <http://www.ohrc.on.ca/english/publications/index.shtml#consultations> (August 29, 2007).

[18] S.O. 2006, c. 30.

[19] The amendment is available on <http://www.e-laws.gov.on.ca>; a review of the full procedure is beyond the scope of this chapter.

[20] The amendment provisions relating to the Ontario Human Rights Commission and Ontario Human Rights Tribunal came into force on June 30, 2008. The provisions relating to the Human Rights Legal Support Centre have not yet been given a proclamation date. The full list of proclamation dates is available online: <http://www.e-laws.gov.on.ca/html/tables/publicstatutesannotations/elaws_t_pu_st_an_t90h19.htm> (August 29, 2007).

OHRC retains carriage of preexisting proceedings (Part IV, ss. 49 to 57). Regulations may also be made to address additional transitional matters as they arise.

Highlights of Procedural Changes

Direct Access Model

A meaningful change is the restructuring of the resolution process from one of investigation, selection and carriage of a proceeding by the OHRC to a "direct access" model. Direct access means that people can commence a proceeding directly with the HRTO and obtain a hearing should the issue not be resolved beforehand. It is expected that this fundamental change will reduce delay, make the resolution of proceedings more accessible and eliminate any conflict of interest related to the current OHRC involvement.

A proceeding commences by way of application and not complaint, as it has been previously the case. A person (s. 34(1)), two or more people jointly (s. 34(1)(4)), a person or organization on behalf of another, where the person alleging discrimination consents (s. 34(5)), or the OHRC (s. 35) may file an application with the Tribunal. The ability of a group to file an application is new and permits entities, such as unions or special interest groups, to file claims directly with the HRTO and is discussed further below.

Limitation Period

The limitation period is one year from the date of the alleged infringement of a right or, where a series of infringements are alleged, one year from the date of the last incident (s. 34(1)). Section 34(2) permits the Tribunal to extend the one-year limitation period under certain circumstances. Previously, a six-month limitation period was in effect.

The Role of the Courts

Changes that involve the courts concern the authority to review a Tribunal decision and to hear and decide a Code infringement where it is part of a civil proceeding. Currently, a party has a statutory right to appeal the Tribunal's decision to the Divisional Court. A **privative clause** in the amendment expressly limits the ability of a reviewing court to change or substitute the Tribunal's decision with its own. Section 45.8 states that the Tribunal's decision is final, and only **patently unreasonable** decisions may be altered or set aside by judicial review. That would require, for example, that the decision under review be found to be unsupported by the facts. The court cannot substitute its own decision where it simply disagrees with the result of the Tribunal. The Tribunal can, when requested by a party, reconsider its own decision (s. 45.7). The failure of the Tribunal to follow its own rules is "not a ground for setting aside" a decision unless it results in a "substantial wrong which affected the final disposition of the matter" (s. 43(8)).

> **45.8** Subject to section 45.6 of this *Act*, section 221.1 of the *Statutory Powers Procedures Act* and the Tribunal rules, a decision of the Tribunal is final and not subject to appeal and shall not be altered or set aside in an application for judicial review or in any other proceeding unless the decision is patently unreasonable.

Counter-balances to the narrowed scope of judicial review include a new selection process for the Commission and the Tribunal appointments mandated under the Act (ss. 27 and 32, respectively), a party's right to an oral hearing, the HRTO's ability to intervene in the proceeding and the availability of legal advice or representation to applicants. These are discussed further in the next section of this chapter. In addition, the OHRC has authority under s. 45.6 to **state a case** to the Divisional Court, where it is a party to a proceeding and believes that a decision or order made by the Tribunal is inconsistent with Commission policy.

There have, in the past, been conflicting decisions regarding the court's ability to hear Code matters and award damages where the allegation arises within a civil proceeding. The amendment expressly permits the court to decide a Code infringement and award damages where the allegation is related to the main issue in the civil proceeding (s. 46.1(1)). Therefore a proceeding for wrongful dismissal, as an example, may include a separate but related allegation of discrimination, and the court can hear both grounds and award monetary compensation. Where a Code infringement is related to a civil action and included in the statement of claim, the person cannot file an application with the Tribunal (s. 34(11) and (12)). A party may want to consider the best forum in which to bring the human rights claim prior to pursuing it. A matter relating solely to an infringement of the Code must be heard by a tribunal with authority to hear the matter.

The Ontario Human Rights Commission

The amendment expands the OHRC, or Commission's, function regarding independence from government, education, policy development and research, and its ability to provide consistency in the application of the Code (s. 29). The changes facilitate independence by having members appointed by the Lieutenant Governor in Council (s. 27(2)), and the Commission will report to the legislature, not the Ministry of the Attorney General (s. 31.6(2)). Reports can be made directly to the public or to whomever the OHRC considers appropriate (s. 31.7) regarding the state of human rights, which facilitate independence, transparency and accountability. The Commission is not constrained by providing information only to government or at its request. The Commission will no longer receive and screen complaints for hearings, investigate all matters or mediate settlements. All adjudicative responsibilities are removed by the amendment.

The OHRC's goal is to ensure compliance with the Code and eliminate discriminatory practices (s. 29). The idea is that increased public awareness through general and specific educational initiatives will pro-actively increase Code compliance and reduce infringements. It is likely, however, that there will be an increase in applications initially. The Commission will provide guidelines on the interpretation and application of the Code. There is also a refocusing of the OHRC on systemic discrimination. Research into systemic discrimination will pinpoint areas, sectors or industries that require remediation, and information and education will then target those identified areas. Guidelines and policies can then be tailored to the problem area.

In addition to authorizing research, the amendment provides the OHRC with authority to request copies of applications and responses filed with the HRTO in order to review them and identify areas of systemic concern (s. 38). Whether research or a series of individual applications with similar facts suggest systemic discrimination, the OHRC has extensive power to make recommendations, co-ordinate remedial programs and activities, initiate reviews, commence proceedings, act as intervenor or conduct inquiries (s. 29). The only qualification is that the action taken must be in the **public interest**, but what constitutes public interest appears to be at the Commission's discretion.

The Commission has broad powers when conducting an inquiry or review similar to those before amendment (ss. 31 to 31.2). Those powers include entry without warrant and production of evidence (s. 31). They may be used, for example, for reviews, pro-active investigation of systemic discrimination or to gather evidence in support of an application. The powers appear broader in the sense that an inquiry can be undertaken on the Commission's own initiative and does not have to be tied to an application. Specifically, the OHRC has authority to promote, assist and encourage groups to participate in programs that will alleviate incidents of tension and conflict based on a prohibited ground (s. 29(e)). That provision expressly refers to the OHRC's initiating a review or inquiry where only conditions that *may* lead to tension or conflict based on the Code are present. This authority suggests that the Commission, for example, may thus insert itself in situations that involve an identified group. It would not require that an application be filed or that discrimination be demonstrated.

Ensuring consistency in the application of the Code relative to HRTO decisions and the drafting of legislation is also part of the Commission's mandate. While its policy guidelines regarding the application of the Code are not binding on the Tribunal, the HRTO may consider OHRC-approved policies when deciding a case (s. 45.5(1)). The Tribunal must consider the policy if requested by a party (s. 45.5(2)). If the Commission believes that a final HRTO decision it was involved in is inconsistent with its policies, it may request that the Tribunal state a case to the Divisional Court (s. 45.6), identified earlier. That procedure is unavailable where the OHRC has not been a party or has not acted as an intervenor. However, the Tribunal is obligated to state a case, in writing, on a question of law only where the Tribunal itself deems it "appropriate" (s. 45.6(2)). The Commission may also review a statute or regulation and make recommendations where any aspect of the law is inconsistent with the intent of the Code (s. 29).

The OHRC retains discretion to initiate an application (s. 35(1)) or intervene (s. 37(1)) in a proceeding where the issue is of public interest. The Commission's use of adjudication to advance its goal of compliance may arise from the performance of any of its functions: education, research, review or investigation. Where the applicant consents, the Commission may intervene as a party in the proceeding and fully participate in the proceeding and lead evidence (s. 37(2)). If the OHRC seeks to intervene under other circumstances, its degree of participation will be determined by the Tribunal (s. 37(1)). An intervenor generally cannot lead evidence or cross-examine as those rights attach only to a party. Alternatively, the Commission may bring its own application in the public interest, even if an individual has independently filed an application. The applications would likely be heard together (ss. 35(2) and (3)).

The Ontario Human Rights Tribunal

The amendment creates a more autonomous adjudicative body and enhances the HRTO, or Tribunal's, authority over the resolution process, procedure and available remedies. Its core values are to increase accessibility, fairness, transparency, timeliness and the opportunity to be heard.[21] It is anticipated that non-systemic applications will take less than one year to reach the hearing stage.[22]

The amendment facilitates autonomy by requiring that adjudicator appointments meet specified criteria, removing the OHRC from the selection process for hearings and limiting court interference in decisions (discussed above). Section 32 requires adjudicators to be appointed by the Lieutenant Governor in Council. The appointment process is to be competitive and requires candidates to be assessed on specified criteria, including the candidate's experience, knowledge or training in human rights law and issues, aptitude for both impartial adjudication, and alternative dispute resolution processes provided for in

---

[21] Online: <http://www.hrto.ca/NEW/about/mandate.asp> (July 8, 2008).

[22] Michael Gottheil, "An Approach to Proceedings Before the Human Rights Tribunal of Ontario — Draft for Discussion Purposes Only" (Paper presented to the Ontario Bar Association, 11 July 2007) at page 8.

the rules (s. 32(3)). By appointing a group of "experts" as adjudicators, the Tribunal's expertise in deciding human rights issues would be expected to surpass that of the courts and thus attract the court's deference to the decision made. Expertise is one of the factors that limits a court's review of tribunal decisions.

The Tribunal is to deal with applications by adopting practices and procedures that "offer the best opportunity for a fair, just and expeditious resolution of the merits of the applications" (s. 40). The HRTO is empowered to make its own rules of practice and procedure, including implementing forms of alternate dispute resolution, such as mediation (s. 43(1) and (3)(a)).[23] Mediation is expected to be available throughout the proceeding and may be recommended by the Tribunal, and a party is able to request, or decline, participation.

The Tribunal can, among other things, intervene in a proceeding to conduct examinations in chief or cross-examinations of a witness or require a party to produce evidence or a witness (s. 43(3)). Moreover, section 44(1) empowers the Tribunal to conduct an inquiry where requested by a party and where it is satisfied that an inquiry is necessary to obtain evidence, where the evidence may assist in a fair, just and expeditious resolution on the merits and where it is appropriate under the circumstances (s. 44). As well, the HRTO has broad power when conducting an inquiry (s. 44), which includes warrantless entry. People are legally obligated to comply with tribunal requests during inquiry (s. 44(10)).

The Tribunal can refer matters arising out of a proceeding to the Commission, where the Tribunal determines the issue may be of interest to the Commission (s. 45.4). The OHRC is not, however, obligated to deal with the matter. The amendment expressly entitles a party to the proceeding to an oral hearing and written reasons (s. 43(2)). Decisions of the Tribunal will be made public.[24]

Remedies under the current act distinguished between a monetary award, or damages, for breach of the Code and monetary compensation for "mental anguish", where the infringement was imposed wilfully or recklessly, to a maximum of $10,000. The amendment eliminates the distinction between those monetary awards, the precondition of wilful or reckless conduct and the "mental anguish" maximum (s. 45.2). It also permits the Tribunal to make an order with respect to a party's future practice, even where the order was not requested by the applicant (s. 45.2(1) and (2)):

> **45.2**(1) On an application under section 34, the Tribunal may make one or more of the following orders ...
>
> 1. An order directing the party who infringed the right to pay monetary compensation to the party whose right was infringed for loss arising out of the infringement, including compensation for injury to dignity, feelings and self-respect.
> 2. An order directing the party who infringed the right to make restitution to the party whose right was infringed, other than through monetary compensation, for loss arising out of the infringement, including restitution for injury to dignity, feelings and self-respect.
> 3. An order directing any party to the application to do anything that, in the opinion of the Tribunal, the party ought to do to promote compliance with this Act.

---

[23] The Tribunal's *2004 Rules of Procedure* are available online: <http://www.hrto.ca/english/rules/2004rules.pdf> (August 29, 2007).

[24] For example, on <http://www.canlii.org>.

In a civil proceeding that includes an ancillary Code infringement, only the first two remedies directly above may be awarded (s. 46.1(1)). Therefore, the remedy sought will be an influencing factor in deciding the preferred forum in which to bring the application where **concurrent jurisdiction** exists.

A group (or person) may want to select the Tribunal where more than one has jurisdiction over the matter. This could arise in a civil proceeding, previously identified, or in a unionized workplace. The union might be seeking a systemic remedy. The union has recourse to the Ontario Labour Board, and arbitrators can hear Code applications. However, the arbitrator would be unable, for example, to amend a collective agreement, which may be the only way to address the systemic issue. Alternatively, a person may choose to file only with the HRTO because it has already decided a case on similar facts. Tribunal decisions are not expressly binding, but consistency would be expected.

Where two or more tribunals have concurrent jurisdiction to hear the application and an application has been filed with both, the HRTO retains jurisdiction over the matter. However, the HRTO would likely defer the application under its rules until the other tribunal has decided the matter. The HRTO will not, as is currently done by the OHRC, look to see whether the application "could or should" have proceeded under another act and dismiss on that basis. Section 45.1 permits the Tribunal to dismiss an application, on a case-by-case basis, only where the other proceeding has resolved the matter on the merits:

> The Tribunal may dismiss an application, in whole or in part, in accordance with its rules if the Tribunal is of the opinion that another proceeding has appropriately dealt with the substance of the application.

The Code currently permits only costs awards against the Commission, under particular circumstances, for the benefit of a respondent. There is no similar provision in the amendment. The Tribunal will be able to award costs against either party to the proceeding pursuant to the SPPA and its own rules. The SPPA permits costs only where the conduct of a party has been "unreasonable, frivolous or vexatious or a party has acted in bad faith" and a tribunal has made rules in respect of costs (SPPA s. 17.1(2) and (4)). In the event of a conflict between the Tribunal's rules, act or regulation and the SPPA, the SPPA is trumped (s. 42(2)).

The enforcement of awards is enhanced by s. 45.9(3), which permits an applicant to apply directly to the Tribunal if the written and signed settlement is breached within six months of the breach. Previously, an applicant seeking enforcement of a settlement had to reapply and, effectively, restart the OHRC process unless the settlement expressly permitted the Tribunal to deal with the issue.

The Human Rights Legal Support Centre ("HRLSC")

The creation of the HRLSC, or Centre, pursuant to the amendment is unique to Ontario's human rights regime. Its mandate is to "establish and administer a cost-effective and efficient system for providing support services, including legal services, respecting applications to the Tribunal under Part IV" (s. 45.12(a)). The purpose is to facilitate access to the HRTO. HRLSC is not an agency of the Crown and is independent of, but accountable to, the government of Ontario (s. 45.11). Information on procedure and process will be readily available to all who inquire and is expected to be available online. Applications may be prepared and submitted through the HRLSC but can be filed directly with the HRTO.

The Centre has authority to establish policies and priorities regarding its function that qualify its mandate. Services will be provided, province-wide

(s. 45.13(2)), "based on its financial resources" (s. 45.12(b)). Thus, financial resources will dictate the level of service available, and there is no right of specific entitlement. Legal assistance, however, will not be dependent on eligibility criteria, such as financial need.[25] While available for information and assistance, the Centre does not screen applications. An applicant is not obliged to use the HRLSC services, and an application can be filed directly with the HRTO.

The amendment, in s. 45.13, does specify particular services that will be provided:

> (1) The Centre shall provide the following support services:
> 1. Advice and assistance, legal and otherwise, respecting the infringement of rights under Part I.
> 2. Legal services in relation to,
>   (i) the making of applications to the Tribunal under Part IV,
>   (ii) proceedings before the Tribunal under Part IV,
>   (iii) applications for judicial review arising from Tribunal proceedings,
>   (iv) stated case proceedings,
>   (v) the enforcement of Tribunal orders,
> 3. Such other services as may be prescribed by regulation.

The delivery and range of availability of services will evolve once operation begins. Helena C. Birt, Transition Director, Human Rights Legal Support Centre, expects that there will be a staffed office located in Toronto and service networks across the province. Summary advice and assistance, substantive legal advice and support, legal representation and post-hearing services and support are anticipated.[26] Summary advice and assistance will include consideration of the merits of the claim, assistance in preparing applications, identifying issues and remedies, as well as preparing supporting documentation. It will also involve contact with the respondent to determine whether settlement is possible. Legal advice and assistance are potentially available at any stage in the proceeding. Partnerships between the HRLSC and existing community clinics and members of the private bar may evolve to augment service where needed. During the pre-hearing stage, representation may be provided by duty counsel or on a continuing solicitor/client basis.[27] Moreover, to assist with the enforcement of monetary awards, the Centre will offer information or advice regarding traditional methods, such as liens and garnishment.

While a respondent will be able to obtain general information or referrals from the HRLSC, legal representation is expected to be unavailable.[28]

Anti-Racism and Disability Rights Secretariats

The precise role of these two secretariats is not fully formed at present, but their function is identified under the act. Each secretariat is to conduct research and make recommendations to the OHRC, educate the public concerning discriminatory practices and other tasks as assigned by the Chief Commissioner, in order to eliminate these forms of discrimination (ss. 31.3(4) and 31.4(4)). Each secretariat will consist of a maximum of six people appointed by the Lieutenant Governor in Council on the advice of the Chief Commissioner (ss. 31.3(2) and 31.4(2)).

---

[25] Helena C. Birt, "The Ontario Human Rights Legal Support Centre: A Brief Introduction". Paper presented to the Ontario Bar Association, July 11, 2007, at p. 9.

[26] *Ibid.*

[27] *Ibid.* at p. 5.

[28] *Ibid.*

CHAPTER SUMMARY

This chapter identified the roles of the Human Rights Commission and the Human Rights Tribunal of Ontario in the human rights resolution process. The Commission has discretionary power to refer a complaint to the Tribunal, and the limits of this discretion are set out in sections 34 and 36 of the Code. The Tribunal is an administrative body and quasi-judicial in nature and may make monetary and non-monetary orders. The Code is remedial in nature.

The sequence of events in the complaint process at the Commission was discussed, including the powers of investigation under section 33 of the Code. The differences between mediation and conciliation were noted and related to confidentiality, appropriateness, and the potential for affecting the decision to refer the matter to the Tribunal or to dismiss under section 36(1). A complainant's right to reconsideration was also explored.

A description of the complaint process at the HRTO was presented. A discussion on intervenors, pleadings, and the pre-hearing conference followed. The type of evidence allowed at an administrative tribunal through the SPPA was briefly explained, and the types of orders available to an adjudicator and the relevant maximum were identified.

The chapter concluded with an overview of pending changes in the human rights resolution process.

GLOSSARY OF NEW TERMS AND KEY CONCEPTS

amicus curiae
A Latin term meaning "friend of the court", referring to an intervenor in a hearing, who may be allowed to make a written submission regarding the ramifications of a complaint.

assented to
When a bill is in its final form and accepted, or passed, by the legislature, it is assented to and becomes law.

case analysis
A report submitted by the investigation officer to the Commission summarizing the facts, issues, and evidence in a complaint. The case analysis will also include the officer's recommendation regarding the referral of the matter for a hearing.

complainant
The party in a human rights complaint who alleges that a right under the Code has been infringed.

concurrent jurisdiction
Where more than one adjudicative body has authority to decide the issue.

panel
One or more members of the Tribunal who adjudicate a hearing.

patently unreasonable
A standard of judicial review that shows the highest level of deference to the decision of an administrative adjudicative body; to set aside a decision, the decision being reviewed must be found to be without factual basis or legal authority.

privative clause
A clause in the enabling statute of an administrative adjudicative body that limits review of its decisions by the court.

public interest
Comprising the public concepts of justice and equality, which promote and advance the common good to the community within the social areas covered by the Code.

reconsideration
The process through which a complainant may request the Commission to reverse its decision regarding the non-referral of a complaint.

respondent
The party in a human rights complaint who is alleged to have infringed a right under the Code.

similar act evidence
A type of evidence allowed at the Tribunal to establish that a pattern of behaviour has occurred.

state a case
A written request to the court for a decision regarding a question of law.

social area
The Code only applies to specified social areas found in sections 1 to 6.

REVIEW QUESTIONS

1. What are the legislative functions of the Ontario Human Rights Commission under the Code?

2. By what criteria can the Commission make a decision to dismiss a complaint? Is the Commission bound to refer the complaint to the Tribunal if the complaint is outside of the dismissal criteria?

3. Distinguish between mediation and conciliation in the resolution process.

4. What types of evidence are admissible at the Tribunal?

5. Describe the two types of orders that can be made by an adjudicator, and give an example of each.

6. Identify the Commission's three objectives, which are included in its mandate.

7. The Commission has referred a complaint to the Tribunal for a hearing. Identify the three obligations the Board of Inquiry seeks to fulfill regarding the complaint.

8. A complainant wants to have a court reconsider the Commission's reconsideration decision. Should the complainant file an appeal or application for judicial review? Will the decision be stayed?

DISCUSSION QUESTIONS

1. In your view, what are the strengths and weaknesses of the present enforcement system?

2. Go to the Ontario Human Rights Commission website at <www.ohrc.on.ca>, and read some of the policies on human rights issues. Select one policy to investigate, and then contact an equality-seeking group that represents members relevant to the policy you have selected. Compose a summary of the group's perspective of the issue, along with any initiatives the Commission has undertaken regarding the matter. Present a discussion summary of your findings.

3. A friend has contacted you because a landlord has refused to rent her an available unit, saying that he doesn't rent to single mothers. What would you advise her to do? Explain the human rights resolution process to her.

4. You were denied a promotion at work that you felt should have been yours. Your supervisor has made questionable references in the past about your ethnic background, and you can't help but wonder if she discriminated against you regarding the promotion. You filed a grievance with the union of which you are a member. The union determined that there were no irregularities with the selection process used by your supervisor. You, however, want to file a human rights complaint. What are the chances of your phone call to the Commission resulting in a complaint being filed? Why?

5. A young woman has recently immigrated to Canada from a country where female genital mutilation, or "FGM" (also known as female circumcision, a procedure that removes part or all of a female's external sexual organs), is a cultural norm. The young woman's parents wish to continue this practice in Canada despite the fact that the young woman

does not consent. Does the young woman have a human rights complaint, and, if so, on what basis?

6. What is the most significant change in the function of the Human Rights Commission pursuant to the upcoming changes to the human rights process?

SUGGESTED READING

Cornish, Mary, et al. *Achieving Equality: A Report on Human Rights Reform* (Government of Ontario, 1992).

WEBSITES
Human Rights Legal Support Centre: <www.hrlsc.on.ca>
Ontario, Ministry of the Attorney General: Human Rights in Ontario, <www.attorney general.jus.gov.on.ca/english/ohrc>
Ontario Human Rights Commission: <www.ohrc.on.ca>
The Human Rights Tribunal of Ontario: <www.hrto.ca>

Aboriginal Rights

Janet I. Mason
BARRISTER AND SOLICITOR

Learning Objectives

After reading this chapter, the reader should be able to:

➢ understand why Aboriginal rights are considered *sui generis*

➢ understand elements of the historical treatment of First Nations by colonists and government and the effect of that treatment on their relationships

➢ appreciate why issues surrounding Aboriginal rights remain relevant today

➢ identify the various ways that an Indian band can acquire Aboriginal title to a tract of land

➢ comprehend the requirements for establishing Aboriginal title under the common law

➢ identify the requirements for establishing an Aboriginal right, other than title, under the common law

TABLE OF CONTENTS

INTRODUCTION

The fact that **Aboriginal** peoples occupied the land prior to the arrival of Europeans distinguishes them from other minority groups in Canada. It also provides the foundation from which Aboriginal rights arise and explains their unique treatment under the law.[1] When the first Europeans arrived in North America, the land was already occupied by tribes of Indians, or Aboriginals, who had been there for thousands of years.[2] When first contact was made between the two groups, the Aboriginal peoples were seen to be "liv[ing] in communities on the land ... participating in distinctive cultures, as they had done for centuries."[3] The Aboriginal population at that time has been estimated to be several million.[4] North American history clearly began long before the first European arrived on its shores.

Aboriginal communities have claimed, and some continue to claim, that they were sovereign nations prior to contact with Europeans and were treated as independent nations by early European colonists. As such, the Indians assert entitlement to certain rights that "encompass all aspects of their culture, including rights to land, traditions, and survival."[5] However, when the British Crown asserted **sovereignty** (i.e., supreme authority) over North America, it was not long before the "new" majority disempowered and marginalized the First Nations.[6] The Crown acquired sovereignty on the basis that it (like France, before ceding its claim) was the first to discover the "vacant" land of North America. It was an accepted practice in Europe at that time to consider land "vacant" where the inhabitants were "insufficiently Christian".[7]

The Canadian government has begun to acknowledge certain Aboriginal rights, but not the sovereignty (or more specifically, the right of self-government), of North America's indigenous population. "Since the *Constitution Act, 1982*,[8] does not explicitly acknowledge an aboriginal right of self-government, such a right does not exist as a matter of Canadian law."[9] Aboriginal rights issues remain unsettled as the federal government and First Nations seek to find a balance between two fundamentally different cultures. The goal is to try to reconcile the Aboriginal rights that flow from a prior occupation of the land with Crown sovereignty so that First Nations can maintain their culture.[10]

---

[1] Shin Imai, *Aboriginal Law Handbook*, 2d ed. (Toronto: Carswell, 1999) at 6 [Imai].

[2] The terms "Aboriginal", "First Nation", and "Indian" are respectfully used interchangeably throughout this chapter for the ease of the reader. These terms refer to the one group of founding peoples of Canada, the North American Indian, who was historically involved with the European colonists. The other two founding peoples, the Métis and Inuit, are identified separately. The words "band" and "tribe" are also used interchangeably to denote a particular Aboriginal community or group. All of these terms are open to debate or objection and may have a narrower, or broader, meaning in certain contexts. The usage in this introductory and general overview of Aboriginal history is as defined above.

[3] *R. v. Van der Peet*, [1996] 2 S.C.R. 507 at para. 30 [*Van der Peet*].

[4] Neal Salisbury, "The Indians' Old World: Native Americans and the coming of the Europeans" (1996) 53 William and Mary Quarterly 435 at 435.

[5] Imai, *supra* note 1 at 6.

[6] While it was originally the British Crown who dealt with Indian matters, it has been the responsibility of Canada's federal government since Confederation. The term "Crown" can be read as federal government.

[7] John Borrows, "Sovereignty's Alchemy: An Analysis of *Delgamuukw v. British Columbia*" (1997) 35 Osgoode Hall L.J. 125, at 132.

[8] Being Schedule B to the *Canada Act 1982* (U.K.), 1982, c. 11 [*Constitution Act, 1982*].

[9] The Constitutional Law Group, *Canadian Constitutional Law*, 3d ed. (Toronto: Emond Montgomery Publications Limited, 2003) at 522 [Law Group].

[10] Statistics Canada, 2001, reports an Aboriginal population of 976,305 comprising 608,850 North American Indians, 292,305 Métis and 45,070 Inuit. Canada's total population, according to the 2001 Census, is 29,630,030. This

All matters concerning Indians are under the power of the federal government as enunciated in s. 91(24) of the *Constitution Act, 1867*[11] and are considered to be *sui generis* (i.e., unique).[12] This *sui generis* nature emerged as a way to more fairly deal with issues arising from the prior occupation of North America by Aboriginal peoples and to allow courts to properly apply common law principles. An Aboriginal right is relevant only to a legislatively, or judicially, identified group within Canadian society who meet certain requirements. Existing Aboriginal rights, which are rights that existed and were not extinguished prior to the enactment of *Constitution Act, 1982*, are specifically protected in s. 35 of *The Canadian Charter of Rights and Freedoms*.[13] This *sui generis* nature also evolved as a way to reconcile disputes over rights. For example, the evidentiary standard in an Aboriginal rights claim is unique in that it permits oral evidence of historical facts, passed down through Aboriginal generations, to be admitted and relied upon in court.

Present-day Aboriginal rights cannot be properly understood without a consideration of the historical context through which they have evolved. A complete history is beyond the scope of this chapter, and only certain events have been selected to illustrate characteristics in a general way. More detailed information can be obtained by referencing the "Suggested Reading" section provided at the end of this chapter. The historical overview included here serves to provide the reader new to the subject with enough contextual background to understand the present law. The focus is on the relationship between Aboriginal peoples and government, whether that government was colonial or Canada's own. The overview also demonstrates that Aboriginal rights issues, generally viewed as consisting of land claims and a desire for Aboriginal self-government, remain unsettled. These issues have roots that can be traced back generations. The particular behaviours and incidents discussed are representative of the relationship between various European groups and First Nations. There was little difference, for example, in the relationship whether it concerned the French and the Huron or the British and the Iroquois. The focus is on the British and their Iroquois allies since the British eventually acquired sovereignty in North America. There were, and are, many tribes across Canada who have experienced similar treatment.

This chapter will begin with a discussion of some of the fundamental differences between the Aboriginal and European cultures. In addition to the First Nations' prior occupation of North America, a variety of factors have affected Aboriginal rights over time. These factors include the cultural differences between European settlers and Aboriginals, disease, the early relationship between settlers and First Nations, and a failure of government to fulfill contractual obligations contained in treaties. Once these issues have been examined, attention will then be given to legislation governing Indians, the content of an Aboriginal land title right, and the current requirements for establishing an existing, but unrecognized, Aboriginal right under the law.

---

means that the Aboriginal population comprises approximately 3% of the total population. Online: Statistics Canada <http://www12.statcan.ca/english/census01/home/Index.cfm> (August 2004). Statistics on Aboriginal peoples collected in the 2006 Census was released in January 2008 <http://www12.statcan.ca/english/census06/release/aboriginal.cfm>.

[11] (U.K.), 30 & 31 Vict., c. 3, reprinted in R.S.C. 1985, App. II, No. 5.

[12] Under this provision, the Inuit would also qualify as "Indian" under federal jurisdiction. However, the federal government does not consider the Métis to be under federal jurisdiction.

[13] Part I of the *Constitution Act, 1982*, being Schedule B to the *Canada Act 1982* (U.K.), 1982, c. 11 [the "Charter"]. For more information on the constitutional protection of Aboriginal rights, see the chapter titled "The Canadian Charter of Rights and Freedoms" in the complete edition of this book.

ABORIGINAL CULTURE

It was European colonists, consisting of the Dutch, French and British, who first formed relationships with the Aboriginal peoples they encountered. At the time of first contact between the groups, Aboriginal tribes lived in civilized and structured communities. Some of these communities were established on particular tracts of land, with hunting and fishing expeditions extending into the surrounding areas. Others enjoyed a nomadic existence that would, for example, follow the buffalo on seasonal hunts. Each Indian tribe was autonomous, although most shared common cultural attributes. The Cherokee and Iroquois, for example, were independent tribes who spoke different languages, but their cultural practices (such as annual celebrations and care of their poor) and spiritual beliefs were similarly based. Trade between bands was common and expanded to include trade with the Europeans when they arrived.

The First Nations people have enjoyed a highly developed social structure.[14] This early culture was generally grounded on a more evolved form of gender equality than that of the Europeans; certain personal attributes were culturally valued, and they embraced a spirituality that included an awareness of the fragility of the environment. Tribes commonly viewed women as having equal status to men. Words that differentiated between genders (e.g., *his* or *hers*) were absent from many Aboriginal languages. Women often sat on band councils and participated in the decision-making process. Band membership was sometimes established through maternal bloodlines, such as in the Gitksan or Wet'suwet'en tribes of British Columbia. The First Nations valued the attributes of self-discipline, adaptability, and humour. Self-discipline and adaptability were necessary for living off the land in a climate that could be harsh and unforgiving. Humour was particularly highly valued because it provided a source of comfort when life was hard.

Indian spirituality included a respect for, and relationship with, the land that they depended on for food and home. Bands regularly changed hunting grounds when the animal population became dangerously low. Many Indians were proficient farmers and knew to rotate crops so as not to deplete the soil. The "Great Spirit" or "Creator" (either term being the equivalent to the Europeans' concept of "God") existed in the land, people, and animals, and no single entity was considered to rank above the other. All entities constituted a temple of the Great Spirit and belonged to it.[15] Thus, a band had a relationship with the land but did not *own* it.

Leadership/Political Structure

The Indians had a political, or leadership, structure comprised of a band council and a community-based judicial system, and groups sometimes warred with neighbouring tribes. There was no central governmental authority for Indian tribes. Generally, each tribe had its own council made up of members of the community.[16] The band could be further divided into "houses" or "clans". Each **house or clan** may have had one or more hereditary chiefs — for example, the Wet'suwet'en band — with each chief being selected by a

---

[14] It is beyond the scope of this chapter, which focuses on the law, to discuss the cultural contributions of the three founding peoples to Canada's broader culture. International recognition of Indian and Inuit art is increasing, and other creative arts are also gaining attention as part of Canada's character.

[15] Ronald Wright, *Stolen Continents: Conquest and Resistance in the Americas*, 10th ed. (Toronto: Penguin, 2003) at 100 [Wright].

[16] *Ibid.*

group of elders. Band chiefs were sometimes replaced, or simply ignored, if they lacked the necessary leadership skills. Political decisions were made by council consensus and not by a simple majority (i.e., a 51% vote in favour of the decision). Since consensus was required, a chief had to be skilled in the art of persuasion. Dissenters could withdraw from the community. Council members that withdrew could leave the band with their supporters and establish a new community. In this way, a war between disagreeing band members could be avoided.

When a crime was committed, the Indians believed that it affected the whole community and not just the victim and offender. A **healing circle**, usually consisting of band elders, would be held where the members and the injured party would speak of the harm suffered. Offenders were expected to take responsibility for their behaviour. The council goal was to design a sentence that would rehabilitate and assist offenders so that they could remain as part of the community. When serious events such as murder occurred, the Indians generally believed in "an eye for an eye" and, historically, retribution was the standard response. Healing circles continue to be held today and are recognized by the courts.

Indian tribes did engage in wars with each other, and prisoners, including colonists, were often adopted by their captors. Inter-tribal wars were common in North America but rarely concerned a dispute over land. They were more likely to be started to effect retribution or achieve personal prestige, or for adoption.[17] Adoption was the most common reason since it was an efficient way to maintain or increase the band's population. Many of the colonists who were adopted were unwilling to return to colonial life even when given the opportunity. They acquired a preference for the Aboriginal way of life.

Written Language and Oral Evidence

The Indians did not have a written language when early treaties were entered into. Band history and important agreements were passed down orally from generation to generation. **Wampum belts** or strings were often used as an oral aid and were made of beads and coloured strings woven into symbolic designs. The Wampum belt's composition of beads and strings represented specific facts that were discussed more fully in the oral commentary that accompanied them. These belts were also used to record the terms of formal agreements the band entered into and then given to the other party to the negotiation. Oral commentary was always required as an accompaniment to the Wampum.

The importance of this oral tradition remains to the present day and is part of the *sui generis* nature of Aboriginal rights. An Aboriginal rights claim often involves evidence of the **oral history** passed on to each generation in order for the court to properly decide the matter. Under standard evidence rules, oral historical evidence is inadmissible. The Supreme Court of Canada decided in *Van der Peet*, however, that oral evidence is admissible in order to determine a land claim or other Aboriginal right: e.g., the right to hunt on a particular piece of land where title is not claimed. If the oral evidence was excluded, the claim would be likely to automatically fail because there would be insufficient evidence to support it. In *Van der Peet* the Aboriginal person had appealed a conviction for selling 10 fish caught under an Indian food fish licence. The accused asserted that the right to sell the fish for money was

---

[17] Olive Patricia Dickason, *Canada's First Nations: A History of Founding Peoples from Earliest Times*, 3d ed. (Toronto: Oxford University Press, 2002) at 63 [Dickason].

an Aboriginal right grounded in the band's history and culture.[18] While the Supreme Court upheld the conviction, it decided that the admissibility of the oral evidence was part of the *sui generis* nature of Aboriginal rights:

> [C]ourts should approach the rules of evidence, and interpret the evidence that exists, with a consciousness of the special nature of aboriginal claims, and of the evidentiary difficulties in proving a right which originates in times where there were no written records of the practices, customs and traditions engaged in. The courts must not undervalue the evidence presented by aboriginal claimants simply because that evidence does not conform precisely with the evidentiary standards that would be applied in, for example, a private law torts case.[19]

Prior to the Supreme Court's acceptance of oral evidence the Indians were unable to fully participate in a judicial system that gave greater consideration to written evidence, such as contracts or treaties. The written agreement, even where it did not reflect the Indians' understanding of the terms or their oral history, was seen to be more binding in court than Wampum belts and their accompanying commentary. This ignored the fact of the First Nations' existence in North America since "time immemorial" and any rights associated with their prior possession of the land.[20] Therefore, even where the terms of the agreement had been presented orally to the Indians in a way that differed from the written agreement, the written agreement superseded any verbal promise.

Status in the Aboriginal Community

Status in the Aboriginal community was commonly based on the distribution of wealth and not the acquisition of wealth. Status did not require that each Indian aspire to own an individual parcel of land. Rather, land was held communally by the band and could not be owned, sold, or given as a gift by an individual. The First Nations also believed in caring for widows and orphans, and ensuring that food and other necessaries were available for everyone in the community. A celebration would be held where the objective was to give away as much as possible to those in the band who were less fortunate. The Indians believed that becoming attached to material items would only lead to unhappiness when those items were lost or no longer of use. Giving wealth away prevented an attachment and also ensured that everyone had what was needed. The obligation of generosity was reciprocal. Often, the same items would be passed along to others each year. Ceremonies and the exchange of gifts with agreements were important cultural events. It was a highly evolved, and alien, social structure that the European colonists encountered upon their arrival. While the Aboriginals may not have had written language or European technology, they certainly were not the "savages" the Europeans called them. It could be said that the social structure of Aboriginal communities had, in fact, evolved beyond the class-based and exploitive European culture of that time.

---

[18] The specific requirements for making a successful Aboriginal title claim are discussed later in this chapter under "Land Claims".

[19] *Van der Peet, supra* note 3 at para. 68.

[20] Wright, *supra* note 15 at 129.

EUROPEAN CULTURE

The Europeans arrived in North America with political and cultural norms very different from those of the Aboriginal peoples they met. The Europeans had lived under a political and social hierarchy and assumed the same structure existed in the Indian communities. Therefore, the Europeans sought to deal with the *top* Aboriginal leader who could sign an agreement on behalf of the tribe. As identified, the Aboriginal population consisted of independent and autonomous bands and each was free to make its own decisions. The Europeans couldn't find a governing Indian tribe through which they could bind all tribes to an agreement.

However, some tribes would occasionally meet to make joint decisions on certain matters. For example, the Iroquois established a confederacy of eventually six separate tribes, later called the Six Nations. This confederacy had leaders from each band who would sit on a special council and come to a consensus regarding issues that affected the well-being of their communities: e.g., whether to side with the British or French or remain neutral during the war for control of the land. The confederacy could be viewed as a governing body over the participating tribes.

European life at the time was difficult for those not born into the privileged classes. Many settlers left for North America to acquire wealth and land — the two commodities denied them at home. The acquisition of wealth and ownership of land was their method of obtaining social status. North America offered a better standard of living and greater independence. The settlers arrived prepared to do whatever it took to ensure they received their share of the land. The Indian communities were soon viewed as the new peasant class, with the European settlers claiming status as the upper or ruling class.

Fundamental differences between Aboriginal and European-based cultures remain today. These differences present unique challenges for the Canadian government and Aboriginal peoples as they try to reconcile them. In June 2004, the Canadian Press reported that an Aboriginal band in British Columbia opposed the government's efforts to relocate an orca whale.[21] The Mowachaht-Muchalaht band believed that the orca contained the former chief's spirit, as his deathbed wish was that his spirit would inhabit an orca, and the orca appeared in the area shortly after the chief's death. The band wanted to act as steward to the orca and requested that the government provide money to support the whale and to conduct a "public education campaign for visitors using our title waters." The band also asked to be involved in the decision to relocate the whale at a "culturally appropriate time." The Department of Fisheries wanted to relocate the orca with its pod after conducting medical tests and believed this to be in the best interests of the whale. Reintegration with the pod would allow the whale to live normally and eliminate the public safety risk the orca presented by its presence at Mooya Bay and Gold River Harbour. While each position shared a concern for the orca, they were not easily reconciled because of fundamentally different perspectives: the government viewed the situation from a scientific standpoint, whereas the First Nations considered it a spiritual matter.

---

[21] Scott Sutherland, "Aboriginal band demands stop to plan to relocate Luna from their waters" *The [Vancouver] Province* (23 June 2004), online: Reunite Luna <http://www.reuniteluna.com/news_release.php?id=514>.

THE EPIDEMICS

Disease epidemics played an important role in the early relationship between the Indians and colonists and facilitated the marginalization of Aboriginal peoples. The isolation of North America's indigenous peoples from European and other populations meant that the Indians were susceptible to new diseases that the Europeans brought with them because the Indians had not acquired any natural resistance to these diseases. The resulting epidemics decimated the Aboriginal population. Eventually, the population of the First Nations became too low to repel the invaders by force. Many council leaders died of disease, leaving the Indians without experienced leadership at times when difficult decisions, such as treaty terms, needed to be made. The matter was further compounded by the fragmentation of Aboriginal peoples — the downside of band autonomy. The independent nature of Indian bands meant that they were vulnerable to the Europeans in the absence of competent leadership and collaboration with other bands.

There were two major epidemics that affected the Aboriginal population. The first occurred in the 16th century and originated in the southern United States. The second epidemic began in 1738 when a British slave ship arrived in South Carolina with a cargo that included smallpox. Half of the Cherokee Nation in the United States died of smallpox, including many of their leaders. The smallpox spread easily with trade between the Europeans and the Indians as well as inter-tribal trade, and it wasn't long before the epidemic had spread north to Montreal. The French colonists in Montreal suggested to the Indians that the smallpox was a deliberate attempt by the British to harm the Aboriginal people. The French hoped that this misinformation would increase support for their side and against the British as each group vied for dominance of the new land.

The French suggestion was indicative of what subsequently happened. The first recorded incident of modern germ warfare seems to have been between the British and the Iroquois. Lord Jeffrey Amherst, who deliberately ignored British obligations under treaties and failed to prevent illegal squatting on Indian land, wanted to be rid of the Indian population once the French were conquered. He was angry about the Indian uprising against settlers, even though the majority killed by the Indians had been illegal squatters. After France ceded its claim to North America, Amherst ordered his men to take the bed sheets used by smallpox victims and give them as gifts to the chiefs they met during parlays. In this way, smallpox spread quickly and further decimated the Iroquois population.

The effect of European diseases on the Indian population led to Britain's ultimate emergence as the ruling power in North America. The Indians lost many great leaders, and dissent within Aboriginal communities became common. Some felt that the Europeans should be resisted and ousted from the land, while others supported co-operation with the invaders. But, more important, the end result was that there were too few Indians left to force the Europeans to leave. The Iroquois leaders who survived the epidemics were left with no choice but to sue for peace with the British in order to survive.

THE EARLY RELATIONSHIP BETWEEN THE EUROPEANS AND INDIANS

The First Nations cautiously welcomed the newcomers and taught them how to survive in the new land. The colonists learned how to travel by toboggan, canoe and snowshoe and were introduced to new crops, such as corn and squash, which they sent home. In exchange, the Indians were able to obtain new technology, such as gunpowder. The British and French entered into trade agreements with the Indians and relied on them as military allies until the French ceded their claim to North America in favour of Britain. Without the help of the First Nations, the Europeans "would not have been able to survive the rigours of the climate, succeed in their business (fishing, whaling, fur trading), or dodge each other's bullets."[22] However, the relationship between the Europeans and the Aboriginal population was often uneasy.[23]

The Europeans were often unconcerned with fairness when trading with First Nations and were dependent on their Indian allies as they attempted to gain control of the land. In their drive to acquire wealth, some Europeans would ensure that the Indians they traded with were drunk before negotiations began. These traders exploited the Indians in their drunken state by obtaining furs at reduced prices. Military alliances between a First Nation and the French or British became common. These alliances were necessary as the Indians soon held the balance of power in North America because the military strength of each group (i.e., French, British and First Nations) was evenly matched. In addition, the native population knew the lay of the land and were adept at making quick military strikes and then fading into the forest. Both the French and British desired alliances with various bands to fight on their behalf in their quest for dominance of North America. In exchange, the First Nation received trade agreements and goods.

France, England and Spain signed the **Treaty of Paris** in 1763. The British emerged as the controlling European presence as France and Spain (who ceded Florida but retained other states) gave up their claims. The result was that Britain held the land east of the Mississippi and north to Canada. The Aboriginal tribes that had allowed Britain to gain power were not mentioned in this treaty. Concerned that more of their land would be taken over by settlers, a group of Ohio Indians led by Chief Pontiac began a war against the British to prevent further encroachment. The British won the war, with Amherst's help, but were aware that their resources for funding wars in North America were depleted. In order to prevent further Indian uprisings over land, two agreements specifically addressed the issue: the first was an agreement between the British and the Iroquois called the **Two Row Wampum** of the Iroquois (which included the terms that each group would not interfere with the other, and each would retain their own customs and law); and the second was the **Royal Proclamation** of 1763 issued by King George.[24]

The Royal Proclamation "portrays Indian nations as autonomous political entities, living under the protection of the Crown but retaining their own internal political authority" and states that the First Nations "were not to be 'molested or disturbed' on their lands."[25] It attempted to define the boundaries of the Indian's land and to prevent settlers from illegally establishing communities on identified land. The Royal Proclamation also stated that only the Crown, and not settlers, could purchase Indian land. This was to prevent the Indians from being exploited by unscrupulous settlers determined to own Indian land. However, the settlers refused to acknowledge the defined bound-

---

[22] Royal Commission on Aboriginal Peoples, *Looking Forward, Looking Back*, Volume 1 (Ottawa: Minister of Supply & Services, 1996); summary online: Indian and Northern Affairs Canada <http://www.ainc-inac.gc.ca/ch/rcap/rpt/lk_e.html> (August 2004) [cited to summary] at 7 [RCAP].

[23] It should be noted that the French, British and Dutch all had separate and independent dealings with First Nations.

[24] Imai, *supra* note 1 at 27. The Two Row Wampum "formed the basis of all ... treaties with other nations including the Dutch, the French, the British and the Americans." Online: Akwesasne <http://www.akwesasne.ca/tworowwampum.html> (August 2004) at 2.

[25] RCAP, *supra* note 22 at 9.

Cayuga Sachem Deskaheh's Last Public Address, 1925

EXHIBIT 23.1

My home is on the Grand River ... where, one hundred and forty winters ago, we had a little sea-shore of our own and a birch-bark navy.

You would call it Canada. We do not ...

We didn't think we would ever live long enough to find that a British promise was not good. An enemy's foot is on our country, and George the Fifth knows it for I told him so, but he will not lift his finger to protect us nor will any of his ministers ...

To punish us for trying to preserve our rights, the Canadian Government has now pretended to abolish our government [and] set up a Canadian-made government over us, composed of the few traitors among us who are willing to accept pay from Ottawa ...

One word more so that you will be sure to remember our people. If it had not been for them, you would not be here. If, one hundred and sixty-six winters ago, our warriors had not helped the British at Quebec ... it would have been a French-speaking people here today, not you. That part of your history cannot be blotted out by the stealing of our wampum belts in which that is recorded.

Source: Passage cited in Ronald Wright, *Stolen Continents: Conquest and Resistance in the Americas*, 10th ed. (Toronto: Penguin, 2003) at 345–46.

---

aries; they burned Indian towns and claimed the land as their own.[26] The British were unable, or unwilling, to enforce the boundaries on behalf of the Indians. After all, the French were no longer a threat to British power in North America, with the result that the Indians were no longer needed as military allies. The Indians were viewed as a barrier to large-scale, European settlement.

However, the British were still concerned about the lack of a dividing line between what are now Canada and the United States. In 1784 the British Crown transferred the Grand River tract of land, located along the western end of the Niagara Peninsula, to the Mohawk and Six Nations. It is interesting to note that this land transfer was made to "his majesty's faithful allies", indicating that the British viewed the Six Nations as an independent nation and not a conquered or dependent nation. The Indian presence on this land provided Britain with a buffer zone between them and the United States. The Iroquois maintained a military presence and would protect the north from southern invaders without putting any European at risk.[27]

As these events unfolded, the Indian bands again split into factions. Some groups believed that the British should be resisted and the land reclaimed. Others believed that they should acculturate to the emerging European economy. Some believed that if they didn't sell their land to the Crown, it would simply be taken from them by force. Joseph Brant was the leader of the Iroquois Confederacy located in Grand River. He advocated participation in the new economy and leased Grand River land, some of the finest agricultural land in Canada, to the white settlers in order to raise money for economic participation. The leases stipulated that the land remained the property of the

---

[26] Wright, *supra* note 15 at 221.

[27] As the border between Canada and the United States was being established, the Iroquois nation ended up being split, with some located on the Canadian side and some on the U.S. side. This, along with other reasons, resulted in two parallel Iroquois Confederacies. One was located on the Grand River, and the other in New York.

Iroquois Confederacy. This stipulation did not prevent the government from subsequently, and arbitrarily, declaring the leases to be irrevocable land concessions by the Iroquois to the British.

Towards the end of the 19th century it became clear that the United States would not invade its neighbour to the north. The Indian buffer states were no longer needed, and the Six Nations were viewed as an obstacle to the government's power over, and claim to, the land now called the Dominion of Canada. By 1867 the Six Nations were left with only 90 square miles of land on the Grand River. The Canadian government asserts that the Grand River is an Indian Reserve. The Iroquois maintain that the Grand River and other remaining lands are national territories similar to the state of Monaco. "Why, [the Indians ask], should a people who have never been conquered by Canada, and have never surrendered their independence, be colonized when other small nations are free? They add that if lands unjustly taken were returned to them, their countries might not be so small."[28]

By the middle of the 20th century, non-Aboriginals were being drawn to cities and no longer threatened Indian land. But the desire for Indian land was not diminished. Industrial growth created the need for electrical power, and dams were the least expensive way of generating that power. It was not unusual for Indian land to be expropriated to build a dam, which reduced construction costs. The result was that "[t]he Iroquois lost more land in fifteen years than they had lost in the preceding century."[29] The factories that sprang up around the dams often polluted the surrounding land and water, contaminating the Indians' traditional hunting and fishing grounds. Aboriginal rights to land remain unsettled to the present day.

THE *INDIAN ACT*

Once the military force of the First Nations was no longer required, the Canadian government decided that the most efficient way of dealing with the "Indian problem" was to assimilate the Indians into the broader Canadian culture. Assimilation could be seen as a way to avoid further land claims or the need for treaties — everyone would simply be Canadian. A variety of methods were used to achieve this goal, including special boarding schools for Aboriginal children, various legislation, and the offer of Canadian citizenship status. Students at Aboriginal residential schools were forbidden to speak their native language or practice their religion, which resulted in the breakdown of family and community bonds. The Canadian government could arbitrarily relocate Aboriginal communities. Registered Indians who volunteered for service in World Wars I and II returned home to find that they were denied the benefits available to non-Aboriginal veterans.[30] Until 1951, it was a criminal offence for Aboriginal peoples to hold feast ceremonies. As well, Quebec didn't allow Indians to vote until 1968, and between 1927 and 1951, it was illegal to raise money for Indian claims, effectively denying First Nations access to Canadian courts. Incentives, such as a small financial payment and ownership of a small piece of land, were held out to the Indians to encourage them to abandon their native roots to become voting members of Canada.[31] Few Indians took the government up on the offer. Today, the issue of self-

---

[28] Wright, *supra* note 15 at 221. Monaco is an independent country bordered by France on three sides and the Mediterranean Sea on the remaining side and covers only 195 hectares (1.95 square kilometres).

[29] *Ibid.* at 347.

[30] RCAP, *supra* note 22 at 14.

[31] Wright, *supra* note 15 at 335.

	EXHIBIT 23.2
Duncan Campbell Scott, Head of Indian Affairs, 1920	

I want to get rid of the Indian problem. Our objective is to continue until there is not a single Indian in Canada that has not been absorbed.

Source: Passage cited in Ronald Wright, *Stolen Continents: Conquest and Resistance in the Americas*, 10th ed. (Toronto: Penguin, 2003) at 340.

government is important as First Nations seek to protect and nurture their unique identity and culture.

The *Indian Act*[32] was an important piece of legislation that promoted the dissolution of Aboriginal culture. Many First Nations view the Act as paternalistic and controlling. In an attempt to legislate cultural assimilation, the Act tried to change Aboriginal concepts of land title, governance, inheritance, family law, economic activity, and community standards. The Act virtually ignored all Aboriginal traditions. Aboriginal women, because of the Act's discriminatory provisions, have voiced criticism. The women allege that the Act places men in leadership positions, imposing a patriarchal regime that perpetuates sexual discrimination and is unfair to women regarding property rights when marital breakdown occurs.

The legislation also governs band elections, the requirements for obtaining Indian status under the law, and the council's decision-making power. The *Indian Act* dictates rules for electing a chief and band council that reflect European culture and not Aboriginal culture. The Act further requires that a leader is chosen by a secret ballot (s. 74), which was not done in Aboriginal society. The Act also provides that the chief and council can be chosen by the band's custom: e.g., through hereditary lineage for the chief or, for the council, to serve for a period of time different from that stated in the Act (s. 2(1)). The Act does not, however, recognize traditional governing bodies, such as the Iroquois Confederacy.

Indian Status

The *Indian Act* defines who is classified as an Indian under the law (ss. 5 to 16) and, therefore, who is entitled to make claims and receive benefits. **Indian status** is assigned when the person shows that he or she is a descendant of a particular band for whom a reserve was established or where the band was a party to a treaty.[33] The person must register in order to obtain Indian status. The Act's classification scheme disregards the different ways by which certain Aboriginal groups established membership. The scheme provided that Indian status travelled exclusively down the patrilineal line (i.e., male descendant line). Some bands, such as the Mohawk and Iroquois, use the

---

[32] R.S.C. 1985, c. I-5; there is other legislation that also governs Indian matters: see, e.g., *First Nations Land Management Act*, S.C. 1999, c. 24; *Department of Indian Affairs and Northern Development Act*, R.S.C. 1985, c. I-6; and the *Indian Oil and Gas Act*, R.S.C. 1985, c. I-7. In 2005, the *First Nations Fiscal and Statistical Management Act*, S.C. 2005, c. 9 was enacted to facilitate economic development relating to taxation and to establish an institute to gather and analyze statistical data concerning First Nations and Aboriginal groups.

[33] Peter W. Hogg, *Constitutional Law of Canada*, Student ed. (Toronto: Thomson Canada Limited, 2002) at 579 [Hogg].

matrilineal line (i.e., female descendant line) for determining membership. An amendment to the *Indian Act* (Bill C-31 in 1985) allowed, among other things, women to regain Indian status where they had lost it by marriage to a non-Aboriginal and removed other discriminatory provisions from the Act. However, Indian status continues to require registration today and remains governed by the Act. Generally, new registrants are required to show that they have two grandparents, on either parent's line of ascent, who meet the descendant requirement (noted above) for registration.

The band also has the option of establishing a **membership or citizenship code** that identifies who can be a band member (s. 10). However, it does not automatically follow that these band members or citizens receive Indian status. Only those individuals who meet the registration requirements are entitled to status and the benefits contained in the *Indian Act*. These benefits include the right to vote in band elections, live on a reserve, and obtain Indian Affairs benefits and applicable tax exemptions. Entitlement to benefits may also be affected, based on whether or not the individual resides on the reserve.

Band Councils

The *Indian Act* allows the **band council** to pass by-laws concerning identified matters on the reserve. The council is required to pass a resolution, which contains the by-law, by a simple majority and the agreement of the chief. By-laws are usually created under the authority contained in section 86 of the Act. Such authority includes the ability to regulate who may reside on the reserve and the ability to enforce fishing and game regulations, taxation, alcohol, licensing and membership codes. However, all by-laws are subject to the approval of the Minister of Indian Affairs before being enacted, which limits the autonomy of the band. For many years, the government regularly withheld approval of submitted by-laws.

Aboriginal Taxation Exemption

Section 87 of the *Indian Act* exempts Aboriginal people's property from taxation but only where specific requirements are met. Exempt property is identified as being the "interest of an Indian or a band in reserve lands or surrendered lands" (s. 87(1)(a)) and the "personal property of an Indian or a band situated on a reserve" (s. 87(1)(b)). The purpose of the exemption is to "preserve the entitlements of Indian people to their reserve lands, and to ensure that the use of their property on their reserve lands is not eroded by taxation."[34] Since sub-section 87(1)(b) applies only to property situated on a reserve, the exemption will not apply to personal property acquired and held in the commercial mainstream. Section 87 is not a general ameliorative provision. "Personal property" is, however, broad enough to include employment income in relation to the payment of income tax.

The interpretation of "situated on a reserve" has been the primary source of litigation under section 87 in regard to income tax. In *Williams v. The Queen*,[35] the Supreme Court of Canada introduced a "connecting factors" test. The factors to be considered in determining whether the property is situated on a reserve concern the examination of the evidence that connects the property to the reserve. It is not necessary that the property be physically on the reserve under all circumstances. Factors will include, where relevant, the following:

[34] Indian and Northern Affairs Canada, *Status Indians and Taxes* <http://www.ainc-inac.gc.ca/pr/info/info113_e.html>.
[35] [1992] 1 S.C.R. 877.

1. The location or residence of the employer;
2. The location and surrounding circumstances of the work performed by the employee, including the nature of any benefit that accrued to the reserve from it;
3. The residence of the employee; and
4. The place where the employee is paid.

Each case is to be decided on its own facts, and structuring one's affairs for proper tax planning reasons is permissible.[36]

Shilling v. M.N.R.[37]

This case applied the connecting factors test in the context of income.

Ms. Shilling was a member of the Rama band, had resided in Toronto for a number of years after living on a reserve and was employed by a Native health centre in Toronto. Ms. Shilling's employment was under contract to an agency. The agency was a sole proprietorship owned by an Indian with its head office located on reserve but unrelated to the band Ms. Shilling belonged to. Ms. Shilling was not employed directly by the health centre itself. This was for tax planning reasons. It was believed that structuring the employment relationship in this way would permit Ms. Shilling to claim the s. 87(1)(b) exemption because all incidents related to employment were "on a reserve" and the health centre benefited the Aboriginal community. Ms. Shilling's salary was wired from the agency's reserve bank to her bank, located on another reserve. The lower court decided that the exemption applied.

The Federal Court of Appeal overturned the lower court's decision because the evidence did not meet the connecting factors test. There was no evidence that the reserve in which the employer-agency was located benefited from Shilling's employment. The appellate court found that there was a lack of evidence regarding where the agency had conducted business during the relevant time period, as there was a suggestion that business may have been conducted off-reserve. Ms. Shilling had not put the employment contract into evidence, making it impossible for the court to know the exact relationship between the agency and the health centre so as to determine against whom Ms. Shilling's legal rights could be enforced should the employment relationship break down. The court identified that the property being located on a reserve other than the one of which the person was a member likely precluded application of the exemption. The court decided that Ms. Shilling's provision of social services to off-reserve people in Toronto did not connect it to a reserve: "[M]erely because the nature of employment is to provide services to Indians does not connect that employment to an Indian reserve as a physical place."[38]

The residency of Ms. Shilling was relevant but not the decisive factor. The "location and nature of her employment" were the primary factors in the decision. The fact that the Aboriginal person resided off-reserve would therefore not, on its own, preclude the application of the exemption. Ms. Shilling's residency simply pointed in the same direction as the other evidence. Her employment was found to be in the commercial mainstream, and the exemption did not apply.[39]

---

[36] Structuring one's financial affairs to *avoid* paying tax(es) is legal; tax *evasion* is not.

[37] 2001 FCA 178 (CanLII) ["*Shilling*"].

[38] *Ibid.* para. 51.

[39] This proceeding asked the appellate court to answer a question of law — i.e., whether the exemption applied. In 2002, the Supreme Court of Canada dismissed Ms. Shilling's application for leave to appeal the court's answer to the question of law. The Crown's subsequent motion to dismiss Ms. Shilling's proceeding claiming exemption was

Creditor Enforcement Exemption

Section 89(1) of the *Indian Act* exempts the real and personal property of an Indian or a band situated on a reserve from "charge, pledge, mortgage, attachment, levy, seizure, distress or execution" in favour of a creditor other than an Indian or a band. Section 90(1) deems property to be on a reserve where it is (a) purchased by Her Majesty with Indian moneys or moneys appropriated by Parliament for the use and benefits of Indians or bands, or (b) given to the Indians or a band under a treaty or agreement between a band and Her majesty. This means that property located off-reserve can still be exempt where section 90(1) applies. Section 90 also applies to the tax exemption in section 87.

McDiarmid Lumber Ltd. v. God's Lake First Nation[40]

The facts concerned the building of a school on the reserve. God's Lake First Nation had engaged a contractor but later defaulted in payment. The creditor obtained default judgment. The creditor then moved to enforce the judgment by seizing the funds in the band's Winnipeg bank account. The band had entered into a treaty with the government in 1909 that included annual grants and funds to maintain schools. A lump sum was paid to the band and deposited into its bank account; the sum included funds for other reasons, such as improving the standard of living on reserve.

The Court decided that payments from the federal government to a First Nation that were deposited in an off-reserve bank in Winnipeg were not "situated on a reserve". The funds were not exempt from seizure by an unpaid creditor under section 89(1). The phrase was to be given its plain and ordinary meaning.

In this case, the band had alternatively submitted that section 90(1) would apply because the payment had been received from the government under an agreement. The issue for the Court was to define the content of "agreement" in the Act. Did it include any or all of a government payment under any agreement so as to deem the payment "on reserve" even if located elsewhere?

The Court began with a statement of the purpose underlying the exemption in the *Indian Act*, finding that its purpose was not to provide a general economic benefit to Indians:

> The Court confirmed in *Williams* that the purpose of the exemptions in ss. 87, 88 and 89 of the *Indian Act* "was to preserve the entitlements of Indians to their reserve lands and to ensure that the use of their property on their reserve lands was not eroded by the ability of governments to tax, or creditors to seize" (p. 885). The purpose is to protect what the Indian band was "given" in return for the surrender of Indian lands. The exemptions are tied to the reserve lands and the Indians' ability to preserve their lands against outside intrusion and diminishment. As Gonthier J. stated in *Williams*, "the purpose of the sections was not to confer a general economic benefit upon the Indians" (p. 885). For example, they do not exempt from seizure or taxation contractual arrangements in the commercial mainstream that amount to normal business transactions, but only "property that enures to Indians pursuant to treaties and their ancillary agreements": *Mitchell*, at p. 138. Only the latter is protected by s. 90(1)(*b*).[41]

---

granted and upheld on appeal: *Shilling v. Canada*, 2004 FCA 16. For cases where income was found to be situated on a reserve see *Williams v. The Queen*, [1992] 1 S.C.R. 877 and *Folster v. The Queen*, [1997] 3 F.C. 269 (C.A.).

[40] [2006] 2 S.C.R. 846, [2006] S.C.J. No. 58.

[41] *Ibid.* at para. 27.

The Court held that "agreement" was to be given a restricted meaning and that the agreement in question must be associated with a treaty.[42] Otherwise, the word "treaty" would not be needed in the provision as a qualifier, and any agreement between government and a band would suffice. The protection against exploitation underlying the exemption applied only to treaty entitlements that were often included in a more detailed, ancillary agreement. Policy reasons for this restricted meaning also favoured that finding. Obtaining credit in order for Aboriginal people to participate in economic pursuits and facilitate self-sufficiency and self-government is necessary as we all live in a credit-based market. The provincial credit regime is an important part of everyday life that applies equally to Indians save for the limited exemption.

The band failed in its claim for exemption because of a lack of evidence. The lump sum form of payment meant that neither the government nor the band could identify what portion of the total received was ancillary to the treaty and likely exempt. The payment was found to be a pool of money for a variety of purposes that included the enhancement of self-sufficiency and living standards in a wide range of areas. The judgment creditor was entitled to seize the funds.

The Métis and Inuit

There are two other quasi-founding Aboriginal groups, the **Métis** and **Inuit**, who do not qualify for Indian "status" and are, therefore, not governed by the *Indian Act*. The Métis are descendants from French colonist and Indian inter-marriages. The descendants from British colonist and Indian inter-marriages were referred to as half-breeds. Descendants from other Indian inter-marriages sometimes registered as non-status Indians. Today, there is little agreement concerning the requirements that identify a person as Métis. The identification of Métis peoples and their associated Aboriginal rights are issues separate from First Nation rights.[43] It is clear, however, that the Métis originated after contact with the Europeans. Therefore, the descendants of Indian inter-marriages did not have the same relationship with the Crown as the First Nations. The blending of the two cultures resulted in the creation of a distinct common culture and ethnic identity that also separates them from the First Nations. The result is that the Métis are treated differently by the government and are referred to as non-status Indians, despite their inclusion as "aboriginal" in the Constitution (s. 35).

A Métis governing council is not established in the same way as one for status Indians. The Métis council is created by the incorporation of a non-profit corporation and governed by the corporation's constitution and relevant legislation concerning not-for-profit organizations. The Métis are not recognized by the federal government as a people under federal jurisdiction and have been denied most federal benefits available to status Indians. The federal government does not include this Aboriginal group within the definition of "Indian" under s. 91(24) of the Constitution. It has been left to the provinces to deal with their particular Métis population and provide benefits.

[42] The Supreme Court also referred to one of its earlier decisions: "This Court has already considered the meaning of "agreement" in section 90(1)(b) and concluded that it should be restricted to agreements that flesh out commitments of the Crown to Indians in the treaty context of the surrender of their homelands": para. 26, referring to *Mitchell v. Peguis Indian Band*, [1990] 2 S.C.R. 85.

[43] For further discussion on Métis issues, see Imai, *supra* note 1 at 83–93. For more information concerning the identification of Métis, see *R. v. Powley* (1998), 58 C.R.R. (2d) 149, [1999] 1 C.N.L.R. 153 (Ont. Prov. Div.), as a starting point.

The Inuit, historically referred to as Eskimo, are the "indigenous peoples of the circumpolar north."[44] There is no formal Inuit registry and, therefore, a non-status/status distinction does not exist. The federal government considers the Inuit to be "Indian" under s. 91(24) of the Constitution. The Inuit population was also reduced by the epidemics. However, the arrival of a significant number of settlers did not occur until the middle of the twentieth century, and this differentiates them from the First Nations. Attempts were made to assimilate the Inuit culture, but recent developments show a willingness of government to establish agreements that respect this unique society.

The creation of the new territory of Nunavut (from part of the Northwest Territories) in 1999 was the result of a negotiated land claim agreement. This agreement allows the Inuit a formal role in making recommendations to the government concerning the land, environmental issues, land use planning, wildlife management, and establishing Inuit status. The territorial government of Nunavut follows the same structure as that of other provinces in Canada (i.e., an elected government leader and Cabinet). While Nunavut can be seen to provide a level of autonomy to the Inuit of that area, this autonomy does not amount to self-governance. In exchange for government protection of Inuit resources and land, the Aboriginal people were required to surrender all Aboriginal claims of any kind.

LAND CLAIMS

Aboriginal rights issues often arise regarding land. First Nations are able to claim a proprietary interest in land by **treaty** right, or because the land has been designated by the federal government as having **reserve** status, or by successfully having a **common law claim** affirmed by the court. A common law claim may assert a right to title of the land or be limited to using the land for a specific purpose. An Aboriginal interest in land is communally held and is a group right for the exclusive possession and use of an identified piece of land. There is no concept of private property within Aboriginal culture. Today, individual band members receive certificates of possession from the band. The certificate can be sold, but the purchaser must be another band member. The band, as a whole, can sell the land only to the federal government, who then transfers the title to the relevant province. This limited ability to sell land represents a fundamental difference between Aboriginal title and the usual form of land ownership in Canada (i.e., fee simple title) that allows the owner to sell the property to anyone. Aboriginal title to land is, however, considered a proprietary interest in the land and not just a licence to occupy the land.[45]

Aboriginal rights to land are not absolute, however, despite Constitutional protection. The government is permitted to infringe on a right where certain requirements for justification of the infringement are met. For example, conservation initiatives that limit an Aboriginal right to fish on an identified portion of land may justify an infringement on the band's fishing rights.[46] Con-

---

[44] Law Group, *supra* note 9 at 512. Most of the Inuit in Canada are located in the Northwest Territories, Quebec, Labrador, and Nunavut. Nunavut was formed in 1999 as a result of a land claim agreement between Canada and the Inuit of the eastern Arctic.

[45] *Delgamuukw v. British Columbia*, [1997] 3 S.C.R. 1010 at para. 113; (1997), 153 D.L.R. (4th) 193 [*Delgamuukw* cited to S.C.R.].

[46] See *R. v. Sparrow*, [1990] 1 S.C.R. 1075 where the Court outlines the test for government infringement on an Aboriginal right and holds that the extinguishment of an Aboriginal right by the Crown must be clear and unequivocal. The test in *Sparrow* was refined in *R. v. Gladstone*, [1996] 2 S.C.R. 723, where the Court enunciated

---

EXHIBIT 23.3

The Report of the Royal Commission

A careful reading of history shows that Canada was founded on a series of bargains with Aboriginal peoples — bargains this country has never fully honoured. Treaties between Aboriginal and non-Aboriginal governments were agreements to share the land. They were replaced by policies intended to ... remove Aboriginal people from their homelands ... suppress Aboriginal nations and their governments ... undermine Aboriginal cultures ... [and] stifle Aboriginal identity. It is now time to acknowledge the truth and begin to rebuild the relationship among peoples on the basis of honesty, mutual respect and fair sharing. The image of Canada in the world and at home demands no less.

Source: Royal Commission on Aboriginal Peoples, *Looking Forward, Looking Back*, Volume 1 (Ottawa: Minister of Supply & Services, 1996), Summary, online: <http://www.ainc-inac.gc.ca/ch/rcap/rpt/lk_e.html> (August 2004) [cited to summary] at 1–2.

---

servation issues would be considered a compelling objective that would be in the best interests of both the band and the broader community. Therefore, conservation would trump, at least temporarily, an Aboriginal right to fish. The government also has a **fiduciary duty**, which is to act in the best interests of Aboriginal peoples in all dealings with First Nations. This duty includes, or can be limited to, consulting with a band before infringing on its right.[47] The obligation to consult was recently expanded in *Mikisew Cree First Nation v. Canada (Minister of Canadian Heritage)*, [2005] 3 S.C.R. 388 where the Supreme Court held that the duty to consult extended to development of land adjacent to that belonging to First Nations, where development projects may affect treaty or land rights.

Treaties and Reserves

A treaty contains an exchange of promises entered into by both parties. The goal is to allow for peaceful coexistence between, and reconciliation of, First Nations and the Canadian community, of which they are a part. Historically, the First Nations entered treaties after being subjected to military force or when they had no way to refuse the government's demands.[48] Before the enactment of constitutional amendments, the government could unilaterally ignore or override a treaty right. The government could assert the belief that settlements did not require the consent of the First Nations and that Aboriginal rights existed only at the pleasure of the Crown. Therefore, a right could be extinguished or limited at the whim of the government. Once the amendments were proclaimed, it gave constitutional status to existing treaty and Aboriginal rights that had not been previously given up by First Nations. It also protects treaties and agreements entered into after 1982. This protec-

---

that "beyond conservation, there could be other 'compelling and substantial objectives'" by which the government could limit an Aboriginal right (para. 69). Other objectives include "pursuit of economic and regional fairness, and the recognition of the historical reliance upon, and participation in, the fishery by non-aboriginal groups, are the type of objectives which can ... satisfy this standard" (para. 75).

[47] The fiduciary duty of the Crown concerning Aboriginal title was held to exist in *Guerin v. The Queen*, [1984] 2 S.C.R. 335. The scope of the duty was enlarged in *Sparrow* to cover "all dealings" with Aboriginal peoples.

[48] Albert L. Hurtado and Peter Iverson, *Major Problems in American Indian History: Documents and Essays*, 2d ed. (Boston: Houghton Mifflin Company, 2000) at 184–85.

> **EXHIBIT 23.4**
>
> **Section 18 of the *Indian Act***
>
> **18.(1) Reserves to be held for use and benefit of Indians** — Subject to this Act, reserves are held by Her Majesty for the use and benefit of the respective bands for which they were set apart, and subject to this Act and to the terms of any treaty or surrender, the Governor in Council may determine whether any purpose for which lands in a reserve are used or are to be used is for the use and benefit of the band.
>
> (2) **Use of reserves for schools, etc.** — The Minister may authorize the use of lands ... for the purpose of Indian schools, the administration of Indian Affairs, Indian burial grounds, Indian health projects or, with the consent of the council of the band, for any other purpose for the general welfare of the band, and may take any lands in a reserve required for those purposes, but ... compensation for that use shall be paid to the Indian ...

---

tion means that the government cannot override a treaty or other right by passing standard legislation.

Disputes often arise around the terms contained in early treaties. Land treaties generally involved terms that required the First Nations to give title of a large piece of land to the government in exchange for payment and the establishment of a reserve. The terms may also permit the band to hunt and fish on land adjacent to the reserve. First Nations believe that written treaties often do not reflect the terms agreed upon or their desire to retain independence. "Aboriginal people ... often say that their understanding, as transmitted through oral tradition, is that an agreement of peace and friendship was established in which they agreed to share the land with the Europeans, not sell it."[49] In practice, the government has generally treated surrendered land as its own, regardless of any Aboriginal right to use it, although such conduct would be limited today.

Treaties are not considered to be standard contracts or international agreements. A contract binds only the parties who sign it, whereas a treaty binds all band members regardless of whether their signature appears on the document. The treaty will also set out rights that apply to everyone in the band. An international treaty requires the legislature to adopt the agreement and proclaim it as a law in order for it to be binding. Indian treaties were not proclaimed. While there is evidence that early treaties contained terminology similar to that of a nation-to-nation agreement, Canada's First Nations are not domestically considered to be sovereign nation states. The Supreme Court of Canada views these treaties as unique documents, to be treated in a special way, which further reflects the *sui generis* nature of Aboriginal rights. For example, where a treaty dispute arises, the court may admit Aboriginal oral history evidence and consider the intentions of the First Nation and the government at the time the treaty was signed.[50]

---

[49] Imai, *supra* note 1 at 69.

[50] See *R. v. Marshall*, [1999] 3 S.C.R. 456, where the Court held that the interpretation of a treaty requires (i) a "generous" interpretation of the terms and, where a term is in doubt, it should be decided in favour of the Aboriginal band; and (ii) the written text is not determinative of the terms contained therein, and the court is required to consider the history and evidence surrounding the Aboriginal understanding of the term that conflicts with the written document. In this way the common intention of the parties at the time the treaty was entered into can be determined.

Reserve land is defined under the *Indian Act*, and the Act governs the land. Her Majesty or, more accurately, the government of Canada, holds title to the land. While designed to protect Aboriginal culture, reserves have had the effect of "isolat[ing] and impoverish[ing]" First Nations because the reserve land is usually too small and has inadequate resources by which to maintain the Aboriginal way of life.[51] The same restrictions on selling reserve land apply: that is, it can be sold only to the federal government. However, because the land is held communally, band consensus is required before any sale can be made. The First Nations' right of title to the land is extinguished when it is sold or given up and cannot be reclaimed.

Common Law Land Title Rights

Many tracts of land in Canada are occupied by Indians and have not been part of any land agreement or treaty. Aboriginal rights are often dealt with by negotiation or mediation between the government and the particular group of founding peoples. Alternatively, the First Nation may begin a proceeding that claims a common law right to title of identified land. British Columbia, for example, has large portions of land where Indian bands reside that have not been dealt with by a treaty or other agreement. The First Nation may seek to claim **Aboriginal title** through the courts. The Supreme Court of Canada in *Delgamuukw* dealt with a common law land title claim. While the Court decided that the matter required a new trial because of a defect in the pleadings and a failure of the trial judge to give proper weight to oral evidence, it did take the opportunity to clarify issues surrounding Aboriginal title under the common law.

Delgamuukw concerned a land claim that covered approximately 58,000 square kilometres in British Columbia. All of the Wet'suwet'en and most of the Gitksan First Nations made two communal claims for title to the land based on historical and present possession of the land and because of spiritual ceremonies that took place there. These ceremonies connected each band to the land. The Aboriginal claim failed at trial and on appeal. Justice McEachern held that there was insufficient evidence to support the inference that "the Indians possessed or controlled any part of the territory, other than for village sites and for aboriginal use in a way that would justify a declaration equivalent to ownership."[52] The Court also decided that any claim to the land had been extinguished by the government's intention to use the land for another purpose that was inconsistent with Aboriginal rights.[53] The majority of the Court of Appeal agreed that a claim for Aboriginal title had not been made out but disagreed with the assertion that Aboriginal rights had been extinguished. The necessary clear and plain intention by the Crown to extinguish such rights was absent from the evidence. However, this did not affect the trial decision concerning the Aboriginal title to the land.

The majority of the Supreme Court of Canada held that Aboriginal title was "the right to use land for a variety of activities, not all of which need be aspects of practices, customs and traditions which are integral to the distinctive cultures of aboriginal societies."[54] The right to title arises because of the band's occupation and possession of the land before the British asserted sovereignty over that land. The date of sovereignty in Canada varies by location. The band can use the land for any use, with one important limit: the land cannot be used in a way that violates the Aboriginal connection to it. For

---

[51] RCAP, *supra* note 22 at 11.
[52] *Delgamuukw, supra* note 45 at para. 18.
[53] *Ibid.* at para. 24.
[54] *Ibid.* at para. 111.

example, if the band asserts title because it has historically occupied and used the land for a special ceremony that forms the basis for obtaining Aboriginal title, the band cannot alter the land in a way that destroys this "physical and cultural" relationship with the land.[55] Therefore, building a shopping plaza on the ceremonial site could be seen to destroy the underlying connection with the land and would be irreconcilable with its historical use.

In order for a First Nation to establish a common law right to Aboriginal title, or joint title with another band, it must fulfill three requirements: "(i) the land must have been occupied prior to sovereignty; (ii) if present occupation is relied on as proof of occupation pre-sovereignty, there must be a continuity between the present and pre-sovereignty occupation; and (iii) at sovereignty, that occupation must have been exclusive."[56] In this case, British sovereignty over British Columbia occurred when the Oregon Boundary Treaty was signed in 1846. Under the common law, possession of the land before and since sovereignty is sufficient to ground Aboriginal title provided title has not been surrendered or extinguished. Evidence of the band's physical occupation of the land could be established in a variety of ways. The band could show that it had Aboriginal laws governing the land, constructed dwelling places on the land, enclosed fields, or cultivated the land, among other things.

Present occupation can be the more likely basis for asserting Aboriginal title because evidence of pre-sovereignty possession can be difficult to acquire. But continuity does not require that there is an unbroken chain of possession dating back to the pre-sovereignty period. The band is required to show a substantial maintenance of the connection between the people and the land even if the occupation and use of the land was disputed in the past or the nature of the occupation changed.[57] This is because the European colonists were unwilling to recognize Aboriginal title and simply took possession of the land they wanted. Applying this requirement too strictly (i.e., demanding an unbroken chain of occupation) would mean that most claims for Aboriginal title would fail for reasons that were beyond Aboriginal control.

Since Aboriginal title contains the right to *exclusive* use, as well as occupation of the land, the band must show that it had the ability to exclude others from the land. Otherwise, the Aboriginal title gained would be greater than that historically exercised. The court must determine exclusive use in the context of the Aboriginal society at the time of sovereignty. Requiring the band to show historical evidence of trespassing laws, for example, would impose a European standard on a society that was organized differently. Even where it is shown that other First Nations were located on the land or used it, exclusivity can be established where the band held the ability to exclude others. This could include evidence of other bands having to obtain permission before being granted access to the land.

OTHER ABORIGINAL RIGHTS TO LAND

Even where a First Nation cannot establish Aboriginal title to a tract of land, it may still have rights over that land in the absence of a land agreement. Other rights can arise "from the social organization and distinctive cultures of

---

[55] *Ibid.* at para. 132.
[56] *Ibid.* at para. 143.
[57] *Ibid.* at para. 154.

aboriginal peoples on that land."[58] These rights are considered inherent rights because they arise from the prior use of the land by the First Nations. The right can include the authority to engage in a particular activity, such as hunting or fishing, on an identified tract of land. The right must be seen necessary for the band's well-being and the continuation of their culture. The band must show that the Aboriginal right asserted is grounded in the "practices, customs and traditions that are integral to the distinctive cultures of aboriginal peoples." The practice, custom and tradition (hereinafter "Practice") must have existed prior to the first Aboriginal contact with the Europeans. This is a different point in time from the date used to determine a land title claim: i.e., the date of sovereignty. This limitation thus excludes cultural attributes that emerged as a result of European influences.

The requirements for establishing an Aboriginal right to use land for a specific purpose were outlined in *Sparrow* and *Van der Peet*. The general test enunciated by the Supreme Court of Canada is to be considered in the context of the particular band, the specific right being asserted, and whether the right is significant for maintaining the band's unique culture. The test has four components: (i) there must be sufficient evidence that the band lived as an organized society at the time the practice originated (e.g., the band had their own territory, name and resources); (ii) the Practice must be integral to the band's culture; (iii) the Practice must have originated prior to first contact with the Europeans; and (iv) while there must be evidence of sufficient continuity in the exercise of the Practice in the intervening time between pre-contact and the assertion of the right, an unbroken chain of continuity is not required. Exclusive possession of the land is not necessary.

While *Sparrow* provided the test to be met for establishing an Aboriginal right protected by section 35(1) of the Constitution, in *Van der Peet* the Supreme Court found that, as a preliminary step, the scope and nature of the Aboriginal right claimed may require definition. This is often relevant where an Aboriginal band or person is found in breach of legislation governing natural resources. The focus is less on identifying the right and more on determining the extent or scope of the right. The applicable test identified three factors that are used to characterize the scope and nature of the right:

1. The nature of the action that the applicant is claiming is done pursuant to an Aboriginal right
2. The nature of the conflict between governmental legislation and the right claimed
3. The ancestral traditions and practices that establish the right

In application, it seems that once the scope and nature of the protected right is identified using factors 1 and 3 above, consideration turns to whether the application of the legislation being challenged infringes the right or whether the right had been extinguished. There is some overlap in the evidence associated with the characterization of the right and the establishment of the right as both relate to pre-contact traditions and practice. In some cases, the establishment of the scope and nature of the right is determinative because the right claimed is not found to exist as framed, and the claim fails. Alternatively, where the claimed right is proved, it may be undisputed that the legislation would infringe the right and that a constitutional doctrine would apply to remedy the infringement; and where the right was previously extinguished, no infringement would be found. It will depend on the particular facts before the court.

---

[58] *Van der Peet, supra* note 3 at para. 74.

In *Van der Peet* the Aboriginal right being claimed was the right to sell fish for money. A band member had been convicted of selling the fish in violation of a fishing regulation. The accused asserted that commercial fishing was part of the distinctive culture of the Stó:lô band in British Columbia, of which she was a member. The Court held that the significance of the particular practice is a factor but will not, by itself, establish an Aboriginal right. The other requirements must also be met. The practice may be exercised in a modern form, such as using a motorboat rather than a canoe for fishing. The practice must be integral (i.e., a practice that makes the particular culture distinctively unique) to the culture of the Aboriginal band asserting the right. Therefore the right is relevant only to the particular band that *successfully* claims it and is not a general right that extends to all First Nations.

The claim failed in *Van der Peet* because the nature and scope of the right was not found to include commercial fishing. The Court held that the practice of exchanging fish for money or other goods was not an integral part of the distinctive Stó:lô culture that existed prior to contact. Prior to contact, the practice of selling fish in exchange for money or goods was only incidental to the main cultural activity of fishing for food.

The case of *R. v. Sappier; R. v. Gray*[59] similarly concerned the characterization of the scope and nature of the Aboriginal right claimed. It also answered the question of whether or not the pre-contact use of a natural resource for survival could give rise to an Aboriginal right.

R. v. Sappier; R. v. Gray

Two members of the Maliseet band and one member of the Mi'kmaq band were charged under provincial legislation with unlawful possession of, or cutting of, Crown timber from Crown land. The timber had been obtained from land traditionally harvested by the two First Nations. The timber was used for personal and not commercial use. The Maliseet had used the timber to construct a home and provide community firewood. The Mi'kmaq had used the timber to craft furniture. At trial, the First Nations members raised the defence of an Aboriginal and/or treaty right to harvest the timber and were acquitted. All of the acquittals were upheld by the provincial Court of Appeal, and the Supreme Court of Canada subsequently dismissed the appeal with reasons. The Supreme Court decided the case on the basis of the scope and nature of the Aboriginal right and found it unnecessary to deal with the treaty right submission.

The Court found that both First Nations had been migratory peoples before first contact with Europeans. They lived by travelling to where wildlife was available for hunting, and they used the waterways for transportation. The evidence demonstrated both bands had used timber for pre-contact domestic needs that included shelter, transportation, fuel and tools.

The Court identified that consideration was to focus on the importance of the actual Practice integral to the pre-contact culture of an Aboriginal people. To do so, the right had to be clearly defined first. A general right to a natural resource would be too broad and beyond the scope of historical practice. Moreover, "[A]n aboriginal right cannot be characterized as a right to a particular resource because to do so would be to treat it as akin to a common law property right." In characterizing Aboriginal rights as *sui generis*, the Supreme Court had, in *Sparrow*, rejected the application of traditional common law property concepts to such rights.

59 2006 SCC 54, [2006] 2 S.C.R. 686 [*Sappier*].

The Court considered the pre-contact Practice of the band in relation to the harvesting and use of timber as relevant to the definition of the content of the right. It is the pre-contact Practice that is central to the *Van der Peet* test for establishing an Aboriginal right to land. Pre-contact Practice required the Court to "grasp the importance of a resource to a particular aboriginal people ... to understand how that resource was harvested, extracted and utilized. These practices are the necessary 'aboriginal' component in aboriginal rights"[60] that are protected under section 35(1) of the Constitution. The Court then considered how the right might have evolved to its present-day form.

The Maliseet and Mi'kmaq's practice had been to use the timber "to fulfill the communities' domestic needs for things such as shelter, transportation, tools and fuel. [The Court defined the aboriginal right asserted as the right to] harvest wood for domestic uses as a member of the aboriginal community."[61] This definition delineated the right in accordance with its historical practice that reflected the way of life or distinctiveness of the particular Aboriginal community.

The use of the word "domestic" in the Supreme Court's decision means that the harvesting or possession of timber for commercial purposes is not included in the right. The phrase "as a member of the Aboriginal community" means that the right is a communal one that cannot be exercised independently by a band member. It was this particularized right that section 35 of the Constitution protected. The right did not provide *carte blanche* authority for the harvesting and use of timber by any band member, for any purpose, at any time and in any location.

Once the scope and nature of the right was defined, consideration turned to the historical exercise of the right and its integrality to the band's distinctive culture. The evidence demonstrated that the First Nations had practised the harvesting of wood for domestic purposes prior to European contact. The question was whether the practice was integral to the distinctive culture of the band. The Court had previously recognized an Aboriginal right based on evidence showing the importance of a resource to the pre-contact culture of an Aboriginal people. The Crown had also conceded in previous appeals that wood had been important to both bands for survival purposes in the pre-contact period and used in many facets of Aboriginal life.

The Court found that the fact that the activity was carried out for the purpose of survival did not automatically preclude it from being found integral to the band's distinctive culture. The notion that the pre-contact Practice upon which the right is based must go to the core of the society's identity — i.e., its single most important defining character — has never been the test for establishing an Aboriginal right. The claimant need only show that the Practice was integral to the Aboriginal society's pre-contact distinctive culture.

The protection afforded Aboriginal rights under section 35 of the Constitution arises from the simple fact of prior occupation of the lands now forming Canada. That underlying fact provides perspective for identifying whether a practice is part of a band's distinctive culture. While the right must be distinctive it is not required to be distinct.

> The focus of the Court should therefore be on the *nature* of this prior occupation. What is meant by "culture" is really an inquiry into the pre-contact way of life of a particular aboriginal community, including their means of survival, their socialization methods, their legal systems, and, potentially, their trading habits. The use of the word "distinctive" as a qualifier is meant to incorporate an element of aboriginal specificity. However, "distinctive"

---

[60] *Ibid.* at para. 22.
[61] *Ibid.* at para. 24.

does not mean "distinct", and the notion of aboriginality must not be reduced to "racialized stereotypes of Aboriginal peoples". ...

... [T]hese were migratory communities using the rivers and lakes of Eastern Canada for transportation and living essentially from hunting and fishing. The Court must therefore seek to understand how the particular pre-contact practice relied upon relates to that way of life. In the present cases, the practice of harvesting wood for domestic uses including shelter, transportation, fuel and tools is directly related to the way of life I have just described. I have already explained that we must discard the idea that the practice must go to the core of a people's culture. ...[62]

The Court held that "harvesting wood for domestic uses was undertaken for survival purposes is sufficient, given the evidence adduced at trial, to meet the integral to a distinctive culture threshold."[63] Based on the evidence provided, the Court decided that the practice of harvesting wood for domestic uses was integral to the pre-contact distinctive culture of both the Maliseet and Mi'kmaq peoples.

The inquiry did not end there. "The nature of the *right* had to be determined in light of present-day circumstances." The practice and uses associated with the right are permitted to evolve to reflect modern means. Otherwise, the right may be effectively vitiated or meaningless. An example would be where the right to harvest timber had to be done using the tools available in pre-contact times.

If aboriginal rights are not permitted to evolve and take modern forms, then they will become utterly useless. Surely the Crown cannot be suggesting that the respondents, all of whom live on a reserve, would be limited to building wigwams. If such were the case, the doctrine of aboriginal rights would truly be limited to recognizing and affirming a narrow subset of "anthropological curiosities", and our notion of aboriginality would be reduced to a small number of outdated stereotypes. The cultures of the aboriginal peoples who occupied the lands now forming Canada prior to the arrival of the Europeans, and who did so while living in organized societies with their own distinctive ways of life, cannot be reduced to wigwams, baskets and canoes.[64]

The right was found to be site-specific, limited to Crown land historically used for the practice and the timber's use limited as identified above. The existence of the specific Aboriginal right was exercisable only within its articulated scope and nature, and protected under section 35(1) of the Constitution.[65]

DISPUTES REGARDING ABORIGINAL LAND

The Indians express valid concerns over arbitrary decisions made regarding their land to the present day. Examples include the communities of Oka, Ipperwash, and Caledonia. Oka brought the land issue to the attention of the Canadian public and provided motivation to improve the land-dispute resolution process although confrontations dated back centuries.

---

[62] *Ibid.* at paras. 45 and 46.

[63] *Ibid.* at para. 46.

[64] *Ibid.* at para. 49.

[65] The Crown had not challenged the submission that legislation regulating the harvesting of timber infringed the Aboriginal right, if so found. The right was not shown to have been previously extinguished: *Ibid.*, para. 60. In this case, the nature and scope of the established right was determinative.

In 1990, the French Canadian resort town of Oka had a land crisis with its Mohawk community.[66] Earlier, in 1945, the Canadian government had set aside land the Mohawk claimed had belonged to it before the British asserted sovereignty. The government did not resolve the issue of the disputed land and the established reserve boundary did not include it. The government allowed the non-Aboriginal town council to take title to a portion of the disputed land in order to build a golf course. The Mohawks submitted a land claim to the government that replied (in 1977) that all claims dating from before the foundation of Canada in 1867 were not its problem.

The 1990 crisis arose when the town council wanted another portion of the disputed land, located beside an Indian cemetery, in order to expand the golf course. The Mohawk community built roadblocks and barricades, patrolled the area and protested the proposed expansion. In July of 1990, while negotiations were underway with the Mohawks, the Quebec police arrived at the request of the Oka mayor. The mayor was in favour of the golf course expansion.[67] The police later charged the roadblock, and gunfire was exchanged. After this exchange, one police officer was dead, but no conclusive evidence was provided as to which side was responsible for the death.[68]

Prime Minister Brian Mulroney subsequently made the army available to Quebec and appointed a mediator. Both Iroquois Confederacies expressed their concern over the government's handling of land claims and cited this as the major cause of the Oka crisis. The Confederacies suggested that negotiations begin between them and the federal and provincial governments in order to resolve the matter peacefully. The Mohawks broke off negotiations when the army moved up to the barricade. The army's relocation was criticized by human rights observers since it violated a prior agreement made by both levels of government.

The army advanced on the Oka Mohawks while other Indians and Canadians protested the government's handling of the crisis and its refusal to hear the First Nations' claim. The army attempted to prevent the reporters located inside the Mohawk stronghold from getting supplies, confiscated film, and otherwise tried to stop them from properly communicating details of the Oka crisis to the world. The Mohawks repeatedly made offers, indicating their willingness to begin a process of resolution and requested that "a joint commission from Quebec, Ottawa, the Iroquois Confederacy, and international human rights organizations [to] preside over the disengagement and judicial process."[69] Quebec declined to participate in a joint commission. Its primary interest seemed to be to use the army to force the Mohawks to surrender. At the beginning of September 1990, Canadian soldiers crept under a fence they had erected and clubbed a Mohawk warrior as he slept in his foxhole. At the end of the month, the 40 or so Mohawks remaining in their stronghold calmly walked out.

Since the Oka crisis, little progress has been made regarding Aboriginal land claims. With regard to Oka, Prime Minister Mulroney appointed a Royal Commission to explore the grievances of the First Nations and discontinued the policy of disqualifying land claims that were based on events prior to 1867. A portion of the disputed land was purchased by the government and transferred to the Mohawk community in 2000. However, "[M]any Mohawks

---

[66] For a more detailed analysis of the Oka crisis, see Wright, *supra* note 15 at 350–75 and Dickason, *supra* note 17 at 326.

[67] *Ibid.* at 353.

[68] *Ibid.*

[69] *Ibid.* at 362.

resented being 'given' what they regard as rightly theirs."[70] More recently, the creation of the new Inuit territory (discussed below) indicates a willingness of government to acknowledge Canada's First Nations to a greater degree. However, many Aboriginal peoples see self-government as necessary for maintaining their unique culture.[71]

The long-awaited report of the Ipperwash Inquiry was released in May 2007 and concerned the death of Mr. Dudley George, an Aboriginal protestor shot by an O.P.P. officer at Ipperwash Provincial Park in 1995. The inquiry concluded that government and the O.P.P. had improperly dealt with the matter and that both levels of government had not established a viable policy for the resolution of Aboriginal land claims. The protest concerned reserve land that had been temporarily appropriated during World War II as a military training site and not returned. Aboriginal people and supporters who were occupying the land in protest believed the appropriated land contained a sacred burial site. Despite persistent attempts to regain the Aboriginal land, 50 years had gone by and the federal government continued to refuse its return.

The Premier and the O.P.P. did not agree on the proper approach to the long-standing land claim protest and occupation, which was not conducive to a peaceful resolution. Members of government made racist comments, and the Premier wanted a speedy resolution to the occupation. The O.P.P.'s plan contained shortcomings, and both sides were wrong in their perceptions of the other's intentions. Cultural insensitivity and racism was evident in the conduct of some police officers. The inquiry concluded that these main factors, along with others, combined to lead to the death of Mr. George.

Since Ipperwash, no steps have been implemented to appropriately deal with the problem that caused the protest or to educate the Canadian public about the facts and delays underlying land claim tension:

> Unfortunately, the issues that were at the heart of the Ipperwash occupation remain to this day. This inexcusable delay and long neglect, by successive Federal governments, are at the heart of the Ipperwash story. ... Research in the course of the inquiry showed that the flashpoints for aboriginal protests and occupations are very likely as intense today as they were at the time of Ipperwash. No one can predict where protests and occupations will occur, but the fundamental conditions and catalyst sparking such protests continue to exist in Ontario, more than a decade after Ipperwash.[72]

The report recommended, among other things, that the government create a Treaty Commission to deal with land claims in a fair and timely way. The standoff in Caledonia, which similarly dates back decades, is a recent example of ongoing conflict and government's failure to implement a regime for the effective and timely resolution of Aboriginal land claims. While inquiries are not binding on government and do not always impact government policies, Parliament has, since the release of the report, introduced a new land claims policy and is considering methods of reducing delay in the resolution of land claims.

---

[70] *Ibid.* at 371.

[71] Imai, *supra* note 1 at 115.

[72] The Ipperwash Inquiry, Press Release, "Commissioner's Statement" (May 31, 2007), online: <http://www.ipperwashinquiry.ca/li/pdf/Commissioner-s_Statement-May31_2007.pdf>; the full report is available online at <http://www.attorneygeneral.jus.gov.on.ca/inquiries/ipperwash/report/index.html>.

CHAPTER SUMMARY

This chapter identified that the prior occupation of North America by Aboriginal peoples is the underlying foundation for Aboriginal rights and their *sui generis* nature. All matters concerning Indians are under the jurisdiction of the federal government. Some factors that have affected the evolution of Aboriginal rights throughout history were discussed. These factors include fundamental cultural differences between the First Nations and European colonists, as well as the effects of epidemics on Aboriginal populations. In addition, the oral tradition of the Indians has become part of the *sui generis* nature of Aboriginal rights in that they are admissible in court when a claim is asserted.

The failure of colonial and Canadian governments to fulfill treaty and other obligations was examined. Aboriginal concern over the treatment of land claims remains relevant today, as illustrated by the discussion of the Oka crisis. The process of attempted assimilation of the First Nations into the Canadian culture was identified as including special schools, various pieces of legislation, and the holding out of incentives to encourage Aboriginal abandonment of cultural roots in exchange for Canadian citizenship. The requirements for status and band councils under the *Indian Act* were explained, and the non-status designation of the Métis and Inuit under the *Indian Act* was identified.

The methods by which a First Nation can ground an Aboriginal title claim were noted as being based on a treaty right or on the land having been designated as an Indian reserve, or by a successful common law claim. Land ownership in Aboriginal culture is a communally held right. Aboriginal title includes the right to exclusive possession and use of an identified piece of land. Such land can be sold only to the federal government and cannot be purchased by the public. The Supreme Court of Canada enunciated the necessary steps for establishing a common law claim to Aboriginal title, and these steps were identified. Where Aboriginal title is not established, the band may have rights to use the land for a particular purpose where certain requirements are met.

GLOSSARY OF NEW TERMS AND KEY CONCEPTS

Aboriginal (or Aboriginal peoples)	Referring to the indigenous peoples or original inhabitants of North America.
Aboriginal title	A communal right for the exclusive use and possession of an identified tract of land by an Indian band based on a history of exclusive occupation dating back to the time before British sovereignty.
band council	The governing body of a particular Indian tribe. The *Indian Act* contains the method for elections, or the tribe can choose a chief and council through custom; the council can pass by-laws that cover specific issues identified in the Act and that apply to their land subject to government approval.
Charter	Section 35 of the Charter specifically protects Aboriginal rights that were not extinguished or surrendered at the time the Charter came into force and prevents the government from unilaterally overriding or ignoring an established Aboriginal right.
common law claim	An Aboriginal rights claim without reference to a treaty or other land agreement. It requires that certain conditions be met but is not restricted to land title claims, and can be a claim for the specific use of an identified tract of land based on historical use.
fiduciary duty	A legal duty whereby a party must act or make a decision that is in the best interests of another party.

healing circle	Used for sentencing under an Aboriginal judiciary regime, the circle consists of a group of community members. The goal of the circle is to provide an opportunity to address the harm suffered by the victim and the community and to design a sentence that rehabilitates offenders and allows them to remain as part of the community.
house or clan	A band may be subdivided into houses or clans; each house or clan can have one or more hereditary chiefs, and each chief is selected by the elders.
Indian Act	Legislation designed to facilitate the assimilation of Aboriginal peoples into the larger Canadian culture. It governs Indian status, council elections, band governance, inheritance, family law, and economic activity.
Indian status	The requirements for acquiring Indian status are contained in the *Indian Act*; only status Indians are able to obtain benefits enunciated in the Act; registration is required before status is assigned.
Inuit	The indigenous peoples of the circumpolar north; they are not status Indians, and the *Indian Act* does not govern them.
membership or citizenship code	The *Indian Act* permits a band to design its own requirements for membership or citizenship in the band. For example, permitting a non-Aboriginal to be a member and live on a reserve is not the same as "status" under the Act and does not automatically entitle the member or citizen to any other benefit.
Métis	Generally speaking, the Métis are descendants from inter-marriages between Europeans and Indians; they are referred to as "non-status" Indians and are not governed by the *Indian Act*. The provincial government deals with Métis issues and benefits.
oral history	The spoken words of Aboriginal peoples concerning historical events and practices that have been passed down from generation to generation; it is admissible as evidence in court.
reserve	Land owned by the government but allocated for the use and benefit of an Indian band, which is subject to the *Indian Act* and any treaty terms. Reserve land can only be sold or surrendered to the federal government.
Royal Proclamation	Signed in 1763 by Britain's King George, this document attempted to establish boundaries around Indian land and also stipulated that this land could be sold only to the government.
sovereignty	The supreme or ultimate authority in a state.
sui generis	Unique or of its own kind. Aboriginal rights are *sui generis* because of the fact of prior occupation by Aboriginal peoples. The methods for establishing these rights and the content of the rights are also unique.
treaty	Generally considered to be a formal agreement made between two nations, but not in the context of the First Nations, since Canada does not recognize them as a nation; thus, it can include any Aboriginal right.
Treaty of Paris	Signed in 1763 by France, Spain and Britain, this document allowed Britain to gain control of North America when the other countries ceded their claims to the land.
Two Row Wampum	An agreement entered into by the Iroquois and British that included terms under which each group agreed not to interfere with the other.
Wampum belts	Used as an aid to oral commentary, they record historical facts and terms in agreements in lieu of written language.

REVIEW QUESTIONS

1. What is the basis for an Aboriginal right to land that does not concern a claim for Aboriginal title? Identify the requirements that must be satisfied for such a common law claim to succeed.

2. What was the purpose of the Royal Proclamation in relation to Aboriginal rights?

3. What facts must be established before a person can be designated as having Indian status?

4. Why are healing circles held in the Aboriginal culture? What is the purpose of an Aboriginal healing circle?

5. How did Indian tribes traditionally make political decisions? Describe the option historically available to a dissenter in the decision.

6. Identify how the Supreme Court of Canada defined "distinctive culture" for the purposes of establishing an Aboriginal right to the use of land, and provide an example that would form part of a band's distinctive culture.

DISCUSSION QUESTIONS

1. An Indian band has allowed the non-Aboriginal spouse of a member to obtain citizenship in the band. Will the spouse be able to obtain benefits under the *Indian Act*?

2. In 1895 a treaty was entered into between an Indian band and the government. The written treaty established an Indian reserve, included compensation for the purchase of other Indian land, and contained a clause that severely limited the band's right to hunt and fish on land adjacent to the reserve. However, the Indians expressed concern during negotiation about the maintenance of their hunting and fishing rights and were verbally assured that these rights would be respected. The hunting and fishing rights met the requirements for establishing a common law claim for an Aboriginal right to use the land for hunting and fishing. Can the band make a common law claim that will override the terms contained in the treaty?

3. An Aboriginal band has Aboriginal title, as of June 1985, to a tract of land located in British Columbia. The provincial government has decided, in 2004, to expropriate the land in order to build an industrial park. Discuss. What difference, if any, would it make if title had been established in 1975 and the provincial government attempted to expropriate the land in 1980?

4. An Indian band in Newfoundland does not have a land agreement that deals with the land it has occupied for generations. What evidence is the band required to produce in order to make a successful common law claim to title of the land? Would it make a difference if a portion of the identified land had been communally and exclusively shared with another independent band?

5. Identify and discuss some of the fundamental differences between Aboriginal and early European cultures.

6. A band had a pre-contact practice of obtaining water from a stream on land it does not have title to. It used the water for survival, cooking, washing and in construction of shelter. The band seeks to bottle and sell the water from the stream and an adjoining lake as a business enterprise. Discuss whether or not the band would be successful in its claim for an Aboriginal right to do so.

SUGGESTED READING

Borrows, John. "Sovereignty's Alchemy: An Analysis of *Delgamuukw v. British Columbia*" (1997) 35 Osgoode Hall L.J. 125.

Cairns, Alan C. *Citizens Plus: Aboriginal Peoples and the Canadian State* (Vancouver: UBC Press, 2000).

Carcone, Janet Mason, & Stanley Gershman. "The Charter of Rights and Freedoms" in Laurence M. Olivo, ed., *Introduction to Law in Canada* (Toronto: Captus Press, 2004).

Constitutional Law Group, The. *Canadian Constitutional Law*, 3d ed. (Toronto: Emond Montgomery Publications Limited, 2003).

Dickason, Olive Patricia. *Canada's First Nations: A History of Founding Peoples from Earliest Times*, 3d ed. (Toronto: Oxford University Press, 2002).

Eccles, W.J. *The Canadian Frontier, 1534–1760 (Histories of the American Frontier)* (New Mexico: University of New Mexico Press, 1965).

Hogg, Peter W. *Constitutional Law of Canada*, Student ed. (Toronto: Thomson Canada Limited, 2002).

Hurtado, Albert L., & Peter Iverson. *Major Problems in American Indian History: Documents and Essays*, 2d ed. (Boston: Houghton Mifflin Company, 2000).

Imai, Shin. *Aboriginal Law Handbook*, 2d ed. (Toronto: Carswell, 1999).

———. *Indian Act and Aboriginal Constitutional Provisions* (Toronto: Carswell, 2004).

Royal Commission on Aboriginal Peoples. *Looking Forward, Looking Back*, Volume 1 (Ottawa: Minister of Supply & Services, 1996).

Salisbury, Neal. "The Indians' Old World: Native Americans and the coming of the Europeans" (1996) 53 William and Mary Quarterly 435.

Wright, Ronald. *Stolen Continents: Conquest and Resistance in the Americas*, 10th ed. (Toronto: Penguin, 2003).

Administrative Law

Irv Ash
SENECA COLLEGE

Learning Objectives

After reading this chapter, the reader should be able to:

- ➤ define administrative law
- ➤ differentiate between the three branches or functions of government
- ➤ elaborate on various concepts of public policy
- ➤ explain the reasons for, the types of, and the functions of agencies
- ➤ compare and contrast agencies and courts
- ➤ identify specific rules and procedures for a specific agency
- ➤ assess the relevant provisions of the *Statutory Powers Procedure Act* as they relate to the rules and procedures of Ontario agencies
- ➤ document how various sections of the *Charter of Rights and Freedoms* have been applied to agency proceedings
- ➤ illustrate and discuss principles that flow from the duty to act fairly
- ➤ distinguish between the remedies of reconsideration, appeal and judicial review that may be available in respect of an agency proceeding
- ➤ outline various concerns in respect of appealing an agency proceeding
- ➤ summarize the various remedies available from an agency proceeding pursuant to judicial review

TABLE OF CONTENTS

INTRODUCTION

In the past 20 years, the number of cases involving administrative law have increased tremendously. The reason for the increase is tied to both the explosive growth of government and the definition of "administrative law". The definition involves government and governmental delegates, the legal restrictions imposed on the government when implementing public policy, and the remedies available to persons "harmed" by the misuse of governmental power. This chapter will attempt, in varying detail, to deal with each component of this definition.

The courts have been given the **jurisdiction**, both **inherent** and **statutory**, to oversee and remedy many governmental actions. This jurisdiction or power derives, in common law, from the *Magna Carta* in 1215 and has been strengthened over the years by various statutes and case law. Further, in Canada, greater jurisdiction has been given to the courts by the constitutional documents that instituted and regulate the country, and by the federal-provincial split of powers. Before delving into various aspects of administrative law, it is necessary to review some aspects of government and the Constitution and to further discuss the concept of public policy and how it is legislated and enforced in our system.

BRANCHES OF GOVERNMENT

Canada has three branches (or functions) of government. The legislative (or parliamentary) branch includes elected Members of Parliament, whether federal or provincial, and the appointed Senate. The major task of this branch is to introduce, debate, and institute new legislation, and amend and/or repeal existing legislation. Once the legislation is enacted and **proclaimed in force**, it is the main duty of the executive branch to ensure compliance with such legislation and subordinate governmental policy instruments that may be in force (regulations and orders-in-council). This is achieved through the work of government ministries, departments, and agencies, as well as through boards, commissions, and tribunals. The third branch of government, the judicial branch, has a basic obligation to interpret the legislation presented before it in specific cases in order to resolve disputes. If there is no specific relevant legislation, the judicial branch must also determine the law to be applied. In addition to this basic obligation to interpret the legislation put before them, there has developed a review component of the courts' powers. The courts oversee not only the appropriate exercise of substantive powers of government (constitutional law) but also the exercise of government's procedural powers (administrative law).

PUBLIC POLICY

In discussing the branches of government in Canada, reference was made to the legislative function, including legislation. It should be noted that almost all legislation is initiated by the governing party. By starting the legislative process and then shepherding it to its conclusion, the governing party is putting into law parts of its governmental or public policy. This is just one facet of public policy that can be defined as a "conscious choice [of government or governmental authority] that leads to deliberate action — the passage of a law, the spending of money, an official speech or gesture, or some observable act — or inaction."[1] If it is conceded that the function of government is to govern, then any action taken by government in governing is public policy.

MECHANICS OF PUBLIC POLICY

Many different paths can be taken in order to achieve what the government of the day perceives as its objectives. A lot of policy is developed internally in the caucus of the elected members of the governing party and through consultation with their advisors (sometimes their constituents) and the civil service. Policy also derives from the party platform prior to elections; it can originate in any number of ways as allowed by that party's internal constitution and is developed in answer to current issues. For example, policy actions can follow from senior ministers floating "trial balloons" at speaking engagements and in media interviews, from public hearings before standing committees of the legislature, or from reports from royal commissions appointed to investigate certain issues. Upon determining the substance of the proposed public policy in a specific area, the government makes it governmental policy or law in a variety of ways that include (a) legislation and (b) orders-in-council properly published in the **gazette**.

After the legislative function has been carried out, the next step is to enforce the legislation. If the legislation is regulatory — that is, it involves control of public and/or private sector operations in the "public interest" — mechanisms will be found to achieve the desired ends. This is also the case for legislation that is operational in nature, such as legislation in respect of delivery of goods and/or services, review and/or advice, the use and conservation of resources, or legislation for disciplinary or other purposes.

Governments continue to enact and enforce more and more regulatory legislation. The main function of the executive branch of government concerns enforcing these laws. That function is often achieved by civil servants working for various ministries in the government, usually in specialized regulatory bodies. It should be noted that under constitutional law, the government can delegate, to bodies it creates, its powers to legislate and enforce laws. Such bodies shall, for the purposes of this chapter, be called agencies (which also includes boards, commissions, authorities, committees, and tribunals). Although administrative law can and does deal with actions of Cabinet ministers and/or other elected members of government, it mostly involves judicial review and/ or appeals (to be discussed later) from agencies.

AGENCIES

There are various reasons why a government would appoint an agency to deal with a specific area, including, but not limited to, the following:

1. Specific expertise can be developed and applied.

2. The magnitude and complexity of government and its attendant workload requires a shift in responsibilities from elected members to such experts.

---

[1] Stephen Brooks, *Public Policy in Canada, An Introduction* at 12.

3. It is more efficient in time and costs to use an agency to deal with recurrent matters.

4. It offers a more precise, yet flexible and timely, way to deal with specific situations than going through the more cumbersome elected bodies.

5. It is a way to distance the government from the public effect of certain decisions or actions.

6. It allows future unforeseen events to be dealt with more efficiently.

Because there are many and diverse reasons why agencies are created, there are many agencies in existence. In 1990, the number in Ontario totalled 485. By 1994, that number had grown to 716.[2]

There are three main types of agencies:

- Advisory — provide information to government that will assist in developing policy or the ongoing delivery of programs. Some examples of Ontario advisory agencies include the Ontario Advisory Council on Senior Citizens and the Ontario Advisory Council for Disabled Persons.

- Operational — main function is to deliver goods and/or services necessary to implement approved government policy or programs. Operational agencies in Ontario include the Workplace Safety and Insurance Board and Ontario Hydro.

- Regulatory — decision-making bodies that control public- or private-sector operations as authorized by their enabling legislation, or the exercise of a licence-review function or an appeal function, with respect to both government and third-party decisions. The Canadian Radio and Telecommunications Commission (CRTC) and the Ontario Human Rights Commission are examples of regulatory bodies.

Agencies may, if empowered, exercise legislative, executive, and judicial functions. As will be discussed, the legislative function includes the ability to make rules and regulations in respect of procedure to be followed before the agency. The executive function includes research and advice on, and administration and enforcement of, government policy. The judicial function allows for adjudication on specific situations and may determine individual rights, privileges and obligations. An agency may have any or all of the above-mentioned powers, which must be specifically delegated by the legislation that establishes the agency.

An agency is established by legislation enacted by the government. That **enabling legislation** will have provisions that may delegate power to the agency in order to carry out certain stated objectives. Such legislation will usually set out general procedures of the agency, such as who has the right to appear before such agency and the jurisdiction and powers of such agency. Further, the agency may be able to make rules and regulations regarding its own procedures. Finally, the legislation will authorize the staffing of the agency and determine who may be eligible to be employed there.

---

[2] Government of Ontario, *Guide to Agencies, Boards and Commissions of the Government of Ontario 1994* (Toronto, Ont.: Queen's Printer, 1995) at 3.

	EXHIBIT 24.1
The Differences between the Courts and the Agencies	

COURTS	AGENCIES
¤ interpret and apply the law	¤ formulate (by regulation), interpret, and apply the law
¤ *stare decisis* applied (inflexible)	¤ no *stare decisis*, although attempts to be relatively consistent (flexible)
¤ formal — specific rules and procedures to be followed	¤ more informal — there may or may not be specific rules and procedures to be followed, but more procedural latitude is allowed
¤ make decisions based strictly on law; no policy or public interest concerns	¤ make many decisions based on public policy
¤ no relationship with parties before them either before or after hearing	¤ likely to have many relationships with parties both before and after adjudication
¤ unlikely to have expertise in area to be decided	¤ usually have expertise in area to be decided

AGENCIES COMPARED TO COURTS

One function of agencies is adjudicative. Agencies may determine rights, privileges, and/or obligations of persons in relation to another person or to a group or to society. An agency acting under such powers has been seen as having a **judicial or quasi-judicial function** that would seem to encroach on the judicial branch of government — that is, the court system.

There is considerable case law on the differences between the courts and agencies. Some agencies do have some similarities to courts, in that both interpret legislation and apply it to specific cases. However, there are differences in the two bodies (see Exhibit 24.1).

One of the most contentious issues in the court–agency comparison is how far the judiciary should go in recognizing agencies' obligations to make decisions based on public interest (or the collective good of society). Public interest is foreign to the courts, which have always looked to individual rights first and foremost. This tension can be observed in the greater or lesser control that the courts have exercised over agencies during the past 50 years, to be discussed later in this chapter.

STEPS TO DETERMINE RULES OF AGENCIES

We shall next examine the legal restrictions imposed on agencies. To determine the specific rules and procedures, or legal restrictions, followed by a specific agency, the following should be reviewed:

1. Enabling statute creating the agency.
2. Regulations pursuant to the enabling statute.
3. If applicable, general legislation that details rules and procedures that apply to certain agencies.

4. The *Charter of Rights and Freedoms*[3] (the Charter).
5. Rules, guidelines and/or directives formulated by the agency.
6. Rules set out in notices issued generally and/or for particular proceeding.
7. An overall common law requirement to "act fairly", and rules derived therefrom.

Each of these steps shall be discussed at some length to clarify how such rules and procedures are found.

Enabling Statute

As we saw above, agencies must be created by government statute that sets up an agency to advise on, operate in and/or regulate a legislated area. Usually, such an enabling statute will detail the composition of the agency, its powers and jurisdiction and, occasionally, some rules and procedures. An agency that is set up under a specific enabling Act may also be named as the relevant agency to hear appeals of issues under different legislation. For example, the Social Assistance Review Board (SARB) and its successor, the Social Benefits Tribunal (SBT), was created pursuant to the *Ministry of Community and Social Assistance Act*,[4] but it is also the appropriate board for the *Family Benefits Act*,[5] the *General Welfare Assistance Act*[6] and the *Vocational Rehabilitation Services Act*.[7] Any general information about rules or procedures for SARB and SBT would initially be found in its enabling Act, and usually not in the other Acts.

Regulations Pursuant to the Enabling Statute

Enabling Acts will have provisions that allow regulations to be made in respect of the rules and procedures to be applied by the agencies. Powers to develop and **promulgate** regulations are often granted to the Governor General in Council (federal Cabinet) or the Lieutenant Governor in Council (provincial Cabinet), depending on whether the enabling Act is federal or provincial. The procedures in respect of SARB and SBT, as an illustration, are prescribed in regulations by the Ontario Lieutenant Governor in Council. Such regulations will usually give details regarding documentation to be provided in a hearing, time limits with which there must be compliance, and other hearing procedures.

Legislation That Establishes Rules for Many Boards

Some provincial jurisdictions (currently Alberta and Ontario) have provisions that govern procedures of numerous agencies set out in one statute. In Ontario, the statute is entitled the *Statutory Powers Procedure Act*[8] (SPPA). Originally enacted in the 1970s to provide "minimum rules for proceedings of certain tribunals", the SPPA was an attempt by the Ontario government to codify the rules and procedures that the court system had developed for administrative agencies over the years, through the common law "duty to act fairly" and its predecessor concept, the "**rules of natural justice**". It was felt that there should be somewhat common rules and procedure for those agencies required to hold a hearing — that is, to exercise a "statutory power of decision".

---

[3] *Constitution Act 1982*, R.S.C. 1985, Appendix II, No. 44, Part 1.
[4] *Ministry of Community and Social Assistance Act*, R.S.O. 1990, c. M.20.
[5] *Family Benefits Act*, R.S.O. 1990, c. F.2.
[6] *General Welfare Assistance Act*, R.S.O. 1990, c. G.6.
[7] *Vocational Rehabilitation Services Act*, R.S.O. 1990, c. V.5.
[8] *Statutory Powers Procedure Act*, R.S.O. 1990, c. S.22.

It is important to note that the SPPA applies to all Ontario agencies unless they are explicitly excluded by the provisions of the SPPA or another statute.

As initially conceived and enacted, the SPPA dealt with such matters as the following:

1. Determining who are the parties to a proceeding.
2. Notice provisions to advise of the case to be met, and providing time to prepare.
3. Requiring public hearings unless there are reasons for private hearings.
4. Appropriate representation of parties at hearing, including examination and possibly cross-examination of witnesses.
5. Powers of agencies to compel evidence.
6. Rules regarding admissibility of evidence.
7. Written decisions to be provided to all participants after the hearing.
8. The need for the agency to compile a record of the proceedings.

All of those matters are part of the common law "duty to act fairly", to be discussed below.

Certain amendments were made in 1994 to the SPPA, under the *Statute Law Amendment Act (Government Management and Services)*,[9] that allow agencies that fall within the SPPA to have more cost-effective and efficient proceedings. Some of the amendments include the following: (a) a general provision allowing any agency under the SPPA to make its own rules and procedures, and to promulgate them in the form of regulations; (b) a recognition of the value, where appropriate, of both written hearings and, especially, electronic hearings by amending the previous rules to allow such hearings; and (c) a provision permitting agencies to have pre-hearing conferences, determine more questions about admissibility of evidence, make interim orders, and have the power to review and vary a decision. More recent amendments to the SPPA in 1999 made certain changes, especially, but not limited to, inserting provisions for the appointment, with the consent of all the parties, of mediators, conciliators and negotiators to facilitate resolution of a matter before a tribunal. This alternative dispute resolution mirrors similar programs instituted in the civil court system to try to resolve matters without going to the time, expense and hard feelings of a court hearing.

Charter of Rights and Freedoms

There are many general statements made in the Charter in terms of individual rights and freedoms. The judiciary has been given the power under the Charter to determine if a person's freedoms or rights have been infringed upon by some governmental law or action (including actions of agencies, as they are creations of governmental law). The judiciary has used various sections of the Charter to review the rules and procedures and, ultimately, the decisions of agencies.

Section 7 of the Charter states that, "Everyone has the *right to life, liberty and security of the person* and the right not to be deprived thereof, except in accordance with the *principles of fundamental justice*." Through a series of decisions, the Supreme Court of Canada (SCC) has read into those italicized words, principles of procedural fairness. Although such principles existed in the common law concept of the rules of natural justice, the Charter has entrenched those principles as part of the basic constitutional law of Canada.

---

[9] *Statute Law Amendment Act (Government Management and Services)*, S.O. 1994 c. 27.

Two leading authors on administrative law,[10] after analyzing the decisions of the Supreme Court of Canada, summarized the principles as follows:

> These [principles] include the rights to notice, and a hearing, and unbiased decision-making and all the other related, procedural rights. One must then ask whether any particular procedural right should be afforded in the specific case. Several limiting factors should be examined. First, the purpose of the impugned legislation should be considered and a balance should be struck between the demands of fairness and efficiency. The competing interests of the state and the individual must be balanced. Second, in extradition matters at least (and perhaps more generally), the Court may ask whether denying the remedy would "shock" the conscience of Canadians or violate the standards of the international community. Third, the nature of the decision-making function will be analyzed. Depending upon where the function resides on the continuum of administrative decision-making, a higher or lower degree of procedural fairness will be required. The closer the decision-maker is to the legislative (or policy) end of the spectrum, the lower the standard of procedural fundamental justice which is required. A higher degree of fairness is required as the decision-maker moves along the spectrum toward judicial or quasi-judicial deliberations.

Agencies have powers to force production of documents or evidence by summons and/or subpoena, or to permit entry of premises to conduct searches by search warrant. They must comply with section 8 of the Charter, which states that such seizures or searches must be reasonable. Various decisions in the courts have determined that individuals have some sort of sliding scale in their right to privacy. The reasonableness of privacy is dependent on the circumstances, such as the purposes of the search and other related factors. Further, certain procedural safeguards usually must be maintained, such as an impartial decision-maker authorizing such search or seizure on reasonable evidence supplied.

Section 13 of the Charter states, "A witness who testifies in any proceedings has the right not to have any incriminating evidence so given used to incriminate that witness in any other proceedings, except in a prosecution for perjury or for the giving of contradictory evidence." This section is not the same as the American Fifth Amendment, which allows a person to not give any evidence that would tend to incriminate oneself. Instead, evidence given by a person may not be used to incriminate that person in a subsequent proceeding.

Section 14 of the Charter states, "A party or witness in any proceeding who does not understand or speak the language in which the proceedings are conducted or who is deaf has the right to the assistance of an interpreter." Further, the interpreter must translate word for word and not summarize the information being translated. Notice that the Charter makes no reference as to who pays for the interpreter, making such issue open for discussion.

Rules, Guidelines, and Directives Formulated by the Agency

Some enabling statutes, such as the Ontario *Workplace Safety and Insurance Act, 1997*,[11] under subsection 159(1) for the Workplace Safety and Insurance Board (WSIB) and subsection 173(1) for the Workplace Safety and Insurance Appeals Tribunal (WSIAT), give specific power to agencies to determine their own practice and procedure. Depending on the statute, the rules the agency makes in respect of practice and procedure may have the force and effect of a regulation. The regulation, however, must be approved by the appropriate Cabinet, and the guidelines to promulgate such rules as regulations must be

---

[10] Jones & de Villars, *Principles of Administrative Law* at 57–58.
[11] *Workplace Safety and Insurance Act, 1997*, S.O. 1997 c. 16, Sch. A.

followed. If, however, the agency has made its rules in a non-statutory form, as described in the next paragraph, such rules must be followed if they are mandatory.

Rules Set Out in Notice Generally or for a Particular Proceeding

For reasons of flexibility, agencies usually have some latitude in determining which rules should apply generally and in a particular proceeding, provided that the overriding concern of fairness is met. This concern is also addressed when determining whether the specific rules are mandatory (must be followed) or directory (may be followed). Although consistency in rules is preferable, it is not necessary to follow all rules if there is a risk of unfair treatment. It is recognized that in these situations agencies have to broadly interpret, and even change, rules as long as no party is prejudiced. On the other hand, if some or all of the parties have acted in reliance upon a specific rule, it would not be correct to amend such rule.

Common Law Requirement to "Act Fairly" and the Rules Derived Therefrom

The six steps to determine the rules of any agency discussed above should be observed through the lens of the court-developed "duty to act fairly" and its predecessor concept, the "rules of natural justice". The rules of natural justice have largely been supplanted by the duty of fairness and, therefore, are not very relevant here. The courts have used the obligation to require anybody to act fairly, as a means to determine a person's rights and obligations. A successful attack, by way of judicial review as discussed later, has been decried by some opponents as interference with agencies' freedom to act in determining the public interest. The reply to this position notes that the courts will only interfere where a party is treated unfairly and where the decision has a sufficiently serious effect on the party. This suggests that the more adverse the effect on the party, the greater the duty to act fairly, as shown by an increase in the procedural protections. But in an emergency, an agency may be entitled to have more flexibility in its procedural protections, at least initially. Therefore, it can be argued that there is a sliding scale of procedural protections mandated on an agency, depending on certain factors that sometimes are recognized by the courts.

Notwithstanding any other requirements, before an agency can make a decision adverse to a person's interest, at a minimum the person should be:

- told of the case to be met; and
- given an opportunity to respond.

Both "notice of the case" and "right to respond" can range, depending on the circumstances, from verbal advice to written notice to provision of documentary evidence in the former situation, and from written to electronic or, most likely, oral hearing in the latter situation. These minimum requirements can be observed in rules adopted by most agencies to be fair to the parties because the courts would likely impose them anyway. However, even if no rules are prescribed for an agency to follow, the duty to act fairly will impose a number of rules on the agency, as outlined in the next paragraphs.

Status

One of the most important preliminary matters to be decided by an agency is who has the status to appear before it. A person who should appear before an agency but is denied an opportunity to appear would be considered unfairly treated. The most likely person to have status as a party to the proceeding is a person who may be seriously affected by the outcome of the proceeding. Factors used to determine whether a person is seriously affected include the subject matter of the proceeding, the person's interest in the subject matter, and the effect that the decision might have on that interest. Using the concept of "serious effect" allows not only persons directly affected, such as a named party or the complainant in a disciplinary proceeding, but members of the public who may have the status of an **intervenor**. This is especially important in an agency environment, where the public interest is so compelling and where the effect of a decision might be far reaching.

Notice

The general principle here states that, except for emergencies, advance notice advising of a proceeding where a decision may be made must be given to all persons who would be affected by the decision. Such notice should be explicit and state the time and place of the proceeding, in order that those persons affected may take action to protect their position. Whether service is verbal, written, or even by newspaper advertisement, it must be effective: the notice must reach the person and be timely enough to permit the person to adequately prepare.

Disclosure

In order for the person affected by the possible decision to have an opportunity to make appropriate submissions, the person should be informed of the case to be met. That includes disclosure of (a) all relevant information that the agency may take into account when rendering a decision, (b) the issues as presented to the agency, and (c) the penalties that could be imposed on the person. A party to a proceeding may very well be entitled to more disclosure than an intervenor. In some circumstances, only partial or even no disclosure is permissible when it involves confidential information or information that would cause harm if released. Disclosure of information must be timely and should be given as soon as reasonably possible in the circumstances.

Adjournments (or Stays)

Even where there is no provision in the enabling statute to allow it, agencies have inherent discretionary jurisdiction to adjourn proceedings to ensure fairness. An agency would likely grant a stay in the following situations: (a) a party received insufficient notice, (b) a party received late or improper disclosure, (c) a new issue is raised in the hearing, requiring time for a party to prepare, and (d) a related matter is being heard in another agency or in court. In determining whether to grant a discretionary adjournment, an agency will usually review factors such as complexity of the proceeding; previous stays, if any; interests of the persons affected; and costs of the stay. If a stay is granted, the agency will likely fix the time and place for the resumption of the proceedings.

Effective Participation (Especially the Right to Counsel)

In order for a party to properly deal with a hearing, such party must be present at the hearing. That means the agency should carry on with a hearing only if all parties are present, unless it is shown that such missing party or parties had effective notice of the hearing but decided not to attend. In almost all circumstances, any person who has a right to appear in a hearing has the right to be represented by counsel who can present the case for the person. An agency may have some discretion, under its enabling Act, to allow counsel. Concerns such as the ability of the parties involved to represent themselves, the nature and complexity of the proceeding (the more complex or serious the matter, the more likely that counsel will be allowed), and the possible consequences of the proceeding are taken into account. If an agency denies use of counsel, it must state its reasons for doing so. Unless the legislation requires it, the counsel does not have to be a lawyer and, in fact, almost all agencies will allow paralegals or laypersons with some specialized knowledge to represent parties in a hearing.

Public or Private (In Camera) Hearings

The general rule for most hearings, whether in court or before an agency, states that they should be public, for reasons of fairness and as a safeguard against covert actions. However, especially for hearings before an agency, there is discretion to have *in camera* hearings for national security reasons or if a person, such as a party or even a witness, could be harmed by a public hearing. In some situations, such as a hearing before the Workplace Safety and Insurance Appeals Tribunal, the hearing is private unless the parties to the proceedings unanimously agree to allow the public to be present. This situation likely has to do with a possibility of embarrassment if evidence as to a worker's physical condition and health became public knowledge.

Evidence

In order to reach a decision, an agency must base all findings of fact upon the relevant evidence. On the whole, the rules of evidence, which are formal and usually strictly applied in court, are much less formal when applied by an agency. Therefore, such uncertain types of evidence as hearsay and somewhat unqualified "expert" evidence will likely be admitted, although in determining whether to admit the evidence the agency must determine its relevance. Even if the evidence is admissible, the agency must also determine the evidence's weight (probative value) and its credibility. If the evidence does not have much value or is not believable, possibly because of contradictions, the agency will likely gloss over the evidence. An agency also has the right to take notice of commonly accepted facts without the need for evidence to prove those facts.

Witnesses

Witnesses before an agency can give evidence in written or oral form, depending on the circumstances and the provisions of relevant legislation. Oral evidence is usually adduced by questions of the party calling the witness, or by members of the agency itself, which often has a wide latitude to participate in an active way, unlike most court proceedings. The difficult issue for most agencies to determine is when a party has the right to cross-examine a witness, which can be done whether the initial submission is in a written or oral form. Although certain acts require cross-examination, an agency has discretionary power to grant it. The party must convince the agency that the party should be given the opportunity to correct or controvert any relevant and prejudicial statement made by the witness. More specifically, cross-examination will be allowed if it is the only means to reveal or test the evidence that goes to the heart of the hearing where there is conflicting and/or contradictory evidence, as if cross-examination provides the best way to assess the credibility of the witness.

Proof

Parties who bring an application to appear before an agency usually carry the burden of proving their case. However, the standard used to determine if the burden has been met is not the **"beyond a reasonable doubt" test** used in criminal court proceedings but, rather, the **"balance of probabilities" test** used in civil court proceedings. In making a finding of fact and the eventual decision, the agency should be reasonably satisfied that the fact occurred, which depends on such factors as the nature of the facts to be proven and the consequences that would flow from the finding of fact. Once the parties with the burden or onus to prove the case have finished their submissions, the other parties have the ability to make a motion for a non-suit (dismissal) without making any submissions. In determining whether to grant the motion, the agency must determine whether the first party made a *prima facie* case. The *prima facie* test, a test that has less of a burden than the balance of probability test the agency will use in making its final decision, requires looking at the evidence in the light most favourable to the parties who presented it. Even if the evidence is weak and not very credible, if there is any evidence at all to support the contentions of the parties presenting the case, the agency should not grant a motion of non-suit.

Evidence by Compulsion

Pursuant to legislation, many agencies are granted powers to obtain relevant evidence in the following ways:

1. exercise of search and/or seizure powers;
2. use of inspection powers; and
3. use of subpoena and/or summons powers, which are subject to section 8 of the Charter.

In respect of search and/or seizure, an authorized person is permitted to pay a surprise visit to search for and/or seize evidence. Prior authorization is given by a person, usually not a member of the agency, but not necessarily a judge. Such person should not have an interest in the proceeding and should be satisfied on reasonable and probable grounds, provided under oath, that it is reasonable to grant such search and/or seizure warrant. The search should not be a general search but should be a search in respect of a specific situation and anything relevant to it.

Inspection orders permit inspectors to view premises for spot audits and to regulate businesses as allowed under the enabling Act. The usual purpose of the inspection is to protect the public interest and is likely to be carried on during reasonable hours.

Documents and/or witnesses can be subpoenaed to require production and/or attendance, respectively. If there is non-compliance, contempt proceedings can be initiated before the appropriate court. If non-compliance is proven beyond reasonable doubt, the offender can be imprisoned unless there is compliance. Certain documents cannot be compelled, most commonly those that are privileged, such as solicitor–client communications for the purposes of obtaining legal advice, and Cabinet or ministerial communications where disclosure would prejudice the public interest. Summonses will be granted to compel a witness to appear if the party requesting it can show that such witness is reluctant to appear, the likely evidence obtained is relevant, and it is unlikely to be obtained in any other fashion than by a summons.

Orders and Decisions

Unless required by the appropriate legislation to be in writing, an oral final order or decision is acceptable. The decision should be given as expeditiously as possible, and some enabling Acts even have a specific time limit for a decision to be handed down. Although it may not be required, agencies usually give reasons for the decision, especially if the decision might be raised in court on appeal or by way of judicial review (to be discussed later). The following are some of the problems that can arise if the reasons for the decision are not included:

1. Lack of reasons may undermine confidence in the agency.
2. The court will disregard the agency's expertise if it is not demonstrated by stated reasons for the decision.
3. The court can derive adverse inferences if there are no reasons to review.
4. A disturbing impression of injustice may be left with those reading the decision.
5. The parties do not know why the decision was made, or if there are any grounds for appeal or judicial review.

Further, if the enabling Act requires reasons to be given, and there are none, the decision is likely null and void. The reasons, as given, should adequately explain how the agency reached its conclusions, whether based on fact, law, or public policy.

Over and above the rules or procedures to be followed by agencies in respect of the duty to act fairly, two other principles, derived originally from the rules of natural justice, are important: the decision-maker must be impartial (no bias), and the decision-maker must not fetter his or her discretion. Not following either principle will likely lead to a successful application for judicial review.

Bias

If, in the exercise of its powers, an agency is found to lack neutrality, has not been impartial and/or has had personal interests in mind, the decision of the agency will likely be null and void. If a member of an agency is found to be biased, that member will be disqualified from hearing the case. Indicators of bias of a member of the adjudicating agency body include the following:

- Pecuniary interest in the proceeding
- Having a friend, business associate, or relative as a party or a witness, unless it is a past and/or distant connection
- Improper conduct at the hearing, such as flippant or derogatory language, expressed feelings of hostility or antagonism, or repeated interference in the proceeding
- Private meetings with one party to the exclusion of others
- Social meetings with parties or witnesses prior to or during the hearing
- A Predetermined view of the issues (although a tentative prior view is acceptable as long as there is an opening for persuasion)

It is important to remember that an appearance of bias or a reasonable apprehension of bias (where a reasonable person would suspect that a member may be influenced by improper considerations to favour one party over another) will likely be sufficient for a court to find bias. Therefore, if a member of an agency board hearing a case believes there may be a possible bias situation, it is best if the member abstains from the decision or, possibly, disqualifies himself from the proceeding. Once that is done, an unbiased member or unbiased panel can be put in place. It should also be noted that certain agencies are, under statute, biased, such as labour arbitration boards with members drawn from management and labour.

Improperly Fettering Discretion

Agencies, in most circumstances, as previously noted, are given wide discretion in such areas as the responsibility to apply rules to each situation as it arises, as long as the agency is fair. Other areas of discretion include determining whether a specific situation is covered by the legislation, which action is warranted, and considerations of public policy applied to specific situations.

An agency must funnel all of its decisions through the obligation to promote the objects of its enabling legislation. If an agency exercises its discretion arbitrarily or dishonestly, the courts may rule that the agency is acting in bad faith and that, therefore, the actions of the agency are reviewable. Bad faith, however, must be proven. Indicators of bad faith, such as discriminating against a specific person for different treatment, or making a decision based on an improper purpose or irrelevant considerations, would go a long way in proving bad faith.

The most likely example of improper fettering of discretion is the application, by an agency, of *stare decisis*, or standing by precedent. Most agencies keep accessible copies of decisions, and it is quite common for appropriate and, sometimes, inappropriate decisions to be submitted to an agency. If the agency bases its decision solely or predominately on a prior decision without proper regard to the actual case before it, a court would likely determine that there has been improper fettering of its discretion. Although consistency is desirable, it is not an all-encompassing obligation for an agency as it is in the judicial branch of government. Further, there are ways to make a decision without making it obvious that *stare decisis* was used.

Not only is it inappropriate to improperly fetter discretion, it is also wrong to not exercise discretion that is conferred on an agency. In the right circumstances, to be discussed in the following section on judicial review, such agency can be compelled to exercise its discretion.

REMEDIES AVAILABLE IF A DECISION OF AN AGENCY IS NOT SATISFACTORY

Once an agency has made a decision, the parties should comply. There are legal mechanisms available to try to ensure compliance. However, depending on certain circumstances, especially when permitted to do so by legislation, a party may be able to have the decision

- reconsidered,
- appealed, or
- reviewed

by making an application of judicial review. Reconsideration involves an agency revisiting a case, after the agency made a decision to look at the case again because of a request to do so. An appeal is requested to allow an appellate body, either an appellate agency or a court, to reconsider the result on the merits of a case because the decision may be "wrong". An application for judicial review is made because there is some question not of the results but of the rules and procedures used to achieve such result. To better understand these options or alternatives that can be exercised, each shall be discussed in turn.

Reconsideration

Under either its enabling Act or some other general legislation, such as the *Statutory Powers Procedure Act*, some agencies are given the power to review or reconsider the decision made and to change it, if appropriate. An example of a reconsideration involving an agency would be the case of an applicant for some type of financial assistance benefits in respect of vocational rehabilitation, who has applied for a hearing with the Social Assistance Review Board. If SARB has made a decision to refuse benefits, the party who was denied has the option to request a reconsideration by SARB, to appeal the decision to court, or to apply for judicial review. In choosing the appropriate option, it is important for the party to assess the reasons for its attempt to have the decision reversed. If the party does not like the decision, but does not have any new evidence or cannot point to errors made by SARB, the party should not take any action. However, if the party has evidence of such errors as relevant evidence not considered, bias, unfair treatment by non-adherence to appropriate procedures, or mistakes of law or fact, the party should select the appropriate option. If a ground such as new evidence exists, it would be best for the party in this example to request a reconsideration. Factors making this the best option include the expeditiousness and the cost of a reconsideration being overwhelmingly more in favour of the party than either of the other options. In other words, it will happen much sooner and costs much less. The appropriate legislation will state the scope of a reconsideration, if any.

Appeal

The second option available to the party in the example would be to appeal the decision. In respect of a decision of SARB, the appeal goes to Ontario Divisional Court. In order to determine if any appeal rights exist against the decision of any agency, either the enabling Act or other appropriate legislation must be consulted. If there are no appeal rights explicitly granted, in respect of an agency's decision, in the legislation, no appeal can be made. Note that the legislation could designate a court, as in the example, or another agency to hear the appeal. For example, decisions from the Workplace Safety and Insurance Board are appealed to the Workplace Safety and Insurance Appeals Tribunal. The following matters in respect of appeals need to be discussed.

Status (Who May Appeal?)

As will be seen in most of the discussion of appeals, one must first and always look at the legislation to determine who can appeal. If the Act states that only a "party" may appeal, or is silent on the matter, then only a party to a proceeding can appeal. However, the legislation could be broader and give status to appeal to such persons as intervenors or, even, some members of the general public. This can be achieved by the use of such phrases as "adversely affected", "aggrieved person" or, even, "interested party". The appellate body has the right to determine if the "appellant" is allowed to appeal under the words of the legislation. Although somewhat unusual because of the possible appearance of bias, some Acts allow the agency to be an appellant.

Scope of Appeal

The scope of appeal, or the grounds upon which an appeal can be heard, is set out in the statute. Such grounds can be that the agency made errors on questions of jurisdiction, law or fact, or some combination of such grounds. In brief, the following points are raised:

- A question of jurisdiction relates to whether the agency did not have the power to hear the case or, if initially having such power, commits some act to lose or exceed such power. Actions taken outside jurisdiction are **ultra vires** (outside the power) and may be rendered null and void.

- A question of law relates to the interpretation and application of the law to the facts of a specific case. Although this appears to be a clear position, there has been much blurring of whether a suggested error is a question of law, fact, or jurisdiction.

- A Question of fact relates to the facts as found or determined by the adjudicator, usually after the perusal of the submissions of witnesses and physical and documentary evidence.

Some case law suggests it is an error of jurisdiction to make a decision where there is a total lack of evidence. Usually issues related to evidence are considered questions of fact. However, if necessary (where an appellate body wants to have the right to grant an appeal even though the Act limits appeals to questions of jurisdiction), it has been decided in some cases to call it an error of jurisdiction. The question of alleged errors and their categorization is even more important for judicial review and shall be discussed further below.

Type of Appeal

Depending on the statute, the appellate body could hear the appeal in a number of ways:

- A hearing *de novo* (a new hearing), where the appellate body would act as a new adjudicator and rehear the matter without any reference to the decision appealed. The parties would be able to submit any and all evidence to support their positions.

- A new hearing where the appellate body has the right to look at and, even, defer somewhat to the decision appealed from.

- Review of a record of the agency that arrived at the decision, without oral hearing of arguments by the party or parties, regarding errors made by the agency that appear on the record. This method is most often used in appeals from a court decision.

Further, the error must be appealable pursuant to the statute granting the appeal rights. In this way of appeal, the agency is required to produce a record that will usually include the following documents: (a) specific decision under appeal, (b) any interlocutory or interim orders, (c) the reasons for the decision, (d) the notice for the original adjudication from which the decision arose, (e) all documentary evidence and (f) the transcript of the proceedings. The first means of appeal is the broadest and, in effect, puts the appellate body in the position of a body hearing the matter for the first time.

The method of appeal will have a direct relationship to the powers of the appellate body to make a decision. If the first way is the type required by statute, the appellate body's decision will replace that of the original agency decision-maker. However, the other ways, especially the third one, will likely mean a return to the agency for a new hearing, although before a new adjudicator(s). To ensure that the new adjudicator does not make the same mistakes, the appellate body may be able to provide directions along with the order for a new hearing.

General Concerns Regarding Appeals

Items such as notice of appeal, leave to appeal (where required), and stay of an agency decision during the process of appeal are all detailed in the enabling Act or other relevant legislation. Normally, rules about the time to file and where to file an appeal are strictly enforced. There is, however, the ability in most circumstances to exercise discretion to extend the time where it would be fair to do so. If leave to appeal is required, a *prima facie* case must be made by the possible appellant of the substance of the arguments supporting the requested appeal. The general position on stays (or holding in abeyance) is that an application for a stay before the appellate body must be granted if the decision has been appealed. Normally, the agency's decision is effective immediately, even if an appeal has been launched; but the appellate body, if granted such power, can order a stay until the decision is made on the appeal.

Two further points should be made about appeals and how they relate to applications for judicial review. First, it is usually better, if the grounds allow it, to launch an appeal rather than make application for judicial review. The powers of the appellate body to possibly hear the case anew and consider the merits of the decision are almost always wider than the reviewing court's power. Second, if the application for judicial review is made while appeal rights exist but have not been explored, the court will almost invariably refuse to hear the application until all appeal rights have been exhausted.

Judicial Review

The third way that a decision of an agency can be challenged is by an application for judicial review. Such application was formerly by the mechanism of a prerogative writ. This method is still available, but other mechanisms now exist to provide similar review. This method shall be considered in detail, including (a) specific remedies available, (b) the grounds for the types of review, (c) statutory provisions to try to limit or even prevent review, and (d) other specific concerns.

Prerogative Writs

Prerogative writs were the mechanisms developed over the centuries by English common law to control arbitrary government action. Initially, they were orders issued by the Crown to oversee and direct the actions of its underlings. Over time, issuance of these writs was transferred to superior courts and became part of their inherent jurisdiction to supervise governmental decisions.

As these writs can be granted on a discretionary basis (similar to equitable remedies), there are certain situations where the court will usually refuse to grant such remedy. As previously discussed, if there is another valid remedy available, such as appeal, the court will likely not grant the application. Another reason to exercise the discretion not to grant a writ is that such grant would be ineffective because it was academic or useless. Other situations where the writ may be refused include where the party objecting and bringing the application has

1. waived or acquiesced knowingly in the agency's error;
2. taken too long to seek this remedy (*laches*); or
3. by his conduct, such as bad faith, become disentitled to review (**clean hands doctrine**).

Generally, the court requires that the applicant for a writ be a person who has a sufficient interest in the proceeding. The application is brought against an agency who, depending on circumstances, may be able to participate actively in the court review, or may only be a neutral friend of the court.

The five prerogative writs still in use, to varying degrees, are *certiorari*, prohibition, *mandamus*, *quo warranto* and *habeas corpus*. Following is a discussion of each of these writs:

□ CERTIORARI

This writ allows the court to quash (basically, stop or nullify) a final decision of an agency on certain grounds, usually errors of jurisdiction made by the agency. Originally part of the superior court's inherent jurisdiction to supervise inferior courts, it was extended over the years to include certain supervisory powers over agencies. It can only be applied once the agency has made the improper decision, and not before that time. Historically, *certiorari* was available if an agency acted judicially or quasi-judicially; however, recent cases have decided that it can also be used to quash decisions of agencies acting administratively. Limitations to the use of this writ include its non-applicability to legislative decisions or delegated legislation or the Crown itself (except for certain situations). However, the writ does apply to public bodies whose power is granted by legislation.

☐ PROHIBITION

Prohibition is essentially the same as *certiorari* in terms of history and its limitations, except that it can be applied for at any stage prior to the making of the final decision. It is used, therefore, to try to prevent something from being done outside the jurisdiction of the decision-maker before the ultimate order or award is made.

☐ MANDAMUS

An application for *mandamus*, if granted, will result in an order by the court to compel an agency to perform a statutorily required duty where the agency has refused to do its duty. If the power an agency is refusing to exercise is discretionary, *mandamus* would likely issue — but only to require such agency to exercise the discretion, not to dictate the way it must be exercised. In order to use this writ the following circumstances must exist:

- The applicant must have status to apply; in this situation, there must be a public duty to act owed by an agency to the applicant.
- An explicit demand has been made to such agency that it act, and there has been a refusal to do so.
- As with all prerogative writs, it does not apply against the Crown or its agents when not acting under a statutory duty.

☐ *QUO WARRANTO*

Rarely applied for, this writ, if granted, will state that a person has no right to hold a public office. It is of little relevance to agency proceedings.

☐ HABEAS CORPUS

This writ, which is centuries old, is used to quash an illegal detention of the applicant. Only the detained persons or someone acting on their behalf can make application. The grounds for granting the writ relate to errors of law or jurisdiction.

Statutory Applications in the Nature of Judicial Review

☐ PROVINCIAL (ONTARIO AND ALBERTA)

Most provinces have legislation to provide potential applicants with an alternative to requesting one of the prerogative writs against provincial agencies. In fact, some of the provinces, including Ontario, have, in effect, abolished some of the prerogative writs. The Ontario statute that accomplishes that task is the *Judicial Review Procedure Act*[12] (the JRPA), specifically section 7, which turns applications for *mandamus*, prohibition, and *certiorari* into an application under the JRPA. The intent of the legislation was to make such applications a summary proceeding with fairly consistent procedures that should be heard by the Ontario Divisional Court. Under section 2(1)(1), an application is made by way of an originating notice to request an order in the nature of *mandamus*, prohibition, and *certiorari*. That provision means that all the law developed under those three specified remedies is still important. The JRPA, in section 2(1)(2), also puts into summary form two kinds of private law remedies (to be discussed later) historically available to applicants. Under the clause, the applicant can request a declaration or an injunction, or both

---

[12] *Judicial Review Procedure Act*, R.S.O. 1990, c. J.1.

remedies, in relation to the exercise or purported exercise of a statutory power of decision. "Statutory power of decision" is defined as the power conferred on an agency by a statute to make a decision affecting the rights, duties or powers of any person, or the eligibility of a person to receive a licence or benefit. Note that the application in replacement of the three prerogative writs is not restricted to the exercise of statutory power. Detailed rules of procedure in respect of the JRPA are set out in the Ontario *Rules of Civil Procedure*. Also note that the definition of "party" includes some groups that are not persons at law and, therefore, likely did not previously have standing to bring an application for a prerogative writ. Alberta has very similar legislation to the Ontario legislation discussed in this paragraph.

□ FEDERAL

In making application in the nature of any of the prerogative writs against an agency under federal jurisdiction, the *Federal Court Act*[13] (the FCA) states that all such applications are in the exclusive jurisdiction of the Federal Court, Trial Division. An exception to this provision provides for applications in respect of 15 specified federal agencies to be in the exclusive jurisdiction of the Federal Court of Appeal. The application for judicial review, so called, is made pursuant to the rules and procedures of section 18.1 of the FCA. As in the JRPA, such applications are meant to be heard in a summary fashion. The section further gives extensive powers to the court to order all the types of relief that could be granted under the prerogative writs, if any of the enumerated errors exists. When the FCA was first enacted, certain wordings allowed for an application for judicial review only if the agency was acting in a judicial or quasi-judicial manner. This led to many cases where the issue was not whether there was an error that could be reviewed, but whether the agency was exercising a judicial or quasi-judicial jurisdiction. Recognizing this problem, the legislators amended the FCA, effective in 1992, to remove the distinction between judicial or quasi-judicial jurisdiction.

Remedies under Private Law

Relief may also exist pursuant to common law and/or equitable remedies awarded through an ordinary action. Specifically, one could simply sue the agency in tort, likely for some form of negligence, although some intentional torts could also support the action. In this situation the claimant alleges that an agency has either committed some intentionally improper action that interferes with that person (intentional tort), or is careless in performing some action that causes damage to the person to whom such agency owes a duty of care (negligence). In order for an action in tort to succeed, the action complained of must be illegal or **ultra vires**. A review of the case law indicates that the court will likely find agencies liable if the elements of the specific tort can be proven. However, the courts have also recognized the need for flexibility for agencies to effectively function. It should also be noted that, historically, there was a limit to which parties could be sued due to "Crown immunity", which basically prevented a person from bringing a tort action against the Crown in an official capacity. Federal and provincial legislation has effectively brought Crown immunity, in most circumstances in this instance, to an end — although strict time limits have been imposed to restrict somewhat the right of action. There is much more material to be discussed about tortious actions that can be brought against agencies, but that is outside the scope of this chapter; however, the relief that can be granted in consequence of a successful action in tort can include the following:

---

[13] *Federal Court Act*, R.S.C. 1985, c. F-7.

☐ DECLARATORY RELIEF

This discretionary relief (also known as declaratory judgment or declaration) is a non-coercive judgment of the court setting out the legal positions of the parties and/or the law applicable to them. Although not binding, since there is no legal way to enforce such a judgment, declarations have become an accepted way for a person to have a court determine if an agency had the power to take certain actions. It is also a very flexible remedy, with few technical requirements to be followed, and can be used in a number of ways. The courts have normally issued declarations against agencies as part of their supervisory function in respect of the legality of some governmental actions. Remember that a declaration can be obtained in summary fashion under the FCA and, with limitations in respect of an exercise of statutory power, under the JRPA.

☐ INJUNCTION

An injunction is a discretionary equitable remedy in which the court can order a party to act or refrain from acting in a certain way, and if there is non-compliance a party would be liable for contempt of court. There are two main types of injunctions, both of which have been used against agencies after a successful tortious action. One type is a mandatory injunction, somewhat similar to *mandamus*, to compel an agency to act in a lawful manner. The other type is a prohibitory injunction, somewhat similar to prohibition, to restrain an agency that acts, or even threatens to act, in an illegal fashion. Further, injunctions are available on an interim basis, without a full-blown trial and, possibly, without notice to the other side. An interim injunction will enjoin an agency until such time as the cause of action is tried and, possibly, a permanent injunction is granted. Standing to bring an action for an injunction, along with Crown immunity issues, must be addressed before an injunction can be successfully obtained. Also, in a similar way to declaratory relief, injunctive relief can be granted under both the FCA, for federal agencies, and under the JRPA, for Ontario agencies.

☐ DAMAGES

In any successful action for tort the court has the obligation to award the common law remedy of damages to compensate the victim for certain types of loss or injury suffered as result of the tort. Once the amount (or quantum) of damages is proven on the balance of probabilities to the court's satisfaction, the court will order the **tortfeasor** to pay such damages. Not only will the innocent party be compensated for losses suffered through no fault of such party, but liability for damages may act as a deterrence to the wrongdoer. The potential for deterrence can clearly be seen in the ability of the court to award punitive or exemplary damages in circumstances where an agency has acted maliciously. These principles in respect of damages have been accepted if a tort action has been successful against an agency. One issue still open for resolution is whether a purely economic loss is compensable. As in the other two private remedies examined above, items such as standing and Crown immunity may be relevant. There is no provision for a summary award of damages in either the FCA or the JRPA.

Although in some jurisdictions it is possible to apply for one or more prerogative writs, to apply for statutory judicial review, and to commence a private law action for one or more of the private law remedies, most persons will likely only make application under the appropriate statute. An application is made in a summary fashion and is, therefore, less costly and more expedient and provides grounds, in most circumstances, at least as broad as the other remedies. Although a discussion of grounds for judicial review can be overwhelming, the following are some concepts to remember.

Grounds for Judicial Review

As previously mentioned, the grounds for most appeals of agency decisions usually relate to the merits or the result of the decision by questioning the findings of fact by the adjudicator. Typically, the grounds for judicial review relate to how the result was achieved and are likely determined by looking for jurisdictional or legal errors made. It is possible that a resourceful court can make what appears to be a possible question of fact into a question of law; however, the grounds for judicial review tend to be very narrow. A vast amount of case law exists on the sole issue of whether an alleged error of an agency is reviewable, but an analysis of the law is beyond the scope of this chapter. However, certain principles can be canvassed.

The major focus of determining proper grounds for judicial review revolves around the statutory power of an agency to take a particular action. Usually the court must determine if the statutory power exists or, if it does exist, whether an agency has either exceeded or has somehow lost its statutory power. This is a search to discover the jurisdiction of the agency. It can also be classified as a question of law because if an agency took an action without the statutory power or the jurisdiction to do so, such action is declared illegal. Determining jurisdiction often requires the reviewing court to interpret appropriate legislation to determine exactly what is an agency's jurisdiction.

As an agency is a creation of its enabling Act and other relevant legislation, understanding the words of all of such legislation is usually the first step the court takes to determine whether an agency has acquired the appropriate jurisdiction. Other initial issues may include whether the agency is validly constituted — that is, has proper appointment and delegation — and whether there has been compliance with all preliminary matters, such as proper notice. Any or all of these issues may be examined in order for the court to determine if the agency has acquired jurisdiction.

If the jurisdiction is properly acquired, an agency's actions can still be reviewed if it exceeds or loses its jurisdiction. Broadly speaking, an agency can exceed or lose jurisdiction in three ways: (a) abuse of discretion, (b) non-compliance with the duty to be fair, and (c) bias. (Refer to material detailed earlier in this chapter for a more comprehensive discussion.) Certain concepts regarding each of the three ways jurisdiction can be lost now follow.

Abuse of discretion can include actions such as the following:

- Exercising a discretionary power in bad faith for improper or irrelevant considerations
- Making a decision with no evidence whatsoever or by ignoring relevant evidence
- Using discretion to obtain an improper result because it is discriminatory or unreasonable, or is made based on a misunderstanding of the law
- Improperly fettering or restricting the exercise of discretion

Notice how an evidentiary problem, which is normally a question of fact, can become an abuse of discretion issue. A reviewing court can find that because there is no evidence to support the exercise of discretion, an agency has lost its jurisdiction and, therefore, the decision is reviewable.

The origins of procedural fairness, or the duty of an agency to be fair to parties before it, derive from the rules of natural justice. These rules of natural justice, developed over the centuries to try to ensure that a party was treated fairly, were initially reserved for agencies acting in a judicial or quasi-judicial manner. The need to characterize the function of an agency was all-important because if an agency was acting in a legislative or executive manner, the rules of natural justice were likely not applicable. However, in most but not all situations, it is no longer relevant to characterize function, since an agency is required to act fairly in most of its functions. The determination of whether an agency has acted fairly is based upon whether the rules flowing from the duty to act fairly, as stated earlier in this chapter, have been followed. Such rules of natural justice are basically the same rules derived from the duty to be fair. Remember that how closely any such rule must be followed is dependent on fairness to the persons involved in the proceeding.

The loss of jurisdiction due to the bias of an agency also derives from the duty to be fair. Various types of bias in respect of agencies are discussed elsewhere in this chapter. It is important to note the problem of whether bias should be judged by the strict objective test used in courts, or by a more subjective standard for agencies that need to consider public policy in coming to decisions. Such public policy obligations may make the actions of an agency appear biased to a party. Many agency members have criticized the courts in going too far to make agency proceedings appear like court proceedings. Different considerations often apply between agencies and courts.

A further ground for review, specifically for an application for an order of, or in the nature of, *certiorari*, is an error on the face of the record. These are errors of law and not jurisdictional errors. The errors are clear and obvious when the record of the proceeding is read; such errors allow the court to quash a decision of an agency. An example of an error of law is an agency incorrectly interpreting and/or applying a statutory provision other than its own enabling legislation. Numerous recent cases have tried to place limitations on which errors of law on the face of the record are quashable by positing tests to be followed. These tests arose to try to deal with "privative clauses", discussed next. The most important test suggests that errors of law that are "patently unreasonable" are errors of jurisdiction and, therefore, reviewable even with a privative clause. This test has been used, and possibly misused, in numerous court decisions to try to determine the ambit of judicial review by way of *certiorari*. Such cases have made it difficult to state a consistent principle to be applied, other than that the test is important in this area, mostly as a way around a privative clause.

Privative Clauses

A privative clause is a statutory provision intended to prevent, or at least limit, the right of the judiciary to hear judicial review applications or even appeals. The legislature's intent in using such a clause derives from a concern that the courts have intervened too readily and in areas better left to an agency's expertise and streamlined procedure. No matter what the specific wording of a privative clause is, it will not prevent a court from reviewing an agency's action based on a jurisdictional error. Therefore, a privative clause will be of use only where there is an error of law on the face of the record. The three common general types of privative clauses in use are as follows:

1. A final and binding clause, or similar wording, that means there is no appeal from an agency's decision, but that still allows the court to determine whether any jurisdictional errors exist if the decision is patently unreasonable.

2. An exclusive jurisdiction clause to the effect that only an agency has exclusive jurisdiction to determine certain matters. This clause has the same basic effect as in item 1.

3. A clause that prevents any application for any prerogative writ or declaration. Again, this clause has the same basic effect as in item 1.

There has been much discussion about whether an agency's decision should be reviewable by the courts and, if so, what the appropriate limits are, if any, to such review. This is yet another issue that threatens to go totally unanswered in the near, and possibly distant, future. There are still other concerns that are usually considered under judicial review.

Other Concerns in Judicial Review

There are always time limits, invariably short, within which to apply for judicial review. Such time limits often are strictly enforced, although there is often some discretion, based on fairness, to extend the time. The time is usually found in the enabling legislation or any rules pursuant to it. A stay of an agency decision is not automatically in place upon making an application for judicial review. It must be specifically and separately applied for to the appropriate court, which must be convinced of the efficacy of granting a stay. The hearing is a review, and not a new hearing, which is why the record, as discussed previously, is so important. This is an absolute necessity where the review application is based on an error on the face of the record. Problems occur in this area when the agency does not have much in the way of transcripts. Usually the winner in an application for judicial review will have costs awarded in its favour.

POSSIBLE TRENDS IN ADMINISTRATIVE LAW IN CANADA

There is a fair amount of tension between those who believe that agencies should have comparative freedom from the courts and those who want agencies to follow many rules and procedures as overseen by courts. On one hand, there is the obligation on agencies to follow and, even, develop public policy, which is or may be foreign to the court's perspective of individual rights. On the other hand, there is the court's traditional role to ensure justice is done and seen to be done. There is a need for the expertise and cost-effectiveness of agencies, but should it be at the expense of fairness to a specific person? There have been relatively recent examples of methods to try to find new ways to resolve issues even before they get to an agency hearing, let alone to court. One example is the use of mediation in some situations before the WSIB. There have been attempts to have a different forum for review than the court, as in the use in a number of provinces of an ombudsperson. This governmental, yet independent, official has the power to scrutinize governmental abuses affecting members of the public. Such investigation includes not only how the result was achieved but the merits of the result. In England, a Council of Tribunals was created to review and approve all rules and procedures adopted by agencies. Such a comprehensive and considered approach to ensure fair rules may mean less need for parties to appear before the court suggesting an unfair rule. Even if some or all of the steps discussed in this paragraph are taken, the cases will still be forthcoming. There are just too many concerns still debated to foresee an early end to the tension.

CHAPTER SUMMARY

In this chapter, the reader discovered a definition of administrative law that led into a discussion of the three branches of government. After a summary review of public policy, the essential characteristics of agencies were introduced.

Specifically, agencies were seen as creations of government that, if empowered to do so, can exercise many of the same functions of any or all of the three branches of government. Various types of agencies and a comparison between agencies and courts followed.

After the concept and uses of agencies were explored, there was a lengthy discussion of the ways to determine what specific rules and procedures are applicable to a specific agency. This discussion included an exploration of such factors as the Ontario *Statutory Powers Procedure Act*; sections 7, 8, 13 and 14 of the *Charter of Rights and Freedoms*; and the "duty to act fairly". The duty to act fairly was first defined and then broken down into some of its component parts to allow the reader to discover how the common law provides at least some procedural protections to parties involved in an agency proceeding. Other common principles of no bias and not fettering the discretion of the decision-maker were also introduced.

The reader was then introduced to the remedies available if there is a complaint or concern regarding an agency proceeding. The remedies are (a) reconsideration by the same agency, (b) appeal to another agency or to court or both, or (c) judicial review to the courts. Substantial details regarding the requirements, procedure, scope, and type of appeal were discussed. Also reviewed were the remedies available under judicial review: (a) prerogative writs, (b) statutory applications, both federally and in Ontario, and (c) private law remedies of tort, declaratory relief, injunction, and damages.

Finally, there was a discussion of possible future trends in administrative law in Canada.

GLOSSARY OF NEW TERMS AND KEY CONCEPTS

balance of probabilities test	The standard used by the trier of fact in a civil proceeding (the judge or the jury, where appropriate) to determine whether the plaintiff or the defendant has won the case. If the evidence is more in favour of one party, even if just barely, then that party should be awarded the decision in the case.
beyond a reasonable doubt test	The standard used by the trier of fact in a criminal proceeding (judge or the jury, where appropriate) to determine whether the accused is found guilty or not guilty. If there is any reasonable doubt that the accused did not commit the offence charged, there must be a finding of not guilty.
clean hands doctrine	A principle of the law of equity that requires someone seeking to invoke an equitable rule to have conducted herself fairly and honourably in the events leading up to the proceeding, and in the proceeding itself.
enabling legislation (act, statute)	A law that permits a person (which for most purposes includes an individual, a corporation, and an agency) to do something that, prior to the law, the person was not permitted to do.
gazette	The name of a publication issued by both the federal and provincial governments in Canada on a regular basis, containing official notices and announcements and in which regulations made under the authority of a statute are first published.
judicial or quasi-judicial (function, manner, jurisdiction)	The authority or power of a court or a body similar to a court (that is, a body with the power to decide a person's rights) to decide matters before it. The rules of natural justice were historically applied to these bodies as well as to court proceedings. These bodies were different from agencies, whose decisions applying administrative jurisdiction were not subject to the rules of natural justice.
inherent jurisdiction (also statutory jurisdiction)	A power or right that is vested in an authority (agency or court) intrinsically, whereas statutory jurisdiction is a power or right that is vested in an authority derived from legislation.
intervenor	A person who is given status to participate in a proceeding even though the person is not a party to the proceeding.

proclaimed in force	A bill does not come into force (or become a statute) automatically when it is passed; it must first be proclaimed in force — that is, officially recognized as a statute.
promulgate	To publish a law.
rules of natural justice	The procedural standards imposed historically under common law in any proceeding where a party's rights may be affected by a decision-maker.
stare decisis	Latin, meaning "following precedent"; a legal doctrine that says that if a prior case is decided in a higher court in the same jurisdiction and on similar facts, then that prior case decision must be followed by subsequent courts.
tortfeasor	A person who commits a tort (a civil wrong excluding an action in contract).
ultra vires	Latin, meaning "outside (or beyond) the power"; an action or a statute that is determined by the courts to be outside the powers assigned to the legislature that enacted it.

REVIEW QUESTIONS

1. What are the three branches of government in Canada?

2. Describe how public policy becomes law in Canada.

3. Where would you find how an agency was created and the powers granted to it?

4. Discuss at least five reasons an agency may be created.

5. Detail the three types of agencies that can exist.

6. Set out five differences between an agency and a court.

7. What are the seven steps to determine which rules and procedures apply to a specific agency?

8. How does the *Statutory Powers Procedure Act* determine rules and procedures to be applied to an Ontario agency?

9. Discuss how four sections of the *Charter of Rights and Freedoms* are used to imply rules to be used in an agency proceeding.

10. What are the two main components or principles that are derived from the "duty to act fairly"?

11. List and explain the three remedies available if there is a problem or concern arising from an agency proceeding.

12. Set out three types of appeal and the scope of each type of appeal.

13. What are the remedies available when it is determined that judicial review will be allowed?

14. Discuss the grounds that must exist before judicial review may be awarded.

15. What is a privative clause, and how is it used to avoid judicial review?

16. List and discuss three methods in which public policy is derived or developed.

17. In order for notice to meet the requirement of the duty to act fairly, how may it be given in order to achieve its ends?

18. What is the usual burden of proof used by agencies to determine whether a case has been proven?

19. How does an agency deal with "hearsay" evidence before it at a hearing?

20. List three ways in which most agencies can obtain evidence by compulsion.

21. List three types of relief available if a person successfully sues an agency under tort law.

DISCUSSION QUESTIONS

1. Agencies are a better way to determine a person's rights than are the courts. Discuss.

2. If an agency is meant to deal with matters in an expeditious and cost-effective manner and with the expertise developed in the agency, is it worthwhile or even appropriate to allow a court to interfere with an agency's decision?

3. Have the various statutory and common law protections imposed on an agency's proceedings placed enough or too many rules on an agency's proceedings?

4. Should there be so many remedies available to a person who is concerned with an agency proceeding?

5. What changes would you make in Canadian administrative law? Why?

6. Why do the philosophies of some incoming governments lead to an expansion of the numbers and powers of agencies, and some lead to a contraction of the numbers and powers of agencies?

7. Discuss the current and future effects of the *Charter of Rights and Freedom* on agencies.

8. List four indicators of bias in an agency and/or an adjudicating member.

SUGGESTED READINGS

Blake, Sara. *Administrative Law in Canada*, 2d ed. (Toronto, Ont.: Butterworths, 1997).

Brooks, Stephen. *Public Policy in Canada: An Introduction*, 3d ed. (Toronto, Ont.: Oxford University Press, 1998).

Finkelstein, Neil, & Brian M. Rogers, eds. *Recent Developments in Administrative Law* (Toronto, Ont.: Carswell, 1987).

Jones, David, & Anne de Villars. *Principles of Administrative Law*, 2d ed. (Toronto, Ont.: Carswell, 1994).

Law Society of Upper Canada. *Administrative Law: Principles, Practice and Pluralism* (Scarborough, Ont.: Carswell, 1993).

———. *Recent Developments in Administrative Law* (Toronto, Ont.: Department of Continuing Legal Education, 1995).

Macaulay, Robert W., & James L.H. Sprague. *Practice and Procedure before Administrative Tribunals* (Toronto, Ont.: Carswell, 1994).

Moskoff, Franklin R., ed. *Administrative Tribunals: A Practice Handbook for Legal Counsel* (Aurora, Ont.: Canada Law Book Inc., 1989).

Swaigen, John. *Administrative Law: Principles and Advocacy* (Toronto, Ont.: Emond Montgomery Publications Limited, 2005).

WEBSITES

University of Toronto Law Library with Administrative Law links:
    <http://www.law-lib.utoronto.ca/resources/topic/admin.htm>

York University Law Library with Administrative Law links:
<http://library.osgoode.yorku.ca/res_web_links_adm.html>

The Canadian Legal Network website, providing links to other sites:
<http://canlaw.net/administrative.htm>

University of Montreal Faculty of Law site with many links to statutes, cases etc.:
<http://www.lexum.umontreal.ca/index-en.html>

Almost every administrative agency has its own website, which usually include the rules and forms used by the agency, a link to its enabling legislation and past decisions made by the agency. Following are a sample of the websites:

Federal agencies
Canadian Radio-television and Telecommunications Commission: <www.crtc.gc.ca>
Immigration and Refugee Board: <www.irb-cisr.gc.ca>
Office of the Commissioner of Review Tribunals CPP/OAS: <www.ocrt-bctr.gc.ca>

Ontario agencies
Workplace Safety and Insurance Board: <www.wsib.on.ca>
Workplace Safety and Insurance Appeal Tribunal: <www.wsiat.on.ca>
Social Benefits Tribunal: <www.sbt.gov.on.ca>
Human Right Tribunal of Ontario: <www.hrto.ca>

25   Alternative Dispute Resolution

Michele Braniff
MEDIATOR

Learning Objectives

At the conclusion of this chapter, the reader should be able to:

➣ understand the meaning of the term "ADR" and appreciate the differences between the various processes of dispute resolution

➣ understand how ADR processes fit into the legal system

➣ understand the role of an arbitrator and appreciate how an arbitration process would work

➣ critically assess key approaches and strategies for interest-based negotiation

➣ distinguish mediation from arbitration and negotiation models, identify the various factors in the selection of an appropriate model for dispute resolution and the choice of the neutral third party

➣ discuss roles and responsibilities of parties, counsel, and the mediator

➣ prepare for a role-play to practise interest-based negotiation and a role-play of a mediation

TABLE OF CONTENTS

INTRODUCTION

During the mid- to late-1990s, Canadian legal systems for dispute resolution adapted rapidly from the traditions of the 19th century directly to the technologies and processes for the new millennium. New systems for electronic filing and tracking of court documents facilitated a shift from a court-centred system for dispute resolution to one that relies on a network of innovative and client-centred procedures for early resolution and settlement of disputes.

The acronym **ADR** is commonly applied in Canada and the United States to refer to a variety of methodologies and processes for dispute resolution outside of the courtroom. ADR, or alternative dispute resolution, is an inclusive description, referring to **negotiation, mediation, arbitration** and a wide variety of hybrid models for dispute resolution. The systems are described as "alternative" because they provide options other than court and litigation; however, these dispute resolution processes are increasingly incorporated into court systems and treated by litigants and their counsel as part of a litigation practice.

Historical Context

Negotiated settlements have historically been part of the litigation system. Over 90 percent of litigated cases would settle without a judicial decision. In the Canadian common law system, like the British system from which it developed, judicial decisions develop out of the consistent application of legal principles based on **precedent**. Canadian business, community, family, and government interaction unfolds in the shadow of a strong civil court system. By and large, often with the assistance of lawyers and other professionals, Canadians can govern their personal and business affairs with a fairly good idea of rights, rules, regulations, and laws. We have a system where people can make agreements that can be relied on and that will be enforced by the courts if necessary. Parties enter into agreements to avoid or to settle disputes.

For hundreds of years, the Canadian law developed through a system where a small proportion of cases would go to trial, but the vast majority would be resolved through a negotiated settlement based on the parties' and their lawyers' best approximation of a judicially determined outcome. Since World War II, the legal system has seen increasing volumes of cases taken to court. A variety of factors are at work, including demographic trends, such as population growth and migration to urban areas; increasingly complex and wider government intervention through statutes and regulations; and more complicated business, government, and social interaction. The litigation system has become more expensive, with longer trial lists.

Increased government intervention has resulted in a proliferation of administrative decision makers in the form of boards and tribunals. These boards are granted statutory powers to administer a wide variety of decisions with respect to labour and employment matters, human rights issues, municipal and land use matters, and insurance and workers' compensation issues. There are limited rights to appeal administrative decisions — usually on the grounds of major misapplication of legal principles or the denial of **natural justice**. Natural justice is the right to hear the other side's case and to cross-examine, defend, and call independent evidence. Administrative tribunals typically have a process much like court but, often, with more relaxed or informal rules of process and with hearings heard by one to three decision makers on the board.

Through the years, statutes have provided for referral of matters to arbitration, either as part of an administrative process or as an alternative to litigation. An arbitration is much like litigation, except that the decision maker, the arbitrator, is most commonly chosen by the parties.

Mediation has perhaps the shortest history as an option to a litigated outcome. Although there are some long-standing traditions of consensus-based and participatory decision making in some Canadian cultures, such as among the Quakers and the North American Indians, mediation began to be more widely available during the 1980s. Community-based mediation projects developed across Canada as a grass-roots response to crimes such as vandalism and neighbourhood scuffles. The first mediation case was a result of the vandalism of some homes in Elmira by a group of boys. This first community mediation was an attempt to provide **restorative justice** through a facilitated meeting between the accused young men and the homeowners who had been vandalized. The concept of restorative justice is one of community equilibrium, accountability, and reparation. Community mediation programs have spread through many cities in Canada, where they operate with trained volunteers to resolve some criminal matters and a wide variety of disputes between neighbours. These programs have helped to create an awareness of and educate the public about mediation and consensus-based processes.

In addition to the grass-roots development of community mediation programs, referral to mediation began to occur with respect to labour and trade union disputes and, also, for family law litigation. Mediation offered a forum for joint problem-solving in an informal setting that moved the parties away from adversarial positions.

Contemporaneously, management studies in business began to encourage more facilitative styles, with emphasis on team development and participatory decision-making processes in the workplace. Workplace decision making evolved from authoritarian, or top–down, models to encompass two-way communication for wider input by staff, consensus-based models for meetings and facilitated approaches to human resources.

Cultural changes were also reflected in advertising and marketing campaigns, which shifted from the hard sell method of buy-what-we-sell and began to embrace the "win/win" approach of listening to the consumer's needs in order to sell what the customer wants. Listening to the customer became a key component in sales and marketing strategies.

By the late 1980s and early 1990s, there was a proliferation, in Canada, of a wide range of models for decision making that included new approaches to negotiation, mediation, facilitative workplace management, and referral of disputes to arbitration and administrative tribunals. These approaches had originally developed on a sector-by-sector basis. The next stage was a consolidation and cross-germination of experience through the recognition of commonalities between the various methodologies and sectors. Practitioners and trainers founded networks and organizations and began to describe themselves as a multidisciplinary profession working in the common field of ADR. A growing backlog of cases in the court systems increased willingness of lawyers and litigators to resort to the more quickly available dispute resolution alternatives of mediation and arbitration. American experimentation with and development of ADR is probably 10 to 20 years ahead of the Canadian experience, and the availability of literature, professional training, and testimonials from the United States accelerated Canadian interest in ADR.

Professional organizations for mediators and arbitrators, at provincial, national, and international levels, have consolidated the interests and presence of ADR practitioners through the development and widespread adoption of codes of ethics and standards for practice and training. ADR is not regulated as a profession by the government or by any professional body; however, organizations such as the Arbitration and Mediation Institute of Ontario and the Ontario Association of Family Mediators have designations for recognition of training and experience that help to define a standard of qualification for their professional members. Many ADR practitioners are professionals

Conflict Resolution Network Canada

EXHIBIT 25.1

Conflict Resolution Network Canada is Canada's largest broad-based conflict resolution organization. It is a national organization and has been active for over 20 years in engaging people in peaceful processes to help build safe and healthy families, communities and workplaces. CR Network Canada describes its promotion of conflict resolution activities as focusing on five strategies: supporting conflict resolution education; encouraging innovation; promoting excellence in conflict resolution practice; influencing public policy; and supporting Canada's international role as a leader for peace and conflict resolution.

The Network has studied the evolution of training activities in Canada and reports tremendous growth in the number of trainers and training organizations in every province and territory in Canada, particularly British Columbia, Saskatchewan, New Brunswick, Newfoundland, and Ontario. In 1988, the Network studied ADR training opportunities and listed 10 to 15 trainers, 2 to 3 associations and organizations, and 4 or 5 academic institutions. In June 1999, the Network's database included over 75 sources of training. The Network estimates that in Ontario alone approximately 2,500 students and 1,500 professionals enrol each year in conflict resolution training. The CR Network Canada website lists 187 private and public institutions offering conflict resolution courses. Prior to 1992, universities and colleges were only marginally involved in ADR training but more recently are designing courses for certificate and both undergraduate and graduate degrees in conflict resolution through faculties of law, social work, education, and environmental studies. The Network reported that in 1999, it was dealing with 38 publishers who produce texts, instruction manuals or other resources in conflict resolution. Most recently, CR Network Canada has partnered with the National Film Board of Canada. The CR Network Canada online bookstore offers over 300 titles about conflict resolution.

The fastest growing fields for ADR training have been identified by the Network as follows: divorce and separation, landlord/tenant, small claims, public policy disputes, victim/offender, restorative justice, land use, environment, workplace, employment, community or neighbourhood disputes, consumer complaints, and insurance.

Source: *The Network: Interaction for Conflict Resolution*, unpublished file data, June 1999; Conflict Resolution Network Canada website: <www.crnetwork.ca>.

qualified and regulated as lawyers, social workers or accountants. For example, the Law Society of Upper Canada, the governing body for lawyers in Ontario, has amended its Code of Ethics to deal with issues facing lawyers in the role of mediator. Conferences and professional and trade publications about ADR have also had a role in developing understanding and innovation for ADR processes and strategies.

The most recent development in the ADR field has been its transition from an alternative to litigation to a part of the litigation system. The professionalization of the field has given ADR credibility. Attorney Generals in the various provinces have been faced with relatively little funding for civil litigation and growing dissatisfaction with inefficient court processes. The less formal, faster and more flexible processes of ADR promise a cost-effective way to deal with case volume through the early resolution of an increased number of court cases. Administrative boards and tribunals have systemized processes that send disputants to arbitration and mediation prior to scheduling of a board hearing. Technological case management and electronic filing and tracking provide an efficient way to incorporate the more client-centred processes of ADR into court and administrative systems. At the approach of the year 2000, a number of provinces have created pilot projects through which alternative dispute resolution has become a component in the court system.

THE DISPUTE RESOLUTION SPECTRUM

Exploring the Dispute Resolution Spectrum

Alternative dispute resolution is the categorization by process or procedure of a variety of methods for the resolution of disputes. Dispute resolution theory offers a systematic comparison of **dispute resolution** models along a **spectrum**. Factors that vary across the spectrum are formality, control of the process by participants rather than by a third party, and the extent of self-enforcement of the rules of process by the parties. Negotiation is participant-controlled without formal rules of practice; parties negotiate without third-party intervention. Mediation relies on a third party to facilitate communication and to provide some formality of process while parties retain the role of substantive decision making. Arbitration allows the parties to select a third party and to agree in advance with respect to the rules of process but delegates the substantive decision-making power to the neutral third party or arbitrator. Administrative boards and tribunals operate similarly to courts but usually follow less formal and more expedited rules of process and procedure. If parties go to court, the dispute will be resolved according to the court rules of procedure, and decisions will be made by a judge appointed by the court. The parties do not have control over the process or over the substantive decision making.

Each process may also be compared along its own spectrum. Parties may negotiate in a very informal setting or may set an agenda, retain legal counsel or defer aspects of their decisions to mutually agreed on experts, such as an accountant or an architect. Both mediation and arbitration involve intervention by a neutral third party, who is usually chosen by the parties. There is a great deal of flexibility with respect to process, and there are med-arb models for dispute resolution in which the parties agree to a process that begins as a mediation but assigns decision making to the mediator to become an arbitrator in the event of an impasse between the parties. Some parties agree to steps for dispute resolution commencing with referral to mediation and provide for appointment of a different party as arbitrator if the mediation is unsuccessful. Rules of practice in some Canadian jurisdictions include an informal pre-trial settlement conference with a judge that has many similarities to mediation.

The availability of a variety of options means that parties can select a process that is most appropriate to their needs. However, even more fundamentally important than selecting an appropriate process is the need for the parties to understand the process and to match expectations for dispute resolution with the model they have chosen. Selection of the appropriate process requires consideration of a number of aspects of the dispute.

Parties to a dispute often measure the outcome or resolution in terms of one of three dimensions: (1) the extent that each party has accomplished his or her substantive goals: that is, a *task-focused analysis*; (2) the effect or repercussions on the relationship, which is a *relationship-focused assessment* of the process; and (3) comfort of the participants with the cost, timeliness, and manner of resolution, which is an *experiential evaluation* of the process.

By way of illustration, picture a soccer or hockey team. If you measure the team's success by standings and number of wins, you are applying a task-focused analysis. A relationship-focused assessment would define a successful team as one with cohesiveness and a strong team spirit. The experiential evaluation looks at whether the team had fun.

In a negotiation, the parties maintain responsibility to manage the task, the relationship, and the experience. In a mediation, the neutral third party manages the process in a manner responsive to both the relationship and the experience in order to facilitate a comfortable setting for the parties to concentrate their efforts on the task. Increasing levels of formality in arbitration and in the courts put less emphasis on the relationship and increased focus on the task. The experience is subject to application of rules that offers predictability rather than responsiveness and may not facilitate timeliness or cost-efficiency.

The spectrum of dispute resolution can be studied in another context by looking at **power, rights,** and **interests** as the three bases for resolving conflict. Power is about using resources to influence or compel compliance by others. Sources of power include physical strength, social status, gender, race, financial status, voting strength, personal charisma, position in an organizational hierarchy. Abuse of power takes the form of physical confrontation or threats, economic sanctions, intimidation. Processes that are power-based include elections, legislation, strikes, and war, while rights are created and defined by laws, regulations, court decisions, policies, agreements, past practices, customs, or conventions. Rights are the subject of adjudicative tribunals, such as arbitration, administrative tribunals, and the courts. In a democratic process, individual rights are often balanced with democratically elected hierarchies of power. Interests are less tangible and measurable and are often explored by asking about needs, concerns, fears, expectations, priorities, assumptions, goals, hopes, and aspirations. The processes include interest-based negotiation and interest-based mediation. Rights-based processes do not usually explore or attempt to accommodate the interests of the parties.

To return to the game analogy, without any rules in a competitive setting, the game can degenerate into a contest of the biggest and strongest — a game about power. If the players agree to play by recognized rules, however, and perhaps choose a referee to arbitrate or enforce the rules, the game would be rights-based. The game can also be played just for fun, for exercise, or to learn skills rather than to compete with another team. Activity may be skills-focused on drills or a game without score keeping. The application and enforcement of rules can minimize risks of abuse of power and maximize the interests of the players, whether those interests are for a competitive contest, for fun, or for exercise or learning.

If there is potential for abuse of power or the perception of vulnerability to an abuse of power, a rights-based and very formal process is appropriate. Where the interests of the parties are significant, they need to be addressed in the dispute resolution process, and the parties should be wary of committing to a formal process that will largely ignore interests.

Negotiation

Negotiation is an interactive process between two or more parties in which they attempt to reach agreement about an exchange of rights, responsibilities, benefits, and obligations in the form of a sale, a settlement, or other bargain. A careful negotiation prior to a sale or at the beginning of a relationship will often result in agreed-on mechanisms that will prevent or de-escalate conflict in the event of a later dispute. It is important to keep in mind that negotiation occurs at the stages of conflict avoidance as well as in the context of dispute resolution.

Negotiation is the simplest and least formal process, and it is not surprising that its effectiveness and efficiency vary widely. Negotiation is a process that is most vulnerable to an abuse of power. Negotiators may focus on rights or interests or may discuss both, and they often have different negotiation styles based on whether the negotiator focuses on task, relationship, or experiential factors. A relationship-oriented individual may be very vulnerable to making too many substantive concessions when confronted with a task-focused negotiator. Negotiators may fail to appreciate experiential elements and end up making non-sustainable agreements because of pressures caused by time deadlines or by unpleasant interaction.

The effectiveness of negotiation can be improved tremendously when a negotiator develops skills and strategies and adopts evaluation criteria for self-

---

EXHIBIT 25.2   **Negotiating Skills and Effectiveness of Lawyers**

Gerald Williams, Associate Dean and Professor of Law at Brigham University in Utah, conducted an experiment to study the negotiating skills and effectiveness of lawyers. The experiment involved 40 experienced and practising lawyers from a midwestern city in the United States who were asked to prepare and conduct settlement negotiations with respect to a personal injury case. All lawyers were given identical facts; they were effected by the same insurance laws and provided the same data about comparable jury trials. They were given two weeks to prepare and told that the results of the negotiation exercise would be published. The lawyers were divided into pairs, with one half representing the injured plaintiff and the other half, the defendant insurance company. Tabulation of the results showed a wide range in opening demands and in settlement amounts, with 3 of 14 negotiating groups reporting an impasse or failure to reach settlement. Plaintiff opening demands varied from a low of $32,000 to a high of $675,000. Counsel for defendant made opening offers ranging from $3,000 to $50,000. Negotiated settlements ranged between $15,000 to $95,000, with little pattern or logic between the opening numbers and the final settlement.

Professor Williams takes the view that many lawyers rely on hard-line tactics for negotiation because they lack adequate training in collaborative models of negotiation. Legal practice and culture traditionally are developed out of an adversarial and aggressive style of negotiation. While many law schools now endorse collaborative and interest-based negotiation styles, the academic setting is more conducive to learning styles based on reading and lecture format with limited opportunity for experiential and practical learning. Williams advocates the adaptation of university classes to nurture the environment required to facilitate opportunities for students to practise skills in order to train and develop highly effective negotiators.

Source: Law Society of Upper Canada, *Alternative Dispute Resolution*, 42nd Bar Admission Course, 1999, Day 9–3; Larry C. Farmer & Gerald R. Williams, "The Rigorous Application of Deliberate Practice Methods in Skills Courses", UCLA/IALS Sixth International Clinical Conference Enriching Clinical Education, online: <http://www.law.ucla.edu/docs/farmer__williams-_deliberate_practice_methods.pdf>; Google.com — "Gerald Williams, University of Utah, negotiation".

---

assessment. A key element to successful use of negotiation is the ability to objectively determine when to continue negotiation until finalization of an agreement and when to abandon or adjourn the negotiation to pursue other alternatives, such as another process for dispute resolution.

Mediation

Mediation is a process in which a neutral third party assists two or more parties to reach a voluntary, negotiated settlement of issues in a dispute. Key elements are that participation of parties is voluntary and that the role of the mediator is to provide structure to the process. In practice, there are a variety of different styles, objectives, and mediation models that are applied to provide structure to the mediation process. Factors of influence are the participants' expectations, the nature of the dispute, and the objectives and style of the mediator. The role of the mediator can be very facilitative and client-centred. Alternatively, the mediator may take a less facilitative role. For example, the parties may select a mediator who has expertise in a particular area, and they may seek the mediator's expert opinion on issues in dispute. Retired judges who mediate usually offer a process in which their opinion is an integral element in the mediation.

An important variable is whether the mediation focuses upon rights or interests. Rights are the clearly defined rules, regulations, laws, and contracts that may be the determining factor in some disputes. Interests are the less tangible motivating elements, perhaps arising from the parties' relationship or the needs, goals, expectations, and assumptions of the individuals involved in the dispute.

Mediation may be described as **interest-based**. The mediator encourages the parties to explore interests, develop a large number of options, and assess the options jointly by objective and mutually acceptable criteria. The role of the mediator is to help the parties express to one another their needs and expectations, and to brainstorm for lots of options, searching for a win/win approach that gives each party as much as possible with as little sacrifice or cost to either side.

By way of contrast, **rights-based mediation** focuses on rules, contract interpretation or the law. It is also called **early neutral evaluation**, or **evaluative mediation**. The mediator evaluates the case in the context of rules, such as the law or generally accepted accounting principles. The expertise and credibility of the mediator are extremely important in this model. Labour mediations, for example, are usually rights-based. In Ontario the pre-trial conference is an evaluative intervention in that the judge listens informally to the facts and legal aspects of a case and makes a preliminary assessment of his or her view of a likely court decision.

Collaborative Law

In recognition of the impact of process upon family relationships in matrimonial disputes, associations of lawyers, in various cities across Ontario and elsewhere, are working towards a less adversarial approach. Lawyers are forming associations for collaborative law based on a commitment to interest-based negotiations and win/win outcomes. Associations of collaborative lawyers agree to participate in training in interest-based negotiation and to establish a process for negotiation. Collaborative law is based on a four-way agreement between the lawyers and their clients to follow a non-adversarial practice. The website for collaborative law, <www.collaborativelaw.ca>, describes the process as "about cooperation not confrontation" and states that the spouses and the collaborative lawyers all work together as a team:

> The Collaborative Family Law Process uses informal discussions and conferences to settle all issues. In the Collaborative Family Law Process both clients will:
> • treat each other with respect;
> • listen to each others' perspectives, interests and concerns;
> • explore all possible choices;
> • let go of the past in order to focus on the future.

Members regard this collaborative style as very different from trial-based law. In fact, a usual term of agreement is that, if the dispute is not settled and clients subsequently decide to take the matter to court, both of the collaborative lawyers will refer the files to different lawyers for the trial preparation and process.

Arbitration

Arbitration involves the appointment or selection of an independent party to make a decision that will be binding and enforceable upon the parties to a dispute. Parties may agree, or may be required by legislation, to arbitrate with a chosen, or a prescribed, procedure and evidentiary requirements to be followed. In comparison to a mediation or negotiation, an arbitration is quite formal, with a rights-based application of rules and safeguards for natural justice and fairness. In addition to substantive decisions about the merits of the case, the arbitrator will interpret the rules for the arbitration process, including regarding admissibility of evidence, assessment of credibility of witnesses and the onus of proof and weight of evidence, and also the timing and order of the advocate's argument and submissions.

Usually, selection of the arbitrator is based on qualifications or expertise with respect to legal or technical aspects of the case. For example, parties in dispute about payment requirements prescribed by contract for architectural services may appoint a lawyer, an architect or, perhaps, an accountant as the arbitrator. The arbitrator may be appointed with instructions to consider expert evidence and render a decision based on that evidence in a process similar to the consideration of evidence by a judge in court. Alternatively, the parties may agree to a process that leaves more room for the arbitrator to apply his or her own expertise in addition to, or instead of, independent expert opinion from the parties' respective technical witnesses.

Arbitrated decisions are generally private and confidential among the parties, and the reasons of the arbitrator are rarely collected or published. Occasionally, one of the parties seeks judicial review of an arbitrated decision and then, because the facts and reasons of the arbitrator are considered by the court, there is a publication by the court-reporting services as part of the court case. Parties will refer matters to arbitration for a consideration of facts, credibility, an expert application of technical matters or for the application of clear legal principles or interpretation of an agreement. Where there is a new point of law to be determined, matters usually are referred to court.

Other Dispute Resolution Choices

There are also many hybrid and partial models that have developed for the resolution of disputes. Parties may refer certain issues to a fact-finder or to an arbitrator or may agree to a sequence of steps so that negotiation, mediation, and then arbitration are explored prior to taking a matter to court.

There is also legislation that appoints boards and tribunals with jurisdiction to make decisions and that may include referral to a mediator or arbitrator as part of a multi-step procedure.

Application of Process to the Legal System

Referral of matters to ADR takes place in one of four contexts:

1. contractual undertaking to use an ADR process;
2. private sector systems design;
3. systems design for public sector disputes; or
4. court-connected dispute resolution system.

The process, procedure, and expectations of the users vary from one context to another and are dependent on the sector in which the dispute occurs.

ADR by Contract

This is the simplest application of an ADR process. For example, a dispute develops, and the parties attempt to negotiate a settlement. Failing resolution, they may then consider process issues and agree to refer their dispute to mediation, **neutral fact-finding,** or arbitration. The referral to an ADR process will usually be confirmed in writing, and the choice of process, date, selection of mediator or arbitrator, and nature of proceedings will be established by agreement of the parties.

ADR by agreement also occurs as part of a conflict avoidance strategy at the formation of legal relationships during contract negotiations. Many business people and their lawyers are including dispute resolution clauses as a standard form in a commercial contract or as part of matrimonial or other settlements. The dispute resolution clause is a commitment to negotiate, mediate, arbitrate, or to use some combination of ADR process prior to taking the other party to court. The clause may specify the process, selection criteria, or method of selecting a mediator, or it may provide detailed procedures for resolution of any dispute. The purpose of such clauses is to create a mechanism for a speedy and cost-effective way to resolve disputes and to minimize negative impact upon the relationship.

Private Sector Systems Design

Business and non-profit organizations may create a policy for employees, staff, or clients that encompasses an ADR procedure in the event of disagreement. Unionized work environments often have legislative remedies available for collective agreement disagreements, negotiation breakdowns, or grievances. An in-house procedure must comply with, and may be complementary to, collective agreement and legislative requirements. Increasingly, workplaces are implementing systems on a voluntary basis. For example, most Canadian universities have harassment policies that map out informal avenues for involvement of specialized staff from a human resources or **ombudsman** office to investigate or interview complainants, witnesses, and respondents. Often there are tiers, with first-stage intervention featuring internal avenues, and a mediation model at an intermediary stage culminating in a more formal hearing process, often including some right of appeal.

As business, academic and non-profit organizations move into more decentralized and team-based structures, their needs increase for flexible, time-sensitive, and informal options for dispute resolution. In simpler and slower-paced times, many organizations coped well with de facto organizational response. Modern organizations, however, are dealing with re-organization, downsizing, dramatic and fast-paced changes and, perhaps, erosion of morale, trust, or employee loyalty. There is increasing workplace diversity with respect to gender, culture, and demographic differences.

Human resources staff increasingly take on a facilitative role within the workplace and, often, act in the capacity of an in-house mediator. A mediator who is on staff with an organization has knowledge of the culture and expectations of the organization but is usually not directly involved with the group or the department where the dispute or complaint began.

In contrast to an adjudicative model based on defined criteria of eligibility or limited areas of complaint, the new systems are designed to collect employee feedback and suggestions on a proactive basis before a situation escalates. The ADR process is often implemented in conjunction with training, team-building, and interest-based negotiation strategies, and as part of a general implementation of consensus-based decision making. ADR processes are also often implemented in response to concern about power imbalances or deadlocks with rights-based systems. Often the design is based on informal, interest-based processes at commencement with progression to rights-based procedures or adjudication.

Systems Design for Public Sector Disputes

Dispute resolution systems for conflict prevention and management are increasingly being implemented by government ministries, agencies, boards, and commissions for municipal, provincial, and federal matters. The system is implemented by statutes or regulations and may require use of arbitration or mediation or other ADR processes for specific types of disputes between non-government parties or with respect to disputes of private organizations or individuals with government ministries or other offices.

The use of mediation and arbitration for labour matters has been widespread across Canada for decades. Legislation stipulates the procedure for referral of collective agreement and grievance issues to mediation and/or arbitration by independent mediators and arbitrators who are not employed by or affiliated with the Labour Board.

In Ontario, in late 1998 and early 1999, the **Ministry of the Attorney General** created a **Dispute Resolution Office** as a resource for design of dispute resolutions systems; assistance to draft dispute resolution clauses in contracts, agreements, policies and legislation; negotiation and mediation training; and support of government groups committed to ADR. The mandate of the Dispute Resolution Office is to encourage the use of ADR by Ontario government offices and to promote dispute resolution processes as "a cost-effective and more responsive means of resolving disputes." The Ontario Dispute Resolution Office works with the Ministries of Agriculture, Education, Intergovernmental Affairs, Environment, and Attorney General and with the Human Rights Commission and the **Financial Services Commission of Ontario.**

Currently in Ontario, there are dispute resolution systems in a wide variety of government departments, ministries, and boards. For example, the Ontario Municipal Board has implemented a process using former and current Municipal Board members as board mediators who offer a rights-based assessment or opinion, encourage informal discussion and debate between the parties, and provide a mediation report and summary sheet that may formalize terms of settlement or refer the matter to a hearing before another board member. The **Workplace Safety and Insurance Board** has been including mediation as part of its return to work (RTW) solutions since February 4, 1999. Mediation is without charge to the worker. The WSIB website advises that mediations usually take about two to three hours with an appeal to the WSIB Appeals branch if dissatisfied with the resolution. The RTW mediator is on staff with the board and works with the workplace parties to help resolve disputes about the return to work of an injured worker using a rights-based model. If the mediation is not successful, the mediator becomes the decision maker and decides possible penalties or impact on benefits. A mediator's decision may be appealed by the parties to the Workplace Safety and Insurance Board.

These ministry initiatives for ADR are different from the client-centred and facilitative models used when parties voluntarily select an uninvolved third-party neutral because the staff mediator is mandated to follow ministry guidelines and, often, has significant power over the parties, including the right to order a settlement in the event of disagreement.

Court-Connected Dispute Resolution Systems

In the 1980s, rules for civil litigation introduced the **pre-trial conference**, which involved a mandatory meeting between counsel and a judge to discuss the merits of a case and to canvas reasonable terms for settlement. Pre-trials generally were scheduled after a case was on a trial list — that is, after examinations for discovery and completion of motions. The pre-trial judge is not the one who will try the case. The settlement discussions are very rights-based and centred on respect for the pre-trial judge's expertise. Cases settle at pre-trial where issues involve matters of law or rule interpretation rather than issues of fact or credibility. Effectiveness of a pre-trial is usually a product of the quality of preparation and expertise of counsel and of the pre-trial judge.

In contrast, various pilot projects and innovative court programs throughout Canada in the late 1990s began to explore earlier and more client-centred dispute resolution systems. The goal was to design a process that would mandate referral to a mediator early in the litigation; however, systems designers wanted to preserve the voluntary nature of mediation. Cost was also a factor,

ADR for Insurance Cases

EXHIBIT 25.3

The Financial Services Commission of Ontario was evaluated independently by the Honourable George W. Adams, QC, and described in his evaluation report as the largest and most comprehensive dispute resolution system of any Ontario administrative board or commission, and a "pioneer on the cutting edge of dispute resolution best practices". The Dispute Resolution Group (DRG) at the Financial Services Commission of Ontario (FSCO) mediates, arbitrates, and resolves personal injury disputes between consumers and no-fault car insurance companies. The process for dispute resolution is contained in the Ontario *Insurance Act* and in a *Dispute Resolution Practice Code* developed by the commission, which are available online at <http://www.fsco.gov.on.ca/english/insurance/auto/drs/resources.asp>.

Mediation

Mediations are conducted within 60 days of an application being registered with the commission. The mediation is the mandatory first step when a person disputes the insurance company's decision about accident benefits. Mediations are conducted by telephone conference or in person, and each mediator conducts about eight mediations per week. Eighty-one percent of claimants have legal counsel for the mediation. The mediator writes a written report at the conclusion of the mediation, indicating whether or not issues have been settled. In 1998, the FSCO reported that 78 percent of all claims settled some or all issues at the mediation stage.

Arbitration

Where the claim is not settled at mediation, the claimant (but not the insurance company) may go to private arbitration, arbitrate through the FSCO, or proceed to the court system. Once a claimant requests arbitration, the insurance company is permitted to raise its own new issues for arbitration. The first step for an FSCO arbitration hearing is the arbitration pre-hearing meeting, where issues are identified, preliminary matters may be resolved, exchange of productions is arranged, and another attempt is made to mediate a resolution. If the matter is not resolved at the pre-hearing, the arbitrator has discretion to set a future date to resume settlement discussions or may ask for a list of witnesses and set the hearing date. The arbitration is a formal hearing, and the arbitrator provides a written decision. In 1998, 87 percent of cases settled before a written decision was issued.

Neutral Evaluation

Where there has been an application for arbitration and the fee has been paid, on application, issues can be referred to an experienced evaluator. On such an application, arbitration is suspended until the evaluation has been completed. The FSCO provides a non-binding opinion of the likely outcome. If the case is not resolved after neutral evaluation, it is fast-tracked for arbitration. The FSCO arbitrator provides a review of the positions of the parties and assesses the probable range of outcomes. In 1998, FSCO received 142 applications for neutral evaluation, and 75 percent of cases that went to neutral evaluation were resolved at that stage in the proceedings.

Appeals

Either party may appeal the decision of the arbitrator, after the hearing. The appeal is to the Director of Arbitrations or her delegates. Appeals are allowed with respect to issues of law but are not allowed with respect to findings of fact.

Source: *Dispute Resolution at the Financial Services Commission of Ontario*, FSCO Brochure, May 1999; Financial Services Commission of Ontario website: <www.ontarioinsurance.com>.

with policy makers favouring user-pay systems rather than building mediation costs into the operational budget of the whole civil litigation system. Emphasis was upon enhancing interest-based settlement discussions and enhancing the preservation of relationships between parties and a speedy, cost-effective, and informal discussion structure.

There was institutional recognition of the essential differences arising in the context of separation, divorce, and family law disputes. Policy makers were concerned about universality and the need to offer funding subsidies where disputants had inadequate resources to pay the costs of mediation. Second, there was recognition of the impact of power imbalances in domestic settings where physical violence could be a significant factor in dispute resolution. Accordingly, mediation models for family law disputes have developed as part of newly designed family courts with heavy emphasis on mediator qualifications and screening for domestic violence. Mediators are trained to use sophisticated questionnaires and to interview spouses separately in order to more easily identify and screen out families where there is a risk of physical violence. Currently, the court system, often through a combination of civil and criminal remedies and sanctions, is the most effective way to deal with physical intimidation and violence.

In Ontario, the **Unified Family Court** in Hamilton operated for over 10 years as a pilot project with totally subsidized family mediation as an in-house program with staff mediators. There are now 17 family court locations where mediation is available. Government funding is available for mediations conducted at court locations, while funding is user-pay for off-site mediations.

The *Ontario Child and Family Services Act* was amended in 2006 to include a directive obliging Children Aid Societies to consider ADR at any stage in the proceedings. Under the legislation, a judge has power to adjourn a case in order to allow ADR to take place.

The Canadian Bar Association Systems of Justice Implementation Committee's Working Group on Dispute Resolution Standards has proposed *Draft Model Guidelines for Court-Connected Mediation Programs*. The study examines standards for selection of mediators both in the family and non-family sectors and recommends separate rosters and special standards for the family mediators to encompass safeguards and screening for domestic violence. The study also notes programs in British Columbia, Alberta, and Ontario that provide mandatory parent education sessions to give information about family and divorce mediation, and about the impact of separation and divorce on children. The sessions emphasize the importance of effective parental communication in facilitating successful transition by children during the separation and divorce process.

Non-family civil litigation is a different venue for the application of ADR to the mainstream court system. Saskatchewan was the first Canadian jurisdiction to introduce an initial mediation session for parties involved in non-family civil litigation. The program consisted of a short mediation session for orientation and public education. There were settlement discussions in the mandatory session, and parties were able to continue the mediation process through a voluntary referral on a per file basis. Amendments were made to the Saskatchewan *Queen's Bench Act* in March 1994 to introduce the pilot project in Regina and Swift Current. The pilot project was evaluated for Saskatchewan Justice by a private and independent corporation through a series of surveys and interviews. The evaluation report found a high level of client and lawyer satisfaction with the program, and an increased understanding of the case by litigants as a result of the session. Some cases settled at the initial session, and a significant proportion of clients whose cases did not settle reported changing their plans to proceed through ADR after an initial decision to use the court process. Fewer lawyers indicated a change in advice about appropriate venue.

Following small pilot projects in Toronto and Ottawa, Ontario introduced a **Mandatory Mediation** Program on January 4, 1999, in the City of Toronto and the Regional Municipality of Ottawa-Carleton. On December 31, 2002, the program was expanded to Windsor, Ontario. The goal of the program is to

---

Collaboration

EXHIBIT 25.4

One of the classic illustrations about collaboration is a fable about two mules tethered together and struggling as one pulls east and the other tugs to the west. Both animals are strong. They are prisoners of their resistance and have been locked in the same spot for hours. Finally, the mules stop in exhaustion. Like most of the animals from traditional fables, they are gifted with communication skills more acute than most humans.

The eastern mule exclaims in righteous frustration, "You stupid mule. We are prisoners here and we are starving to death. I want to be able to move! I am hungry!"

The western mule mocks him: "What do you think I am trying to do? Just lift your head and look to the west!"

The eastern mule is impatient: "I cannot imagine why I would want to look or go to the west when there is a huge stack of grain to the east!" But he turns his head and, looking to the west, realizes that there is also a stack of grain to the west!

The mules look silently to the east and to the west and then, nodding knowingly to one another, walk easternly together and eat contentedly and then, move in harmony towards the setting sun, to complete their repast.

---

provide an accessible and affordable alternative to court processes. The Ministry of the Attorney General website explains:

> Many parties negotiate during the course of litigation. Over 90 percent of all lawsuits settle before getting to the trial stage. Under the Ontario Mandatory Mediation Program, cases are referred to a mediation session early in the litigation process to give parties an opportunity to discuss the issues in dispute. With the assistance of a trained mediator, the parties explore settlement options and may be able to avoid the pretrial and trial process.

The Mandatory Mediation Program has been implemented in Ontario by a revision to the **Ontario Rules of Civil Procedure**, involving a co-operative venture between members of bench, bar, the public, and ministry staff. This collaboration has the potential to become a model for consensus-based government policy reform. It also represents a fundamental shift in the basic tenets of the civil justice system.

An evaluation of the mandatory mediation programs in Toronto and Ottawa submitted to the Civil Rules Committee on March 12, 2001, concluded that the program "demonstrated positive impact on the pace, costs and outcomes of litigation".[1]

The Evaluation of the Ontario Mandatory Mediation Program concluded that

> [m]andatory mediation under the Rule has resulted in significant reductions in the time taken to dispose of cases. Mandatory mediation has resulted in decreased costs to the litigants. Mandatory mediation has resulted in a high proportion of cases (roughly 40% overall) being completely settled earlier in the litigation process — with other benefits being noted in many of the other cases that do not completely settle. In general, litigants and lawyers have expressed considerable satisfaction with the mediation process under Rule 24.1.[2]

---

[1] Robert G. Hann & Carl Baar, with Lee Axon, Susan Binnie and Fred Zemans, *Evaluation of the Ontario Mandatory Mediation Program (Rule 24.1): Executive Summary and Recommendations* (Toronto, Ont.: Queen's Printer, March 12, 2001), online: <http://www.attorneygeneral.jus.gov.on.ca/english/courts/manmed/execsummary.asp>.

[2] *Ibid.*

Mandatory mediation has been implemented in the context of **case management**. Case management involves computerization and tracking of court files in order to impose judicial scrutiny with respect to time frames. Historically, the rules have imposed time frames for various stages of litigated proceedings; however, enforcement has been almost non-existent. High volumes of court cases, backlogs and waiting lists for trials, and a non-centralized system requiring one litigant to apply to court to enforce timeliness, plus a cultural expectation of long delays, have mitigated against any viable enforcement mechanisms to keep parties on track. New technologies and high consumer dissatisfaction with the costs and delays of the court provide method and incentive to streamline and fast-track cases for settlement or trial.

Litigants must schedule a mediation session within 90 days from the date when the first **Statement of Defence** is filed. Permission of a **Case Management Master** or judge is required for any extension of time. Parties select a mediator, or, if they fail to do so, a mediator is appointed from a roster of private-sector mediators. Fees are prescribed in the rules on a user-pay basis, with legal aid or other financial relief available through a financial eligibility test available for impecunious litigants. Cases that do not settle during mediation proceed through the traditional path to trial.

Mediators are selected by a **local mediation committee** comprising representatives from the judiciary, lawyers, mediators, members of the public, and the Ministry of the Attorney General. Mediators apply to be considered and will be selected for the roster upon satisfactory demonstration that they have appropriate mediation experience, training, educational or professional background and understanding of the civil justice system.

Case law has developed on procedural points after motions to decide where, when and how the mediation should proceed. Perhaps of greater practical significance than the body of case law is the impact that mediation has had on the legal culture. At the beginning of the pilot project, lawyers would behave in mediation in much the same way as at a trial — often taking charge of the process, orchestrating clients's involvement in the process and limiting input to matters of evidence and seeking to persuade the mediator of their case. As lawyers have worked with the mediation process through its first few years, they have begun to recognize the importance and difference of the role of the client in this informal process.

PROCESS AND PROCEDURE

The ADR options most commonly applied for dispute resolution are negotiation, mediation and arbitration. Each has its own key characteristics with respect to process and procedure, and a range of areas where there is flexibility for parties to modify or customize formalities and expectations.

Negotiation

Negotiation is a very informal process for dispute resolution. The parties retain responsibility and control over the substantive issues in dispute and also with respect to the interaction, agenda and process. Negotiation is as old as language and civilization itself, pre-dating the development of both currency and barter economies. However, in recent years, there has increasingly been a study and focus on effective strategies for negotiation. The concept of **principled negotiation** or **win/win negotiation**[3] has been analyzed and taught in

---

[3] Strategies developed and explored by Roger Fisher, William Ury & Bruce Patton in *Getting to Yes: Negotiating Agreement Without Giving In*, 2d ed. (New York: Penguin Books, 1991).

workshops and books in various forums, including primary schools, sales and marketing seminars, management training courses, and law schools.

The strategy of principled or interest-based negotiation is based on joint problem solving, brainstorming, and creativity. In contrast, **positional bargaining** occurs when parties deliberately take an opening position from which they intend to make marginal concessions. This is the bargaining of the flea market, where the buyer offers $100 for the antique chair ticketed with a price of $250. Positional bargaining can be confrontational or adversarial and is usually measured by attributing success to the party who makes the fewest or least expensive concessions.

In contrast, principled negotiation begins with an inquiry rather than a contest. It is based on listening to the other party rather than on dominating. The strategy is to find out about the underlying interests of each party: what are the assumptions, concerns, fears, hopes, priorities, expectations, values, beliefs? Interest-based negotiators attempt to transcend the task of dividing the pie by redefining it into a bigger pie.

For example, two sisters are fighting over an orange. The choice seems to be to give the orange to one or the other or to cut it in half. The interest-based strategy is to find out why. As it turns out, one sister wants to eat the fruit and the other wants the zest in order to bake a cake. Based on this information, each sister can have everything she wanted from the whole orange if one keeps the fruit and the other, the zest.[4]

Whereas the positional negotiator faces an adversary across a chasm of differences, the principled negotiator looks at the process as a journey rather than a destination. The view from the top of the mountain is very different and problematic when each party is standing at the peak of a different mountain. Building bridges from mountain top to mountain top can be expensive and impractical. The principled negotiator uses listening and active communication skills to travel with the other party from the base of the mountain. The analysis is often symbolically represented by a diagram of two overlapping triangles. (See Exhibit 25.5.) The interests of each party forms the base of the triangle. The party's position is like the peak of a triangle. Metaphorically, the new triangle formed by the overlapping areas is a new set of options for joint decision making — a new mountain to climb together.

The principled negotiator is one who shifts the process from one of persuasion or competition to an inquiry. The first step is to listen to the other person's perspective. The inquiry is most effectively launched with journalistic and **open questions** — Where? How? When? What happened? Parties should be cautious with "why" questions because they often generate a very defensive response. An alternative approach may be to ask what the person expected to happen or what assumptions had been made.

Active listening requires a concentrated response to another person — often through reading facial expression and body language and repeating back what the person has said. For example, in response to a loud and expressive description of the events leading up to a rear-end collision, the listener can acknowledge the emotional and substantive content of the story by words such as the following: "So you are quite angry that the car did not seem to slow down at all before it ran into the back of your vehicle!" Repeating back what has been heard gives the storyteller the opportunity to clarify and correct: "No, I was more stunned and shocked then angry. I did not get angry until I went over to the vehicle to talk to the driver and noticed the strong smell of alcohol."

---

[4] *Ibid.* at 73.

| EXHIBIT 25.5 | Negotiation: A Process of Building Bridges |

The interests of the parties to a dispute can be represented by points on a page.

Position "A"

Position "B"

Upon inquiry, the parties discover the underlying interests that have motivated each party to take the positions. They explore hopes, aspirations, concerns, fears, values, priorities, assumptions, values, goals, needs. When parties move away from the black-and-white adversarial world of positions, they discover many shared interests. Interest-based negotiation works with the triangle of shared interests and acknowledges with respect areas of different interest.

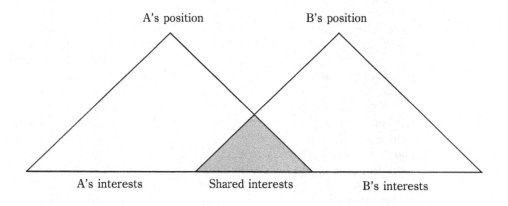

Acknowledgment is an extremely important part of listening. A listener who acknowledges that he or she has heard the other party can set an extremely respectful and courteous tone for interaction. The next step is to seek clarification. In order to minimize misunderstanding, the listener should make no assumptions. Questions of clarification emphasize the inquiring nature of the interaction.

Closed questions and leading questions are more appropriate for a debate or the cross-examination of a courtroom. **Closed questions** invite a "yes" or "no" answer, while leading questions attempt to undermine the other person's credibility or to identify logical weaknesses or inconsistencies in the story. These are techniques more suited to persuasion than to an objective inquiry.

The principled negotiator is hard on the problem but soft on the people.[5] He or she is committed to a process of joint problem solving, and interaction is based on mutual respect and a willingness to show flexibility and adaptability. The process begins with each person listening to the other's story. The next stage is to identify the goals, assumptions, expectations, fears, interests, values, and concerns of those involved. The investigative part of the inquiry provides a foundation of mutual understanding to develop an atmosphere for brainstorming.

---

[5] *Ibid.* at 11.

Brainstorming is non-judgmental and unstructured. Instead of finding *the* solution, parties look for numerous options, all of which are charted or written down. Sometimes a very impractical idea can be a jumping-off point for a simple and elegant option. Parties can emphasize the collaborative nature of the brainstorming idea by using a whiteboard or flip chart, or by sharing paper notes at a round table, or by sitting side by side rather than across from one another.

The next step is to evaluate the options using objective criteria. At this point, the parties can review the list of interests as criteria to measure the various options. For example, in a court environment, the parenting issues facing a separating couple can become a custody battle. Principled negotiation would begin with an inquiry about what the children and the adults need and prefer. The parents would confirm shared values and explore some of the differences in expectation, discipline styles, and work schedules. The list of interests may include the following:

- Quality time with both parents
- Consistency in key expectations for behaviour and responsibility of children
- Time with parents rather than a third party babysitter, where possible
- Assistance with math homework
- Time for creative play
- Getting the children to school on time

As the parties acknowledge shared values, the needs of the children, and the strengths of each parent, there is potential to develop solutions that allow a balance between the two parental households so that the influence and care of the respective parents are complementary. Where one parent bases the day on routine and schedule and the other is a free spirit, they could take positions and may be tempted to attack each other's personal qualities with labels such as "anal retentive" or "completely irresponsible". Alternatively, they could jointly inquire into a way to schedule time and agree on standards in both parents' homes that would encourage following and learning scheduling in one home with an expectation for the child to be self-regulating and responsible for timekeeping at the other home. With shared understanding and common goals, the parents can brainstorm for options and jointly select solutions that build a better nurturing environment. Collaboration makes available resources from both parents that collectively will give the children a richer learning and loving environment than either parent could provide alone.

Interest-based negotiation is a process in which parties commit to a respectful and listening interaction in order to jointly resolve the substantive problem. The principled negotiator recognizes that there is value in accommodating the other's interests. The process tends to happen naturally where parties have a strong and valued relationship. The adversarial process, on the other hand, tends to sweep people into the shadows of their differences. Interaction can be very unpleasant and counter-productive. In contrast, the principled negotiator respects and acknowledges the interests of the other party in the context of joint problem solving.

The essence of the positional bargainer is the caricature of the salesman who could (and would) "sell coal in Newcastle" or "blocks of ice on Baffin Island". Marketing strategies in the 1990s focused on listening to customers and offering ways to satisfy their needs. The market has become more sophisticated as it has evolved from "buy what I sell" to a customer-focused model.

The principled negotiator does not measure success as a contest to be won or lost. The Harvard Negotiation Project developed a measuring standard to plan and assess interest-based negotiated settlements.[6] **BATNA** is the Best Alternative to a Negotiated Agreement. While consumers are usually fairly sophisticated in comparison shopping before they negotiate the purchase of large-ticket items, parties to a dispute often fail to accurately assess their alternatives. For example, a person may want to buy a used vehicle and prefer the colour blue. If she knows that she can buy a grey used car of the same make, model, and relative conditions for $12,000 and have it painted blue at a cost of $2,500, this information can provide a relevant context to measure the success of her negotiation to buy the blue car of her dreams. The salesman may be nice or unpleasant, may make a ridiculous trade-in offer, or may offer to split the difference between his asking price and her best offer. Interaction can be distracting and may make the negotiation process look successful or unsuccessful. Unfortunately, negotiators often measure success by the interaction. However, if our car buyer knows her BATNA, she will not pay a whole lot more than $14,500 to buy the blue used car. She may prefer to buy blue than to arrange for a paint job, but she probably will not be willing to pay an extra $10,000 to buy the blue vehicle.

In the context of dispute resolution, parties often fail to appreciate the full measure of the BATNA. They may also need to look at the **WATNA** — the Worst Alternative to a Negotiated Agreement. The interaction may have costs in the form of timing, delay, legal fees, costs that are usually significant. There may be relationship costs. Before parties come to the negotiation table, they should make a thorough and accurate assessment of the best (and the worst) alternative to a negotiated agreement.

In order to ensure a final and binding settlement, negotiating parties must reach agreement on key points and document their agreement through a binding and enforceable contract.

Mediation

Mediation is a dispute resolution process in which the parties invite a mutually agreed upon third party or mediator to take responsibility for the interaction. The mediator looks after the process, often establishing and enforcing **ground rules** for courteous and respectful behaviour, taking charge of the agenda, and looking after scheduling of meetings. Typical ground rules include the following: each party will listen to the other without interrupting; there will be no name-calling; parties will try to be brief; parties will be courteous.

The mediator may

- confirm that each party has authority to settle the dispute on the day of the mediation session;
- ask the parties to address one another by first name;
- encourage parties to treat the process as a joint problem-solving session or inquiry
- suggest that parties try to persuade one another rather than present a case to the mediator.

The mediator may provide a written agenda, or **terms of mediation**, to set the tone of interaction and/or may verbally outline the intended steps or stages of the mediation session. A mediation may be scheduled to begin and end in one day or may be scheduled with shorter sessions over a period of time.

The agenda may include arrangements for exchange of documents or other disclosure at a set date prior to the mediation. Some mediators use fur-

---

[6] *Ibid.* at 100–1.

niture or room arrangements to set the tone of the interaction through use of a round table, a whiteboard or flip chart, or separate rooms. A **break-away room** can be used to facilitate discussion (if more than one person represents each side) or to allow separate discussion by each party with the mediator. Some mediators conduct a mediation session with all parties together for the entire session. Other mediations may involve joint sessions plus time out for discussion in separate rooms. There is also a **shuttle style of mediation** in which the mediator meets separately with each party.

The mediator will also provide guidance to ensure that all necessary persons attend, or are represented, at the mediation. In some contexts, parties will bring legal counsel or other expert advisors to the mediation session. Alternatively, lawyers may not attend the mediation session, but multiple mediation sessions may be scheduled to facilitate access to legal advice for each party in between sessions. It is part of the function of the mediator to ensure that all **stakeholders**, the key participants in a dispute, have a voice in the mediation process. For example, if two tenants in a shopping mall have a dispute, it may be necessary to include the landlord in the mediation process if options for resolution include matters that would require changes to the lease or location within the shopping mall. Stakeholders may attend the mediation session, or the process may utilize telephone access or arrangements to adjourn for input from the absent stakeholder. Ideally, questions about presence and voice of stakeholders are anticipated and discussed as part of the agenda on a proactive basis.

Before delegating responsibility for process and interaction, parties should be very clear in their expectations about the role of the mediator. Just as musicians celebrate their art in the sounds of classical, jazz, country, polka, rock and roll, or rap music, mediators can be compared across a range of roles, styles, and preferred processes.

Some mediation models are extremely client-centred processes in which the role of the mediator is to be responsive to the needs of the parties. Essentially, the mediator will identify choices at an experiential and relationship level and with respect to the tasks. The mediator will facilitate effective communication and better listening by each party and will help the parties to generate creative problem solving. The intervention of a third-party facilitator can improve the resolution experience and focus the parties on joint problem solving rather than on a contest or competition. This type of mediation is often called a **joint problem solving** or **facilitative mediation** and is often used in a family, community, or workplace setting where the parties have a strong and trusting relationship but are dealing with controversial task-focused issues and concerns about preserving the relationship and minimizing experiential unpleasantness.

The role of the mediator in the facilitative model is often to assist with data problems, such as lack of information, misinformation, or data collection or evaluation. The mediator can bring focus to elicit data, set up a structure for information exchange so that the parties can either resolve differences in value or look for areas of agreement that accommodate their differences in perspective. The facilitative or joint problem-solving mediation is typically used in an interest-based mediation.

The different approaches to mediation of the various models can be illustrated by looking at a simple fact situation. A horse rancher dies. There is a will, and it provides a scheme of division giving one-half of the horses to the eldest son, one-quarter to the middle son, and one-fifth to the youngest son. The estate consists of 19 horses.

The facilitative mediator would meet the sons at the ranch, riding in on her own horse and, removing the saddle and bridle, would lead her horse to pasture with the 19 estate horses. She would encourage discussion and

---

EXHIBIT 25.6   **Narrative Mediation**

Recognition of the role of story has been an important and recent development in the field of counselling and therapy and has been introduced as a style of mediation. This is a very client-centred process. The mediator goes beyond the stories of each party and searches for the areas of discrepancy between the different stories and for patterns that underlie the stories. The philosophy of narrative mediation is based on a model of human behaviour in which actions and interaction are driven by old stories that have been playing over and over again, with modifications, through various events and transactions. The narrative mediation is a forum where the parties are guided to find new stories and to re-write their expectations. People tend to base expectations of what others will do in the future on behaviours from the past. A new story offers a new explanation of past interactions and may inspire different and more functional expectations and interaction for the future.

---

negotiation among the three sons, and let them decide a method for choosing the horses. The mediator has facilitated the choosing process because now the sons are able to apply a formula to a herd of 20. The oldest son can take one-half or 10 horses; the second son would take one-quarter or 5 horses; and the youngest son would choose one-fifth or 4 horses. The mediator rides away on her own horse, which was the 20th in the pasture.

The *rights-based mediation* would encourage discussion about entitlement, laws, and rules and may look at birth order, and investment of time, effort, or money in the ranch by each of the sons. The task-focused application of legal criteria to assign horses among the three sons could take place either with or without consideration of the relationship or the experiential effects. The mediator could work with the 19-horse herd, or she could lend her horse to the herd to facilitate the division.

However, the dispute may involve issues beyond the legalities or rules of interpreting entitlement of the will or the challenge of fractioning a live herd of animals according to a formula. Sometimes there are emotional or psychological complications arising out of the relationship or history. There may be differences in values or disputes relating to social justice, fairness and concepts of right and wrong.

Therapeutic or healing mediation heavily emphasizes relationship and community. Examples include workplace facilitations to deal with transition, change, downsizing, or harassment programs. Community-based mediation programs may offer this kind of process for neighbourhood disputes. The mediator who applies a therapeutic or healing model may ask the sons about their relationship with their deceased father and with each other.

Transformative mediation strives to encourage the parties to appreciate positive aspects of the relationship and to offer recognition of one another's points of view. Studied and advocated by Bush and Folger in their book, *The Promise of Mediation*, this model strives to empower the parties and to afford opportunities for disputants to see themselves and each other differently. The mediator may inquire about how the sons each feel about horses and ranching, or ask whether there were daughters in the family. In a *transformative mediation*, the mediator sees her role as being to shift paradigms and question assumptions of the parties.

The **restorative justice model** is used in victim-offender mediation programs that provide an informal and healing dimension to the criminal justice system. This model can be complementary with a transformative approach. A restorative model could be used in a situation where the conflict between the brothers has escalated into a threatening confrontation, perhaps involving an assault or complaint to the police.

Historically, the setting of disputes was often determinative of the model so that healing or transformative approaches were applied in community mediation programs, and insurance disputes were often determined in a rights-based model. As mediation develops as a profession, there is a wider academic study of theory and growing cross-germination of ideas.

Selection of the mediator is a key element of the resolution process, and it should be appropriate for the nature of the dispute and meet the expectations of all stakeholders. Parties who are more knowledgeable and sophisticated will enhance their chances of the resolution of the dispute by working effectively together in choosing the mediator and providing input to the mediator with respect to process for interaction.

Mediator experience and competence can be assessed by evaluating the mediators' professional or academic background, training in mediation, and mediation experience. Mediation is a multidisciplinary field, and mediators may have education or credentials in a wide variety of fields, such as law, social work, labour relations, human resources, behavioural sciences, religious ministry, or teaching. Mediation training is offered privately by a number of well-respected practitioners and also through academic institutions, such as universities or colleges. Parties should also make sure that they are comfortable with the mediator to ensure a satisfactory interaction and an environment that is conducive to settlement discussions.

Participation or interaction of the parties will vary, depending on the role of the mediator and the model of mediation. Where the mediation is rights-based and the mediator is making recommendations or an assessment to be used to assist the parties in negotiation, the parties will participate through advocacy and models of persuasion. In contrast, other mediation models require participation through active listening and effective communication. It is the role of the mediator to set the tone of the parties' participation, often either by conducting an inquiry through open-ended questions, **reframing** and other strategies, or by helping the parties to engage in an inquiry.

By way of analogy, if we compare a settlement agreement to a fishing expedition, the mediator-centred models are ones in which the parties come along on the fishing expedition, but the mediator catches the fish. In the transformative, restorative justice, and therapeutic models, the mediator gives step-by-step instructions to bait the hook, to cast, when and how much to reel in the line, and where to hold the net. The parties and mediator have "gone fishing together" but may not have learned enough to be able to go fishing alone in the future. The most facilitative models are ones where the mediator teaches the parties how to fish.

Parties who have a strong relationship of mutual respect may work together most effectively with a very facilitative model. Where the parties wish to preserve a relationship but have areas of distrust or diffidence to one another, they need a facilitative mediator who has the skills and resources to intervene at key points and redirect the interaction. Disputes are often complex. One party may have an intricate understanding about how to navigate the eddies, currents, and bends of the river while the other party knows where to find the fish. They may have fishing skills but not be able to apply those skills together at this river. In life, as in rivers, the fish may not always be found in the most easily accessible waters. The role of the mediator is to take charge of the fishing expedition. Different mediators have different approaches to the teaching, guiding, and intervention components of the fishing expedition.

Some parties simply want a resolution; they may have no interest in the joys of the fishing trip, no need to scrutinize the healthiness of the live fish, or concern about whether the river is polluted. They will go to the market and buy some fish. Arbitration is the choice. Currently, there is no settlement equivalent to the ease and comfort of simply ordering fish from a restaurant menu.

There are some parties and some disputes for whom any mediator with a minimum amount of training and experience will be able to help reach a settlement. There are other parties and situations that could not be successfully mediated even by someone possessing the essence of divine or secular wisdom. However, most situations are between the two extremes.

The substantive outcome of a mediation is a settlement that is negotiated by the parties. Accordingly, the finality of a mediated agreement is achieved in the same way as a negotiated agreement: that is, by way of a valid and enforceable contract, signed by both parties.

Arbitration

Arbitration is a more formal process in which the parties select, or are bound by the appointment of, a neutral third party to make a substantive decision to resolve the dispute. The arbitrator also takes responsibility to ensure compliance with rules of evidence and procedure that may be imposed by statute or be agreed upon in advance by the parties.

Typically, rules of evidence and procedure are more relaxed but based on the court process. Provincial legislation generally provides a framework for the process but permits parties to contractually modify and amend.

Arbitration is a rights-based, adversarial model. It meets the fundamental criteria of natural justice: each party has the right to be heard, and the right to hear and to reply to the case against him. Decisions are based on evidence and on principles of law.

The arbitrator will give each party an opportunity to present evidence, usually through witnesses and by way of documents that are agreed upon as evidence by the parties or are identified by the witnesses. Witnesses usually swear or affirm, and, therefore, there is additional formality in the form of an oath or promise "to tell the whole truth and nothing but the truth." The decision maker will weigh evidence by its credibility. Evidence may be conclusive or may be sufficient to shift the onus of proof to the other party. For example, written contracts that are signed and witnessed provide more conclusive proof about the terms of a contract than oral evidence of each person's recollection of what was in agreement. One party may produce in evidence a dinner roll containing a nail that he swears came from the other party's bakery. Such evidence shifts the onus to the bakery to establish that the dinner roll came from some other baker or that the nail was inserted in the dinner roll after it left the bake shop.

An arbitrator will respond to objections of the party and make rulings or decisions about evidence or procedure. The arbitrator will hear submissions by the party on matters of process and, before completion of the arbitration, about the merits of the case. The arbitrator may make a decision immediately or may adjourn and provide a decision later. Usually, there will be written reasons for the decision.

An arbitrator will make findings of fact based on the weight and credibility of the evidence presented. The arbitrator does not purport to find the truth or to discover what happened. An arbitrated decision is an assessment of the evidence and the submissions presented at the arbitration. Accordingly, technicalities and presentation are very important. Parties often seek legal advice or representation for an arbitration. They may require experts to provide evidence as to the appropriate interpretation or assessment of the evidence. Experts provide written reports that are usually exchanged prior to the arbitration and, on consent of the parties, accepted as evidence at the arbitration.

Often the arbitration process is structured much like a civil trial, but parties may, by agreement, create or amend the process to best suit their needs. For example, they may jointly select an expert to conduct an inspection of a piece of technical equipment or a building, and to decide whether the equipment complies with design specifications. Often, accountants are selected to arbitrate matters involving forensic accounting issues and may be asked to apply generally accepted accounting principles to analyze financial statements. In a trial, a judge would hear expert evidence from accountant witnesses for both parties and make an assessment based on that evidence.

The finality of an arbitration is enforced by legislation and judicial cases that have significantly limited situations where a court will overrule or set aside arbitrated decisions. A party who does not like an arbitrated decision has limited recourse for appeal, and non-compliance or non-payment may result in application of the court remedies for collection. However, because there are additional costs to import an arbitrated decision into the court process, most disputants avoid arbitration if they anticipate the possibility of a collection or compliance problem.

Selecting the Appropriate ADR Model

The key factor for selection of an ADR model is that the parties have some insight about the nature of the dispute and the context of their interaction and relationship. The advantage of ADR models are that the spectrum offers a range of dispute resolution models and, therefore, parties can select the model that is most suitable to their needs. One of the key elements causing dissatisfaction with the civil justice system is that it fails to meet the expectations of litigators. People look forward to their "day in court" but fail to appreciate the time, resources, and energy consumed by the court system. Choice of ADR model should be based on meeting the expectation and needs of the parties with respect to interaction (timing, cost, comfort), the relationship, and the substantive matters.

APPLICATION OF THEORY

The communication strategies inherent in effective principled negotiation and mediation are life skills best explored through experiential learning models. People communicate and negotiate from a very young age and develop a preference for those methods and techniques that appear to be effective in the environment in which they function. The study of ADR is an examination of process issues that separately examines key elements such as interaction, relationship development, and substantive decision making. The relevance of interests, rights, and powers varies depending on circumstance and perspectives of participants.

Role-plays are an effective experiential learning device through which students can practise negotiation or mediation strategies with coaching and the opportunity to debrief. The fact situation is described in an instruction sheet, and each actor is provided with separate and confidential instructions as to interests, concerns, or challenges that will determine how his or her script will unfold in the role play. Students are asked to act out the role-play as realistically as possible with a view to exploring and assisting fellow students to explore the emotional and experiential elements of the role-play situation. The role-play attempts to provide a realistic and non-threatening simulation of a potential real-life negotiation or communication opportunity.

CHAPTER SUMMARY

In this chapter, the reader was introduced to Alternative Dispute Resolution as a field that focuses on the process of finding agreement between disputing parties. The chapter explored the history and development of ADR and the way it fits into the court process and into various other venues for resolving disputes.

The chapter then examined the process and design characteristics of negotiation, mediation, and arbitration and compared the venues and situations where each form of ADR may be used. The similarities and differences of the different forms of ADR were studied and compared.

Next, the chapter examined the forms of ADR in terms of process design in the context of selection of a form of ADR by private agreement and implementation in the public sector, through private process design and recent developments of ADR programs as part of the court process.

The chapter concluded with a practical application and examination of negotiation and mediation strategies. There are opportunities for practising these strategies through role-plays based on real-life negotiation and mediation situations.

GLOSSARY OF NEW TERMS AND KEY CONCEPTS

active listening

A strategy for responsive communication that involves attention to body language, facial expression, and questions of clarification. Active listening is accomplished through an empathetic acknowledgment of both the emotional and verbal content of the message.

ADR

An acronym of alternative dispute resolution, ADR refers to dispute resolution processes other than the civil court system. The term encompasses negotiation, mediation, arbitration, and other hybrid or similar processes for dispute resolution. The term "ADR" also refers to the multidisciplinary field of study about dispute resolution that focuses on the process, procedure and methodology of resolving disputes.

arbitration

A process for dispute resolution in which a neutral third party is selected or appointed to make a decision for parties to a dispute to resolve some or all of the issues in contention.

BATNA

An acronym for the Best Alternative to a Negotiated Agreement, BATNA is a measuring standard estimated by an inquiry into the costs, risks, and available resources for a negotiator's most attractive plan of action other than resolution through negotiation with this party. The negotiator measures the expected outcome of Plan B as a way to decide whether or not to continue with the negotiation of Plan A. (Compare **WATNA**.)

brainstorming

A collaborative and creative activity that is usually most effective in groups, to generate a wide choice of options in an open and non-judgmental environment.

break-away room

An additional and private room that is used in the mediation process to facilitate private communication between the mediator and a participant or participants, or among participants, where matters can be dealt with in confidence and without disclosure to others involved in the process.

case management

In the civil justice court system, this is a system of computerization and tracking of court files in order to provide supervision of time frames by a judge or other officer of the court.

Case Management Master

In the Ontario case management system, this is the judicial officer appointed by the court to deal with the procedural issues arising from non-compliance with time sanctions of the rules of practice.

closed questions

Queries that are phrased to elicit a yes or no, either/or response.

dispute resolution spectrum	A metaphor used in the study of ADR to describe the processes of dispute resolution in comparison to one another, like colours through a prism.
Dispute Resolution Office	A newly created department of the Ministry of the Attorney General in Ontario to encourage use of ADR by Ontario government offices.
early neutral evaluation	A dispute resolution process, or component of the process, in which a neutral third party provides an expert opinion as to the likely outcome of the issues in dispute. The process is similar to arbitration.
evaluative mediation	A dispute resolution process in which the neutral third party makes a substantive assessment of the issues in dispute in order to encourage the parties to reach settlement. This process is most effective where parties have high confidence in the expertise and competence of the neutral party.
facilitative mediation	A mediation model in which the neutral third party intervenes, predominantly with respect to communication and agenda, and takes a minimal role with respect to evaluation or involvement with the substantive matters in dispute.
Financial Services Commission of Ontario	The administrative body under the *Insurance Act* in Ontario that has responsibility to regulate insurance companies and provide a resolution process for insurance disputes.
ground rules	The basic agreements in a mediation about courtesy and respect to which the mediator asks the parties to agree in order to provide an environment conducive to effective communication and respectful negotiation.
healing mediation	Also referred to as **therapeutic mediation**, this is a mediation model in which the neutral third party intervenes at a level designed to improve the health or balance of the relationship or to change the perspectives or attitudes of one or more parties to the dispute.
interest-based mediation	A mediation model that includes or focuses on an inquiry into the interests of the parties.
interests	The intangible factors that motivate human behaviour, individually and in groups, such as concerns, values, hopes, assumptions, priorities, expectations, fears, needs.
joint problem solving	A mediation model that takes a very practical approach to the issues in dispute to encourage the parties to find mutually acceptable objective criteria and options for a resolution of their differences. Goals of the process are often equated with satisfaction of needs.
local mediation committee	Pursuant to the Mandatory Mediation Program in Ontario, a committee for a judicial district, with responsibility to select and monitor the mediators on the local roster. The committee consists of members of the community, lawyers, judges, mediators, and a representative of the Ministry of the Attorney General.
mandatory mediation	A court-connected process for dispute resolution that requires parties to attend a mediation session. There are significant sanctions for non-attendance. The process is voluntary in that, while attendance is mandatory, participation is not evaluated.
mediation	A process for dispute resolution through which a neutral third party facilitates communication between parties to a dispute in order to attempt to reconcile their differences and broker a settlement of some or all issues in dispute.
Ministry of the Attorney General	In provincial government, the office of the Cabinet minister in charge of the civil and criminal court systems.
natural justice	A principle of administrative law based on democratic notions of basic fairness that include the right to hear what is said against the person, the right to reply by way of evidence, and argument before a decision will be made in a hearing or quasi-hearing.
negotiation	An informal process for dispute resolution in which parties communicate for the purpose of bargaining with one another.
neutral fact-finding	A process in which a neutral third party is chosen by parties or appointed to investigate and make findings of fact as part of a resolution of issues in dispute.
neutral evaluation	A process introduced in 1996 as part of the arbitration process for insurance disputes dealt with by the Financial Services Commission of Ontario.

ombudsman	An office created in government or private organizations to provide a safe space or user-friendly environment for the investigation of complaints. Usually an ombudsman has responsibility to safeguard individual rights in the context of a real or perceived power imbalance between the potential complainant and the larger organization.
Ontario Rules of Civil Procedure	The very detailed rules for civil litigation passed by regulation that prescribe the forms, time requirements, rights, and responsibilities for the procedures involved in bringing a dispute through the civil court system in Ontario.
open questions	A strategy for communication that relies on journalistic questions that encourage story-telling response rather than simply yes or no answers.
positional bargaining	A competitive or adversarial bargaining process in which parties deliberately take an opening posture from which they intend to make concessions.
power	In the context of dispute resolution, the use of resources to influence or compel compliance by others. Sources of power include physical strength, charisma, social status, wealth, status, position. Abuse of power takes the form of physical confrontation, threats, economic sanction, or intimidation.
precedent	A legal decision. Canadian common law has developed historically from the judicial tradition of following earlier legal decisions so that cases that are similar are decided according to similar legal principles.
pre-trial conference	In civil court cases, an informal meeting between lawyers and a trial judge in which the judge makes a substantive assessment of the issues in dispute in order to encourage the parties to reach settlement. The judge who attends the pre-trial is usually not the same judge who would be hearing the case at trial.
principled negotiation	A process of bargaining and communication in which one or more parties listen to both sides of the dispute in order to attempt to reach a settlement based on mutually acceptable objective criteria. (Also referred to as **win/win negotiation**.)
reframing	A communication strategy for active listening in which the listener repeats back what he or she has heard. The technique may be used for clarification or to distill the message by verbalizing the emotional content. Sometimes, in the context of a mediation, the mediator will re-phrase a message by one party into a content that the other party will be willing or able to hear and acknowledge.
restorative justice	A concept of fairness based on notions of balance and healing that views relationships and social institutions in terms of an ecosystem; restorative justice does not seek revenge or punishment but, rather, reconciliation and assumption of responsibility.
restorative justice model	A mediation model often used in victim-offender reconciliation or neighbourhood disputes that seeks reconciliation, healing and the assumption of responsibility for rectification of hurt or damage.
rights	The fundamental freedoms and protections guaranteed in a democratic society. Rights are created by laws, regulations, agreements, court decisions, policies, past practices, customs, and conventions.
rights-based mediation	A mediation process that focuses on the legal issues between the parties as provided by law, contract, or convention.
shuttle style of mediation	A mediation process in which the parties to a dispute communicate indirectly through the mediator rather than speaking directly to one another. The mediator shuttles from party to party. This method is used where there are significant power imbalances or where the emotional overlay makes person-to-person contact untenable to one or both parties.
stakeholders	Those persons or organizations who may be affected by the resolution of a dispute, either by a potential benefit or risk.
statement of defence	The pleading, filed and served in response to the claim against the defendant, that summarizes the law and facts upon which the defendant will rely at trial.
terms of mediation	The process for a mediation as outlined verbally or in writing by the mediator.

therapeutic mediation	Also referred to as **healing mediation**, this is a mediation model in which the neutral third party challenges the parties to improve the health or balance of the relationship or to change the perspectives or attitudes of one or more parties to the dispute.
transformative mediation	A mediation model that acknowledges human capacity for growth and development in response to change. Transformative mediation casts the role of mediator to empower the parties by facilitating opportunities for participants in the mediation to see themselves and each other differently.
Unified Family Court	A court system for family disputes that has jurisdiction over all family matters. The traditional system limits jurisdiction of provincially appointed judges who cannot determine matters of property or divorce. The unified family court system provides streamlined and one-stop-shopping for family law matters.
WATNA	An acronym, the **Worst Alternative to a Negotiated Agreement**; a measuring standard estimated by an inquiry into the costs, risks, and available resources for a negotiator's least attractive plan of action other than resolution through negotiation with this party. The WATNA is often used to complete the cost/benefit analysis that begins by an inquiry into his or her **BATNA**.
win/win negotiation	A process of communication and bargaining in which one or more parties makes a commitment to look for settlement options that provide benefits and solve the problems to both sides to a dispute. The term is used to distinguish the process from the win/lose competitive bargaining of **positional negotiation**. (Win/win negotiation is also referred to as **principled bargaining**.)
Workplace Safety and Insurance Board	The administrative board in Ontario that was created by statute to administer issues of safe work environments, return to work, and compensation for injured workers. Formerly, these responsibilities were held by the Workers' Compensation Board. New legislation has changed the emphasis from compensation to that of safety and prevention.

REVIEW QUESTIONS

1. How is mediation different from arbitration?

2. Compare rights and interests in the context of ADR.

3. In what situations do parties typically negotiate?

4. What are the key characteristics of mediation?

5. Compare interest-based and rights-based mediation.

6. What happens if collaborative law negotiations break down and the matter goes to trial?

7. What is the role of an arbitrator?

8. Name and summarize the four contexts in which disputes are referred to an ADR process.

9. Compare interest-based negotiation to positional bargaining.

10. How can participants measure the settlement options when they are negotiating or mediating?

11. What is the basis for an arbitrator's decision?

DISCUSSION QUESTIONS

1. What considerations are relevant in selecting a dispute resolution process where there is a power imbalance or potential for an abuse of power?

2. What are some factors parties should consider in the selection of a mediator?

3. In what circumstances would parties choose arbitration rather than mediation?

4. Compare public sector mediation models to private mediations.

5. What are the challenges in assessing BATNA or WATNA when the alternative to a negotiated agreement is litigation?

SUGGESTED READINGS

Bush, Robert A.B., & Joseph P. Folger. *The Promise of Mediation* (San Francisco: Jossey-Bass Inc., 1994).

DeBono, Edward, *Conflicts: A Better Way to Resolve Them* (Toronto, Ont.: Penguin Books, 1991).

Fisher, R., & S. Brown. *Getting Together* (New York: Viking Penguin, 1989).

Fisher, R., & W. Ury. *Getting to Yes: Negotiating Agreement Without Giving In* (Boston: Houghton Mifflin, 1981).

Fisher, Roger, & Danny Ertel. *Getting Ready to Negotiate: The Getting to Yes Workbook* (New York: Penguin Books, 1995).

WEBSITES
Conflict Resolution Network: <www.crnetwork.ca>
Collaborative Family Lawyers of Canada: <www.collaborativelaw.ca>
Financial Services Commission of Ontario (FSCO): <www.ontarioinsurance.com>
Ontario Ministry of The Attorney General: <www.attorneygeneral.jus.gov.on.ca>
ServiceOntario e-Laws: <www.e-laws.gov.on.ca>
Workplace Safety and Insurance Board (WSIB): <www.wsib.on.ca>

26   Health Care Law in Canada

Sharon McCleave
SENECA COLLEGE

Learning Objectives

After reading this chapter, the reader should be able to:

➢ explain the legislative structure surrounding health care delivery at the federal and territorial/provincial levels

➢ summarize how precedent influences court proceedings in medical law

➢ classify various forms of legal consent found in the medical setting, including the use of the *emergency doctrine*

➢ predict situations where the disclosure of a patient's medical information would be required

➢ relate how the power of a medical health officer is similar to police power when dealing with the public and issues of communicable diseases

➢ identify the criteria that allow supervised injection facilities to be exempt from the laws regarding possession defined in the *Controlled Drugs and Substances Act*

➢ summarize the legal status of voluntary euthanasia, non-voluntary euthanasia, involuntary euthanasia, and assisted suicide

➢ compare and contrast the *living will* and the *advance directive*

➢ identify how common law has come to shape the status of abortion in Canada

TABLE OF CONTENTS

THE PROVISION OF HEALTH CARE AND HEALTH CARE LAW

Medical treatment for Canadians is largely covered by government funds, and medical care is therefore considered a publicly funded entity. Generally speaking, it means that any Canadian that is insurable has access to basic medical care that will be financially covered by a provincial or territorial health plan.

In actuality, roughly 70 percent of Canada's health care costs are publicly covered and the remaining 30 percent is paid for through the private sector. For example, the cost of services such as pharmacy, physiotherapy, dentistry, chiropractic, optometry, acupuncture and ambulance transportation are *generally* not assumed by provincial or territorial health care insurance plans.

The Canada Health Act

The *Canada Health Act* (CHA) is a federal Act that provides the legislative framework for public health care insurance throughout the country. It carefully outlines the parameters in which each province and territory determines its public health care policy. In return for adhering to the binding principles of the CHA, the federal government makes financial contributions to each provincial and territorial health care insurance plan. The binding principles of the CHA legislation are intended to make certain that all insurable Canadians have equal access to essential medical care without burdensome "out-of-pocket" costs. The core guiding principles of the CHA are *public administration, comprehensiveness, universality, portability*, and *accessibility*. (See Exhibit 26.1 for their definitions.)

Individuals in Canada are able to obtain provincial or territorial health insurance if they are Canadian citizens or permanent residents. In New Brunswick, Quebec, Ontario and British Columbia, a three-month "eligibility period" exists for permanent residents before coverage becomes active. Some people will decide to purchase private insurance during this time. For refugees arriving in these provinces, however, emergency and essential services will be provided to them at the expense of the province during the three-month

---

EXHIBIT 26.1	Program Criteria of the *Canada Health Act*

Public Administration: This refers to the management of public health care. Provinces and territories are obligated to provide insured medical services to all qualified citizens on a non-profit basis. All records of activity are publicly audited, and the provision of care must meet the guidelines of the individual provincial or territorial governments.

Comprehensiveness: Each province and territory must cover *all* medical services that have been determined to be publicly funded.

Universality: All insured persons of a province or territory are entitled to publicly funded health care on equal terms and conditions.

Portability: There are a few considerations regarding portability. If a person moves from one province to another, the home province is obligated to cover any medical costs until the new province assumes responsibility at a time not to exceed three months. Individuals who are absent from the province for a period of time are entitled to remain covered under the province's insurance plan during their absence.

Accessibility: This refers to the ability to receive care by insured individuals. All insured Canadians have a right to medical care that is reasonably available and without discrimination on the basis of socio-economic status, age, or state of health.

period. It is important to note that while most residents are provided for by their province or territory, some special populations in Canada receive funding for medical care *directly* from the federal government. These individuals include First Nations people, the Royal Canadian Mounted Police, inmates of federal prisons, and military personnel.

The *Canada Health Act* (CHA) was established in 1984 and was the result of a long evolution of health care policies and strategies in the country. By the beginning of the 20th century, organized medical initiatives were seen in a variety of settings: overcrowding in new urban centres generated public health Acts; unions created trust funds to cover the costs of work injuries; and hospital care was ensured by religious charities to those unable to afford private physicians. In 1947, the Saskatchewan government, under the leadership of Tommy Douglas, passed the *Saskatchewan Hospitalization Act* to ensure publicly funded hospital care to the province's residents. It was the initial step in Canada to ensure care for all, irrespective of financial means. Federal involvement in sharing medical costs was fully established 10 years later with the *Hospital Insurance and Diagnostic Services Act* (HIDS Act). By 1961, all provinces and territories had adopted a collaborative agreement with the federal government to share the costs of hospital care and diagnostic procedures.

Canada's health care system required more refining, however, because only the cost of hospital care was covered, and the cost of out-patient treatment was not. The *Medical Care Act*, introduced by Lester B. Pearson's federal government in 1966, changed that. The Act established cost-sharing between federal and provincial bodies to cover medical treatment in *and* out of the hospital. During the era of the *Medical Care Act*, however, user fees and extra billing by physicians were still permitted. User fees were extra costs imposed on the patient for the use of medical services. Extra billing, on the other hand, was a practice used by physicians to charge patients for care above and beyond what they were to receive from the government-run insurance plan. When the CHA evolved out of the *Medical Care Act*, it required the practices of user fees and extra billing to be eliminated.

Overall, the federal Act sets the legal boundaries within which provinces and territories deliver health care. If individual jurisdictions do not adhere to the five guiding principles of the CHA or do little to halt the use of extra-billing or user-fee practices, the federal government is obligated to intervene and impose penalties. Generally, the federal government is keeping a relatively close eye on the preservation of the five guiding principles of the CHA, but this is changing. As a result of increasingly escalating health costs, the federal government has been less likely to impose penalties on jurisdictions that do not discourage extra billing and user fees. Since the late 1990s, the federal government has also halted penalties placed on jurisdictions that have allowed private health care clinics to open. Another increasing trend is the **delisting** of health care services, leaving more medical treatments to be covered privately. While it means the jurisdictions that decide to delist forgo a certain amount of federal financial assistance, it is a decision that is still thought to be economically advantageous.

Health Care Law

The law as it pertains to health follows the common law tradition in which *stare decisis* or precedent governs court decisions. Within this framework the judge-made *law of torts* applies. Quebec offers an exception: health law in this province is governed by the *Civil Code of Quebec*, and tort law is replaced by the *law of obligations*.

CONSENT TO TREATMENT

According to common law in Canada, individuals have a right to self-determination and consent to medical treatment. In other words, they have the right to refuse unwanted physical interference. When a medical act is performed on someone without consent, it is considered a battery (or, in this situation, **medical battery**).

The issue of consent is particularly noteworthy in today's medical environment. At one point in time, the physician/patient relationship was one of paternalism and authority: the physician "knew what was best" and the patient complied without asking questions. Today, patients are expecting more control in the planning of their care. The physician/patient relationship is becoming more collaborative and egalitarian as patients become more informed of their health through mass media, the Internet, and consumer advertising for pharmaceutical drugs. The result is that consent, now more than ever, is a factor the health care professional cannot overlook before administering medical treatment.

The essence of consent is that it must be voluntary, informed (based on accurate knowledge), obtained without coercion or deceit, and related to a specific procedure. In the medical field, consent may be expressed or implied. Consent by a parent is also considered appropriate in the case of the treatment of minors. In *certain* circumstances, consent is not required at all.

It is important to note that even though most examples given in this chapter depict the interactions between patient and physician, in reality these laws are generally applicable to all in the health care field: nurses, nurse practitioners, medical technicians, rehabilitation specialists, and home-care providers, to name a few.

Express Consent

Express consent is considered given when a patient explicitly asks for a treatment or authorizes a procedure to be undertaken. Express consent may be *verbal*, where a patient may ask for the removal of a mole or an annual flu shot, or it may also be *written*, as in the case of signing documents for a surgical procedure.

Implied Consent

Implied consent is not a verbal or written consent but is determined by the physician according to patient behaviour. If the patient conducts him/herself in a way that allows the physician to proceed with treatment, the physician presumes consent is given. It is certainly the most common form of consent seen in daily interactions between physician and patient. Typical examples include a patient holding out his arm to have his blood pressure checked, or removing his shirt so the physician can listen to his heart. Implied consent is also seen when a patient takes a requisition form from a physician to a clinic to have his ankle X-rayed.

Although the implied consent is very common, whether it has actually been given is open to interpretation. In tort law, when a patient's implied consent *cannot* be determined to be reasonably affirmative, an action of medical battery may be successful. It is the physician's responsibility to understand and interpret the cues of implied consent with accuracy.

Informed Consent

Informed consent describes the patient's awareness about a procedure before it is undertaken. For example, if a patient is in need of a hip replacement, the physician is required to state what the surgery involves, the risks, and the expected outcomes.

In the case of a surgical procedure, the consent is for the specific operation indicated. If the surgeon performs the operation and decides to undertake a secondary procedure because it "might be useful", he or she is vulnerable to legal liability. For example, a physician, during a surgical procedure to remove a patient's adenoids (small lymph nodes in the sinuses), decided to also remove the tonsils. While the physician argues the intent was to simply prevent the possibility of tonsillar infections in the future, the patient did not consent to the latter surgery. The physician therefore committed the tort of medical battery. It is also technically possible to charge the physician with a criminal offence of having committed an assault, although this is rare.

Surgery, however, can uncover situations that the physician or patient might not have anticipated. Therefore, if a surgeon discovers an unexpected and potentially dangerous medical condition during an operation, he/she is allowed to perform an extended procedure (or the extra-required surgery) for the sake of the patient's life. For example, a surgeon performs an operation to remove a cancerous tumour. During the procedure, she notices the cancer has spread to nearby lymph nodes. Realising the cancer has spread (or *metastasized*), she removes the infected lymph nodes at the same time. By carefully determining that the removal was necessary for health and safety of the patient with metastatic cancer, the extended procedure would be defendable in the court of law.

The Treatment of Minors

Medical care to those under the age of majority (18 or 19 years old, depending on the province) is provided with consent being obtained in a variety of ways.

A child up to the approximate age of six is determined to be an *infant*, and consent to treatment is obtained from parents or guardians. Parents cannot *refuse* consent to medical intervention if the treatment is necessary for the health of an infant. If this should happen, the infant is put under the care of the state and the treatment is performed. The most common example is parents' refusal to a procedure that conflicts with their religious beliefs (see Exhibit 26.2). The law recognizes parents' right to practise their religion but

---

When Treatment Is in Conflict with Patient's Religious Beliefs   EXHIBIT 26.2

Sheena was a premature infant. At one month of age, and after a variety of medical treatments her parents had consented to, Sheena's hemoglobin level dropped. Fearing for the life of the infant, the physicians requested consent to perform a blood transfusion. The parents were Jehovah's Witnesses and refused consent. A hearing was subsequently granted on short notice, and the Provincial Court (Family Division) put the infant under the wardship of the Children's Aid Society for 72 hours. A blood transfusion was given and her condition improved to a degree, but her health care team determined she was also in need of surgery. The wardship was extended for a further 21 days, and the surgery, with the necessary blood transfusions, was completed. The infant was then returned to the care of her parents.

Sheena's parents appealed the decisions on the basis of section 2(a) of the *Charter* (everyone has the fundamental freedom of conscience and religion) and section 7 of the *Charter* (everyone has the right to life, liberty and security of the person). The appeal was dismissed by the trial judge on the grounds that "neither s. 2(a) nor the liberty interest of s. 7 permits parents to endanger the lives of their children."

Source: *B.(R.) v. Children's Aid Society of Metropolitan Toronto*, [1995] 1 S.C.R. 315.

does not allow them to impose their beliefs on the infant in need of medical care.

Minors are youth between the approximate age of six and the age of majority. While this group is loosely divided between "immature" and "mature" minors, the division is ambiguous and open to interpretation by the courts. It is generally assumed that in life-threatening situations, life-saving medical procedures will be implemented even though the youth does not wish it. In other situations, the needs of the minor will be recognized with the understanding that the youth is old enough to comprehend the repercussions of the decision he has made. For example, a minor would have grounds to refuse to take medication for hyperactivity in spite of her parents wanting her to. However, if she wanted to refuse chemotherapy for the treatment of cancer, her parents could "step in" and provide consent for the life-saving therapy.

The Emergency Doctrine

If the patient is unable to give consent to treatment for whatever reason, a health care provider may intervene and provide medical treatment if necessary for the preservation of life. Termed the **emergency doctrine**, it allows health care providers to perform a procedure in an attempt to save a patient's life when the patient is unable to communicate. An example of this might be when a patient is unconscious after a motor vehicle accident and a paramedic applies a brace to the victim's injured neck.

MEDICAL NEGLIGENCE

When a physician performs a medical act without consent, the physician is liable for the intentional tort of battery. The tort of **medical negligence** occurs when the practitioner, who is established as the caregiver in the patient/physician relationship, performs a medical act that causes undue harm to the patient.

Negligence can occur in various aspects of medical care, whether it be relating to the diagnosis, the proper referral to specialists, the recording of medical documents, communication with the patient, or the very treatment itself (see Exhibit 26.3).

EXHIBIT 26.3	Factors in the Consideration of Medical Negligence

¤ Did the physician perform in a way that is consistent with accepted standards of the profession?

¤ Was the physician reasonably informed about the most recent clinical procedures in his or her field?

¤ Did the physician decide to perform a procedure that was beyond his or her clinical competence?

¤ Did the physician adequately inform his or her patient about the risks and the possible outcomes of a procedure?

¤ Was the physician competent in referring the patient to an appropriate specialist or someone able to provide a second opinion when needed?

¤ Did the physician make a diagnosis that reasonably determined the type of disorder and urgency for emergency care?

Standard of Care

In a negligence action, the plaintiff (patient) must prove that the defendant (physician) failed to meet the standard of care expected of an ordinarily competent physician in a given situation. If the patient proves the failure to meet the standard of care, the physician is in **breach of the duty of care**. Generally, a physician must possess and use a degree of skill or care expected of physicians in any given medical situation. The standard of care test does not require the physician to be flawless in the exercise of his or her skills — or to put it another way, he or she does not have to be at the top of the medical school graduating class. At the same time, he or she should not be at the bottom, either. The physician is also not liable for an error of judgment if it was one that an ordinarily competent physician might have made.

The test used to determine the standard of care is objective: Did the physician meet the generally accepted standards of practice expected ordinarily of a practitioner in a similar community in similar cases? If he or she did, then the duty of care has not been breached and there can be no negligence. If the physician is a specialist, then the standard is that of the ordinary, prudent specialist. Again, the specialist does not have to be the best in the world, but he or she should be meeting the standards of an ordinarily competent and skilled specialist. If an ordinary physician is providing treatment that specialists normally provide, he or she is not expected to meet the standards imposed on a specialist.

Causation-in-Fact

When a physician is accused of negligence, the plaintiff has the burden of proof. In other words, if a patient has suffered illness or disability from the treatment provided by the physician in question, the patient must prove that it was the *direct* result of the physician's negligence. Physicians are not liable just because a patient does not respond well to treatment.

The patient can prove negligence through such means as medical documents, test results, and expert witnesses. If it is determined that the physician performed a negligent act, an award of monetary damages is made to the plaintiff. Some factors may affect the outcome of the claim; therefore, the plaintiff needs to be aware of them.

Limitation of Actions

Provincial law dictates how much time a plaintiff has to commence a lawsuit. Depending on the province or territory, this amount of time may be one or two years after the plaintiff begins to notice the negative health effects of the physician's negligent actions. If the claim is made too late, the action will not be allowed to proceed because the time limit for bringing a lawsuit has expired.

Mitigation of Loss

Patients who have received negligent treatment still have a responsibility to care for themselves. When a physician offers treatment to alleviate the illness due to negligence, it is in the best interest of the patient to consent and comply. If the patient refuses, the monetary award will be reduced as a result.

Contributory Negligence

In some cases, the patient's lifestyle behaviours are considered. If the court determines that the patient does not typically demonstrate good, healthy lifestyle behaviours, the award for negligent behaviour by the physician is reduced. An example of this might involve a patient whose arm, after being treated for a fracture, fails to heal properly or not heal at all. The physician might have been negligent in not setting the bone properly; but if the patient

---

EXHIBIT 26.4   **Assessment of Causation-in-Fact**

Mrs. Snell, a 70-year-old woman who was "legally blind" in the right eye, consented to cataract surgery performed by Dr. Farrell. He injected a local anaesthetic into the eye and noticed retrobulbar bleeding, a condition that can progress to a hemorrhage and cause permanent damage to the eye. Dr. Farrell palpated the eye, waited 30 minutes, and determined it was safe to proceed with the surgery.

By the end of the procedure, there was more blood in the eye and Mrs. Snell was in considerable pain. The blood took approximately nine months to clear, and by this point, the optic nerve had atrophied, leaving Mrs. Snell completely blind in the right eye.

Expert witnesses could not state with certainty that the hemorrhage had occurred as a direct result of the surgery since Mrs. Snell was moderately hypertensive and a diabetic, two factors that also predisposed her to retrobulbal hemorrhage. However, they also stated that whenever a bleed occurs (other than the modest amount from administering the anaesthetic), surgery should not proceed. The judge accepted evidence from Mrs. Snell that during the procedure she heard Dr. Farrell tell another physician that he would have to hurry the operation (presumably to complete the procedure before the bleeding became too severe).

Mrs. Snell's claim was upheld and Dr. Farrell was found liable for negligence. The trial judge noted that although the expert witnesses could not determine when the actual hemorrhage might have occurred, the surgery should not have proceeded at all when there was blood in the eye. He found the doctor's decision to quickly complete the operation before the blood accumulated to be negligent. He concluded, on the basis of sound probabilities, that Mrs. Snell had proven her case.

Source: *Snell v. Farrell*, [1990] 2 S.C.R. 311.

---

chooses to play sports and attempt heavy labour with his cast on, these factors will *contribute* to the poor healing that originated with the physician's poor casting technique. Here, the patient will have his damage award reduced to the extent that his own acts made the situation created by the physician worse than it otherwise would have been.

Quantification of Damage Award

If a patient has been subject to medical negligence, how much should the damage award be? In the late 1970s, a series of cases in the Supreme Court of Canada laid the framework for determining or quantifying the monetary award to the plaintiff.[1]

In the case of a negligent act that creates a temporary illness or inconvenience, common law dictates a monetary amount consistent with previous settlements. Each case is unique, however; and so, considerations is given to the type of illness and the specific effects on the individual. For example, it is not likely that a temporary infection from a surgery will receive more compensation than the complete loss of limb function. In another situation, the loss of nerve function in a finger would be considered more debilitating to a musician than to a marathon runner.

When debilitating damage has been done that results in the patient needing ongoing medical care for the rest of his/her life, a lump sum payment may be made. Such an award is determined upon a complex series of consider-

---

[1] See the following: *Andrews v. Grand & Toy Alberta Ltd.*, [1978] 2 S.C.R. 229, 3 C.C.L.T. 225, [1978] 1 W.W.R. 577, 8 A.R. 182, 83 D.L.R. (3d) 452, 19 N.R. 50; *Teno v. Arnold*, [1978] 2 S.C.R. 287, 3 C.C.L.T. 272, 83 D.L.R. (3d) 609, 19 N.R.1; *Thornton v. Board of School Trustees of School District No. 57 (Prince George)*, [1978] 2 S.C.R. 267, 3 C.C.L.T.257, [1978] 1 W.W.R. 607, 83 D.L.R. (3d) 480, 19 N.R. 552.

ations (e.g., the estimated life expectancy of the patient, the type of care needed over the patient's remaining life span, etc.). The exception to this might occur if an out-of-court settlement is made. In this case, the award called a structured settlement would be paid in instalments over the course of the remaining life of the plaintiff. While this approach creates an assured, tax-exempt income, the overall amount of an out-of-court settlement is usually less than the lump sum agreement.

If a patient dies as a result of medical negligence, the dependants of the deceased are provided with the financial means to cover the immediate funeral and other associated expenses. Dependants may also receive a sum for the loss of care, guidance and companionship. As one lawyer quipped, if you injure someone, it is cheaper if the person dies than if the person lives and require treatment and care.

PATIENT CONFIDENTIALITY

Medical personnel are under strict ethical rules to maintain patient confidentiality. Put another way, physicians, nurses, pharmacists, paramedics, etc. *all* have a **duty of non-disclosure**. The patient/practitioner relationship is deeply compromised if the patient is unable to disclose personal information without fear of exposure. The **fiduciary relationship** that exists between patient and health care provider requires the health practitioners to act in good faith in the patient's interest and, thus, assures trust and confidence — key components to successful medical care. Patient confidentiality is also protected by provincial privacy legislation that protects patient charts in the medical setting. Federally, the *Personal Information Protection and Electronic Documents Act* (PIPEDA) has many similarities to provincial and territorial Acts, but it is limited to commercial medical practices only (e.g., physiotherapists, dentists, pharmacists, and physicians working outside of the hospital in private practice). Between PIPEDA at the federal level and comprehensive privacy Acts at the provincial level, patient confidentiality is protected by law *irrespective* of whether the setting is private or public.

When Disclosure Is Required

Although laws have been set up to protect patient confidentiality, there are situations when it would be appropriate (or required) for the health care provider to turn over medical files for scrutiny.

Public Health Authorities

Provinces have public health policies that require physicians to report certain communicable diseases or situations that can prove to be harmful to an individual when discovered (see Exhibit 26.5). The duty of disclosure in these circumstances is important for monitoring the spread of illness and overall public safety. The information is a vital component to containing an outbreak and providing data for medical research. Each province and territory has a register of reportable diseases; and while these registries are similar in many ways, there are also geographical variations according to epidemiologic trends. It varies across jurisdictions as to what type of information is provided to public health authorities. Most jurisdictions require identifiable information (like the name and address of the infected person). Occasionally, a patient with a communicable disease such as tuberculosis will have his or her occupation provided to the local public health authority.

In the three territories and in Prince Edward Island, Alberta, and British Columbia, members of the public are also required to report if they know someone with a communicable disease or who has died from one. There are

---

EXHIBIT 26.5

Reportable Diseases

The following are some examples of reportable diseases common to most jurisdictions in the country. The list is by no means exhaustive as there are many rare and tropical diseases not considered here.

COMMUNICABLE DISEASES	SEXUALLY TRANSMITTED DISEASES
¤ Anthrax	¤ Chlamydia
¤ Botulism	¤ Gonococcal infections (i.e., gonorrhea)
¤ Chicken pox (in population clusters)	¤ Genital herpes
¤ Foodborne illnesses (i.e., "food poisoning")	¤ HIV/AIDS
¤ Hepatitis (all forms)	¤ Syphilis
¤ Meningitis (all forms)	
¤ Pertussis (whooping cough)	
¤ Rabies	
¤ Rubella (German measles)	
¤ Toxoplasmosis	
¤ Tuberculosis	
¤ Waterborne illnesses	
¤ Yellow fever	

---

more jurisdictions (e.g., Alberta, Newfoundland, and Prince Edward Island) that are now requiring *contact notification* as well. For example, family members in contact with an individual newly diagnosed with tuberculosis would need to be notified of that person's condition.

Legal Authorities

In recent years there has been a growing concern regarding the number of stab wounds and gunshot injuries presenting in hospital emergency departments. This has created a conflict of interest between legal authorities and medical professions. While legal authorities would like to have the information on and from the victim in order to prosecute the perpetrator, medical personnel have different priorities. Physicians are primarily concerned with breaching patient confidentiality, but they are also concerned that victims would avoid treatment, knowing their identity would be disclosed to police by the attending practitioner.

In spite of these concerns by the medical profession, Ontario introduced the *Mandatory Gunshot Wounds Reporting Act* in September 2005, requiring health care professionals to report the name of the victim and the hospital providing the care. The Act calls for an oral disclosure of the incident as soon as it is possible without causing undue disruption of hospital activities. Disclosure of the patient's name is required irrespective of the circumstances: the wound may be from a criminal act or a hunting accident or may be self-inflicted. The Act also has a provision to protect reporting facilities from proceedings for damage after a disclosure has been made. It does not, however, require the hospital to detain a patient who has sought treatment for a gunshot wound. In September 2007, Saskatchewan introduced a similar *Gunshot and Stab Wounds Mandatory Reporting Act*. This Act requires, however, that the identity of any victim presenting at a hospital in Saskatchewan with a gunshot or stab wound be provided to the police.

Lastly, to ensure the health and safety of all Canadians, the physician is also obligated by law to report those who are considered unsafe drivers, who are committing acts of child abuse, or who are being sexually abused by another health care practitioner.

Patient Consent to Disclosure
Sometimes patients will request that information from their medical history be shared. Such a situation may arise when the patient needs documents to be sent to another physician, health care provider, or insurance company. The patient who expressly consents to the sharing of information also has the right to qualify what information gets released. However, if the patient selects what can be divulged in a way that will alter or misrepresent his or her condition, the physician is not required to comply with the instructions. For example, a patient may wish to apply for life insurance and asks for all of his records to be sent *except* for an abnormal test result he recently received. In this situation, the physician would be in no way obligated to fulfill the patient's request to selectively disclose his medical records.

In a Court of Law
The medical information about a patient, if needed in a court of law, must be supplied by the physician or the person who compiled the medical record. If the health practitioner refuses, the practitioner may be summonsed to give evidence orally, or to provide medical records, or to both. If the practitioner fails to answer the summons, he or she may be found in contempt and be fined or jailed.

Patient Access to Records
A patient's medical chart is the property of the physician in charge or of the clinic the patient visited. However, this does not mean the contents of the file are within the complete control of the health care provider (see Exhibit 26.6). In the modern medical context where patients have more control over decisions of their treatment protocol, it is also a patient's right to see what is contained in the file. The physician is, therefore, obligated to allow the patient to see what has been written about the diagnosis and treatment. Medical documents can be difficult to understand by those untrained in the field, however.

EXHIBIT 26.6

Patient's Right of Access to Records

Margaret MacDonald asked her physician for copies of the medical documents found in her file. Dr. Elizabeth McInerney complied by providing copies of the records she wrote herself but did not copy the documentation prepared by other physicians. The reasoning was that those particular documents were the property of the other physicians and that it would be unethical to copy them without their knowledge.

While the documents are the property of the physicians who prepared them, patients are entitled to access all information contained in their medical file. In upholding the fiduciary physician/patient relationship, it is the responsibility of the physician to not only maintain patient confidentiality but also patient trust. With this trust comes the obligation to reveal information about the patient's case.

Mrs. MacDonald had applied for an order to have her entire chart released, and the Court awarded her request.

Source: *McInerney v. MacDonald*, [1992] 2 S.C.R. 138

For this reason, physicians or hospitals usually incorporate procedures that allow the patient to view charts while a health care professional is present. In this way, the information can be shared in a way that is in proper context and understood by the patient.

In rare circumstances the physician may determine that the well-being of a patient might be jeopardized if the patient has access to the medical file. If this is the case, a patient has a right to seek a court order for the release of the documents. In this situation, the physician will be asked to defend the position of non-disclosure in the court of law.

The Rules of Professional Conduct for lawyers and for paralegals requires medical information received in respect of a client to be shown to the client, even where a medical practitioner directs that it not be revealed. The proper position for a lawyer or paralegal is to refuse to accept the medical report under those conditions. Where revelation of the information to the client might harm the client, the lawyer or paralegal should encourage the client to review the record first with the medical practitioner.

PUBLIC HEALTH AND THE LAW

Public health law is found in provincial and territorial statutes. Federally, there are two key public health Acts: the *Quarantine Act* and the *Department of Health Act*.

The new *Quarantine Act* was given Royal Assent in 2005. The change in the Act was in large part a result of the SARS outbreak in 2003; it provides the Government of Canada with enhanced power at entry points to check the spread of **communicable disease** entering the country. The new Act includes extended power to appoint appropriate health officers, divert transportation vehicles to other landing points, and establish detaining facilities to hold or quarantine individuals.

The *Department of Health Act* is in place for the preservation of health among Canadians. It provides the minister with such responsibilities as overseeing the safety of consumer products, health promotion, research, and the protection of health of those travelling by air, sea, or rail.

Within provinces and territories, medical health officers (MHOs) are afforded many rights and privileges to ensure the health of their communities. They are provided with these powers so that they can locate carriers of communicable disease and ultimately work to contain the spread of the illness. There are laws regarding the power to enter facilities, detain patients, examine patients, and isolate them if necessary.

Entering a Facility to Examine

Under public health law, a health officer can enter a private residence to examine those suspected (on reasonable grounds) of carrying a contagious illness or sexually transmitted disease. While jurisdictions across Canada have specific stipulations on the power to enter, generally a warrant or written authority provided by a chief health officer is required. In Ontario, a medical health officer entering a room *specifically* used as a dwelling place requires the consent of the occupant.

Those refused to be examined or to adhere to the directives of public health officials face fines and/or incarceration. Individuals who *knowingly* spread communicable diseases (i.e., with criminal intent) may be charged under the *Criminal Code* and dealt with accordingly:

> 180.(1) Every one who commits a common nuisance and thereby
> (a) endangers the lives, safety or health of the public, or
> (b) causes physical injury to any person,

is guilty of an indictable offence and liable to imprisonment for a term not exceeding two years.

221. Every one who by criminal negligence causes bodily harm to another person is guilty of an indictable offence and liable to imprisonment for a term not exceeding ten years.

273.(1) Every one commits an aggravated sexual assault who, in committing a sexual assault, wounds, maims, disfigures or endangers the life of the complainant.

Closing a Facility, Isolation, and Quarantine

The widespread authority of MHOs allows them to close buildings and gathering places in an attempt to contain a suspected or known illness that threatens to become an **epidemic**. Examples of facilities include public gathering places, entertainment venues, places of worship, schools, daycare centres, and campgrounds.

In all jurisdictions, MHOs also have the power to **isolate** and **quarantine**. Isolation may involve containment at a hospital or the prevention of movement in and out of residence. Isolation is enforced when a person or persons are known to be infected with a communicable disease. The MHO may quarantine an individual or group of people if they have been — or suspected to have been — exposed to a communicable disease but have not yet presented with signs and symptoms of illness. Detaining powers are often for the recalcitrant individual who does not wish to co-operate with the investigative process. The law allows for the MHO to detain an individual, if necessary, for medical examination, treatment, and the prevention of the spread of disease.

Supervised Injection Facilities

In 2003, Vancouver became the first Canadian city to open a supervised (or *safer*) injection facility (SIF) for injection drug users (IDUs). The centres provide safe areas, supervised by medical staff, for IDUs to inject using sterile equipment. The centres were created in an attempt to decrease public drug use, accidental overdose, and the spread of infectious illness, such as HIV/ AIDS and hepatitis C, through needle-sharing. With medical staff present, the SIF also acts as an area for safe injection education and obtaining health information.

The facilities are legally sanctioned areas for the safe injection of pre-obtained illicit drugs *on the condition* that the IDUs participate in ongoing research and evaluation regarding SIF's effectiveness in reducing overdose-related deaths, blood-borne illness, and public drug use. Medical staff and "research subjects" (the IDUs) are exempt from the laws regarding possession defined in the *Controlled Drugs and Substances Act* (CDSA) *only* when they are within the interior borders of the SIF. Furthermore, the illicit drugs permitted at the centre may only be of the kinds that are injected.

Under current regulation, only the IDU can inject himself or herself when on the premises. Anyone requiring assistance cannot recruit injection from medical staff, nor have a friend assist with the injection if done within the parameters of the site.

EUTHANASIA AND REFUSING TREATMENT

The issue of terminating a life that is considered in some way futile is very complex. Common law in Canada offers concrete parameters in some situations but presents variable legal outcomes in other cases involving the termination of life. It is an area of moral and ethical concern that is likely to generate more debate in the future for many reasons. Individuals are living longer, leaving them more susceptible to incapacitating chronic illness that greatly affects their quality of life. Patients are also more informed about their care, and they expect to contribute to the medical decision-making of their own health. Finally, with the increasing technological advances in medicine, the prolongation of life is more feasible, albeit at a financial cost.

Euthanasia and Assisted Suicide

In health care and health care law, "euthanasia" and "assisted suicide" are two of the terms used to describe the cessation of life.

Euthanasia may be defined as voluntary or involuntary. **Voluntary euthanasia** is the act of one individual deliberately ending the life of another as a means to eliminate suffering. It is performed on the consent of a **competent** individual or as the result of a valid advance directive. A competent patient is one who is able to understand the current situation, the repercussions of any decision he or she makes regarding the state of his or her health, and who has the ability to communicate such a decision. When life support is withdrawn from a competent patient, it is voluntary euthanasia; when it is withdrawn from an **incompetent** patient or in the absence of consent, it is called **non-voluntary euthanasia.**

Involuntary euthanasia is also an act of terminating a life to end suffering, but it is performed *against* the wishes of a competent individual or contrary to the terms of a valid advance directive. This is considered the same as manslaughter or murder.

All situations of euthanasia involve an individual engaging in a method that *actively* terminates the life of another as a means to end suffering: an example would be the injection of a lethal dose of medication to the patient in question.

Assisted suicide, on the other hand, occurs when a health care professional or other person *provides* medical information or specific tools to an individual so that that individual obtains the capacity to end his or her own life. (See Exhibit 26.7.)

EXHIBIT 26.7

Right to Assisted Suicide

Sue Rodriguez was a 42-year-old woman who suffered from the progressively debilitating neurological disease, ALS (amyotrophic lateral sclerosis). By the end-stage of the disease she would be confined to bed on a respirator and nourished by way of gastrotomy. Rodriguez wanted the right to be able to take her own life when her condition became unbearable for her. She requested that a physician provide her with the technical means to commit suicide because in the last stage of her illness she would be too physically disabled to undertake the task unaided. Rodriguez took her case to the Supreme Court on the basis that section 241(*b*) of the *Criminal Code* breached her rights according to sections 7, 12, and 15 of the *Charter*. She argued that as a physically disabled person, she had lost the fundamental right to decide her life course because she did not have the physical ability to take her own life. Assisted suicide would return to her the physical means already afforded to able persons. In spite of her arguments, the Supreme Court upheld section 241(*b*) of the *Code* and dismissed her application. It was determined that section 241 had an important role in the preservation of the sanctity of life, and according to Justice Sopinka, its integrity was particularly necessary to protect vulnerable individuals "who might be induced in moments of weakness to commit suicide."

Sue Rodriguez took her life four months after the trial, apparently assisted by an anonymous physician.

Source: *Rodriguez v. British Columbia (Attorney General)*, [1993] 3 S.C.R. 519

Right to Refuse Treatment

EXHIBIT 26.8

Nancy B. was a 25-year-old woman with Guillain-Barré syndrome. The disease left her permanently paralyzed and on mechanical ventilation in order to remain alive. After living as a quadriplegic for four years, Nancy made a request to her physician to remove her ventilation. He refused her request on the basis that it would be unethical and unlawful for him to do so.

The court realized Nancy B. was mentally competent and her request for the removal of the ventilator was a conscientious refusal of treatment. Justice Jacques Dufour made the following statement (at p. 394):

> Sections 222 to 241 of the Criminal Code deal with different forms of homicide. What I have just reviewed is sufficient to conclude that the person who will have to stop Nancy B.'s respiratory support treatment in order to allow nature to take its course, will not in any manner commit the crimes prohibited by these sections. The same goes for s. 241, aiding suicide. I would however add that homicide and suicide are not natural deaths, whereas in the present case, if the plaintiff's death takes place after the respiratory support treatment is stopped at her request, it would be the result of nature taking its course.

Five weeks after the court's decision, the mechanical ventilation was removed and Nancy B. died peacefully.

Source: *Nancy B. v. Hôtel-Dieu de Quebec* (1992), 86 D.L.R. (4th) 385; 69 C.C.C. (3d) 450 (Que. Sup. Ct.).

As stated in section 241 of the *Criminal Code*, both euthanasia and assisted suicide are illegal in Canada:

> Every one who (a) counsels a person to commit suicide, or (b) aids or abets a person to commit suicide, whether suicide ensues or not, is guilty of an indictable offence and liable to imprisonment for a term not exceeding fourteen years.

Refusing Treatment by a Competent Individual

While euthanasia or the active administration of a procedure that would end life is illegal, the *refusal of treatment* by an individual is not only legal but also a fundamental right according to section 7 of the *Charter*. Because of this, a competent patient who decides he or she does not want life-prolonging procedures (without being influenced or coerced) is entitled to have the treatment *withheld* or *withdrawn*. The treatment in question might be the supply of hydration/nutrition, surgery, pharmaceutical intervention, or the sustaining of life by mechanical ventilation.

Life-Prolonging Treatment for the Incompetent Patient

Every day, physicians are faced with patients who are so severely ill that they remain alive only by medical life-support. Although they are incompetent and cannot consent (i.e., they remain in a **persistent vegetative state**), it is not too uncommon for the physician to withhold or withdraw life-supporting measures. In common law, there is no precedent that clearly defines a legal framework for the termination of life-support for an individual who will in no way benefit or recover from the treatment. However, there have been cases in other Commonwealth countries that have *shaped* common law in Canada to be tolerant of this current practice. The Law Reform Commission of Canada has also released a document entitled *Euthanasia, Aiding Suicide, and Cessation of Treatment*. The paper endorses the practice of withholding or withdrawing life-support from a patient whose outcome is futile and encourages a firm legal position to be created in which physicians can work. Since its release in 1982, there have been no changes in Canadian law, but the proposed recommendations have not been rejected. So, while the termination of life-support of incompetent patients is done in the course of current medical practice, it is done on the basis of sound medical and ethical reasoning — not in accordance with defined law.

The Living Will

Some individuals have drawn up a living will in anticipation of an illness that will render them incompetent to participate in medical decision making. A **living will** is a document that indicates the circumstances under which a patient would want life-prolonging measures to cease. In other words, the individual defines when life-support for him or her should terminate. The living will has been useful in some cases, but the nature of the document leaves itself open to interpretation. For example, the directive is applicable only when the *specific* condition for which life-support is provided is experienced: a directive to halt life-support after a heart attack will raise questions by medical staff if the person is on life-support after a motor vehicle accident. Another area of conflict arises when a family member or loved one challenges the will and wants to overturn it. Finally, living wills are not always made apparent to health care staff. No wishes can be adhered to if there is no knowledge that directives exist.

The Advance Directive

The **advance directive** is a document that received legal recognition in many jurisdictions as a result of the 1990 case *Malette v. Shulman*. Like the living will it is a document intended for the physician should the individual become incompetent. Unlike the living will, however, the advanced directive describes what *treatments* the individual prefers as well as when treatment should cease. The advance directive consists of two parts: (i) the *instruction directive* clarifies what treatments are preferred and what are not, and (ii) the *proxy directive* identifies a person designated to negotiate treatment options on behalf of the patient who has become incompetent.

EXHIBIT 26.9   **When Treatment Becomes a Battery**

Georgette Malette was unconscious and rushed to the hospital in Kirkland Lake after being involved in a car accident. The accident, which took the life of her husband, left Malette with serious injuries. Upon arrival at the hospital, a nurse discovered a card in Malette's possession. The card stated that Malette was a Jehovah's Witness and that under no circumstances should a blood transfusion be administered. Dr. Shulman was made aware of the document.

While in hospital, Malette's condition began to deteriorate due to the profuse bleeding she was suffering. In spite of the specific instructions indicated on the card, Shulman ordered and administered a blood transfusion himself on the basis that it was his responsibility to preserve the life and health of his patients.

Malette made a successful recovery and brought an action against the physician and hospital staff. It was decided that with the knowledge of the instruction card she was carrying, the *emergency doctrine* was not applicable. The court determined that the physician has committed the tort of battery, and the plaintiff was awarded $20,000.

Source: *Malette v. Shulman* (1990), 72 O.R. (2d) 417; [1990] O.J. No. 450 (C.A.).

In the best situation, the advance directive increases communication between the individual drawing it up and his or her loved ones. Furthermore, there is less ambiguity for the treating physician regarding the degree of intervention the patient wants should he or she become seriously ill. As can be expected, the more details the document provides, the more valuable it becomes. Generally, the advance directive allows for the individual to determine how much medical intervention to be provided (i.e., from "prolong life" to "provide comfort care *only*") to treatment options such as dialysis, mechanical breathing, pharmaceutical intervention and blood transfusions.

REPRODUCTIVE HEALTH AND THE LAW

Few areas of law feature as many "hot buttons" as the law relating to human reproduction. While the state has been removing itself from the bedrooms of the nation since the 1960s, issues concerning the right to reproduce, and the right not to, continue to be matters of dispute.

Sterilization

Common law contemplates a variety of situations regarding the sterilization of an individual. Considerations are made regarding competence of the individual, consent to the procedure, and the reasons for the surgery to be performed.

Consent to Sterilization by the Competent Individual
Sterilization for the purpose of contraception is certainly an option for the competent adult. If the individual is married, he or she has the right to opt for sterilization without the consent of his or her spouse, as confirmed by section 15 of the *Charter*. If a patient wishes to be sterilized and the physician does not feel it is in the patient's best interest, the physician is not compelled by law to perform the procedure. In keeping with standards of medical practice, however, the physician is obliged to refer the patient to another physician who will more likely meet the patient's needs.

Sterilization of the Incompetent Individual
Common law is not as definitive when sterilization involves an incompetent individual. If a mentally challenged individual is able to understand the connection between intercourse, pregnancy, and the consequences of sterilization, he or she is able to make decisions regarding his or her reproductive health and consent accordingly. However, if a patient is so mentally challenged that sterilization cannot be understood, the involuntary procedure must be done with great care.

To sterilize an incompetent patient simply to prevent the genetically damaged individual from having children is **eugenic sterilization** and is completely illegal. *Occasionally*, the Supreme Court of Canada will recognize the therapeutic sterilization for the physical or mental protection of the patient, and the Court uses the **parens patriae** jurisdiction solely to ensure the health and safety of a vulnerable individual. Unfortunately, therapeutic sterilization is not governed by a consistent set of guidelines in common law. It might be safe to say that sterilization would be warranted if a uterine tumour in the incompetent patient was threatening to metastasize (spread to nearby tissue), or the patient was *so* emotionally vulnerable and mentally compromised that a pregnancy would have detrimental psychological effects on her.[2]

2 See *E. (Mrs.) v. Eve*, [1986] 2 S.C.R. 388.

Rights of the Fetus

When a fetus is *in utero* (unborn), it does not have rights nor is it considered — legally — a person.[3] This is confirmed by section 223(1) of the *Criminal Code* which states the following:

> A child becomes a human being within the meaning of this Act when it has completely proceeded, in a living state, from the body of its mother, whether or not (a) it has breathed; (b) it has an independent circulation; or (c) the navel string is severed.

On occasion section 223(1) has resulted in unfortunate consequences, particularly when a mother takes drugs or engages in harmful lifestyle behaviours during pregnancy that ultimately affect the health of the unborn child. In the case of *R. v. Drummond*,[4] the circumstances were particularly noteworthy. Brenda Drummond was acquitted of attempted murder after shooting a pellet gun into her vagina just before she came to term. The baby was fortunate to have survived the ordeal, being born alive a few days later with a pellet lodged in his head.

A certain amount of legal protection *does* exist for the neonate when it is being delivered. Section 242 of the *Criminal Code* states that a pregnant woman is guilty of an indictable offence if she fails to obtain assistance for a birth she wishes to conceal or with the intent that the child shall not live. Section 238(1) of the *Criminal Code* states that a person is guilty of murder and liable to imprisonment for life when causing the death of a newborn in the act of birth. However, as subsection (2) clarifies, the charge *does not* apply to an individual that causes the death of the newborn in order to save the life of the mother.

Abortion

Section 287 of the *Criminal Code* states that an individual who, by any means, procures a miscarriage in another woman is liable to imprisonment for life. A pregnant woman who, by any means, induces the miscarriage of her own fetus is liable to imprisonment for a maximum sentence of two years. The *Criminal Code* makes exceptions, however. It states that a hospital-based physician, under the guidance of a therapeutic abortion committee, may perform a therapeutic abortion if the pregnancy is likely to endanger the life or health of the mother. There is ambiguity here, however, as the term "health" is not clarified. The therapeutic abortion committee then, depending on ethical leanings, can wield considerable power over the decision to grant an abortion to the woman in need.

In 1988, the Supreme Court of Canada reduced the significance of section 287 in the case involving Henry Morgentaler, a Canadian physician wanting to perform legal and accessible abortions. The Supreme Court of Canada held section 287 impeded upon section 7 of the *Charter of Rights and Freedoms*. As Chief Justice Brian Dickson stated, "Forcing a woman, by threat of criminal sanction[,] to carry a foetus to term unless she meets certain criteria unrelated to her own priorities and aspirations, is a profound interference with a woman's body and thus a violation of her security of the person." Since then the federal government has failed to implement any legislative framework controlling abortion practices. In other words, there is no *criminal* regulation of the practice. Most jurisdictions today cover medical abortion by provincial and territorial health care insurance plans. Women have access to the procedure through hospitals, public health care clinics, and a few private centres. Unfor-

---

[3] See *Tremblay v. Daigle*, [1989] 2 S.C.R. 530. This case also addresses the lack of precedent that supports the rights of the father to veto a woman's decision to have an abortion.

[4] (1996) O.J. No. 4597.

tunately, even today, women who live in remote areas or who cannot afford quick access to a private clinic are subsequently unable to exercise the right to abortion.

Wrongful Birth

Wrongful birth is a tort that results from the negligence of a physician prior to delivery that results in the birth of a disabled child. Wrongful birth does not mean the physician performed a procedure that caused disability in the newborn. It pertains to a physician's knowing that a child is likely to be born disabled and failing to disclose this information to the parents. The parents are able to make the claim on the basis that they were uninformed of the situation and were therefore unable to consider therapeutic abortion as an option.

The increasing effectiveness of amniocentesis, ultrasound, and genetic testing are making the tort of wrongful birth a more common occurrence. The physician must also be continually aware of the medications prescribed to the pregnant woman and alert her to any chance that teratogenesis (birth defects) might result. Lastly, wrongful birth may be alleged if the physician does not carefully consider the chance of a newborn inheriting a condition that has been recognized in previous births by the mother.

In every wrongful birth case, when presented in the court of law, the prosecution must prove the physician had a reasonable degree of knowledge about the outcome of the birth and failed to disclose that to the parents.[5] The prosecution must also prove the birth was a direct result of the physician's failing to disclose the likely outcome of the newborn's health. In other words, the parents would need to demonstrate that, had they known about the disability of the child, they would have opted for therapeutic abortion. If the preventable birth of a disabled child is determined to inflict undue hardship on the parents and offspring, an award is made to the prosecution.

MENTAL HEALTH LAW

The law protecting the rights of patients with mental illness is different than the law for patients receiving general medical care. In the field of mental health, patients who are very ill are frequently unable to make decisions about their treatment that is in their own best interest or in the best interest of others around them. Therefore, the issues most frequently encountered in mental health law generally involve involuntary hospitalization and treatment without consent.

There are challenges in mental health law. While the *Charter of Rights and Freedoms* ensures Canadians the right to liberty and freedom from involuntary detainment, patients with severe mental illness are at risk to themselves and others if care is not implemented. Those who advocate for patients' rights claim that any sort of involuntary hospitalization is imposing and authoritarian. They suggest that uninvited treatment violates tenets of the *Charter* and removes the liberty and dignity of the patient. Sections 9 and 15 are considered when addressing the rights of those requiring involuntary committal:

9. Everyone has the right not to be arbitrarily detained or imprisoned.

15.(1) Every individual is equal before and under the law and has the right to the equal protection and equal benefit of the law without discrimination and, in particular, without discrimination based on race, national or ethnic origin, colour, religion, sex, age or mental or physical disability.

---

[5] See *Arndt v. Smith*, [1997] 2 S.C.R. 539.

Conversely, those who adhere to human needs principles suggest that a legal framework for involuntary care is necessary for the immediate safety of the patient *and* for the benefit of the patient's long-term rights and freedoms. Certainly, untreated mental illness contributes to homelessness, fills shelters, overtaxes supportive housing projects, and creates overwhelming challenges for the families of those who are ill.

While those with less severe psychiatric disorders can voluntarily enter into care and be protected by common law, those with severe illness (e.g., bipolar disorder, major depression with suicidal tendencies, schizophrenia) fall within the guidelines of *statutory law*. The management of mental health patients by statute creates a fine balance between acknowledging patients' rights according to the Charter, **lawful compulsion**, and issues regarding consent to treatment.[6]

Involuntary Admission to Hospital

For those whose judgment and reasoning are impaired by mental illness, *lawful compulsion* or committing a patient to psychiatric care is admissible. The patient can be committed for medical assessment and thereafter for treatment, but each of these steps requires a certificate of committal to be completed by one or more physicians. In cases of involuntary committal, the patient is given certain rights. A tribunal review is available to all psychiatric patients involuntarily committed for the purpose of evaluating the admission criteria and discharge plans. The review board is necessarily a neutral body, with the sole purpose of deciding whether the treatment of the patient was fair, ethical, and in the patient's best interest.

Criteria for Committal

While there are some differences between the provinces in determining if a patient should be involuntarily hospitalized, some criteria are consistent throughout the country. All jurisdictions require the patient to meet a *dangerousness standard*, which determines if the patient is to be a threat to the physical safety of himself or herself or others. In Ontario, Saskatchewan, Manitoba and British Columbia, the dangerousness criteria also include the patient's risk of impending mental or physical *deterioration*. Another basis for involuntary admission is *inappropriateness for voluntary treatment*. In this situation, the patient's reasoned thinking and judgment are so greatly impaired a conscientious decision for voluntary treatment is impossible. Finally, all jurisdictions require a *diagnosis of mental disorder* to be made.[7]

Variations between jurisdictions exist. In the Yukon Territory, British Columbia, Saskatchewan, Manitoba, Quebec, Prince Edward Island, New Brunswick, and Newfoundland, "dangerousness" has come to encompass *nonbodily* or *psychological* harm. In Saskatchewan, Manitoba, and British Columbia, criteria for admission also requires the patient *to be in need of treatment*.

The rights of those who are mentally ill, while for the most part protected, are monitored by advocacy groups throughout the country, who ensure section 15 of the *Charter* is upheld by medical authorities. Patients with severe mental illness *can* be committed involuntarily, but they have access to a tribunal board, ombudsmen or similar advocacy groups, legal council, or any designated representative to ensure that the rights *and* well-being of all involved are preserved.

---

[6] See *Fleming v. Reid* (1991), 4 O.R. (3d) 74 (C.A.).

[7] The actual definition of "mental disorder" varies across jurisdictions. The most serious mental disorders, however, are *all* included within this otherwise arbitrary definition.

Because it is generally the most serious disorders that demand involuntary committal, it is rare for those with mild disorders to be detained against their will.

MEDICAL MARIJUANA IN CANADA

The use of marijuana for medical purposes became legal in Canada in 2001. (The process of legalization began in the late 1990s after Terry Parker, who suffered from grand-mal epilepsy, was found not guilty of growing and using marijuana for medicinal reasons.) Health Canada's *Medical Marijuana Access Division* (MMAD) regulates the use of medical marijuana, and the legislation is described in the *Marijuana Medical Access Regulations*.

The Application Process

A patient can be prescribed medical marijuana by a family doctor or medical specialist. Both patient and physician complete application forms, and the patient supplies his or her photograph with the documents. The application provided by the physician includes the patient's diagnosis, the dosage required, and the predicted course of treatment. The forms are resubmitted annually in order to provide Health Canada ongoing information regarding the progression of the treatment.

The types of illness deemed manageable by marijuana are indicated by categories. "Category one" conditions are those that create extreme pain, seizures, or cachexia (weight loss, fatigue and nausea, seen with terminal illness). The conditions include spinal injury or spinal cord disease, multiple sclerosis, epilepsy, severe arthritis, HIV/AIDS, and cancer. "Category two" illnesses are not specifically identified but are conditions that have been debilitating to the patient and that have not responded to any traditional therapy.

Obtaining Medicinal Marijuana

During the application process, the patient selects how he or she will obtain the marijuana and provides the appropriate data to Health Canada. Medical marijuana can be sent out at monthly intervals by Health Canada, grown by the patient, or produced by a grower designated by the patient. For plants to be grown by the patient or designate, strict rules apply. The seeds must be obtained from Health Canada, and the applicant needs to declare where the plant will be grown, how many plants will be cultivated, how the product will be securely stored, and give assurance the plants will be away from daycare centres, schools, or playgrounds. If the patient designates a grower (who must be over 18 years of age), similar rules apply. Designate growers may grow plants at the patient's residence or their own, but in both cases the method of production and procedures regarding security are maintained. Patients using marijuana are provided with an authorization card that allows them to have in their possession one month's supply of dried product at any given time. Growers are also provided with authorization to possess, as well as with a licence to grow and process limited quantities of the plant for medicinal purposes.

CHAPTER SUMMARY

Most medical treatment for Canadians is publicly funded so that any Canadian that is insurable has access to basic medical care, which is financially covered by a governmental health plan. The *Canada Health Act* (CHA) is a federal Act that provides the legislative framework for public health care insurance throughout the country. The law as it pertains to health follows the common law tradition. In Quebec, the *Civil Code of Quebec* and the *law of obligations* provide the legislative framework for medical law.

Consent to treatment is necessary for medical care, or a charge of medical battery may be laid. In the case of negligence, the physician has failed to provide an adequate standard of care. One of the core functions of the health care practitioner is to maintain patient confidentiality; however, the physician is obligated to release certain medical information to public health authorities, legal authorities, and in the court of law.

Medical health officers are afforded the right to enter buildings and examine individuals who are thought to have a communicable disease. They also carry the power to detain, isolate, and quarantine an individual or individuals as a means to contain the spread of disease.

Euthanasia is illegal in Canada, but common law has been tolerant in the cessation of life-support to those who are in a persistent vegetative state or whose treatment outcome is futile. Individuals, however, have the right to refuse treatment.

Unborn fetuses do not hold legal rights, and they are not considered by law to be human beings until they are born alive. Abortion is covered by public health insurance, and it is within a woman's rights to opt for the procedure — with or without the consent of a spouse or partner. Wrongful birth is a tort that results when a physician, knowing that a child will likely be born disabled, fails to disclose this information to the parents.

Mental health law has specific stipulations for seriously ill patients. While those with less severe psychiatric disorders can voluntarily enter into care and be protected by common law, those with severe illness fall within the guidelines of *statutory law*. The criteria for involuntary admission to hospital vary from jurisdiction to jurisdiction.

The use of marijuana for medical purposes was legalized in Canada in 2001. The *Medical Marijuana Access Division* of Health Canada carefully regulates the application process, production, distribution, possession, and use of marijuana for therapeutic use.

GLOSSARY OF NEW TERMS AND KEY CONCEPTS

advance directive	A document prepared by an individual that outlines the type of treatment desired and when treatment efforts be terminated should the person become incompetent.
assisted suicide	The voluntary termination of one's life using the knowledge, means, or both of another individual.
breach of the duty of care	The failure to perform a professional obligation or act to an accepted level or standard of care.
communicable disease	An infectious agent or toxic product that can be transmitted from person to person or animal to person.
competent	A person who is of sound mind and is therefore able to make, act accordingly upon, and understand the consequences of decisions regarding his or her health and medical treatment.
delisting	The elimination of a medical service from a provincial or territorial health care insurance plan so that the patient must pay for the service out-of-pocket.
duty of non-disclosure	The professional obligation to hold a patient's medical information in confidence
emergency doctrine	A provision that allows a health care professional to perform treatment that is considered to be life-saving on an incompetent patient (and therefore without consent).
epidemic	An outbreak of an infectious illness in a community or population that is widespread or greater than what would normally be expected.

eugenic sterilization	A surgical procedure on an individual that eliminates reproductive capacity. In this situation it is done to eliminate the continuation of genetic traits or behaviours determined to be unwanted or "substandard".
fiduciary relationship	In medicine, a relationship between health care provider and patient in which the practitioner is responsible for ensuring the patient's trust and confidence in good faith.
incompetent	A person who is not of sound mind and is therefore unable to make, act upon, and understand the consequences of decisions regarding his or her health and medical treatment. Incompetence also applies if the individual has been threatened or coerced into a particular decision.
involuntary euthanasia	The act of ending a life by one person to eliminate suffering of a competent individual who does not wish the procedure to be carried out.
isolate	To separate and contain an individual or individuals known to have a communicable disease in order to prevent the spread of illness.
lawful compulsion	The compelling or inducement by legal authority to carry out a required act.
living will	A document made by a competent individual indicating when life-prolonging treatment be terminated in the event he or she becomes incompetent.
medical battery	The intentional violation of a patient's right for the purpose of delivering medical care.
medical negligence	A tort that resulted from a medical act performed by a physician that causes undue harm to the patient.
non-voluntary euthanasia	The termination of life by one person as a means to end the suffering of another who is incompetent, or when consent has not been obtained.
parens patriae	Latin, meaning "father of his country". It refers to the government's duty to act as the ultimate guardian for those who are unable to care for themselves as a means to ensure their health and safety.
persistent vegetative state	A condition that involves the absence of higher brain function. While the reflexes for breathing, heart rate, blood pressure, and digestion remain, the patient has no awareness of the external environment at all. In other words, the patient remains alive by the presence of basic neurological functioning only.
quarantine	To separate and contain an individual or individuals suspected or known to have been exposed to a communicable disease but are not yet showing signs and symptoms of the illness.
voluntary euthanasia	The termination of one's life by another as a means to end suffering. The individual wishing the act has provided consent to have it carried out.

REVIEW QUESTIONS

1. Identify ways the provincial and territorial management of health care has begun to deviate from the standards originally set out in the *Canada Health Act*.

2. At the scene of a motor vehicle accident, paramedics splint the broken leg and administer oxygen to an unconsciousness woman. What is the legal basis that allows them to do this without her consent?

3. Identify situations where a physician would be required to disclose the medical information of a patient.

4. A patient provides consent to have his medical history released. Under what circumstance can the physician refuse her patient's request?

5. A client seeks counsel, complaining about the actions of his physician. What criteria would a lawyer use to determine whether or not the physician was negligent in the case? How would a lawyer determine the physician's actions were that of negligence and not battery?

6. Explore situations where the *Quarantine Act* and the *Department of Health Act* would apply. How would public health legislation treat an outbreak of meningitis in Ontario differently from a group of infected individuals in a ship off the coast of Vancouver Island?

7. A drug addict who possesses and uses street drugs is not arrested for injecting drugs at an SIF. Outline why he is able to do this, and state what criteria he must follow to avoid arrest.

8. What criteria would a physician consider before admitting a patient to a psychiatric ward on an involuntary basis?

9. A patient is refusing treatment in the psychiatric ward of a hospital. Outline the course of action that would typically occur in such a situation. What rights does the patient have?

10. A client tells her lawyer she was charged with possession of marijuana but claims she needs it for a medical condition. What are the requirements to grow, possess, and use medicinal marijuana legally?

DISCUSSION QUESTIONS

1. List some common situations in which personal privacy and the obligation of confidentiality conflict with other private or public interests. Analyze and resolve legal issues that arise from such conflicts.

2. Assisted suicide and obtaining assistance for injecting drugs at SIFs are illegal. Discuss how the law is in conflict with the rights of disabled persons.

3. Explore Saskatchewan's and Ontario's mandatory reporting Acts for gunshot and stab wounds. What are the advantages and disadvantages of this Act according to the legal and medical professions?

4. Using web resources that support and oppose the practice of euthanasia, debate the ethical and legal dilemmas that arise with this issue. Discuss the advantages and disadvantages that have been seen with the practice in the Netherlands.

5. More and more medical services are being delisted from provincial and territorial health care insurance plans. Debate whether this trend is a benefit or liability to Canada's public health care system. Will privatization ensure health care by decreasing wait times for treatment, or does it jeopardize the core values in which the *Canada Health Act* is based?

SUGGESTED READING

Caulfield, Timothy A., & Barbara von Tigerstrom. (Eds.). *Health Care Reform and the Law in Canada: Meeting the Challenge* (Edmonton, Alta.: University of Alberta, 2002).

Downie, Jocelyn, Timothy Caulfield, & Colleen Flood. (Eds.). *Canadian Health Law and Policy*, 2d Ed. (Markham, Ont.: Butterworths, 2002).

Eaves, D., J.R.P. Ogloff, & R. Roesch. *Mental Disorders and the Criminal Code: Legal Background and Contemporary Perspectives*. (Burnaby, B.C.: Simon Fraser University, 2000).

Sneiderman, Barney, John C. Irvine, & Philip H. Osborne. *Canadian Medical Law: An Introduction for Physicians, Nurses, and other Health Care Professionals* (Scarborough, Ont.: Carswell, 2003).

Sport and the Law

Susan Haslip
ALGONQUIN COLLEGE

Learning Objectives

After reading this chapter, the reader should be able to:

➤ describe how sport is organized in Canada

➤ understand how the high performance sport system fits within the international sport movement

➤ explain how the organization of sport relates to the jurisdiction of sport in Canada

➤ identify the areas where sport and the law intersect in Canada

➤ identify some challenges arising with the funding of sport in Canada

➤ explain factors informing the under-representation of identified groups in sport

➤ describe how human rights instruments affect sport

➤ explain how sport is affected by policies and law on official languages

➤ explain how doping is dealt with in the Canadian sport system

➤ describe how disputes are dealt with in the Canadian sport system

TABLE OF CONTENTS

INTRODUCTION

Sport, while operating by its own set of rules and principles, does not exist in a vacuum. While there is no distinct "sports law"[1] *per se*, sport and the law do intersect. This chapter explores a number of these points of intersection in the Canadian amateur sport system. As such, it does not canvass "professional" sport (i.e., the National Hockey League, the Canadian Football League, the National Football League, motor sport racing). The chapter starts with an overview of the organization of sport in Canada and a consideration of how the domestic sport system fits within the international sport movement. Issues impacting the "high performance" sport system in the area of funding, including the adequacy of funding, the impact of the federal tobacco policy and the *Income Tax Act* are explored. Factors informing the **under-representation** of women, visible minorities, **Aboriginal peoples** and **athletes with a disability** (or disabilities) are explored. The intersection of other policies and laws, including instruments related to human rights, official languages, doping and dispute resolution are canvassed.

ORGANIZATION OF AMATEUR SPORT

"Sport" in Canada can best be understood when viewed as *a* component of a *physical activity spectrum*. The *Minister's Task Force on Federal Sport Policy*, for example, defines "sport" as "one part of a physical activity spectrum that includes play, fitness activities, recreational sport, organized competitive sport and high performance sport"[2] (see Exhibit 27.1). While terms such as "play" and "fitness activities" are commonly understood, distinctions between "recreational", "competitive" and "high performance" sport levels may not be as well-known and are outlined at Exhibit 27.2.

The entire sport structure is premised on the ideal of attaining Olympic status. If one envisions a pyramid, leisure-type activities are located at the bottom of the pyramid while international competition is located at the top. The higher one moves up the pyramid, the higher the level of performance. National Sport Organizations (NSOs) (and, by extension, their respective Provincial Sport Organizations (PSOs)) form part of the international sport movement — a "complex, multi-layered, interdependent entity" (see Exhibit 27.3). An appreciation of where domestic sport organizations fit within the international sport movement is important in order to appreciate not only where high performance sport fits within that structure but also to appreciate how the international sport federations impact domestic sport organizations.

The international sport movement comprises a number of bodies, including non-governmental organizations (NGOs). The Olympic Movement is one such NGO.[3] This movement consists of the International Olympic Committee (IOC) and the International Paralympic Committee (IPC), the National Olympic Committees (NOCs) and National Paralympic Committees (NPCs) of each country (i.e., the Canadian Olympic Committee, the Canadian Paralympic Committee), and international sport federation (ISF) bodies (i.e., the International Amateur Boxing Association). The IOC is *the* key player, responsible for delegating the control and development of a given sport to the appropriate interna-

---

[1] John Barnes, *Sports and the Law in Canada*, 3d ed. (Toronto: Butterworths, 1996) at 2, n4.
[2] Minister of State Fitness and Amateur Sport, *Sport: The Way Ahead — The Report of the Minister's Task Force on Federal Sport Policy* (Ottawa: Minister of Supply and Services Canada, 1992) at 22. (Task Force Report)
[3] *Ibid.* at 131.

EXHIBIT 27.1

Sport in Canada

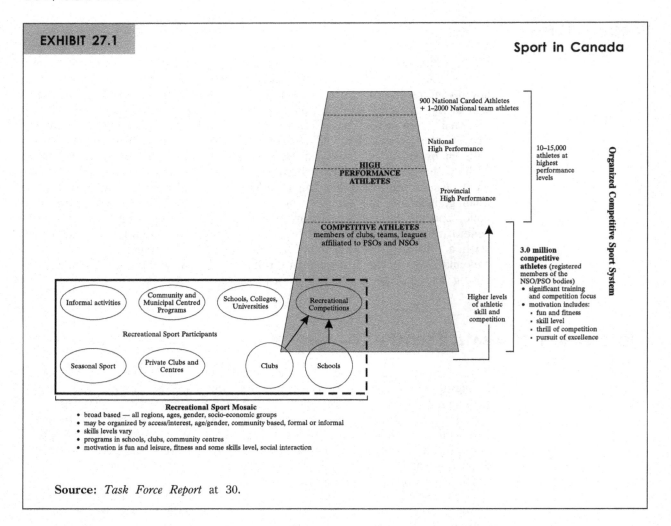

900 National Carded Athletes
+ 1–2000 National team athletes

National
High Performance

**HIGH
PERFORMANCE
ATHLETES**

10–15,000
athletes at
highest
performance
levels

Provincial
High Performance

COMPETITIVE ATHLETES
members of clubs, teams, leagues
affiliated to PSOs and NSOs

Organized Competitive Sport System

**3.0 million
competitive
athletes** (registered
members of the
NSO/PSO bodies)
• significant training
and competition focus
• motivation includes:
  ‣ fun and fitness
  ‣ skill level
  ‣ thrill of competition
  ‣ pursuit of excellence

Higher levels
of athletic
skill and
competition

Informal activities

Community and
Municipal Centred
Programs

Schools, Colleges,
Universities

Recreational
Competitions

Recreational Sport Participants

Seasonal Sport

Private Clubs and
Centres

Clubs

Schools

Recreational Sport Mosaic
• broad based — all regions, ages, gender, socio-economic groups
• may be organized by access/interest, age/gender, community based, formal or informal
• skills levels vary
• programs in schools, clubs, community centres
• motivation is fun and leisure, fitness and some skills level, social interaction

Source: *Task Force Report* at 30.

EXHIBIT 27.2

Description of Sport Levels

CHARACTERISTIC	LEVEL		
	RECREATION	**COMPETITIVE**	**HIGH PERFORMANCE**
Level of Play	informal (i.e., pickup game) to more organized (i.e., university, college, seasonal sport)	extensive involvement in organized sport (i.e., member of team affiliated with national sport organization)	high performance (i.e., at provincial, national and international levels)
Key Motivating Factor	fun, leisure, fitness, social interaction	fun, fitness, excitement of competition, desire to improve skills, pursuit of excellence	pursuit of excellence
Skill Level	some, usually obtained during participation	elevated athletic skill and competition	highest level acquired through extensive training, skill, competition

Source: *Task Force Report* at 30.

Organization of Sport Community

EXHIBIT 27.3

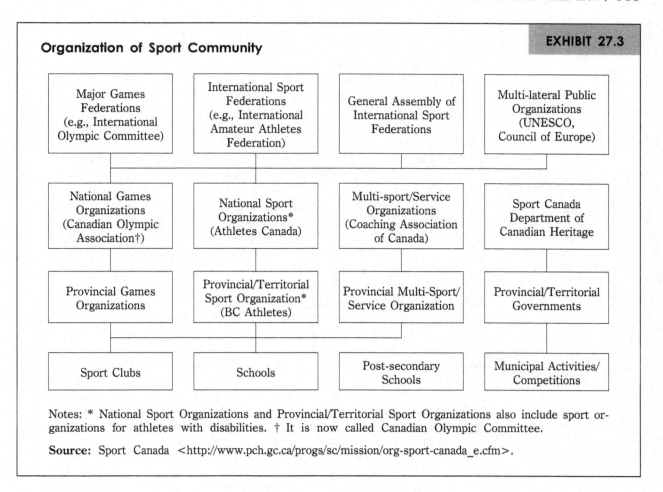

Notes: * National Sport Organizations and Provincial/Territorial Sport Organizations also include sport organizations for athletes with disabilities. † It is now called Canadian Olympic Committee.

Source: Sport Canada <http://www.pch.gc.ca/progs/sc/mission/org-sport-canada_e.cfm>.

tional sport federation and NOCs. International sport federations serve as a governing force for the control and development of their respective sports at an international level. An NSO, in turn, is required to comply with the rules of its ISF. The Canadian Amateur Boxing Association (a national sport organization or NSO), for example, is influenced by, and must comply with, the rules of its respective international federation, the International Amateur Boxing Association (or its more commonly known French acronym, the AIBA). Similarly, a provincial sport organization (or PSO), such as the Ontario Amateur Boxing Association, is influenced by and must comply with the rules of its NSO. Failure to comply with the rules of a governing body means that the governing body likely will not recognize the non-complying organization. In high performance sport, recognition is equated with existence. It follows, therefore, that non-recognition is typically fatal. An organization that is not recognized is ineligible for competition, as competitions are limited to recognized bodies. A competition that includes athletes from unrecognized bodies is considered "contaminated". Athletes from a recognized organization that compete with a "contaminated" athlete themselves become contaminated.

REGULATION OF SPORT

"Amateur" (i.e., "non-professional") sport in Canada is affected at a variety of levels by a variety of laws. The starting point when considering legislative regulation of any area is the *Constitution Act, 1867*. Sections 91 and 92 of this

Act set out the areas within federal and provincial jurisdiction, respectively. These sections are silent, however, when it comes to sport. Despite this silence, private and community organizations that fall within provincial jurisdiction have typically taken a lead in the area of sport development and participation. Constitutional authority for such involvement stems from the provinces having exclusive jurisdiction over areas such as education, property and civil rights, municipal institutions, public lands and general matters of a merely local or private nature (sections 93, 92(13), 92(8), 92(5) and 92(16), respectively).[4] Pursuant to this authority, for example, provincial legislation affecting the area of sport and recreation is enacted.[5] Federal government jurisdiction in the area of sport stems from one of a number of areas, including the exercise of federal "spending power" in order to complement provincial or private contribution[6] or where the matter in issue involves a matter of "national or international significance".[7] Other rationales include sections concerning Parliament's residual authority to enact laws for the peace, order and good government of Canada, trade and commerce, tax, military, criminal law, immigration and citizenship (*Constitution Act, 1867*, sections 91, 91(2), 91(3), 91(7), 91(27) and 91(25) and 95, respectively).

While these constitutional rationales for federal government involvement in sport have existed since 1867, the federal government's support of amateur sport dates from the early 1960s, with the enactment in 1961 of the *Fitness and Amateur Sport Act* (Bill C-131)[8] (FASA) and the creation of the Fitness and Amateur Sport Branch of what was then the Department of National Health and Welfare. (The FASA was subsequently repealed and replaced in 2003 by the *Physical Activity and Sport Act*.[9]) The Fitness and Amateur Sport Branch consisted of a sport unit and a recreation unit. The former unit funded "mainstream" high performance sport organizations (i.e., NSOs), while the recreation unit funded disability-based sport organizations. Federal involvement in sport at that time was fuelled by concerns with the general fitness levels of Canadians, stemming in large part from Canada's results in high performance international competition. An agreement reached between the provinces and territories resulted in a provision in the Act concerning a "federal–provincial agreement" whereby the federal government would contribute funding to sport at the provincial level.[10] A sport organization looking to avail itself of this funding needed to establish that it had a PSO responsible for its sport.[11] Further funding was available where it could be shown that a sport had a NSO responsible for it.[12] The effect of this was that the provinces and territories focused on sport development, from a community level of participation, which includes recreation, to a level of athletic excellence just below national team standards, while the federal government directed its energies to high performance sport at national and international levels.

---

[4] *Supra* note 1 at 10.

[5] Stephen Bird, for example, references a May 1985 publication of the Ontario Ministry of Tourism and Recreation that listed almost 100 Acts and Regulations that affect recreation in Ontario. See: Stephen Bird, *Recreation and the Law*, 2d ed. (Toronto: Thomson Canada, 1997) at 5.

[6] *Supra* note 1 at 11.

[7] *Ibid.*

[8] R.S.C. 1985, c. F-25 (repealed by the *Physical Activity and Sport Act*, S.C. 2003, c. 2, s. 39).

[9] S.C. 2003, c. 2 (Bill C-12). The Act received Royal Assent on 10 March 2003 and the majority of the Act came into force 15 June 2003 (P.C. 2003-941 12 June 2003). (Registration SI/2003-129, 2 July 2003.)

[10] B. Schrodt, "Changes in the Governance of Amateur Sport in Canada" (May 1983) 14:1 *Canadian Journal of History of Sport* 1 at 6.

[11] *Ibid.*

[12] *Ibid.*

In 1993, responsibility for high performance sport was transferred from the Fitness and Amateur Sport Branch of the Department of National Health and Welfare to Sport Canada, a branch of the identity sector of the Department of Canadian Heritage. Paragraph 4(2)(f) of the *Department of Canadian Heritage Act* provided at that time that the Minister of Canadian Heritage had jurisdiction for, among other things, "the encouragement, promotion and development of amateur sport".[13] While the federal focus remains largely the same, the reference to "amateur" was deleted by way of an amendment provided for in the *Physical Activity and Sport Act*.[14] The position of Secretary of State (Amateur Sport), attached to the Department of Canadian Heritage, created in 1998, took on responsibility for high performance sport. The latter position has subsequently been replaced under Prime Minister Paul Martin's government by a Minister of State (Sport) (Stan Keyes). As at 2007, Sport Canada is listed as a branch of the International and Intergovernmental Affairs and Sport Sector within this same department.[15] The Honourable Helena Guergis is presently the Secretary of State (Foreign Affairs and International Trade) and (Sport).[16] Sport Canada's mission as at 2007 "is to enhance opportunities for all Canadians to participate and excel in sport. This is achieved by enhancing the capacity of the Canadian sport system, encouraging participation in sport and enabling Canadians with talent and dedication to achieve excellence in international sport."[17]

The Canadian Sport Policy, released by the federal government in May 2002, outlines four goals to be achieved by 2012:

1. *Enhanced Participation*, demonstrated by the involvement in quality sport activities at all levels and in all forms of participation of a "significantly higher proportion of Canadians from all segments of society";

2. *Enhanced Excellence*, demonstrated by an expanded pool of talented athletes and the systematic achievement of world class results "at the highest levels of international competition through fair and ethical means" by Canadian athletes and teams;

3. *Enhanced Capacity*, as illustrated by having "the essential components of an ethically based, athlete/participant-centred development system ... in place", which are "continually modernized and strengthened as required"; and

4. *Enhanced Interaction*, whereby "the components of the sport system are more connected and co-ordinated as a result of the committed collaboration and communication amongst the stakeholders".[18]

In an effort to achieve these four goals by 2012, Sport Canada provides financial support through three primary programs, two of which include separate sub-components:[19]

---

[13] S.C. 1995, c. 11.

[14] Online: Canada's Parliament <http://www.parl.gc.ca/37/1/parlbus/chambus/house/bills/government/C-54/C-54_3/90184 b-2E.html#20>.

[15] Online: Sport Canada <http://www.pch.gc.ca/progs/sc/index_e.cfm>.

[16] Online: Canadian Heritage <http://www.pch.gc.ca/pc-ch/min/guergis/portfolio_e.cfm>.

[17] Online: Canadian Heritage <http://www.pch.gc.ca/progs/sc/prog/index_e.cfm>.

[18] Online: Sport Canada, *The Canadian Sport Policy*, "Towards the Vision" <http://www.pch.gc.ca/progs/sc/pol/pcs-csp/ 2003/4_e.cfm>.

[19] Online: Sport Canada <http://www.pch.gc.ca/pgm/sc/pgm/index-eng.cfm>.

1. Sport Support Program
   * National Sport Organization (NSO) component;
   * Multisport Service Organization (MSO) component; and
   * Project Stream component.

2. Hosting Program
   * International Major Multi-Sport Games component;
   * International Single Sport Events component;
   * International Strategic Focus Events component; and
   * Canada Games component.

3. Athlete Assistance Program (AAP)

Sport Canada supports a number of initiatives, including mainstream and disability-based sport organizations at a national level (i.e., the Canadian Amateur Boxing Association, the Canadian Wheelchair Basketball Association); multi-sport/multi-service organizations (i.e., the Canadian Olympic Committee, the Canadian Paralympic Committee); and national sport centres. Sport Canada contributes some funding for "major Games" (i.e., the Olympic Games, Paralympic Games) and the hosting of major single-sport events. Some athletes receive funding through the "Athlete Assistance Program". The federal government has also injected monies to develop Olympic and Paralympic champions for upcoming Olympic Games into the Canadian Olympic Committee's "Excellence Fund".[20] The federal contribution is illustrative of the federal government's championing of partnerships and, in particular, the corporate sponsorship of national sport organizations, events and programs. Sport Canada also provides funding for a number of other initiatives, including for Aboriginal people. Initiatives in this area include the Aboriginal Sport Circle (Circle), a "national body" of Aboriginal persons that represents the interests of Aboriginal people in sport, the North American Indigenous Games (NAIG) and Aboriginal coaching initiatives.

Athletes with a Disability

Some persons with disabilities participate in the **mainstream sport** system, while others participate in a **parallel sport system** for athletes with a disability. There are three main global movements, and each movement is focused on a major Games: the Paralympics, the Special Olympics and the World Games for the Deaf. Each movement has an international body that is responsible for co-ordinating its major Games. Domestic development of **sport for athletes with a disability** has reflected the three-pronged international movement. In addition, disability-specific (i.e., amputee, blind) *multi*-sport organizations were created (i.e., the Canadian Amputee Sports Association, the Canadian Blind Sports Association). In some cases a sport organization developed around a specific sport — i.e., the Canadian Association for Disabled Skiing.

Since 1993, a number of sports for Paralympic athletes in Canada have been integrating with mainstream NSOs whereby sport for athletes with a disability becomes an integral part of either all or almost all aspects of the operation of the mainstream sport organization. In addition to the Paralympic movement, the Special Olympics are devoted to athletes with intellectual disabilities. Minimum disability requirements exist to participate in these Games. The Canadian Special Olympics organization has made a concerted effort to

---

[20] See, for example, Martin Cleary, "Project Delivers future Olympians $7.4 million in funding" *The [Ottawa] Citizen* (11 December 2003) B3; and Pierre LeBrun, "Potential medal winners in line for extra cash" *The [Ottawa] Citizen* (26 February 2003) C2.

forge partnerships with mainstream sport organizations in an effort to access more sport-specific technical expertise for training programs for athletes, as well as additional opportunities for competition. The Canadian Deaf Sports Association generally has supported the existence of the World Deaf Games — a parallel sport system for the deaf operated by the deaf. Sport Canada's long-awaited Policy on Sport for Persons with a Disability was made publicly available in June 2006.[21]

Aboriginal Sport

Aboriginal athletes may participate in the mainstream sport system, the disability sport system or an Aboriginal sport system. Another long-awaited policy, Sport Canada's Policy on Aboriginal Peoples' Participation in Sport (Aboriginal Sport Policy), was made publicly available in May 2005.[22] The North American Indigenous Games (NAIG), for example, a "segregated, developing high performance event for Aboriginal athletes"[23], are a component of that system. The NAIG provide

> a culturally appropriate competition venue for a large number of junior Aboriginal athletes to express and enhance their cultural heritage. For Aboriginal community sport leaders and athletes, the NAIG provides an incentive and focus for community sport development and leadership participation. For Aboriginal athletes with high performance potential, NAIG training and competition provide an opportunity to improve skills in readiness for Canada Games team selection trials.[24]

As at 2007, a total of six NAIG have been held: Edmonton, Alberta (1990); Prince Albert, Saskatchewan (1993); Duluth, Minnesota (1995); Victoria, British Columbia (1997); Winnipeg, Manitoba (2002); and Denver, Colorado (2006). The 2008 NAIG is to be held in the Cowichan Valley, British Columbia.

CONTROVERSIES

Adequacy of Support

Funding levels for amateur sport in Canada are a contentious issue among high performance athletes. The "See You In Athens" advertisement was illustrative of this concern. The advertisement depicted athletes living in poverty and carrying a sign that reads "hungry for gold":

> With nearly seventy percent living below the poverty line, what do our athletes have to do next? Beg? The harsh reality is, in the four years leading up to the games, most won't be able to afford proper nutrition, housing, equipment, or even basic essentials like a coach. What kind of country treats their athletes this way? Well, certainly not the Americans, Australians, or Germans. The See You In Athens Fund is a non-profit organization that puts money directly in the hands of athletes who need it.[25]

A further concern arises in light of the considerable funding differences between the mainstream sport system, the sport system for athletes with a disability and the Aboriginal sport system and the athletes participating in

---

[21] Online: Sport Canada, *Policy on Sport for Persons with a Disability*, HTML version <http://www.pch.gc.ca/progs/sc/pol/pwad/tdm_e.cfm> and pdf format <http://www.pch.gc.ca/progs/sc/pol/pwad/pwad_e.pdf>.

[22] Online: Sport Canada <http://www.pch.gc.ca/progs/sc/pol/aboriginal/index_e.cfm>.

[23] Aboriginal Sport Circle, *Aboriginal Sport Development: The Role of Coaching Development, the NAIG and Provincial/ Territorial Aboriginal Sport Bodies* (October 1998) [unpublished] at 7.

[24] *Ibid.* The Canada Games are a biennial celebration of Canadian sport that targets youth under 20 years of age. Athletes from other provinces and territories compete.

[25] See, for example, the advertisement in the *Ottawa Citizen* (19 July 2003) at C5. See also Wayne Scanlan, "Athletes' advocates talking tough" *The [Ottawa] Citizen* (19 March 2003) D1, D7.

those respective systems. Differences are evident, for example, in the three systems with respect to the funding of sport organizations and sport programming and support for major Games and coaching initiatives.

Impact of Tobacco Policy and Legislation on Funding of Sport

Despite the federal government's recognition of, and emphasis on, corporate sponsorship of national sport organizations and events, Sport Canada proceeded to introduce its controversial *Federal Government Policy on Tobacco Sponsorship of National Sport Organizations* (Tobacco Policy) in March 1985.[26] The Tobacco Policy preceded the enactment of, and is entirely independent of, federal tobacco legislation. While the Tobacco Policy is concerned with the prohibition of tobacco sponsorship, the *Tobacco Act*[27] places restrictions on the size, placement and content of sponsorship advertisements by tobacco companies.

The Tobacco Policy provides that

> ... effective immediately, all national amateur sport bodies funded in part by the federal government will be required to desist from associating in any new or renewed sponsorship arrangements with the tobacco products industry. The federal government will withhold all funds from *national amateur sport organizations* associating in any sponsorship, promotional or other financial support arrangements (e.g., advertising) with the tobacco products industry *for events or programs **predominantly** involving **amateur** athletes*.[28] [emphases added]

The policy also provides that a sponsorship contract in existence at the time the policy went into effect would be permitted to run to completion; however, federal funding would be withheld from any sport organization that opted to continue such a contract beyond its expiry date.

While the Tobacco Policy may appear to be well-intentioned, it is clearly designed to make tobacco sponsorship unattractive and to have the effect of restricting the corporate sponsorship of national sport. The policy, however, may not be as limiting as it first seems as there appear to be several loopholes. For example, the policy purports to withhold funds from *national sport organizations*. Explicit reference in the policy to NSOs is significant, as it suggests that while those organizations and their respective programming would be caught by the policy, the policy would likely *not* apply to other bodies receiving federal funding (i.e., national sport centres, major games organizations and athletes receiving funds through the Athletes Assistance Program). The policy's explicit reference to *predominantly amateur* athletes is also relevant, as the policy presumably would not apply to a national sport organization whose membership consisted predominantly of *professional* athletes (provided the organization satisfied all other funding criteria). This policy would also likely not apply to an organization that does not use the word "amateur" to describe its athletes. The latter point, however, could be contested, given that there is relatively little distinction today between an "amateur" and a "professional" athlete.

---

[26] Online: Sport Canada <http://www.pch.gc.ca/progs/sc/pol/tabac-tobacco/index_e.cfm>.
[27] S.C. 1997, c. 13. Bill C-71 (the *Tobacco Act*, with the exception of two subsections, came into force on Royal Assent, 25 April 1997).
[28] *Supra* note 26.

Sport and Charitable Status under the Income Tax Act

"Charitable" status in law is dependent on the common law rather than statute law. The starting point is the preamble to the *Statute of Charitable Uses*.[29] The definition was then succinctly captured by Lord Macnaghten in an 1891 decision commonly referred to as the *Pemsel* decision:

> "Charity" in its legal sense comprises four principal divisions: trusts for the relief of poverty; trusts for the advancement of education; trusts for the advancement of religion; and trusts for other purposes beneficial to the community, not falling under any of the preceding heads.[30]

Sport is not specifically identified in any of these four categories and is, thus, not specifically recognized as having charitable status at common law. This is not to say that sport cannot be a means by which to achieve a recognized charitable purpose in law (i.e., as a part of a general program that promotes participation as a means by which to improve certain physical conditions or overall healthy recreation) or that it does not form part of an overall educational program (i.e., universities, schools).

From the government's perspective, sport for the sake of sport does not qualify for charitable status. As a result, a donation made to a sport organization is not tax exempt, and the recipient organization is unable to issue an official tax receipt. Thus, fundraising attempts by sport organizations have historically proven to be challenging.[31] The federal government, in recognition of the limits posed by this challenge and in an attempt to provide non-profit national organizations that promote amateur sport across Canada with some form of tax relief, amended the *Income Tax Act* in 1972 to provide an equivalent-to-charitable status for Canadian Amateur Athletic Associations (CAAA) (s. 248, s. 149(1)(l)). An organization seeking to qualify for charitable status must apply to be registered — and, if approved, receives the status of a Registered Canadian Amateur Athletic Association (RCAAA). Four types of organizations are eligible for RCAAA status: national sport organizations, multi-sport national and international events (i.e., the Olympics), legacy facilities and multi-sport training centres. In order to apply for RCAAA status, the organization in question completes the required form (T1189). In order to obtain the status of an RCAAA, the organization must satisfy the definition of a CAAA (i.e., it must be created under a law in force in Canada, be a resident in Canada and satisfy the definition of a non-profit organization at paragraph 149(1)(l) of the *Income Tax Act*). In addition, the CAAA's main purpose and function must be to promote amateur athletics in Canada on a "nation-wide basis".

Revocation of status as a *registered* Canadian Amateur Athlete Association is a cause for concern. An RCAAA's status may be revoked for a variety of reasons. While an RCAAA is able to channel its funds to another organization — i.e., a provincial organization — the decision to do so must be that of the RCAAA and not attached as a condition to the donation. An RCAAA that accepts a gift or donation made on the condition (either express or implied) that the recipient RCAAA make a gift or donation to another person or association may, therefore, lose its status (ss. 149(1)(l), 168(1)(f)). An RCAAA may also lose its status where it issues a tax receipt to someone for the payment for a service — i.e., a fee paid to a coach. The basis for this is that there exists a distinction in law between a "gift", for which a receipt may be issued,

---

[29] 1601, 43 Eliz. I, c. 4.

[30] *Com'rs for Special Purposes of Income Tax v. Pemsel*, [1891] A.C. 531 at 583.

[31] A charitable organization can issue an official donation receipt to the donor; the donation is exempt from income tax by the recipient, and the donor may claim tax relief (*Income Tax Act*, R.S.C. 1985 (5th Supp.), c. I-1, ss. 110.1, 149(1) and 118.1, respectively).

and payment for a service that does not qualify as a gift and would, therefore, be ineligible for a tax receipt.

The 2006 Federal Court of Appeal decision on *A.Y.S.A. Amateur Youth Soccer Association v. Canada Revenue Agency*[32] upheld the decision of the Minister of National Revenue to refuse to recognize a sport body, the Amateur Youth Soccer Association of Ontario, as a registered charity on the basis that the promotion of sport was not recognized as a charitable purpose.

A unanimous Federal Court of Appeal wrote the following:

> In formulating this status in 1972, Parliament must be taken to have been aware that no association which has, as its main purpose, the pursuit of amateur sport could qualify as a charity under the common law, and hence, under the Act. That is the background against which Parliament opted to provide a charity-like treatment for amateur athletic associations, but only with respect to those which met the requirements specified in paragraph 248(1).
>
> This brief legislative history shows that Parliament has put its mind to the tax treatment of amateur sports associations and that it was willing to forgo federal tax dollars to promote amateur sport in Canada, but only if the funds were to be expended on a country-wide basis. Parliament did not want to assist in the funding of these associations if the beneficiaries were to be limited to a province or region.
>
> In my view, this scheme precludes the possibility that an amateur sport association be treated as a charity under the Act. Parliament gave these associations a special status under the Act subject to specific terms and conditions. It follows that Parliament must be taken to have occupied the field respecting the tax treatment of amateur sports associations, regardless of their status in the law of charity. Indeed, as this case illustrates, to hold otherwise would frustrate Parliament's clearly expressed intent to limit the federal funding of amateur sports associations to those which operate nationally.
>
> I, therefore, conclude that regardless of the state of common law, the Act forecloses the possibility that an association such as the appellant, whose primary purpose is the pursuit of amateur sport, can be registered as a charity under the Act. ...[33]

The FCA's decision was appealed to the Supreme Court of Canada, which granted leave to appeal. The appeal was dismissed.[34]

Justice Rothstein, writing for eight judges, noted that the fact that an organization did not qualify as an RCAAA was not tantamount to a finding that the organization could not be characterized as a charity within the meaning of the *Income Tax Act*. Put another way, Justice Rothstein did not perceive section 248(1) of the *Income Tax Act* as setting out a complete code for determining whether or not a sport organization was eligible for charitable status. As a result, the fact that the A.Y.S.A.'s mandate was not nation-wide and thus rendered it ineligible for RCAAA status did not mean that it may not qualify as a charity. As a result, Justice Rothstein had occasion to examine the common law test of charity and whether or not the A.Y.S.A. qualified as a charity. Ultimately it was determined that the A.Y.S.A. did not qualify as a charity because its purposes and activities were not considered charitable.[35]

Justice Abella, on the other hand, considered the definition of RCAAA as evidence that Parliament had intentionally excluded other amateur athletic organizations from qualifying for such status and therefore was of the opinion

---

[32] 2006 FCA 136.

[33] 2006 FCA 136 at paras. 20–23.

[34] 2007 SCC 42; available online: <http://scc.lexum.umontreal.ca/en/2007/2007scc42/2007scc42.html>.

[35] 2007 SCC 42 at paras. 1–45.

that resort to the common law test of whether the A.Y.S.A. qualified as a charity was unnecessary.[36]

Commencing in 2007, the Government of Canada now allows a non-refundable tax credit on eligible amounts of up to $500 paid by parents to register a child in an eligible program of physical activity.[37]

UNDER-REPRESENTATION

Sport Canada's *Strategic Directions* established a series of goals in relation to its strategic objectives for the period 1998–2001. One of the goals identified was "to increase access and equity in sport for targeted under-represented groups."[38] The groups identified were women, Aboriginal peoples, visible minorities and athletes with a disability. This goal is reflected in the *Physical Activity and Sport Act* (PASA) (which, it will be recalled, repealed the *Fitness and Amateur Sport Act*). The PASA's objectives include to "encourage, promote and develop physical activity and sport in Canada" (s. 5). The Act's object also provides that "[t]he Minister may take any measures that the Minister considers appropriate to further those objects, and in particular may ... (m) facilitate the participation of under-represented groups in the Canadian sport system" (s. 5(m)).

Sport Canada's website in 2007 listed 10 strategic directions — none of which specifically referenced increasing access and equity in sport for these targeted under-represented groups:

- Strengthen Sport Leadership
- Provide Strategic Support for High Performance Programming
- Promote Technically Sound Sport Development
- Enhance Opportunities for Sport Participation
- Maximize the Benefits of Hosting
- Promote Linguistic Duality in the Canadian Sport System
- Strengthen the Ethical Foundation of Sport
- Expand the Body of Knowledge about Sport
- Strengthen Sport Canada Program and Policy Evaluation
- Harmonize the Canadian Sport System[39]

The fact that these 10 strategic directions do not make specific reference to increasing access and equity in sport for women, Aboriginal peoples, visible minorities and athletes with a disability, however, is not to suggest that one or more of these directions could not be employed to support such efforts. The strategic direction of enhancing opportunities for sports participation, for example, could be considered to support such ends.

Women

The *Sport Canada Policy on Women in Sport* dates to 1986. It provides that Sport Canada will work in co-operation with other levels of government and agencies to "increase participation opportunities for women in all forms of competitive sport."[40] In pursuit of its strategic objective to increase access and

---

36 2007 SCC 42 at paras. 46–59.

37 See Canada Revenue Agency, *Children's Fitness Tax Credit* <http://www.cra-arc.gc.ca/whatsnew/fitness-e.html>.

38 Sport Canada, *Strategic Directions (1998–2001)* (Ottawa: Sport Canada, 1998).

39 Sport Canada, *Mission* <http://www.pch.gc.ca/progs/sc/mission/index_e.cfm>.

40 Sport Canada, *Sport Canada Policy on Women and Sport* (Ottawa: Sport Fitness and Amateur Sport, 1986), online: <http://www.pch.gc.ca/progs/sc/pol/femmes-women/index_e.cfm>.

equity for women, Sport Canada identified as a strategic objective the provision of "leadership and support to achieve equitable opportunities for female athletes, coaches, officials and leaders."[41] While national sport organizations are required to satisfy national "gender equity standards", the "depth and expression" of that commitment varies considerably.[42] According to the Canadian Association for the Advancement of Women and Sport (CAAWS), for example, "inequities in funding and participation opportunities available for women in sport"[43] continue to exist.

The CAAWS seized the opportunity presented by debate surrounding the introduction of a new sport Act to address the issue of gender equity in sport. The CAAWS submitted a request to the House of Commons subcommittee on sport to amend Bill C-54 to include a provision requiring "universities and national sport programs to give equal opportunity and funding for women and men."[44] Following an agreement reached between the CAAWS and then Secretary of State (Amateur Sport) Paul DeVillers, CAAWS agreed to withdraw its demand for the inclusion of this provision. Bill C-54 was reintroduced as Bill C-12 and then enacted as the *Physical Activity and Sport Act*. The key factor informing this agreement was a written commitment from DeVillers that Sport Canada would create "an accountability framework that clearly articulates how existing national standards are to be applied in such areas as funding, coaching and staffing if national sport bodies are to continue to receive funding."[45] According to CAAWS Chair Shawnee Scatliff, "[t]he new accountability framework will smooth out those differences and nudge negligent sports organizations in the right direction."[46] The CAAWS will have a hand in the development and implementation of the accountability framework, including input into the consequences that flow to national sport bodies that fail to satisfy the terms of the accountability framework. DeVillers also promised CAAWS that the government will use the national women's sport strategy currently being developed by the CAAWS to develop a federal program to promote increased physical activity among girls.[47] This latter initiative is timely given that a February 2003 survey found that 67 percent of the women surveyed are too busy to play a sport, while the daughters of 46 percent of the women surveyed recently stopped playing a sport.[48]

The Sport Funding and Accountability Framework (SFAF) is the mechanism employed by the Department of Canadian Heritage to identify which National Sport Organizations and Multi-Sport and Service Organizations are eligible for various Sport Canada funding/contribution programs, in which areas, at which level and under which conditions. The SFAF III is the third edition of the SFAF and covers the funding cycle running from April 1, 2005, through to March 31, 2010.[49]

The SFAF consists of four steps: eligibility, assessment, funding and accountability. The eligibility criteria for NSOs and MSOs are set out in separate documents. The NSOs eligibility criteria are used to create a list of NSOs eligible for assessment by Sport Canada under the SFAF III. In order to

---

[41] Wayne Kondro, "Imposed sport equity 'not appropriate'" *The [Ottawa] Citizen* (24 May 2002).

[42] *Ibid.*

[43] *Ibid.*

[44] *Ibid.*

[45] Wayne Kondro, "Women withdraw gender equity demand" *The [Ottawa] Citizen* (6 June 2002).

[46] *Ibid.*

[47] *Ibid.*

[48] Joanne Laucius, "Many women too busy to play a sport: survey" *The [Ottawa] Citizen* (11 April 2003) A14.

[49] Online: Sport Canada, *Sport Funding and Accountability Framework III (SFAF III): 2005–2010* <http://www.patrimoinecanadien.gc.ca/progs/sc/prog/cfrs-sfaf/sfafelig2005_e.cfm>.

determine if an NSO is eligible for funding, the entity is assessed against a series of criteria. The criteria are designed to determine whether an NSO has "reached a requisite level of development and capacity enabling them to provide technically and ethically safe and sound sport programs and activities that are accessible to all Canadians."[50]

In order to enter the SFAF process and qualify for funding for the 2005–2010 funding cycle, an NSO must complete and submit an eligibility application. This requirement applies to all NSOs, even those that have previously received funding. It is important to note that a determination that an NSO satisfies the eligibility criteria is not tantamount to a finding that the organization will be funded but rather means that the NSO is able to access the next step in the SFAF process (assessment). The assessment stage entails an evaluation of an NSO's size, scope, performance and potential. NSOs are then ranked with respect to contribution of the organization to goals outlined in the Canadian Sport Policy in four areas — participation, excellence, capacity and interaction. Funding levels, in turn, are informed by the assessment scores and tied to the achievement of "National Accountability Standards" as well as compliance with contribution guidelines. A funding decision is made by the responsible minister once the SFAF process is complete.[51]

The first of the four steps, eligibility, consists of three sections: general criteria (Section A), national scope (Section B), and international scope (Section C). In order for an NSO to be considered "eligible", it must satisfy all of the Section A criteria and all criteria in either Section B or Section C. NSOs completing the Section C criteria are to complete it for both mainstream disciplines and disciplines for athletes with a disability. The onus is on the NSO to providing supporting documentation where required. One of the Section A (general) criteria, which must be satisfied by all NSOs in order to be considered for funding, is A13:

> The NSO has a formal policy or policies demonstrating commitment to equity and access, notably for women, persons with a disability and Aboriginal peoples as athletes, coaches, officials, volunteers and leaders.[52]

However, Annex A13 provides that where an NSO exceeds 40 percent female participation or representation in all areas (i.e., athletes, coaches, officials, volunteers and leaders), the NSO is not required to have a formal policy on women and sport.[53]

Aboriginal Peoples

It is undisputed that Aboriginal peoples are under-represented in the Canadian sport system. This is both ironic and troubling given that sport is "deeply rooted in the cultural history of [...] indigenous peoples"[54] and directly related to the cultural experience of indigenous peoples.[55]

While the reasons for Aboriginal under-representation in the Canadian sport system are complex, a few reasons will be briefly canvassed here. A key consideration when discussing such under-representation is a lack of sport programming, facilities and equipment. This absence is attributable, in

---

[50] *Ibid.*

[51] *Ibid.*

[52] *Ibid.*

[53] *Ibid.*

[54] *Supra* note 2 at 153.

[55] Alwyn Morris, "The Olympic Experience: An Aboriginal Perspective" 9–11 at 9 in T. Taylor, ed., *How You Play the Game: Papers from the First International Conference on Sports and Human Rights (September 1–3, 1999)* (Australia: Human Rights Council of Australia, 2000).

considerable part, to the absence of funding for such initiatives. The area of **Aboriginal sport** has virtually been ignored by all levels of government. While the federal government has "jurisdiction" over Indians pursuant to subsection 91(24) of the *Constitution Act, 1867*, it has, until relatively recently, taken very little interest in Aboriginal sport. The federal government, however, has generally adopted the position that Aboriginal sport initiatives did not qualify as "high performance" sport and, thus, were outside the jurisdiction of the federal government. Historically, most provinces have taken the position that Aboriginal sport fell within the federal government's exclusive jurisdiction and, thus, was not a provincial concern. This issue as to responsibility for Aboriginal sport remains unresolved.

"Pro-active" federal government involvement in the area of Aboriginal sport dates to the 1970s when the government, recognizing the absence of opportunities for sport and recreation in Aboriginal communities, initiated several projects designed to assimilate Aboriginal peoples into the mainstream sport system. In an effort to assist Aboriginal athletes to compete in the mainstream sport system, the federal government in 1970 introduced a two-year pilot project that provided funding to Aboriginal associations in five provinces (Alberta, Manitoba, Saskatchewan, British Columbia and Québec) through to 1972.[56] Sub-objectives included broadening the participation base of Aboriginal people, increasing both the quality and diversity of opportunities for Aboriginal people and raising the level of performance in Aboriginal communities.[57] Interest in the two-year initiative spread to Aboriginal groups in other provinces and, ultimately, resulted in the creation of a Native Sport and Recreation Program (NSRP) in 1972. The NSRP, a five-year program structured to aid Aboriginal organizations develop sport and recreation programs,[58] was extended for an additional year (1977–1978). A review conducted that year verified that "sport and recreation [were] integral components of indigenous culture and that the program had facilitated community development significantly."[59] A further two-year extension was granted (1978–1980), and funding was approved for 1980–1981. The funds for that year, however, were not advanced, and the NSRP program was eliminated without notice to, or consultation with, Aboriginal peoples.[60]

The unceremonial demise of the NSRP was apparently owing to a difference in vision. The federal government appears to have supported the development of a segregated sport system that would then be "integrated" into the mainstream system — in other words, Aboriginal athletes would train to attain a level of performance that would enable them to compete in competitive events in mainstream sport with, generally, non-Aboriginal Canadians. This vision, however, kept the sport programming focus on mainstream sport. Aboriginal sport organizations envisioned a model that allowed Aboriginal athletes to participate in the mainstream sport system, if they so desired, but also sought to provide a meaningful alternative — a segregated parallel sport system that included "sport" *and* more "traditional" elements, such as the powwow. The segregation aspect is significant: (i) it provides "for sufficient participation numbers to more equitably meet the needs of Aboriginal young people showing an interest and talent for sport[...]", and (ii) "Aboriginal

---

[56] *Supra* note 2 at 153.

[57] *Ibid.*

[58] *Ibid.*

[59] *Ibid.*

[60] V. Paraschak, "Knowing Ourselves Through the 'Other': Indigenous Peoples in Sport in Canada" in R. Jones & K. Armour, eds., *Sociology of Sport: Theory and Practice* (Essex: Longman, 2000) 153–66 (at 15). Copy of original from Paraschak on file with writer. All page references are to copy on file with writer.

athletes benefit most from early developmental experiences that occur in the supportive environment that retains an Aboriginal orientation."[61]

Following the demise of the NSRP program in 1981, with the exception of the Arctic Winter Games, there were no further attempts at a federal level to develop sport programming in Aboriginal communities until the early 1990s.[62] Renewed federal interest in the 1990s coincided with a series of reports acknowledging the importance of sport to Aboriginal peoples and the under-representation of Aboriginal people in the Canadian sport system: the May 1992 Minister's Task Force Report on Federal Sport Policy,[63] the 1996 report of the Royal Commission of Aboriginal Peoples[64] and a 1998 report of a Sub-Committee of the Standing Committee on Canadian Heritage tasked with studying sport in Canada.[65]

In addition to lack of funding for programming initiatives, remote geographic locations pose challenges for some communities. Aboriginal people living **off-territories** frequently face the challenge of insensitive programs and staff. Stereotypes and **racism**[66] also present barriers. A lack of qualified physical activity and recreation leaders for Aboriginal people and a dearth of Aboriginal coaches present further barriers to Aboriginal participation. Barriers to the development of Aboriginal coaches include difficulties accessing the National Certification Coaching Program, the location of Aboriginal communities, a curriculum that does not address the reality of Aboriginal peoples, and the under-representation of Aboriginal course conductors.[67]

Aboriginal people and their descendants have likened sport to "the strongest type of medicine" because of its "preventative nature",[68] and are championing sport as a mechanism to address "many of the social ills facing Aboriginal people"[69] and the "heightened health risks"[70] faced by Aboriginal youth. While the federal government does contribute funding to Aboriginal sport, it does so in conjunction with access and equity initiatives and not as a right. A contemporary interpretation of the "medicine chest" clause in Treaty No. 6 (and an oral clause in Treaties 7, 8, 10 and 11) may support the inclusion of sport and recreation opportunities.[71] In addition, existing Aboriginal and treaty rights, such as rights flowing from the medicine chest clause in the above-noted treaties, are entrenched in Canada's *Constitution Act, 1982*. If a contemporary interpretation of the medicine chest clause supports sport opportunities, this would mean that an Aboriginal right to sport exists — and is constitutionally entrenched in Canada's Constitution. This line of argument has

---

[61] Aboriginal Sport Circle, *Aboriginal Sport Development*, *supra* note 15 at 7.

[62] *Supra* note 2 at 154.

[63] *Ibid.*

[64] Royal Commission on Aboriginal Peoples, *Bridging the Cultural Divide: A Report on Aboriginal People and Criminal Justice in Canada* (Ottawa: Supply and Services Canada, 1996).

[65] Canada, *Sport — Leadership, Partnership and Accountability — Everybody's Business* (Ottawa: House of Commons, 1998) at 129.

[66] Saskatchewan Interagency Committee for the Elimination of Racism from Sport and Recreation, *Eliminating Racism from Sport and Recreation: A leader's resource* (Saskatoon: The Agency, 1995), online: The Leisure Information Network <www.lin.ca/resource/html/racism.htm>.

[67] Aboriginal Sport Circle, *Aboriginal Sport Development*, *supra* note 15 at 5–6.

[68] Alwyn Morris, *Aboriginal Sport Circle Presentation* (Corner Brook, Newfoundland, 1999) at 9.

[69] *Ibid.*

[70] *Ibid.* at 2.

[71] Susan Haslip, "A Treaty Right to Sport?" (June 2001) 8:2 Murdoch Univ. L. Rev., online: Murdoch University Electronic Journal of Law <http://www.murdoch.edu.au/elaw/issues/v8n2/haslip82.html>; and Susan Haslip & Victoria Edwards, "Does Sport Belong in the Medicine Chest?" in Vicky Paraschak & Janice Forsyth, eds., *Proceedings of the 2002 North American Indigenous Games Research Symposium* (Winnipeg: University of Manitoba, 2003).

interesting ramifications, given that case law supporting the existence of incidental rights may be used to support the existence of incidental rights to
coaching and the existence of sport/recreational facilities.[72]

As noted earlier, the federal government released its long-awaited policy concerning sport and Aboriginal peoples in 2005: *Sport Canada's Policy on
Aboriginal Peoples' Participation in Sport* [*Aboriginal Sport Policy*].[73]

The *Aboriginal Sport Policy* contains a number of strengths. A key starting
point in a consideration on the strengths of the *Aboriginal Sport Policy* is the
existence of the policy itself. The existence of the policy is illustrative of the
ability of Aboriginal and non-Aboriginal Peoples working together to produce a
document that confirms and clarifies Sport Canada's — read this as the federal
government's — intentions concerning the increased participation of Aboriginal
Peoples in sport, recreation and physical education.

The interrelationship between the *Aboriginal Sport Policy* and the *Canadian Sport Policy* (also published by Sport Canada, in 2002) is also an important strength as it illustrates that the *Aboriginal Sport Policy* does not exist
in a vacuum. The *Aboriginal Sport Policy* states that it is guided by the principles in the *Canadian Sport Policy*.[74] One of these principles describes sport
as based on equity and access.[75] The *Aboriginal Sport Policy*'s focus on
increased participation opportunities for Aboriginal Peoples in sport, recreation and physical education provides an example of this commitment in
process. To this end the *Aboriginal Sport Policy* provides that it "aims to
ensure that the vision of the CSP [Canadian Sport Policy] is inclusive; that it
has the power to enhance the experience of — and access to — sport for all,
including Aboriginal Peoples living in Canada."[76] Reference in these policies to
increased participation opportunities for Aboriginal Peoples is related to the
goal of increasing access and equity in sport — a goal confirmed in the *Physical Activity and Sport Act* (citation omitted) enacted in 2003. Reference in both
policies to the barriers faced by Aboriginal Peoples in relation to meaningful
participation in sport,[77] including socio-economic barriers (the significance of
which is discussed in further detail below), is important since it provides
express recognition of these barriers.

The fact that this explicit recognition of barriers appears in a policy document (*Canadian Sport Policy*) endorsed by the federal/provincial/territorial ministers responsible for sport is significant since it provides a baseline from
which to move forward rather than revisit whether such barriers exist.

An additional strength of the *Aboriginal Sport Policy* is its reference to
diversity. This policy provides that while economies of scale dictate the need
for having core organizations serving the "general population",

> *An inclusive sport system serving a diverse population will, by necessity, include
> organizations, programs and events that serve distinct populations.*[78] [emphasis
> added]

The strengths identified in the *Aboriginal Sport Policy* can be utilized to
assist in dismantling the barriers faced by Aboriginal Peoples in relation to

[72] See Haslip, "A Treaty Right to Sport?", *ibid.*; and Haslip & Edwards, *ibid.*
[73] Sport Canada, *Sport Canada's Policy on Aboriginal Peoples' Participation in Sport*; online: <http://www.pch.gc.ca/progs/sc/pol/aboriginal/index_e.cfm>.
[74] Ibid., p. 2.
[75] Sport Canada, *The Canadian Sport Policy*, p. 13; online: <http://www.pch.gc.ca/progs/sc/pol/pcs-csp/2003/polsport_e.pdf>.
[76] *Supra* note 72, p. 1.
[77] *Supra* note 72, pp. 4–5; note 74, pp. 9–10.
[78] *Supra* note 72, p. 2.

participation in sport, recreation and physical education. This being said, however, the effective and meaningful operationalization of statements made by the Government of Canada in both its Aboriginal Sport Policy document and the Canada Sport Policy document concerning Aboriginal peoples require careful monitoring and assessment. By way of example, the *Aboriginal Sport Policy* document provides that "Sport Canada will develop and implement an Action Plan for the Policy on Aboriginal Peoples' Participation in Sport."[79] As of fall 2008, however, this document does not appear to be publicly available from Sport Canada.[80]

Visible Minorities

When this chapter was first written, it was observed that Sport Canada did not have a policy on visible minorities in the Canadian sport system. As of fall 2008, Sport Canada still has not made such a policy publicly available. In pursuit of its strategic objective to increase access and equity for visible minorities, however, Sport Canada indicated it would provide leadership and support to foster the inclusion of visible minorities in the Canadian sport system.[81] The reasons for the under-representation of visible minorities in the Canadian sport system are complex. One factor, however, is racism. An article in the *Ottawa Citizen* reported on a number of incidents in which racial slurs were alleged to have been advanced against athletes in the Ontario Hockey League (OHL). A Sault Ste. Marie Greyhounds player, for example, left his club after learning from teammates that a coach had used a racial slur when referring to him. The player returned following the coach's resignation. The same article also refers to an incident during the 2000–2001 season in which a member of the Barrie Colts received a two-game suspension for a racial slur directed at a Kingston Frontenacs player. A second Barrie Colts' player received a four-game suspension for a comment he reportedly directed at a Sault Ste. Marie Greyhounds goaltender.

The incidents in question are troubling — particularly in light of the fact that "a memo posted in every OHL team's dressing room details the league's policy on harassment, abuse, taunting and slurs based on race and national or ethnic origin."[82] While a policy document will clearly not in and of itself solve the problem of racism in the Canadian sport system, it would serve as an example of much-needed government leadership in this area. The absence of a policy on visible minorities and sport may itself be interpreted as sending a message. Given that slurs concerning sexual orientation are also commonplace in sport, *quare* why reference to sexual orientation is omitted from the policy?

Athletes with a Disability/Disabilities

According to a 1991 Health and Activity Limitation Survey conducted by Statistics Canada, 4.2 million Canadians were living with a disability. Of that 4.2 million, 65 percent (or 2.7 million) were under the age of 65. A 2001 Statistics Canada's Survey provides that 12.4 percent or 3.6 million Canadians have disabilities related to activity and functional limitations.[83] While the latter

[79] Supra note 72, "Implementation", online: <http://www.pch.gc.ca/progs/sc/pol/aboriginal/2005/4_e.cfm>.

[80] For further discussion concerning the Aboriginal Sport Policy and challenges related to its implementation, see Susan Haslip, "A Consideration of Sport Canada's Policy on Aboriginal Peoples' Participation in Sport", Aboriginal Sport Forum Presentation — Barriers to Aboriginal Sport Panel, November 2005, Ottawa.

[81] Kondro, *supra* note 28.

[82] Donna Spence, "Player returning, but Greyhounds' boss quits over racial slur" *The [Ottawa] Citizen* (11 March 2003) B1, B2.

[83] Statistics Canada, "Participation and Activity Limitation Survey: A profile of disability in Canada", *The Daily*, December 3, 2002.

statistic suggests that the number of Canadians with disabilities had declined in the previous decade, there is no reason to believe that the challenges experienced by persons with disabilities have declined. Despite advances made, persons living with a disability or disabilities continue to experience barriers to their full participation in community life. The sport universe is a microcosm of that community life. As such, the physical and attitudinal barriers faced by persons with disabilities in day-to-day life are also experienced by persons with disabilities in the sport world. Athletes with disabilities continue to be under-represented in the Canadian sport system. The federal government has acknowledged this under-representation and promised to "provide leadership and support to increase access and equity in sport for athletes with a disability."[84]

The area of sport for athletes with a disability is complex, and issues arising are multifaceted. One component of this complexity is that the sport community for athletes with a disability is somewhat fragmented. In addition to dealing with issues of gender and race, divisions exist within different disability groups and within the same disability group owing to the severity of the disability. In addition, the sport structure for athletes with a disability is in a state of flux. There is a movement, for example, towards the **integration** of some disability-based sport organizations into their mainstream counterpart. **"Reverse integration"** is also a challenge, where athletes from the mainstream sport system compete in a sport, such as wheelchair basketball, that was conceived for athletes with a disability. At a high performance level, eligibility and classification are key considerations. The three major Games movements (i.e., the Paralympics, Special Olympics and Deaf Sport) each have minimal disability requirements to determine eligibility. Classification systems for athletes based on the type and/or severity of disability exist at the Paralympics. These systems, however, are the subject of controversy. Possible manipulation of divisioning of Special Olympians is also open to dispute.

Sport Canada has made some contributions in the area of sport for athletes with a disability or with disabilities. Inequities in both representation and funding remain. As noted above, Sport Canada's Policy on Sport for Persons with a Disability was released in June 2006. The policy contains a number of strengths, not the least of which is the existence of the policy itself. As is the case with the policy on Aboriginal sport, the Policy on Sport for Persons with a Disability provides that "Sport Canada will develop and implement an Action Plan for its Policy on Sport for Persons with a Disability."[85] As at fall 2007, however, such a document does not appear to be publicly available from Sport Canada.

HUMAN RIGHTS LEGISLATION

Human rights legislation (i.e., provincial human rights codes and the *Canadian Charter of Rights and Freedoms*[86]) also impact the domestic sport system. An interesting case in point is that of Sikh boxer Pardeep Singh Nagra. Nagra was an Olympic hopeful vying for a place on Canada's national team for the 2000 Olympics in Sydney, Australia, in the light-flyweight division (48 kilogram weight class). Nagra is a practising Sikh and, pursuant to the

---

[84] Sport Canada, *Strategic Directions, supra* note 26.

[85] Sport Canada, *Policy on Sport for Persons with a Disability*, "6.0 Policy Implementation and Evaluation", online: <http://www.pch.gc.ca/progs/sc/pol/pwad/6_e.cfm>.

[86] *Canadian Charter of Rights and Freedoms*, Part I of the *Constitution Act, 1982*, being Sch. B to the *Canada Act 1982* (U.K.), 1982, c. 11.

requirements of that faith, is required to "maintain unshorn hair".[87] Nagra's beard, however, worn pursuant to this tenet of his faith, conflicts with the rules of his sport. However, the rules of the International Amateur Boxing Association (more commonly known as the Association Internationale de Boxe Amateur — AIBA), the international sport federation responsible for boxing, require boxers to be clean-shaven. A finding that a boxer is clean-shaven is a component of a successful medical examination at the "weigh in" stage prior to the start of the tournament. Failure to satisfy this threshold results in a boxer being declared ineligible to box. An exception is made for boxers who wear a thin moustache not extending beyond the upper lip. The rules of the Canadian Amateur Boxing Association (CABA), the National Sport Organization responsible for the sport of boxing in Canada, reflect those of its international sport federation, the AIBA. Similarly, the rules of the Ontario Amateur Boxing Association (OABA), the Provincial Sport Organization responsible for the sport of boxing in Ontario, reflect those of its national federation, the CABA.

The OABA, citing the CABA's rules, attempted to prevent Nagra from competing in a provincial qualifying tournament since he was not clean-shaven. Mr. Nagra filed a successful complaint with the Ontario Human Rights Tribunal, which decided that the no-beard rule was contrary to Nagra's rights, and that he could compete if he wore netting over his beard during the competition.[88] Success at this tournament qualified Nagra for the 1999 national championships hosted by the CABA in Campbell River, B.C. The national tournament was a qualifying tournament for membership on the Sydney 2000 Olympic team. This time the CABA took up the fight, arguing that since the CABA's and the AIBA's rules make no exceptions for persons wearing beards, Nagra was in breach of that rule and was ineligible to fight. Nagra sought and obtained an interim order from Justice Somers on December 1, 1999, permitting Nagra to fight at the B.C. tournament.[89]

Justice Somers' decision presented a problem for the CABA. Failure to comply with the court order meant that the CABA could be found in contempt of court. It also meant that Nagra would likely launch a claim for damages due to lost opportunity. Compliance with the court order, however, meant that the CABA would likely face sanctions and repercussions for breach of the rules of its international body. Further, otherwise eligible boxers competing against Nagra could find themselves declared ineligible under the so-called **contamination rule** for fighting with a boxer declared ineligible. The CABA opted to postpone the light-flyweight class in Campbell River until the national intermediate championships in January 2000 in St. Catharines, Ontario. In the interim, it sought and obtained the AIBA's reaction. The AIBA agreed that it if Nagra obtained a court order requiring him to box, the AIBA would not impose sanctions against the CABA to the extent that a court ordered that the CABA's rules be altered. A court order issued from Justice Low on January 12, 2000, declared the CABA's rule prohibiting the wearing of a beard where the boxer did so for "legitimate and bona fide religious reasons" to be "inconsistent with the principles and tenets of Canadian human rights law and

[87] Anne Lowthian, Executive Director, World Sikh Organization, *Ontario Today*, Canadian Broadcasting Corporation Radio (2 December 1999) from 12:31 p.m. to 12:41 p.m. reported by Bowdens Media Monitoring Ltd., Ottawa, Ontario.

[88] J. Christie, "Ministers offer support to boxer" *The Globe & Mail* (9 December 1999), online: *The Globe and Mail* <http://www.globeandmail.com/>. The Ontario *Human Rights Code*, for example, provides that

> Every person has a right to equal treatment with respect to services, goods and facilities, without discrimination because of race, ancestry, place of origin, colour, ethnic origin, citizenship, creed, sex, sexual orientation, age, marital status, same-sex partnership status, family status or disability (R.S.O. 1990, c. H.19, s. 1).

[89] *Nagra v. Canadian Amateur Boxing Assn.* (1 December 1999), Ottawa 99-CV-180990 (Ont. Sup. Ct.).

the Canadian Charter of Rights and Freedoms"[90] and ordered the CABA to permit Nagra to fight at the upcoming tournament in St. Catharines.[91] The CABA neither consented to nor opposed the court order, and no one from the CABA attended the hearing.[92] While the decision ensured that Nagra would be able to fight, he faced opposition outside the ring. Nagra reported that he felt unsafe while preparing for a fight in St. Catharines, Ontario, in January 2000 and that he was threatened by a man carrying a razor and scissors during the national championships.[93] Pursuant to an agreement reached between counsel for both parties, the CABA requested that the AIBA amend its rule concerning boxers and beards and encouraged its provincial organizations (branch members) to follow Justice Low's order. It also provided notice of an amendment to its impugned rule at its 2000 Annual General Meeting.

OFFICIAL LANGUAGES

The *Treasury Board Policy on Official Languages*[94] and the *Official Languages Act*[95] also impact upon the domestic sport system in Canada. Treasury Board policy, for example, provides that

> [i]t is government policy that federal institutions providing grants or contributions to voluntary non-governmental organizations for activities, projects or programs involving service to a public composed of members of both official language communities must take the necessary measures to ensure that the recipients of public funds respect the spirit and the intent of the Official Languages Act when serving the public.[96]

The objective behind this policy is

> [t]o ensure that when grants or contributions are made to voluntary non-governmental organizations serving the members of the public of both official language communities, communications with and services to the public are provided in both official languages in accordance with the spirit and intent of Part IV of the Official Languages Act.[97]

Sport Canada, a branch of the identity sector of the Department of Canadian Heritage, is subject to the *Official Languages Act* (Part IV of this Act, ss. 21–31).

> Where it is determined that an activity, project or program that receives financial assistance is national in scope and provides services to the general public of both linguistic communities, the relevant federal institution is required to ensure that the recipient organization will:
>
> (a) make any announcements to the public concerning the activity, project or program in both official languages;
> (b) actively offer services to members of the public in both official languages;

---

[90] *Nagra v. Canadian Amateur Boxing Assn*, [2000] O.J. No. 850 (Sup. Ct.) (QL).

[91] *Ibid.*

[92] *Ibid.*

[93] No author, "Bearded boxer faced threat at B.C. tourney" *The [Ottawa] Citizen* (3 February 2000) B5.

[94] Sport Canada's website references *Treasury Board Policy on Official Languages* at <http://www.patrimoine canadien.gc.ca/progs/sc/pol/lang/index_e.cfm>. The text of the policy as it appears on the Treasury Board website is available at <http://www.tbs-sct.gc.ca/pubs_pol/hrpubs/offlang/chap1_4-1_e.asp>.

[95] R.S.C. 1985 (4th Supp.), c. 31.

[96] *Supra* note 67.

[97] *Ibid.*

(c) make available in both official languages any documents for the general public relating to the activities, projects or programs;

(d) encourage members of both official language communities to participate in the activities, projects or programs; and

(e) organize activities, projects or programs, when appropriate, in such a manner as to meet the needs of the two linguistic communities.[98]

In light of these requirements, most organizations funded by Sport Canada are required to sign a contribution agreement that sets out the requirements the recipient organization must satisfy in order to receive funding. One such requirement concerns official languages whereby organizations agree to provide services in both of Canada's official languages.

The depth and expression of the commitment to official language requirements, however, varies. Several athletes from national sport organizations, for example, brought their language-related concerns to the attention of then Secretary of State (Amateur Sport) Denis Coderre. Coderre raised his concerns and, in response to these concerns, the Office of the Commissioner of Official Languages commenced an investigation into allegations that French-speaking athletes were unable to develop to their full potential within current sport programs. The Commissioner's first report, released in June 2000, found that these allegations could be readily supported.[99] As a result, 16 recommendations were advanced as part of a strategy to ensure that the Canadian sport system fully reflected Canada's two official languages. Fifteen of the sixteen recommendations were directed at Sport Canada, while the remaining recommendation was directed at the Treasury Board. The Commissioner's follow-up report, issued in June 2003, found that Sport Canada had complied with three of the fifteen recommendations and had partially implemented nine others. Sport Canada failed to address three of the recommendations. The recommendation made to the Treasury Board was partially implemented.[100]

A study funded by the Department of Canadian Heritage, *Linguistic Barriers to Access to High Performance Sport Study — 2005*, notes that Sport Canada's Canadian Sport Policy provides that "linguistic duality is an essential feature of the sports system and that all persons, regardless of language or culture, should be able to participate in this system." The funded report further provides that "the Canadian Sport Policy is aimed at eliminating language barriers imposed on Francophone athletes by providing them with essential services in their own language, such as coaching[...]" and notes that "Sport Canada consulted with the Office of the Commissioner of Official Languages in the course of formulating this policy."[101]

As noted above, the Sport Funding and Accountability Framework (SFAF) consists of four steps. The NSOs eligibility criteria is used to create a list of NSOs eligible for assessment by Sport Canada under the SFAF III. In order to determine if an NSO is eligible for funding, the entity is assessed against a series of criteria. In order to enter the SFAF process and qualify for funding

---

[98] *Ibid.*

[99] Office of the Commissioner of Official Languages, *Official Languages in the Canadian Sports System*, vol. 1 (Ottawa: Public Works and Government Services Canada. 2000), online: <http://www.ocol-clo.gc.ca/docs/e/sport1_e.pdf>.

[100] Office of the Commissioner of Official Languages, *Official Languages in the Canadian Sports System: Follow-Up — Getting a second wind!* (Ottawa: Public Works and Government Services Canada, 2003) at 1, online: <http://www.ocol-clo.gc.ca/docs/e/SportEng.pdf>; see also No Author, "Sport body still getting failing grade in French" *The [Ottawa] Citizen* (12 June 2003) B10.

[101] Mira Svoboda, Senior Consultant, EKOS Research Associates & Peter Donnelly, Ph.D., Director, Centre for Sport Policy Studies University of Toronto, 2006 <http://www.canadianheritage.gc.ca/progs/sc/pubs/obstacles_linguistiques-linguistic_barriers/index_e.cfm>.

for the 2005–2010 funding cycle, an NSO must complete and submit an eligibility application. This requirement applies to all NSOs, even those that have previously received funding. It is important to note that a determination that an NSO satisfies the eligibility criteria is not tantamount to a finding that the organization will be funded but rather means that the NSO is able to access the next step in the SFAF process (assessment).

The first of the four steps, eligibility, consists of three sections: general criteria (Section A), national scope (Section B) and international scope (Section C). In order for an NSO to be considered "eligible" it must satisfy all of the Section A criteria. One of the Section A (general) criteria that must be satisfied by all NSOs in order to be considered for funding is A12:

> The NSO has a formal policy on Official Languages that complies with Sport Canada contribution guidelines on Official Languages.[102]

Annex A12 clarifies that "[a] policy on Official Languages should include how the organization commits to promoting Canada's two official languages within its operations. This policy should extend to the delivery of services in both French and English to athletes within the sport system and to communications with the public."[103] Annex A12 further provides that those NSOs that did not receive funding in 2003–2004 are required to submit a copy of their policies or procedures demonstrating compliance with guidelines.[104]

DOPING

In 1991 Sport Canada introduced a policy on doping in sport. Following two further reviews of the policy in 1998 and 1999, the *Canadian Policy on Doping in Sport* (Doping Policy) came into effect on January 1, 2000.

The Canadian Policy Against Doping in Sport (2004) replaces all previous anti-doping policies (including the 1991 and 2000 versions).[105] This policy provides that doping "involves Prohibited Substances or Prohibited Methods that are designed to enhance sporting performance, pose a real or potential risk to the health and integrity of Athletes and/or are unethical."[106]

The 2004 anti-doping policy in sport is the basis for the Canadian Anti-Doping Program administered by the Canadian Centre for Ethics in Sport (CCES). This program, in turn, is comprised of "General Principles and Rules and Standards for Canadian Sport Organizations, their affiliated members and their Participants who are responsible for implementing it, and is intended to be the basis for any related or complementary policies of Governments."[107]

The policy "commits to the implementation of the mandatory and other portions of the World Anti-Doping Program, including the World Anti-Doping Code, the mandatory International Standards and the Models of Best Practice."[108]

As a condition of receiving federal government funding, NSOs and MSOs are required to adopt the Canadian Policy Against Doping in Sport and to

---

[102] Sport Canada, *Sport Funding and Accountability Framework III (SFAF III): 2005–2010*, online: <http://www.patrimoinecanadien.gc.ca/progs/sc/prog/cfrs-sfaf/sfafelig2005_e.cfm>.

[103] *Ibid.*

[104] *Ibid.*

[105] Sport Canada, *The Canadian Policy Against Doping in Sport*, online: <http://www.pch.gc.ca/progs/sc/pol/dop/index_e.cfm>.

[106] *Ibid.*

[107] *Ibid.*

[108] *Ibid.*

respect the designated authority of the CCES on all anti-doping matters. NSOs and their PSO/TSO affiliates are also obligated to implement anti-doping measures to the extent required by their respective international sport bodies.[109]

The policy applies not only to athletes but also to coaches, doctors and other support staff (i.e., Athlete Support Personnel) and to National Sport Organizations. The basis of the policy's application to individuals is "the contractual relationship which exists between Sport Organizations and their members or Participants through those individuals' agreement to participate in sport according to its rules. Sport Organizations committed to doping-free sport will adopt the POLICY and the General Principles and Rules and Standards of the Canadian Anti-Doping Program as part of their governing documents and thus as an important part of the rules of sport and the rights and obligations governing their members and Participants."[110] Additional information concerning the Canadian Anti-Doping Program may be obtained from the Canadian Centre for Ethics in Sport website (http://www.cces.ca).

The consequences of an athlete tested positive for doping include being stripped of his or her medal(s). Canadian athletes have seen their medal status change. Ben Johnson, for example, was stripped of his gold medal for the 100-metre final at the 1988 Summer Olympics in Seoul, for which he also set a world record, after reportedly tested positive for the anabolic steroid stanozolol.[111] Beckie Scott, a member of Cross Country Canada, saw her medal status change from bronze to gold after the gold and silver medalists were stripped of their medals after reportedly testing positive for a banned blood doping agent.[112]

While issues around performance enhancement in the mainstream sport system are relatively well-known, similar issues arising in the sport movement for athletes with a disability "[remain] unknown and [receive] little publicity".[113] Many Canadians, for example, while familiar with the Johnson situation, would likely be unfamiliar with the fact that, in 1995, "a high-profile Canadian wheelchair athlete was caught by Canadian sport officials using the banned substance stanozolol".[114] Yet it is arguably the case that athletes with a disability may have even more incentive to participate in doping practices:

> In able-bodied sport, centimeters and hundredths of a second can mean the difference between financial glory or no rewards at all. In comparison, athletes with a disability find few financial rewards and public adulation is sparse. Nevertheless, competing (and winning) provides strong personal rewards. Self esteem as an athlete, developing a renewed sense of independence and control, and coping with a disability, all appear to be linked to athletic excellence. These reasons may in fact be more powerful than any financial gain, and an athlete with a disability may be more willing to sacrifice a great deal simply for the opportunity to see [him]/herself as competitive and worthy, in an effort to claim or reclaim a stronger sense of self-esteem and self-worth.[115]

---

[109] *Ibid.*

[110] *Ibid.*

[111] See, for example, No author, "I'm still the best, Ben says" *The [Ottawa] Citizen* (25 September 2003) C7.

[112] See, for example, No author, "Skier Scott set to celebrate medal upgrade" *The [Ottawa] Citizen* (21 October 2003) B3; Dan Barnes, "Five hundred and one days later, a silver lining for Beckie Scott" *The [Ottawa] Citizen* (30 June 2003) D1, D2; Jim Morris, "Canadians find IOC stance on Scott gold mystifying" *The [Ottawa] Citizen* (20 December 2003) C5.

[113] See, for example, David Legg & Daniel S. Mason, "Autonomic Dysreflexia in Wheelchair Sport: A New Game in the Legal Arena?" (1998) 8 Marq. Sports L.J. 225 at 227.

[114] *Ibid.*

[115] *Ibid.* at 236.

There are also some unique doping issues that arise in the world of athletes with a disability. **Autonomic dysreflexia**, for example, entails the self-infliction of bodily harm by athletes to obtain "a naturally-occurring bodily response"[116] — a boost of adrenaline that permits athletes to enhance performance.[117] Self-infliction takes many forms, including distending the bladder by ingesting fluids, clamping or obstructing the catheter, excessively tight leg strapping or tightening, or deliberately inflicting trauma to the lower limb,[118] deliberately twisting or sitting on a scrotum or extended sitting in a race chair or race equipment to raise blood pressure.[119] A spinal cord injured athlete, for example, self-inflicts an injury in an area where he or she does not receive a pain sensation and receives the "benefit" of an adrenaline rush, without the pain.[120] The risks involved with this practice are significant due to elevated blood pressure associated with the desired adrenaline rush. Responses include "cerebral [hemorrhage], blindness, aphasia, seizure, cardiac dysrythmia, retinal [hemorrhage], apnea, cardiac arrest and death".[121]

A number of reports have noted that upwards of 90 percent of wheelchair quadriplegia athletes intentionally induced an autonomic dysreflexia response in order to enhance performance.[122] Despite increased vigilance, however, as at 1998, there were no documented cases of this activity in a sport setting.[123] Legg and Mason posit that, given the prevalence of this form of boosting and given the gain to be provided by boosting, the absence of detection is likely attributable to inadequate control mechanisms and judges concerned about falsely accusing an athlete.[124]

DISPUTE RESOLUTION

Conflict in sport is inevitable.[125] The inevitable nature of conflict is attributed to a variety of factors, including the "'enormous ambition' attached to participating in sport, the scarcity of available opportunities and resources and the great diversity of backgrounds and experiences among participants, nationalities and regions in Canada."[126] Conflicts arise, for example, between an athlete and his or her national sport organization, a coach and a national sport organization and/or an athlete and a coach over issues such as team selection criteria, disciplinary matters and linguistic rights. A conflict may also arise between a national sport organization and its respective international sport federation.

Given the inevitability of conflict in sport, it is surprising to find that little concern was given to the need for a dispute resolution system for sport in Canada until the early 1990s. In 1994, an Alternative Dispute Resolution (ADR) Committee recommended an independent dispute resolution system for sport. The Centre for Sport and the Law introduced such a program in Febru-

---

[116] *Ibid.* at 228.

[117] *Ibid.*

[118] *Ibid.* at 231.

[119] *Ibid.* at 233, n36.

[120] *Ibid.* at 228.

[121] *Ibid.* at 231.

[122] *Ibid.*

[123] *Ibid.* at 231, n29.

[124] *Ibid.* at 235, n43.

[125] Bruce Kidd, News Conference with the Secretary of State for Amateur Sport and Others at 4 (5 January 2000) (transcript available from Media Q Inc.).

[126] Susan Haslip, "A Consideration of the Need for a National Dispute Resolution System for National Sport Organizations in Canada" (2001) 11(2) Marq. Sports L.J. 245 at 247–48 citing Kidd, *supra* note 80.

ary of 1996, but this disbanded in 1997 as a result of federal government funding cutbacks. In January 2000, then Secretary of State (Amateur Sport) Denis Coderre expressed a desire to develop a national dispute resolution system for the high performance sport community. An ADR Work Group was formed and charged with drafting a report that outlined options for a national ADR system. The Work Group's Report, presented to Coderre in June 2000, identified the need for such a system to deal with "widely acknowledged" problems in Canada's high performance sport community.[127]

The *Physical Activity and Sport Act* provides for the creation of such a centre — the Sport Dispute Resolution Centre of Canada. The Centre's purpose is to provide an ADR service for sport disputes for the sport community (s. 10(1)(a)). The Centre has the jurisdiction to hear a variety of disputes, including those among sport organizations and between a sport organizations and those connected with it, including members of the organization (s. 10(2)). The Centre includes a dispute resolution secretariat and a resource centre (s. 9(1)).

CHAPTER SUMMARY

The intersection of sport and the law in Canada presents an interesting dynamic. As the overview of the Canadian sport system suggests, national sport organizations are affected by the rules of their respective international sport federations. Provincial sport organizations are, in turn, impacted by these rules and organizations. Domestic sport organizations are also impacted by a variety of policies and legislation. Sport Canada, the federal body responsible for high performance sport at a national level, has made considerable advances in addressing doping issues and providing for a national body with jurisdiction to hear sport-related disputes. Despite these advances, the federal government also appears to have dropped the ball in some areas, including addressing the under-representation of women, Aboriginal peoples, visible minorities and persons with disabilities in the Canadian sport system. Improvements are still required in the area of official languages. Additional challenges faced by the domestic sport system include concerns with the funding of sport — particularly as it relates to sport for Aboriginal peoples and for athletes with a disability(ies). The federal Tobacco Policy presents considerable obstacles to fundraising efforts by national sport organizations. While amendments to the *Income Tax Act* providing for Registered Canadian Amateur Athletic Associations are of some benefit to sport organizations, restrictions accompanying such status limit a National Sport Organization's flexibility. The intersection of human rights instruments and sport suggests that sport organizations need to be vigilant and take a leadership role in anticipating possible conflicts with their rules and in playing a pro-active role in ensuring that their rules reflect and respect human rights norms.

GLOSSARY OF NEW TERMS AND KEY CONCEPTS

Aboriginal sport	Sport delivered, where possible, at all levels (i.e., national, provincial/territorial, regional, local) by and for Aboriginal peoples.
Aboriginal peoples	Defined in the *Constitution Act, 1982*, as the Indian, Métis, and Inuit people of Canada.

[127] Haslip, *supra* note 91 at 263.

athletes with a disability	Athletes with a physical, sensory and/or intellectual disability. This phraseology is important since it places emphasis on the *athlete* and not the disability.
autonomic dysreflexia	The self-infliction of bodily harm by athletes to obtain an adrenaline boost to enhance performance.
contamination rule	A rule in high performance sport providing that where a competition is not formally recognized or sanctioned by its respective sport body, a participant in such a competition is considered "contaminated". As a result of this status, any athlete competing with a "contaminated athlete" is also considered "contaminated".
integration	A process of planning and providing for opportunities for athletes with a disability and/or sport for athletes with a disability to work together with non-disability-based (i.e., mainstream) sport organizations.
mainstream sport	The "traditional" sport system.
off-territory	A term used in reference to Aboriginal peoples in Canada living in urban and rural areas that are outside of reserves created by the federal government.
parallel sport system	A separate venue for sport that operates separately from the mainstream sport system. Examples include sport systems for Aboriginal peoples and athletes with a disability or disabilities.
racism	Prejudicial or stereotypical acts, attitudes, comments or institutional structures that lead to discrimination or harassment directed towards a group on the basis of its ethno-cultural background, perceived racial origin or colour.
reverse integration	Where athletes from the mainstream sport system compete in a sport conceived for athletes with a disability.
sport for athletes with a disability	Training and competition for athletes with a disability as well as related support systems.
under-representation	A situation where an identifiable group of persons in a sphere such as sport are not represented in proportion to their representation in the general population. Examples include women, Aboriginal peoples, visible minorities and athletes with a disability.

REVIEW QUESTIONS

1. Identify areas where sport and the law intersect in Canada.
2. Explain how sport is organized in Canada.
3. Describe how the organization of sport in Canada relates to jurisdictional responsibility for sport.
4. How does the Minister's Task Force on Federal Sport Policy define "sport"?
5. Describe the difference between recreational, competitive and high performance sport.
6. How does the high performance sport system fit within the international sport movement?
7. Identify government initiatives for Aboriginal sport.
8. Describe the importance of the North American Indigenous Games to Aboriginal peoples.
9. Identify challenges facing sport organizations seeking to raise funds in Canada.
10. Identify concerns arising with the funding of sport in Canada.

11. What is the Tobacco Policy? Explain how this policy impacts national sport organizations.

12. What benefits accrue to Registered Canadian Amateur Athletic Associations?

13. How can an RCAAA lose its status?

14. Identify groups currently under-represented in the Canadian sport system.

15. What general pronouncements has the federal government made concerning addressing the under-representation of these groups?

16. How did the Canadian Association for the Advancement of Women in Sport respond to the proposed *Physical Activity and Sport Act*? What was the basis for this response? How was the matter addressed?

17. Outline the history of the federal government's involvement in sport for Aboriginal peoples.

18. What is reverse integration?

19. How do human rights instruments impact on sport in Canada?

20. Explain the dilemma faced by a national sport organization where human rights law conflicts with the policies of its international sport federation.

21. How do federal initiatives, such as legislation and policy on official languages, impact the national sport system?

22. Which body is responsible for monitoring doping in the Canadian sport system?

23. Identify a concern with doping unique to athletes with a disability.

24. Identify the organization that has legislative jurisdiction to deal with disputes arising in sport in Canada. What sort of disputes can be heard through this organization?

25. Identify and describe a concern arising with the introduction of the Aboriginal Sport Policy.

DISCUSSION QUESTIONS

1. Does the law have a place in the Canadian sport system?

2. Is the expenditure of tax dollars to support a select group of high performance athletes justifiable?

3. Were advertisements promoting the "See You in Athens" effort appropriate?

4. Should a sport organization be able to circumvent the federal tobacco policy by not using the word "amateur" to describe its athletes?

5. Should concerns with access and equity be addressed by government at the level of high performance sport?

6. Can parallel sport systems be justified?

7. Justice Low declared the Canadian Amateur Boxing Association's (CABA) rule prohibiting the wearing of a beard where the boxer did so for bona fide religious reasons to be inconsistent with the principles of human rights instruments (i.e., human rights codes, the Charter) and

ordered the CABA to permit Mr. Nagra to fight at the upcoming tournament in St. Catharines. Explain how you would have decided that case.

8. Describe the significance of the judgment of Justice Rothstein in *A.Y.S.A. Amateur Youth Soccer Association v. Canada Revenue Agency*, 2007 SCC 42; online: <http://scc.lexum.umontreal.ca/en/2007/2007scc42/2007scc42.html>.

SUGGESTED READINGS

GENERAL

Barnes, John. *Sports and the Law in Canada*, 3d ed. (Toronto: Butterworths, 1997).
Bird, Stephen. *Recreation and the Law*, 2d ed. (Scarborough: Thomson, 1997).
Canada. *Canadian Sport Policy* (Hull, Québec: Sport Canada, 2002).
Canada. *The Canadian Sport Policy: Federal-Provincial/Territorial Priorities For Collaborative Action 2002–2005* (Hull, Québec: Sport Canada, 2002).
Canada. *Towards A Canadian Sport Policy: Report on the National Summit on Sport* (National Summit on Sport — Ottawa, April 27–28, 2001) (Ottawa: Public Works and Government Services Canada, 2001).
Canada, Sport Canada. *Strategic Directions (1998–2001)* (Ottawa: Sport Canada, 1998).
Canada, House of Commons. *Sport — Leadership, Partnership and Accountability — Everybody's Business* (Ottawa: Sub-Committee on the Study of Sport in Canada, 1998) (Chair: Clifford Lincoln).
Crossman, Jane, ed. *Canadian Sport Sociology* (Scarborough: Thomson, 2003).
Holman, Margery, Dick Moriarty & Janice Forsyth, eds. *Sports, Fitness and the Law: North American Perspectives*, 2d ed. (Toronto: Canadian Scholars' Press, 2001).
Minister of State Fitness and Amateur Sport. *Sport: The Way Ahead — The Report of the Minister's Task Force on Federal Sport Policy* (Ottawa: Minister of Supply and Services Canada, 1992).
Schrodt, B. "Changes in the Governance of Amateur Sport in Canada" (May 1983) 14:1 *Canadian Journal of History of Sport* 1.

Website

Sport Canada: Home, <http://www.pch.gc.ca/progs/sc/index_e.cfm>; Strategic Directions, <http://www.pch.gc.ca/progs/sc/mission/index_e.cfm>

ABORIGINAL SPORT

Canada. *Policy on Sport Canada's Policy on Aboriginal Peoples' Participation in Sport* (Hull, Quebec: Public Works and Government Services Canada, 2005).
Haslip, Susan. "A Consideration of Sport Canada's Policy on Aboriginal Peoples' Participation in Sport". Paper presented at 2005 Aboriginal Sport Forum — Ottawa 2005, in Vicky Paraschak & Janice Forsyth, eds., *Aboriginal Sport Forum Proceedings* (Ottawa: Sport Canada, 2006).
Haslip, Susan. "A Treaty Right to Sport?" (June 2001) 8:2 Murdoch Univ. L. Rev., online: Murdoch University Electronic Journal of Law <http://www.murdoch.edu.au/elaw/issues/v8n2/haslip82.html>.
Haslip, Susan, & Victoria Edwards. "Does Sport Belong in the Medicine Chest?" in Vicky Paraschak & Janice Forsyth, eds., *Proceedings of the 2002 North American Indigenous Games Research Symposium* (Winnipeg: University of Manitoba, 2003).
King, C. Richard, ed. *Native Americans and Sport* (Armonk, N.Y.: M.E. Sharpe, 2004).
Morris, Alwyn. "The Olympic Experience: An Aboriginal Perspective" 9–11 at 9 in T. Taylor, ed., *How You Play the Game: Papers from the First International Conference on Sports and Human Rights (September 1–3, 1999)* (Australia: Human Rights Council of Australia, 2000).
Paraschak, Vicky. "Knowing Ourselves Through the 'Other': Indigenous Peoples in Sport in Canada" in R. Jones & K. Armour, eds., *Sociology of Sport: Theory and Practice* (Essex: Longman, 2000) 153.
———. "The Native Sport and Recreation Program, 1972–1981: Patterns of Resistance, Patterns of Reproduction" (1995) 26:2 *Canadian Journal of History of Sport* 1.
Robinson, Laura. "Native runners honoured decades after relay" *The [Ottawa] Citizen* (3 November 2003) A2.

ATHLETES WITH A DISABILITY
Canada, Sport Canada. *Policy on Sport for Persons With A Disability* (Hull, Quebec: Public Works and Government Service Canada, 2006).
Canada (Statistics Canada). Participation and Activity Limitation Survey: A profile of disability in Canada, *The Daily*, December 3, 2002.
DePauw, Karen P., & Susan J. Gavron. *Disability and Sport* (Champaign, Illinois: Human Kinetics, 1995).
Gregson, Ian. *Irresistible Force: Disability Sport in Canada* (Victoria: Polestar, 1999).

DISPUTE RESOLUTION
Sport Canada. *A Win-Win Solution: Creating A National Alternate Dispute Resolution System For Amateur Sport in Canada* / Report of the Work Group to the Secretary of State (Amateur Sport) (Hull, Québec: Secretary of State (Amateur Sport) = secrétaire d'état au Sport amateur, 2000).
Corbett, R., H. Potter & H.A. Findlay. *Administrative Appeals — A Handbook for Sport Organizations* (Edmonton: Centre for Sport and Law, 1995).
Haslip, Susan. "A Consideration of the Need for a National Dispute Resolution System for National Sport Organizations in Canada" (2001) 11:2 Marq. Sports L.J. 245.
———. "Just Do It? A Consideration of Alternative Dispute Resolution and Amateur Sport" in *Proceedings of the Conflict Resolution Symposium: 2000* (Ottawa: Carleton University, 2001).
———. "Takin' my ball and goin' home: Amateur Sport and ADR" (Spring 2000) *Canadian International Institute of Applied Negotiations News* 12.
———. "Leveling the Playing Field: A Consideration of the Need for an Alternative Dispute Resolution System for High Performance Sport in Canada" (April/May 2000) 11:2 For the Record 3.
Haslip, Susan, & Victoria Edwards. "Parent Contracts — A Mechanism for Playing Nicely Together?" (Spring 2002) Canadian International Institute of Applied Negotiations News 8.
———. "Putting the Fun Back into Sport: Parent Contracts as a Mechanism for Managing Conflict — Are We There Yet?" in *Proceedings of the Conflict Resolution Symposium: 2001* (Ottawa: Carleton University, 2001).

Website
ADRsportRED: <http://www.adrsportred.ca/>.

DOPING
Canada. *Canadian Policy Against Doping in Sport* (2007), online: <http://www.pch.gc.ca/progs/sc/pol/dop/index_e.cfm>.
Canada, Sport Canada. "Canadian Policy on Doping in Sport", online: <http://www.pch.gc.ca/progs/sc/pol/dop/index_e.cfm>.
Canada, Sport Canada. *Canadian Strategy for Ethical Conduct in Sport: Policy Framework* (24 May 2002), online: <http://www.pch.gc.ca/progs/sc/pol/eth2002/StEthic.pdf>.
Hatch, Hilary Joy. "On Your Mark, Get Set, Stop! Drug-Testing Appeals in the International Amateur Athletic Federation" 16 Loyola L.A. Int'l & Comp. L.J. 537.
Legg, David, & Daniel S. Mason. "Autonomic Dysreflexia in Wheelchair Sport: A New Game in the Legal Arena?" (1998) 8 Marq. Sports L.J. 225.

Website
Canadian Centre for Ethics in Sport: <http://www.cces.ca>

OFFICIAL LANGUAGES
Canada, Sport Canada. "Treasury Board Policy on Official Languages", online: <http://www.patrimoinecanadien.gc.ca/progs/sc/pol/lang/index_e.cfm>.
Canada, Sport Canada. *Sport Funding and Accountability Framework III (SFAF III): 2005–2010*, online: <http://www.patrimoinecanadien.gc.ca/progs/sc/prog/cfrs-sfaf/sfafelig2005_e.cfm>.
Office of the Commissioner of Official Languages. *Official Languages in the Canadian Sports System*, vol. 1 (Ottawa: Public Works and Government Services Canada, 2000), online: <http://www.ocol-clo.gc.ca/docs/e/sport1_e.pdf>.
———. *Official Languages in the Canadian Sports System: Follow-Up — Getting a second wind!* (Ottawa: Public Works and Government Services Canada. 2003) at 1, online: <http://www.ocol-clo.gc.ca/docs/e/SportEng.pdf>.

Svoboda, Mira & Peter Donnelly. 2006. *Linguistic Barriers to Access to High Performance Sport Study — 2005*, online: Sport Canada <http://www.canadianheritage.gc.ca/progs/sc/pubs/obstacles_linguistiques-linguistic_barriers/index_e.cfm>.

Website
Department of Canadian Heritage: <http://www.patrimoinecanadien.gc.ca>

TOBACCO
Canada, Sport Canada. "Federal Government Policy on Tobacco Sponsorship of National Sport Organizations" (March 1985), online: <http://www.pch.gc.ca/progs/sc/pol/tabac-tobacco/index_e.cfm>.

WOMEN
Canada, Sport Fitness and Amateur Sport. *Sport Canada Policy on Women and Sport* (Ottawa: Sport Fitness and Amateur Sport, 1986), online: Sport Canada <http://www.pch.gc.ca/progs/sc/pol/femmes-women/index_e.cfm>.

Smith, Lissa, ed. *Nike is a Goddess: The History of Women in Sports* (New York: Atlantic Monthly Press, 1998).

Website
Canadian Association for the Advancement of Women and Sport and Physical Activity: <www.caaws.ca>

CASES OF SIGNIFICANCE
United Kingdom
Com'rs for Special Purposes of Income Tax v. Pemsel, [1891] A.C. 531.

Canada
A.Y.S.A. Amateur Youth Soccer Association v. Canada Revenue Agency, 2006 FCA 136.
A.Y.S.A. Amateur Youth Soccer Association v. Canada Revenue Agency, 2007 SCC 42.
Nagra v. Canadian Amateur Boxing Assn. (1 December 1999), Ottawa 99-CV-180990 (Ont. Sup. Ct.).
Nagra v. Canadian Amateur Boxing Assn., [2000] O.J. No. 850 (Sup. Ct.) (QL).

RELEVANT LEGISLATION
Domestic
Canadian Charter of Rights and Freedoms, Part I of the *Constitution Act, 1982*, being Sch. B to the *Canada Act 1982* (U.K.), 1982, c. 11.
Constitution Act, 1982, being Sch. B to the *Canada Act 1982* (U.K.), 1982, c. 11.
Department of Canadian Heritage Act, S.C. 1995, c. 11.
Fitness and Amateur Sport Act, R.S.C. 1985, c. F-25 [repealed].
Income Tax Act, R.S.C. 1985 (5th Supp.), c. I-1.
Official Languages Act, R.S.C. 1985 (4th Supp), c. 31.
Ontario *Human Rights Code*, R.S.O. 1990, c. H.19.
Physical Activity and Sport Act, S.C. 2003, c. 2.
Tobacco Act, S.C. 1997, c. 13.

International
Olympic Charter, online: Olympic Movement <http://multimedia.olympic.org/pdf/en_report_122.pdf>

Family Law

Laurence M. Olivo
SENECA COLLEGE

Learning Objectives

After reading this chapter, the reader should be able to:

➣ understand what areas are generally considered part of family law in Canada

➣ appreciate the extent to which economic, social, and cultural factors shape family law

➣ appreciate the extent to which family law has evolved in the past few decades, and be aware of the forces that have led to that evolution

➣ understand the contractual nature of the engagement and of marriage

➣ know the requirements of a valid marriage

➣ know what constitutes a common law relationship and, generally, know what consequences flow from such a relationship

➣ know what the grounds for divorce are, and the consequences that flow from divorce in respect of custody, support, and property division

➣ be aware of situations where a marriage might be subject to annulment instead of divorce

➣ understand and apply concepts that determine custody, support, and property division

➣ trace the process whereby a child might proceed from being a child in need of protection to becoming a Crown ward being placed for adoption

➣ distinguish among the different routes to adoption

TABLE OF CONTENTS

INTRODUCTION: THE SCOPE OF FAMILY LAW

In Canada, most people consider "family law" to be basically about divorce, and of course, divorce *is* a big part of family law. However, family law can best be understood by thinking of families as going through a sort of life cycle. At various stages in the cycle, legal issues arise that are part of family law. Here is an overview.

Family Formation

At this stage, when a couple decides to form a permanent relationship, there are social and legal changes in their status that affect their rights and responsibilities. If they marry, certain legal rights and liabilities follow. If the couple intends to form a permanent relationship without the formalities of an engagement or marriage, there are still legal consequences that will flow from this arrangement, although they will differ in some respects from the consequences of marriage. Family formation rules will affect families that are composed of same-sex partners, with or without children. Further, while we usually assume that a family is based on a conjugal (sexual) relationship, that may not always be the case. Thus, we will often have to consider as a "family" other kinds of permanent relationships: for example, a single adult raising an adopted child or an unrelated child, or two siblings living together.

Family Dissolution

If the partnership between the couple does not work out and they decide to end it, then it becomes necessary to deal with the consequences of the termination. If the parties were formally married, then they will probably wish to have their union formally terminated by a divorce, although they need not do so unless one or the other wishes to remarry. However, even if they decide to live separately without divorcing, decisions will have to be made about the care and support of the couple's children, the support of a spouse who is not able to be self-supporting, and how the property acquired during the marriage is to be disposed of. In many respects the law dealing with the dissolution of a family resembles the law relating to the dissolution of a business partnership. As we will see later, the legal similarity between dissolutions of families and partnerships is not an accident.

Family dissolution, where a couple separates and each party goes his or her own way, is what most people understand "family law" to be about; indeed, most lawyers who practise in this area spend much of their time attending to separation, divorce, and its consequences. However, there are other ways in which destructive forces can cause families to become dysfunctional and to disintegrate. This situation gives rise to legal rights and remedies that are different from those that arise when spouses decide to dissolve their family unit.

Child Protection

While adults are presumed to be competent to protect their own interests, the law recognizes that children are not able to protect themselves when destructive forces begin to affect a family. Where the adults in a family, for whatever reason, are unable to properly care for a child, or they neglect or abuse a child, the law may step in to declare that child to be in need of protection. This usually happens when the parents or other adults responsible for the child's care are unable to provide proper care. The law's intervention here is independent of any decision by spouses to end their relationship. Intervention is entirely dependent on whether or not the child is in some danger that triggers the operation of the law. Child protection legislation is designed to protect the child, at first, within the family unit, which often means providing assistance to the family as well as to the child. If this approach does not work, then the state reserves the right to protect the child by removing it from a dysfunctional family, and placing it in a family, or in another social setting, where the child will be protected and cared for.[1]

There is another aspect of child protection that is relatively new and is not necessarily connected to family dissolution or dysfunction. While traditional child protection law is concerned with ensuring that children do not come to harm in the face of obvious situations of danger, new initiatives in this area focus on ensuring that children have equal access to benefits that all children should have. For example, recent developments have focused on the right of children to education and treatment that will meet their particular needs, rather than focusing on merely giving access to whatever education or treatment might be available.

Adoption

When a family has been dissolved by divorce, or is non-existent, or has become non-functional for other reasons, social and legal decisions have to be made so that children will continue to receive care and nurturing within a family setting, if possible. In divorce situations, this problem is often dealt with by giving one parent custody of the child, but having both parents remain involved with the child. Where neither parent is able, nor prepared, to care for a child, then the law allows for the child to be adopted into another family; at that point, the child ceases to be a member of its former family and becomes, legally, the child of the adopting family.

ORIGINS OF CANADIAN FAMILY LAW

So far, we have described some of the subjects and issues that are the concern of family law. We now turn to examine some of the historical, social, cultural, and legal forces that give rise to family law in Canada.

The Role of the Family in Society

To understand how family law developed, it helps to examine the role of the family in society in Britain and Europe from the end of the Middle Ages to the present, as this was the place and time in which family law as we know it developed. The family — often in its extended form, including more than one generation under one roof — was the basic unit of society. It performed many functions now performed in whole or in part elsewhere: e.g., education and the care of old, sick, and disabled members. Then as now, the family also functioned as an economic unit, organizing its resources and members to maximize wealth.

The family unit was rigidly structured. The oldest male member usually directed the family and controlled its female and more junior members. Both society and the law saw a husband and wife as one person — and that person was the husband. As head of the family, he could determine to whom, and in what trade, his son was to be apprenticed; he could determine what land should be bought or sold; he could decide the type and level of education his children would receive, and he was in charge of religious training and belief, as well. It is important that he could also decide whom his children could marry — it was his choice, not his wife's, and certainly not his children's.

His word was law within the family. Any opposition could be met with various forms of corporal punishment that might today be considered crimi-

---

[1] The idea that the child should not be taken from the family except as a last resort is beginning to give way to the idea that physical protection of the child should take precedence over the preservation of a poorly functioning family. This trend is observable in amendments to child protection legislation passed in Ontario in 1999.

nal assault. The ultimate penalty was expulsion from the family. In an age before social-welfare institutions, becoming disconnected from one's family had serious consequences, both economic and social. This was particularly so for women, whose economic needs, until the Industrial Revolution, were primarily met by performing domestic work within the family, not by working outside the home. There were not, prior to the 20th century, many jobs available for women outside the home: if we look at European literature from before the 20th century, we see few women described as working outside the home, unless they are unmarried — and even then, there was an expectation that marriage would put an end to such employment.[2]

In literature, the woman who was beyond marriageable age and still single was often seen as pitiful or laughable: occupying economically marginal positions, or reduced to the role of economic dependant of other family members. No one would argue that the role of "spinster" or "maiden aunt" was desirable or glamorous or that it conferred high social standing or economic clout.[3] An exception to this was the single woman who controlled wealth: a rich woman who did not marry actually had an advantage over a rich woman who did marry. Until the 1880s, in most North American jurisdictions, a married woman lost the right to own and control her property — her property rights passed to her husband on marriage. A single woman, on the other hand, had the same rights over property as a man. Generally, however, a woman acquired wealth and status as either a daughter or a wife, in a family setting, but rarely as a person in her own right.

A Marriageable Woman as a Form of Moveable Sexual Property

Prior to this century, a woman's economic value to the family resulted from her ability to maintain the family unit by providing domestic services and by providing heirs. Her skills and potential here determined, in part, her marriageability, as did whatever wealth she might bring with her in the form of a **dowry** (which made her an economically more attractive proposition over other competitors; after all, any marriageable woman could be expected to be able to bear children and run a house). A woman without a dowry had diminished opportunities for marriage. She could expect either not to marry or to marry someone relatively undesirable: someone of lower social or economic status than her own family's, or someone old or unpleasant, or both.

The importance of a dowry reflected the family's strategy in arranging a marriage for a daughter. What a father hoped to do was make an economically advantageous match for his daughter (i.e., that her economic needs, currently met by the father, would now be met by her husband) and for his own family by creating an economic alliance with another family. This was a common practice among European royalty, who married their children to the children of kings of other countries in order to reinforce diplomatic or other political alliances between nations. On a smaller scale, a farmer might make a match for his daughter with the son of an owner of adjacent land, with a view that the two farms might eventually be combined to form a more powerful economic unit.[4]

---

[2] Well into the 20th century in North America, women schoolteachers were required to resign their positions when they married.

[3] The role of widow, however, might indeed confer high status, which came not from widowhood but from the status of the widow's deceased husband and the wealth that he left her. Ultimately, it could be said that the widow's status came from the fact that she had been a married woman.

[4] This discussion of economic factors in marriage arrangements applies to the middle and upper classes. The poor did not have an economic surplus to provide dowries for daughters. Conversely, this gave more freedom to a woman from a poor family, as economic factors played a much smaller role in choosing a mate. Did poorer women then get to marry for love or have more control over choosing a mate? Perhaps, although unlike the middle and upper

In this environment, the senior male relative arranged the marriage and had to consent to the arrangement. Men and women did not choose their own mate; romantic love or magnetic attraction was not a factor to be considered, and certainly it was not the basis for the choice. It might well be the case that the bride and groom did not even meet until shortly before the marriage. Again, an examination of European literature reveals that love relationships often feature men and women who are unmarried and unlikely to marry each other, or who are married but not to each other. The relationship of Romeo and Juliet is a good example of the impossible relationship where love is front and centre, but marriage unlikely.

Physical attractiveness was a plus, but not a requirement. A woman's chastity and her ability to bear children, however, were extremely important, although verifying these qualities before marriage was difficult. Chastity had a symbolic and practical importance. A chaste woman was assumed to be obedient and controllable: good qualities in a wife. A woman chaste at the time of marriage might also be assumed to be chaste after marriage, providing exclusive sexual services for her husband. This was not just a question of loyalty and obedience. In a world where wealth was centred on the family and passed on to younger generations within a family by inheritance, it became important to know that the heirs were, biologically, the husband's heirs. We can think of wives, in this context, as the conduit through which family wealth could be transmitted over time and preserved within the family over time.

To conclude the overview of a woman's position in a traditional family, her value lay in domestic and breeding skills, which made her a marriageable commodity that her senior male relative could dispose of to his, and the family's, benefit as if she were a piece of moveable sexual property to be transferred to the highest bidder.

Sources of Canadian Family Law

English Family Law Underlying Family Law in Canada

Early Canadian family law, like much else legal, was inherited from England. What follows is a quick overview of English common law in the premodern period. The most significant thing about English family law was that there was not much of it. As the family structure was **patriarchal**, many of the decisions affecting its members were not legal matters at all but were left to the father as lawmaker and decision maker. The power, to be sure, was not unlimited: a father could not kill a disobedient family member without being punished by the state's legal system. Such law as there was often served to back and support the senior male decision maker and, generally, to preserve the structure of the family against forces that might subvert it.

A principal rule here was the common law doctrine referred to as the **unity of personality**. It defined a married couple as a unitary body. This meant that a husband and wife were one person for the purpose of the law in family-related matters and that control of the person was vested in the husband. In family matters, therefore, so long as her husband lived, the wife had no legal control over family property or over children. She could not sue or be sued in her own name, and she was bound by her husband's decisions in legal matters. This effectively allowed a husband to add legal powers over the family to the economic and other power that he already enjoyed.

---

classes, the poor did not leave evidence in the form of written records, such as marriage contracts, deeds, or correspondence.

The woman was in no better position as a daughter than she was as a wife. As noted earlier, her father had the right to dispose of her in marriage. While technically, as a matter of the law of marriage, she had to freely consent to the marriage, enormous economic and social pressures could be brought to obtain that consent. Once a woman was disposed of in marriage, control over her passed from her father to her husband, who then had legal control as a result of the unity of personality doctrine. This was reinforced by the fact that at law, his wife's property passed into his control during marriage. He could sell it, keep its profits and did not have to account to anyone. Similarly, the dowry the wife brought into the marriage became his property or the property of his family.

The family, once formed, could not be dissolved. As a basic social structure, the family could not be subjected to destruction without causing social chaos. Further, there were strong Christian religious rules that supported this view by prohibiting divorce. Prior to 1857 in England, it was not possible to obtain a divorce from any English court to terminate a marriage. In cases of serious abuse by a husband, a wife could apply to church courts (called **ecclesiastical courts**) for a *divorce mensa et thoro*. This decree permitted a wife to reside separately from her husband but only if he was abusive. She might also obtain an order for **alimony**, an allowance to be paid her by the husband, permitting her to live, as the case law said, "modestly and in retirement", often at a greatly reduced standard of living.

If a wife was difficult to control, the law offered no specific remedy, as the husband was expected to control and discipline her himself; indeed, the law countenanced this by granting him, among other things, the right of physical chastisement (now known as spousal assault) to control her. In this context, there was no need to apply for court orders. The husband had enough power and authority to do the job himself.

But there were other legal forces that gave a husband a good deal of control over his wife, and made it very difficult for her to find a better life without him. First of all, until 1857 there was no legal divorce. Only in rare instances and only where parties were wealthy and influential enough, could they terminate a marriage, and then only by an Act of Parliament.

If she chose to leave her husband where the law gave her no right to do so, she had to find some way to meet her economic needs. A deserting wife was not entitled to any support payments (unless she had the court's permission to separate and could meet the tests for alimony). Economics dictated that she find another man to support her. However, the law created great difficulty for any man prepared to do this: Any man who enticed her away or offered her shelter and support could be sued by her husband for damages for the tort of harbouring his wife or enticing his wife away. Any man who offered the wife a sexual relationship (whether she had left her husband or not) could be sued for the civil tort of **criminal conversation** for interfering with the husband's sexual monopoly over his wife. Lastly, even her children were not hers. Children, at common law, were seen as the property of the father, and decisions about them were not based on what was best for the child but on whose property the child was. Unless the father was clearly a physical danger to the children, he was presumed to have a right to custody and control over them; and the wife, in these circumstances, would have no rights at all.

Early Canadian Family Law

From the English common law described above, family law in Canada evolved. There were some immediate differences. First, the *Constitution Act, 1867* divided legislative power between the federal government and the provinces. One of the results of this was that the power over family law was split between the provinces and the federal government. The federal government has power to determine what is required for a valid marriage and may make divorce law, including law governing support and custody issues, when a couple is obtaining a divorce. The provinces have an independent and separate power to make laws to determine how family property issues are resolved, and they have a concurrent or shared power over custody and support where the marriage has broken down but the parties will not divorce. This division of power has been the source of much confusion: different provinces have made up different rules covering support, custody, and property issues that reflect local conditions or values within the particular province. Because there was a lack of agreement in the provinces about divorce, this resulted in a stalemate that prevented forming a consensus that would tolerate a federally enacted national divorce law.

In matters of divorce, in 1857, England abolished the ecclesiastical courts as a relic of the Middle Ages and established its first divorce court. This was never a big issue in Canada, however, as ecclesiastical courts were never established here; however, neither were divorce courts, at least initially, because of the opposition of Roman Catholic Quebec to divorce in any form. What happened instead was that individual provinces asked the federal government to pass a Divorce Act that would apply to that province alone. This was done, for example, in Ontario, in the early 20th century. The first Acts were cautious: allowing a husband a divorce for a wife's adultery; later, a wife was allowed a divorce on the husband's cruelty; still later, the grounds of cruelty and adultery were made grounds for either to divorce. It is important to note that while divorce was available in courts in some provinces, it was still necessary for Quebec residents, until 1968, to apply to Parliament to dissolve their marriage. Also, divorce was not available on no-fault grounds. One spouse had to prove that the other had committed some kind of legally recognized matrimonial offence, such as cruelty or adultery.

Support in family breakdown situations was still tied to fault. Blameworthy wives would not receive support on a divorce. Nor would they receive alimony if they separated, unless the husband was blameworthy and the wives were innocent of wrongdoing and were prepared to take the husband back in the marriage relationship.

For poorer women who were deserted by their husbands, provincial legislation provided for a simple court application to provide support; amounts awarded under this statute were generally lower than alimony awards, reflecting a differential application of the law dependent in part on the social class of the applicant.

Matters with respect to property improved for married women in the 1880s, both in England and Canada (except Quebec, where the reforms came in the early 20th century). An Act called *The Married Woman's Property Act* allowed married women to continue to own and control property free of their husband's control. This, of course, was only of use to the small minority of women who actually had property to own and control.

Under this Act, a couple deciding, on consent, to separate could do so without a court order. Also, they could enter into an agreement to deal with post-separation matters, including support, child custody, and property division.

The unity of personality theory was imported to Canada and, with modifications, survived until the mid-20th century. Wives had limited rights to sue or be sued. Spouses could not sue each other, except to dissolve marriages; nor could they give evidence against each other in criminal cases. The unity of personality doctrine also gave the husband control over children, and meant that a wife could not gain custody of children. However, by the beginning of the 20th century, the idea that children were more than miniature adults was gaining currency, and with it came the idea that custody should be determined in accordance with the best interest of the child, not the property rights of the father.

Current Trends in Canadian Family Law

As a consequence of the rise of the women's movement in the late 1960s, pressure began to be applied to change and modernize family law in Canada by making family law rules apply equally to men and women.

In the first wave of reform in the 1970s, the focus was on elimination of legal rules that discriminated on the basis of sex; in the later stages, there was an emphasis on discriminatory effects of law that might, on its face, be gender neutral. The elimination of the unity of personality doctrine and the abolition of the action for criminal conversation are examples of the first type of reform. Laws to make support enforcement easier and to set minimum child-support standards are examples of the later stages of the reform process.

While the actual laws vary from province to province, some clear trends have emerged that are reflected in the current law discussed in the rest of this chapter:

1. Since 1968, there has been a Canada-wide *Divorce Act*. The courts now recognize marriage breakdown as the basis for a divorce without anyone having to be at fault, although a fault basis for divorce is still available.

2. Support is generally based on need of the recipient and the ability of the payer to pay; who was, or was not, a "bad spouse" is not material. Men, as well as women, are eligible to receive support.

3. There is a growing concern with ensuring that support payments, once ordered, continue to be paid. Many provinces, and the federal government, have enacted legislation to assist recipients in enforcing support rights.

4. There is a consensus that child support amounts are often inadequate. There are now federal child-support guidelines that fix child support by use of a formula that takes into account expenses, the region of the country where the child lives, parental income, and other factors. This has resulted in standardized support awards, although there is some room for judicial discretion. The main purposes of the guidelines are to reduce the amount of litigation on this issue and raise the amount of money given in child support awards. It is likely that most provinces will adopt or adapt child support guidelines for provincial child support proceedings in the future.

5. Following the successful introduction of child support guidelines, a draft spousal support guideline is now circulating among family lawyers to be considered for use in spousal support claims under the *Divorce Act*. If adopted, it will likely also be used with support applications under provincial family law legislation. Some lawyers are beginning to use the guidelines in their practices, even though they are not binding. Once spousal support guidelines become part of the law, it is likely that spousal support, like child support, will cease to be a contentious issue in family breakdown cases.

6. Custody is determined according to what is best for a child. There is a growing movement to ensure that the non-custodial parent's access rights are respected and enforced. Safeguards are also available to make it easier to retake a child abducted by the non-custodial parent. Under proposed amendments to the federal *Divorce Act*, the distinction

between "custody" and "access" will be ended, and the law will then speak of "shared custody" or "parenting orders". It is believed that this change in language will help to eliminate the idea of winners and losers in custody cases, where the "winner" gets custody and the "loser" gets access. Instead, by using the term "shared custody", it is hoped that parents will see custody as a shared responsibility after, as well as before, divorce. However, it appears that in most cases one parent will have dominant responsibility, so the change may be no more than linguistic.

7. Property is no longer dealt with in terms of who owned or had title to it. Generally, if property was acquired or owned during the marriage, there is an assumption that each spouse contributed to its acquisition, and each should share in its value at the time of separation, no matter which of them actually owned the property.

8. While family law usually deals with rights and remedies for married couples ending their marriage, many of these rights are now available to same-sex couples, as well as men and women who are cohabiting in permanent relationships, though not married to each other.

9. Since about 1990, same-sex couples have been treated more and more like heterosexual couples, first in informal unions and later in marriage unions. Courts in seven provinces by 2004 had held that refusing gay and lesbian couples the right to marry violated their equality rights under s. 15 of the *Charter of Rights and Freedoms*. As a result, the federal government referred the matter to the Supreme Court of Canada, on a **reference**, asking if it would be valid for the federal government to change the law to permit gays and lesbians to marry. The Supreme Court, in December 2004, in *Reference Re Legal Capacity for Marriage*,[5] held that the federal government, which has the power to determine who may marry, could legislate to permit gay and lesbian marriages. In January 2005, the prime minister announced that the government would introduce amendments to the federal *Marriage Act* to permit same-sex unions. The legislation was introduced and became law in July 2005. Some provinces, notably Alberta, have said that they will use the power to issue licences and regulate the ceremony of marriage to refuse to issue licences to same-sex couples and refuse to sanction or recognize such marriages. This is unlikely to be successful, as once the federal government has determined that same-sex unions are valid, the provinces are unlikely to be able to prevent such marriages without violating the equality rights of same-sex couples.

10. Various attempts have been made to reduce the conflict in matrimonial disputes. Mandatory mediation is now a required part of the litigation process in many provinces. Increasingly, child custody cases require the use of neutral assessors to make recommendations to the court on custody, and the trend is to push for joint custody, rather than to reinforce the winner-take-all approach that characterized custody disputes in the past. More recently, some family lawyers have begun to develop an approach called collaborative family law. The lawyers and their clients agree to negotiate a settlement without going to court. As long as the negotiations continue, neither party can resort to the courts. It is only when the negotiations break down that the parties can move

---

[5] [2003] S.C.C.A. No. 329, December 9, 2004.

the dispute to court. The lawyers involved in the negotiations agree not to represent the parties in court. The cost of engaging new lawyers is perceived to strongly encourage the parties not to let the negotiations fail.

FAMILY FORMATION

Normally, the law does not pay much attention to family formation, as couples are expected to be able to do this without much assistance. The processes of courtship and marriage arrangements are seen as social and emotional, rather than legal. But there are legal rules that underlie the processes, and they usually emerge when the processes get into difficulty.

The Engagement

The **engagement** or **betrothal** is an exchange of promises by a man and a woman to marry. In earlier times, the promise could be made by parents on behalf of children, even when the children were minors; however, in the case of minors, the promises would have to be confirmed when the children reached the age of majority. In the absence of parents making formal arrangements, men and women come to an agreement on their own. The engagement is a formalization of the agreement, usually with the man giving a ring to the woman. The ring functions like a deposit on goods, requiring the recipient to hold the goods off the market until the time stipulated for making the final payment and taking delivery. In this case, a woman who accepts the ring is actually promising not to marry anyone else, removing herself, so to speak, from the market.

All of this is academic until one of the parties breaks off the engagement. Then the question arises, "Who gets to keep the ring?" It used to be the case that the person who wrongfully broke off the relationship forfeited the right to keep the ring or other engagement gift from the other party. However, modern legislation has eroded this rule[6] in many jurisdictions.

Marriage

Historically, the marriage ceremony was social, cultural, and religious in nature, although it has legal aspects as well. In a country like Canada, with a multicultural population, the ceremonial requirements are kept to a minimum. There must be someone to perform the ceremony or at least to supervise it. There must be formal witnesses (usually two), and the couple must publicly state that they are taking each other as spouses and that they freely consent to doing so.

The law requires, in most provinces, that persons seeking to marry obtain a licence, usually through their local municipal office. Alternatively, they may go through a religious process of having **banns** published. This requires that someone announce the intention of the parties to marry at a religious service. The exact procedure is not specified, to allow individual religions to publish banns in accordance with the custom of that religion. The purpose of both the licence and the banns is to permit objections to be made to the marriage, on the ground that one or both parties is not entitled to marry.

The question of entitlement turns on a number of factors. The persons marrying must be both over the age of majority, although minors may marry

---

[6] For example, see s. 33 of the Ontario *Marriage Act*, which says that the fact that the donor broke off the relationship is not a factor to be considered in determining the ownership of gifts given in contemplation of marriage.

in some circumstances with parental consent. The couple must have the mental capacity to understand what a marriage is, to know that the event they are attending is their marriage ceremony, and to give consent to marry. Any prior marriages for either must have been terminated by death or divorce. The couple also may not marry if they are too closely related.

At the time of marriage both parties must have the capacity for sexual intercourse, although consummation of the marriage by sexual intercourse is not a requirement, provided both parties do not insist on consummation.

Spouses who go through a marriage ceremony without having met all of the requirements for marriage may find that their marriage is void.

Marriage law in Canada does not seem to contemplate **polygynous** or **polyandrous** marriages, even though there are large numbers of residents who practise religions that permit such marriages. The law here is very complicated, but it would appear that a resident of Canada who was married polygamously in a country where **polygamous** marriages are permitted has made a valid marriage. If the same person sought to marry polygamously in Canada, that marriage would likely be void on the ground that such marriages are not legally permitted in Canada. The barrier to polygamous marriages may violate the *Charter of Rights and Freedoms* by interfering with the free exercise of religion, including the right to marry according to the rules of one's own faith.

As of July 2005, the amendments to the *Marriage Act* now permit gay and lesbian couples to marry anywhere within Canada. Accordingly, provinces will be required to issue marriage licences to gay and lesbian couples. However, the Act also permits the clergy of any faith that does not recognize the rights of gays and lesbians to marry to refuse to perform religious marriage ceremonies for gay and lesbian couples.

Common Law Relationships

What used to be called "living in sin" by your grandmother has now become an acceptable form of behaviour for many Canadians. While the majority of couples who form permanent relationships still marry, a large minority of men and women enter into long-term relationships, living together in a monogamous sexual relationship, raising children, buying houses — doing everything married spouses do, except go through a marriage ceremony.

We refer to this type of relationship as one of **cohabitation**, and the partners are referred to as **unmarried spouses.**

This type of relationship has sometimes been described as a common law relationship, although technically it is not that: a common law relationship is one where the couple represents to others that they are married, when in fact they are not. In these circumstances the "spouses" would acquire some spousal rights at common law. The breakthrough for unmarried spouses came with modern family law legislation, which, first of all, gave the children of such unions the same rights of support and inheritance[7] that children of marriages have. Second, the law recognized that unmarried spouses were obliged to support each other if the relationship ended, provided the parties had lived together for several years.[8] There are still some differences in legal remedies for married and unmarried spouses: in order to claim an interest in property

---

[7] The idea that the child of unmarried parents was, at law, the child of no one, with no right to inherit from his or her parents, has been superseded by provincial legislation. All children now have the rights that only legitimate children previously had. "Bastard" still remains a term of abuse, but it has no legal significance. See, for example, Ontario's *Children's Law Reform Act*, R.S.O. 1990, c. C.12, s. 1.

[8] For example, s. 29 of the Ontario *Family Law Act* requires that the parties cohabit for not less than three years to be eligible for support if cohabitation ends.

under family law rules in most jurisdictions, it is necessary to be married; for unmarried spouses, property rights must be determined under usual common law rules, as if the common law spouses were unrelated strangers.

It also appears that the rights of unmarried spouses are being extended to **same-sex couples**.

FAMILY DISSOLUTION

When spouses decide that their relationship has come to an end, it is necessary for them to deal with spousal and child support, child custody, and property division, and then terminate their relationship by divorce (if they were in a marriage relationship). They may deal with all these matters, except divorce, by voluntarily negotiating a **separation agreement**, or, if they cannot agree, they can apply to the courts for remedies or agree to have a private arbitrator decide the issues.

Domestic Agreements

In addition to using a separation agreement after a relationship ends, it is also possible to determine some matters before marriage if the spouses decide to enter into a **marriage contract**, or, if they are not intending to marry, a **cohabitation agreement**. The terms of all of these types of agreements are enforceable. However, there are some limits to the use of marriage contracts and cohabitation agreements: the spouses are not permitted to decide custody issues, although they may in a separation agreement. The reasoning behind this is that one cannot decide who will get custody of a child not yet born, as this would not be in a child's best interest. As well, most lawyers advise against setting down detailed rules about who does what in a marriage.

Marriage contracts and cohabitation agreements are unusual in most parts of Canada, at least for young couples starting their first marriage or cohabitation arrangement. The reason for this is that these agreements focus on what happens when the relationship breaks up. Most young couples, for reasons of sentiment, find this distasteful or even ominous. Further, most young couples do not have any money or assets to warrant drafting an agreement. However, for older couples, previously married and now entering into a second marriage or permanent relationship, marriage contracts are more common. Spouses here often have assets and children from earlier marriages, whose interests they would like to protect.

Divorce and Annulment

There are two ways to formally terminate a marriage — divorce or annulment. A marriage is terminated by annulment only when the marriage is not valid. Marriages can be invalid because the spouses did not freely consent to marry, they were too closely related, one of them was still married to someone else, or the ceremony was defective in some material way. In these examples, the marriages would be *void ab initio*: the defects were external and made the marriages void from the very beginning. They could not be subsequently validated.

There is another type of invalid marriage that is not *void ab initio* but merely voidable by one party or the other. This means that the marriage is considered valid as long as neither party complains of the defect. For example, if a couple chooses not to consummate the marriage, the marriage is valid if neither makes an issue of non-consummation. However, if one party is unwilling or unable to have sexual intercourse and the other spouse is not prepared to accept the situation, the dissatisfied spouse can ask to have the marriage annulled by the court. A court order, declaring a marriage annulled, results in a marriage that is a **nullity** — that is, it is deemed never to have been a marriage.

Annulment by a court is not the same as a religious annulment. Some religions that do not permit their members to divorce may consider religious annulments where there is some question that the marriage was not valid. These religious annulments may meet the internal requirements of a particular religion, and the spouse in an annulled marriage is free to remarry in his or her own religion, without violating religious rules about divorce. However, for the marriage to be legally annulled, the spouses must apply to a court for an order declaring the marriage to be a nullity. A marriage that is annulled by a court is deemed never to have been a marriage at all; in other words, the person is considered as having never been married and is, therefore, thought of as free to marry. A marriage annulled by a religious body has no legal significance. In the eyes of the state, the spouses are still legally married until they obtain a nullity or a divorce decree from a court.

In earlier times, when divorces were difficult to obtain, couples might engage in ingenious arguments in order to have a marriage declared a nullity. Nullity proceedings are much more unusual today because it is generally simpler to treat one's marriage as valid and to obtain a divorce.

Until 1968 in Canada, there were different divorce laws for each province that was prepared to allow divorce. Generally, the courts allowed for divorce when one spouse had committed a matrimonial offence. In 1968, a Canada-wide *Divorce Act* was passed that allowed for divorce on an additional ground: marriage breakdown where the spouses had been living separately for more than three years. Additionally, it was also possible to obtain custody and support along with a divorce.

In 1986, the federal divorce laws were again streamlined — the many grounds of divorce were reduced to one: marriage breakdown by reason of adultery, cruelty, or separation for more than one year. The current Act also contains provisions to encourage mediated settlements, and where there is a support or custody order as well, the Act permits the former spouses to vary a support order if circumstances change after the order was made. The next revisions to the *Divorce Act* will likely focus on new ways of dealing with custody and access to children to reduce conflict between divorcing parents over issues involving the children. It is also likely that the *Divorce Act* may require adjustments to dissolve same-sex marriages.

Support and Support Enforcement

Under current federal divorce law, divorcing spouses may obtain support for themselves or for their dependent children. Under the law of most provinces, spouses who separate because of marriage breakdown may also apply for support on the basis of marriage breakdown before they file for divorce, or without ever filing for divorce. In most provinces, who caused the breakdown is not relevant. What is relevant is whether a dependant has a need for support where the other spouse is able to meet the need. (Children receiving support are assumed to be in need and unable to meet the need themselves.)

There are some trends that have emerged in recent years. Dependent spouses, unless they are unemployable, are expected to become self-supporting. This has meant, in many cases, that a wife would be expected to become self-supporting within several years of the breakup of the marriage by obtaining job training so that support would be time limited and function as a training allowance. The fact that many women in this position also have the responsibility for children means that they have child care burdens on top of training for, finding, and keeping employment. A consequence of this pattern is that women have more responsibility and less income than was the case while they were married. Men, freed from day-to-day child care responsibilities, appear to have more options and room to manoeuvre economically than their ex-wives do, in part as a result of the fact that spousal support that they pay is often time limited.

Another trend emerging is concerned with guaranteeing that child support is adequate. American and Canadian data suggest that after marriage breakdown, children and their mothers often find themselves with a falling standard of living, while the former husband, after an initial drop in income, begins to recover his standard of living. This has resulted in two legal initiatives: support enforcement and child support guidelines.

Starting in the 1980s, a number of Canadian jurisdictions began to confront the problem of support orders in default. Data showed that in most cases support orders were honoured for the first few months but that, as time went on, payments were likely to become sporadic and then stop, resulting in billions of dollars in back support going uncollected because the recipients, being support dependants, did not have the resources to hire a lawyer to enforce the order. Support recipients in these circumstances often ended up on welfare, with the result that the support payer passed his obligations to the state. In answer to this, Manitoba, followed by other provinces, passed legislation establishing government offices that would monitor and enforce support obligations, using conventional judgment-enforcement techniques, such as **garnisheeing** wages, seizing and selling property of the debtor, and jailing debtors for non-payment. The federal government, for its part, has enacted legislation that permits access to federal data banks so that enforcement agencies can more easily locate debtors and garnishee tax refunds, wages of federal civil servants, and other federal payments otherwise due to the support payer.[9]

The enforcement initiative has had some impact on defaulters, but determined non-payers continue to hinder collection of support debts. The "second generation" of support-enforcement legislation aims at increasing efficiency of collection by deducting support debts directly from wages before there is a default by the payer. This works in the same way as income tax withholding, where income tax is deducted from the taxpayer's wages without the taxpayer having any choice in the matter.[10]

With respect to child support, the federal government has implemented a formula-based method of determining child support that is intended to reduce judicial discretion to determine the amounts of support, and to result in higher and more realistic support awards for most families. It is still too early to tell whether the goals will be achieved in full.

Custody

The custody of children, determined on the basis of property rights in children until the mid-19th century, is now determined on the basis of a broad legal concept — "the best interest of the child". This development took hold in the late 19th century as part of social and cultural changes that began to recognize childhood as a distinct psycho-social stage in human development. Previously, children who survived infancy were often thought of as miniature adults and were assumed to be more resilient than they perhaps were.

---

[9] The two federal acts are the *Garnishment and Pension Diversion Act* and the *Family Orders and Agreements Enforcement Assistance Act (Canada)*.

[10] This approach has been incorporated into Ontario enforcement legislation, *The Family Support Plan Act*, ss. 3.1–3.13 (now *The Family Responsibility Act*).

In its early stages, "the best interest of the child" was interpreted to mean that the mother, as the family member responsible for raising and nurturing children, was most likely to obtain custody and child support. In later years, the courts have, at least in theory, become more gender neutral in awarding custody; however, most custody orders are still made in favour of women, reflecting the fact that women are still primarily responsible for child rearing in Canadian society. It is quite clear that the "best-interest" principle focuses on the psycho-social needs of the child, rather than on merely material needs. Whoever can give the child the most material things does not necessarily win custody.

Custody can be awarded by a court granting a divorce or, in the absence of divorce proceedings, the court may act under provincial legislation. In the latter case, many provinces permit anyone to apply for custody — the right of custody is really a child's right and, therefore, in appropriate cases the choice should not be restricted to competing parents.

The process of deciding custody has become more sophisticated. There is a growing movement towards the use of child-custody assessments by child psychologists and other "experts", on which the court relies in making its decisions. As well, the courts and legislation encourage the use of mediation and other forms of **alternative dispute resolution** for all family law matters, but especially for custody. To some extent, this protects the child from being involved directly in the conflict and anger that often results from court proceedings. The courts, experts in legal decision making, are not necessarily expert in making decisions about how a child's psycho-social needs are to be met. Many judges have embraced assessments willingly, though there has been some criticism that the courts have abandoned their duty to make legal decisions, which are now effectively being made by psychologists and social workers.

One area of reform in the custody area arose as a result of a serious problem in a small minority of cases: child abduction by the non-custodial parent. This can be a particular problem if the abducting parent has ties or connections outside Canada, in which case it is difficult to obtain the child's return, as the custodial parent often has to fight a long-distance court battle in a foreign jurisdiction. Part of the remedy for this has been that most Canadian provinces have, by legislation, agreed to enforce *The Convention on Civil Aspects of International Child Abduction* (also called the Hague Convention). Canada has signed the covenant and is a participating state, although provinces must agree to enforce the covenant within each province, as this is a provincial rather than federal jurisdictional matter. The result of this is that children wrongfully brought into a province from abroad will be quickly returned to the custodial parent as a result of the provincial Attorney General taking immediate action. Other nations that have signed the convention will return children wrongfully taken or retained in their country to Canada. Additionally, the definition of "kidnapping" in the *Criminal Code of Canada* has been expanded to include child abduction from a parent with lawful custody.

Property Settlement

At common law, marriage conferred no special property rights on spouses. The general rules prevailed: if a party could show that he or she owned or had title to an asset, then the asset belonged to the owning spouse. The law of equity, which softened the harsh effect of common law rules, recognized that a non-owner could acquire rights in an asset by contributing to the creation, improvement, or acquisition of the asset in a concrete way, usually by contributing money or money's worth. However, this rule did not recognize the indirect contribution a spouse might make, for example, by attending

---

Illustration of the Partnership Asset-Sharing Model

EXHIBIT 28.1

¤ Wife enters marriage with $10 in assets, and leaves with $100 in assets.

¤ Husband enters marriage with $50 in assets, and leaves with $200 in assets.

> Her "profit" is $100 − $10 = $ 90
>
> His "profit" is $200 − $50 = $150

¤ For equalized sharing of the assets, the spouse with the lesser profit is entitled to one-half the difference between the profits of both of them:

> (the greater profit) minus (the smaller profit)
> = the difference between the two profits
> = $150 − $90 = $60

¤ The difference is then divided into two equal parts: $60 ÷ 2 = $30

¤ The difference is subtracted from the greater and added to the lesser profit, so that both leave the marriage with "equal profits":

> Greater profit: $150 − $30 = $120 (final equalized profit)
>
> Lesser profit: $90 + $30 = $120 (final equalized profit)

---

to domestic matters and freeing up the other spouse to make money and buy assets.

Opponents of the common law approach have argued that marriage is an economic partnership, where each partner carries out partnership activities that together result in the creation of partnership wealth that both partners should share, regardless of who legally owns the assets. The rationale for this approach is expressed in the Ontario *Family Law Act*, section 5(7):

> The purpose of this section is to recognize that child care, household management and financial provision are the joint responsibilities of the spouses and that inherent in the marital relationship there is equal contribution, whether financial or otherwise, by the spouses to the assumption of these responsibilities, entitling each spouse to the equalization of the net family properties (of both of them)....

The arguments for equal sharing of "partnership assets" on marriage breakdown have generally prevailed, and provinces generally have followed the approach illustrated in the passage noted above. The Ontario legislation illustrates how the scheme works: it requires each spouse to note the value of the assets each has on entering marriage and on leaving the marriage. (See Exhibit 28.1 for an application.) If the value has increased, then it is presumed that the increase, or profit, is due to joint efforts and is to be shared with the other spouse so that both spouses leave with equal partnership wealth.[11] Most of these legislative schemes have provisions to safeguard against equal distributions in circumstances where that would be unfair.

---

[11] The actual legislative scheme is somewhat more complicated; see the Ontario *Family Law Act*, R.S.O. 1990, ss. 4–16.

CHILD PROTECTION

While child-custody issues arise as a consequence of divorce or separation, there are other times where the welfare of children becomes the concern of the law — either because the child or the child's family has become so dysfunctional that society deems it necessary to interfere with the child and his or her family.

Generally speaking, the law recognizes the right of families to be free from state interference. Because of this, much of child protection law is concerned with striking a balance between the right of families to be free of the state, and the right of the state to step in where the situation warrants. When the children's rights movement arose in the 19th century (at the same time as, and as part of, movements to prevent cruelty to animals), its adherents tended to be paternalistic and interventionist, imposing middle-class, Anglo-Canadian standards on immigrant, native, and working-class families. Since that time, the balance has shifted, and principles underlying child protection are much more respectful of varying community standards and ways of doing things. The shift is illustrated by the principles set out in section 1 of Ontario's *Child and Family Services Act*:[12]

Paramount purpose

(1) The paramount purpose of this Act is to promote the best interests, protection and well being of children.

Other purposes

(2) The additional purposes of this Act, so long as they are consistent with the best interests, protection and well being of children, are:
1. To recognize that while parents may need help in caring for their children, that help should give support to the autonomy and integrity of the family unit and, wherever possible, be provided on the basis of mutual consent.
2. To recognize that the least disruptive course of action that is available and is appropriate in a particular case to help a child should be considered.
3. To recognize that children's services should be provided in a manner that,
   i. respects a child's need for continuity of care and for stable relationships within a family and cultural environment,
   ii. takes into account physical, cultural, emotional, spiritual, mental and developmental needs and differences among children,
   iii. provides early assessment, planning and decision-making to achieve permanent plans for children in accordance with their best interests, and
   iv. includes the participation of a child, his or her parents and relatives and the members of the child's extended family and community, where appropriate.
4. To recognize that, wherever possible, services to children and their families should be provided in a manner that respects cultural, religious and regional differences.
5. To recognize that Indian and native people should be entitled to provide, wherever possible, their own child and family services, and that all services to Indian and native children and families should be provided in a manner that recognizes their culture, heritage and traditions and the concept of the extended family.

---

[12] R.S.O. 1990, c. C.11, as am. by S.O. 2007, c. 9, s. 25.

As a result of some notorious cases of child abuse where the child had been left with the family and had died, a number of provinces are re-examining the point at which a child should be removed from home. Ontario, for example, in 1999 amended its child protection legislation to make physical protection of the child a higher priority.

"Child in Need of Protection"

This broad term describes a child who is at risk of serious mental or physical harm either caused by family members or that family members or caregivers are unable to prevent. The term also includes a child in need of medical or psychiatric care, where that care is not otherwise provided and where serious harm might result if it is not. The category also covers children who are uncontrollable and who have committed serious offences but who are not subject to the *Youth Criminal Justice Act* because they are under 12 years of age.

Where a child is believed to be in need of protection, child care workers or the police are required, in extreme cases, to take the child to a place of safety and to commence court proceedings to have the child declared in need of protection. In the first instance, if the child is found to be in need of protection, the court will make an order designed to treat the child in the family setting. Usually the supervision of this process is given to a **Children's Aid Society**.

Wardships and Adoptions

If the child is successfully treated, the child protection order is allowed to lapse, and the child is returned to his family. However, if the child has no family or other caregiver or if the court finds that the family is too damaging and harmful for the child, the child is made a ward of the state either as a Children's Aid Society ward or, if the matter is more serious, as a Crown ward. If a child has been made a Crown ward and cannot be returned to the family setting, the child is required to be put up for adoption. Often such children are beyond preschool age and cannot be adopted easily. Such children may go into a foster family or a group home prior to adoption: if, indeed, they are ever adopted.

Adoption of Crown wards is only one kind of adoption. There are also adoptions of newborns and "step-parent" adoptions. Newborn adoptions arise where a woman has given birth to a child and has decided not to keep the child. There are elaborate procedures to ensure that proper consent has been given so that the birth mother cannot try to reclaim the child after the child has gone to the adoptive home. In some provinces, Children's Aid supervises these adoptions. In others, the jurisdiction may be shared with private licensees who charge a fee for the adoption service (but not for the child, as we are not yet at the stage where we are willing to treat children as property for purchase).

Step-parent adoptions typically involve a person adopting the child of his or her spouse, where that child is the product of the spouse's former marriage or of an earlier relationship. These adoptions are typically privately arranged, and are minimally supervised by the state or the courts.

CHAPTER SUMMARY

In this chapter, the reader was given a general overview of family law in Canada. While focusing on divorce and family dissolution, we also examined child welfare and adoption. General principles and trends were identified, and the reader was cautioned that, aside from divorce law, most of family law is provincial. While there is much similarity, there is substantial variation in the law of the 10 provinces and the territories.

The chapter discussed family law in the context of social and cultural values and assumptions surrounding the family. The origins of family law in English common law were examined, including limits on divorce, and the requirement of bad behaviour by a husband as a prerequisite for very limited remedies for a wronged wife.

Current trends in family law were then identified, including family law remedies being available without having to prove who is at fault, a growing concern with the adequacy of child support both in terms of amount, and in terms of certainty that payments will be made over time. The law is also expanding remedies to include couples who are in a permanent relationship, though not married. There is also a trend towards defining "family" in a more inclusive way, to include, among other things, same-sex couples. Last, there is a trend towards treating spousal property as if it were partnership property, to be shared equally if the "partnership" dissolves.

Contemporary family law was then examined following the sequences in a family's "life cycle", from formation to dissolution. The legal aspects of betrothal and marriage were examined and compared to so-called common law relationships. This was followed by an examination of the law relating to divorce and annulment, support, and custody, both in the context of divorce and provincial legislation. Lastly, we examined developments in the law relating to property distribution on dissolution of a marriage.

The chapter then turned to child protection and child welfare, identifying the principles under which this law operates today and examining the child-protection process through several stages, culminating in adoption. This type of adoption was distinguished from newborn and "step-parent" adoptions.

GLOSSARY OF NEW TERMS AND KEY CONCEPTS

alimony
An award of support payable to a wife whose husband has engaged in matrimonial misconduct; as a condition of receiving alimony, the wife has to be prepared to forgive the husband and take him back, although the courts softened this requirement in later years. Alimony has been replaced as a remedy by statutory-support provisions in the *Divorce Act*, and in provincial legislation.

alternative dispute resolution (ADR)
The latest trend in settling disputes by negotiation, rather than by fighting it out in court. Many members of the bar and the public have jumped on the ADR bandwagon as a panacea. However, if the parties do not have equality of bargaining power (often the case in family breakdown), ADR can result in the weaker party doing far worse than it might do after a court fight.

banns
A public announcement of an intention to marry, made at a religious service.

betrothal
An agreement, contractual in nature, to marry at a later date. The social and cultural event we call an engagement is the outward sign of what has legally occurred.

Children's Aid Society
An organization, originally a private, voluntary, charitable group, that is given statutory powers and government funding to protect children in many Canadian jurisdictions.

cohabitation
A situation where a man and a woman live in a permanent, sexually monogamous, marriage-like relationship, without being formally married.

cohabitation agreement
A form of domestic agreement that permits those intending to cohabit to agree on issues relating to property and support if the relationship ends.

criminal conversation
Neither criminal, nor a conversation, this is a legal wrong done to a husband by another man who has sexual intercourse with his, the husband's, wife. This tort was abolished by statute in most jurisdictions by the 1970s.

dowry	A contractual payment, enforceable in law, to the parents of a groom by the parents of the bride. Dowries are no longer part of the arrangements in most European and North American marriages, particularly where the bride and groom choose each other rather than have their parents choose for them. The payment may be seen as a contractual inducement to purchase akin to the manufacturer's rebate offered by some car manufacturers on slow-moving models. In societies where women have a very high economic value, a groom's family might have to pay a "bride price" for the right to marry the bride.
divorce mensa et thoro	An order from the old ecclesiastical courts that would permit spouses to cease to live together, in circumstances of serious abuse or violence, where it was impossible for them to continue doing so. They were still legally married, however, and could not re-marry unless one spouse died.
ecclesiastical courts	A system of English courts that dealt with the affairs of the Church of England, the legal rights and liabilities of the clergy and, in a limited way, with some family law matters. These courts were abolished in 1857 in England, and were never introduced to Canada.
engagement	*See* **betrothal**.
garnisheeing, garnishment	A method of enforcing a judgment for the payment of money by requiring a third party who owes money to the judgment-debtor to pay that amount, or a part of it, to the court for the benefit of the judgment-creditor.
marriage contract	Also called an **ante nuptual** agreement. The same thing as a cohabitation agreement, except that the parties intend to marry. *See* **cohabitation agreement**.
nullity	Usually refers to a court order declaring a marriage to be null and void. Such a marriage is said to be a nullity.
patriarchal	Usually used to describe a pattern of authority in society in which males have the most power and authority. A patriarchal family, therefore, is one in which the father is the principal authority and decision maker.
polygamy	The union of one man with two or more women, or one woman with two or more men, to form a family unit.
polygynous/polyandrous	A polygynous marriage is one where a man may have more than one wife at a time. A polyandrous marriage is one where a wife may have more than one husband.
reference	a procedure by which the Government of Canada refers important legal or factual questions to the Supreme Court of Canada and asks the Court to give the government its opinion.
same-sex couple	Two homosexuals or lesbians who cohabit in a long-term conjugal relationship that resembles that of a heterosexual couple.
separation agreement	An agreement whereby spouses who are ending their marriage decide terms about issues related to support, custody, and division of property.
unity of personality	A common law doctrine that defined a married couple as one person in law, with the authority over that person vested in the husband. The effect of the doctrine was to deprive a married woman of most legal rights, including legal control of her property and children.
unmarried spouses	"Spouse" usually means a married person; but where a couple has formed a long-term relationship that looks like a marriage relationship without a formal marriage ceremony, the term "unmarried spouse" is used to describe the members of this relationship.
void ab initio	"Void from the very beginning."

REVIEW QUESTIONS

1. Explain how the law and customs relating to marriage and divorce in the premodern period supported the family as an economic unit.

2. What is alimony? How does it differ from modern law related to spousal support?

3. What are some of the requirements of a valid marriage?

4. When is a marriage dissolved by a divorce decree? When by a nullity decree?

5. What are some of the current problems with the laws of spousal and child support?

6. What is the general principle applied to determine custody disputes?

7. What is the rationale for equalizing the spouses' shares in family property when the marriage ends?

8. Describe the steps that might be taken with a child whose parents are alcoholic and physically abusive.

9. What are the different types of adoption, and how do they differ?

10. Describe new developments with respect to the following:

    (a) Ensuring that child support is paid regularly as ordered by the court
    (b) Making the determination of child support fairer and more equitable

11. Suppose Margaret, who is separated from Gary, does not want Gary to see the kids. They have not yet divorced, and there is no court order in respect of custody. She decides to move with the kids back to England without telling him. What rights does Gary have?

12. What is "collaborative divorce", and what is its purpose?

13. What is "shared custody"?

DISCUSSION QUESTIONS

1. How do the structure and operation of the traditional family explain the following legal rules?

    (a) The unitary personality doctrine
    (b) The tort of criminal conversation
    (c) The tort of harbouring and/or enticement
    (d) Divorce *mensa et thoro*
    (e) Alimony

2. An unrelated man and woman may form a family unit. Should an unrelated man and man or an unrelated woman and woman be allowed to form a family unit recognized by law? Should a brother and sister, or parent and child, form family units recognized by law? What criteria should we use to define a family? What kind of legal recognition should be given?

3. John and Mary are in a custody dispute regarding their child Henry, age 13. John is a workaholic, who travels a lot and earns a very good living. He will be able to give Henry lessons and summer camp and can afford a housekeeper to look after Henry when he is not there. He is a very

loving dad and shares an interest in sports and outdoor activities with Henry.

Mary will have to return to work and will not be earning as much as John. Until the marriage ended, she did almost all of the child rearing and has a strong, warm, and loving relationship with Henry. Henry confides in her and finds her easier to talk to than his dad. Mary will continue to live in the family home if she gets custody.

How would you apply the "best-interest" test to determine who should get custody?

4. Miranda is quite wealthy, in love with Mel, and wants to marry him. Mel is a musician, has no money, and doesn't earn very much. He is reluctant to marry because of the differences in wealth; however, he finally agrees. During the marriage, Mel stops working and lies around all the time watching soap operas on T.V. He also drinks and physically abuses Miranda. Miranda continues to work and brings in all the family income; she also has to look after the house as Mel feels that is "women's work". After six months, Miranda has had enough and ends the marriage. Mel is now asking to have their family property divided into equal shares.

Miranda objects to the equal division. What arguments can she make that might persuade a court not to make an equal division?

5. Jerrold, age 11, has been picked up by the police while wandering downtown at 2:00 a.m. His parents are drunk, as usual, and the police discover they are unaware of his absence. Jerrold is generally bedraggled and unkempt. When he shows up at school, which is not often, he is inattentive and disruptive. On physical examination, there is evidence of active tuberculosis, a highly infectious disease.

   (a) What criteria should apply to this case in considering whether Jerrold is a "child in need of protection"?

   (b) Bearing in mind the principles underlying child protection legislation, what would you put in the child protection order?

   (c) Assuming that Jerrold cannot, in his interests, be returned to his family, what happens?

6. If we permit same-sex marriages in Canada, should we also permit polygynous marriages (where a husband may marry more than one wife) or polygamous ones (where a wife may marry more than one husband)?

7. "An engagement ring is just a ring." Discuss.

SUGGESTED READINGS

Consolidate Ontario Family Law Statutes and Regulations, Annual ed. (Toronto, Ont.: Carswell).

Kronby, Malcolm. *Canadian Family Law*, 9th ed. (Toronto, Ont.: John Wiley & Sons Canada, 2006).

MacDonald, J., & L. Ferrier. *Canadian Divorce Law and Practice*, 2d ed. (Toronto, Ont.: Carswell, 2000).

WEBSITES

Ministry of the Attorney General Ontario: <http://www.attorneygeneral.jus.gov.on.ca/english/family/>

• "Family Arbitration": <http://www.attorneygeneral.jus.gov.on.ca/english/family/arbitration/>

Department of Justice: <http://canada.justice.gc.ca/eng/pi/sup-pen/grl/lawsr-loisr.html>

• *Federal Child Support Guidelines*
<http://canada.justice.gc.ca/eng/pi/sup-pen/grl/fcsg-lfpae.html>

• *Spousal Support Advisory Guidelines: A Draft Proposal*
<http://canada.justice.gc.ca/eng/dept-min/pub/ss-pae/proj/toc-tdm.html>

Women and the Law

T. Brettel Dawson
CARLETON UNIVERSITY

Jennifer Quaile
CARLETON UNIVERSITY

Learning Objectives

At reading this chapter, the reader should be able to

> explain the feminist critique of law as containing gender bias in rules, processes, and attitudes and the argument that law is socially constructed around categories such as gender and race

> cite actual instances of gender bias in the law on the part of judges and legislatures, as well as some of the historic breakthroughs made by women in relation to their legal status

> describe the range of the equality guarantees in Canadian law

> understand that different meanings have been suggested for "equality" in law and that different legal tests or principles are attached to them

> understand and identify processes of law and social change related to the positions of women in Canadian society and the contradictory and complex nature of legal reform as it affects women

TABLE OF CONTENTS

INTRODUCTION: THE GENDER ISSUE IN LAW

In her influential book, *Feminism Unmodified*, **feminist** legal theorist Catharine MacKinnon commented that "at the heart of every women's initiative for civil equality from suffrage to the [U.S.] equal rights amendment" has been the "simple notion that law respond to women as well as to men" and that women "participate in defining the terms that create the standards, and be a voice in drawing the lines."[1] As readers of this book will already be aware, law plays an important role in our society: it regulates conduct, provides benefits, or imposes restrictions, and provides an avenue for resolving disputes and obtaining remedies. Law is powerful in our society; it is also a place in which competing conceptions of social and legal relationships and ordering are articulated and contested. It is important, then, that law — its rules, its judges, and its processes — are not affected by bias. Australian legal academic Professor Margaret Thornton is not alone, however, in suggesting that "[s]o successful has been the prevailing ideology of law as a neutral arbiter of disputes and as a positive instrument of social change, rather than as a primary determinant of social relations, that little attention has been directed to the possibility that the form of law itself might be flawed."[2] Madam Justice Bertha Wilson, the first woman to be appointed as a judge of the Supreme Court of Canada, echoed this concern in a public lecture in 1990 in which she said:

> many studies have found overwhelming evidence that gender-based myths, biases and stereotypes are deeply imbedded in the attitudes of many male judges, as well as in the law itself ... in some areas of law ... a distinctly male perspective is clearly discernable [*sic*] and has resulted in legal principles that are not fundamentally sound, and should be revisited as and when the opportunity presents itself.[3]

These sorts of problems constitute the "gender issue in law". Identifying these problems and issues, and working creatively and persistently to change them, has defined the project of feminist legal scholarship. In a 1988 article in the *New York Times*, entitled "Feminist Scholars Spurring Rethinking of Law", Tamar Lewin observed that "in a flood of recent articles in legal journals, feminist scholars are proposing a basic rethinking of everything from the doctrine of negligence to the criminal laws about rape." She quoted Professor Martha Minow, of Harvard Law School, who commented, "In many cases, the legal framework doesn't allow us to do justice. Where that's true, we have to change the framework. That's what good lawyering is, feminist or not."

In this chapter, we explore the implications of the "gender issue in law", the idea that law has a gender dimension and can affect women and men differently and, indeed, that it can affect different groups of men and women differently depending on their class, race/ethnicity, and family status. Understanding the gender issue in law can assist us in examining and responding to legal and social issues involving women. In the next section, we examine some of the history of women's inequality in Canadian law; in identifying some important breakthroughs for women, we also explore the complexity of law and social change and ask some difficult questions about how positive these changes were and for whom. Our examples include the historic restrictions on married women's ability to own property, the exclusion of women from the right to vote, and the struggle for women to be permitted to become lawyers. A com-

---

[1]   Catharine MacKinnon, *Feminism Unmodified* (Cambridge, Mass.: Harvard University Press, 1987) at 228.
[2]   Margaret Thornton, "Feminist Jurisprudence: Illusion or Reality" (1986) 3 Aust. J.L. & Soc. 5 at 8.
[3]   Madam Justice Bertha Wilson, "Will Women Judges Really Make a Difference?" (1990) Barbara Betcherman Lecture, Osgoode Hall Law School.

mon issue in these examples was whether women were "legal persons". For many years, women were considered "non-persons" in law and, as such, had no power, rights, or capacity in law. The struggle to change this situation was one of the defining features of the women's movement in the first 30 years of this century.

In the third section of the chapter, we examine the impact that gender-biased judicial attitudes and legal rules have had on women's efforts to be included in legal standards and to have law respond to them equally and fairly. We will see that profoundly sexist views of women have affected legal outcomes throughout the years and, sadly, continue to do so. In the fourth section of the chapter we explore the scope and meaning of sex equality guarantees in Canadian law. A case study on pay equity in the federal public service brings together many of the themes of the chapter, including the need to look at law in relation to social and economic dynamics and to place formal legal processes in the context of workplace and policy-based processes. We conclude the chapter by outlining several current equality issues and asking readers to identify the equality problems at stake and the ways in which differing approaches to equality affect how we respond to these problems, and to articulate and argue for what they believe are just and appropriate ways to resolve them.

THE STRUGGLE FOR WOMEN TO BECOME LEGAL PERSONS

We would like to think that we have gone a long way from the days when employed women had to leave their jobs when they married (or more recently, when employed married women had to leave their jobs when they became pregnant), or when married women could not own property, or obtain custody of their children. We would also like to think we are a long way away from the time when women were not considered to be **"legal persons"**, could not vote, go to university, or become doctors, lawyers, or members of Parliament. The breakthrough case which established that women were "legal persons" was a 1929 decision of the Judicial Committee of the English Privy Council Court. The case involved the question of whether women were included in the term "persons" who were eligible to be called as senators. The Canadian Supreme Court had decided that women were not persons and that the framers of our Constitution could not possibly have meant to include women in the term. The Privy Council reversed this decision. This was the famous "persons case". The Lord Chancellor, Lord Sankey, echoed our hopes of progressive movement to a more equal society when he commented that the exclusion of women from public office was "a relic of times more barbarous than ours."[4] Interestingly, much before this, in 1917, an Alberta court had refused to accept the argument that women were not legal persons. A person convicted of vagrancy was appealing his conviction because it had been made by a woman magistrate. The Court expressed the view that it was "returning to the more liberal and enlightened view of the middle ages in England and passing over the narrower and more hardened view, which ... by the middle of the 19th century had gained ascendancy."[5] What the Alberta Court made clearer than the Privy Council was that the legal status of women is not "natural" or "inevitable" but reflects social choices and changes over time and according to social context. Nevertheless, such optimism aside, it

---

[4] *Edwards v. Attorney General for Canada*, [1930] A.C. 124.
[5] *R. v. Cyr*, [1917] 3 W.W.R. 849.

remains true that barriers to women's equality have not all been eliminated at the end of this century.

Of course, many formal barriers to women's legal capacity and full participation in our society have been removed. In this section we look at three examples of such change. We outline the changes and move on to examine a number of difficult questions that these breakthroughs also raise. It is clear that the gradual elimination of legal barriers affecting women was not only, or at all, the result of enlightened and progressive motivations. Moreover, the changes in women's legal status did not improve the social and economic position of all women equally and contemporaneously. These examples also suggest that the barriers and inequalities experienced by women were not individual problems or the result of irrational or atypical actions; rather, they were problems ingrained in systems of thought, rules, and legal processes. The examples in the next two sections of the chapter make clear what U.S. feminist legal scholar Deborah Rhode meant when she commented that the "three core assumptions of feminist critical theories are that gender is a central category for analysis, that equality between women and men is a crucial social objective and that equality for all women cannot be achieved without fundamental social transformation."[6]

Married Women and Property

Prior to the mid-19th century, married women could not own property. Marital property law was predicated on the concept of "legal unity", in which a woman lost her separate legal identity and capacity when she married. The legal rationale for this was explained by Sir William Blackstone, a leading law commentator in the 18th century, who regarded it as a self-evident principle of law that "by marriage the husband and wife are one person in law; that is, the very being or legal existence of the woman is suspended during marriage, or at least is incorporated into that of the husband, under whose wing, protection and *cover* she performs everything...."[7] In practice this meant that a married woman could not own property and that all property in the family unit belonged to her husband. The story is told of a prominent suffragist in England, Millicent Garrett Fawcett, who had her purse snatched on a London street. When the charge against the young thief was read out in court, it stated that he had stolen "from the person of Millicent Fawcett a purse containing [a sum of money], being the property of Henry Fawcett" who was her husband. Similarly, even after a marriage had broken down in fact (a divorce in law could only be obtained by private Act of Parliament at one time), an estranged husband could claim any assets or income earned by his wife because they legally belonged to him.

The *Married Women's Property Act*s in the 1880s in the United Kingdom and in Canada (although New Brunswick's initial legislation was much earlier in 1851) changed the law to permit married women to own property. The Acts also ensured that husbands no longer held claim to their wives' property upon marriage.

The struggle for the law to be changed had been long and hard fought. On its face it looked to be a victory for the women's movement. However, researchers have compellingly demonstrated that the legislative motivations for the enactment of the *Married Women's Property Act*s were not primarily to enhance the legal status of women. Rather, they were motivated by other

---

[6] Deborah Rhode, "Feminist Critical Theories" (1990) 42 Stanf. L. Rev. 617.

[7] W. Blackstone, *Commentaries on the Laws of England*, Book I (Chicago: University of Chicago Press, 1979), c. 15 at 442.

interests, particularly those of creditors.[8] Similarly, the state was motivated to introduce the legislation out of its own interests in limiting the costs of social assistance rather than in order to protect women or promote women's equality. Sociologist Jane Ursel has pointed out that the state needed to "minimize the number of dependents upon the public purse."[9] This happened to coincide with women's desire to own their own property. Thus, the state and women held only a shared interest in dismantling laws which had always been costly to women and had gradually become costly to the state. With the reform of marital property laws, women were given more power over family finances. These laws, however, were not intended to allow women to become more independent or equal, but only to provide them with "some economic security in case of their husbands' death or desertion."[10] It should be noted too that the concept of equal division of marital property on marriage breakdown did not occur until the Family Law Acts in the 1970s and 1980s.

This example makes it evident that assumptions regarding women's subordinate role in marriage were structured into legal rules. Changes to marital property rights for women were heavily influenced by economic and political factors, and indeed the changes were not motivated by an interest in achieving women's equality. They may well have led to greater economic security for some women of more advantageous class positions (who had always had some protection through the use of family trusts), yet it is questionable whether, for example, working class married women actually gained from the *Married Women's Property Act*s. Similarly, even today with laws providing for division of marital property on marriage breakdown and the so-called "clean break principle" of spousal independence upon divorce, women may receive an ambiguous benefit. In our society, income rather than property assets is the main source of economic wealth and security; however, income is not normally divided. Spousal support on marriage breakdown is very limited. Finally, provincial legislation providing for property division on marriage breakdown does not apply to property on Indian reserves and hence does not benefit aboriginal women living on such reserves.

Women and the Vote

In 1997, it seems amazing that Canadian women in this century could not vote in federal, provincial or local elections. In 1916, Manitoba, Alberta and Saskatchewan were the first provinces to extend the franchise to non-aboriginal women.[11] Ontario and British Columbia extended to non-aboriginal women the right to vote provincially in 1917.[12] The last province to award the franchise to women was Quebec in 1940.[13] The federal franchise was awarded

---

[8] See, e.g., Norma Basch, *In the Eyes of the Law: Women, Marriage and Property in Nineteenth Century New York* (Ithaca, New York: Cornell University Press, 1982).

[9] Jane Ursel, *Private Lives, Public Policy: 100 Years of State Intervention in the Family* (Toronto, Ont.: Women's Press, 1992) at 300.

[10] Sandra Burt, "Legislators, Women, and Public Policy", in Sandra Burt, Lorraine Code, and Lindsay Dorney, eds., *Changing Patterns: Women in Canada* (Toronto, Ont.: McClelland & Stewart, 1988) 126 at 130.

[11] Manitoba: *An Act to Amend the "Manitoba Election Act"*, 6 Geo. V, c. 36; Alberta: *The Equal Suffrage Statutory Law Amendment Act*, 6 Geo. V, c. 5; Saskatchewan: *An Act to Amend the Statute Law*, 6 Geo. V, c. 37, s. 1.

[12] Ontario: *The Ontario Franchise Act*, 1917, 7 Geo. V, c. 5. Women could not, however, be elected to the Legislative Assembly, nor could they hold office until 1919: *Women's Assembly Qualification Act, 1919*, 9 Geo. V, c. 8. British Columbia: *Provincial Elections Act Amendment Act, 1917*, 7–8 Geo. V, c. 23.

[13] *An Act Granting to Women the Right to Vote and be Eligible as Candidates*, 4 Geo. VI, c. 7. The right to vote in local elections was delayed until 1941: *An Act to Amend the Cities and Towns Act*, 5 Geo. VI, c. 41; and *An Act to Amend the Municipal Code*, 5 Geo. VI, c. 69.

to all non-aboriginal women in 1918,[14] but it was not until 1960 that aboriginal women were given an unrestricted right to the vote federally. Quebec was the last province to extend the provincial franchise to aboriginal men and women when it did so in 1969.[15]

Race was a major factor in restrictions on the vote in Canada. Federal suffrage legislation continued to discriminate after 1918 on the basis of race and ethnicity. Until 1948, Canadians of Chinese, Japanese, and East Indian ethnic origins were not allowed to vote unless they were war veterans.[16] Legislation also prevented "Eskimos" (as the Inuit had been called) from voting until 1950. The *Indian Act* (1876), 39 Vict., c. 18 provided in section 3(12) that "the term 'person' means an individual other than an Indian, unless the context clearly requires another construction." The *Electoral Franchise Act* (1885), although including (status) Indians within its definition of "person" went on to exclude from the right to vote a wide range of "Indians", a restriction repeated in the 1890 Act.

We are familiar with the suffrage movement and the efforts of the women's movement in advocating for the vote at the beginning of this century.[17] Gaining the right to vote was such an important issue for women because the right to vote is fundamental to full citizenship; participation in the political process is a basic political right of citizens in a democracy. What seems to us to be a straightforward matter of justice, however, is anything but in terms of the history of women and the vote. Today in equality struggles, we still often hear the refrains of arguments used against giving women the vote. In Quebec, Cardinal Villeneuve's views were influential. In March 1940, he listed four reasons that women should not vote: (1) suffrage would militate against the family unit; (2) women would be exposed to the passions of elections; (3) most women in Quebec did not want the vote; and (4) social reforms could be achieved by women's organizations outside of politics.[18] Nellie McClung, a prominent suffragist, mocked such views in her essay, "Hardy Perennials", commenting on one of these kinds of arguments in the following terms:

> There is [an argument against giving women the vote], that if women were ever given the chance to participate in outside affairs then family quarrels would result ... [but] father and son have been known to live under the same roof and vote differently, and yet live! If a husband and wife are going to find cause to quarrel they will find cause for dispute easily enough, and will not be compelled to wait until election day.[19]

The vote was won, albeit slowly and unevenly. Gaining the right to vote was a high-priority issue for middle-class women. The majority of women who

---

[14] *An Act to Confer the Electoral Franchise upon Women*, 8–9 Geo. V, c. 20 gave to non-aboriginal women the right to vote in federal elections.

[15] Some of the dates of provincial enfranchisement of aboriginal persons were: British Columbia (1949), Manitoba (1952), Ontario (1954), Saskatchewan (1960), New Brunswick and Prince Edward Island (1963).

[16] In 1924, the federal government had awarded the franchise to approximately 4,000 Native Indians who were war veterans (Joseph Krauter and Morris Davis, *Minority Canadians: Ethnic Groups* (Toronto, Ont.: Methuen, 1978) at 75). In 1917, the *Military Voters Act*, S.C. 1917, c. 35 extended the federal vote to all Canadian men and women on active duty, including Indians. The *Dominion Elections Act* S.C. 1920, c. 46, s. 29(1) gave the vote to "Indians who served in the World War (later extended to the Second World War as well) but excluded Indians ordinarily resident on an Indian reservation."

[17] A number of women played a leading role in the Canadian suffrage movement, most notably Nellie McClung, Emily Murphy, Alice Jamieson, Louise McKinney, Irene Parlby, and Emily Stowe.

[18] Catherine L. Cleverdon, *The Woman Suffrage Movement in Canada* (Toronto, Ont.: University of Toronto Press, 1974) at 257.

[19] Nellie McClung, *In Times Like These* (Toronto, Ont.: University of Toronto Press, 1972) at 5.

were active in the leading suffrage associations, and who led the suffrage movement, had relatively high social positions; many were professionals such as doctors and educators and 60 per cent of the female suffragists held jobs. Carol Bacchi has noted that this is a "rather exceptional number" given that in 1911, only 14 per cent of women in Canada were employed for wages.[20] Labour groups and organized farm women's groups in the Western provinces also actively worked towards the enfranchisement of women through their own organizations. However, few ever joined the ranks of the suffrage societies, perhaps because of political differences.[21] Yet their enduring struggle should not be under-emphasized — after all, the prairie provinces were the first to grant the franchise to non-aboriginal women.

As in the case of married women's property, however, a number of competing interests were in motion around allowing women to vote. One lucid exchange on the topic appears in the historical record of the parliamentary debates. In 1929, Agnes McPhail, who had been Canada's first woman M.P. when she was elected in 1921, rose in the House of Commons to challenge the government of the day, which was claiming credit for first granting women a partial right to the federal vote in the *War Times Election Act*, 1917, S.C. 1917, c. 39. She said,

> I am astounded that [credit should be claimed] for the Conservative party for giving the franchise to women. I do not know of anything more scandalous except the *War Time Elections Act*, of which it was a part, than the manner of granting the franchise to women in 1917. Does the hon. member ... and his party not know that it was the starvation and the fighting and the going to jail and the forcible feeding suffered by the suffragettes of Great Britain, and to a lesser extent of the United States, that gave the franchise to Canadian women? [At which point some hon. members laughed. Agnes McPhail continued:] Hon. members do not show good sense in laughing at that. It is true; it is not a thing to be laughed at. The Conservative government ... gave votes to women in 1917, but not to all women. That would be too risky ... they gave votes to women who they thought would vote for them at that particular time ... they gave votes to some women, not to all women, and not because they were intelligent, but because they had a husband or a brother or a son fighting at the front. Whether war time or not, it was a very stupid way of extending the franchise to women.[22]

This initial law had indeed not been in any way a victory for the suffrage movement; its intention was merely to allow men fighting the war overseas to have a sort of "proxy" vote through their female relatives. Of course, that such a matter was legislated provides a clear insight into just how important and fundamental the right to vote was regarded as being, albeit for men. Catherine Cleverdon has quoted the Secretary of State as noting that the soldiers' female relatives were "likely to vote in such a way ... as they themselves would do upon our shores."[23]

McPhail clearly pointed out the distinct reasons for granting some women the vote in 1917. Obviously, the state's reasons for granting suffrage to women were not predicated on a desire to ensure full citizenship rights for women. Legislative change regarding women and the vote took a slow and uneven path. As in changes regarding marital property, its inception was not

---

[20] Carol Bacchi, "Divided Allegiances: The Response of Farm and Labour Women to Suffrage", in Linda Kealy, ed., *A Not Unreasonable Claim, 1880–1920s* (Toronto: The Women's Press, 1974) 89 at 91.

[21] *Ibid.* at 90.

[22] Canada, House of Commons, *Debates & Proceedings* (Hansard) (19 March 1929).

[23] Catherine L. Cleverdon, *The Woman Suffrage Movement in Canada* (Toronto: University of Toronto Press, 1974) at 125.

Lawyer Firsts	**EXHIBIT 29.1**

¤ In 1897, Clara Brett Martin was called to the Bar in the Province of Ontario, and was simultaneously admitted to practise as a solicitor. She was the first woman in the entire British Empire to be admitted to the practice of law. Certainly, the path was opened for other women to enter the legal profession.

¤ In 1912, Mabel French was the first woman to gain the right to practise law in two provinces (New Brunswick and British Columbia).

¤ In 1924, Vera Parsons became the first woman criminal lawyer in Ontario, and the first woman lawyer to appear before judge and jury. She was also one of the first women lawyers with a disability; she had polio and used a cane. It was not until 1941 that Quebec granted women the right to be admitted to the practice of law. Access to the legal profession was delayed for women of racial minorities.

¤ In 1946, Greta Wong Grant was the first Chinese-Canadian lawyer in Canada.

¤ Delia Opekokew was the first Native woman to be admitted to the Bar in Saskatchewan (1979), and also the first in Ontario (1983).

¤ In 1984, Marva Jemmott was appointed as a Queen's Counsel, the first black woman to receive this honour.

¤ In 1992, Paule Gauthier became the first woman president of the Canadian Bar Association.

grounded in any desire to grant all women full and equal political participation. Assumptions about women's rightful place in society informed restrictive legislation, and impeded women's efforts to gain the vote. This is a recurrent theme in much of the history of women and the law.

Canada's First Woman Lawyer

In 1897, Clara Brett Martin was called to the Bar in the Province of Ontario, and was simultaneously admitted to practise as a solicitor. She was the first woman in the entire British Empire to be admitted to the practice of law. Her accomplishment did not come without a struggle and the support of senior politicians including the Premier, Oliver Mowatt. In 1891, she petitioned the Law Society of Upper Canada (the governing body for lawyers in the province) for permission to become a student member; such membership was a prerequisite to articling as a clerk, attending lectures, and sitting the exams required to receive a certificate of fitness to practise as a solicitor. The Law Society denied her petition, interpreting its governing statute as permitting only men to be admitted to the practice of law. Clara Brett Martin succeeded in having her case raised in the Ontario legislature and legislation was ultimately passed to permit women to become solicitors.[24] In order to implement this legislation, the Law Society was required to alter its regulations; initially it refused to do so, deeming it "inexpedient". However, in a narrow vote (12 for; 11 against) and after various machinations, rules for admitting women were eventually approved. Clara Brett Martin then registered as a **student-at-law**. Partway through her study, she decided that she wanted to be admitted as a barrister as well as a solicitor (at the time, the profession of law was divided into two branches) She was once again faced with a struggle with the Law Society. In 1895, legislation was passed to allow women to be called to the bar.[25] Once

---

[24] *An Act to Provide for the Admission of Women to the Study and Practice of Law*, 1892, 55 Vict., c. 32 (Ont.).

[25] *An Act to Amend the Act to Provide for the Admission of Women to the Study and Practice of Law*, 1895, 58 Vict., c. 27 (Ont.).

again, the Law Society resisted drawing up the necessary regulations; eventually it altered its regulations in 1896.

Throughout her studies, she was "dogged with various degrees of scrutiny, harassment and ridicule." The following quote demonstrates her motivation: "If it were not that I set out to open the way to the bar for others of my sex, I would have given up the effort long ago. You would not believe how many obstacles I have had to overcome single-handed."[26] She maintained an active interest in women's issues and in women's rights generally throughout her career as a lawyer. She remained single. Her health began to decline by 1920, and she died in 1923 at the relatively young age of 49.

Clara Brett Martin has been regarded as a pathbreaker and role model for women wishing to enter the legal profession. However, in 1989, a letter written by Martin in 1915 to the Attorney General was found in the archives of the Law Society of Upper Canada. In the letter, Martin made comments which were clearly and unequivocally anti-Semitic, casting aspersions on the real estate transactions of Jewish individuals and requesting that the Attorney General take legal action. These views show that although she was sensitive to aspects of sexism, Martin was clearly not so mindful of discrimination against Jews. The discovery of her letter led to a storm of controversy over Martin's stature in women's legal history. Law professor Constance Backhouse reminds us that Martin's anti-Semitism is a telling example of how we can perpetrate certain forms of discrimination while at the same we are struggling for the elimination of other forms.[27]

JUDGING AND GENDER

In this section of the chapter, we examine the impact that gender-biased judicial attitudes and legal rules have had on women as litigants or participants in the legal process. In the last section, we discussed examples which focused on the role of legislation and legislative change in influencing women's equality. The roles of politicians, leaders of the legal profession, and women's activists were touched upon. However, in understanding the scope of the gender issue in law, it is vital to include the role of judges. It is judges who articulate, interpret, and apply legal principles to fact situations brought before them by litigants unable to settle their disputes. It is judges who interpret legislation and provide remedies. It is judges who control the courtrooms. Their world views and assumptions — and their gender biases — play a very significant role in determining the scope and pace of legal change for women.

Of course, the "official" version of how judges do their jobs[28] is that they are objective, impartial, and neutral in reaching their decisions.[29] Many written judgments and transcripts of oral remarks suggest, however, that in practice judges have allowed gender bias to influence their decision making. Sometimes this can be seen as the product of individual bias; other times, the

[26] Buffalo Express (1896), undated clipping, archives of the Women's Law Association of Ontario as quoted in Constance Backhouse, " 'To Open the Way for Others of My Sex': Clara Brett Martin's Career as Canada's First Woman Lawyer" (1985) 1 C.J.W.L. 1 at 22.

[27] Constance Backhouse, "Clara Brett Martin: Canadian Heroine or Not?" (1992) 5 C.J.W.L. 263–79.

[28] To further explore ideas about judging, refer to Hon. Bertha Wilson, "Will Women Judges Really Make a Difference?" (1990) 28 Osgoode Hall L.J. 507; J.A.G. Griffiths, *The Politics of the Judiciary*, 2d ed. (London: Fontana, 1981); Peter Russell, *The Judiciary in Canada: The Third Branch of Government* (Toronto, Ont.: McGraw-Hill Ryerson, 1987).

[29] See also Mary Jane Mossman, "Feminism and Legal Method: The Difference it Makes" (1987) 3 Wisconsin Women's L.J. 147, and (1986) 3 Aust. J. L. & Soc. 30.

Judicial Firsts

EXHIBIT 29.2

- In 1916, Emily Murphy was the first woman to be appointed as police magistrate in the British Empire. Her initial jurisdiction was the City of Edmonton. However, it was later extended throughout Alberta. She presided over a women's police court where cases were heard in the absence of men.
- In 1917, Helen Gregory McGill was appointed as Judge of the Juvenile Court in Vancouver, British Columbia.
- In 1934, Helen Kinnear became the first woman in the British Commonwealth to be appointed as King's Counsel — an honour granted to senior, respected members of the legal profession. In 1943, Kinnear was appointed as County Court Judge, and became the first woman lawyer in the British Empire to be appointed to a superior court judgeship.
- In 1971, Mabel Van Camp became the first woman appointed to the Ontario Supreme Court.
- In 1973, Jean Folster was the first Native woman to be appointed as a magistrate in Manitoba.
- In 1975, Agnes Sempler of the Northwest Territories was the first aboriginal woman to be appointed as Justice of Peace.
- In 1976, Rosalie Abella became the first Jewish woman to be appointed as judge in the Ontario Provincial Court.
- In 1982, Bertha Wilson was the first woman to be appointed to the Supreme Court of Canada.
- In 1987, Canada had its first black woman judge, when Corrine Sparks was appointed to the family court in Nova Scotia. In 1979, she had been the first black woman to graduate in law school in Dalhousie University, Nova Scotia.
- In 1991, Terry Vyse became the first aboriginal person, man or woman, to be appointed as judge in Ontario when she was appointed to the Provincial Court of Ontario;
- In 1993, Maryka Omatsu became the first woman of Japanese ancestry to be appointed as Judge of the Ontario Provincial Court.
- In 1994, Rose Boyko, a T'Sekani woman from British Columbia, became the first aboriginal woman appointed by the federal government to a superior court, when she was appointed to the Ontario High Court.

statements made by the various judges reflect the dominant thinking or views of the time. Also of concern is where a judge, without overt bias, applies a rule into which bias is already built. This section discusses a number of examples of problematic, even appalling, judicial comments; what may be most unsettling, though, is that while some comments are from long ago, some are very recent indeed. And, while some of these comments may seem absurd, quaint, or even ridiculous, we need to remember that they had an impact on individual outcomes and systemic responses to women.

Judicial Attitudes to Women: Gender Bias

In 1977, a 21-year-old man was convicted in Toronto of a criminal charge of unlawfully confining an 18-year-old woman. He had gone to a house with a knife in his hand, broken down a door, ripped the telephone off the wall, and forcibly seized the woman. He was on probation for similar offences at the time of these events. The trial judge, Judge Bewley, sentenced him to six months in prison. In so doing, he made the following comments about the young woman and her friends:

> There is a girl here, or a couple of girls, young nubile females, who've been around a bit, eh? They've travelled from Ontario to here, they're a free floating type of female, young for their age, very nubile, very attractive, surely, but, I suppose, basically I have to look at it this way, still impressionable,

still stupid ... you know women don't get much brains before they're thirty anyway ... but at the age of eighteen or so, they make some stupid mistakes, mostly because we males who know better, lead them into it....

I found him technically guilty of unlawful confinement, you know, but I'm not too sympathetic towards these stupid girls. There's no big deal, right? It isn't as if he held up ... an innocent driver, getting away from something or threatened a policeman with a knife or something. He's demonstrating his manhood to a little girl eighteen years of age, who's probably half inclined to think he's a man by showing a knife, so big deal, eh?

So, I could give him five years, but I don't think under the circumstances of this case, I'd be entitled to give him five years, because as we clearly have said before, he got mixed up with a silly, little bunch of girls who mean well, they got scared because he was proving himself a macho man, was going to haul one of them out and talk to her even if she got scared and ran into the bedroom, so we've got a bunch of clucking females running around, and they are all so scared that they have to call the Police.[30]

These comments show a very patronizing and disrespectful view of young women. They paint a very different picture of events from that recorded in the facts of this man's criminal conduct. They also display a distressing acceptance that, somehow, violent conduct by men towards women is not very serious. (Similarly, in 1982, Members of the House of Commons had to apologize for an outburst of disbelieving laughter when a parliamentary report on battered wives was tabled in Parliament.[31]) The direct impact of Judge Bewley's attitude in the cited case was more lenient sentencing than one might expect; the indirect impact on the young women hearing these comments was likely profound.

These comments were not unprecedented, nor were they the last of this kind. Remarks made in December 1989 by Judge Bourassa, a territorial court judge in the Northwest Territories, raised similar concerns. He was quoted by the *Edmonton Journal* as saying, "The majority of rapes in the Northwest Territories occur when the woman is drunk and passed out. A man comes along and sees a pair of hips and helps himself. That contrasts sharply to the cases I dealt with before (as a judge in southern Canada) of the dainty co-ed who gets jumped from behind."[32] The judge later said that he regretted his remarks and a Judicial Inquiry recommended against disciplinary action. In another Northwest Territories case, Mr. Justice Mark De Weerdt ruled in 1990 that "a man who beat his wife deserved a lighter sentence because she provoked him" by wearing a lewd T-shirt. The shirt, showing cartoon polar bears engaged in a sexual act, could be seen as "implying the possibility, if not the actual promise of sexual perversity and promiscuity." In his ruling, Judge De Weerdt said that the T-shirt's implication "could be understood by the other spouse as an imminent threat that she might commit adultery." Such a threat would be "calculated to arouse alarm, fear, and anger in that other spouse, with clearly foreseeable consequences," he said. Instead of a prison sentence, the judge imposed a fine of $1,000. Again, a ready tolerance of male violence against women found its way into a judicial outcome.

A remark made by Judge Denys Dionne during an assault and weapons trial in the Montreal suburb of Longueuil on 27 January 1989, which came to light early in 1990, is also instructive of gender bias on the part of judges. It was reported that Judge Dionne interjected during argument with the comment, "Rules are like women, they are made to be violated." A lawyer

---

[30] *R. v. Tourangeau* (25 August 1977), unreported (B.C. Provincial Court, Vancouver). See further, M.E. Atcheson, M. Eberts and B. Symes, *Women and Legal Action* (Ottawa: CACSW, 1984), at 40–42.

[31] House of Commons, *Debates*, 12 May 1982, 17334; 13 May 1982, 17368; 14 May 1982, 17423–424.

[32] *Edmonton Journal* (20 December 1989).

involved in the case responded, "Exactly." An official complaint was made against the judge by the Quebec Ministry of Justice to the Quebec Judicial Council. *The Globe and Mail* reported the proceedings of the hearing on 13 February 1990. In explanation, the judge argued that he had made the remark sarcastically to dismiss an argument advanced by a defence lawyer. An audio recording revealed that a lawyer was stressing how "all good principles of law have their exceptions" when Dionne interjected with the comment. He testified to the panel that he first heard the controversial remark about 30 years ago from a respected Quebec jurist. A witness, Crown prosecutor Michel Breton, who was in court when Dionne uttered the 1989 comment, said he considered the remark a "farce" or a "quip" made in impatience to the defence lawyer: "It was something I've heard before," he said. "I was not surprised and I didn't notice any surprise in the courtroom."[33] How deeply entrenched — and normalized — such comments may be is suggested by this comment and indeed by Judge Dionne's testimony that he had originally heard the remark from a "respected jurist". In June 1990, the disciplinary committee ruled that the comment by Judge Dionne was "sexist, in extremely bad taste and unacceptable coming from a judge." It also said that the comments tarnished the image of justice and could lead people to believe that some judges are prejudiced and incapable of rendering impartial decisions. Dionne was to be "severely reprimanded" but not removed from the bench; the goal of the reprimand would be to make sure that the judge realized such statements are wrong and will not be tolerated.

A similar inquiry was held in 1993 into comments made by Judge Frank Allen, a Manitoba provincial court judge. He received a reprimand from the Manitoba Judicial Council in relation to a range of remarks dating back to 1985 when he had commented, while sentencing a man who had threatened to kill his former girlfriend and himself, "I can tell you from 60-odd years of experience that there isn't any woman worth the trouble you got yourself into." In 1989, Judge Allen had reprimanded a female lawyer who was seeking an adjournment because her nursing infant was running an extremely high fever and throwing up antibiotics, and she herself was feeling unwell. The judge suggested that she find a replacement "who is not trying to be a mother and a lawyer at the same time." The Council concluded that judges do not have the right to make such sexist comments, but held that Judge Allen's remarks did not prove that he was incompetent. Of course, this raises the question of whether one can be a good judge (or a good lawyer) if one is profoundly sexist and antipathetic to women's rights to equality and respect. Certainly, Ontario Provincial Court Judge Walter Hryciuk crossed the line. He was ordered removed from the bench in 1993 for sexual misconduct following an inquiry which accepted allegations by two female Crown attorneys that he had sexually harassed and touched them, made lewd remarks, and had forced his tongue into one of the women's mouth during an unwanted kiss.

Very recently indeed, in March 1996, the Canadian **Judicial Council** held a hearing to investigate comments made by Judge Jean Bienvenue of the Quebec Superior Court, who had presided over the trial of a woman accused of murdering her husband. During the trial, he told the woman that by slashing her husband's throat, she made him suffer more than the victims of the Nazi gas chambers: "the Nazis did not eliminate millions of Jews in a painful and bloody manner," he said, "they died in gas chambers without suffering." Female violence to men appears to be judged by a different standard than male violence to women. The judge also said that women can "become more

---

[33] Eric Siblin, *Canadian Press Newswire*, 11 April 1990.

depraved than men" and referred (in French) to the woman as a "négresse" which, in French, is a pejorative term equivalent to describing Blacks as niggers.

These comments and actions by judges became public due to media reporting and when complaints were made to Judicial Councils which oversee the conduct of judges. In 1992, the Canadian Bar Association (CBA) initiated a Task Force to inquire into gender bias in the legal profession. This Task Force was chaired by now-retired Supreme Court Justice, Hon. Bertha Wilson. In its far-ranging report, the Task Force recommended, *inter alia*, parental leave policies for female and male lawyers, flexible work arrangements, workplace equity, sexual harassment policies, commissions to investigate gender-based complaints against judges, and mandatory courses on gender and racial bias for all newly appointed and sitting judges. Following the submission of the Task Force Report, the CBA passed a resolution at its meetings of February 1994, recognizing inequalities in the legal profession, and initiated a process directed towards establishing a similar inquiry into racism in the legal profession.

Public and Private Roles

Clara Brett Martin's struggle to become the first woman lawyer showed us that opposition to women having a public or professional role was legally and socially entrenched. In provinces other than Ontario, women went to court to argue that prohibitions on them becoming lawyers should be set aside. The responses by judges included outrage, incredulity, and implacable opposition. One telling example comes from the case of Annie MacDonald Langstaff, a resident of Quebec who petitioned the Quebec Superior Court in 1915, after her application to take the preliminary bar examination was refused because she was a woman. Mr. Justice Saint-Pierre rejected her petition and blustered:

> I would put within the range of possibilities though by no means a commendable one, the admission of a woman to the profession of solicitor or to that of *avoue*, but I hold that to admit a woman and more particularly, a married woman as a barrister, that is to say, as a person *who pleads cases at the bar before judges or juries in open court and in the presence of the public*, would be nothing short of a direct infringement upon public order and a manifest violation of the law of good morals and public decency.
>
> Let us for a moment picture to ourselves a woman appearing a defending or prosecuting counsel in a case of rapt (sic) [rape] and putting to the complainant the questions which must of all necessity be asked in order to make proof of the acts which are of the essence of the crime or which are equally necessary to meet and repeal the charge. No woman possessing the least sense of decency could possibly do so without throwing a blur upon her own dignity and without bringing into utter contempt the honour and respect due to her sex.

A classic statement in this genre was made in the United States by Justice Bradley in the 1879 case of *Bradwell v. Illinois*. His views were later cited and accepted in Canadian cases. In *Bradwell*, Myra Bradwell, who had legal education and published a successful legal newspaper in Chicago, was petitioning the court to be permitted to become a practising lawyer. She based her case on the U.S. Constitution which provided that no state should make laws abridging the "rights or immunities of citizens", which Bradwell took to include the economic right to practise a profession. Her case went all the way to the U.S. Supreme Court which dismissed her petition. In the words of Justice Bradley:

> Civil law as well as nature herself has always recognised a wide difference in the respective spheres and destinies of man and woman. Man is or should

be, woman's protector and defender. The natural and proper timidity and delicacy which belongs to the female sex evidently unfits it for many of the occupations of civil life. The constitution of the family organization, which is founded in the divine ordinance, as well as in the nature of things, indicates the domestic sphere as that which properly belongs to the domain and functions of womanhood.

Interestingly, 60 of the leading lawyers of Chicago petitioned the state governor to appoint her a Notary Public while her case was pending in the Supreme Court. And, three years after the decision, Bradwell did become an honorary member of the bar.[34]

A more contemporary example of women's aspirations to a public, professional role being rebuffed is the story of comments made to Bertha Wilson upon starting law school. The exchange took place in 1954 between Wilson and one of her male law professors. He sneered at her, "Why would someone like you, at age 31, with a husband to look after you, want to study law?" She replied that she wanted to study law "as part of a liberal education", to which the professor replied, "Look, my dear, we have no room here for dilettantes. Why don't you just go home and take up crocheting?"[35] We can be glad that she did not take this particular advice!

A romantic paternalism is also apparent in many of the cases which refused to allow women to vote or study at university. In an 1863 English case, *Chorlton v. Lings*, women's efforts to register to vote in a city election were challenged and rebuffed by the Court. One of the judges, Sir James Easte Willes, rationalized his refusal to permit women to vote in the following terms:

> What was the cause of the exclusion of women, it is not necessary to go into: but admitting that fickleness of judgment and liability to influence have sometimes been suggested as the ground of exclusion, I must protest against it being supposed to arise in this country from any under-rating of the sex either in point of intellect or worth. That would be quite inconsistent with one of the glories of our civilisation — the respect and honour in which women are held. This is not a mere fancy of my own but will be found in Seldon, in the discussion of the origin of the exclusion of women from judicial and like public functions, where the author gives preference for this reason, that the exemption was founded upon motives of decorum, and was a privilege of the sex.

Despite protestations of respect for women, a thread of case law exists in which women were clearly grouped together with children in assessing legal capacity. For example, in the 1873 case of *Daniels v. Clegg*, a United States court, when concerned with the standard of diligence required of a 20-year-old woman, decided that she should not be required to conform to the standards of the "reasonable man", the accepted standard in assessing conduct. Rather, concessions were to be made for her because of "the incompetency indicated by her age and sex ... which was less in degree, it is true than in the case of a mere child; but the difference is in degree only, and not in principle." Similarly in the 1867 Irish case of *The Queen v. Crosthwaite*, a case concerned with whether a woman was included in the term "persons" in a municipal voting Act, one of the judges, Baron Deasy, stated that:

> [T]he general policy of the law is to exclude [women] from any such intervention ... partly on the supposition that such subjects are beyond their cognizance, as requiring a judgment superior to that which they possess, and

---

[34] See, generally, Martha Minow, "Forming Under Everything That Grows" (1985) Wisconsin L.R. 819 at 846–50.

[35] David Vienneau, "Speaking Her Mind: Supreme Court Judge Bertha Wilson" *Toronto Star* (13 September 1990) D1, D3.

partly on the ground that it is inconsistent with the delicacy and modesty of their sex, that they should be mixed up in the strife and turmoil of a contested election. (at 472)

> ... That the law in recognising the distinction of the sexes assumes a greater worthiness in the male than in the female, is manifest in the law of descent; that it has regard to the infirmity of bodily strength and ability in the female, by rendering her incompetent for some offices and privileges, or incapacitating her from the discharge of duties thereto belonging, cannot be questioned. Again, that she is subject to incapacities from a presumed inferiority of discretion and judgment, seems also certain: a woman was not admitted as a witness in a case of villeinage against a man; and the reason assigned is, because of her "fragility."

In the same case, Baron Fitzgerald wholeheartedly agreed with his judicial brother, and added for himself that he could:

> have no doubt that in substance the reason of the Common Law still applies; and that the course of education and mental training to which women, happily for us and themselves, are subject, does render them far less fit than men for the administration of public affairs. ... Having regard to every one of the reasons of Common Law, the subordination of sex, the inferiority of bodily ability, and the mental inferiority in the sense explained ... I am not sorry ... to come to the conclusion that this judgment ought to be reversed.

More blunt still were comments arising out of the effort made in 1869 by Sophia Jex-Blake and six other women, together known as the "Edinburgh Seven", to study at the Edinburgh Medical School. Their efforts were rebuffed by the University and the full weight of the law was used in support. Lord Neaves, a member of the full bench of the Scottish Court of Session which heard the women's appeal in 1873, had little apparent hesitation in supporting the expulsion of the women from the School. In his decision he stated:

> It is a belief, widely entertained that there is great difference in the mental constitution of the two sexes, just as there is in their physical conformation. The powers and susceptibilities of women are as noble as those of men; but they are thought to be different, and, in particular, it is considered that they have not the same power of intense labour as men are endowed with. If this be so, it must form serious objection to uniting them under the same course of academic study. ... A disregard of such an inequality would be fatal to any scheme of public instruction, for, as it is certain that the general mass of an army cannot move more rapidly than its weakest and slowest portion, so a general course of study must be toned and tempered down to suit the average of all the classes of students for whom it is intended; and that average will always be lowered by the existence of any considerable numbers who cannot keep pace with the rest.
>
> Add to this the special acquirements and accomplishments at which women must aim, but from which men may easily remain exempt. Much time must, or ought to be, given by women to the acquisition of a knowledge of household affairs and family duties, as well as to those ornamental parts of education which tend so much to social refinement and domestic happiness, and the study necessary for mastering these must always form a serious distraction from severer pursuits, while there is little doubt that, in public estimation, the want of these feminine arts and attractions in a woman would be ill supplied by such branches of knowledge as a University could bestow. ... [this] case certainly affords no ground from subverting the constitution of our universities, or affecting the dignity and weight which belong to the highest honour attending the medical profession....
>
> Any change which would incur the risk of lowering the standard that now exists, and which we have seen exemplified in so many of our great physicians and professors, is infinitely to be deprecated, and such a danger, I think would be incurred by the revolution in the medical teaching of our universities that has here been attempted to be brought about; while at the

same time it would otherwise affect and in my opinion, deteriorate our Universities in a way unknown to any period of their history.

These comments contain a disturbing set of assumptions about women, and clearly sought to assign women to a separate, private sphere. The assumptions made included that men were superior to women in mental and physical ability, that only men were (or should be) involved in public (important) matters, and that women were "less worthy" than men. Their inclusion in university study would lower presumptively rigorous standards and undermine the professions, to say nothing of injuring women's health and well-being. Ethel Benjamin, who was the second woman to become a lawyer in the British Empire (she was admitted in New Zealand in May 1897), placed at the top of her law school class and in reply to queries as to whether her health had been affected replied, "No, my health did not suffer in the least. Do I look like an invalid?" Suffragist Nellie McClung also reminded her readers in 1916 that the same men who recoiled from the idea of women leaving the "sacred precincts of home" had their offices "scrubbed by poor women who do their work while other people sleep." McClung suggested that it was "the thought of women getting into comfortable and well-paid positions which wrings their manly hearts."[36] Justice Brennan of the U.S. Supreme Court added another insight in a 1973 case which considered sex classifications involving dependents' benefits for servicemen and women. He commented in *Frontiero v. Richardson*, that "there can be no doubt that our nation has a long and unfortunate history of sex discrimination. Traditionally, such discrimination was rationalized by an attitude of 'romantic paternalism' which, in practical effect, put women, not on a pedestal, but in a cage."

The Scope of Legal Rules

Many of the comments included in this section of the chapter have identified the gender bias of individual judges. But what if the rules themselves are not neutral in their effect or formulation but are themselves gender biased? Of course, the legal rule that only "persons" could vote, be lawyers, go to university, or be called to the Senate of Canada, which underlay many of the cases discussed so far, is a prime example of a rule being the source of discrimination. What has obscured that point for us today is that it seems so clear that it was the judges' interpretation and application of the rule that led to discrimination against women in many cases. However, there is no shortage of other examples of rules which contain prejudice. A good example is found in the 1985 N.W.T. case of *R. v. Oquataq*. This was a sexual assault case. The accused was challenging restrictions contained in the *Criminal Code* which restricted his right to ask questions of the complainant about her sexual conduct with other people on other occasions. These restrictions related to the law of evidence (which determines what information can be admitted in a trial). The restrictions were designed to counteract the role of stereotype and myth in the trial process. However, Mr. Justice Marshall held that the restrictions were unconstitutional. In so finding he made the following extraordinary admission:

> Although relating chastity to likelihood of consent [to sexual activity] is unfair, it has comprised part of the carefully balanced evidentiary process. ... The question of the proper evaluation of such evidence is a difficult one. It is a question of logic — what is legally relevant, what is logically probative of the issues with which we are dealing. ... Now then, in logic, is willingness to consent to have intercourse outside of marriage or established relationships ... is [such] sexual indulgence logically probative of consent on a particular

---

[36] McClung, *supra* note 22 at 56.

occasion? ... Does it mean, the girl [sic] was more likely to have consented? [In my view] it is logically probative. The problem with this assumption is that it denies both autonomy and dignity to women ... [but] our test for judicial truth is based on probabilities ... it may show rank prejudice; but we use it.[37]

Similarly, judges may follow the logic of existing reasoning to reach a result — but fail to notice that the reasoning on which it is based excludes the experiences or understandings of women and, as a result, denies them an appropriate legal remedy. Four examples of this can be given. The Manitoba Court of Appeal held in 1986 that to consider sexual harassment to be sex discrimination was "amazing". Instead, the judges opined, if not all women in a workplace were harassed, the attention given to some women, must be because they are attractive, not because they are women.[38] The Supreme Court of Canada later reversed this ruling, holding that sexual harassment was indeed sex discrimination. The Manitoba Court of Appeal also rejected the defence of self-defence raised to a murder charge against a battered aboriginal woman, Lyn Lavallee, referring to it as "fanciful".[39] The decision met a similar fate in the Supreme Court of Canada, which accepted that evidence of the "battered woman syndrome" was admissible to support a defence to such a charge. A third example is the ruling of the New Brunswick Court of Appeal that touching a woman's breast should not be considered to be a sexual assault. The judges reasoned that breasts are "secondary sexual characteristics", in the same manner as a man's beard is a secondary sexual characteristic. They reasoned that only the touching of genitalia should be considered "sexual" assault in order to avoid "absurdity" and to preserve the ability of a man to "steal a goodnight kiss".[40] The Supreme Court of Canada reversed this ruling, accepting that breasts have a sexual meaning in our society. The final example is of a trial court judge in Ottawa, who acquitted a man charged with threatening serious bodily harm. He had written explicit letters to three cheerleaders of a football team in which he had made it clear that he knew where they lived and would have sexual intercourse with them even if he had to rape them. The trial judge held that this was not a threat to cause the women serious bodily harm.[41] This ruling too, was reversed on appeal.

Another aspect of the problem of gender bias in legal rules is when law, as a result of excluding women's experiences, has failed to develop appropriate legal frameworks. The prime areas in which this kind of problem exists is in the area of pregnancy. An example is provided by a case which involved the criminal prosecution of two midwives, who were alleged to have been negligent in their actions during a childbirth resulting in the death of the foetus prior to completed birth. In this 1991 case, the legal question was whether the foetus could be characterized as a "person" within the scope of the criminal offence. Legal reasoning built around the idea of the centrality and separateness of individuals forced the analysis to focus on whether the foetus was a legal person or not to the exclusion of the surrounding events — namely, childbirth and the intimate connectedness of the foetus with its mother.

[37] Marshall J in *R. v. Oquataq* (1985), 18 C.C.C. (3d) 440, at 450 (N.W.T.).
[38] *Janzen v. Platy Enterprises* (1986), 43 Man. R. (2d) 293.
[39] *R. v. Lavallee* (1988), 52 Man. R. (2d) 274.
[40] *R. v. Chase* (1984), 40 C.R. (3d) 282.
[41] *R. v. McGraw* (8 November 1988, Dist. Ct. of Ont., Flanagan, D.C.J.); also reproduced in (1989) 21 Ottawa L. Rev. 201.

The result of the case (an acquittal) is less important here than the insightful argument made to the Supreme Court by an intervenor in the case, the Women's Legal Education and Action Fund (LEAF). It argued:

> Traditionally legal method proceeds by analogy and distinction, making it tempting to compare the relationship between a pregnant woman and her fetus to relations already mapped by law. However, there are no adequate analogies to pregnancy and childbirth and attempts to find them distort reality. Had women not been excluded from participation in the legal system, the unique relationship between the woman and her fetus and the experience of pregnancy in the life of women — hardly new facts — might have engendered their own fundamental legal concepts and doctrines, as elaborate as doctrines dealing with commercial partnerships for example.

The point that LEAF was making — independently of the merits of the case — was that the legal principles and forms of reasoning simply didn't fit the situation and that appropriate principles, concepts, and doctrines to deal with it had not been developed within a legal system that took men and men's life cycles as the norm.

WORKING TOWARDS EQUALITY IN LAW AND LIFE

On 17 April 1985 the equality rights section of the 1982 *Canadian Charter of Rights and Freedoms* came into effect. The Charter sets the standard for all legislation and government action in Canada. The *Canadian Charter of Rights and Freedoms* sets out a range of guaranteed rights. If a piece of legislation or other government action is thought to be inconsistent with Charter rights, it can be challenged in the courts. If the judges agree, they can strike it down or give a remedy which removes the inconsistency and upholds the basic right.

Section 15(1) sets out the scope of equality rights in the following terms:

> Every individual is equal before and under the law and has the right to the equal protection and equal benefit of the law without discrimination, and in particular, without discrimination based on race, national or ethnic origin, colour, religion, sex, age or mental or physical disability.

Section 15(2) clarifies that "any law, program or activity which has as its objective the amelioration of conditions of disadvantaged individuals or groups" is not precluded by the main equality clause. This subsection is important for claims to equality because there is a recognition that special treatment is required to alleviate inequalities which stem from discrimination. It recognizes that differential treatment may be necessary given the "historical realities" of the position of individuals or groups in society. Section 28 of the Charter guarantees the rights and freedoms set out in the Charter equally to "male and female persons".

While the Charter covers government action in the form of legislation and the actions of government officials, the actions of private individuals and corporations in relation to employment, services, and accommodation are regulated by provincial human rights legislation. Federally regulated employers, including the federal government itself as employer, are governed by the *Canadian Human Rights Act* 1976–77, c. 33, s. 1. The purpose of this Act is to:

> extend the laws in Canada to give effect, within the purview of matters coming within the legislative authority of Parliament, to the principle that every individual should have an equal opportunity with other individuals to make for himself or herself the life that he or she is able and wishes to have, consistent with his or her duties and obligations as a member of society,

without being hindered in or prevented from doing so by discriminatory practices based on race, national or ethnic origin, colour, religion, age, sex, marital status, family status, disability or conviction for an offence for which a pardon has been granted.

In Ontario, the current *Human Rights Code*, which has its roots in legislation that came into effect in 1958 and 1961, has been extended over the years to protect people against discrimination based on race, ancestry, place of origin, colour, ethnic origin, citizenship, creed, sex (including sexual harassment and pregnancy), sexual orientation, age, marital status, family status, handicap, and the receipt of public assistance.

A wide range of more specific legislation addressing the legal situation of women (among other groups) also exists (e.g., pay equity laws, employment equity laws, family laws, and provisions in the *Criminal Code*). Often municipal by-laws and collective agreements prohibit certain forms of discrimination. The national bodies of trade unions in Canada have had a longstanding commitment to equality guarantees. At the international level, Canada is a signatory to several international conventions and treaties which commit the country to seeking to achieve certain standards. Of particular interest is the United Nations *Convention on the Elimination of All Forms of Discrimination Against Women* (which was adopted by the UN in 1979 and came into force in 1981). Thus, from the loftiest international levels to the most mundane of municipal regulation, a commitment to equality, including sex equality, has been steadily included in Canadian law. This may prove to be one of the most useful and enduring breakthroughs of the century; the prevalence of equality as a current legal concept certainly means that an understanding of the concept and an ability to use it are essential parts of the gender issue in law. That said, there are many different conceptions of what equality means and different approaches to achieving equality. At its minimum, of course, equality means the right to be free from discrimination and to be able to participate and contribute to society as a full citizen. Before we move to discuss these points theoretically, we include a case study which raises many issues related to equality legislation, approaches to equality and the processes involved in claiming equality in Canada.

Human Rights Legislation and Gender: Pay Equity

For many years, women in the labour force have been paid less than men. Data on wage differences by gender were first collected by Statistics Canada in 1967: the average earnings of women working on a full-time, full-year basis was 58 per cent of those of their male counterparts. In 1993, women earned 72 per cent of male earnings.[42] To what can we attribute the gendered wage gap? How is it that women are paid less than men? Different arguments exist on this point. Some argue that men earn wages which are sufficient to provide for the needs of their families. The so-called "family wage" allows women to stay home, raise children, and maintain the family. If women enter the paid labour force, they do so only to earn some extra money for the family; therefore, lower wages are justified. Others believe that pay inequities between men and women reflect the fact that women do work that is worth less. This would imply that secretarial work is worth less than janitorial work. A third position, human capital theory, posits that women have not invested in their own development in terms of education, training, and skills. According to this line of reasoning, women are paid less because they have not learned the skills nor obtained appropriate education which would lead to higher wages.

---

[42] Statistics Canada, Housing, Family and Social Statistics Division, Target Groups Project, *Women in Canada: A Statistical Report*, 3d ed. (Ottawa: Statistics Canada, 1995) at 86.

Legislature Firsts

EXHIBIT 29.3

¤ In 1917, Louise McKinney and Roberta MacAdams became the first women elected to a provincial legislature (Alberta).

¤ In 1921, Mary Ellen Smith was the first woman in the British Empire to serve as a Cabinet minister. She was the "Minister without Portfolio" in the British Columbia legislature. In 1920, women were granted the right to hold political office and to sit in Parliament.

¤ In 1922, Agnes McPhail became the first woman member of parliament in the federal House of Commons.

¤ In 1928, the Supreme Court of Canada ruled that women were not among the "qualified persons" eligible to be called to sit as senators. This decision was reversed by the English Privy Council in 1929. Cairine Wilson was the first woman Senator in 1930.

¤ In 1949, Nancy Hodges became the first woman Parliamentary Speaker in the Commonwealth when she was appointed Speaker in the British Columbia legislature.

¤ In 1957, Ellen Fairclough was the first federal Cabinet minister; she was appointed as the Secretary of State.

¤ In 1971, Margaret Birch became the first woman Cabinet minister in Ontario.

¤ In 1972, Rosemary Brown became the first black woman to be elected to a Canadian legislature when she was elected as a New Democratic Party member in British Columbia.

¤ In 1973, Muriel Ferguson became the first woman Speaker of the Senate.

¤ In 1980, Jeanne Sauvé was appointed the first woman Speaker of the House of Commons. In 1984, she was the first woman appointed as Governor-General of Canada.

¤ In 1980, Alexa McDonough was the first woman to lead a provincial party when she was elected leader of the Nova Scotia New Democratic Party. The first woman leader of a political party was Thérèse Casgrain who led the Co-operative Commonwealth Federation in Quebec in 1951.

¤ In 1984, Anne Clare Cools was the first black woman to be appointed to the Senate of Canada.

¤ In 1988, Ethel Blondin was the first aboriginal woman to be elected to the federal Parliament; in 1993, she was the first to be appointed to the federal Cabinet when she became Minister of State for Youth and Training.

¤ In 1990, Audrey McLaughlin became the first woman in North America to lead a major political party (New Democratic Party).

¤ In 1990, Zanana Akande became the first black woman elected to the provincial legislature in Ontario.

¤ In 1993, Jean Augustine became the first black woman to be elected to the House of Commons, when she was elected Liberal Member of Parliament for a Toronto riding.

¤ In 1993, Catherine Callback became the first woman elected as provincial premier, when she led the Liberal Party to victory in Prince Edward Island.

There are several assumptions beneath these claims. Underlying the notion of the male family wage are the assumptions that male wages are indeed sufficient to provide for female dependents, and that women ought to be dependent on men to provide for them. These assumptions are contradicted by evidence which shows that most women work in the labour force out of economic necessity, and not because of the desire to earn pocket money. The dual-income family has become an economic necessity: to support a household, 60–80 hours of paid work per week are required.[43] The argument

---

[43] Canadian Advisory Council on the Status of Women, *Expanding Our Horizons: The Work of the Canadian Advisory Council on the Status of Women and its Context* (Ottawa: CACSW, 1993) at 73.

that women have invested less in their education is easily refuted. Women who are university graduates and are employed full-time earn only 75 per cent as much as their male counterparts.[44]

It becomes apparent, then, that wages are assigned by gender. Again, several explanations have been suggested for how this takes place. One argument is that the difference is a result of pure wage discrimination on the basis of gender, where women do comparable work to that of men yet are paid less. Another suggestion is that it is due to the occupational sex-segregation of the labour force whereby women are concentrated in a narrow range of low-paid occupations. Certainly, the segregated labour force is a crucial explanatory factor of the wage gap and female-dominated jobs remain under-valued and under-paid. In 1990, women's share of the 10 lowest-paying occupations was 73 per cent while their share of the 10 highest-paying occupations was only 20 per cent.[45] Women are held in female-dominated jobs by processes that "reproduce class and gender; processes deeply rooted in ideas about women's domesticity and women's employment."[46] Wage differences are explained as a function of the gender division of labour, and the division of labour is a function of wage differences.[47] Women, then, are caught up in a vicious circle.

The fact that women in the labour force earn less than men is a serious problem which has long-term impacts on women. Consider that the wage gap leads to a "pension gap" between women and men because pensions are based on earnings while in the paid labour force. Lower earnings increase the chance of living in poverty in old age. In 1993, women aged 65 and over had incomes which were only 63 per cent of their male counterparts.[48] Lower earnings also translate into lower unemployment insurance benefits when maternity or parental leave is taken or upon job loss. It is a matter of gross unfairness to women that they are paid less than men by virtue of their sex. As Wilson points out, "few women earn enough to support themselves or their dependents on their own."[49] Single-parent families headed by women are especially likely to have low incomes. In 1993, 60 per cent of these families had incomes which were below the Low Income Cut-offs established by Statistics Canada.[50] For example, in 1992 these families spent more than 55 per cent of their income on food, clothing, and shelter.[51]

Social policy, legislation, and economic practices combine to reproduce the gendered wage gap. Not surprisingly, then, the wage gap varies according to factors such as women's marital status, age, and education. Consider that, statistically, marriage weakens women's earning potential: in 1993, the average annual earnings of single women of all age groups was 96 per cent of their male counterparts while married women earned only 68 per cent of men's average earnings.[52] The wage gap also generally increases with age. While

---

[44] Statistics Canada, 1995 at 87.

[45] Canadian Advisory Council on the Status of Women, *Work in Progress: Tracking Women's Equality in Canada* (Ottawa: CACSW, 1994) at 8.

[46] S.J. Wilson, *Women, Families, and Work*, 3d ed. (Toronto, Ont.: McGraw-Hill Ryerson, 1991) at 95.

[47] Martha MacDonald, as cited in Pat Armstrong & Hugh Armstrong, *Theorizing Women's Work* (Toronto, Ont.: Garamond Press, 1990) at 59.

[48] Statistics Canada, 1995 at 92.

[49] Wilson, 1991 at 95.

[50] According to Statistics Canada, "families or individuals are classified as 'low income' if they spend, on average, at least 20 percentage points more of their pre-tax income than the Canadian average on food, shelter, and clothing" (Statistics Canada, 1995 at 86).

[51] *Ibid.* at 85.

[52] *Ibid.* at 87.

women aged 15 to 24 earn on average 91 per cent of male earnings, those aged 55 and over earn only 69 per cent of male wages.[53] As for the effect of education on the wage gap, at all levels of educational attainment, women's earnings are less than those of men. Women with less than a high school education earn only 65 per cent of their male counterparts, while those with a university degree earn 75 per cent.[54]

Given that a serious and pervasive wage gap exists, the problem shifts to finding principles and processes which would be effective to close the gap. The term **"pay equity"** has been coined to express the aspiration to remedy this problem. Although we are now familiar with the term, it is interesting to note that it did not even exist at the beginning of the 1980s. By the end of the decade, however, pay equity was being called "the working women's issue of the 1980s."[55] Various legislative initiatives concerning pay equity have been taken. Federal legislation covers employees of federal departments, agencies, and corporations under federal jurisdiction; all other workers are covered by provincial legislation. Pay equity legislation was first introduced in the 1950s and 1960s by both the federal government and by the provinces. Its principle was "equal pay for equal, or 'substantially similar' work."[56] This legislation proved to be ineffective because the concept of "substantially similar" work was narrowly interpreted by the courts — minor differences were sure to be found when comparing work. On the other hand, international standards for pay equity were first introduced in 1948 by a United Nations policy, the International Labour Organization's (ILO) Convention 100. This policy called for "equal remuneration for men and women workers for work of equal value." This principle was a broader interpretation of pay equity. But it was not until 1972, after the women's movement had re-emerged as a political force in the late 1960s, that the Canadian federal government endorsed this principle and committed itself to amending its legislation to conform to the ILO standards.

The first provincial jurisdiction to introduce equal pay for work of equal value was Quebec in 1975. Two years later, the federal government introduced its pay equity legislation for federal workers in the *Canadian Human Rights Act*, and Labour Canada became responsible for enforcing standards of pay equity. The amendment to the Act reads:

> 11.(1) It is a discriminatory practice for an employer to establish or maintain differences in wages between male and female employees employed in the same establishment who are performing work of equal value.

As a result of this amendment, it became possible for individuals or groups to initiate complaints to the Canadian Human Rights Commission to rectify pay inequities. This approach is a complaint-based process rather than a "proactive approach", like that contained in Ontario's *Pay Equity Act*, 1987 which established a system of job comparison and salary adjustment and required all employers in the public sector and all private sector employers of more than 100 employees to achieve pay equity in their workplaces.

However, even with federal, provincial, and international standards in place, progress has been very slow in achieving wage improvements for women. Indeed, it is estimated that if pay increases continue at the present rate it will take another 60 years before women can expect to earn as much

---

[53] *Ibid.* at 97.

[54] *Ibid.* at 95.

[55] Debra J. Lewis, *Just Give Us the Money: A Discussion of Wage Discrimination and Pay Equity* (Vancouver: Women's Research Centre, 1988) at 221.

[56] See e.g., *Female Employee Fair Remuneration Act*, S.O. 1951, c. 26.

as men.[57] This figure helps to us to see that, important as law is in establishing standards and removing barriers, it is not sufficient by itself to affect change in social and economic structures. A combination of social, political, and legal action is needed. In the area of "pay equity", we have a good example of law being joined by the women's movement and labour unions in a multi-pronged strategy. These groups have the resources, knowledge, and the mandate to struggle for effective change. They also represent the constituencies affected by the problem.

Unions and unionization are important for several reasons. Unions improve wages for their members, and through grievance procedures, and monitoring and communication functions are able to take collective action for individual workers who would otherwise have very little individual bargaining power.[58] The wage gap is less for unionized than for non-unionized workers.[59] However, unions represent only 31 per cent of all paid women workers while the unionization rate for men is higher at 38 per cent.[60]

The lengthy struggle for pay equity by federal government employees is one example of the specific role that both political and legal action have in addressing the issue of pay equity. Federal pay equity legislation was intended to address wage discrimination on the basis of gender; the basic principle is "equal pay for work of equal value", and it allows women's jobs to be compared to men's jobs. One of the first collective complaints to the Canadian Human Rights Commission (CHRC) was filed by the union representing federal government employees, the Public Service Alliance of Canada (PSAC). This complaint was made in 1979 on behalf of women librarians who earned 20 per cent less than their male counterparts. The Treasury Board, the employer of all federal government workers, was adamantly opposed to the principle of pay equity. Besides increasing the amount paid out for wages, it might undermine their control of job classification.[61] The employees had two alternatives: the political approach to strike over pay inequities or the legal approach of taking their case to the CHRC. They chose the latter approach, and two years after the initial demand was delivered to the Treasury Board, a negotiated settlement was reached in favour of the employees. With the assistance of the CHRC, librarians received wage adjustments amounting to $2.3-million. Although the librarians were successful, the Treasury Board refused to add clauses concerning equal value into the collective agreement with other groups of employees. Seventy-five per cent of all women in the public service are concentrated in four lower-echelon categories: secretarial, clerical, administrative, and program management. Almost half are in clerical jobs.

By 1984, the PSAC had filed complaints on behalf of the clerical group, of which 80 per cent were women. This time, however, Treasury Board was not about to risk losing the case before the CHRC and announced that a joint union-management committee would undertake a study to investigate pay inequity, and work towards achieving equal pay. This study took over five years to complete, and only with the PSAC's threat to reactivate its complaints before the CHRC did Treasury Board finally announce the results of

[57] Canadian Advisory Council on the Status of Women, 1993 at 75.
[58] Morley Gunderson & Leon Muszynski, *Women and Labour Market Poverty* (Ottawa: Canadian Advisory Council on the Status of Women, 1990) at 129.
[59] Wilson, 1991 at 102.
[60] Statistics Canada, 1995 at 77.
[61] See, generally, Rosemary Warskett, "Political Power, Technical Disputes, and Unequal Pay: A Federal Case" in Judy Fudge & Patricia McDermott, eds., *Just Wages: A Feminist Assessment of Pay Equity* (Toronto, Ont.: University of Toronto Press, 1991) at 172–92.

the study and the payments which would be made. The payments made in 1990, however, fell short of the results of the study and in 1992 the Treasury Board announced that it would not comply with the retroactive pay requirements of the *Canadian Human Rights Act*.

PSAC continued to pursue the issue through the CHRC. In 1996 the CHRC ruled that the original study results were valid and should be used as the basis for determining compensatory awards. The PSAC estimates that the federal government could owe up to $1.5 billion in back pay to 80,000 clerical workers, encompassing six job groups: clerks, secretaries and typists, data processors, librarians, hospital services staff, and educational support staff. Unless this matter is settled, a hearing before the Human Rights Tribunal is scheduled to determine how the wages of workers in female-dominated jobs are to be increased. The study guidelines suggest that a clerk earning $13 per hour doing comparable work to male-dominated jobs earning an average of $14 per hour should receive an increase in wages to $14. However, the Treasury Board is expected to argue that the adjustment would discriminate against men who earn below the average $14 pay rate.[62]

This issue and case example demonstrates the importance of legal standards, union-based action, and sheer persistence in the cause of justice and equality for women. It would be difficult to envision an individual worker having the resources to struggle for pay equity over a period of 11 years against the federal government. However, it also demonstrates the limitations of pay equity legislation. The Treasury Board took unilateral action to avoid compliance, and used its resources to extend the complaint process, causing delay and expense. Perhaps the final lesson of this example is that law does not operate in a vacuum, but is very much part of a wider social, political, and economic environment. Accordingly, just changing the law will not mean that the problem is solved.

Meanings of Equality

In the previous parts of this section, we have outlined the legislation which contains equality guarantees in Canadian law. We have also explored the operation of one of these guarantees in practice — the pay equity guarantee in the federal *Canadian Human Rights Act*. Readers should, then, have a good idea about what the law provides and a sense of the context in which it applies. In this section and the next, we turn to a more theoretical discussion, but a discussion which has very real and immediate application: what does "equality" mean in Canadian law — what is an equality problem? — and how can we achieve equality in life and law for women?

There are different conceptions of equality which in turn lead to differing approaches to *achieving* equality. Does it mean that no distinctions are to be made between groups of persons, or does equality require that some distinctions be made in some circumstances? If we take some differences into account, is that a form of "special treatment" or an exception to a general equality standard? Is it even possible to identify the ways in which women and men are different or the same in order to identify whether they are being treated similarly to each other? On the other hand, is it more meaningful to think of inequality as arising from being in a disadvantaged or oppressed social position — being a member of a group which receives fewer benefits or suffers harms or exclusion based on perceptions about the worth and social role of that group? If we think of equality in that way, equality would mean the removal of disadvantage and would lead us to focus on social structures rather than only individual circumstances.

[62] See, e.g., "PS hits new barrier in $1.5B pay-equity claim" *The Ottawa Citizen* (21 March 1996) A1.

Another set of debates about equality focuses on the objectives of equality-seeking. One school of thought advocates **"formal equality"** — where all overt or obvious distinctions or restrictions are removed from the law. In this approach, the key thing is to provide individual equality of opportunity and the removal of formal barriers. One example of formal equality is gender neutrality in the drafting of legislation or in the formulation of legal rules. Under this line of thinking, equality is satisfied by changing the legal standard of conduct from "reasonable man" to "reasonable person" and by assuming that the standard now includes women too. Similarly, the crime of "rape" was changed to "sexual assault" and phrased to include women as perpetrators. Obscured in the change, of course, is the fact that the overwhelming number of perpetrators are men and rape is a serious social problem involving the exercise of unequal power by men over women. Of course, formal equality can sometimes be very effective. An unequal rule that only men can administer wills, do certain jobs, access athletic facilities and so forth, can be equalized by allowing both men and women to do these things without distinction. This has been called a "liberal approach" to equality. It has three central features: it focuses on the individual rather than on social systems; it considers that the state should have the very limited role of responding to complaints; and thirdly, it places faith in the neutrality of the "rule of law".[63]

A different school of thought advocates **"substantive** or **result equality"** where the focus is on equality of outcome or equality of condition. This approach critiques formal equality, noting that "treating those who are unequal in terms of power and resources as though they are the same allows certain disparities to persist, while an illusion of fairness is created."[64] Under this approach, the focus shifts from only procedures and intentions, to institutions and structural forms of discrimination. Rules or standards which have a disparate impact on women are considered problematic, whether or not they are written in gender-neutral terms. The focus, then, is on whether a law, policy, or practice operates to the detriment of women or has a particular impact upon them that differs from the impact on men. Under this approach, "discrimination is interpreted as the subordination of an individual by virtue of her or his membership in a particular class of persons or the subordination of a social group."[65]

These two main approaches to equality have given rise to distinct legal principles of equality. The approach of "formal equality" has fostered two principles: the "similarly situated test" of equality and the differential or special treatment modification of this strict form of equality. The "similarly situated test" was at one time the most common perception of equality. It regards equality as meaning that everyone should be treated in the same way. Likes should be treated alike; those who are unalike should not be treated in the same manner. Of course, it is difficult to be sure of the ways in which people are the same or different and to ascribe importance to these characteristics. This approach also assumes a standard against which being the same or different can be assessed. The question here is, Who sets the initial standard? Experience in law with this approach suggests that the standard has been set based on existing norms; in law, as we have seen, these norms have tended to be defined from men's experiences. Feminist Diana Majury has commented that in an unequal world, dominant groups inevitably set the standards for

---

[63] See, generally, Colleen Sheppard, "Equality, Ideology and Oppression: Women and the Canadian Charter of Rights and Freedoms" in C. Boyle et al., *Charterwatch: Reflections on Equality* (Toronto, Ont.: Carswell, 1986) at 195.

[64] *Ibid.* at 204.

[65] *Ibid.* at 216.

"equality"[66] Women, then, must show that they are the same as men and ought to be treated in the same way. A variation on this approach is the so-called "differences" or "special treatment" principle, pursuant to which women can be provided with accommodation for their biological differences from men (e.g., pregnancy, childbirth, and lactation).

The "substantive equality" approach has fostered the principle of a contextual approach to equality or an anti-subordination approach to equality. The third principle of equality arising from the aspiration to achieve substantive equality is the "contextual" or "anti-subordination principle" of equality. Here the focus shifts away from assessing sameness and difference to seeking to identify the impacts of policies, procedures, or rules. In its more radical form, it focuses on experiences "that happen almost exclusively to women ... the most sex-differential abuses of women as a gender" and it poses equality questions as "questions of the distribution of power" in our society. Under this approach, women's "sex-segregation into poverty", "the range of issues known as violence against women", and "the difference sex makes" rather than the sex difference become the focal points for defining equality issues and what solutions are necessary.[67] In its less radical form, there is "some contextualized discussion and some focus on disadvantage and inequality."[68] The Supreme Court of Canada has moved in this direction, turning away from the "similarly situated" test as being inconsistent with the objectives of the Charter. In the case of *Andrews v. The Law Society of British Columbia*,[69] Mr. Justice McIntyre commented:

> The mere equality of application of similarly situated groups or individuals does not afford a realistic test for a violation of equality rights. For, as has been said, a bad law will not be saved merely because it operates equally upon those to whom it has application. Nor will a law necessarily be bad because it makes distinctions.... Consideration must be given to the content of the law, to its purpose, and its impact upon those to whom it applies and also upon those whom it excludes from its application.

In Canada, then, a substantive view of equality is being developed.

Current Equality Issues for Discussion

Child Support

Following marriage breakdown, the determination of child support is based on the principle that both parents have an equal responsibility towards their children and should contribute "in accordance with their own means to the needs of the children."[70] The onus is on the custodial parent (usually the mother) to ask for child support. Levels of child support are often a bargaining chip in divorce negotiations; they can easily be bargained away. Under the provisions of the *Income Tax Act* S.C. 1970-71-72, c. 63, any payments made to a custodial parent for the maintenance of her children are required to be included in her income. A corollary to this provision allows the non-custodial parent to deduct these same support payments from his income for income tax purposes.

---

[66] See, generally, Diana Majury, "Equality and Discrimination According to the Supreme Court of Canada" (1990–91) 4 C.J.W.L. at 407.

[67] See, generally, the work of Catharine MacKinnon, in particular, "Difference and Dominance: On Sex Discrimination" in *Feminism Unmodified* (Cambridge, Mass.: Harvard University Press, 1987) 32 at 40–42. See also Diana Majury, "Strategizing In Equality" (1987) 3 Wisconsin Women's L.J.

[68] See, generally, Diana Majury, "Equality and Discrimination According to the Supreme Court of Canada" *supra* note 66.

[69] [1989] 1 S.C.R. 143.

[70] Federal/Provincial/Territorial Family Law Committee, 1991: 5.

Suzanne Thibaudeau, a custodial mother of two children, stopped paying taxes on her child support payments in 1988. In 1992, she argued in the Tax Court of Canada that by imposing a tax burden on money which she was to use exclusively for the benefit of her children, the *Income Tax Act* infringed her right to equality guaranteed by section 15(1) of the Charter of Rights. At the trial level, she was unsuccessful. The judge ruled that the court which had awarded support payments to Thibaudeau had accounted for the effects of income tax when it determined the amount of the payments. Thus, the judge concluded that there was no violation of Thibaudeau's equality because the payments had been "grossed up" in the routine operation of the family law system. Her appeal to the Federal Court in 1994 was successful. Mr. Justice Hugessen pointed out that although adverse tax effects could and should have been corrected when determining support amounts, this is "not always, or even usually" the case. He concluded that the *Income Tax Act* violated the rights of custodial parents to equality before and under the law albeit on the basis of family status rather than sex.

The government appealed this decision to Canada's highest court, the Supreme Court of Canada. In May 1995 the Federal Court's ruling was reversed. The majority of the Supreme Court judges (which did not include the two woman judges) commented:

> The purpose of s. 15(1) is to protect human dignity by ensuring that all individuals are recognized at law as being equally deserving of concern, respect and consideration. Consequently, it is the effect that an impugned distinction has upon a claimant which is the prime concern under s. 15(1). Here, the group of single custodial parents receiving child support payments is not placed under a burden by the inclusion/deduction regime. Although there may be some cases in which the gross-up calculations shift a portion of the payer's tax liability upon the recipient spouse, one cannot necessarily extrapolate from this that a "burden" has been created, at least not for the purposes of s. 15(1).

The Court also ruled that the *Income Tax Act* operates at the "level of the couple" and was designed to minimize the tax consequences of support payments, thereby "promoting the best interests of the children" by ensuring that more money is available to provide for their care:

> If anything, the inclusion/deduction regime confers a benefit on the post-divorce "family unit." The fact that one member of the unit might derive a greater benefit from the legislation than the other does not, in and of itself, trigger a s. 15(1) violation, nor does it lead to a finding that the distinction in any way amounts to a denial of equal benefit or protection of the law.

In essence, the Court ruled that any unfair displacement of the tax liability between the custodial and non-custodial parents "lies in the family law system", not in the *Income Tax Act*. As such, the majority concluded that the *Income Tax Act* did not discriminate against custodial parents. As readers may be aware, the federal government responded to the public outcry at this decision with new rules for the taxation of child support in its 1996 Federal Budget.[71] Under these rules, child support paid under orders or agreements made after 1 May 1997 will no longer be taxed as income to the recipient, or be tax deductible for the payer. Guidelines accounting for the new tax rules will be introduced to aid in setting consistent and fair child support awards. New enforcement mechanisms, including suspension of passports and permitting

---

[71] "The New Child Support Package" (Ottawa: Government of Canada, 6 March 1996).

arrears for child support to be deducted from federal public service employee pension benefits are contained in legislation introduced in the House of Commons on 30 May 1996.

Sexual Assault and Therapy Records

Hubert Patrick O'Connor, a bishop of the Roman Catholic Church, was charged in 1991 with two counts of rape and two counts of indecent assault on four of his former students, as a result of incidents which occurred while he was the principal of a Native residential school in Williams Lake, B.C., in the 1960s. At his trial, O'Connor argued that his lawyers should have access to the entire medical, counselling, and school records of the four students. He justified this on "the need to test the complainants' credibility, as well as to determine issues such as recent complaint and corroboration." The court agreed and ordered the Crown prosecution to disclose all files from therapists, counsellors, psychologists, or psychiatrists with whom the women had sought treatment concerning sexual assault or sexual abuse. In 1992, the Crown applied to the British Columbia Supreme Court for directions regarding the disclosure order. The women who had brought the charges were not prepared to comply with the Court order. The judges expressed surprise at the fact that the Crown was not complying with the order.

One Crown counsel, Wendy Harvey, argued that disclosure of medical and therapeutic records would "revictimize the victims", and suggested that the order to disclose "exhibited gender bias".

The B.C. Supreme Court upheld the lower court order to disclose the records. The Crown appealed to the Supreme Court of Canada; LEAF intervened in this case, arguing that personal records should not be used in sexual violence cases to attack women's credibility. To allow records to be produced is a direct violation of women's right to equality. As Karen Busby notes, requests for personal records are made "almost exclusively in sexual violence cases."[72] Requests are made under the assumption that women frequently lie about sexual violence "out of vindictiveness, malice or delusion." Furthermore, a law requiring disclosure of personal records would have a disproportionate impact on women. For example, as Busby notes, counsellor-patient relationships would be undermined, attention would be distorted away from the incident at hand towards whether the "complainant is worthy of the law's protection", and women's reporting of sexual assault would likely be discouraged. The majority of the Supreme Court of Canada ruled in favour of records disclosure, holding that defendants in sexual assault cases need only establish that counselling records are "likely to have relevance" for a judge to order that they be produced. A process was established by which judges would review and assess records in the exercise of judicial discretion.

A spokesperson for a rape crisis centre in Ontario has remarked that since the Supreme Court decision, the percentage of women at her centre who decide to report their sexual assault to police has dropped from 36 per cent to 15.[73] In essence, women are forced to choose between laying criminal charges and seeking professional help for themselves.[74] Some rape crisis centres have resorted to keeping only minimal records. Other "more defiant groups" have shredded documents.[75]

---

[72] Karen Busby, "Supreme Court decisions on the use of personal records in sexual assault cases — what it means for women" *Leaf Lines* 7, 1996 at 4.

[73] "New bill restricts access to records" *The Globe and Mail* (31 May 1996) A1.

[74] *Ibid.* at A3.

[75] *Ibid.* at A1.

Regarding it as an "urgent" problem, the Minister of Justice announced on 31 May 1996 that he plans to introduce legislation that would restrict access to records. It would be impermissible for lawyers to launch "fishing expeditions" to see whether there is something in the records that would damage the credibility of the victim. Courts would be required to establish relevance of therapy records, and would restrict access to only those parts of the records that are deemed important to the case. In addition, defendants would be allowed to ask for counselling records at the trial stage only, not in the preliminary hearing. A provincial court judge rather than a justice of the peace would be able to issue subpoenas for such records. The Minister of Justice commented that it was important to "balance the rights of the accused with the equality and privacy rights given to victims by the Charter of Rights and Freedoms."[76]

The Legal Curriculum

Legal education is a critical space where ideas and attitudes about law are shaped. As Elizabeth Schneider has pointed out, "law schools transmit our first messages about what is permissible in law."[77] In 1988, the Faculty Council at a major Canadian law school passed an "Equality Resolution". It stated in regard to teaching and learning at the Law School that:

> The faculty and students, in order to continue and expand efforts to promote freedom from discrimination both within the Law School and in society at large, undertake to consider the following measures in relation to teaching and learning:
> (a) inclusion in teaching materials of works or references to works that demonstrate the impact of law on groups that are or have been subjected to discrimination, or inclusion in teaching materials of explanations for the omission of such works or references;
> (b) placement of teaching materials that support or exhibit discrimination within a context that identifies their discriminatory nature and that invites open and critical comment on it;
> (c) use of language in the classroom, in written materials, and in examinations that is free from discriminatory stereotypes and references;
> (d) use of other measures, such as holding seminars about non-discriminatory teaching materials and methods, which demonstrate continuing sensitivity to the problems faced by individuals and groups subject to discrimination; and
> (e) a heightening awareness of the existence of systematic discrimination.

CONCLUSION

In her CBC Massey Lectures in 1990, renowned Canadian scientist Ursula Franklin outlined a theory which she called "Franklin's earthworm theory of social change." She suggested that "social change will not come to us like an avalanche down a mountain. Social change will come through seeds growing in well-prepared soil — and it is we, like the earthworms, who prepare the soil." Being able to identify and analyse problems of gender bias in processes, rules, and personnel involved in the legal system is an important step in being able to work for change in that system. What is also important, however, is imagination — being able to envisage what an equal and just society and legal

---

[76] *Ibid.*

[77] Elizabeth Schneider, "Task Force Reports on Women and the Courts: The Challenge for Legal Education" (1988) J. Legal Educ. 38 at 88.

system would look like. The legal imagination is the seed for change; understanding is our preparation and consistent tending and work in the soil will help change to grow and bear fruit.

CHAPTER SUMMARY ───────────────────────────────

This chapter has outlined and analysed legal breakthroughs for women, examined the problems of gender bias in judging and legal rules, and explored the meanings and applications of equality guarantees contained in Canadian law, most particularly as they affect women's equality. One of the themes of the chapter has been that law changes in complex and inconsistent ways; change is often slow and contested. Law does not by itself cause or cure complex social inequalities. In the end, law is a terrain of struggle in which contested meanings and visions of society are debated. Law, then, plays an important role in the struggles to eliminate gender bias and achieve women's equality. However, it is not the only — or even the most important — place to begin. Our questions have moved beyond "adding women" into law; the focus is much more on the structure and operation of law and the "simple notion that law respond to women as well as to men."[78] We hope that in reading this chapter, readers have developed historical and substantive knowledge of the gender issue in law. We hope, too, that they have been equipped with analytical and theoretical skills with which to identify, debate, and act on issues.

GLOSSARY OF NEW TERMS AND KEY CONCEPTS ──────────

feminist
"If we conceive of feminism as more than a frivolous label, if we conceive of it as an ethics, a methodology, a more complex way of thinking about, and thus more responsibly acting upon, the conditions of human life, we need a self-knowledge that can only develop through a steady, passionate attention to all female experience. I cannot imagine a feminist evolution leading to radical change in the public/private realm of gender that is not rooted in the conviction that all of women's lives are important; that the lives of men cannot be understood by burying the lives of women; and that to make visible the full meaning of women's experience, to reinterpret knowledge in terms of that experience, is now the most important task of thinking" Adrienne Rich, "Towards a Woman-Centred University", in *On Lies, Secrets and Silences* (New York: MacMillan, 1980).

legal person
"Legal personality refers to the particular device by which the law creates or recognizes units to which it ascribes certain powers and capacities. ... A legal system must be provided with a basic unit before full legal relationships can be devised which will fulfill the primary purpose of organizing social facts. The legal person is the unit or entity adopted." G. Paton, *Textbook on Jurisprudence*, 4th ed. (London: Oxford University Press, 1972) at 392.

Judicial Council
A panel of senior judges which oversees the conduct of judges.

pay equity
Term which refers to legislation and policies designed to implement the principle of equal pay for work of equal value and eliminate the wage gap between male and female workers.

formal equality
An approach to equality where the focus is on equality of opportunity and the removal of overt distinctions between men and women in legislation and policy. Associated with the "similarly situated" test of equality.

───────────────

[78] MacKinnon, *supra* note 1.

student-at-law | Another term used to describe a law student who is completing his or her practical bar admission training and his or her articled clerkship. See also **articling clerk**, above.

substantive equality | An approach to equality where the focus is on equality of outcome or equality of condition. Associated with the contextual, disadvantage-focused test of equality.

REVIEW QUESTIONS

1. What are three examples of ways in which women have been discriminated against in Canadian law?

2. What was the "Persons Case", and what is its significance?

3. When did women in Canada receive the right to vote?

4. Who was Canada's first woman lawyer?

5. In what ways can "gender bias" be present in judicial opinions? Why does gender bias matter?

6. What action can be taken when a judge demonstrates gender bias?

7. What is the *Canadian Charter of Rights and Freedoms* and what equality guarantees are contained within it?

8. What other guarantees of equality exist in law?

9. What reasons can explain the wage gap between men and women in the Canadian workforce? What are some of the consequences of unequal pay for women?

10. What does the term "pay equity" refer to?

11. What different meanings can be given to the term "equality"? Explain the differences between "formal equality" and "substantive equality".

12. Which legal principle of equality has been adopted by the Supreme Court of Canada?

DISCUSSION QUESTIONS

1. How important do you think the *Married Women's Property Act*s were? How significant is it that interests other than women's equality influenced the legislation?

2. What arguments can be made to challenge the views of Cardinal Villeneuve against giving women the right to vote?

3. The example of Clara Brett Martin reminds us that struggles to gain equality for women have sometimes benefited "particular" women rather than all women. Do you think that these limited and partial breakthroughs nevertheless pave the way for all women to gain benefits? Or do you think that they maintain rather than challenge or change the *status quo*? Can you think of other examples or potential issues?

4. Should courses on gender and racial bias be mandatory for all judges, or might this requirement conflict with judicial independence?

5. What remedies are appropriate for judges who are found to have made sexist or racist comments?

6. In an English case in 1979, *Jeremiah v. Ministry of Defence*, the senior judge of the Court of Appeal, Lord Denning, dismissed a claim by a male worker that an exception made for women that relieved them from having to work overtime in a dirty area of a munitions factory constituted sex discrimination against him. One of the reasons for his decision was that Mr. Jeremiah had little regard for "chivalry or the women's hair-dos ... a woman's hair is her crowning glory, so it is said. She does not like to have it disturbed, especially when she has just had a 'hair-do'." What critique can you make of Lord Denning's comments in light of the discussion in this section?

7. What might a legal system that was structured around women's lives as well as men's lives look like? Can you think of examples?

8. There are two models of pay equity legislation. One is "complaint-based"; the other is "proactive". Which model do you think holds the most promise for remedying the inequality in wages faced by women in the labour force?

9. Use the various approaches to equality to identify whether the fact situation in the Thibaudeau case raises an equality problem. If it does, what kind of an equality problem is it?

10. Do you agree with the Supreme Court of Canada's conclusion that section 15 of the *Charter of Rights and Freedoms* had not been violated by the *Income Tax Act*? What factors did the Supreme Court take into account? What other factors might it have taken into account?

11. Use the various approaches to equality to identify whether the fact situation in the O'Connor case raises an equality problem. If it does, what kind of an equality problem is it?

12. The Charter also contains a right to "life, liberty and security of the person" (s. 7) and a right to a full and fair defence to a criminal charge (s. 11(d)). Does a case like O'Connor raise a problem of balancing equality rights with these rights? How should such a situation be approached?

13. Why might a commitment to "equality" in legal education be important? Are there any objections to this goal? In what areas might legal education be unequal?

14. How would you implement the "Equality Resolution"? What concrete changes do you think might need to be made in a law school or in a law course?

SUGGESTED READINGS

Boyd, Susan, & Elizabeth Sheehy. *Canadian Feminist Perspectives on Law: An Annotated Bibliography of interdisciplinary Writings* (Toronto, Ont.: Resources for Feminist Research, 1989). (Second edition in preparation)

Canadian Journal of Women and the Law (1985–current).

Chunn, Dorothy, & Joan Brockman, eds. *Investigating Gender Bias: Law, Courts and the Legal Profession* (Toronto, Ont.: Thompson Educational Publishers, 1993).

Dawson, T. Brettel, ed. *Women, Law and Social Change: Core Readings and Current Issues*, 3d ed. (North York, Ont.: Captus Press, 1998).

MacKinnon, Catharine. *Feminism Unmodified* (Cambridge, Mass: Harvard University Press, 1987).

Razack, Sherene. *Canadian Feminism and the Law* (Toronto, Ont.: Second Story Press, 1991).

Smart, Carol. *Feminism and the Power of Law* (London: Routledge, 1989).

Task Force on Gender Equality. *Touchstones for Change: Equality, Diversity and Accountability* (Ottawa, Ont.: Canadian Bar Association, 1993).

Williams, Patricia. *The Alchemy of Race and Rights* (Cambridge, Mass: Harvard University Press, 1991).

Children, Youth, and the Law

David Turner
UNIVERSITY OF VICTORIA

Learning Objectives

After reading this chapter, the reader should be able to:

➢ understand how and where the law treats children and youth differently than adults
➢ understand notions of children's rights
➢ identify key legal areas and processes affecting children and youth
➢ identify key legal issues for children and youth

TABLE OF CONTENTS

INTRODUCTION

The Victorian saying, "Children should be seen and not heard" is still used in Canada today by some traditional families. It illustrates the persistent relative powerlessness of many children in relation to their parents and other authorities. In principle, the law recognizes that children and youth should be accorded a voice and special rights. This chapter explores the law and rights applying to children and youth in contemporary Canada, and identifies key issues and legal gaps.

HISTORICAL OVERVIEW

Contemporary North American media prominently feature stories about child and youth issues: in particular, youth crime, child abuse, learning disabilities, child poverty, and adoption. It is easy to forget that the law, and society in general, essentially ignored children until the past century. Children were viewed as miniature adults, inheriting the social status and occupations of their families. If they were poor, their labour was usually required and, often, exploited on the farm or in the mine, factory, or workhouse; if wealthy, they were protected by guardians, nannies, and private tutors, and their estates (inherited lands and money) were held in trust.

The mid-19th century saw the beginnings of **special protection** in England (on whose law our common law is based), primarily to cushion the negative impacts of industrialization. For example, the *Factories Act* prohibited young child labour, and the *Schools Act* initiated public education on a limited basis. In the United States, the first juvenile justice system emerged in the 1890s, with special laws, courts, and correctional facilities. Shortly thereafter a juvenile justice system developed in Canada, along with private children's aid societies to protect orphaned, abandoned, or neglected children. The next two decades saw the development of the first "child welfare" laws across the provinces: Ontario's *Children's Protection Act*, the *School Act* of British Columbia and the first *Juvenile Delinquents Act* at the federal level.

Until the current era of State intervention, parents — especially fathers — had total control over the welfare, discipline, and religious education of their children. The prohibitions in the criminal law for killing or maiming a child, or depriving the child of the necessities of life, were often ignored, so children were at their parents' mercy. Even today this parental power, though tempered, is reflected in Canadian law. Section 43 of the *Criminal Code* allows, as a defence to what might otherwise be a charge of assault, for a parent or guardian or teacher (*in loco parentis*) to exercise reasonable force in correcting or disciplining a child. (Note, though, that in most provinces and territories, teachers are now prohibited from using corporal punishment in public schools.) Also, in family law, children in custody disputes are still "awarded" to either parent as if they are owned as property by them: the concept of parent rights still has priority.

The view gradually prevailed that when parents failed in their responsibility of caring for their children, the state (or its agencies) was entitled to intervene to protect them. It became accepted that children required different treatment than adults. Law in Canada has, since the mid-20th century, evolved to become an instrument of social policy and redistribution of social resources, rather than being simply a regulator of private commercial affairs. One result has been state powers to intervene to protect vulnerable children and youth. Social welfare legislation, such as the Canada Health and Social Transfer (formerly Canada Assistance Plan) allowed federal cost sharing for provincial child protection, child care, and education programs. Impetus was given to the expansion of comprehensive child welfare laws and social services for children in every province and territory.

More recently, legal and political questions have resurfaced about the changing roles of parent, child, and state. A backlash has emerged against some kinds of State intervention into what is viewed as the private sanctuary of the family. Traditional political ideologies have harnessed this resentment against "state interference". An effort to reassert parental (or state) rights over children and youth has also re-emerged in calls for harsher penalties under the *Youth Criminal Justice Act*.[1] Likewise, the credibility of statements of children when testifying to sexual or physical abuse by their parents in criminal or child welfare law has been challenged. Law is attempting to balance competing rights and interests.

JURISDICTION

As mentioned in an earlier chapter, the Canadian Constitution (ss. 91 and 92 of the *British North America Act, 1867*) lists how the powers to make laws are divided between the federal and provincial governments. Fairly random division has led to a patchwork of responsibility where child law is concerned. For instance, criminal law is the prerogative (that is, lies within the jurisdiction) of the federal government. So, criminal law dealing with youth over 12 and under 18 is the same across Canada. The *Juvenile Delinquents Act* was replaced in 1984 by the *Young Offenders Act* and, in April 2003, the *Youth Criminal Justice Act*, which is the current instrument of youth justice across the country. However, the administration of justice is provincial: youth justice courts and correctional services are administered by each province, so the actual justice that youths receive may vary.

Civil law is the prerogative of the provinces, which means that matters such as child welfare, education, health, mental health, and family law (except divorce, which is federal) may differ among the provinces. Later in this chapter we will summarize the main principles that are shared across the country.

Jurisdictional differences also arise through issues of age. For instance, in British Columbia a "child" under the *Family Relations Act*[2] is a young person under 19, but a child under the federal *Divorce Act*[3] is a person up to the age of 16. The duration of child maintenance (financial support by parents) after marriage breakdown might differ, depending on which statute is used. A "child" for child welfare purposes is under 18 in Quebec, but under 19 in British Columbia.

First Nations children on reserves are subject to another complication of jurisdiction. Aboriginal affairs are legally controlled by the federal government under the *Indian Act*, yet the child welfare law and services for those children remains a provincial responsibility. A serious gap has long existed, especially as bands have tried to gain local control of welfare services.

---

[1] S.C. 2002, c. 1 (assented to 19 February 2002, proclaimed in force April 1, 2003).
[2] R.S.B.C. 1996, c. 128.
[3] R.S.C. 1985, c. 3 (2nd Supp.).

HOW LAW TREATS CHILDREN DIFFERENTLY

The notions of limited **"capacity"** (the competency to make informed decisions) and **"dependency"** (that children are vulnerable and require guardians or the state to protect them) are historical concepts still in operation today. They account for the emergence of special laws, rights, and policies dealing with children and youth.

Many legal rules in Canada are age-related, on the assumption that maturity, and its accompanying responsibility or privilege, arrives (or is sufficiently consolidated) at a particular chronological time in a young person's development. Change from child **status** to legal status as an adult comes at the **age of majority**, which is 18 in most provinces. Voting, entering into binding contracts, and consenting to marriage are all examples of the privilege of majority. What is confusing is the variation in legal age for different activities:

- The age at which young people may drive is 16, but 19[4] is the legal age for the consumption of alcohol and buying cigarettes, and the age at which a young person ceases being a "child" under the protection legislation.[5]

- A fetus is not recognized as a "person" under the *Charter of Rights and Freedoms*, yet it can be a "child in need of protection" under the child welfare Acts of some provinces.

- Federally, consent in criminal law to sexual activity applies at the age of 14 — except in the case of anal intercourse, when a young person must be 18.

- A child must be over 12 to be held criminally responsible.[6] In most provinces, only a youth 14 or over can be assumed to understand the nature of the oath in testifying, without an inquiry being made as to the child's capacity.

- Within the *Criminal Code*, age requirements can be different for similar offences. For example, it is an offence to unlawfully abandon or expose a child under 10 so that "its [sic] life is or is likely to be endangered" — yet the necessaries of life must be provided to all under 16.[7]

- Civilly, minors (young people under the age of majority) cannot be held liable for breaches of contracts. The exceptions are for purchases of food, clothing, and necessaries, and beneficial services such as an apprenticeship contract.

These discrepancies within child laws of each province and across Canada can be explained by different historical developments, objectives, jurisdictions, and application of the public or politicians' values.

Another outcome of the notion that children are vulnerable and have special needs is the establishment of a separate court. In British Columbia, for example, this is the Family Division of the Provincial Courts (see Exhibit 30.1). This court deals with child protection, custody, maintenance and access in Family Court, and with young offenders matters in Youth Justice Court. Family Court and Youth Justice Court are still open and public in British Columbia, though they are often located apart from regular provincial courts. Cases may be held in a closed hearing if it is in the child's best interests. In

---

4 Except in Alberta, Quebec and Manitoba, where legal drinking age is 18.
5 *Child, Family and Community Service Act*, 1996, c. 46.
6 *Youth Criminal Justice Act*, 2002, s. 2(1).
7 *Criminal Code of Canada*, R.S.C. 1985, c. C-46, ss. 215 and 218.

EXHIBIT 30.1
Family Courtroom Layout

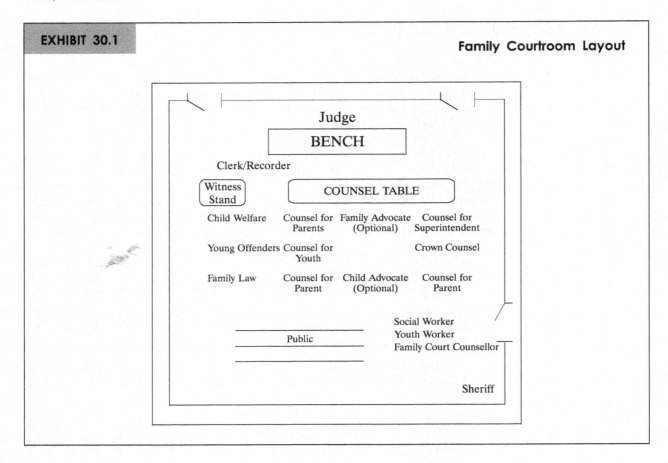

Ontario, all members of the public, except the parties, are excluded from Family Court, though media can attend with restrictions on publishing names and identifying information on the child or youth.

ISSUES OF CHILDREN'S RIGHTS

The concept of children's rights, as distinct from the rights of adults, has arisen in law in fairly recent times as the notion of vulnerability has gained acceptance. The major rights of children can be classified as follows:

Legal and Administrative Rights

In theory, children and youth enjoy many of the same rights as adults. These include those set out in the *Charter of Rights and Freedoms*: legal rights such as representation by counsel; anti-discrimination rights; and rights to fairness in court processes and bureaucratic decision making. In reality, at the federal level, the *Youth Criminal Justice Act* is one of the few statutes that clearly delineates legal rights for youth. It should be noted that several Human Rights Codes, including British Columbia's *Human Rights Code*, are limited in scope to adults over 19 in prohibiting discrimination in public facilities, tenancy, and employment. This may be seen as violating the Charter provision on age equality (s. 15) and could be open to future legal challenges. To date, few child cases have proceeded to the higher courts on Charter challenges, except in the case of young offenders appealing transfer of their criminal case to the ordinary courts.

In many provinces, an ombudsman has jurisdiction to review the **administrative fairness** of decisions by government ministries dealing with children. In British Columbia, this has recently been extended to cover two other authorities: school boards governing schools and municipalities responsible for parks, recreation, and public facilities, such as libraries and community centres. The creation of external **accountability mechanisms** for children's rights and services established by provincial statutes, such as the Office of the Children's Lawyer in Ontario, the Child Advocate in Alberta and the Office of the Representative for Children and Youth[8] in British Columbia, means that decisions that affect children by adults such as teachers, social workers, and foster parents are more open to public scrutiny.

Rights to Social Services
The provision of services for children and their families, such as social services, health care, child care, family support, and education, are found in distinct statutes, such as Ontario's *Child and Family Services Act*,[9] British Columbia's *Employment and Assistance Act*,[10] and Manitoba's *Public Schools Act*.[11] However, as will be discussed below, it is questionable whether children have rights to demand those services, other than the right to basic provision. Provision of preventative services, such as those provided by counsellors, homemakers, and child care workers, is at the discretion of bureaucrats[12] and is subject to funding as politicians in government choose.

Rights to Standards of Care
Ideally, children and youth should have the legal right to a particular standard of care in their own or relatives' homes, as well as in state facilities, such as foster homes, child care and treatment centres, schools, and correctional institutions. Minimal community standards of parental care are enforced through the child protection legislation of each province. Certain state facilities, such as daycare centres and hospitals, are licensed, and some schools are accredited, while foster homes are monitored by social workers. Correctional centres and care facilities are inspected by offices of government — such as the Deputy Ombudsman for Children and Correctional Inspectorate in British Columbia, or the Office of Child and Family Service Advocacy in Ontario — but usually only after receiving specific complaints.

More jurisdictions are considering incorporating principles of rights to services and standards for children in the care of the state. Ontario's *Child and Family Services Act*[13] includes a section on rights, ranging from the right to reasonable privacy and possession of personal goods to meals that are well-balanced and of good quality; from age-appropriate clothing to "the right to be consulted and heard whenever significant decisions are made respecting education, religion, medical treatment, and discharge, placement, and transfer plans." B.C.'s *Child, Family and Community Service Act*[14] reflects these rights

---

[8] This replaced the combined offices of the former Children's Commissioner and Child and Youth Advocate.
[9] R.S.O. 1990, c. 11.
[10] S.B.C. 2002, c. 40.
[11] R.S.M. 1987, c. P250.
[12] See David Turner, "Children's Rights to Service in Canada", in David Turner and Max R. Uhlemann, *Holding Governments Accountable for Children's Rights: The Canadian Experience*, ch. 4, pp. 132–62 (Victoria, B.C.: Sedgewick Society for Consumer and Public Education, School of Social Work, University of Victoria, 1990).
[13] R.S.O. 1990, c. 11, Part V.
[14] R.S.B.C. 1996, c. 46.

for children but adds an additional right: "to receive guidance and encouragement to maintain their cultural heritage."

Children not in the care of the state may require similar protection, but no province has yet enacted a general Bill of Rights for *all* children.

Obstacles to Implementation of Child Rights

There are several ambiguities, contradictions, and obstacles to the implementation of child rights.

Competing Concepts of Child Rights

The concept of child rights is often viewed as competing with other rights, such as parental authority or the State's right to social control and law and order. In 1989, the United Nations passed a resolution on the Convention of the Rights of the Child,[15] which is intended to be morally binding on the nations that signed the document. It sets out a series of principles for states to adopt and to implement in all legislation and policies dealing with children. These principles include not discriminating against children and ensuring that all social welfare institutions, courts, and administrative and legislative bodies use the best interests of the child as the primary consideration in all their actions concerning children.[16]

Do Canada's laws and social policies conform to this principle? It remains to be seen whether the recent *Youth Criminal Justice Act* will continue to reinforce the pattern, established by the *Young Offenders Act*, of putting the protection interests of society over the needs and interests of young persons. Holding young offenders "responsible" by substantial imprisonment in youth and adult correctional facilities may not be in their "best interests". But youth are seen as threatening the law-and-order attitudes held by many members of the public, so the call for even tougher sentences is what is receiving attention. Likewise, most levels of family income assistance paid by law or regulation are well below the poverty line across Canada; this seems to violate Article 27.1 of the U.N. resolution, which reads, "States Parties recognize the right of every child to a standard of living adequate for the child's physical, mental, spiritual, moral and social development." The United Nations has recently condemned Canada's rates of child poverty. But many Canadians see this as purely a parental responsibility, in which government has no justification for interfering.

Child Rights versus Child Needs

The *Youth Criminal Justice Act* is one of the few laws specifying children's and youth's automatic right to counsel. Their legal rights are thus protected, but some argue it is at the expense of their interests. The right to due process may interfere with the need of young persons for swift and meaningful consequences for their illegal behaviour. Legal defences and technicalities may widen the gap between the "legal" and "moral" guilt of youngsters who are still developing a social value system.

Others, however, see these rights as a protection against the abuses of the earlier *Juvenile Delinquents Act*,[17] where children and youth were imprisoned as criminals (delinquents) for such *status offences* as being beyond the control of their parents or running away from foster homes.

---

[15] Resolution of the United Nations General Assembly: Convention on the Rights of the Child, December 1989.
[16] Idem, Article 3.
[17] R.S.C. 1970, c. J-3.

Enforceability

One person's rights necessarily impose duties on another person. In most cases, governments have great discretion in the provision of services to children, even where certain "rights" are mandated by law. For example, do children have a right to protection? They probably do but in a limited fashion: a government or private child welfare agency may have the obligation to investigate child abuse allegations, but the apprehension (removal) of the child or the provision of preventative services to the child and the child's family is purely discretionary, and rarely enforceable by the courts. Do children have a right to an education? Most laws compel parents to have their children attend school between certain ages, but children do not necessarily have the right to an individualized education. It is often at the discretion of the province, school board, or particular school as to what actually happens in the classroom.

Access to Rights

Cutbacks to public services directly affect children, yet, as non-voters, it is a challenge to have their voices echo in the legislative chambers of Canada. There is a great need for **advocacy** when new laws or changes to existing laws are being considered. Legal advocates are sometimes available on individual family matters affecting children, such as custody battles; but in British Columbia, their appointment has been at the discretion of judges or the Attorney General.[18] Now many jurisdictions are developing permanent advocacy and review mechanisms, such as an Ombudsman for Children, who monitors the ministries dealing with children, or the recent Office of the Representative for Children and Youth in British Columbia,[19] which deals with complaints on behalf of children in the child welfare system. Ontario has the Office of the Children's Lawyer employing social workers to investigate custody and access or education complaints. In Quebec, Youth Protection Committees monitor child welfare and corrections complaints — in particular, rights violations.

KEY SUBSTANTIVE AREAS

There are several areas of law that deal centrally with children and their interests. Although most areas are under provincial jurisdiction (with the prime exception of young offenders) and vary in detail, there are common principles and processes that are outlined here.

Child Welfare

This area of civil law is in the jurisdiction of the provinces, though certain programs for child care are cost-shared with the federal government through the Canada Assistance Plan (which is currently under political review). The principle is that families have the responsibility to care for and raise their children within certain limits. The state, as represented by a provincial authority (ministry, superintendent's or director's office or private children's aid society), is legally empowered to protect children who are at risk or whose standard of care fails to meet minimal community levels. The process is triggered by *a complaint or report* (see Exhibit 30.2), usually from a neighbour, teacher, or physician, who believes a child is in need of protection. This need is legally defined in each child welfare statute, and usually includes physical and sexual abuse, and neglect. But apart from statutes in Ontario, Alberta,

[18] *Family Relations Act,* R.S.B.C. 1996, c. 128.
[19] *Representative for Children and Youth Act,* S.B.C. 2006, c. 29.

EXHIBIT 30.2   **Child Welfare Process**

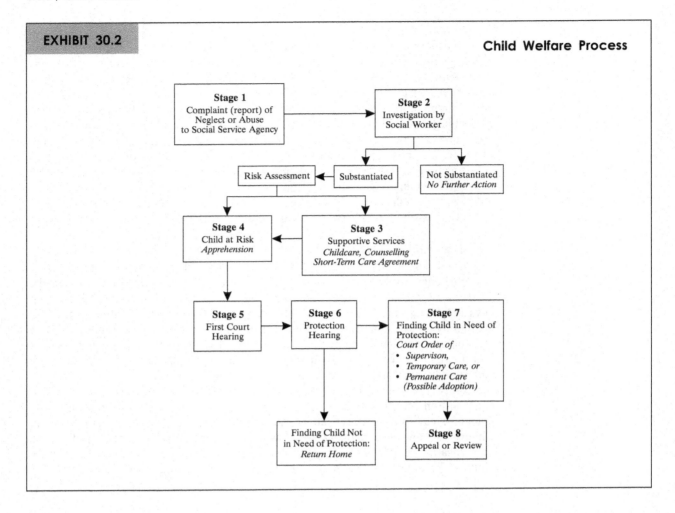

and British Columbia, most are vague and interventionist.[20] For instance, New Brunswick's definition includes "living in unfit or improper circumstances",[21] which encompasses a variety of "evils" and lifestyles whose interpretation depends on the social worker's or judge's values. The three jurisdictions mentioned above, by contrast, have closely defined circumstances for intervention, including clarification of "emotional abuse or neglect".

The next stage[22] is the *investigation* of the veracity of the complaint by a social worker. If it is, in the social worker's judgment, substantiated, supportive services, such as a child care worker, counselling, or a voluntary care agreement with the parents may be offered. If the child is at risk, the social worker will usually protect by an "*apprehension*" or "*removal*": taking the child into care. In some jurisdictions, the "offending" parent can be ordered to leave the home and to refrain from contact with the child until the issue is reviewed by a court. The worker or police officer may remove the child without a warrant or court order if the child's safety or well-being is

---

[20] Dick Barnhorst & Bernd Walter, "Child Protection Legislation in Canada" in Nicholas Bala, Joseph Hornick & Robin Vogel, eds. *Canadian Child Welfare Law: Children, Families and the State* (Toronto, Ont.: Thompson Educational Publishing, 1991) at 21.

[21] *Family Services Act*, S.N.B. 1980, c. F-2.2, s. 31(1).

[22] For details on the various stages, see David Turner & Max R. Uhlemann, "Child Protection and the Legal Process" in *A Legal Handbook for the Helping Professional*, 3d ed. (Victoria, B.C., 2007), c. 3, or Bala, *supra* note 19.

in immediate danger,[23] and may enter any premises, vehicle, or vessel by force, if necessary. The child then is taken into *temporary care* and placed in a reception centre or foster home, and the situation is reviewed by the Family Court in a short time (within seven days in British Columbia). The state or agency presents the case for review through its counsel. Parents or relatives are notified by the social worker and may contest through their lawyer. The child is not usually separately represented except in exceptional circumstances. The court can order health and psychiatric assessments to assist in its deliberations. If the judge decides there is prima facie evidence that protection is required (in British Columbia, the requirement is reasonable grounds to believe the child is in need of protection), the case is set for a full *protection hearing*, a process that can be quite adversarial if contested. A child may be represented by a separate counsel, known as a *Family Advocate*, but budgets for this are very limited.

Child welfare is civil, so the standard of proof is on the balance of probabilities. This means the court decides whether the evidence shows the child is more likely to be in need of protection than not. Family Court can be less formal in its procedures than other courts. In fact, since abuse often happens in the privacy of families, without witnesses, the civil doctrine of *res ipsa loquitur* (let the matter speak for itself) can apply, which allows the circumstances to be taken into account in assessing causation of injury. For instance, where no witness saw the injury being inflicted, if, in the mind of a reasonable person, the bruising and other circumstances are consistent with non-accidental injury, then the court can assume the child was intentionally abused. If the child is found to be in need of protection, then the court can make a *court order* of supervision, or temporary or permanent custody (care or wardship) to the state or agency. Supervision allows the social worker to monitor the care of the child back at home. A custody (care) order suspends or terminates parental rights. Permanent wards can be adopted out, but if over 12 years old, they must consent.

Most child welfare legislation emphasizes "the best interests of the child", though many jurisdictions expand this to ensure that the safety and well-being of the child remain the paramount considerations. The interpretation of this depends largely on the judgment of the social worker, reviewable by the judge whenever an apprehension takes place. Any appeals are to the Supreme Court of the province.

British Columbia, along with some other provinces, such as Alberta, has recently been considering court orders of secure care for children who

(a) have an emotional or behavioural condition that presents a high risk of serious harm or injury to themselves, and

(b) are unable or unwilling to take steps to reduce that risk.[24]

Secure care controversially bridges the philosophies of child welfare and youth justice. This is a place where some child care professionals believe there is a treatment gap, especially since youth corrections and control under the *Youth Criminal Justice Act* are not available for children under the age of 12. Others reject this approach as unnecessarily stigmatizing children, arguing that secure care is similar in nature to imprisonment with enforced treatment. These critics view it as responding to the demand for greater social control by parents and the state over the non–criminal behaviour of children in politically conservative times.

---

[23] British Columbia's *Child, Family and Community Service Act*, R.S.B.C. 1996 c. 46, s. 30.
[24] *Secure Care Act of British Columbia*, Bill 25, 2000, s. 2.

Youth Justice[25]

Across Canada, the same law and process apply to youth (12 to 18 years old) in conflict with the criminal law. The reason is that both the *Criminal Code* and *Youth Criminal Justice Act* (YCJA), which replaced the *Young Offenders Act* in 2003, are federal. Each province has a separate provincial process for dealing with youth who violate provincial statutes (such as liquor offences) or municipal by-laws (such as skateboarding in prohibited areas). Children under 12 are not dealt with as criminals but are referred to the child welfare system.

The philosophy of the YCJA establishes the principles and tone that courts, police and correctional services are expected to follow in dealing with young offenders. It is a tricky balancing act between often competing principles[26] that address the goals of the justice system, the rights of young persons and of victims of their crimes.

The goals are outlined in section 3 of the YCJA as follows:

1. To prevent crime by addressing the circumstances underlying a young person's offending behaviour

2. To rehabilitate young persons who commit offences and reintegrate them into society

3. To ensure that a young person is subject to meaningful consequences for his or her offence in order to promote the long-term protection of the public

Furthermore, the YCJA states that the criminal justice system for young persons must be separate from that of adults and must emphasize the following:

1. Rehabilitation and reintegration

2. Fair and proportionate accountability that is consistent with the greater dependency of young persons and their reduced level of maturity

3. Enhanced procedural protection to ensure that young persons are treated fairly, and that their rights, including their right to privacy, are protected

4. Timely intervention that reinforces the link between the offending behaviour and its consequences

5. The promptness and speed with which persons responsible for enforcing this Act must act, given young people's perception of time

The YCJA goes on to state that within the limits of fair and proportionate accountability, the measures taken against young persons who commit offences should achieve the following:

1. Reinforce respect for societal values.

2. Encourage the repair of harm done to victims and the community.

3. Be meaningful for the individual young person, given his or her needs and level of development, and, where appropriate, involve the parents, the extended family, the community and social or other agencies in the young person's rehabilitation and reintegration.

---

[25] For details, see Jim Hackler, "Youth Justice and the Legal Process" in David Turner & Max R. Uhlemann, *supra* note 21 at 284–315; see also ch. 8.

[26] *Youth Criminal Justice Act*, S.C. 2002, c. 1, s. 3.

4. Respect gender, ethnic, cultural and linguistic differences and respond to the needs of Aboriginal young persons and of young persons with special requirements.

Young persons have rights and freedoms in their own right, such as a right to be heard in the course of and to participate in the processes, other than the decision to prosecute, that lead to decisions that affect them; and young persons have special guarantees of their rights and freedoms. Victims should be treated with courtesy, compassion and respect for their dignity and privacy and should suffer the minimum degree of inconvenience as a result of their involvement with the youth criminal justice system. Victims also should be provided with information about the proceedings and given an opportunity to participate and be heard, and parents should be informed of measures or proceedings involving their children and encouraged to support them in addressing their offending behaviour.

First and less serious offenders are to be dealt with by alternative (called extra-judicial) measures, including police cautions, pre-charge screening (diversion from court) or community-based programs, such as work service for the victim or community. Youth Justice Committees from the community can be used to recommend appropriate extra-judicial measures. However, the Youth Justice Court can now use adult measures in responding to violent or repeat young offenders over 14 (which usually means lengthier jail sentences that can end up in the adult correctional system). Institutional custody is possible if there is no reasonable alternative or combination of other measures available. It would be discussed in a pre-sentence report prepared by a youth worker (see below). The judge or youth worker may call a conference of professionals and community members involved with the young person to give advice on appropriate measures or sentences. This conference might recommend that **restorative justice** processes be utilized.

The needs of the youth and the responsibility of parents are counterbalanced by the need to protect society. Ideally, incarceration (imprisonment) is a last resort but has gained more prominence as community and preventative resources have been reduced by many provincial governments. Youth enjoy full legal rights, including Charter rights, in this justice model, apart from the right to trial by jury, which is not available at Youth Justice Court. The most used Charter rights are the following:

1. Being informed of the reasons for arrest
2. The right to remain silent
3. The right to consult a lawyer without delay

Youth are also entitled to consult a parent or appropriate adult in deciding whether or not to make a statement to police, and they cannot be coerced by the police's power or authority.

The young offender process begins in a fashion similar to that of the adult system (see Exhibit 30.3), with *a report of an alleged crime*. A police *investigation* follows, which may or may not lead to the arrest of a young person. If charged, the youth may be held in detention for the next Youth Justice Court hearing, released with a notice to appear in Youth Justice Court, or issued a summons and returned home. This decision is at the **discretion** of the police at this stage. Crown Counsel (the prosecutor) ultimately decides whether or not the youth will be prosecuted in court and the nature of the charges. Crown may decide, because of the circumstances of the offence and/or the social history of the youth, to use alternative measures (diversion), such as community service, a warning, or victim-offender mediation. A youth

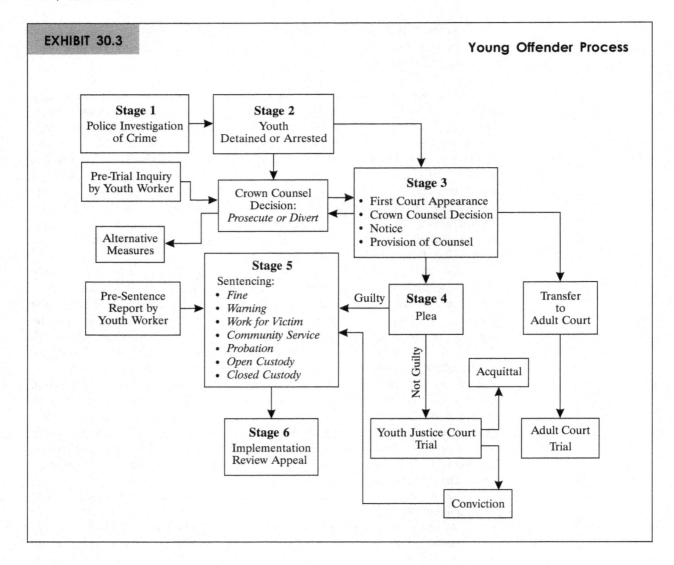

EXHIBIT 30.3

Young Offender Process

worker (probation officer) may provide a social study on the youth's background, called a *pre-trial inquiry*, to assist Crown Counsel in this decision.

If a youth has been arrested and held in a youth detention facility, the youth must appear before a court or justice of the peace within 24 hours for consideration of bail ("judicial interim release", in legal terminology) or continued detention (remand). At this *first appearance*, the youth's age is also at issue to determine that the court has jurisdiction. When the youth has had opportunity to fully instruct counsel, a *plea* of "guilty" or "not guilty" may be entered. A guilty plea leads to a sentencing hearing, and a youth worker may be asked to prepare a pre-disposition (sentence) report for the judge. A "not guilty" plea results in a trial date being set. The format of a *trial* is the same as in the adult criminal courts, apart from the prohibition on publishing identifying details.

The *Youth Criminal Justice Act* delineates a range of penalties, from warnings and fines through probation and compensation to the victim, to "open" and "closed" (secure) custody in a correctional facility, to a maximum of three years (six years for first-degree murder). Before incarceration is ordered, the court must consider the recommendations of a youth worker (probation officer) in a pre-disposition report, which is based on considerations that may include the impact of the offence on the victim; the youth's social history, including family, school and employment; and the Youth Justice Court record of the youth. Probation is a community alternative to imprisonment under the supervision of a youth worker. It may include conditions of social control, such as a curfew; reporting to the youth worker; a "red zone" (an area of the community that the youth can enter only with permission) or direction as to where the youth must live; and conditions of social support, such as counselling or alcohol treatment. Violation of conditions may result in a return to court for further sentencing. Secure custody is incarceration in a youth jail. Unlike the adult system, a reduction in sentence for good behaviour is not automatic. Open custody can be a camp setting, residential treatment, centre or closely supervised correctional group home. For serious crimes, a youth over 14 may be transferred, after a hearing initiated by the Crown, to the adult court for trial and/or sentencing. The youth cannot be publicly identified in Youth Justice Court. A conviction results in a Youth Justice Court record, which is removed after a period of time following completion of the disposition (sentence). Appeals on indictable offences are to the Court of Appeal or on summary offences to the Supreme Court of the province.

The YCJA introduced some innovations in direction, process, and intended outcomes. They include the following:

- A stated goal is to reduce the present over-reliance on incarceration for non-violent young persons. This remains to be seen.

- Youth aged 14–16 accused of serious or violent crimes (known as **presumptive offences**) will be dealt with in Youth Justice Court instead of being transferred to ordinary adult court. Such youth can be subject to preliminary hearings, and if the Crown successfully applies to the court, they will receive adult sentences upon conviction for indictable offences that an adult is liable to a sentence of imprisonment of more than two years. A maximum youth sentence for first-degree murder is six years in custody followed by four years of supervision. This compares with an adult sentence of life imprisonment.

- The YCJA and the system rely on communities, families, parents and others to adopt multi-disciplinary approaches to prevent youth crime by dealing with its underlying causes, responding to the needs of young persons, and providing guidance and support to those at risk of criminal offending. This goes against the current trend in many provinces to cut back social services.

- Youth Justice Courts will have powers of trial by jury presided over by specially appointed Superior Court Judges. Preliminary hearings, as in the adult system, will also be available.

- Provisions have been made in the YCJA for five new youth sentences: a reprimand; an intensive support and supervision program order; a program attendance order; a deferred custody and supervision order; and an intensive rehabilitative custody and supervision order. However, the availability of a number of these new sentences would be dependent on the establishment of programs by the provinces. Some critics argue that provincial funds would be drained away into expensive custodial facilities rather than creative community services.

Health Services

The right to life, liberty, and security of the person in the *Charter of Rights and Freedoms* reflects the right to life as stated in Article 6 of the U.N. Convention on the Rights of the Child and, in Article 24, to the "highest attainable standard of health and to facilities for the treatment of illness and the rehabilitation of health." Section 7 of the Charter was used in the highly publicized British Columbia case[27] of a seven-year-old hydrocephalic boy whose parents refused consent to replace a drain shunt in his skull. Medical opinion asserted that failure to do this would lead to physical deterioration and subsequent death. The British Columbia Superintendent intervened to protect the child and appealed to the Supreme Court of British Columbia. The court overturned the lower court decision and ordered the operation, finding that parents could not be allowed to determine the future quality of life for their son.

Concerning jurisdiction, the *Constitution Act* of 1867 does not specifically mention health. Life and health protection provisions under the federal *Criminal Code* have already been mentioned. The *Medical Care Act* of 1968 establishes programs that will be cost-shared with all the provinces. These include most health areas, such as hospitals, physician services, immunizations, health promotion, and mental treatment. Insured services for children depend on their parents being registered; but, again, the age definition of "child" varies among provinces: 18 in Saskatchewan, 19 in Manitoba, and 21 in Alberta.

Consent by children to medical and mental health treatment is a key issue. Only New Brunswick and British Columbia have clear legal provisions about this. The New Brunswick legislation[28] allows children of 16 and above to enjoy the same consent rights as adults; and rights of consent extend to those under 16 if, in the opinion of two physicians, the children understand the nature and consequences of the intended medical treatment and if allowing them to consent to it is in their best interests. British Columbia goes further by allowing a child (under 19) to give effective consent to health care, without the parent's knowledge or consent, under the following conditions: The health treatment provider (usually a physician) must have explained "the nature and consequences and the reasonable foreseeable benefits and risks"; he or she must be satisfied the child or youth understands and has concluded that the health care is in the child's best interests.[29] In other provinces, parental consent is required unless the child (under 18 in Saskatchewan, for instance) is in immediate danger. This authority can be overruled by the courts.

Unless clearly contrary to the child's best interests, Canadian courts and laws have been generally reluctant to interfere with parents' rights in this area, especially with consent to mental health treatment or admission to a facility. In Ontario, the *Mental Health Act*[30] presumes that children under 16 are not competent to consent, but they can apply for review. The age of medical consent in Quebec is 14. In British Columbia, children under 16 admitted voluntarily to a mental health facility by parents or relatives must, upon admission or as soon as they become capable of comprehension, be informed of reasons for their detention and be informed of rights to counsel, *habeas corpus* (the right to have their detention reviewed by a court), and rights to a board or tribunal review. Young people over 16 have the capacity to request admission in their own right.[31] Many other provinces are silent on these issues of age and consent, leaving physicians cautious about administering medical treatment, such as contraception, to children under 16.

---

[27] Re S.D. 1983, 34 R.F.L. (2nd) 34 B.C.S.C.

[28] *Medical Consent of Minors Act*, R.S.N.B. 1973, c. M-6.1, s. 2.

[29] *Infants Act*, R.S.B.C. 1996, c. 223, s. 17.

[30] R.S.O. 1990, c. M.7, s. 5.

[31] *Mental Health Act*, R.S.B.C. 1996, c. 288.

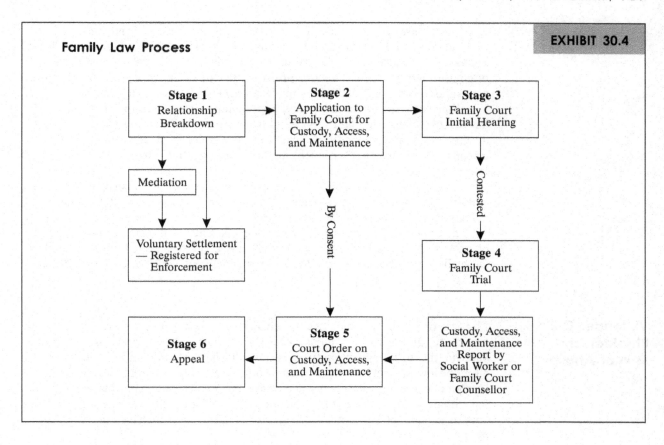

Family Law Process

EXHIBIT 30.4

Stage 1 Relationship Breakdown

Stage 2 Application to Family Court for Custody, Access, and Maintenance

Stage 3 Family Court Initial Hearing

Mediation

By Consent

Contested

Voluntary Settlement — Registered for Enforcement

Stage 4 Family Court Trial

Stage 6 Appeal

Stage 5 Court Order on Custody, Access, and Maintenance

Custody, Access, and Maintenance Report by Social Worker or Family Court Counsellor

Family Law

Family law is civil and under the jurisdiction of the provinces, apart from the granting of divorces. Brief comments will be made on those issues that affect children and youth, such as custody and access, guardianship, maintenance, and family violence. These issues can also arise as part of a *Divorce Act* action under federal law, or as part of a marriage or common-law separation under provincial family laws. *Custody* is the physical care and control of a child and normally includes the legal components of guardianship, such as the right to determine medical treatment, education, and religion. *Access* means the right to visit a child, usually exercised by the parent not having custody. Where parents are co-operative, courts can order joint or shared custody. (See Exhibit 30.4.)

Upon the breakdown of a marriage or common-law relationship, the parents can privately agree on the custody arrangements for the children, and this can be registered in the courts for enforcement. Disputes can be resolved by alternative methods, such as family mediation, where a neutral third person helps the parents to resolve the dispute in the interests of the children. Litigation (court action) involves an *application* to the Family Court at the provincial level or Divorce Court at the supreme level in each province. Both are civil hearings where the court is obligated by law to act in the child's best interests. The "best interest" criteria are similar and set out in provincial family law statutes or the *Divorce Act*. They usually include health and emotional well-being, special needs, love, affection, training and education, financial resources, stability and security, and the child's views, whenever appropriate.[32]

[32] *Family Relations Act*, R.S.B.C. 1996, c. 128, s. 24.

A *contested hearing* is much like a trial, with the parties bringing witnesses, such as psychiatrists or friends, to support their position. The court determines the capacity of each parent to provide for the child's best interests, often through a custody report prepared by a social worker or family court counsellor. The court will then make a *custody order*, which can be enforced. Violations can result in the police apprehending and returning a child to the lawful custodian, and interference with court-ordered custody rights may constitute a criminal offence.[33] Courts can also order civil restraining orders or criminal peace bonds to prevent parents and relatives without custody from interfering with or harassing children.

Courts can also order and enforce *maintenance* (financial support) for children. Child support guidelines on maintenance amounts were introduced in amendments to the *Divorce Act* in 1997. In some jurisdictions, children under 19 can apply for maintenance from their parents.[34] If parents are incapable of providing maintenance, it may constitute child welfare grounds or support an application for income assistance for independent youth aged 16 to 19 years old.

Violence: Child Physical and Sexual Abuse

Physical or sexual violence against children by their parents or caregivers may constitute grounds for criminal charges, child welfare apprehension or civil suits in the tort (civil wrong) of assault and battery. Recently, children (often after becoming adults) have been both suing their parents, caregivers or teachers in residential schools and treatment centres for damages, and reporting them to the police for criminal action. The *Criminal Code* contains a special section on such offences against children, including sexual exploitation by persons in a position of authority or trust.

There are special rules of evidence and process for criminal cases of child sexual abuse.[35] Child victims under 18 may be allowed to testify outside the courtroom, watched by the accused on closed circuit television or from behind a screen. Videotaped evidence of victims under 18 years old may be admitted under certain conditions, as long as it is verified in court and the child is open to cross-examination. Videotaped evidence can also be presented at the sentencing stage as part of a victim-impact statement (a report to the court from the victims as to the impact of the crime on their life). Crown counsel and victim services can be useful in preparing children to testify.

Adoption

Adoption law is of provincial jurisdiction and is civil in nature. An *adoption order* permanently transfers the relationship (including rights and responsibilities) of parent and child from the biological (birth) parents to the parents adopting the child. The adoptive parents gain full custody and guardianship. Birth mothers can *consent* to an adoption 11 days after the child's birth in British Columbia. The voluntary consent can then only be withdrawn if clearly within the best interests of the child. Other jurisdictions allow a period of grace for such revocations. Disclosure of information identifying the birth parents is prohibited without their consent, unless release is essential for the health and well-being of the adopted child or adult. Most provinces have developed Adoption Registries that allow birth parents and adult adopted children who seek identifying information to do so. If requests match, then

[33] *Criminal Code of Canada*, R.S.C. 1985, c. C-46, s. 282.
[34] See *Family Relations Act*, note 31, s. 88.
[35] See Nicholas Lang, Timothy Stokes, and Laurie J. Soloway, "Family Violence and the Criminal Court System", ch. 8 in David Turner & Max R. Uhlemann, *supra* note 21.

reunions can be arranged. This is the "passive" registry model. In several provinces, "active" registries will now conduct searches for adoptee applicants over 19, with a discreet attempt to contact the birth parents to see if they consent to disclosure for a reunion. British Columbia's proposed new Act, currently being debated in the legislature, would allow automatic disclosure at 19 unless a veto is filed.

A couple can adopt children privately, through the provincial government Ministry of Social Services or Children's Aid Society, or from a spouse's former relationship. In the first two instances, the Ministry in British Columbia will have a social worker conduct an *adoption study* after six months to determine whether the adopting parents are fit to adopt. Ontario prohibits private placement for adoption, except through approval of the Director of Child Welfare. Persons over 12 years old must consent to their adoption. Until recently, in British Columbia, a couple had to be married to adopt a healthy child. British Columbia's new Act[36] removes restrictions and allows gay and common-law couples and single people to adopt, and results in more open contact between child and birth parents. An Application to Adopt is made to the Supreme Court, usually in documentation form only, accompanied by the superintendent's (or director's) or society's report.

Education

Each province has its own *Education or School Act* that regulates the conduct of students and teachers, who follow a curriculum set by the provincial government. Common provisions include the following:

1. The compulsory attendance of students from 6 or 7 years old to 15 or 16, unless receiving approved home instruction.

2. A prohibition on corporal punishment.

3. Rules for the discipline and review of student behaviour, including the power of principals to suspend for a maximum fixed period, and of the school board to expel — usually after a hearing.

4. Parent rights to request an exemption to religious exercises. Note that some provinces have only denominational (religious) public school systems.

5. The rights of schools to maintain confidential student records. Some provinces give parents full rights of access to those records.

6. Processes for disciplining teachers for professional misconduct. Several provinces have established separate Colleges of Teachers for certification and professional discipline.

Issues of student rights to freedom of speech and expression and issues of access and integration are recently bringing Charter implications into school law. Section 23 allows parents of the French or (chiefly in Quebec) English linguistic minority the right of instruction for their children in that language, where the numbers of children warrant it. However, this does not include the right to French immersion for English-speaking students. Only a few provinces mention vaguely a child's right to an appropriate education. Saskatchewan states that children between 6 and 12 have a right to receive instruction appropriate to their grade. Ontario's *Education Act* provides for compulsory special education programs, directed by a placement committee and reviewed by a Special Education Tribunal.

---

[36] *Adoption Act*, R.S.B.C. 1996, c. 5.

LEGAL ISSUES FOR CHILDREN

Children's law is difficult to pull together, being dispersed as it is in numerous Acts. Past law reform commissions[37] have proposed a comprehensive Bill of Children's Rights, such as a Charter for Children, to reflect in more specific detail in Canada the spirit of the U.N. Convention. The proposed bill, which was not passed, included the power of courts to order that specific services to children and youth be provided by governments. This would have overcome the present problem of the inability of parents and children to legally demand appropriate services that remain at government discretion, for the most part.

Within each province there is often a complex web of ministries, services and agencies serving children and youth. Families and children find this bureaucracy difficult to navigate. Legislation is required to consolidate and rationalize this delivery, perhaps in a single, comprehensive government ministry.

While all children are unique and require equal treatment in law, several groups are seriously disadvantaged and need special consideration.

Aboriginal Children

The status of First Nations in Canada and their political goals of self-government demand that the law deal differently, and in culturally more appropriate ways, with Aboriginal children. It is recognized that native children are disproportionately represented in our state care and youth correctional systems. In order to change this, new legal and social mechanisms are required. Bands across Canada are taking over their own child welfare, youth justice, and education programs. Child welfare laws are recognizing the importance of preserving an Aboriginal child's cultural heritage and involving the child's Aboriginal community in the decision about her future. Youth justice is involving tribal circles for decision making, and experimenting with such traditional penalties as banishment. Native custom adoption is gaining recognition, and native schools are developing as part of, or separately from, public education.

Ethnic Minority Children

Like Aboriginal children, other racial minorities are over-represented in care and correctional systems in some provinces. Cultural sensitivity in the law and in the process and in the treatment of minority children is still lacking. Perhaps community cultural standards are not being considered, despite the provision in section 27 of the Charter, which urges that the Charter be interpreted in a way "consistent with the preservation and enhancement of the multicultural heritage of Canadians." Only children in care in some provinces — and those in court who are entitled to an interpreter — clearly have rights to maintain their cultural heritage. However, many school boards are finally developing race relations by-laws and policies.

Children in Poverty

According to many reports,[38] including the community panel on the new *Child Welfare Act* in British Columbia, poverty has been viewed as a crucial factor in child abuse, neglect, and ill-health. Yet human rights protections do not prohibit discrimination on the basis of socio-economic status. Nowhere

---

[37] For instance, the British Columbia Royal Commission on Family and Children's Rights (1975) chaired by Justice Berger.

[38] *Making Changes: A Place to Start* (Victoria, B.C.: Ministry of Social Services, 1994); and *Child Poverty in Canada, Report Card 1995: Campaign 2000* (Toronto, Ont.: Family Services Association, 1995).

in Canada are family welfare (income assistance) rates anywhere near the accepted poverty cutoffs. There are insufficient child care spaces for parents and children who require them. Some argue that Canada is contravening the spirit of the U.N. Convention.

Children with Special Needs

Where access of a child with a disability to a regular classroom is concerned, several cases challenging **segregation** (separate education) have occurred across Canada. In Nova Scotia, a student won a case against segregation to a special classroom for children with disabilities.[39] The Supreme Court of Canada ruled that integration was not automatic but that the decision between integration and segregation was to be made on the basis of the child's best interest.[40] The *Schools Act* of New Brunswick stands alone in insisting that exceptional students be placed with non-exceptional students within regular classroom settings to the extent considered practicable by the school board.

Because of jurisdictional differences, the laws for children across Canada remain inconsistent and patchy. Canadian society is experiencing a conflict of values in determining the degree to which children and youth should enjoy rights independent of their parents or guardians. As with all law, this incorporation of rights and principles into law for children is dynamic and tries to reflect current values and social demands.

LAWS PERTAINING TO PROFESSIONALS
WORKING WITH CHILDREN

Professionals working with children and youth need to know about child rights and special laws so that they can act as fair and reasonable persons *in loco parentis*, and as advocates. Criminal record checks are now routinely required for persons employed to work with children, and many jurisdictions maintain registries of child abusers. The *Criminal Code* and professional codes of ethics for social workers, nurses, psychologists, teachers, and child care workers prohibit the exploitation of children.

CHAPTER SUMMARY

This chapter explored briefly the extent to which children and youth are provided, and have been provided in the past, with rights and protections in Canadian law. Key areas of law and process affecting the status of children and youth were discussed, and some common principles identified. Obstacles to rights and key issues were touched on, together with identified groups of children requiring special protection.

GLOSSARY OF NEW TERMS AND KEY CONCEPTS

accountability mechanisms

Processes in law that allow for the review or monitoring of decisions or services provided by an authority such as a government ministry. The Ombudsman Office is a major example.

---

[39] *Elwood v. Halifax County-Bedford District School Board* (1987), N.S.S.C. unreported.
[40] *Eaton v. Brant County Board of Education* (1997), 1 S.C.R. 241.

administrative fairness Rules of fairness in the decision-making process, such as the right to receive reasons for a decision and to appeal it.

advocacy Literally meaning "speaking to", the skill of assisting often disempowered persons, such as children, to put their case across to an authority or to speak on their behalf and represent their interests in partisan fashion. Lawyers are the most formal type of advocate.

age of majority The age when the law assumes a child ("minor" or "infant") has attained the capacity and competency to act fully and legally as an independent adult.

capacity The legal ability to be competent to understand the implications of one's decisions.

consent Agreeing to a choice, an offer, or a proposed treatment in an informed way. Like "capacity", it is crucial for children and for persons suffering from mental disability.

dependency The notion that children are vulnerable and require parents, guardians or the state to protect them.

discretion The ability to make a choice without an obligation in law. It usually concerns the unrestricted ability of a government official to offer a service or not.

in loco parentis Latin for "in the place of a parent", meaning a person who is legally acting as a parent or substitute, such as a teacher or foster parent. Section 43 of the *Criminal Code* gives special disciplinary powers to such persons.

presumptive offences Serious offences (murder, attempted murder, manslaughter, and aggravated sexual assault) where youth aged between 14 and 16 are presumed to require an adult sentence upon conviction after a preliminary hearing has been successfully applied for by the Crown. The Youth Justice Court can now impose an adult sentence.

restorative justice A process for resolution of criminal acts where offenders face the victims and hear of the impact of their crime. It may result in apology and compensation. The process might be mediated by community members assisted by police and justice personnel. Models include group conferencing, sentencing circles and First Nations healing circles.

secure care A court order under child welfare legislation where children with identified problems, such as addictions, can be cared for and treated in a controlled, often closed, setting to protect them from harming themselves.

segregation The practice of separating children with special needs into special classrooms or schools.

special protection Special provisions and processes for children in law beyond what a competent adult might receive or be subject to, based on the notion of the vulnerability of children.

status The legal position of a child in relation to parents or the state. Children in care have wardship status.

REVIEW QUESTIONS

1. Why are there different ages identified in laws for the various changes in status and services for children and youth?

2. Identify three categories of children's rights and the major differences between them.

3. What obstacles exist to the full implementation of independent rights for children and youth?

4. Where does the right to be provided with counsel exist?

5. Identify the key principles in child welfare and young offenders law.

6. Why do certain groups of children require special protection?

7. Identify where the principles of child welfare and youth justice overlap.

8. Under the provisions of the *Youth Criminal Justice Act*, identify the different ways young offenders accused of serious crime might be dealt with.

DISCUSSION QUESTIONS

1. Discuss how far the equality rights in section 15 of the Charter apply to children and youth in reality.

2. Discuss potential conflicts in society or family life if children were to have full rights independent of their parents.

3. What rights does the reader, as a student, have in college classes? How is this different from public education at a primary or secondary level?

4. Exercises

   (a) Imagine that you are a social worker investigating an allegation of child abuse. Identify and discuss some key facts you would want to know before apprehending a particular 10-year-old child. Explain to the child in understandable words the key steps in the process of coming into care. If you have time, you may wish to attend Family Court locally and interview a social worker.

   (b) Imagine that you are a youth worker preparing a pre-disposition report on a young offender. Identify and discuss what key information you would need in recommending a sentence to the court. Examine sections 41 and 42 of the *Youth Criminal Justice Act*, and explain the sentencing options to the youth. You may wish to visit Youth Justice Court and interview a youth worker.

   (c) Imagine that you are a family court counsellor or social worker preparing a custody and access report on an eight-year-old child. Identify and discuss the key factors that the court would take into account in its decision. Explain these to the child. You may wish to visit Family Court locally and interview a family court counsellor or social worker.

5. Exercise: In small groups, examine recent newspaper articles on young offender cases and the recent changes in the *Youth Criminal Justice Act*. Each group should explore how far these cases and reforms apply or change the existing balance of criteria and principles listed under the section "Youth Justice". Students should identify whether they agree or not, and why, with the proposed amendments.

6. Discuss how far children's rights might be compromised under the application of the secure care provisions.

7. Some Provinces have recently suggested that the principle of deterrence should be incorporated into the principles of the *Youth Criminal Justice Act*. Discuss whether you agree or not, exploring potential implications of incorporation.

8. Discuss how far the laws of your province that affect children and youth are in accordance with the following principles taken directly from the United Nations Declaration of the Rights of the Child:

Principle 1 The child shall enjoy all the rights set forth in this Declaration. Every child, without any exception whatsoever, shall be entitled to these rights, without distinction or discrimination on account of race, colour, sex, language, religion, political or other opinion, national or social origin, property, birth or other status, whether of himself or of his family.

Principle 2 The child shall enjoy special protection, and shall be given opportunities and facilities, by law and by other means, to enable him to develop physically, mentally, morally, spiritually and socially in a healthy and normal manner and in conditions of freedom and dignity. In the enactment of laws for this purpose, the best interests of the child shall be the paramount consideration.

Principle 3 The child shall be entitled from his birth to a name and a nationality.

Principle 4 The child shall enjoy the benefits of social security. He shall be entitled to grow and develop in health; to this end, special care and protection shall be provided both to him and to his mother, including adequate pre-natal and post-natal care. The child shall have the right to adequate nutrition, housing, recreation and medical services.

Principle 5 The child who is physically, mentally or socially handicapped shall be given the special treatment, education and care required by his particular condition.

Principle 6 The child, for the full and harmonious development of his personality, needs love and understanding. He shall, wherever possible, grow up in the care and under the responsibility of his parents, and, in any case, in an atmosphere of affection and of moral and material security; a child of tender years shall not, save in exceptional circumstances, be separated from his mother. Society and the public authorities shall have the duty to extend particular care to children without a family and to those without adequate means of support. Payment of state and other assistance towards the maintenance of children of large families is desirable.

Principle 7 The child is entitled to receive education, which shall be free and compulsory, at least in the elementary stages. He shall be given an education which will promote his general culture and enable him, on a basis of equal opportunity, to develop his abilities, his individual judgement, and his sense of moral and social responsibility, and to become a useful member of society.

The best interests of the child shall be the guiding principle of those responsible for his education and guidance; that responsibility lies in the first place with his parents.

The child shall have full opportunity for play and recreation, which should be directed to the same purposes as education; society and the public authorities shall endeavour to promote the enjoyment of this right.

Principle 8 The child shall in all circumstances be among the first to receive protection and relief.

Principle 9 The child shall be protected against all forms of neglect, cruelty and exploitation. He shall not be the subject of traffic, in any form.

The child shall not be admitted to employment before an appropriate minimum age; he shall in no case be caused or permitted to engage in any occupation or employment which would prejudice his health or education, or interfere with his physical, mental or moral development.

Principle 10 The child shall be protected from practices which may foster racial, religious and any other form of discrimination. He shall be brought up in a spirit of understanding, tolerance, friendship among peoples, peace and universal brotherhood, and in full consciousness that his energy and talents should be devoted to the service of his fellow men.

SUGGESTED READINGS

Bala, N. *Youth Criminal Justice Law* (Toronto, Ont.: Irwin Law, 2003).

Bala, N., J.P. Hornick, H.N. Snyder, & J.J. Paetsch, eds. *An International Comparison of Problems and Solutions* (Toronto, Ont.: Thompson Educational Publishing, 2002).

Bala, N., M.K. Zapf, R.J. Williams, R. Vogl, & J.P. Hornick, eds. *Canadian Child Welfare Law: Children, Families and the State*, 2d ed. (Toronto, Ont.: Thompson Educational, 2004).

British Columbia, Ministry for Children and Families. *Know Your Rights Under the Child, Family and Community Service Act: A Guide for Young People in Care* (Victoria, B.C.: Author, 1998).

Howe, R.B., & K. Covell. (eds.) *A Question of Commitment: Children's Rights in Canada* (Waterloo, Ont.: Wilfrid Laurier University Press, 2007).

Doyle, S., T. Farrell, & A. Sheppard. *For the Record: The Youth Criminal Justice Act: A New Law for Canadian Youth, A New Collaborative Approach*, 2d ed. (St. John's, Nfld.: Public Legal Information Association of Newfoundland, 2003).

Justice for Children and Youth. *Age Based Laws/Rights*, online: <www.jfcy.org/agebased.html>.

Payne, J., Q.C., & M. Payne. *Canadian Family Law*, 2d ed. (Toronto, Ont.: Irwin Law, 2006).

Turner, D., & M.R. Uhlemann. *A Legal Handbook for the Helping Professional*, 3d ed. (Victoria, B.C.: Sedgewick Society for Consumer and Public Education, School of Social Work, 2007). [Especially Chapter 3, "Child Protection and Legal Process"; Chapter 4, "Children's Rights to Services in Canada"; Chapter 5, "Aboriginal Self-Determination and Child Protection Law"; Chapter 6, "Adoptions"; Chapter 7, "Family Law"; Chapter 9, "Youth Justice and the Legal Process"; and Chapter 13, "Education and the Law"]

Umbreit, M.S. "Victim-Offender Mediation in Criminal Conflict: Toward Restorative Justice", in E. Kruk, ed., *Mediation and Conflict Resolution in Social Work and Human Services* (Chicago: Nelson-Hall Publishers, 2000).

Vogl, R., & N. Bala. *Testifying on Behalf of Children: A Handbook for Canadian Professionals* (Toronto, Ont.: Thompson Educational, 2001).

For information on child welfare legislation, see

British Columbia

British Columbia. *YCJA: British Columbia*, 2d ed. (Victoria, B.C.: BC Government, 2004). This pocket guide provides detailed information for practitioners in British Columbia. Based on *Moving Forward: Pocket Guide to the Youth Criminal Justice Act Canada* developed by the Nova Scotia Department of Justice, it applies across Canada, since criminal legislation is a national responsibility.

Ontario

Geigen-Miller, M. *It's Time to Break the Silence: Creating Meaningful Access to Rights and Advocacy Services for Young People in Care in Ontario* (Toronto, Ont.: Defence for Children International, 2003).

Zuker, M.A., R.C. Hammond, & R.C. Flynn. *Children's Law Handbook* (Toronto, Ont.: Carswell, 2006).

General

Canada. *Child Welfare in Canada 2000*, online: <http://www.hrsdc.gc.ca/en/cs/sp/sdc/socpol/publications/reports/2000-000033/page00.shtml>

Nicholas Bala, Michael Kim Zapf, R. James Williams, Robin Vogl, & Joseph P. Hornick (eds.). *Canadian Child Welfare Law: Children, Families, and the State*, 2d ed. (Toronto, Ont.: Thompson Educational Publishing, 2004).

WEBSITE

Canadian Coalition for the Rights of Children: <www.rightsofchildren.ca>

Estate Planning

DeeAnn M. Gonsalves
SENECA COLLEGE

Learning Objectives

After reading this chapter, the reader should be able to:

- ➢ understand what a will is
- ➢ appreciate the advantages of making a will
- ➢ understand the legal and formal requirements for making a will
- ➢ identify the information required to prepare a will
- ➢ identify the key clauses in a will
- ➢ understand the execution requirements of a will
- ➢ understand how a will can be amended or revoked
- ➢ demonstrate an awareness of intestacy laws
- ➢ understand what a power of attorney for property is
- ➢ understand what a power of attorney for personal care is
- ➢ understand the legal and formal requirements for making powers of attorney
- ➢ appreciate the limitations of a power of attorney
- ➢ understand how a power of attorney can be revoked
- ➢ demonstrate an awareness of what may happen when someone becomes incapacitated without having made a power of attorney

TABLE OF CONTENTS

INTRODUCTION

It has been said that in life there are only two certainties: death and taxes.[1] The area of estates law, particularly that of estate planning, provides us with an opportunity to address these certainties. The act of estate planning can benefit everyone, from the smallest to the largest estate holder.

What Is an Estate?

An **estate** is all of the property, both real and personal, that someone has an interest in. Estate property may be in the possession of the owner or owed to him or her.

What Is Estate Planning?

Estate planning is the process of organizing one's affairs with respect to the preservation, management and distribution of his or her property during an incapacity or upon death. Estate planning includes the preparation of documents that may assist with the management of the estate of the deceased or incapacitated person. The estate planning process includes choosing someone to handle the estate. It also often includes structuring one's affairs to minimize taxes, probate fees, and other costs and to provide for loved ones.

Common Estate Documents

The most common estate documents are a **will** and powers of attorney for property and personal care. In some cases, additional documents are required for trusts, private corporations, or other entities.

WILLS

What Is a Will?

A will is a written document that sets out a person's directions for the management and distribution of his or her property upon death. A will may also appoint someone, commonly known as an **executor** in the case of a male appointee and an **executrix** in the case of a female appointee, to be in charge of the estate.[2]

The Advantages of Making a Will

Controlling the Disposition of Your Estate

A will allows its maker, known as the **testator** in the case of a male and the **testatrix** in the case of a female, to control the disposition of his or her estate to his or her beneficiaries following his or her demise. A will sets out a plan for the executor to follow with respect to the management and distribution of estate assets, the payment of debts, and other matters. A will specifies who shall receive estate assets. Without a will, government legislation dictates who the heirs are. If those heirs are of the age of majority, they will inherit at the time of the death. With a will, the payment of inheritances can be postponed, beyond the age of majority, through the use of trusts. Such **testamentary trusts** can also be used to benefit some disabled and spendthrift beneficiaries.

---

[1] Benjamin Franklin, 1789, in a letter to M. Leroy.

[2] Given that many estate terms are specifically masculine or feminine, the author has been unable to use gender-neutral terms in some parts of this text.

Choosing an Executor and Beneficiaries

In order to administer the estate, the will should appoint an executor or executrix. In some jurisdictions, terms such as **personal representative** or **estate trustee with a will** are used. One or more persons may be appointed as executor. Some testators appoint a trust company to act as their executor.

An executor obtains his authority to act directly from the will. With a will, an executor may commence his or her duties immediately following the testator's death.

Without a will in place, someone is said to die intestate. Intestacy laws in each province set out who should be appointed to manage the intestate estate. This person is commonly known as the **administrator** of the estate if they are a male and as the **administratrix** if they are a female. In some jurisdictions they are known as the personal representative or the **estate trustee without a will**. In an intestacy, administration of the estate cannot begin until a grant of **letters of administration**; or, in some provinces, such as Ontario, a **certificate of appointment of estate trustee without a will** is obtained from the court.

In his will the testator names the person or persons who are to receive his assets upon his death. These people are known as beneficiaries. Beneficiaries often include family members, friends, and charities.

A will allows the testator to specify which items of property each **beneficiary** shall receive. When drafting a will, care should be taken to name an alternate beneficiary to inherit in the event that the original beneficiary predeceases the testator.

Without a will, provincial legislation sets out how an estate will be divided. There is a commonly held misconception that legally married spouses will automatically inherit each other's estates, thereby dispensing with the need for a will. In most provinces and territories, this is not the case. Where the deceased is survived by a spouse and children, the estate or some portion of it is divided between the spouse and the children. For a more detailed look at provincial and territorial intestacy laws, please consult the table of provincial and territorial intestacy laws set out in Exhibit 31.1. Note that the table sets out legislation only for legally married spouses.

Intestacy and Matrimonial Property Legislation

A well-drafted will can circumvent provincial intestacy laws. Without a will or with a poorly drafted will, an estate or part of it must be distributed in accordance with provincial intestacy laws.

In some cases, a well-drafted will, in conjunction with a domestic contract, such as a marriage contract, can avoid the application of legislation regarding the division of matrimonial property upon the death of a spouse. Couples embarking upon a second marriage later in life may use a will, combined with a domestic contract, to preserve the bulk of their estate for their children from their first marriages while still providing for each other.

In most jurisdictions, couples in a common law relationship are not legally entitled to a share of their partner's property upon the partner's death.[3] However, a couple in a common law relationship may execute wills leaving property to each other.

---

[3] In British Columbia, the *Estates Administration Act* provides that after two years of residing together, common law spouses have the same rights on intestacy as married spouses.

In Manitoba and Nova Scotia, the provincial *Vital Statistics Act*s provide that common law spouses can register their domestic partnership to obtain the same rights as married spouses under intestacy laws.

EXHIBIT 31.1			Summary of Canadian Intestacy Legislation

PROVINCE/ TERRITORY	LEGISLATION	SPOUSE & ONE CHILD	SPOUSE & TWO OR MORE CHILDREN
Alberta	*Intestate Succession Act*	$40,000 to spouse with remainder divided equally between the spouse and child	$40,000 to spouse plus 1/3 of the remainder with the other 2/3 divided equally among children
British Columbia	*Estate Administration Act*	$65,000 to spouse with remainder divided equally between spouse and child	$65,000 to spouse plus 1/3 of the remainder with the other 2/3 divided equally among children
Manitoba	*Intestate Succession Act*	All to spouse[1]	All to spouse[1]
New Brunswick	*Devolution of Estates Act*	Marital property[2] to spouse with remainder of property divided equally between spouse and child	Marital property to spouse plus 1/3 of the remainder with the other 2/3 divided equally among children
Newfoundland	*Intestate Succession Act*	All property divided equally between spouse and child	1/3 of property to spouse with the other 2/3 divided equally among children
Northwest Territories	*Intestate Succession Act*	$50,000 to spouse with the remainder divided equally between spouse and child	$50,000 to spouse plus 1/3 of the remainder with the other 2/3 divided equally among children
Nova Scotia	*Intestate Succession Act*	$50,000 to spouse (or house and contents) with the remainder divided equally between spouse and child	$50,000 (or house and contents) to spouse plus 1/3 of the remainder with the other 2/3 divided equally among children
Nunavut	*Intestate Succession Act*	$50,000 to spouse with the remainder divided equally between spouse and child	$50,000 to spouse plus 1/3 of remainder with the other 2/3 divided equally among children
Ontario	*Succession Law Reform Act*	$200,000 to spouse with the remainder divided equally between spouse and child	$200,000 to spouse plus 1/3 of remainder with the other 2/3 divided equally among children
Prince Edward Island	*Probate Act*	All property divided equally between spouse and child	1/3 of property to spouse with the other 2/3 divided equally among children
Quebec	*Quebec Civil Code*	One-third to spouse and remaining two-thirds to child	1/3 of property to spouse with the other 2/3 divided equally among children
Saskatchewan	*The Intestate Succession Act, 1996*	$100,000 to spouse with the remainder divided equally between spouse and child	$100,000 to spouse plus 1/3 of remainder with the other 2/3 divided equally among children
Yukon Territory	*Estate Administration Act*	$75,000 to spouse with the remainder divided equally between spouse and child	$75,000 to spouse plus 1/3 of the remainder with the other 2/3 divided equally among children

[1] If the surviving spouse is not the biological parent of the child or children, then the spouse receives the greater of $50,000 or one-half of the estate; the spouse will also get one-half of the remainder while the other one-half goes to the child or is shared equally among the children, if there is more than one child: *Intestate Succession Act*, C.C.S.M. c. I85, s. 2(2).

[2] Marital property as defined in *Marital Property Act*, S.N.B., 1980, c. M-1.1.

Providing for a Common Disaster

Most wills contain a special provision known as a "**common disaster clause**". This clause is included in order to address the situation where both spouses die within a short time of each other. An example of a common disaster clause is contained in paragraph 8(e) of the sample will set out in Exhibit 31.2. The clause states that, in order to inherit under the will, the surviving spouse must outlive the deceased by 30 or more days. Thirty days is the figure that is usually used to reflect an assumption that if someone survives an accidental injury by more than 30 days, they are unlikely to die from their injuries. The will usually provides for an alternate beneficiary to inherit in the event that the surviving spouse dies before the 30-day period has concluded.

Without a will or with a will that does not contain a common disaster clause, the family of the spouse who first succumbed to his or her injuries would not inherit anything from their family member's estate. By way of an example, assume that a childless couple, who had not yet made their wills, was involved in a serious car accident. Unfortunately the accident resulted in the death of the husband at the scene of the accident. The wife died two hours later. As the wife outlived her husband, she inherited the husband's entire estate upon his death. As a result of her death, her next of kin — her parents or, if they had predeceased her, then her siblings — inherited her entire estate. The wife's estate also included the husband's estate. The husband's family did not receive any part of his estate as the wife had outlived him, albeit by only two hours. As well, in Ontario and in some other provinces, probate tax would have to be paid twice on the husband's assets. The tax would have to be paid to probate his estate over to his wife and again on her entire estate, which now includes his estate. If the couple had children surviving them, the children would inherit their parents' estates. There would still be an advantage to having a common disaster clause, as the estates could be directly probated to the children, resulting in probate tax being paid only once on each estate.

Some provinces have legislation in place to provide for a more equitable distribution of property where spouses die simultaneously. It should be noted, however, that simultaneous death is a rare occurrence. In Ontario, section 55 of the *Succession Law Reform Act*[4] provides that where the spouses die simultaneously or in circumstances rendering it uncertain which of them survived the other, each spouse's property shall be disposed of as if he or she had survived the other. In the example above, if the husband and wife had died at precisely the same time, the husband's estate would pass to his family, and the wife's estate would pass to her family, as each spouse would be deemed to have survived the other.

Family Law Provisions for Beneficiaries

If someone receives an inheritance, as a result of an intestacy or from a poorly drafted will, he or she may have to share the earnings on their inheritance with their estranged spouse. Matrimonial property legislation, such as Ontario's *Family Law Act*,[5] provides that inheritances are generally excluded from a spouse's net family property and, therefore, are not subject to division or equalization upon a marriage breakdown. However, any earnings generated by an inheritance, such as interest, dividends, or capital gains, constitute part of a spouse's net family property. These earnings are subject to division or

---

[4] *Succession Law Reform Act*, R.S.O. 1990, c. S.26.
[5] *Family Law Act*, R.S.O. 1990, c. F.3.

EXHIBIT 31.2

A Sample Will

LAST WILL AND TESTAMENT OF
ELIZABETH LOUISE COLLINS

THIS IS THE LAST WILL of me, Elizabeth Louise Collins, also known as Liz Collins, of the City of Brampton, in the Regional Municipality of Peel, and Province of Ontario.

Part I
Initial Matters

Interpretation

1. In interpreting this will it is my intention that the headings are intended only as guidelines and are not to be interpreted as being part of the text of this my will.
2. Children as referred to in this will shall mean my son, Jason Oliver Collins, and my daughter, Angela Louise Collins.

Revocation of Prior Wills

3. I REVOKE all wills, codicils, and other testamentary dispositions that I have made before the time of signing this will.

Appointment of Executor

4. I APPOINT my spouse, namely Robert Allen Collins, to be the Executor of my will. In this my will and in any codicil to it I refer to my Executor and my alternate Executor as my Estate Trustee.
5. If my Estate Trustee should:
   (a) predecease me, or
   (b) survive me but die without having proved this my will,
   (c) be unable or unwilling to act, or
   (d) cease to be a resident in Canada, or shall be absent from Canada in any calendar year for a period or periods, the aggregate of which is one hundred and eighty (180) days or more, then I APPOINT my brother, namely Austin Cory Reynolds, to be the alternate Executor of my Will, to act in his place.

Organ Donation

6. I direct my trustee to donate any organs that can be of any use for transplant purposes.

Cremation

7. It is my wish to have my remains cremated and scattered from the bow of my sailboat on Lake Ontario with Vivaldi's *The Four Seasons* playing in the background.

Part II
Disposition of Estate

8. I give all of my property, both real and personal wherever located, including all property over which I have a general power of appointment, to my Estate Trustee upon the following trusts:

Payment of Debts
(a) to pay:
   (i) my debts and cremation expenses, and
   (ii) the expenses of administering my estate and the trusts created by this will and any codicil to this will

Legacy and Bequest
(b) to transfer to my daughter, Angela, my diamond engagement and wedding rings.
(c) to pay the sum of $1,500 to the Canadian Cancer Society.

Memorandum
(d) to distribute all personal and household items in accordance with a memorandum that I may leave among my personal papers or attached to a copy of this will

A Sample Will

EXHIBIT 31.2 (continued)

Residue

(e) to pay or transfer the residue of my estate to my spouse, namely, Robert Allen Collins, if he survives me by a period of at least thirty days.

(f) If my spouse should predecease me, or survive me but die within a period of thirty days after my death, to divide the residue of my estate equally among my children surviving me and to pay or transfer to each child who has attained the age of 25 years, as of the date of my death, his or her share of my estate.

(g) to pay to my spouse, should he survive me, an allowance to meet his basic needs during the thirty days following my death. During that time my spouse shall have full use of all of my household items, furnishings, and personal goods.

Trust for Children

(h) If any child of mine is entitled to a share of my estate but has not yet reached the age of 25 years as of the date of my death, I direct my Estate Trustee to do as follows:

    (i) to hold such child's share and invest it;

    (ii) to use the income and capital, or so much thereof as my Estate Trustee in his uncontrolled discretion considers advisable to or for the care, maintenance, education, support, or advancement of such child which may include payments to the custodians of the children for such purposes; and

    (iii) to pay or transfer the balance in such share to such child when the child attains the age of 25 years.

Any income not so used in any year and the income derived therefrom shall be accumulated (but only for a period not exceeding twenty-one years from the date of my death) by investing the same and the resulting income therefrom and such accumulations shall be added to the share or interest from which they arose and devolve therewith.

(i) If any of my children should predecease me, leaving issue alive at the date of my death, his or her share is to be equally divided among such issue by representation in equal shares per stirpes.

(j) If any of my children should predecease me, leaving no issue surviving him or her or the date of my death, the share of my Estate to which such deceased child would otherwise be entitled shall be divided equally among his or her other surviving siblings alive at the date of my death.

Share of Minors and Incapable Beneficiaries

(k) Except as set out in paragraphs 8(f) and (h) herein, if any person should become entitled to any share in my estate while he or she is incapable of executing a release or has not yet attained the age of 25, the share of such person shall be held and kept invested by my Estate Trustee and the income and capital or so much thereof as my Estate Trustee in his absolute discretion considers necessary or advisable shall be used for the benefit of such person until he or she attains the age of 25 or in the case of any incapacity on the part of my beneficiary, until the beneficiary is no longer incapable.

Custodians and Guardians for the Children and their Property

(l) If Robert Allen Collins predeceases me or at the time of my death has been found to be mentally incapable of caring for our children, and we have any children who have not yet attained the age of majority, I appoint my brother, Matthew Lawrence Reynolds, to have custody of my children and to the extent that I am capable of so doing, I also appoint Matthew Lawrence Reynolds to be the guardian of my children's present and future property during their infancy.

It is my wish that my custodian and guardian make an application within 90 days from the date of my death, as provided for in the *Children's Law Reform Act*, or in any successor or similar legislation thereto, to have custody of my children and to be appointed as the guardian of any property that my children had at the time of my death or that they may acquire after my death.

EXHIBIT 31.2 (continued)

A Sample Will

(m) I direct my Estate Trustee, at his discretion, to pay, from the trust established in Paragraph 8(h) of this will, to my custodian, such amounts as my custodian may require from time to time for the maintenance of a home for my children and to pay the cost of clothing, feeding, and educating my children, it being my wish that the resources of my estate be made available to the custodian in order that there be no financial or physical burden placed upon him by reason of his undertaking to look after my children.

Part III
Powers of Estate Trustee

9. For all purposes contained in this my will I give to my Estate Trustee the following powers:

Power of Sale
(a) to sell any part of my estate not consisting of money at such time or times, in such manner, and at such time or times, in such manner, and upon such terms and either for cash or credit, or part cash and part credit as my Estate Trustee deems advisable;

Power not to Convert Estate
(b) to postpone the conversion of my estate, or any part or parts thereof for such length of time as my Estate Trustee may think best;

Retain Investments
(c) to retain any portion of my estate in the form in which it may be at the time of my death (notwithstanding that it may not be a form of an investment in which trustees are authorized to invest trust funds, and whether or not there is a liability attached to any such portion of my estate) for such length of time as my Estate Trustee deems advisable, and my Estate Trustee shall not be held responsible for any loss that may happen to my estate by reason of so doing;

Division of Assets in Specie
(d) upon any distribution of my estate or any part thereof or the setting up of any trust or fund established under this my will or any codicil hereto to distribute or set aside assets in specie; for the purpose of any such distribution or setting aside, to place such value on all assets from time to time forming part of my estate as shall seem just and proper to my Estate Trustee in his uncontrolled discretion and any such valuation shall be absolutely final and binding and conclusive on all beneficiaries hereunder; and upon any distribution or setting aside to determine to whom or to what trust specific assets shall be given or allocated and to distribute or set aside the same subject to the payment of such amounts as shall be necessary to adjust the share of the various beneficiaries;

Power to Borrow
(e) at any time and from time to time to borrow money upon the security of all or any assets of my estate in such manner, on such terms, and conditions, for such length of time and for such purposes connected with my estate as my Estate Trustee deems advisable, and such borrowing may be from any person or corporation notwithstanding that such person or corporation may be a member of my family or a beneficiary or trustee under my will, and the person or corporation from whom my Estate Trustee borrows shall be entitled to receive and be paid for his, her or its own benefit such interest as my Estate Trustee has decided upon; and

Elections Under the Income Tax Act
(f) to make any elections, determinations and designations under the *Income Tax Act* which in his discretion or on the advice of a professional tax advisor he deems advisable.

A Sample Will

EXHIBIT 31.2 (continued)

Family Law Act

10. I hereby expressly state that all property and income, including but not limited to interest, dividends, and capital gains, from property given under the terms of this my will to any beneficiary at the time of my death shall be excluded from the net family property of such beneficiary for all purposes of the *Family Law Act* as amended from time to time or any similar or successor legislation.

IN TESTIMONY WHEREOF I have to this my last will and testament, written upon this and the three preceding pages of paper, subscribed my name this   day of   , 200   .

SIGNED, PUBLISHED AND DECLARED)
By the said testatrix,)
Elizabeth Louise Collins,)
as and for her last will and)
testament, in the presence of)   _____
us, both present at the same)   Elizabeth Louise Collins
time, who at her request,)
in her presence and in the)
presence of each other, have)
hereunto subscribed our names)
as witnesses.)

WITNESS: WITNESS:
_____   _____

Name: _____   Name: _____

Address: _____   Address: _____

_____   _____

Occupation: _____   Occupation: _____

---

equalization upon a marriage breakdown, unless the will in which the gift was made contains a clause excluding such earnings from a division of matrimonial property. An example of such a clause can be found in paragraph 10 of the sample will contained in Exhibit 31.2. In most cases a family law clause should be included in a will.

Provisions for Minors and Special Beneficiaries

A will can be used to appoint a temporary custodian and guardian for a minor child. The child, following the death of his or her custodial parents, usually resides with the temporary custodian named in the will. The custodian must apply to the local family court for an order granting him or her permanent custody. A will can suggest permanent custodians but cannot make the final appointment as custody of a child must always be determined in regard to what is in the child's best interests. A suggestion made in a will years ago may or may not be what would be in the child's best interests upon the deaths of his or her custodial parents. A court makes that determination following the loss. The parent's suggestions, as set out in his or her will, are, however, strongly considered by the court in making its decision.

A will can also be used to suggest a guardian for a minor child's property. Children generally do not have a great deal of property, although many children do have their own bank accounts from funds given to them on birthdays and other special occasions. Some children have an income from modelling, acting or other part-time jobs. Upon the death of a parent, a child may be entitled to Canada Pension Plan survivor benefits. Minor children often require a guardian to collect these benefits on their behalf. The suggested guardian must apply to the local family court for an order granting him or her guardianship of the child's property. Many people appoint the same person(s) to be their children's custodians and guardians. In some cases, however, it may be desirable to appoint different people to handle each responsibility.

Without a will, children receive their inheritances when they reach the age of majority. With a will parents can raise the age of inheritance to a higher age, such as 21, 25, or 30, or have the money paid out in stages. In paragraph 8(f) of the sample will contained in Exhibit 31.2, the age of inheritance has been raised to age 25. However, in paragraph 8(h)(ii) of the sample will, the trustee of the children's inheritance has been given the power to encroach upon, meaning to use, some of the funds for the children's education and other purposes deemed worthy by the trustee.

A will can be used to set up a trust fund to assist a beneficiary with special needs. For example, a parent of a child with a severe mental impairment could use his or her will to set up a trust to permit funds to be available for the child's needs. In some situations a trust can be set up to provide funds that may be used for the child's needs while still preserving the child's access to government programs and benefits.[6] In other cases, trusts could be established for beneficiaries with substance abuse or gambling problems. In these circumstances the trust could be structured to pay the beneficiary's rent or provide them with a monthly income in place of a one-time inheritance payment.

Cost and Time Savings

A will speaks from the moment of death. It contains instructions for the executor to follow. In some cases, an entire estate can be administered using the will alone, without having to get a grant from the court.

Without a will someone must, in most cases, apply to the court for a grant permitting him or her to administer the estate. In some jurisdictions, it can take weeks to obtain a court grant. As well, in order to obtain a grant from the court, probate tax must be paid on the value of most estate assets. Dying with a will in place can save the estate and the beneficiaries time and money.

Financial and Tax Planning

A will provides the testator with an opportunity to do some tax planning. Spousal trusts and **rollovers** can be used in a will to defer the payment of taxes. A will can also be used to make special provisions for any business that the testator owns.

With a will, the testator leaves behind a plan for the management of his or her estate. Instructions can be given as to the types of investments to be

---

[6] In Ontario, an absolute discretionary trust, known as a Henson trust, preserves the right of a disabled person to continue receiving benefits despite being a beneficiary under a discretionary trust. The trust is named after Leonard Henson, who made such trust provisions for his disabled daughter. When the Ontario Ministry of Social Services revoked Miss Henson's benefits as a result of the trust, the Henson family successfully challenged the ministry's actions and had Ms. Henson's benefits reinstated.

made. If there is no will or if the will does not set out the estate trustee's powers regarding investments, the estate trustee must adhere to provincial trustee legislation. In a will the testator can instruct the executor as to whether assets should be sold immediately or held until a later time. Without a will, property may have to be sold, under less than favourable market conditions, in order to liquidate estate assets to satisfy provincial intestacy laws. With a will, the property could be rented out and sold later on when the market is more favourable.

DRAFTING A WILL

Legal Requirements for Making a Will

There are three legal requirements for making a will. The testator must, subject to a few exceptions, be of the age of majority. He or she must also possess **testamentary capacity** and have knowledge of and approve the contents of the will.

Age Restrictions and Exceptions

Most legislation concerning wills provides that you cannot make a will unless you have reached the age of majority. There are some exceptions to the rule. For example, in Ontario, the *Succession Law Reform Act* permits persons under 18 to make a will if they are married or have been married or if the will is made in contemplation of marriage.[7] Someone under 18 who is a member of the regular Canadian Forces or on active service or is a sailor at sea or in the course of a voyage may also make a will.[8]

Testamentary Capacity

In order to make a valid will the testator must be mentally capable of doing so. The courts have set out four characteristics that demonstrate capacity.[9] These four characteristics are as follows:

1. The testator understands the nature of the activity that he is engaged in. At a minimum he should understand that he is making a will to dispose of his property following his death.

2. The testator understands the extent of his property.

3. The testator is aware of his "moral obligations". The term "moral obligations" refers to those persons that society would normally expect someone to leave their estate to, such as spouse and children. The testator may not be required to leave his estate to such persons; however, he should have turned his mind to those "obligations" when making his will.[10]

4. The testator understands the consequences of his will. For example, if he has four adult children and if his will instructs the executor to divide the estate among three of the children, the testator must understand

---

[7] *Succession Law Reform Act*, R.S.O. 1990, c. S.26, ss. 8(1)(a) and (b).
[8] *Succession Law Reform Act*, R.S.O. 1990, c. S.26, ss. 8(1)(c) and (d).
[9] *Banks v. Goodfellow* (1870), L.R. 5 Q.B. 549.
[10] Unless a marriage contract is in place, in most jurisdictions if the will does not provide for a spouse, the spouse can elect in place of the will to claim an equalization of net family property. A testator is not usually required to name his adult children in his will. A child in those circumstances will have a claim against the estate only if the deceased was supporting him or her.

that one of his children will not receive anything from the estate. In such a case it is recommended that the testator include in his will the reason for excluding one of the adult children.

Knowledge and Approval of the Contents of the Will

The testator must know what is in his will and must approve such contents. The testator should read his will prior to signing it. The testator's signature at the end of his will should confirm his knowledge and approval of the contents of the will. Many lawyers have testators initial the bottom of each page of the will to indicate that they have reviewed the will and to prevent the unscrupulous insertion of supplementary pages into the will in which gifts are made that the testator did not authorize.

Information Required to Draft the Will

Executors and Trustees

The appointment in a will of an executor, sometimes known as an estate trustee with a will or a personal representative, is not legally required. However, it is standard practice to appoint at least one executor in a will to manage the estate upon the testator's death. The testator may name more than one executor to act. It is recommended that an alternate executor or executrix be named in the will so that he or she can be replaced in the event that he or she predeceases the testator, is unable or unwilling to act, or moves outside the province.

The executor, unless the will states otherwise, is the trustee of the entire estate. The testator should also provide the names of any additional trustees to be named in the will. For example, there may be a trust established in the will for the testator's minor children. The testator may appoint the executor as trustee of this trust fund or may appoint another trustee to manage the children's trust. If a trust is to remain in place for a number of years, some testators appoint a trust company to act as the trustee.

Care should be taken in choosing an executor. Testators should choose someone that they trust to follow their instructions and manage their property and financial affairs. It is advantageous to choose someone with knowledge of the testator's affairs. Age and ability to deal with others should also be considered. Someone likely to remain in Ontario is a factor to consider to avoid the possibility of any trust in the will becoming a foreign trust. To deal with this possibility an alternate executor should always be named.

Assets

The testator should provide instructions concerning the disposal of his assets upon death. There may be gifts of specific items of property to specific persons; these are known as **bequests.** There may be gifts of money to specific persons; these are known as **legacies.** Instructions should be given as to the transfer of any assets into trusts. The testator may also leave instructions as to how his assets should be invested or sold.

Memorandum

Quite often a testator has collectible items that he wishes to leave to various friends and family members. Instead of putting these instructions in a will, the testator may draft a legal or a **precatory memorandum** dealing with such gifts. Only a legal memorandum is legally binding on the executor and the estate. A legal memorandum must be prepared before the will and be referred to and incorporated into the will. A legal memorandum can be changed only if the will is changed.

A precatory memorandum, on the other hand, is not legally binding; however, it does provide the executor with a statement of the testator's wishes in regard to the division of his property. A precatory memorandum can be prepared and changed at any time and does not need to be mentioned in the will.

Children

If a testator has minor children, he should provide the names of suggested custodians and guardians. He should also specify at what age children should inherit property. If a testator does not have any children of his own, he may still want to specify an age of inheritance in his will if he wants to postpone the payment of a minor's inheritance beyond the age of majority. This might be necessary if there is a possibility that a minor might inherit property from the testator through a parent who is a direct beneficiary of the testator.

Trusts

The testator should give instructions for any trusts that are to be set up in his will. Trusts may be established for minor children, charities, some disabled beneficiaries or for other purposes. The name of the trustee will be required, along with the names of any alternate trustees. The beneficiaries and alternate beneficiaries of the trust should be specified. The terms of the trust will need to be known, including the duration of the trust and any investment and encroachment instructions concerning the trust.

Funeral Instructions

Some testators wish to provide funeral, burial, cremation, or organ donation instructions in their wills. Although such instructions may be set out in a will, they are strictly advisory in nature and are not legally binding on the executor. The executor has the final word as to the disposal of the deceased's remains. If a testator desires a certain type of funeral, burial or cremation, he should consider prearranging it and should make his wishes known to his family. In regard to organ donation or the donation of one's body for scientific research, many provinces permit their residents to register their intentions in this regard, in some cases, through the renewal of their driver's licence. On a practical note, a will is not the best place in which to leave such instructions as the will is often not located or read until after burial or cremation has taken place.

Standard Powers

Most wills provide the executor with a set of standard powers, such as the power to hold assets, to sell assets, to convert assets, and to borrow and lend estate funds, and to place a value upon estate assets at their discretion. Examples of such standard powers are found in paragraph 9 of the sample will set out at Exhibit 31.2.

TYPES OF WILLS

Formally Attested Wills

The most common form of a will is the **formally attested will**. Such a will is generally typewritten and is signed by the testator in the presence of at least two witnesses who attest to its execution. Attestation is defined as signing one's name, as a witness, to the execution of a document. **Execution** refers to signing — in this case, the signing of the will.

As with all wills, a formally attested will must meet the legal requirements for a valid will, noted earlier. In addition, there are four formal requirements that a formally attested will must meet in order to be valid. These requirements are as follows:

1. The will must be in writing. Wills cannot be made by recording instructions on videotape, CD, cassette tape, DVD or by e-mail. Electronic signatures are not valid for the purposes of a will.

2. The will must be signed by the testator at the end of the will. In Ontario there are provisions in place for someone to sign a will for the testator as long as it is signed in the testator's presence and under his direction.[11] There are also special provisions for the signing of a will by someone who signs with an "X" and for blind or illiterate persons.

3. A formally attested will must be witnessed by two or more persons. The testator signs the will in the presence of the witnesses, who each sign in the presence of each other and the testator. Witnesses must be of the age of majority and should not be a beneficiary or the spouse of a beneficiary.[12] It is *always* prudent to have an **affidavit of execution** sworn by one of the witnesses following the execution of the will. An affidavit of execution confirms that the proper witnessing procedures were followed. The affidavit should be stored with the will as it must be given to the court when the will is submitted for a grant of probate following the testator's death. A sample affidavit of execution form is contained in Exhibit 31.3.

4. The last formal requirement of a will is that it have a disposing intention. This means that the testator's intention, in regard to his will, was that it would be used upon his death to dispose of his property. In some cases, courts have been asked to declare letters from testators to their lawyers, in which they suggest instructions for the disposal of their estate, to be wills. The courts, in such cases, must decide if the letter simply gave instructions for the lawyer's consideration or was intended to actually dispose of the property as a will.

Holograph Wills

In many jurisdictions, a testator may make a legally binding **holograph will**. A holograph will is a will that has been made entirely in the testator's own handwriting and signed by him. Such a will does not require any witnesses.

As with all wills, a holograph will must meet the legal requirements, noted earlier, for a valid will. In regard to formal requirements, the holograph will must be made in the testator's own handwriting and signed by him. The holograph will must also have a disposing intention. Although it is not a legal requirement to do so, it is a good idea to date a holograph will.

Military Wills

Some legislation, such as Ontario's *Succession Law Reform Act*, relaxes the usual formal requirements of a will for members of the Canadian Forces on active service or for a sailor at sea or in the course of a voyage.[13]

Such wills, even if typewritten, do not require any witnesses. At the time of death, in order to validate such a will, a certificate of active service must be obtained from the appropriate forces.

---

[11] *Succession Law Reform Act*, R.S.O. 1990, c. S.26, s. 4(1)(a).

[12] In Ontario, s. 12(3) of the *Succession Law Reform Act*, R.S.O. 1990, c. S.26, may be used to validate a gift made to a beneficiary or spouse who witnessed the will if said person can show the court that he or she did not exercise any improper or undue influence.

[13] *Succession Law Reform Act*, R.S.O. 1990, c. S.26, s. 5(1).

Affidavit of Execution of Will or Codicil

EXHIBIT 31.3

**ONTARIO
SUPERIOR COURT OF JUSTICE**

IN THE MATTER OF THE EXECUTION OF A WILL OR CODICIL OF *(insert name)*

AFFIDAVIT

I, *(insert name)*, of *(insert city or town and county or district, metropolitan or regional municipality or residence)* make oath and say/affirm:

1. On *(date)*, I was present and saw the document marked as Exhibit "A" to this my affidavit executed by *(insert name)*.

2. *(Insert name)* executed the document in the presence of myself and *(insert name of other witness and city or town, county or district, metropolitan or regional municipality of residence)*. We were both present at the same time, and signed the document in the testator's presence as attesting witnesses.

SWORN/AFFIRMED BEFORE)
me at the   of   )
in the   of   )
this   day of   , 20   .)
)   _____
)
)
)
)

_____
A Commissioner for Taking Affidavits *(or as may be)*

NOTE: If the testator was blind or signed by making his or her mark, add the following paragraph:

WARNING: A beneficiary or the spouse of a beneficiary should not be a witness.

3. Before its execution, the document was read over to the testator, who (was blind) signed by making his or her mark. The testator appeared to understand the contents.

Indian Act Wills

Under the federal *Indian Act*,[14] the federal government may accept any written instrument signed by an Indian, indicating his or her wishes regarding the disposition of his or her property, as a will. Such a will has to be approved by the Minister of Indian Affairs following the testator's death.

Split Wills

In some cases, where permitted by law, a testator may choose to prepare two wills, only one of which will be submitted to the court for a grant of probate. The will prepared for submission to the court deals only with those assets for which a grant of probate, known in Ontario as a **certificate of appointment of estate trustee with a will**, is required for disposal of the asset.[15] For example, real estate held solely in the testator's name would be included in this will.

---

[14] *Indian Act*, R.S.C. 1985, c. I-5, s. 45.

[15] In Ontario, Form 74.4.1 under the Rules of Civil Procedure entitled an Application for a Certificate of Appointment of Estate Trustee with a Will (Individual Applicant), limited to assets referred to in the will, should be used.

The other will would cover assets for which a court grant is not required. Such assets might include household furnishings or shares in a privately held corporation. By the use of **split wills**, probate tax can be reduced. Caution must be exercised when drafting split wills in order to ensure that one will does not revoke the other will. The use of standard will clauses that revoke all previous wills must be avoided in split wills; otherwise, the last will executed may revoke the first will made in the pair of split wills.

Foreign and International Wills

If someone has property outside of Canada, it may be necessary to have, in addition to a will made in Canada, a will made in a foreign jurisdiction to cover the assets in that country. Care must be taken in drafting such wills in order to ensure that they can co-exist. The standard revocation clause should not be included in co-existing wills. In some cases a single will, called an international will, can be used to cover all of the testator's assets in different countries. There is a United Nations Convention, of which Canada is a signatory, that provides a Uniform Law on the Form of an International Will. Unfortunately, the list of signatories to the convention is short. To ensure that an international will made under the convention will suffice, the list of countries that have signed the convention must be reviewed.

EXECUTION OF A WILL

Formal and Legal Requirements

As set out earlier, in order for a will to be legally valid, all of the applicable legal and formal requirements must be met.

Witnessing Requirements and Restrictions

A formally attested will must be attested to by at least two witnesses, who must be of the age of majority. The witnesses should be of sound mind, and they should not be beneficiaries under the will or spouses of a beneficiary. Executors, provided that they are not a beneficiary, may witness a will.

Affidavit of Execution

Following the execution of the will, one of the witnesses should swear an affidavit confirming that the proper procedure for witnessing the will was followed. In most cases, it is prudent to have the affidavit of execution prepared as close in time to the signing of the will as possible as it may be difficult to track down witnesses in the future. (See Exhibit 31.3 for a sample affidavit of execution form.)

Safekeeping of the Will

The lawyer who drafts the will usually stores the original will in a fireproof file cabinet in her office. The lawyer has a duty to keep the client's property, including the client's will, safe. In some jurisdictions, wills may also be stored with the local Estates Court for a small fee.[16]

AMENDING A WILL

Alterations

If a will must be altered prior to its execution and if the production of an amended will is impossible, then the alteration should be neatly printed on the will and the testator and the witnesses should write their initials next to the change. If part of the will is to be deleted prior to its execution, the part of

[16] In Ontario, the *Estates Act*, R.S.O. 1990, c. E.21, s. 2, establishes a wills depository with the courts.

the will to be deleted should be neatly crossed out and the testator and the witnesses should write their initials next to the deletions.

If the will is altered after its execution, then the alteration should be neatly printed on the will and the testator and at least two witnesses should sign their full signatures at or near the changes. Any part of the will that is to be deleted should be neatly crossed out, with the testator and at least two witnesses signing their full signatures at or near the deletions. These methods of alteration should be used for minor changes only.

Codicils and New Wills

A **codicil** is a document made after a will that alters part of the will. Codicils are usually made for minor changes to the will, such as the substitution of an executor when the original executor has died. The codicil may be made on a holograph or a formally attested basis. The codicil should be dated and should specify the change in the will and then confirm all other terms of the will. Caution should be exercised in using codicils as the original will and the codicil will become public record if a court grant is sought. If, for example, you are replacing one beneficiary with another beneficiary, you may not want the original beneficiary to know that they were named in the will at one time. When changes of this nature are required the testator should consider making a new will.

REVOKING A WILL

Intentional Revocation

A will may be revoked by making a new will provided that the testator has the mental capacity to make a valid will. A will can also be revoked by a written declaration to revoke the will. In some jurisdictions, a will can also be revoked if the testator burns, tears, or otherwise destroys the will with the intention to do so. The testator may destroy the will himself, or instruct another person under his direction and in his presence to destroy it.[17]

Automatic Revocation and Exceptions

In many jurisdictions, including Ontario, marriage automatically revokes a will subject to some exceptions. If the will was made in contemplation of the marriage, states this fact and names the testator's fiancée, the will remains valid after marriage. As well, a surviving spouse may, within the one-year period following the deceased's death, elect to have a will remain valid that was executed prior to the marriage.[18]

Effect of Divorce on the Will

If someone divorces after the execution of his will, the will is still valid. However, the appointment of his former spouse as his executor is no longer valid unless the will sets out a contrary intention. In regard to gifts made to the former spouse in the will, the former spouse is treated as if she had predeceased the testator, effectively removing her from the will, unless a contrary intention appears in the will.

---

[17] *Succession Law Reform Act*, R.S.O. 1990, c. S.26, s. 15(d).

[18] *Succession Law Reform Act*, R.S.O. 1990, c. S.26, s. 16. In one case when the husband died, the wife was able to elect in favour of a will made prior to the marriage when the couple had been in a common-law relationship. This was of benefit to the wife as her share under the will was larger than what she would have received under intestacy provisions, which would have had a greater share going to his children from his first marriage.

INTESTACY

Intestacy Defined

Intestacy refers to the situation where someone has died without a valid will in place. An intestacy results when someone never made a will or when someone made a will, but the will is not valid. For example, there may have been an error in the execution of the will, or the testator may have lacked testamentary capacity when he made the will.

Legislation Concerning Intestacy

Every province and territory has legislation setting out how an estate will be divided in the event of an intestacy. In most cases, such legislation provides that, where there is a surviving spouse, that spouse in entitled to the bulk of the estate. Where there is a surviving spouse and children, most legislation provides that some portion of the estate is to be divided between the surviving spouse and the deceased's children. In Ontario, for example, *Part II* of the *Succession Law Reform Act* provides that where the deceased's estate is valued at more than $200,000, the surviving spouse (the term "spouse" in that part of the legislation referring only to legally married spouses[19]) receives the first $200,000 of the estate. This is referred to as the preferential share. If there is one child, then the child and the spouse equally share the portion of the estate over $200,000. This portion of the estate is known as the distributive share. Where there are two or more children, the spouse receives one-third of the distributive share and the children equally share the remaining two-thirds. If a child predeceases his parents, that child's **issue** (or descendants) stand in their parent's place with respect to the division of the estate. The term "issue" refers to one's direct descendants. A summary of the provisions for spouses and children regarding an intestacy is provided in Exhibit 31.1. In some cases a surviving spouse may fare better financially by making an election for an equalization of net family property instead of accepting the inheritance under the intestacy provisions. The surviving spouse should consult a lawyer to discuss his or her options.

Intestate Distribution Where There Is No Surviving Spouse

Where the deceased does not have a surviving spouse, legislation sets out the division of his or her estate. In Ontario, for example, when the deceased does not have a surviving spouse, his or her estate is divided equally among his or her children. If the deceased does not have any children or other descendants, such as grandchildren or other issue, and his or her parents are still alive, then the parents inherit the estate. If the parents predeceased the **intestate**, then his or her siblings share the estate. If any of the siblings predeceased the intestate, leaving issue, then their issue share the sibling's share by representation **per stirpes**, meaning that such issue take their parent's share, divided equally among themselves. If there are no surviving siblings, the next in line to share in the estate are the deceased's nieces and nephews. They share the deceased's estate equally without representation for their issue. In summary, the following persons are those in line to inherit where the deceased did not have a surviving spouse:

1. The deceased's children
2. The deceased's other issue, such as grandchildren or great grandchildren
3. If there are no issue, the deceased's parents

---

[19] In some provinces, a person other than a legally married spouse may qualify to receive a preferential share of the estate.

Table of Consanguinity — Showing Degrees of Relationship by Blood

INSTRUCTIONS

Place the subject/decedent for whom you need to establish relationships in the blank box. The labelled boxes will then list the relationship by title to the subject and the degree of distance from the subject.

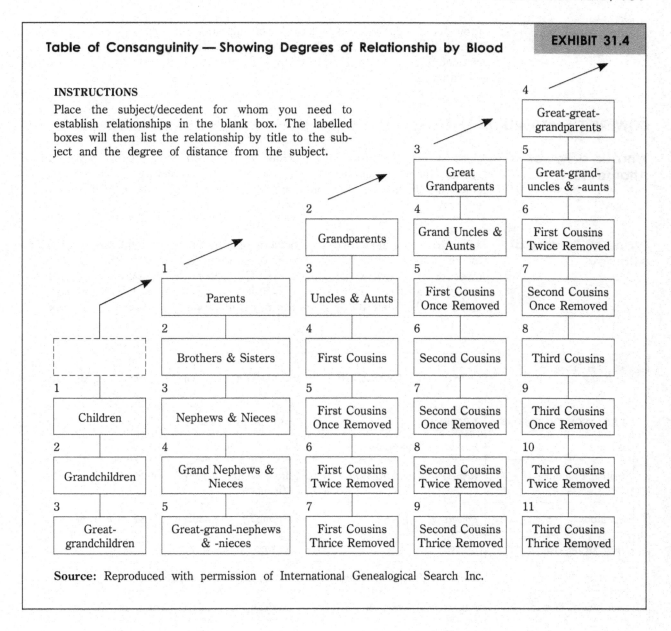

Source: Reproduced with permission of International Genealogical Search Inc.

4. If there are no issue or surviving parents, the deceased's siblings
5. If there are no surviving siblings, the deceased's nieces and nephews

If none of the aforementioned relatives survived the intestate, then the estate is divided equally among the deceased's closest next of kin. A table of **consanguinity** may be used in order to determine the degree of closeness of the surviving next of kin to the deceased. A table of consanguinity is contained in Exhibit 31.4. The table is to be used only where there are no surviving nieces or nephews; it can be used to determine the degree of closeness of a particular relative. Relatives of the same degree of closeness to the deceased share equally in the estate. For example, assume that the deceased was survived by a first cousin, a grand uncle, and a second cousin. Using the table of consanguinity you would find that the first cousin and the grand uncle are both four degrees of distance from the deceased. Being the closest living relatives, they would equally share the estate. The second cousin, at six degrees of distance, would be excluded. If the intestate has no living next of kin, in most cases, his or her estate becomes the property of the provincial government. In such cases the deceased's estate **escheats** to the provincial government.

POWERS OF ATTORNEY

What Is a Power of Attorney?

A power of attorney is a legal document in which one person, known as the **grantor**, appoints another person, known as the **attorney**, to have power to act on his or her behalf concerning his or her property and/or personal care decisions.

Types of Powers of Attorney

There are three main types of powers of attorney: a general power of attorney for property, a continuing power of attorney for property, and a continuing power of attorney for personal care. The rules, terminology, and forms for powers of attorney vary from jurisdiction to jurisdiction. For a summary of names of Canadian powers of attorney for property legislation, see Exhibit

EXHIBIT 31.5	Summary of Canadian Powers of Attorney for Property Legislation	
PROVINCE/TERRITORY	**LEGISLATION**	**DOCUMENT NAME**
Alberta	*Powers of Attorney Act*	Enduring Power of Attorney
British Columbia	*Representation Agreement Act*	Representation Agreement for Property or Finances
Manitoba	*Powers of Attorney Act*	Springing or Enduring Power of Attorney
New Brunswick	*Property Act*	Power of Attorney
Newfoundland	*Enduring Powers of Attorney Act*	Enduring Power of Attorney
Northwest Territories	*Powers of Attorney Act*	Springing or Enduring Power of Attorney
Nova Scotia	*Powers of Attorney Act*	Enduring Power of Attorney
Nunavut	*Powers of Attorney Act*	Springing or Enduring Power of Attorney
Ontario	*Substitute Decisions Act*	Power of Attorney for Property
Prince Edward Island	*Powers of Attorney Act*	Power of Attorney
Quebec	*Quebec Civil Code*	Mandate given in anticipation of Incapacity[1]
Saskatchewan	*The Powers of Attorney Act, 2002*	Enduring Power of Attorney
Yukon	*Enduring Power of Attorney Act*	Enduring Power of Attorney

[1] The mandatary must apply to the court for certification of the grantor's incapacity.

Summary of Canadian Powers of Attorney for Personal Care Legislation

EXHIBIT 31.6

PROVINCE/TERRITORY	LEGISLATION	DOCUMENT NAME
Alberta	*Personal Directives Act*	Personal Directive
British Columbia	*Representation Agreement Act*	Representation Agreement for Health Care
Manitoba	*Health Care Directives Act*	Health Care Directive
New Brunswick	*Infirm Persons Act*	Power of Attorney for Personal Care
Newfoundland	*Advanced Health Care Directives Act*	Advance Health Care Directive
Northwest Territories	None	None
Nova Scotia	*Medical Consent Act*	Authorization to give medical consent
Nunavut	None	None
Ontario	*Substitute Decisions Act, 1992*	Power of Attorney for Personal Care
Prince Edward Island	*Consent to Treatment and Health Care Directives Act*	Health Care Directive
Quebec	*Quebec Civil Code*	Mandate given in anticipation of Incapacity
Saskatchewan	*The Health Care Directives and Substitute Decision Makers Act*	Health Care Directive
Yukon	None	None

31.5; for a summary of the names of Canadian powers of attorney for personal care legislation, see Exhibit 31.6. In some cases multiple powers of attorney, in different jurisdictions, may be required.

General Power of Attorney for Property

A general **power of attorney for property** is a legal document wherein someone gives another person or persons, known as the attorney or attorneys, power over all of his or her property and authorizes them to make decisions concerning such property. The attorney can act on the grantor's behalf concerning his or her property and can do almost anything in regard to such property that the grantor could do. The attorney, for example, can make decisions for the grantor in regard to his or her bank accounts, other investments, real estate, and most other types of property.

A general power of attorney for property is effective upon execution and is often used for one specific transaction. Such a power of attorney cannot be used during a subsequent incapacity. An example of a situation where a general power of attorney would be of assistance is where the owner of a property will be outside of the country at the time of the closing of the sale of the property. The owner can give a general power of attorney for property to someone to sign the sale-closing documents on his or her behalf.

A general power of attorney for property ends when a grantor terminates it or upon any termination date set out in the document itself. The general power of attorney for property will also terminate upon the death of the attorney or the grantor or upon the incapacity of the grantor or of the attorney (where an alternate attorney has not been named).

Continuing or Enduring Power of Attorney for Property

Most powers of attorney for property are continuing powers of attorney for property. They may also be known as enduring powers of attorney. These powers of attorney state that the attorney may continue to act for the grantor if he or she subsequently becomes mentally incapacitated. The advantage of having a continuing power of attorney for property is that it permits the attorney to continue to act if the grantor becomes mentally incapable of managing his or her property after the power of attorney has been made.[20]

Power of Attorney for Personal Care

A **power of attorney for personal care**, where recognized by law, is a legal document in which someone, called the grantor, gives someone else, namely, the attorney, the power to make personal care, health, and treatment decisions for her if she becomes mentally incapable of making such decisions on her own. An attorney using a power of attorney for personal care can make health care, diet, medical treatment, grooming, safety, and other personal care decisions for the grantor. A power of attorney for personal care is sometimes referred to as an advanced health care directive. The power of attorney for personal care may include a **living will**.

DRAFTING A CONTINUING POWER OF ATTORNEY FOR PROPERTY

Formats and forms for use as a power of attorney for property vary from jurisdiction to jurisdiction. Legislation for a particular jurisdiction should be consulted. In Ontario, for example, there is no prescribed form to use. Exhibit 31.7 shows a format that is routinely used to make a Continuing Power of Attorney for Property.

The Grantor

The grantor is the person making the power of attorney for property.

Age Restrictions Concerning the Grantor

The grantor of a power of attorney for property must be of the age of majority. In Ontario he or she must be 18 years of age or older.

Mental Capacity of the Grantor

In Ontario, the *Substitute Decisions Act, 1992*,[21] sets out the factors to be considered in order to determine if a person is capable of giving a continuing power of attorney for property. Under section 8(1) of the *Substitute Decisions*

---

[20] Note that in Newfoundland a power of attorney automatically terminates if the donor becomes incompetent. In Quebec the power of attorney document must be homologated by the court in order to come into effect.
[21] *Substitute Decisions Act, 1992*, S.O. 1992, c. 30.

Continuing Power of Attorney for Property

EXHIBIT 31.7

THIS CONTINUING POWER OF ATTORNEY FOR PROPERTY is given by Elizabeth Louise Collins, of the City of Brampton, in the Regional Municipality of Peel.

Appointment and Authorization

1. I APPOINT my spouse, Robert Allen Collins, to be my attorney for property. I authorize my attorney to do, on my behalf, anything that I could do if capable, except make a will, subject to any conditions and restrictions contained herein. I also authorize my attorney to exercise his powers under this power of attorney for the benefit of any person that I am under a legal obligation to provide for.

Substitution

2. If the above appointed attorney refuses to act, or is unable to act by reason of death, court removal, resignation, or incapacity, then I SUBSTITUTE AND APPOINT my brother, namely Austin Cory Reynolds, to act as my attorney in place of my attorney appointed in paragraph one herein and I authorize him, if required to act as my attorney, to do, on my behalf, anything which I could do if capable, except make a will, subject to any conditions and restrictions contained herein.

Continuing Power

3. It is my intention that this document be a continuing power of attorney for property under the *Substitute Decisions Act, 1992*, as amended, and any successor or similar legislation and it is my intention that this continuing power of attorney be used during any subsequent incapacity.

Authorization

4. I appoint my attorney as my legal representative for all purposes of the *Income Tax Act* (Canada) and I authorize my attorney to examine, settle, liquidate and adjust all or any accounts pending between me and any person including any accounts and income tax matters with the Canada Revenue Agency.

Litigation Guardian

5. I direct that my attorney shall be authorized to act as my litigation guardian if one is required to commence, defend or represent me in any court proceedings.

Family Law Act Consent

6. If my spouse seeks to dispose of or encumber any interest in a matrimonial home in which I have a right to possession under Part II of the *Family Law Act*, or any successor or similar legislation, I authorize my attorney for me and in my name to consent to the transaction, if it would be in my best interests to do so.

Conditions and Restrictions

7. I direct my attorney to utilize my financial resources to allow me to remain in my house as long as possible despite any incapacity on my part.

Gifts and Donations

8. I authorize my attorney to make reasonable gifts to my family and very close friends and to make charitable donations in my name, from my property, subject to the guiding principles set out in the *Substitute Decisions Act, 1992*.

Effective Date

9. This continuing power of attorney for property shall come into effect at the time of execution.

Revocation

10. I revoke any prior Continuing Power of Attorney for Property given by me.

EXHIBIT 31.7 (continued)	Continuing Power of Attorney for Property

Compensation

11.   I authorize my attorney to take annual compensation from my property in accordance with the fee scale prescribed by regulation for the compensation of attorneys pursuant to the provision of the *Substitute Decisions Act, 1992* as amended and its regulations or any succeeding or similar legislation.

EXECUTED at   this   day of   , 20   , in the presence of both witnesses, each present at the same time.

We, the witnesses to this power of attorney, have signed this power of attorney in the presence of the grantor and in the presence of each other on the date shown herein. Neither one of us has any reason to believe that the grantor is incapable of giving a continuing power of attorney for property.

_____
Elizabeth Louise Collins

WITNESS: WITNESS:

_____) _____

Name: _____) Name: _____

Address: _____) Address: _____

_____) _____

Occupation: _____) Occupation: _____

Act, 1992, a person is capable of giving a continuing power of attorney for property if he or she

(a)   knows what kind of property he or she has and its approximate value;
(b)   is aware of obligations owed to his or her dependants;
(c)   knows that the attorney will be able to do on the person's behalf anything in respect of property that the person could do if capable, except make a will, subject to the conditions and restrictions set out in the power of attorney;
(d)   knows that the attorney must account for his or her dealings with the person's property;
(e)   knows that he or she may, if capable, revoke the continuing power of attorney;
(f)   appreciates that unless the attorney manages the property prudently, its value may decline; and
(g)   appreciates the possibility that the attorney could misuse the authority given to him or her.

The Attorney

The grantor can appoint one or more persons of the age of majority to be their attorney(s). Although the appointee is called an attorney, he or she does not have to be a lawyer. If two or more attorneys are named, they are to act jointly, unless the power of attorney provides otherwise. An alternate attorney or attorneys may be named to act as attorney in the event that the original attorney has died, resigned, or is unable to act. The attorney named should be someone who is capable of acting in that capacity. As the attorney will be entrusted with overseeing and managing all of the grantor's property, someone who is responsible, trustworthy, and able to manage money should be chosen. The attorney must keep an account of the grantor's property and financial dealings. The power of attorney may provide that an attorney is to be compensated or may state that the attorney has agreed not to be compensated for his or her efforts.

Commencement Date

Unless it stated otherwise, the power of attorney is effective from the date that it is signed even though the grantor may be capable of managing his or her affairs. If the attorney uses the power of attorney while the grantor is still capable, he or she does so as agent of the grantor and should obtain input from the grantor as to all decisions made.

A continuing power of attorney stipulates that in the event that the grantor subsequently becomes incapacitated, the power of attorney will continue to be effective. A grantor may execute a power of attorney and store it in a safe place, intending it to be used only if she becomes incapable of managing her own affairs. In some cases the grantor will store the power of attorney with a third party, such as a lawyer, and leave written instructions with the document indicating when it should be used. For example, the grantor might direct that the power of attorney should be used only if the grantor directs so in writing or her doctor certifies that she is incapable of managing her own property. The power of attorney document itself may include a condition that it will only come into effect upon any incapacity of the grantor as certified by his or her doctor. The document may set out the definition of "incapacity" or remain silent as to the definition, in which case the definition of "incapacity" contained in the legislation that governs powers of attorney would be used. In Ontario, the *Substitute Decisions Act, 1992* defines incapacity in section 6 of the act as the situation whereby "[a] person is incapable of managing property if the person is not able to understand information that is relevant to making a decision in the management of his or her property, or is not able to appreciate the reasonably foreseeable consequences of a decision or lack of decision."[22]

Limitations, Conditions, and Restrictions in the Continuing Power of Attorney for Property

An attorney under a continuing power of attorney for property can act on behalf of the incapable person for all matters in respect of property that the incapable person could do if capable, except make a will. The attorney should obtain a copy of the grantor's will to ensure that the grantor does not dispose of property that has been bequeathed in the will unless the disposition of such property is necessary to meet the needs of the grantor. An attorney cannot use a power of attorney to carry out any of the grantor's functions of an office, such as sitting as a director or replacing the grantor as estate trustee on someone's estate.

The attorney is bound by any conditions and restrictions set out in the power of attorney itself. A condition is a requirement that must be met before the power of attorney can be used. For example, the power of attorney might say that an assessment of incapacity must be made before the power of attorney can be used. The power of attorney may also contain restrictions. A restriction is a limitation placed on the attorney's authority. For example, the grantor may state in the power of attorney that his or her cottage should not be sold unless it is absolutely necessary to do so in order to meet the grantor's financial needs.

---

[22] *Substitute Decisions Act, 1992*, S.O. 1992, c. 30.

In all cases, attorneys are fiduciaries and must utilize their powers diligently, with honesty and integrity and in good faith for the grantor's benefit.

DRAFTING A POWER OF ATTORNEY FOR PERSONAL CARE

Formats and forms for use as a power of attorney for personal care vary from jurisdiction to jurisdiction. Legislation for your jurisdiction should be consulted. In Ontario, for example, there is no prescribed form to use. Exhibit 31.8 shows a format that is routinely used to make a Power of Attorney for Personal Care.

The Grantor

The grantor is the person making the power of attorney for personal care.

Age Restrictions Concerning the Grantor

Legislation concerning powers of attorney for personal care establishes the minimum age of the grantor. In some cases an actual age is stipulated, whereas in other jurisdictions a test of maturity is used to determine the age at which someone can make a personal care power of attorney. In Ontario, the grantor of the power of attorney for personal care must be 16 years of age or older.

Mental Capacity of the Grantor

The grantor must be mentally capable of making a power of attorney for personal care. There is a lower threshold of capacity to meet than that required for the granting of a power of attorney for property. In the case of a power of attorney for personal care, the *Substitute Decisions Act, 1992*, in section 47(1), provides that the grantor will be considered capable of making a power of attorney for personal care if he or she has the ability to understand whether or not the proposed attorney has a genuine concern for his or her welfare and appreciates that the attorney may need to make decisions for him or her.

The Attorney

A grantor can appoint one or more persons to be his or her attorney under a power of attorney for personal care. Although named as attorney, the appointee does not need to be a lawyer. In different jurisdictions the attorney may be known by a different term, such as proxy, representative, agent, deemed guardian, or substitute decision maker.

Legislation concerning powers of attorney for personal care sets out the minimum age of an attorney. In Ontario, the attorney acting on a power of attorney for personal care must be at least 16 years of age or older. Section 46(3) of the *Substitute Decisions Act, 1992* states that the attorney cannot be someone who provides health care, residential, social, training or support services to the grantor for compensation, unless the attorney is also the spouse, partner or relative of the grantor. The grantor can appoint one or more attorneys. If two or more attorneys are appointed, they shall act jointly unless the power of attorney provides otherwise. The grantor may also name an alternate attorney to act in the event that the original attorney dies, resigns or becomes incapable of acting as the attorney. The attorney must keep a record of the decisions made by him or her.

Attorneys acting on a power of attorney for personal care are not compensated, although the power of attorney may provide for the reimbursement of out-of-pocket expenses.

Power of Attorney for Personal Care

EXHIBIT 31.8

THIS POWER OF ATTORNEY FOR PERSONAL CARE is given by Elizabeth Louise Collins, of the City of Brampton, in the Regional Municipality of Peel.

Appointment

1. I APPOINT my spouse, Robert Allen Collins, to be my attorney for personal care pursuant to the *Substitute Decisions Act, 1992* and any succeeding or similar legislation.

Authority

2. In accordance with the *Substitute Decisions Act, 1992*, I authorize my attorney to make decisions, on my behalf, concerning my personal care, and to give or refuse consent on my behalf to any treatment to which the *Health Care Consent Act, 1996* applies.

Substitution

3. If my attorney refuses to act, or is unable to act by reason of death, court removal, incapacity or he has resigned or he is not available to act when there is the necessity for a decision to be made to which the *Health Care Consent Act, 1996* applies concerning my personal care or treatment then I SUBSTITUTE AND APPOINT my brother, Austin Cory Reynolds, to act as my attorney for personal care.

Reimbursement for Expenses

4. All expenses incurred by my attorney for personal care in carrying out his duties, including obtaining any assessment of my capacity, shall be payable by me or my attorney for property out of my assets.

Living Will Clause

5. My attorney should be guided by my desire that if I have a terminal condition from which there is no possibility whatsoever of recovery, I direct that lifesaving procedures be withheld or withdrawn and that I be permitted to die with dignity. I do, however, direct that I be given medication and/or treatment to alleviate pain. I indemnify my attorney from any liability he may incur in reliance upon my directions contained in this clause of my power of attorney.

Conditions or Restrictions

6. None

Revocation

7. I revoke any prior power of attorney for personal care given by me.

EXECUTED at _____ this _____ day of _____, 20___ in the presence of both witnesses, each present at the same time.

We are the subscribing witnesses to this power of attorney for personal care. We were both present and saw it executed by the grantor on the above noted date. Neither one of us has any reason to believe that the grantor is incapable of giving a power of attorney for personal care. We have both attained the age of majority and neither of us is a spouse or child of the grantor or considered in law as her spouse or child and neither of us is a person whose property is under guardianship or who has a guardian of the person.

_____
Elizabeth Louise Collins

WITNESS: WITNESS:

_____)   _____

Name: _____)   Name: _____

Address: _____)   Address: _____

_____)   _____

Occupation: _____)   Occupation: _____

Commencement Date

A power of attorney for personal care cannot be used unless the grantor is incapable. In some cases, due to illness or side effects of medication, the grantor may alternate between capacity and incapacity. The grantor may be capable of making some decisions but not others. Section 45 of the *Substitute Decisions Act, 1992* provides that a person is incapable of his or her own personal care "if the person is not able to understand information that is relevant to making a decision concerning his or her own health care, nutrition, shelter, clothing, hygiene or safety, or is not able to appreciate the reasonably foreseeable consequences of a decision or lack of a decision."

Limitations, Conditions, and Restrictions in the Power of Attorney for Personal Care

As mentioned above, the attorney can act under a power of attorney for personal care only in the event of incapacity on the part of the grantor to make personal care decisions. The power of attorney itself may stipulate conditions. For example, the grantor may set out some instructions in regard to certain types of treatment or the withholding of treatment. For example, a grantor may state that, in the event that there is no chance for her recovery, she does not wish to be resuscitated. On the other hand, the grantor may direct that all means for treatment, including experimental treatments, should be used to allow her to live as long as possible. As lawyers are not medical professionals, to ensure that the grantor's instructions in this regard are correct, the grantor should be advised to consult with his or her doctor or with an expert in bioethics.

EXECUTION OF POWERS OF ATTORNEY

In the case of both types of powers of attorney the document must be in writing, signed by the grantor and witnessed by at least two witnesses.

Witnessing Requirements

Legislation concerning the execution of a power of attorney varies from province to province and territory. In some provinces one witness to the execution of the power of attorney is permitted, while in other provinces, such as Ontario, both types of powers of attorney require two witnesses, who must be 18 years of age or older. The grantor must sign the power of attorney in the presence of the two witnesses, who both sign in the presence of each other and the grantor. In Ontario, the following people cannot act as witnesses:[23]

(a) The attorney or the attorney's spouse or partner[24]
(b) The grantor's spouse, partner, child, or someone the grantor treats as his or her child
(c) Someone under 18
(d) Someone who has a guardian of the grantor's property (which means that someone has been appointed by a court to represent the grantor due to his or her own mental incapacity)

[23] *Substitute Decisions Act, 1992*, S.O. 1992, c. 30, s. 10(2) for property and s. 48(2) for personal care (which refers back to s. 10(2)).
[24] The *Substitute Decisions Act* defines "spouse" as a person of the opposite sex to whom the person is married or has lived common law with for at least a year, or with whom the person has a child or has entered into a cohabitation agreement. "Partner" is defined as a person of the same sex if the two have lived common law for at least a year or have a child together or have entered into a cohabitation agreement or have lived together for at least one year and have a close personal relationship that is of primary importance in both person's lives.

(e) Someone who has a guardian of the person (which means that someone has been appointed by a court to make personal care decisions for the grantor due to his or her own mental incapacity)

In Ontario, the legislation provides that a court may declare a power of attorney to be effective in some cases, even though a non-permitted witness has acted.

TERMINATION AND REVOCATION OF POWERS OF ATTORNEY

A power of attorney may be revoked by the making of a new power of attorney provided that the grantor is mentally capable of doing so. The grantor, if mentally capable of doing so, may also revoke an existing power of attorney using a signed written revocation, which has been witnessed by two or more people. The death, resignation, or mental incapacity of the attorney may also terminate a power of attorney if there is not a joint or an alternate attorney named to act. The death of the grantor also terminates a power of attorney. If a court order is made appointing a guardian for the grantor, the power of attorney is terminated. A power of attorney cannot be revoked by destruction.

INCAPACITY WITHOUT A POWER OF ATTORNEY

In the event that someone has not made a power of attorney and becomes incapacitated, depending upon which decisions need to be made, there may be legislation in place to address such person's need for assistance. Under Ontario's *Health Care Consent Act*,[25] anyone who is hospitalized or is receiving care or undergoing treatment at a facility covered by the Act must consent to any procedure or treatment. If the patient is incapable of giving consent, the Act sets out who can give consent on the patient's behalf. Section 20 of the Act establishes a hierarchy of persons who are given the authority to make health care and treatment decisions for individuals incapable of doing so. A person appointed by the court as the person's guardian is first in line to give consent on that person's behalf, followed by the person's attorney appointed under a power of attorney for personal care. If the person does not have a guardian or an attorney, then the person's spouse or partner (including a common law partner of one year) is first in line to consent on the person's behalf, followed by the person's child or parent.

If someone becomes incapacitated without having a power of attorney in place, one or more persons can apply to the court to become the guardian of the person and the guardian of his or her property. The guardian of the person makes personal and health care decisions while the guardian of the property makes decisions in regard to his or her property.

In some cases, under legislation in some jurisdictions, a court application may not be required in order to become the guardian of someone's property. In Ontario, if a person is assessed as being incapable of managing his or her own affairs (for example, when the person enters a psychiatric hospital), a copy of the assessment is forwarded to the Office of the Public Guardian and Trustee, who becomes the Statutory Guardian of the person's property. A close family member or friend may apply to the Office of the Public Guardian

---

[25] *Health Care Consent Act, 1996*, S.O. 1996, c. 2, Sched. A.

and Trustee to take over as statutory guardian of the person's property. A management plan as to how the proposed guardian would manage the incapable person's affairs must be filed. In some cases, security may have to be posted in order for someone to be permitted to act as the person's guardian. There is no equivalent procedure for substitute personal care decision-makers. For personal care decisions, a power of attorney for personal care or a court order or use of the *Health Care Consent Act* is required. Note that, in some cases, a person deemed to be incapable of managing his or her own affairs may appeal that decision to the Consent and Capacity Board unless her or she has included special provisions in a power of attorney for personal care waiving the right to appeal.[26]

In a situation where someone poses a threat to his or her own life or health, there may be mental health legislation in place that could be used to have a doctor order to commit the person to a hospital for an assessment. Where the person does not have a doctor, someone may be able to appear before a justice of the peace for a warrant for the person's committal for an assessment.

CHAPTER SUMMARY

In this chapter the reader was introduced to estates law and the concept of estate planning. The key documents of an estate plan, particularly a will and powers of attorney, were examined. The advantages of making a will were explored. The process of making a will, including the legal and formal requirements and information required to make a will, were also covered. There was an examination of the different types of wills, and special attention was given to the requirements for execution of a valid will. The process of amending and revoking wills was also covered. Intestacy, the state of dying without a valid will in place, followed the will provisions in the chapter. A table was given setting out intestacy provisions across the country.

Powers of attorney for property and powers of attorney for personal care were defined. The factors to be considered in drafting powers of attorney were considered for each type of power of attorney; the requirements for execution of powers of attorney were also explored. The process of terminating and revoking powers of attorney was also covered. Some attention was given to the situation wherein someone without a valid power of attorney becomes incapacitated and unable to manage his or her affairs and is unable to make personal care decisions. In this context, statutory and court appointed guardians were discussed.

The chapter contained examples of some key estate planning documents, including a will, an affidavit of execution of a will, a continuing power of attorney for property and a power of attorney for personal care.

---

[26] Special provisions are not routinely included in a power of attorney. However, if a person suffers from a condition that could progress to a state where they are in denial of their condition, they might choose to include special provisions that permit the use of reasonable force to have them assessed and set out a waiver of any appeals of a capacity assessment.

GLOSSARY OF NEW TERMS AND KEY CONCEPTS

administrator   A male person appointed by a grant of the court to administer an intestate estate.

administratrix   A female person appointed by a grant of the court to administer an intestate estate.

affidavit of execution   A document sworn by a witness to a will that states that the proper witnessing procedure was followed. The affidavit also states that the witness believes that the testator is over 18 years of age.

attorney   A person named by the grantor in a power of attorney to act for the grantor by managing his or her property and/or making personal care decisions.

beneficiary   The recipient of a gift made in a will or a person for whom trust property is held.

bequest   A gift of a specific item of personal property made in a will.

certificate of appointment of estate trustee with a will   A document issued by the court that certifies that the will is the last valid will of the deceased and confirming the appointment of the estate trustee.

certificate of appointment of estate trustee without a will   A document issued by the court appointing someone to administer the intestate estate.

codicil   A document made after a will that alters a will.

common disaster clause   A provision in a will to deal with the situation wherein two people die within a short time of each other.

consanguinity   The degree of relationship between persons descended from a common ancestor.

escheat   The situation where ownership of the deceased's property passes to the provincial government.

estate   All of the property, both real and personal, that someone has an interest in.

estate planning   The process of arranging one's affairs for his or her death or incapacity and setting out instructions regarding the management of his or her property upon incapacity or after death.

estate trustee with a will   The executor or executrix named in a will.

estate trustee without a will   The person appointed by the court to manage an intestate estate.

execution   The proper signing of a legal document, usually in the presence of witness(es).

executor   A male person appointed in a will to manage the estate following the testator's death.

executrix   A female person appointed in a will to manage the estate following the testator's death.

formally attested will   A will that has been executed in the presence of at least two witnesses.

grantor   A person who is making a power of attorney.

holograph will   A will, valid in certain jurisdictions, that has been made entirely in the testator's own handwriting and signed by him or her.

intestacy   The situation where someone dies without having a valid will.

intestate   A person who has died without a valid will, or condition of having died without a valid will.

issue   Those persons who have all descended from a common ancestor.

legacies   Gifts of money set out in a will.

letters of administration   A court grant appointing someone to administer an intestate estate.

living will   A document containing instructions for medical treatment and health care or the withholding of such treatment or care. Usually part of a power of attorney for personal care.

military wills	Wills made by members of the Canadian Forces on active service or by sailors at sea.
per stirpes	The process whereby a deceased beneficiary's direct lineal descendants are entitled, by representation, to equally share the original gift that the beneficiary was entitled to.
personal representative	In some jurisdictions, the executor or executrix is termed the personal representative.
power of attorney for personal care	A legal document in which the grantor names someone to be his or her attorney to make health and personal care decisions for him or her in the event that he or she is incapable of doing so.
power of attorney for property	A legal document in which the grantor gives someone, namely the attorney, the power to make financial decisions for the grantor.
precatory memorandum	A memorandum containing the testator's wishes regarding the disposition of assets, or giving funeral, burial or other instructions. It is not legally binding.
rollover	A term used in estate and income tax law to describe the transfer of property from one person to another without the property being taxed as it normally would be when it is transferred. Spouses are permitted to roll over property from one to the other without it being taxed until the recipient spouse sells the property or dies.
split wills	The situation where someone makes two valid, co-existing wills, only one of which will be submitted to the court for probate.
testamentary capacity	The state of being mentally capable of making a will.
testamentary trust	A trust set up in a will to take effect upon death.
testator	A male person who makes his will.
testatrix	A female person who makes her will.
trustee	A person appointed in a trust instrument to manage trust assets on behalf of the beneficiaries of the trust.
will	A written document that sets out the directions for the management and distribution of a person's property following that person's death.

REVIEW QUESTIONS

1. Explain three advantages of making a will.

2. Why might a testator make more than one will?

3. Describe three situations where someone under the age of majority may be legally permitted to make a will.

4. List three factors that a testator should consider when choosing an executor.

5. Set out the four characteristics that illustrate whether someone has testamentary capacity to make a will.

6. Explain the witnessing procedure for a formally attested will.

7. What are the legal requirements for a valid holograph will?

8. How does a legal memorandum differ from a precatory one?

9. Describe two ways in which a will can be amended.

10. What are some ways in which a will can be revoked?

11. What is a continuing power of attorney for property?

12. What is a power of attorney for personal care?

13. Explain two ways in which a power of attorney can be revoked.

14. What happens to an intestate estate if there are no living next of kin?

DISCUSSION QUESTIONS

1. Ingrid, an Ontario resident, would like to make a will. She has a common law spouse named Oscar. Ingrid and Oscar have been together for 10 years. They do not have any children together. Ingrid has a son, Michael, from her previous marriage. She is divorced. Her eldest son, Angelo, predeceased her. Angelo is survived by two daughters: Karen, who is 12, and Kendra, who is 10. The net value of Ingrid's estate is $400,000.

   (a) Describe how Ingrid's estate would be divided if she died intestate.

   (b) Ingrid calls her lawyer on a Friday afternoon. She is leaving for a vacation in Tahiti the next day and is worried that she does not have a will. Is there anything that Ingrid can do about a will before she goes on vacation?

   (c) Michael is 15 years of age. Ingrid is worried as to what would happen to him if she died. What should she put in her will to deal with her concerns?

   (d) Ingrid would like to state in her will that her body may be donated for scientific research and that her organs may be used for transplant purposes. Discuss whether or not it is a good idea to put such clauses in a will.

   (e) Assume that Ingrid made a will leaving Oscar $100,000. Two years later, she and Oscar separate. Does Ingrid need to do anything with her will?

2. Marvin is divorced. He has two children, aged 7 and 8. He wants to make a will, but he has a number concerns, set out below, which must first be addressed.

   (a) Marvin plans to name his best friend, Roger, as his estate trustee. He is, however, worried that Roger may move to Argentina to be with his family. In that case, he would not want him acting as estate trustee. What should be done in the will to cover this possibility?

   (b) Marvin has sole custody of the children. He has heard that he needs both a custodian and a guardian. Explain the difference.

   (c) Marvin has heard that children inherit money at 18 unless other provisions are made for them. What can he do in his will to postpone the children's age of inheritance?

   (d) If Marvin is able to tie up the children's money until they are older, he is afraid that they would not be able to attend college or university. How could he ensure in his will that the money would be available for such purposes?

   (e) Marvin is worried that the children might end up in unhappy marriages and be required to share their inheritances and any earnings on such inheritances with their estranged spouses. Is there anything that can be put into Marvin's will to avoid this possibility?

3. Norman has heard that he should have powers of attorney to protect his assets and to have someone make decisions for him if he is incapable of doing so.

(a) What are two types of powers of attorney that Norman should consider making?

(b) Describe some of the advantages of each type of power of attorney.

(c) Explain the difference between conditions and restrictions, and give an example of each.

(d) What might happen if Norman becomes incapable without having made powers of attorney?

SUGGESTED READINGS

Best, Jeanne, & Dawn Dudley Oosterhoff. *Willing and Able. A Practical Guide to Powers of Attorney in Ontario*, 2d Ed. (Belleville, Ont.: Essence Publishing, 2004).

Botnick, David. *Wills for Ontario*, 15th Ed. (North Vancouver, B.C.: Self-Counsel Press, 2001).

Carter, Tom. *Wills Guide for Canada* (North Vancouver, B.C.: Self-Counsel Press, 2001).

Fazakas, Derek. *Wills and Estates*, 2d Ed. (Toronto, Ont.: Emond-Montgomery, 2004).

MacGregor, Mary L. *Preparation of Wills and Powers of Attorney, First Interview to Final Report*, 3d Ed. (Toronto, Ont.: Canada Law Book Inc., 2004).

Sweatman, Jasmine. *Guide to Powers of Attorney* (Toronto, Ont.: Canada Law Book Inc., 2002).

VIDEO

Advocacy Centre for the Elderly. *The Issues Behind Signing a Power of Attorney* (Toronto: Advocacy Centre for the Elderly, video, October 2000).

32

Estate Administration

DeeAnn M. Gonsalves
SENECA COLLEGE

Learning Objectives

After reading this chapter, the reader should be able to:

➢ identify the estate trustee
➢ understand the responsibilities of the estate trustee
➢ appreciate some of the potential difficulties that the estate trustee may face
➢ understand how to obtain a court certificate
➢ understand how to calculate estate administration tax
➢ identify the tasks involved with the distribution of the estate
➢ appreciate how to deal with some key creditors
➢ demonstrate an awareness of dependants' relief legislation
➢ demonstrate an awareness of matrimonial property legislation
➢ appreciate the possible challenges to a will

TABLE OF CONTENTS

INTRODUCTION

It has been said that "death pays all debts".[1] Many an estate executor has wished that this proverb were true. The reality is that our debts outlive us. The executor of an estate must deal with the deceased's debts as part of the administration of an estate. Dealing with a deceased's creditors is but one of the many tasks that an executor must attend to as part of the administration of an estate.

What Is Estate Administration?

Estate administration refers to the steps that must be taken following a death in order to deal with the deceased's remains, assets, and liabilities.

THE ESTATE TRUSTEE

Estate Trustee With a Will

If the deceased left a valid will, the document should be reviewed to determine if one or more estate trustees are named. The estate trustee with a will is the person named in the will to administer the estate. It is not a requirement of a valid will that an estate trustee be named. In most cases, however, one or more estate trustees are named in a will. The estate trustee with a will is more commonly known as the **executor**, for a male appointee, and the **executrix**, for a female appointee. In Ontario, however, legislation has changed the terminology to be used from executor or executrix to **estate trustee with a will**. Many financial institutions, however, still commonly use the term *executor*.[2]

Where there is an executor or executrix named in the will, that person receives his or her authority to act from the will itself immediately upon the death of the testator. If more than one executor is named in the will, they must be unanimous in their decisions, unless the will contains a majority clause.

If the executor has predeceased the deceased, any co-executors may act alone, although they will have to provide proof of the death of the other executor to the institutions that they deal with. If there is only one executor named in the will and he predeceases the deceased, the will should be reviewed to determine if an alternate executor has been named to act in his or her place. If an alternate executor has not been named, then by the process of **devolution**, the executor named in the deceased executor's will becomes the executor of both estates.

Estate Trustee Without a Will

If a will does not name an executor or if the deceased died intestate, meaning that he or she did not leave behind a valid will, then someone must apply to the court to be appointed as the estate trustee without a will. The estate trustee without a will is more commonly known as the **administrator**, in the case of a male appointee, and the **administratrix**, in the case of a female appointee. In order to be appointed as the estate trustee, the applicant must apply to the court for a **certificate of appointment of estate trustee without a will**, known in some jurisdictions as **letters of administration**.

---

[1] From a 17th century proverb first included in T. Fuller, *Gnomologia*, 1732.

[2] Given that many estate terms are specifically masculine or feminine, the author has been unable to use gender neutral terms in some parts of the text.

INITIAL RESPONSIBILITIES OF THE ESTATE TRUSTEE

Dealing with the Deceased's Remains

The estate trustee should review the deceased's will, driver's licence, and any organ donor card in order to determine if the deceased left any instructions regarding body donation for science or organ or tissues donation. If no instructions were left in this regard, the deceased's spouse or, if there is no spouse, the deceased's next of kin will be asked to make any decisions in this regard.

The estate trustee is responsible for the disposal of the deceased's remains. If the deceased died intestate or the will does not name an estate trustee, then the deceased's next of kin becomes responsible for the disposal of the remains. The decision must be made as to whether the deceased should be cremated, interred in the ground or entombed in a **mausoleum**. The estate trustee or next of kin will also make any funeral or memorial service arrangements. The deceased may have left instructions concerning such matters, but such instructions are only **precatory** in nature, meaning that they are simply an expression of the deceased's wishes and are not legally binding on the executor. As there are laws concerning the disposal of human remains, the deceased's final instructions in this regard cannot be legally binding. For example, if the deceased wanted to be interred in his favourite car, this would not be legally possible in most jurisdictions.

The estate trustee in planning the funeral should bear in mind the lifestyle to which the deceased was accustomed. If the executor spends an excessive amount on funeral expenses, he or she may become personally liable for such costs.

Minor Children and Dependants

The estate trustee must make arrangements for the deceased's minor children and dependants. If the deceased was the child's remaining custodial parent, the will, if there is one, should be reviewed to determine whether the deceased appointed a temporary **custodian**. In Ontario, such appointments are valid for 90 days following the death of the custodial parents. During that time, the temporary custodian should apply to the local family court in order to be appointed the permanent custodian of the child.[3] The courts will make an order based on what is in the child's best interests, taking into consideration the deceased's wishes as expressed in the will. Whether or not there is a will in place, any person can apply to the court for custody of the children.

A minor child also requires a **guardian of property**. If there is a will, it should be reviewed to determine if the deceased named someone to be the temporary guardian of the child's property. Quite often, the will names the same person as custodian and guardian. The proposed guardian must apply to the local family court for an order appointing him or her as the guardian of the child's property.[4] The guardian may have to post a bond with the court in order to secure his or her actions. Once appointed, the guardian can take control of the child's property, which may include bank accounts and other investments. The guardian should also arrange for the payment of any benefits the child may be entitled to, such as Canada Pension Plan survivor benefits.

The estate trustee must consider the financial needs of any dependants following the testator's death. She should review the will to determine what provisions have been made for dependants. The estate is responsible for the support of the deceased's dependants. In some cases the deceased's will

---

[3] *Children's Law Reform Act*, R.S.O. 1990, c. C.12, s. 61.
[4] *Children's Law Reform Act*, R.S.O. 1990, c. C.12, s. 47.

directs that a testamentary trust be set up for minor children or other dependants. The trust must hold and invest the beneficiaries' inheritances until they are a stipulated age. However, it is common for the trustee to be given the authority to use some of the trust funds to pay for a child's education or for other worthy expenses.

Locating and Reviewing the Will

As soon as possible following the death of the deceased, his or her last will should be located. The deceased's papers can be reviewed to determine if a will is among them. If a copy of a will is found, it will probably say on the copy where the original will is stored. A will prepared by a lawyer is usually stored in the lawyer's office. If a will is not found, it is wise to contact all of the lawyers that the deceased dealt with over his or her lifetime in order to determine if they are in possession of a will. In some jurisdictions, such as Ontario, a will may also be held on deposit at the deceased's local Estates Court. The estate trustee can ask the court to check its registry to determine if they are holding a will made by the deceased. In many cases where a will cannot be found, an advertisement looking for anyone with knowledge of a will of the deceased is published. In Ontario such advertisements routinely appear in the Law Society of Upper Canada's weekly *Ontario Reports* bulletin.

If a will is found, it may or may not have an affidavit of execution with it. If it does not have an affidavit of execution, the lawyer who prepared the will should be asked to prepare one as soon as possible as it will be required for an application for probate from the court.

Locating and Reviewing any Relevant Contracts

The deceased's papers should be reviewed to determine if he or she entered into any contracts that may affect the disposition of the estate. Such contracts could include a domestic contract, such as a marriage contract, cohabitation agreement, or separation agreement. If the deceased owned a business, he or she may be a party to a partnership or shareholder agreement that could affect the estate.

Locating and Securing the Assets

The estate trustee is responsible for locating and securing the deceased's assets. He or she must investigate the deceased's affairs to ensure that all assets are found. The executor or administrator is responsible for the safekeeping of the assets. The executor may have to arrange to have locks changed, a safety deposit box rented, insurance limits reviewed and ownership documents updated. The estate trustee will also have to call in any loans made by the deceased, as receivables form part of the estate. An inventory of all assets should be made. Some estate trustees find it helpful to take photos or make a video of the deceased's assets.

Keeping Accounts

The estate trustee must document all estate transactions, particularly in regard to financial matters. All incoming and outgoing monies must be strictly accounted for. The estate trustee should retain receipts for all estate transactions. The estate trustee could be called upon at any time to provide **accounts** to beneficiaries, creditors, and the court.

COURT CERTIFICATES

Determining Whether a Certificate Is Required

If there is a valid will that appoints an estate trustee, the estate trustee should consider whether the will itself is sufficient to administer the estate. In such cases a certificate from the court will not be required. This could result in substantial savings to the estate as **estate administration tax** would not have to be paid. Some financial institutions accept a will, along with a death certificate and a signed agreement to indemnify the institution if the funds are wrongly paid out, in place of a court certificate. The executor should check with the financial institutions holding the deceased's assets to determine their policy in this regard. Some institutions will accept such documentation in place of a certificate if the estate is valued at under $20,000.

Without a will most financial institutions require a court certificate in order to transfer the deceased's assets to the estate. However, if the estate was fairly small, and the sole beneficiary is the deceased's spouse, the financial institution may permit a transfer to the spouse without a will upon receipt of a death certificate and an indemnification from the surviving spouse.

Obtaining Court Certificates

Certificate of Appointment of Estate Trustee With a Will

A **certificate of appointment of estate trustee with a will** is a document granted by the court. The certificate confirms that the will submitted to the court is the last valid will of the deceased. It also validates the appointment of the estate trustee. The certificate is referred to in some jurisdictions as a grant of probate or **letters probate.**

A certificate of appointment of estate trustee with a will provides proof to anyone relying on the certificate that this is the deceased's last will and that the person acting as executor has been approved by the court. Once a certificate is granted, if a later will is found, the estate trustee is not liable for having acted under the earlier will as long as he or she diligently searched for a later will.

The procedure for obtaining a certificate of appointment of estate trustee with a will varies from jurisdiction to jurisdiction. In Ontario there is a prescribed application form that must be completed. A sample application form is found in Exhibit 32.1. The application form solicits information regarding the name, address, and marital status of the deceased. Questions are also asked about the will, any codicils, and whether any witnesses to the will are beneficiaries of the estate. The value of the estate must be set out. The person applying to be the estate trustee must swear that he or she is of the age of majority and that he or she does not know of any later will. The person must also swear that he or she will faithfully administer the estate and render a complete and true account of the administration of the estate. A Notice of Application must also be completed. A sample Notice of Application is found in Exhibit 32.2. The Notice of Application must be served on all of the beneficiaries and contingent beneficiaries named in the will. The beneficiaries and contingent beneficiaries must also receive a copy of the portion of the will dealing with their gift. Residuary beneficiaries, being those beneficiaries named to receive the residue of the estate, must receive a copy of the entire will. If any of the beneficiaries are minors, the application must be served upon their parent or guardian and, also, upon the Office of the Children's Lawyer. If there are beneficiaries who are mentally incapacitated, the application must be served upon their attorney or guardian. If the mentally incapable person does not have an attorney or a guardian, then service should be made upon the Office of the Public Guardian and Trustee. If a charity is named as a beneficiary the charity and the Office of the Public Guardian and Trustee must be served.

Once the application has been made to the court, the court registrar reviews its registry to determine if the court is in possession of a more recent will. The court also searches to see if an application has been commenced in another jurisdiction. If the court does not find a more recent will and there are no other applications pending and no one has filed a notice of

EXHIBIT 32.1	Application Form for a Certificate of Appointment of Estate Trustee With a Will

FORM 74.4
Courts of Justice Act
APPLICATION FOR CERTIFICATE OF APPOINTMENT OF ESTATE TRUSTEE
WITH A WILL (INDIVIDUAL APPLICANT)

ONTARIO **SUPERIOR COURT OF JUSTICE** at Brampton	**APPLICATION FOR CERTIFICATE OF APPOINTMENT OF ESTATE TRUSTEE WITH A WILL (INDIVIDUAL APPLICANT)** *(Form 74.4 Under the Rules)*

This application is filed by (*insert name and address*)

Brown & Hudson, Barristers & Solicitors, 6 Apple Avenue, Brampton, Ontario, L6X 3L4, Telephone: 905-453-2222

DETAILS ABOUT THE DECEASED PERSON

Complete in full as applicable

First given name	Second given name	Third given name	Surname
Elizabeth	Louise		Collins

And if the deceased was known by any other name(s), state below the full name(s) used including surname.

First given name	Second given name	Third given name	Surname
Liz			Collins

Address of fixed place of abode (*street or postal address*) (*city or town*)	(*county or district*)
17 Queen Street, Brampton, Ontario, L6X 7T4	Peel

If the deceased person had no fixed place of abode in Ontario, did he or she have property in Ontario? ☐ No ☐ Yes	Last occupation of deceased person Teacher

Place of death (*city or town; county or district*) City of Brampton; Regional Municipality of Peel	Date of Death (*day, month, year*) 31/07/2008	Date of last will (marked as Exhibit "A") (*day, month, year*) 03/12/2007

Was the deceased person 18 years of age or older at the date of the will (or 21 years of age or older if the will is dated earlier than September 1, 1971)? If not, explain why certificate is being sought. Give details in an attached schedule.	☐ No ☒ Yes

Date of codicil (marked as Exhibit "B") (*day, month year*) N/A	Date of codicil (marked as Exhibit "C") (*day, month, year*) N/A

Marital status ☐ Unmarried ☒ Married ☐ Widowed ☐ Divorced

Did the deceased person marry after the date of the will? If yes, explain why certificate is being sought. Give details in an attached schedule.	☒ No ☐ Yes

Was a marriage of the deceased person terminated by a judgment absolute of divorce, or declared a nullity, after the date of the will? If yes, give details in an attached schedule.	☒ No ☐ Yes

Is any person who signed the will or a codicil as witness or for the testator, or the spouse of such person, a beneficiary under the will? If yes, give details in an attached schedule.	☒ No ☐ Yes

Application Form for a Certificate of Appointment of Estate Trustee With a Will

EXHIBIT 32.1 (continued)

VALUE OF ASSETS OF ESTATE

Do not include in the total amount: insurance payable to a named beneficiary or assigned for value, property held jointly and passing by survivorship, or real estate outside Ontario.

Personal Property	Real estate, net of encumbrances	Total
$ 200,000	$ 100,000	$ 300,000

Is there any person entitled to an interest in the estate who is not an applicant? ☐ No ☒ Yes

If a person named in the will or a codicil as estate trustee is not an applicant, explain.

If a person not named in the will or a codicil as estate trustee is an applicant, explain why that person is entitled to apply.

If the spouse of the deceased is an applicant, has the spouse elected to receive the entitlement under section 5 of the *Family Law Act*?
If yes, explain why the spouse is entitled to apply. ☒ No ☐ Yes

AFFIDAVIT(S) OF APPLICANT(S)
(Attach a separate sheet for additional affidavits, if necessary)

I, an applicant named in this application, make oath and say/affirm:

1. I am 18 years of age or older.
2. The exhibit(s) referred to in this application are the last will and each codicil (where applicable) of the deceased person and I do not know of any later will or codicil.
3. I will faithfully administer the deceased person's property according to law and render a complete and true account of my administration when lawfully required.
4. If I am not named as estate trustee in the will or codicil, consents of persons who together have a majority interest in the value of the assets of the estate at the date of death are attached.
5. The information contained in this application and in any attached schedules is true, to the best of my knowledge and belief.

Name *(surname and forename(s))*	**Occupation**
Collins, Robert Allen	Firefighter

Address *(street or postal address)*	*(city or town)*	*(province)*	*(postal code)*
17 Queen Street	Brampton	Ontario	L6X 7T4

Sworn/Affirmed before me at the City

of Brampton

in the Regional Municipality

of Peel

this _____ day of _____ , 20 ____

_____
Signature of applicant

A Commissioner for taking Affidavits *(or as may be)*

Name *(surname and forename(s))*	**Occupation**

Address *(street or postal address)*	*(city or town)*	*(province)*	*(postal code)*

Sworn/Affirmed before me at the _____

of _____

in the _____

of _____

this _____ day of _____ , 20 ____

_____
Signature of applicant

A Commissioner for taking Affidavits *(or as may be)*

Source: Ontario Court Services Website, <http://www.ontariocourtforms.on.ca/english/civil/>.

EXHIBIT 32.2

Notice of Application

FORM 74.7
Courts of Justice Act
NOTICE OF AN APPLICATION FOR A CERTIFICATE OF APPOINTMENT OF ESTATE TRUSTEE
WITH A WILL

ONTARIO

SUPERIOR COURT OF JUSTICE

IN THE ESTATE OF ELIZABETH LOUISE COLLINS, also known as LIZ COLLINS, deceased.
(insert name)

**NOTICE OF AN APPLICATION FOR A
CERTIFICATE OF APPOINTMENT OF ESTATE
TRUSTEE WITH A WILL**

1. The deceased died on July 31, 2008.

2. Attached to this notice are:

   (A) If the notice is sent to or in respect of a person entitled only to a specified item of property or stated amount of money, an extract of the part or parts of the will or codicil relating to the gift, or a copy of the will (and codicil(s), if any).

   (B) If the notice is sent to or in respect of any other beneficiary, a copy of the will (and codicil(s), if any).

   (C) If the notice is sent to the Children's Lawyer or the Public Guardian and Trustee, a copy of the will (and codicil(s), if any), and if it is not included in the notice, a statement of the estimated value of the interest of the person represented.

3. The applicant named in this notice is applying for a certificate of appointment of estate trustee with a will.

APPLICANT

Name	Address
Robert Allen Collins	17 Queen St., Brampton, Ontario L6X 7T4

4. The following persons who are less than 18 years of age are entitled, whether their interest is contingent or vested, to share in the distribution of the estate:

Name	Date of Birth *(day, month, year)*	Name and Address of Parent or Guardian	Estimated Value of Interest in Estate*
Angela Collins	18/01/1998	Robert Allen Collins 17 Queen Street Brampton, Ontario L6X 7T4	Beneficiary of $3,000 jewellery

* Note: *The Estimated Value of Interest in Estate may be omitted in the form if it is included in a separate schedule attached to the notice sent to the Children's Lawyer.*

5. The following persons who are mentally incapable within the meaning of section 6 of the *Substitute Decisions Act, 1992* in respect of an issue in the proceeding, and who have guardians or attorneys acting under powers of attorney with authority to act in the proceeding, are entitled, whether their interest is contingent or vested, to share in the distribution of the estate:

Name and Address of Person	Name and Address of Guardian or Attorney*
N/A	

* *Specify whether guardian or attorney*

6. The following persons who are mentally incapable within the meaning of section 6 of the *Substitute Decisions Act, 1992* in respect of an issue in the proceeding, and who do not have guardians or attorneys acting under powers of attorney with authority to act in the proceeding, are entitled, whether their interest is contingent or vested, to share in the distribution of the estate:

Name and Address of Person	Estimated Value of Interest in Estate*
N/A	

* Note: *The Estimated Value of Interest in Estate may be omitted in the form if it is included in a separate schedule attached to the notice sent to the Public Guardian and Trustee.*

7. Unborn or unascertained persons may be entitled to share in the distribution of the estate. *(Delete if not applicable)*

8. All other persons and charities entitled, whether their interest is contingent or vested, to share in the distribution of the estate are as follows:

Name	Address
Robert Allen Collins	17 Queen Street, Brampton, ON L6X 7T4
Canadian Cancer Society	2 Main Street, Brampton, ON, L6X 8W1

Notice of Application

EXHIBIT 32.2 (continued)

9. This notice is being sent, by regular lettermail, to all adult persons and charities named above in this notice (except to an applicant who is entitled to share in the distribution of the estate), to the Public Guardian and Trustee if paragraph 6 applies, to a parent or guardian of the minor and to the Children's Lawyer if paragraph 4 applies, to the guardian or attorney if paragraph 5 applies, and to the Children's Lawyer if paragraph 7 applies.

10. The following persons named in the Will or being a member of a class of beneficiaries under the Will may be entitled to be served but have not been served for the reasons shown below:

Name of person (as it appears in will, if applicable)   **Reasons not served**

If paragraph 10 does not apply insert "Not Applicable."

DATE:

· · · · ·

Source: Ontario Court Services Website, <http://www.ontariocourtforms.on.ca/english/civil/>.

objection to the issuance of a certificate of estate trustee, the court will go ahead and issue a certificate of estate trustee with a will. It may take four to six weeks to obtain a certificate from the court. A copy of a certificate of appointment of estate trustee with a will is included in Exhibit 32.3. The original will is an exhibit to the certificate. Notarial copies of the certificate should be made as they will be required by most of the financial institutions that the estate will be dealing with.

Other Certificates

If the deceased obtained a certificate of estate trustee with a will or probate of a will from another Canadian province or territory or the United Kingdom or any British possession, that certificate and the will, if there is one, may be submitted to an Ontario court for **resealing**. The resealed certificate may be used to deal with the deceased's Ontario assets.

If the deceased obtained a certificate of estate trustee with a will or probate of a will from a jurisdiction outside of Canada, the United Kingdom or a British possession, that certificate and the will may be submitted to an Ontario court to facilitate the granting of an ancillary certificate. The ancillary certificate, also known as an **ancillary grant**, may be used to deal with the deceased's Ontario assets.

If the estate is involved in litigation, a **certificate of appointment of estate trustee during litigation** may be obtained. A court order is required for such a certificate. The estate trustee during litigation may perform routine estate administration tasks but cannot distribute the estate without a court order.

If the sole estate trustee dies intestate or becomes incapable of administering the estate, then someone will have to apply for a certificate of appointment of succeeding estate trustee with a will in order for the estate administration to be completed.

Certificate of Appointment of Estate Trustee
Without a Will

Where the deceased did not leave a valid will, someone must apply to the court in order to be appointed as administrator of the estate. In Ontario

| EXHIBIT 32.3 | Certificate of Appointment of Estate Trustee With a Will |

FORM 74.13

Courts of Justice Act

CERTIFICATE OF APPOINTMENT OF ESTATE TRUSTEE WITH A WILL

ONTARIO

SUPERIOR COURT OF JUSTICE

IN THE ESTATE OF ELIZABETH LOUISE COLLINS ,

deceased,

late of   the City of Brampton, Regional Municipality of Peel

occupation   Teacher

who died on   July 31, 2008

certificate of appointment
of estate trustee with a will

Applicant	Address	Occupation
Robert Allen Collins	17 Queen St., Brampton, ON L6X 7T4	Firefighter

This CERTIFICATE OF APPOINTMENT OF ESTATE TRUSTEE WITH A WILL is hereby issued under the seal of the court to the applicant named above. A copy of the deceased's last will (and codicil(s), if any) is attached.

Date _____

_____

Registrar

Address of court office

7755 Hurontario Street, Brampton, ON L6V 2M7

Source: Ontario Court Services Website, <http://www.ontariocourtforms.on.ca/english/civil/>.

this person is known as the **estate trustee without a will**. The **certificate of appointment of estate trustee without a will** is required in order to provide someone with the authority to administer the estate. Legislation prescribes who should apply to be the estate trustee without a will. In Ontario the deceased's surviving spouse, including a common law spouse, and the deceased's next of kin have the first right to apply to be the estate trustee.[5] More than one person may be appointed to act.

If the original estate trustee without a will dies or becomes incapable of completing the administration of the estate, a certificate of appointment of succeeding estate trustee without a will may be required.

If the estate trustee without a will obtained the court certificate, also known as letters of administration, from another Canadian province or territory, or from the United Kingdom or a British possession, the estate trustee

---

[5] *Estates Act*, R.S.O. 1990, c. E.21, as amended, s. 29(1).

can ask an Ontario court to reseal the original certificate so that it can be used to administer the deceased's Ontario assets.

If the estate trustee without a will obtained the certificate from somewhere other than Canada, the United Kingdom, or a British possession, he or she must apply for a certificate of appointment of a foreign estate trustee's nominee as estate trustee without a will in order to deal with the deceased's Ontario assets. As there is no will, the nominee for estate trustee must be an Ontario resident.

Estate Administration Tax

In order to obtain a certificate from the court, probate tax must be paid in all Canadian jurisdictions. Such fees vary greatly across the country and are known in some places as **probate fees**, probate taxes, court fees or, in the case of Ontario, as an **estate administration tax**. The tax is based on the value of the deceased's estate subject to a few exclusions and deductions. If the value of the estate is unknown, an estimate may be made and tax paid to the court on that basis. If an estimate is given, an undertaking must be made to the court to provide the true value of the estate within six months, and to pay any additional tax or to apply for a refund of tax if the value of the estate given was too low or too high. (See Exhibit 32.4 for Canadian estate administration/probate tax rates.)

Estate Administration Tax Inclusions, Exclusions, and Deductions

☐ INCLUSIONS

Each jurisdiction varies as to which items must be included in the value of the estate for estate administration tax purposes. In Ontario, for example, most of the deceased's Ontario assets must be included in the value of the estate. There are very few exclusions and deductions. The only permitted deduction is an encumbrance, such as a mortgage, on any real property that is included in the estate for estate administration tax purposes.[6]

☐ EXCLUSIONS

There are some items that are excluded from the value of an estate for estate administration tax purposes. Insurance, such as life insurance, that is payable to a named beneficiary or assigned for value is excluded. This exception also applies to RRSPs, RRIFs, and pension plans with a named beneficiary. Any assets held in **joint tenancy**, such as real estate or joint bank accounts, are excluded as they pass to the joint owner by right of survivorship and do not form part of the estate. Property located outside of Ontario is also excluded. Such property will be dealt with in its own jurisdiction. A ***donatio mortis causa***, being a gift made in contemplation of death and conditional upon death, is also excluded as it is, technically, property given away while the deceased, albeit close to death, was still alive. Real property cannot be the subject of a *donatio mortis causa*.

☐ DEDUCTIONS

Each jurisdiction has its own laws as to what can be deducted from the value of the estate for estate administration tax purposes. In Alberta, for example, all of the deceased's debts can be deducted from the value of his or her property at the time of his or her death. Other provinces permit some deductions, such as funeral expenses. In Ontario, there is only one allowable

---

[6] *Estate Administration Tax Act, 1998*, S.O. 1998, c. 34, Sch., s. 1.

EXHIBIT 32.4		Canadian Estate Administration/Probate Tax Rates

PROVINCE / TERRITORY	ESTATE VALUE	PROBATE TAX RATE[1]
Alberta	Up to $10,000 $10,001 – $25,000 $25,001 – $125,000 $125,001 – $250,000 Over $250,000	$25 $100 $200 $300 $400
British Columbia	Up to $25,000 Over $25,000 $25,001 – $50,000 On value over $50,000	$0 $208 (administration fee) $6 per $1,000 (or 0.6%) $14 per $1,000 (or 1.4%)
Manitoba	Up to $10,000 On value over $10,000	$70 $7 per $1,000 (or 0.7%)
New Brunswick	Up to $5,000 $5,001 – $10,000 $10,001 – $15,000 $15,001 – $20,000 On value over $20,000	$25 $50 $75 $100 $5 per $1,000 (or 0.5%)
Newfoundland & Labrador	Up to $1,000 On value over $1,000	$60 $5 per $1,000 (or 0.5%)
Northwest Territories	Up to $10,000 $10,001 – $25,000 $25,001 – $125,000 $125,001 – $250,000 Over $250,000	$25 $100 $200 $300 $400
Nova Scotia	Up to $10,000 $10,001 – $25,000 $25,001 – $50,000 $50,001 – $100,000 On value over $100,000	$74.76 $187.97 $312.92 $875.76 $14.79 per $1,000 (or 1.479%)
Nunavut	Up to $10,000 $10,001 – $25,000 $25,001 – $125,000 $125,001 – $250,000 On value over $250,000	$25 $100 $200 $300 $400
Ontario	Up to $1,000 If estate is over $1,000, on the first $50,000 On value over $50,000	0 $ 5 per $1,000 (or 0.5%) $15 per $1,000 (or 1.5%)
Prince Edward Island	Up to $10,000 $10,001 – $25,000 $25,001 – $50,000 $50,001 – $100,000 On value over $100,000	$50 $100 $200 $400 $4 per $1,000 (or 0.4%)
Quebec	Notarial wills Non-notarial wills: natural person/corporation	0 $93/$104
Saskatchewan	For all amounts	$7 per $1,000 (or 0.7%)
Yukon Territory	Up to $25,000 Over 25,000	0 $140

[1] Fees are subject to change at any time. Check current legislation to ensure accuracy.

deduction. Only an encumbrance against any real property that is included in the value of the estate can be deducted. Other debts cannot be deducted. Assume that an Ontario resident died owning a car worth $15,000, with a car loan outstanding in the amount of $12,000. The estate trustee would have to include the full $15,000 value of the car in the estate's value even though there is a $12,000 debt associated with the vehicle. Credit card debt, in Ontario, also cannot be deducted from the value of the estate. In Ontario, therefore, the value of the estate for estate administration tax purposes is the value of the estate at the date of death less the outstanding balance on any encumbrance on real property that is included in the value of the estate. In some instances, if an Ontario resident has a number of consumer debts, he or she might consider replacing them with a mortgage that would be deductible from the value of the estate for estate administration tax purposes.

Posting Security

In most cases, if a certificate of estate trustee without a will is required, the court will demand that security be posted. The court wants to ensure that any beneficiaries or creditors who suffer losses as a result of any wrongdoing by the estate trustee can be compensated. In Ontario, section 35 of the *Estates Act* states that "every person to whom a grant of administration, including administration with the will annexed, is committed shall give a bond to the judge of the court..."[7]

☐ ESTATE ADMINISTRATION BONDS

Where there is not a will there is a presumption that security is required.[8] Such security is usually posted in the form of an **estate administration bond**. An estate administration bond is a promise by the estate trustee to fulfill his or her estate obligations and a promise by the estate trustee and a third party to compensate beneficiaries and creditors who suffer a loss if the estate trustee does not fulfill those obligations. Administration bonds can be purchased from some insurance, fidelity, or guarantee companies. The bond must be maintained in place until the estate is wound up. There is an annual premium for the bond, and the bond must be made payable to the court. In the event that a claim is made against a bond, the bond funds will be paid into court. The beneficiaries and creditors who have suffered a loss are then able to make a claim to the court for compensation. When an administration bond is purchased, it only needs to be in the amount of the estate.

☐ SURETIES

Instead of purchasing an estate administration bond, the estate trustee may post security with the court by providing sureties. A **surety** is a person who promises to pay money in the event that the principal, in this case the estate trustee, fails to perform his or her duties. If the estate is worth more than $100,000, two sureties must each pledge an amount equal to the value of the estate, thereby providing security equal to two times the value of the estate. In the case of an estate worth less than $100,000, one surety is sufficient.[9] If necessary, application can be made to the court to reduce the

[7] R.S.O. 1990, c. E.21, s. 35. Note that administration in this context of this section refers to the situation where there is an intestacy.
[8] In some circumstances where there is a will, security must still be posted: for example, if the estate trustee is not named in the will, or he or she is not a Canadian resident. However, in many cases the court may make an order reducing or dispensing with a bond.
[9] *Estates Act*, R.S.O. 1990, c. E.21, ss. 35 and 37, and Rule 74.11 of the Ontario *Rules of Civil Procedure*, R.R.O. 1990, Reg. 194.

amount of security required if posting all of the security required would cause hardships.

In some cases the court does not require security. If the estate trustee is a government body, such as the Office of the Public Guardian and Trustee, a bond is not required.[10] If the estate trustee is a trust company, the practice of the court is to waive the bond requirement.

In some cases, the court will not require a bond, or an application can be made to dispense with a bond. Where the deceased died intestate leaving behind a spouse and an estate worth less than the $200,000 preferential share, a bond will not be required if a satisfactory affidavit regarding the deceased's debts is filed with the court.[11] Where all of the beneficiaries are of the age of majority, are mentally capable, and they all consent to dispense with a bond, the court may dispense with the bond. The court, however, must be satisfied that the deceased's debts have been or will be paid from the estate.

CREDITORS OF THE ESTATE

The estate cannot be distributed to the beneficiaries until all of the outstanding debts of the deceased and the estate have been paid.

Locating Creditors

The estate trustee must ascertain the deceased's debts. All debts should be verified. Valid debts must be paid, and any questionable debts should be challenged. The estate trustee will need to review the deceased's records and incoming mail, including e-mail, in order to ascertain what the debts are. Inquiries should also be made at the deceased's banks and other financial institutions to determine if there are any outstanding loans, credit cards, or lines of credit. The estate trustee should also inquire as to whether there is credit life insurance on any of the outstanding debts.

Advertising for Creditors

In many cases, the estate trustee will advertise in a newspaper in the area where the deceased resided for creditors of the estate to come forward. If the deceased died intestate, it is common practice to advertise for creditors. In Ontario, if an advertisement for creditors has not been placed in regard to an intestate estate, the estate trustee must wait at least a full year before distributing the estate. If an advertisement is placed, the estate trustee can distribute the estate before the year is up. In some cases, even where there is a will, it is wise to advertise for creditors. An advertisement should be placed if the estate trustee is uncertain as to whether all of the deceased's creditors have been identified. In the case of the death of a business owner, it would be wise to advertise because the estate trustee, unless he or she was involved in the day-to-day activity of the business, may not be aware of all of the creditors. In all cases, advertising relieves the estate trustee from liability for debts that were not identified because the advertisement itself gave notice to all creditors to come forward and make their claims. If, however, the estate trustee is the sole beneficiary of the estate, the estate trustee may not advertise for creditors, as such creditors can trace their debt to gifts made to beneficiaries.

Advertisements for creditors are made in accordance with the local practice in the jurisdiction where the deceased resided and/or worked. In Toronto,

---

[10] *Estates Act*, R.S.O. 1990, c. E.21, s. 36(1).
[11] *Estates Act*, R.S.O. 1990, c. E.21, s. 36(2).

Ontario, for example, the practice is to insert an advertisement for creditors, on at least two separate occasions, in a major daily newspaper, at least one week apart. Creditors are given at least one month from the date of the first publication to come forward with their claims.

Canada Revenue Agency

A creditor common to most estates is the Canada Revenue Agency, once known as Revenue Canada. Everyone who dies has at least one income tax return that must be completed.

Final Income Tax Returns

In every estate, there is at least one income tax return to be completed for the deceased. The most common tax return to be done upon death is the terminal income tax return. This is the final income tax return for the deceased. This return is used to report the deceased's income from January 1st of the year of death up to and including the date of death. A regular T1 income tax form is used. The usual income tax deductions and personal tax credits may be claimed. There are, however, some differences from the usual income tax return. For example, medical expenses may be claimed for a 24-month period that includes the date of death. While alive, someone can claim medical expenses only for a 12-month period. As well, any capital losses can be deducted from the deceased's income. This practice is not permitted during a person's lifetime. During one's lifetime, he or she may deduct capital losses only from capital gains. Personal tax credits can be claimed for the full year even if the deceased passed away on January 1st.

The due date for the filing of the terminal income tax return is the later of April 30th of the year following the date of death or six months after the date of death. Thus, if the deceased died in November or December, the return would be due six months from the date of death. In all other cases the terminal income tax return would be due no later than April 30th of the year following the date of death. For example, if the deceased died on February 15th, Year 0, the terminal income tax return must be filed no later than April 30th, Year 1.

In some cases, certain types of income may be reported on an alternate income tax return, such as a rights or things return. An example of a right or thing would be income or dividends that have been declared or earned but not paid as of the date of death. If, for example, a worker who was paid only at the end of each month died on February 15th, his February pay would be a right or thing that could be included on a separate tax return. There are situations where other optional tax returns could be filed: for example, if the deceased was receiving income from a **trust** or he or she was a partner or a sole proprietor of a business. It is to a taxpayer's advantage, where possible, to file multiple income tax returns. By doing so, income can be spread out into smaller amounts over various returns and taxed at the lower rates used for lower incomes. As a result, the overall tax bill should be lower. As well, personal tax credits can be claimed on every income tax return filed. In some cases foreign tax returns or corporate tax returns must also be filed. The estate itself must file a T3 trust income tax return each year until it is wound up.

Deemed Disposition Upon Death

In addition to including income from the deceased's employment, investments, and other sources on the deceased's terminal income tax return, any capital gains that would arise from a disposition of all capital property upon death must be included. When someone dies, all the property that person owned at the time of death are deemed to be sold. This is called a **deemed**

disposition of property. In the case of capital property, this may result in a capital gain or a capital loss. Capital property is, in a general sense, property that is not used up during the deceased's lifetime. Examples of capital property include real estate, shares in a corporation, some jewellery, and antiques. The estate trustee calculates the gain in the value of the deceased's property by subtracting the net cost of the asset from its fair market value as of the date of death. The resulting figure is called the **capital gain** or, in the event of a negative figure, the capital loss. A capital gain must be reported for income tax purposes. A capital loss may be reported. Capital losses may be deducted from capital gains, or on the terminal income tax return they may be deducted from the deceased's income.

Where a person's assets are left to the surviving spouse or to a true **spousal trust**, there is an exemption from the deemed disposition upon death rule. In such cases, the assets are rolled over from the deceased's estate to the spouse or to a true spousal trust on a tax-deferred basis. Capital gains will not be realized on these assets until the spouse disposes of them or dies. In most cases taxes deferred are taxes saved as the surviving spouse will likely be in a lower tax bracket at the time of his or her death.

Capital Gains

When an item of capital property appreciates in value, if it is sold (or, in the case of death, is deemed to be sold) there is a resulting capital gain. Assume, for example, that someone purchased shares in Canadian Ore Company for $500 five years before her death. When the shareholder died the shares were worth $1,000. At the time of death, the deceased is deemed to have sold all of her property, including the shares in Canadian Ore Company. The deemed sale price is the fair market value of the shares as of the date of death. Accordingly, if the shares were worth $1,000 at the time of death, the estate trustee would subtract the share's cost price of $500 (no adjustments have been made for fees, commissions, or other costs), resulting in a capital gain of $500. In Canada at this time, only 50 percent of a capital gain has to be included in someone's income for income tax purposes. Therefore, from the $500 capital gain, the sum of $250 (50% of the capital gain) would be reported as income on the terminal income tax return.

For certain types of property, including qualified family farm property and certain Canadian small businesses, there is a $750,000 enhanced lifetime exemption from capital gains in certain situations.

Clearance Certificates

After the final income tax return(s) for the deceased and the estate have been submitted, the estate trustee should apply to the Canada Revenue Agency for a **clearance certificate**. This certificate provides proof that the required tax returns were submitted and that any outstanding taxes, penalties or interest have been paid. Once the certificate has been received, the estate trustee is absolved of any liability for unpaid income taxes. If the estate trustee is the sole beneficiary, a clearance certificate is not usually required since creditors, including the Canada Revenue Agency, can trace assets to the beneficiaries.

Other Creditors

The estate trustee must deal with all of the deceased's creditors. Such creditors could include banks, credit card companies, landlords, car leasing companies and others. If someone claims that the deceased owed him or her money at the time of death, the estate trustee must demand corroborating evidence before considering any payment to such a creditor. The estate trustee should always verify amounts owed, obtain receipts for payment, and request the return of any deposits paid by the deceased. In some cases, a deposit for services will have been required. As the deceased no longer needs the services, the deposit should be paid to the estate. Inquiries as to credit insurance should also be made. For example, many mortgagors purchase mortgage insurance. The proceeds of such insurance will usually pay the outstanding balance of the mortgage in the event of death. There may also be credit insurance on some of the deceased's credit cards.

INSURANCE AND OTHER BENEFITS

Life Insurance Policies

The deceased may have a life insurance policy through his or her place of employment. He or she may also have purchased insurance privately. If there is a designated beneficiary on such policies, the policy death benefit does not become part of the estate and need not be dealt with by the estate trustee. However, as the estate trustee possesses information concerning the deceased and the death, the estate trustee usually assists with the redemption of life insurance policies and other benefits. The insurance company should be contacted in order to determine what is required to pay out the death benefit. At a minimum the insurer usually requires the original insurance policy, a funeral director's statement of death, and the completion of its own claimant's statement.

Canada Pension Plan Benefits

There may be employee and government death benefits to which the estate is entitled. If the deceased contributed to the Canadian Pension Plan, an application should be made for the death benefit. If the deceased left behind a spouse and/or dependent children, an application should be made on their behalf for survivor benefits.

Other Death Benefits

Depending on the deceased's circumstances and the circumstances surrounding the deceased's death, there may be other death benefits available to the estate and/or the survivors. If the deceased died as a result of a motor vehicle accident, there may be automobile insurance benefits available. If the deceased died as a result of a workplace accident, there may be worker's compensation benefits available.[12] Some employee health and pension plans also provide death and survivor benefits. The estate trustee should contact the deceased's employer and/or benefit provider to determine whether there are any such benefits available.

IDENTIFYING AND LOCATING BENEFICIARIES

The estate trustee must determine who the beneficiaries of the estate are. If there is a will, the will should be reviewed as a starting point to determining beneficiaries. Without a will, inquiries must be made as to possible beneficiaries. In some cases birth, death, and marriage records may need to be searched.

---

[12] In Ontario, in the event of death resulting from a workplace accident, there may be benefits available to the estate and the surviving family from the Workplace Safety and Insurance Board.

Recognition of illegitimate children

The estate trustee has a duty to identify and locate all beneficiaries. Inquiries should be made by the estate trustee to determine if there are any children born outside of the deceased's or any beneficiary's marriage. Illegitimate children are fully recognized at law. There is no distinction, in estate legislation, as to whether children were born within or outside the confines of marriage. The deceased's will, however, may contain a clause excluding any children born out of wedlock. The will could also exclude illegitimate adult children by defining children to include only those named in the definitions or interpretations sections of their will. An example of such a clause might be as follows:

> Children as referred to in this will shall mean my son, Jason Oliver Collins, and my daughter, Angela Louise Collins.

Half-siblings

Half-siblings who share one parent are considered at law to be full-blooded relatives. If the will or intestacy laws provide for a share of the estate to go to a sibling, half-siblings would be included to the same extent as full-blooded siblings.

Alternate Beneficiaries

For every gift made in a will, an alternate beneficiary should be named. The alternate beneficiary would replace the original beneficiary if that beneficiary predeceased the testator. One or more alternate beneficiaries may be named.

Lapses

If an alternate beneficiary has not been named in a will and the beneficiary has predeceased the testator, the gift is said to **lapse**. The property that is the subject of the lapse becomes part of the **residue** of the estate. The residue will be distributed to the residuary beneficiaries.

Anti-lapse Provisions

In some cases, where the beneficiary is a child, grandchild, or sibling of the deceased, the law provides, through **anti-lapse provisions**, that the gift will not lapse but will pass to the deceased beneficiary's heirs, usually meaning the beneficiary's spouse and/or children.[13]

Gifts made to a charity do not lapse. If the charity no longer exists at the time of death, the estate trustee can apply to the court using the **cy-près doctrine** to have the court make an order permitting the gift to be given to a charity with a similar purpose. The Office of the Public Guardian and Trustee must be served with such an application.

DISTRIBUTING THE ESTATE

Once an estate trustee has attended to the deceased's debts and other estate matters, he or she can arrange for the distribution of the estate.

According to the Will

The estate trustee, in distributing the estate, must follow the provisions of the deceased's will unless there is a court order authorizing him or her to do otherwise. Gifts given outright in the will to beneficiaries who have reached the age of majority should be given. The estate trustee should always secure a written release from a beneficiary before paying out an inheritance. If

[13] *Succession Law Reform Act*, R.S.O. 1990, c. S.26, s. 31.

a beneficiary is under the age of majority, there may be a trust set out in the will into which the minor's inheritance should be paid. In the event that the will does not contain instructions for a testamentary trust and the beneficiary is a minor, the share will have to be paid by the estate trustee into court until the minor is of the age of majority. The public accountant of the court will arrange for interest to be accumulated on such funds.

Ademption and Abatement

If the subject of a gift no longer exists at the date of death, the gift is said to have adeemed. When **ademption** has occurred, the gift cannot be made. The estate trustee cannot substitute other property for the lost item. For example, Marie stated in her will that her niece, Sylvia, was to receive her emerald ring. However, Marie lost the ring three years before her death. The gift would adeem and Sylvia would not receive the ring or anything in its place.

Sometimes there is not enough money in the estate to pay the creditors and the beneficiaries. If this situation occurs, the estate trustee must abate some of the beneficiaries' legacies in order to obtain the necessary funds to pay the creditors. The beneficiaries' legacies will be reduced. Gifts of residue are the first in line to be reduced or used entirely to pay creditors. If the residue is insufficient to pay the creditors, then general legacies, followed by **demonstrative legacies** and **specific legacies**, are reduced or taken to pay creditors. The last gift to abate is a gift of real property, also known as a devise.

The order of **abatement** of gifts is as follows:

1. Residue is the first part of the estate to be abated in order to pay creditors.
2. General legacies then abate.
3. Demonstrative legacies abate next.
4. Specific legacies abate last, with real estate devises being the final specific legacy to be abated.

An example of a situation where abatement would occur would be a case where the estate consisted of a car, a bank account containing $10,000 and cash of $10,000. The estate's creditors in this case are owed $14,000. The deceased's will left the car to her brother and $10,000 from her bank account to a friend. As the creditors must be paid first, the friend's demonstrative legacy of $10,000 would have to be reduced by $4,000 to pay the creditors. As there was no residue in the estate and no general legacies, the demonstrative legacy had to be abated. As the abatement of the gift of the bank account was sufficient to pay creditors, the specific legacy was passed on intact. The deceased's brother received the car, and the friend received the balance of $6,000 from the account.

Trusts and Life Interests

The executor must establish any testamentary trusts set out in the will. Assets may need to be liquidated to obtain the funds required for such trusts. There may also be life interests granted that will have to be respected. For example, the deceased's will may give the surviving spouse a **life interest** in her late husband's house. She then has the right to use the property until her death. If she does not live there, she may rent out the property.

Investing

The will itself may contain instructions or suggestions as to how to invest the assets of the estate. If the will is silent in this regard or the deceased died intestate, the *Trustee Act* for the deceased's jurisdiction sets out the standard to be followed by the estate trustee. In Ontario, for example, a trustee, including an estate trustee, must invest funds as a prudent investor would.[14]

Intestate Distribution

If a will cannot be found, the law presumes that the deceased never made a will or that he or she had a will but destroyed it. Where the deceased died without a valid will in place, the provincial or territorial intestacy laws must be adhered to. On occasion, even with a will, there may be a partial intestacy. This situation could occur where a will does not contain a residue clause. The executor would have to follow provincial or territorial intestacy laws to distribute the residue of the estate in such a case.

DISTRIBUTION OF PARTICULAR ASSETS

Bank Deposits

In most cases, the deceased will have been the owner of one or more bank accounts at the time of death. If the deceased had a joint bank account, the surviving owner of the account, in most cases, automatically becomes the sole owner of the account by right of survivorship.[15] The surviving owner should provide the bank with proof of death of the deceased and request that the account be put into the surviving owner's name alone.

The estate trustee should contact the deceased's banks to determine if they require a certificate of estate trustee in order to transfer the deceased's funds. In most cases, the estate trustee will set up an estate bank account. The deceased's accounts should be closed and the funds transferred to the estate bank account. If there is a certificate of appointment of estate trustee, the bank will generally require the certificate, proof of death and a letter requesting the closure of the account and the transfer of funds to the estate bank account. Without a certificate the bank will need a notarized copy of the will, proof of death, and an indemnity in favour of the bank, signed by the estate trustee, promising that if the funds are wrongly paid out the estate trustee will be liable for their repayment. Some banks also require a declaration of transmission. A declaration of transmission is a document from the estate trustee that sets out information about the deceased, the deceased's death, and the deceased's debts. A letter should be sent to the bank inquiring whether the deceased held any other accounts or investments, including Guaranteed Investment Certificates (GICs), other investments certificates, RRSPS, RRIFS or locked in pension funds with the bank. The letter should also request information as to whether there are any outstanding loans, credit cards, lines of credit or other debts with the bank. The estate trustee should also ask if the deceased has a safety deposit box at the bank.

Real Property

Real property, including land, houses, cottages, and condominiums, is one of the most complex estate assets to deal with. If the deceased owned any real property, the estate trustee must make inquiries as to various matters concerning the property. There are searches to be done, consents to be obtained

---

[14] *Trustee Act*, R.S.O. 1990, c. T.23.

[15] In some cases, even though the account is joint in the sense that it has two or more owners, it may not be a true joint account. For example, an elderly parent may put an adult child on as a signatory to the account to help with banking, but the child never deposits funds to, or uses, the account otherwise. The estate trustee in such a situation will have to determine if it was a true joint account passing solely to the child named on the account, or whether the account funds should become part of the estate.

and special documents to be prepared. The assistance of a lawyer regarding transfers of real property to and from an estate is recommended.

If there is a mortgage on the property the estate trustee should make inquiries to determine if there is insurance on the mortgage that would pay the outstanding balance on the mortgage. If a person inherits a property with a mortgage on it, that person receives the property subject to the mortgage.[16]

A subsearch of the title of the property should also be arranged to determine the names of the owners on title. The subsearch will also reveal whether there are any mortgages or other encumbrances on title. The manner in which title to the property is held should also be noted. If, for example, the property is owned in joint tenancy, in most cases, title to the property automatically passes to the remaining owner(s) upon the death of the other owner. Property held in joint tenancy usually does not become part of the deceased's estate. However, if the property is a matrimonial home held in joint tenancy with someone other than the surviving spouse, the joint tenancy is severed at the time of death and the deceased's share of the property becomes part of the estate.

Real property laws vary from province to province and territory in Canada. Accordingly, the law that must be utilized is that of the province or territory where the property is located. In Ontario, for example, there are currently two systems of land registration: the registry system and the land titles system. The laws for each system differ. For example, in the registry system, if the deceased left a valid will, the will itself may be used for the transfer of the property. A certificate of appointment of estate trustee with a will is not required. However, in the land titles system, in most circumstances, even where there is a will, a certificate of estate trustee is required to transfer the property.[17]

Corporate Shares and Bonds

The deceased may have owned shares in a public or a private corporation at the time of his or her death. The estate trustee may require the assistance of a transfer agent or stockbroker to assist with the transfer of shares. The estate trustee should ask what is required for the transfer of the shares to the estate trustee or, in some cases, directly to a beneficiary. The estate trustee will also need to determine the value of the shares as of their date of purchase and as of the date of death for estate administration and income tax purposes. A stockbroker can assist with the valuation. The documentation required to transfer shares usually includes the share certificates endorsed by the estate trustee, a notarized copy of the certificate of appointment of estate trustee, a declaration of transmission from the estate trustee setting out information about the deceased and the deceased's debts in order to permit the transfer, a letter of direction from the estate trustees to the agent confirming their agreement to the transfer, and a guaranty of the estate trustee's signature proving that it is indeed the signature of the estate trustee. The estate trustees can have their signatures guaranteed by their banks. In some cases, particularly if the estate trustee is not in possession of the share certificates, a power of attorney to transfer the shares may be required. If there is a will, in some instances, the transfer agent may be able to transfer the shares without a certificate of estate trustee. However, not all transfer agents will do so. Without a will, a certificate of estate trustee is

---

[16] Forms of property other than real property are usually inherited on a debt-free basis. For example, if someone inherits a car with a loan outstanding on it, the estate pays off the loan.

[17] Under the Ontario *Land Titles Act*, R.S.O. 1990, c. L.5, a certificate of estate trustee is not required in the land titles system where the land registrar waives the certificate and the value of the estate is under $50,000.

almost always required in order to transfer shares due to the fact that, in the absence of a will or a certificate of estate trustee, there is no one authorized to represent the estate.

The deceased at the time of death may have owned corporate bonds. The bond itself generally sets out the face value, the interest rate, and when the interest is to be paid. The documentation required to transfer corporate bonds is the same as the documentation set out above for shares, with the exception of the shares themselves. For bonds, the bonds endorsed by the estate trustee or a power of attorney to transfer the bonds is required.

Canada Savings Bonds

The estate trustee should search for any Canada Savings Bonds that the deceased may own. The deceased's pay stubs may indicate that he or she had been purchasing Canada Savings Bonds through payroll deductions. The Bank of Canada can provide information as to any bonds owned by the deceased. If the deceased had Canada Savings Bonds worth $200,000 or less and the recipient of the bonds or their proceeds will be the deceased's spouse, a certificate of estate trustee is not required. If the recipient is not the deceased's spouse, a certificate is not required if the bonds are worth under $20,000. In order to transfer or pay out the bonds, the Bank of Canada will require a notarized copy of the will, if there is one; the bonds; proof of death; a letter of direction from the estate trustee(s) indicating their consent to the redemption or transfer of the bonds; and the bank's completed Form 534C.

Registered Retirement Savings Plans

The deceased may have a Registered Retirement Savings Plan (RRSP) or a Registered Retirement Income Fund (RRIF). The estate trustee should review the plan documents and statements to determine if there is a named beneficiary. The deceased's will should also be reviewed to determine if a beneficiary has been named in the will. The latest named beneficiary is the beneficiary. The beneficiary will receive the full proceeds of the RRSP, although, in most cases, the proceeds of the RRSP will be taxable on the deceased's final income tax return as a result of the deemed disposition of assets upon death. The estate has to pay the income tax on the RRSP proceeds from other assets.

The income tax consequences of RRSPs should be taken into consideration during the estate planning process. If, for example, the deceased had two children and she left a GIC worth $50,000 to one child and named her other child as the beneficiary of her $50,000 RRSP, assuming that there were no other assets, the child receiving the RRSP would receive $50,000. The child receiving the GIC, however, would receive less than the full $50,000 because some of the GIC funds would have to be used to pay the income taxes that were incurred as a result of the inclusion of the value of the RRSP funds on the deceased's final income tax return.

The RRSP funds must be included in the deceased's income as a result of the deemed disposition of assets upon death. As income tax has yet to be paid on such funds, the accumulated funds must now be reported and income tax be paid on them. During one's lifetime, RRSP contributions are deducted from income for income tax purposes, and the funds accumulate on a tax-deferred basis. RRSP funds are taxed only when they are withdrawn from the fund or upon the death of the fund owner. Depending on the deceased's tax bracket, the child receiving the GIC might, for example, receive only $30,000 because the sum of $20,000 would have to be used to pay income taxes. The deceased could have named the estate as beneficiary of the RRSP. If the children were named as equal beneficiaries of the estate, the funds to pay the income tax on the RRSP would be taken out of the estate itself, and the remaining funds from both the GIC and the RRSP would be divided equally between the two children. The only disadvantage of this course of action is that the value of the RRSP would have to be included in the estate, thereby increasing the amount of estate administration tax payable.

There is an advantage, in some circumstances, to naming the estate as the beneficiary on an RRSP, as the beneficiaries under the will would not have to share any income generated by their inheritance with their spouse upon any marriage breakdown if the deceased's will contained the standard family law clause.

If the beneficiary of the RRSP or RRIF is the deceased's spouse, including most common law spouses, a rollover of the deceased's RRSP/RRIF funds into the surviving spouse's RRSP is permitted. This rollover has the advantage of postponing income tax payable on the RRSP until the surviving spouse removes funds from the plan or dies. Taxes deferred are usually taxes saved. By the time the surviving spouse cashes in the RRSP or dies, he or she will usually have retired and may be in a lower tax bracket than the deceased may have been in at the time of the deceased's death.

In order to cash out or transfer the RRSP, the holder of the plan will require proof of death, a completed claimant's statement, and a copy of the certificate of appointment of estate trustee, if there is one. If there is no certificate but there is a will, a copy of the will is required.

Other Assets

The deceased likely owned other property at the time of his or her death. He or she likely owned some clothing, jewellery, furniture, household appliances and other items. The deceased's will should be consulted to determine how these assets should be distributed. Some wills give the estate trustee discretion to dispose of clothing and other items of nominal value as he or she sees fit, including making a donation of same to a charitable organization. Without a will, such items often have to be sold by estate auction or otherwise, with the proceeds going into the estate to be distributed in accordance with intestacy laws. For special items of value, such as jewellery, collectibles or antiques, the estate trustee may have to obtain valuations from qualified appraisers. If the deceased owned a motor vehicle at the time of death, the local Ministry of Transportation should be consulted in order to determine what documentation will be required for the sale or transfer of the vehicle. The insurer of the vehicle should be advised of the death.

ESTATE TRUSTEE COMPENSATION

On Consent

An estate trustee is entitled to compensation for his or her efforts in administering the estate. Some jurisdictions have legislation setting out the rates of compensation. Other jurisdictions rely on the common law principles of compensation. In Ontario, the *Trustee Act*[18] states that a trustee, guardian or personal representative is entitled to such fair and reasonable allowance for the care, pains and trouble, and the time expended in and about the estate, as may be allowed by a judge of the Superior Court of Justice. The *Trustee Act* also provides that the amount of compensation may be settled, although the estate is not before the court in an action.[19] In some cases this permits the estate trustee and the beneficiaries of the estate to reach an agreement, outside of the courts, as to estate trustee compensation. Such an agree-

[18] R.S.O. 1990, c. T.23, s. 61(1).
[19] *Trustee Act*, R.S.O. 1990, c. T.23, s. 61(2).

ment would not be possible if the deceased died without a will and there were minor children involved because the Office of the Children's Lawyer usually requires the court to approve such compensation.

Where the quantum of estate trustee compensation can be agreed upon by the parties, the estate trustee should provide the beneficiaries with a summary of the funds entering and leaving the estate along with a list of estate expenditures. A statement of proposed compensation should also be included. The estate trustee should include a breakdown of the proposed distribution of the estate. The estate trustee also sends each beneficiary a release form with the statements. If the beneficiary agrees with the estate summary, proposed estate trustee compensation, and proposed distribution of the estate, he or she signs the release and returns it to the estate trustee. An estate trustee should never pay out estate funds to beneficiaries without first obtaining a signed release. Minor and incompetent beneficiaries cannot give a valid release. In those cases, a passing of accounts before the court may be necessary.

In some cases an estate trustee does not take any compensation for his or her work. If the estate trustee is the sole beneficiary of the estate, it would not be in the estate trustee's best interests to take executor's compensation, which is considered to be taxable income. Such income must be reported on the executor's annual personal income tax return. Inheritances, on the other hand, are not taxable income. If the estate trustee is a close family member and does not wish to take funds out of the estate, he or she may waive compensation, preferring to act out of natural love and affection.

If an estate trustee is also a beneficiary, unless the will says otherwise, there is a presumption, albeit a rebuttable one, that the estate trustee will not take compensation because the inheritance is compensation enough.

Passing of Accounts Although it is easier, quicker, and less expensive to have the estate trustee's accounts and compensation approved by the beneficiaries, such a procedure cannot always take place. On occasion, a formal **passing of accounts** is required through the courts to approve the executor's accounts and compensation and permit the estate to be closed. If a beneficiary, for example, refuses to approve the executor's accounts, the executor will have no choice but to have the courts pass the accounts.

The passing of accounts in court is a process whereby the estate trustee submits his or her accounts, estate statements, and request for compensation to the court for scrutiny by a judge. Original receipts and statements, collectively known as "vouchers", must be available for review by the judge. Any trustee, including an estate trustee, can apply to the court to pass their accounts. As well, anyone who appears to have a financial interest in the estate can ask the court for an order that an estate trustee pass his or her accounts.[20] Such an order could be sought by beneficiaries, contingent beneficiaries, creditors or other parties who appear to have a financial interest in the estate.

The estate trustee's accounts should include a statement of the original assets in the estate, along with statements of **capital receipts** and disbursements, and revenue receipts and disbursements. Capital receipts include property that came into the estate, such as real estate. **Capital disbursements** relate to the payment of property out of the estate, such as the payment of estate administration taxes or the payment of legacies to beneficiaries. The accounts must also include a statement of revenue receipts and one of reve-

---

[20] Rule 74.15(1)(h) of The Ontario *Rules of Civil Procedure*, R.R.O. 1990, Reg. 194.

nue disbursements. **Revenue receipts** relate to monies earned by the estate on its assets, such as bank account interest. **Revenue disbursements** relate to funds spent to maintain income-generating property. An example of a revenue disbursement would be the payment of a bank service charge. The accounts should include a summary page of capital and revenue receipts and disbursements, along with a statement of investments, a statement of unrealized assets left in the estate, and statements of the proposed distribution of the estate, as well as the estate trustee's proposed compensation. If there are any liabilities to the estate that remain to be dealt with, they should be set out on a statement as well. The accounts are accompanied by a Notice of Application setting out the court date and an affidavit verifying the accounts. The application and the affidavit must be served on everyone who appears to have an interest in the estate, along with a blank notice of objection form inviting the recipient to object to the accounts. The judge at the passing of accounts will scrutinize the statements and determine if items have been properly appropriated between capital and revenue. The judge will determine if the compensation claimed by the estate trustee is reasonable and will make an order regarding the accounts and the executor's compensation. Although the court determines each case on its own merits, there are five factors that the court considers in determining executor's compensation:[21]

1. The size of the trust
2. The care, responsibility and risks assumed by the trustee
3. The time spent by the trustee carrying out his or her responsibilities
4. The skill and ability displayed by the trustee
5. The results obtained and the degree of success associated with the trustee's efforts

Over the years the courts have developed an informal tariff that they apply to compensation for estate trustees. This tariff is used in Ontario and other jurisdictions where compensation has not been fixed by legislation. The estate trustee is generally awarded compensation comprising the following:

1. The sum of 2.5% of the capital receipts of the estate
2. The sum of 2.5% of the capital disbursements of the estate
3. The sum of 2.5% of the revenue receipts of the estate
4. The sum of 2.5% of the revenue disbursements of the estate

Many people equate executor fees with the sum of 5 percent of the value of the estate. While not strictly accurate, in a straightforward estate that is administered in a very timely fashion, the executor may only have capital receipts and disbursements to deal with as revenue receipts and disbursements generally accrue in a more drawn out estate. If capital property entered the estate at the time of death and was distributed soon thereafter, the estate trustee would claim 2.5 percent of capital receipts plus 2.5 percent of capital disbursements for a total of 5 percent. If the estate is a particularly complex one, the estate trustee can also ask the court to award a care and management fee totalling two-fifths of 1 percent of the value of the estate. In some cases, the executor and the testator sign a compensation agreement predetermining the amount of estate trustee compensation. Trust companies that have been asked to act as estate trustee have the testator sign a compensa-

[21] *Laing Estate v. Laing Estate*, (sub nom. *Logan v. Laing Estate*) 11 E.T.R. (2d) 268 (Ont. Div. Ct) which was affirmed by the Ontario Court of Appeal at 41 OR (3d) 571.

tion agreement, with the rate of compensation usually being more than the usual tariff applied by the court. If there is more than one estate trustee, the trustees themselves must decide how the fee will be shared.

Unless there is an accusation of fraud, accounts passed by the court should not be re-examined at a later date.

Releases

Once the accounts have been approved by the court, the estate trustee can distribute the estate in accordance with the distribution statement presented to the court and in accordance with the deceased's will or the intestacy laws. Prior to paying the beneficiaries their inheritances, the estate trustee should have each beneficiary sign a release acknowledging that the beneficiary accepts the proposed distribution as his or her inheritance and absolves the estate trustee from liability. If the court has approved the proposed distribution, releases are not required.

ESTATE LITIGATION

The three most common types of estate litigation involve claims for support by dependants of the deceased, matrimonial property claims against the estate, and challenges to the will.

Dependants' Relief Claims

Who Are the Dependants?

Dependants are those persons when the deceased was supporting or was obligated by law to support at the time of his or her death. Support is given a broad interpretation. It includes not only the payment of financial support but other situations where support is less visible, such as the situation where a couple resided together and both purchased groceries and other household items. When one dies, the other loses the support of the deceased towards family purchases. Each jurisdiction has its own legislation setting out provisions for dependants to seek support from the estate. In Ontario, Part V of the *Succession Law Reform Act*[22] governs dependant's relief. Such legislation generally includes spouses, both married and common law, and same-sex spouses. Under Ontario legislation spouses are considered common law if they cohabited continuously for three or more years or were in a relationship of some permanence and had a child together. Under Ontario legislation other potential dependants include children, both natural and adopted, and those the deceased had a settled intention to treat as his or her own child. Children conceived as of the date of death but not yet born may be dependants upon their birth. Parents of the deceased, or grandparents and someone who demonstrated a settled intention to treat the deceased as their child, may also be dependants. Siblings may be dependants as well.

The person claiming dependant's relief from the estate must be a member of one of the categories of dependants set out above. As well, the deceased must have been supporting the alleged dependant at the time of death or have been under a legal obligation to support the dependant. Spouses have a legal obligation to support each other unless they have signed a domestic contract relieving each other from such an obligation. Parents are obligated to support their children, and adult children are obligated to support their parents under the Ontario *Family Law Act*.[23] There is no obligation at law to support one's siblings. However, if the deceased was supporting his or

---

[22] R.S.O. 1990, c. S.26.

her sibling, there may be a continuing obligation to do so. In some instances there may a court order or agreement that obligated the deceased to pay support. Whether or not such support was being paid, there is an obligation to the dependants in whose favour the order was made. The order can be enforced against the estate.

Making the Claim

The dependant claims support from the estate by commencing an application in the Superior Court of Justice in the county where the deceased lived. The application can be brought by the dependant or, in the case of a minor, by the dependant's parent. In some cases the Ministry of Community and Social Services brings an application on behalf of someone who is receiving social assistance benefits. The applicant must file an affidavit that sets out the grounds for the claim. The application must be made within six months from the date that the certificate of estate trustee was granted.[23] The court considers the claimant's assets, income, present and future needs, health, and other factors when setting the quantum of support. The court may grant temporary and/or permanent relief. Support may be ordered to be paid in a lump sum or by ongoing payments, which may be limited to a certain time period or may be ordered to be paid indefinitely. If support is ordered to be paid indefinitely and the dependant's circumstances change — for example, the dependant remarries — the estate can apply for a variation of the original order to reduce or end the support payments.

Matrimonial Property Legislation Claims

Every jurisdiction has family law legislation stipulating how assets should be divided upon a marriage breakdown. Marriage breakdown generally includes separation, divorce, and death. Some legislation, such as Ontario's *Family Law Act*,[24] contains property division provisions that apply only to legally married spouses. Legislation in some other jurisdictions also applies to common law spouses.[25]

Notifying the Surviving Spouse

If the deceased was married at the time of death, the estate trustee should advise the surviving spouse, in writing, that he or she should seek independent legal advice in regard to any claims that he or she might have against the estate. The estate trustee should not distribute any part of the estate in the six months following the deceased's death without obtaining the consent of the surviving spouse.

Election by the Surviving Spouse

A surviving spouse should consult with a lawyer to determine whether it would be in his or her best interests to elect an **equalization of net family property**. If the deceased's will provides that the surviving spouse is to share the estate with other beneficiaries, it may be financially advantageous for the spouse to decline his or her share under the will and elect an equalization payment. If, for example, the deceased had children and died intestate, and the estate is worth more than the preferential share ($200,000

---

[23] *Succession Law Reform Act*, R.S.O. 1990, c. S.26, s. 61.

[24] R.S.O. 1990, c. F.3, Part II covers the division of property.

[25] In Manitoba and Nova Scotia, common-law partners can register their partnership under the provincial *Vital Statistics Act*s to obtain the same property rights as legally married spouses. In British Columbia, the *Estates Administration Act* provides that after two years of residing together common law, spouses have the same rights on intestacy as legally married spouses.

in Ontario), it may be to the surviving spouse's advantage to elect an equalization of family property. Generally speaking, the surviving spouse is entitled to one-half of the difference in the net family property of the deceased and the surviving spouse's. For example, if the deceased's net family property was $400,000 and the surviving spouse's net family property was $100,000, the surviving spouse would be entitled to an equalization payment of $150,000. If the spouse were left only $100,000 under a will, then an equalization would be more favourable. However, in these circumstances, if the deceased died intestate, then the spouse would be better off financially to take the preferential share of $200,000 plus a portion of the distributive share of the estate, such share varying depending on whether there is one child, or two or more children.

There are certain items that each spouse can deduct or exclude from their net family property, such as property (other than the matrimonial home) owned on the date of marriage, damages received for personal injuries, and inheritances. A spouse's property is valued as of the day before the date of death in order to include assets such as the cash value of life insurance policies and property held in joint tenancy.

The surviving spouse, under Ontario's *Family Law Act*, has six months from the date of death to elect to make an equalization of net family property.[26] An election form is filed with the Ontario Estate Registrar, and a court application is commenced. The spouse will also have to file an affidavit and a financial statement with the court. The estate trustee will have to file a financial statement for the estate.

Challenges to the Will

Improper Execution

In order to be valid a will must be signed by the testator. If it is a holograph will, it must also be entirely handwritten by the testator. If it is a formally attested will, it must have been signed by the testator in the presence of two or more witnesses, who both sign in the presence of each other and the testator. An affidavit of execution sworn by one of the witnesses is generally sufficient evidence of proper execution. On occasion, however, solemn proof of the will's execution is required. Such proof is provided by having one of the witnesses testify under oath in court as to the will's proper execution. Sometimes a will is invalid because it was witnessed by only one person. On other occasions it is discovered that both witnesses were not present when the testator signed the will. A will that has not been properly executed may be set aside. The burden of proving proper execution of the will is placed upon the **propounder** of the will. The propounder is the person trying to uphold the will's validity.

Lack of Testamentary Capacity

At the time of giving instructions for the will and at the time of signing the will, the testator must possess the testamentary capacity to make a will. This generally means that the testator must be aware that he or she is making a will; the testator knows the extent of his or her property; and the testator understands the consequences of his or her will and his or her moral obligations.[27]

If a person who appears to have an interest in the estate believes that the testator did not have the requisite testamentary capacity to make a will, that person can ask the court to set aside the will. The testator's prior will

[26] *Family Law Act*, R.S.O. 1990, c. F.3, s. 7(1).
[27] *Banks v. Goodfellow*, (1870) L.R. 5 Q.B. 549.

would then become the binding will. If there was no prior will, the estate would then be distributed in accordance with intestacy laws.

Lack of Knowledge and Approval of the Will's Contents

In order for a will to be valid, the testator must have had knowledge of, and have approved, the will's contents. Lawyers generally ensure that this is done by mailing a draft of the will to the client along with written instructions to the testator to read over the will to ensure that it meets with their approval. At the signing of the will the lawyer also reviews the will with the testator and has the testator initial the bottom of each page before signing the will.

In some cases there is both a lack of testamentary capacity and a lack of knowledge and approval of the will's contents.

Undue Influence

If a testator was subjected to **undue influence** by someone to make and execute a will, the will is invalid. The undue influence may be physical or emotional. Undue influence occurs when the testator is pressured or coerced by someone to sign a will that does not reflect his or her true wishes. In order to set aside the will on the grounds of undue influence, the person impugning the will must prove on a balance of probabilities that the testator was unduly influenced to sign the will. The **impugner** is the party that is trying to strike down the will. Undue influence may be suspected, for example, where the testator makes a new will, leaving the bulk of his or her estate to his or her new caregiver. The caregiver may have arranged the appointment with the lawyer and attended with the testator to ensure that he or she was included in the will. In these circumstances, the testator may have been unduly influenced to make the new will. The testator may have believed that he or she would be mistreated or abandoned by the caregiver if he or she did not change the will or make a new will.

CHAPTER SUMMARY

In this chapter the reader was introduced to the main elements of estate administration. There was a discussion of the roles and responsibilities of estate trustees with or without a will. Some attention was given to the responsibilities of the estate trustee, including dealing with the deceased's remains and dependants. The importance of locating and reviewing the deceased's will, contracts, and assets was covered. The process of obtaining court certificates, including the calculation of estate administration tax and the provision of administration bonds, was also examined. Finding and paying estate creditors, including the Canada Revenue Agency, is discussed. Insurance, particularly life insurance and other benefits such as Canada Pension Plan benefits and allowances, were examined. The steps in identifying and locating beneficiaries were given. Difficulties with the distribution of the estate, including lapses, ademption, and abatement, were also covered. Other areas of responsibility, such as investing and intestate distribution, were briefly examined. Some instruction was given as to the distribution of particular assets, such as real property, shares, bonds, bank deposits, and RRSPS. The process of passing accounts on consent and in court were discussed. The chapter concluded with a look at three common areas of estate litigation: dependant's relief claims, matrimonial property legislation claims, and challenges to the will.

GLOSSARY OF NEW TERMS AND KEY CONCEPTS

abatement	The process whereby residue and gifts made under a will are reduced in order to pay estate creditors.
accounts	Records of the property entering and leaving the estate.
ademption	The situation where the subject of a gift made in a will no longer exists at the date of death. For example, a testator leaves a car to his nephew in his will, but the car is sold before the testator's death.
administrator	A male appointed by the court to administer an intestate estate.
administratrix	A female appointed by the court to administer an intestate estate.
ancillary grant	The court grant given where the estate trustee has a will and a court certificate from outside of Canada, the United Kingdom and any British possession.
anti-lapse provisions	Legislation that permits a deceased beneficiary's heirs to take their inheritance where the beneficiary has predeceased the testator. In Ontario the anti-lapse provisions apply to a beneficiary's child, grandchild, or sibling.
capital disbursements	Property leaving the estate.
capital gain	The increase in the value of property from the date of purchase to the date of disposition.
capital receipts	Property coming into the estate.
certificate of appointment of estate trustee with a will	A document granted by the court that certifies that the will is the last valid will of the deceased and that confirms the appointment of the estate trustee.
certificate of appointment of estate trustee without a will	A document granted by the court appointing someone to administer the intestate estate.
certificate of estate trustee during litigation	A document appointing an estate trustee, by court order, to act for the estate during estate litigation. This trustee cannot distribute the estate without a court order.
clearance certificate	A certificate from the Canada Revenue Agency that confirms that all of the deceased's income tax returns have been filed and that any taxes, interest, or penalties have been paid.
custodian	The person appointed to have custody and care of minor children.
cy-prés doctrine	Provision whereby a gift made in a will to a charity may be redirected by the court to another charity with similar purposes to the original charity where the original charity no longer exists.
donatio mortis causa	A gift made in contemplation of death and conditional upon the donor's death occurring.
deemed disposition	The situation where the deceased is considered to have disposed of all of his or her property at the time of his or her death for income tax purposes.
demonstrative legacy	A gift to be paid from a specific source. For example, "I leave to my niece $5,000 from my investment account at ABC Bank Ltd."
devolution	The situation where an executor dies, and his or her executor takes over the administration of an estate.
equalization of net family property	The process whereby spouses determine the net value of their property as of the date of marriage and the valuation date (in estate situations, the day before the date of death). If the value of the deceased's net family property is greater than the surviving spouse's, the surviving spouse may elect an equalization of net family property in place of a gift under a will or the application of intestacy distribution laws.
estate administration bond	A promise by the estate trustee to fulfill the estate obligations, and a promise by the estate trustee and a third party to indemnify any beneficiaries and creditors who have

suffered a loss as a result of any failure by the estate trustee to carry out his or her duties.

estate administration tax	A tax that must be paid to the court based on the value of the deceased's estate when obtaining a certificate of estate trustee from the court.
estate trustee with a will	The person named in the will to administer the estate.
estate trustee without a will	The person appointed by the court to administer an intestate estate.
executor	A male person appointed in a will to administer the estate.
executrix	A female person appointed in a will to administer the estate.
guardian of property	The person appointed to manage someone else's person or property. For example, a minor child requires a guardian of property.
impugner	The person trying to strike down the will.
joint tenancy	A method of holding title to property whereby if one owner dies the remaining joint owners automatically become the owner(s) of the property by right of survivorship.
lapse	The situation that occurs where a beneficiary has predeceased the testator and an alternate beneficiary has not been named in the will.
letters of administration	A court grant appointing someone to administer an intestate estate.
letters probate	A court grant confirming the appointment of an executor named in a will to act and confirming the validity of the will as the last valid will.
life interest	The situation where someone is granted the use of a property for the remainder of his or her life.
mausoleum	An above ground tomb.
passing of accounts	The process whereby a trustee submits his or her records, statements, accounts, and receipts to the court for approval.
precatory	Precatory requests or directions are an expression of the testator's wishes regarding his or her estate. These requests or directions are not legally binding.
probate fees	A tax charged by the court on the value of the estate when obtaining a certificate of estate trustee from the court.
propounder	The person trying to uphold the will.
resealing	The application of the Ontario court seal to a certificate of estate trustee with or without a will made in another province, the United Kingdom, or a British possession.
residue	The part of the estate remaining after all legacies have been paid.
revenue disbursements	Money spent to maintain an income-generating property.
revenue receipts	Income generated by estate assets.
specific legacy	A gift of a particular item: for example, my Rolex watch to my son.
spousal trust	A trust in favour of a spouse where all of the income must be paid only to the spouse during the spouse's lifetime, and no one else is entitled to any of the capital during the spouse's lifetime.
surety	Someone who promises to pay money if the estate trustee fails to carry out his or her duties properly.
trust	A relationship wherein property is transferred from one person, the settlor or testator, to another person, the trustee, to be held by the trustee for the benefit of a third party, namely the beneficiary. The relationship is governed by the instrument that establishes the trust and by the legislation and case law governing trusts.
undue influence	The situation wherein a testator was emotionally or physically coerced by someone to make or change his or her will such that it no longer reflects the testator's wishes.

REVIEW QUESTIONS

1. How does an estate trustee with a will differ from an estate trustee without a will?

2. What type of funeral arrangements should an estate trustee make?

3. How can you find someone's will?

4. Describe a situation where an estate asset could be transferred without a court certificate.

5. Calculate the estate administration tax that would have to be paid in your jurisdiction on an estate with a net value of $500,000.

6. What is the purpose of an estate administration bond, and how can the estate trustee post security for the administration of the estate?

7. Describe two situations in which the court might dispense with an administration bond.

8. Why would an estate trustee advertise for creditors?

9. Describe two income tax returns that the estate trustee may file.

10. Provide an example of ademption.

11. Why might it be necessary for the estate trustee to pass his or her accounts in court?

12. When should a spouse consider electing an equalization of net family property?

13. Who could be eligible to make a claim for dependant's relief?

14. What is undue influence?

15. What is abatement?

16. Explain estate trustee compensation.

DISCUSSION QUESTIONS

1. Rachel died intestate on October 15, Year 1. She was survived by her spouse, James, and three children: Carol, age 22; Jeremy, age 19; and Ellen, age 15. Rachel had the following assets at the time of her death:

    *   a house worth $200,000 held in joint tenancy with James
    *   a condominium in New York, New York, U.S.A., worth $200,000
    *   life insurance of $100,000 payable to her estate
    *   RRSP worth $50,000 payable to James
    *   a sole bank account with $20,000 in it
    *   Canada Savings Bonds worth $10,000
    *   a car worth $10,000
    *   household items valued at $10,000

        Her only debt is a $5,000 car loan.

    Answer the following questions:

    (a) Calculate the value of the estate for estate administration tax purposes.

    (b) Explain what has been excluded from the estate for estate administration tax purposes.

(c) Explain what has been deducted from the estate for estate administration tax purposes.

(d) Calculate the estate administration tax to be paid, assuming that she died in Ontario.

(e) Who will be the beneficiaries of the estate, and what proportion of the estate will each beneficiary receive?

(f) Who can be appointed as estate trustee?

(g) What matters should be considered for Ellen?

(h) Will a court certificate be required for the transfer of all of the assets? If not, explain.

(i) If Rachel owned an antique desk that she purchased for $1,000 a few years ago, and at the time of her death it was worth $5,000, what would be the income tax treatment of that asset?

2. Allen, an Ontario resident, died on March 2nd, Year 0. He was survived by his spouse, Kelly. They did not have any children. In his will, Allen left Kelly $100,000. At the time of his death, the net value of his estate was $500,000. Answer the following questions:

(a) Should Kelly consider electing an equalization of net family property? Why or why not?

(b) If Kelly decides to make an election, how long does she have to act?

(c) If Kelly decides to make an election, what date will be used as the property valuation date?

(d) What effect would an election by Kelly have on the gift left to her in the will?

(e) What effect would an equalization by Kelly have on the gifts made in the will to other beneficiaries?

3. Frank recently passed away. He was single without dependants. His will leaves his car to his friend Joe. It also leaves $5,000 from his ING Investment Account to his friend Gretchen and $3,000 to his friend Helen. He leaves the residue to his friend William. At death Frank's car is worth $5,000, his ING Investment account has $5,000, and he has $2,000 in loose cash. He owes a credit card debt of $3,000. Describe how the estate will be paid out.

SUGGESTED READINGS

Fazakas, Derek. *Wills and Estates*, 2d Ed. (Toronto, Ont.: Emond-Montgomery, 2004).

Gibbs, Karen M., et al. *The Practical Guide to Ontario Estate Administration*, 4th Ed. (Toronto, Ont.: Carswell, 2001).

Spenceley, Robert. *Estate Administration In Ontario: A Practical Guide* (North York, Ont.: CCH Canadian Limited, 1996).

Intellectual Property Law

Teresa Cheung
BARRISTER AND SOLICITOR

Alex Wellington
RYERSON UNIVERSITY

Learning Objectives

After reading this chapter, the reader should be able to:

➢ define intellectual property, and differentiate the main types of intellectual property

➢ appreciate the importance of intellectual property in contemporary society

➢ recognize the main sources of intellectual property law in Canada

➢ understand the importance of international treaty obligations

➢ know the crucial aspects of patent protection

➢ know the crucial aspects of copyright protection

➢ appreciate the differences between copyright and neighbouring rights

➢ know the crucial aspects of trademark protection

➢ understand the differences between registered marks (statutory) and unregistered trademarks (common law), and the benefits of registration

➢ identify the kind of activities that constitute infringement of intellectual property rights

➢ appreciate the significance of legal protection for trade secrets and confidential information

➢ recognize the range of remedies available in the context of intellectual property litigation

➢ summarize the various remedies that can be granted in intellectual property cases

TABLE OF CONTENTS

INTRODUCTION

The Meaning of Intellectual Property

The phrase "intellectual property" (IP) refers to creations or products of the mind, intangible and incorporeal items, which can be created, owned, and exploited exclusively by an owner (or someone authorized by an owner) for commercial advantage. Such proprietary creations can be inventions; methods; processes; compounds; compositions; literary, artistic, and musical works and performances; and compilations. Intellectual property protection can apply to an almost bewildering array of entities, as can be seen from selective examples: radios, cameras, televisions, exercise machines, mechanical pencils, computer programs, recipes, periwinkle extract, vaccines, antibiotics, and cell lines generated from spleen tissue. Symbols, names, images, and designs used in association with goods and services in trade and commerce are also forms of intellectual property in that they are intangible elements that hold commercial value for the owner.

Intellectual property generates "property rights" that are legally protectable, yet differ in important ways from other property rights, such as those for real property (land and what is attached to land, e.g., houses) or personal property (everything else). The most familiar items that have long attracted intellectual property protection are books, which are protected under copyright law, and mechanical devices (such as a mousetrap), which are protected under patent law. When an author takes pen to paper (or clicks on a keypad to open up a screen) and produces an original work that is then published (or fixed in tangible form), she is legally entitled to prevent others from copying her work without her authorization. The book itself is the carrier of intellectual property, but the book as an object can be bought and sold by many persons without infringing the author's intellectual property rights. Someone who steals the book itself will be committing a theft of property but will not be committing an intellectual property infringement. However, if someone takes the book and photocopies it, or a substantial portion of it, and then sells the photocopy, that person will be infringing the author's copyright. Thus, the book as a literary work subject to copyright protection is distinct from the book as a physical object, or a piece of personal property.

With tangible property, one person's exclusive possession prevents others from making use of the item of property, and the consumption by one person typically prevents simultaneous consumption by others. In terms used by economists, property is both excludable and rival. Most intellectual property, in contrast, is non-rival, since ideas and information can be consumed by many simultaneously. Without legal protection, intellectual property would not naturally be excludable, either. There is normally an inherent "scarcity" with physical property, but not so with intellectual property. Legal protection, in effect, creates an artificial "scarcity" by building legal fences around creations and inventions that provide their creators and inventors with control over how, by whom, and when, the creations and inventions are to be used, or merely accessed. The presumption is that creators and inventors would be reluctant to invest their time, energy, and expertise if others could simply "copy" their creations and inventions without a comparable investment.

Society's rationales for legal measures to protect intellectual property include the following: (i) to appropriately reward creators and inventors for their labour; (ii) to induce potential creators and inventors to produce a social benefit, by providing an incentive; and (iii) the determination, following a calculation of social benefits, that, overall, society will be better off with intellectual property protection than without. Among the benefits society is expected to realize are those arising from technological advancement and innovation and from the transfer and dissemination of technology. There are many public policy debates over where the boundaries are to be drawn between what is legally protected as privately ownable intellectual property and what falls into the "public domain" or the "common heritage of humanity".

The Evolution of Intellectual Property

Intellectual property was formerly thought to be a dry, dense, and overly technical subject in the domain of lawyers or the legally trained. In today's society, intellectual property has become the subject of intense public scrutiny, a *cause célèbre* hotly debated on the editorial pages of newspapers and on blogs, even generating extensive lobbying campaigns on Facebook, the social networking site.[1]

Intellectual property has become a pervasive feature of market economies in the information age and a prominent source of wealth in the knowledge society. International intellectual property agreements have expanded the reach of fundamental intellectual property norms and harmonized substantive legal rules across different countries and legal traditions. The earliest multilateral treaties concerned with intellectual property protection date from the late 1880s — the *Paris Convention for the Protection of Industrial Property* (1883) and the *Berne Convention for the Protection of Literary and Artistic Works* (1886). Canada is a signatory to both those conventions, as well as to the more recent *Rome Convention on the Protection of Performers, Producers of Phonograms and Broadcasting Organizations* (1961). Adherents to international agreements commit themselves to the principle of "**national treatment**", or non-discrimination, ensuring that each country grants the same rights to foreign citizens, residents, and corporations as it grants to its own citizens, residents, and corporations. By becoming a signatory to an international agreement, member countries such as Canada commit themselves to adopt domestic legislation that implements those international commitments.

Canada has signed one of the most high-profile contemporary global agreements, the *Trade-Related Aspects of Intellectual Property, Including Trade in Counterfeit Goods* (TRIPs), administered by the World Trade Organization (Annex 1C to the *World Trade Agreement* of 1994). TRIPs was negotiated at the Uruguay Round of the General Agreement on Tariffs and Trade (GATT). It sets minimum standards for levels of intellectual property protections, as well as enforcement procedures, remedies, and processes for dispute resolution. In addition, the North American Free Trade Agreement (NAFTA), signed by Canada, Mexico, and the United States, includes provisions governing intellectual property protection. See Exhibit 33.1, which shows selected international agreements dealing with intellectual property protection.

Most forms of intellectual property in Canada and around the world are protected under the legal regimes of copyright, patents, and trademarks. Other intellectual property statutes less frequently encountered in Canada are the *Industrial Design Act*, the *Integrated Circuit Topography Act*, and the *Plant Breeders' Rights Act*[2] (See Exhibit 33.2). The common law also protects trade secrets. This chapter focuses predominantly on the legal regimes protecting copyright, patents, and trademarks. Trade secrets are briefly discussed as well.

---

[1] The advocacy coalition, Fair Copyright for Canada, launched an innovative Facebook campaign, spearheaded by legal scholar Michael Geist, in response to Bill C-61, which included amendments to the *Copyright Act*. The bill was initially scheduled to be introduced by the minority Conservative government in December 2007, but was withheld until June 2008. The campaign generated a remarkable response (attracting about 40,000 supporters) and attracted substantial media coverage: <http://www.facebook.com/group.php?gid=6315846683>.

[2] *Industrial Design Act*, R.S.C. 1985, c. I-9; *Integrated Circuit Topography Act*, S.C. 1990, c. 37; *Plant Breeders' Rights Act*, S.C. 1990, c. 20.

EXHIBIT 33.1   International Agreements on Intellectual Property

INTELLECTUAL PROPERTY AGREEMENTS

¤ World Intellectual Property Organization (WIPO) Internet Treaties (1996)
  - WIPO Copyright Treaty
  - WIPO Performances and Phonograms Treaty

¤ Rome Convention/International Convention for the Protection of Performers, Producers of Phonograms and Broadcasting Organizations (Neighbouring Rights) (1961)

¤ Madrid Agreement/Madrid System for the International Registration of Marks (1891)

¤ Berne Convention for the Protection of Literary and Artistic Works (1886)

¤ Paris Convention for the Protection of Industrial Property (1883)

- -

INTELLECTUAL PROPERTY-RELATED TRADE AGREEMENTS

¤ Security and Prosperity Partnership (SSP) Negotiations: North American Free Trade Agreement (NAFTA) + (ongoing)

¤ NAFTA (1994)

¤ Canada–U.S. Free Trade Agreement (1989)

¤ General Agreement on Tariffs and Trade (1947/1994)
  - Uruguay Round (1986–1994)
    - Word Trade Organization Agreement (1995)
    - Trade-Related Aspects of Intellectual Property Rights (TRIPs) — Annex 1C to Marakesh Agreement Establishing the World Trade Organization (GATT 1994)

Canada has had domestic laws dedicated to intellectual property protection for a very long time. The first British intellectual property laws were the *Statute of Monopolies* of 1624 (dealing with patents) and the *Statute of Anne* of 1790 (dealing with copyright). Lower Canada enacted an initial patent law in 1824, followed by one in Upper Canada two years later.[3] The first *Patent Act* proper was passed in 1869.[4] As for copyright law, Lower Canada enacted an initial law in 1832, replaced subsequently by very different laws and culmulating in the most recent *Copyright Act*, which may soon be amended further.[5] The Province of Canada passed a trademark law in 1860 that was soon repealed and replaced with the *Trade Marks and Designs Act* of 1861, which underwent several crucial transformations before the current *Trademarks Act* was passed.[6]

---

[3] W.L. Hayhurst, "Intellectual Property Laws in Canada: The British Tradition, the American Influence and the French Factor" (May 1996) 10 *Intellectual Property Journal* 265.

[4] Current patent legislation: *Patent Act*, R.S.C. 1985, c. P-4.

[5] Current copyright legislation: *Copyright Act*, R.S.C. 1985, c. C-42.

[6] Current trademark legislation: *Trade-marks Act*, R.S.C. 1985, c. T-13. The official name of the existing Canadian law includes a hyphen in the word "trade-mark".

				EXHIBIT 33.2
Protection Provided by Intellectual Property Legislation in Canada				

COPYRIGHT ACT	INDUSTRIAL DESIGN ACT	INTEGRATED CIRCUIT TOPOGRAPHY ACT	PATENT ACT	PLANT BREEDERS' RIGHTS ACT	TRADE-MARKS ACT
Originality, not copied, results from author's skill and judgment; ideas not protected (expression only)	Originality, not copied, novel design *or* new use for old design	Creator is typically owner (unless employee)	Utility	New variety of plant	Distinctive mark
Fixation in material form necessary	Functional articles mass produced	Application within 2 years of design's use	Novelty	Distinct	Use in Association with wares or services
Design for mass-produced items (more than 50 functional items) not protected	Functional features or principles of construction not protected	Complementary to patent protection for circuit itself	Non-obviousness	Uniform	Mark — Common law and registered
Author usually first owner of copyright	Ideas not protected; colour not protected	N/A	Patentable subject matter	Stable	Certification mark
Registration not required	Registration required		Scientific theorems or principles not protected		Distinguishing guise
Term of protection: Life of Author plus 50 years.	Term of protection: 10 years	Term of protection: 10 years	Term of protection: 20 years	Term of protection: 18 years	Registration valid for 15 years (Registered Trademark)

SOURCES OF INTELLECTUAL PROPERTY LAW

The Constitution   For patent and copyright law, there is an explicit constitutional basis; for trademark law, the constitutional basis is mostly inferred. Sections 91(22) and (23) of the *Constitution Act, 1867* expressly stipulate that the legal regimes for patents and copyright fall under federal jurisdiction. Jurisdiction over trademarks is shared between the federal and provincial governments. The overlap in federal and provincial jurisdictions can be inferred from the exclusive provincial power over property and civil rights in section 92(13) of the Constitution, and from the federal power to regulate (international and inter-provincial) trade and commerce found in section 91(2). The sources of law governing trademarks derive from both the federal *Trade-marks Act* and at common law. The *Trade-marks Act* covers matters pertaining to the registration of trademarks, infringement of registered trademarks, and passing-off of unregistered trademarks.

Common Law Basis for Trademark Law and Trade Secrets Law

Trademark owners can enforce common law rights associated with their trademarks or trade names by bringing a passing-off action in the superior courts at the provincial level. Owners of trade secrets, or of confidential information, can rely upon the common law in cases of misappropriation. These topics are discussed in more detail below.

COPYRIGHT LAW

Defining "Copyright"

In Canada, copyright protection is derived exclusively from the *Copyright Act*. A copyright owner is given the exclusive right to produce or reproduce, to perform, or to publish a work or any substantial part of a work in "any material form". The aspect of "any material form" conveys the concept of media neutrality, which enables copyright protection to adapt to future technological advancements. Copyright includes the following economic rights:

- To translate the work
- To convert a dramatic work into a novel or other non-dramatic work
- To convert a work into a performance
- To make a sound recording or film by which the work may be mechanically reproduced or performed
- To communicate the work to the public by telecommunications
- To reproduce, adapt, and publicly present the work as a cinematographic work
- To rent out a computer program or sound recording

Purposes of Copyright Protection

The Supreme Court of Canada has interpreted the purpose of the *Copyright Act* as twofold: to encourage the production and dissemination of artistic and intellectual works as a matter of public interest, and to justly reward the creators of works as an incentive for the creation of artistic and intellectual works.[7] Given that continual technological advancements generates new methods of access to and reproduction of creative works in mass quantities, these dual purposes are often at odds, as is illustrated by the cases summarized in Exhibits 33.3, 33.4, 33.5, and 33.6.

Who Is an Author and Who Is an Owner?

Interestingly, the concept of "author" is not specifically defined in the *Copyright Act*, although the term is understood to refer to the maker of a creative work. The general rule is that the first copyright owner of a work is the author of the work. Ownership can then be transferred by the author through written assignment. An exception to the general rule is where the work was produced in the course of employment, in which case, the copyright is owned by the employer (as per s. 13(2) of the Act). The exception does not apply to freelancers; simply paying a freelancer to produce a work does not entitle the

---

[7] *Théberge v. Galerie d'Art du Petit Champlain Inc.*, 2002 SCC 34, [2002] 2 S.C.R. 336.

Impact of Technology Copyright	EXHIBIT 33.3

The *Robertson v. Thomson Corp.* case illustrates the impact of technological advances on the competing rights of copyright owners. The case explores the extent of copyright ownership in freelance articles acquired by *The Globe and Mail* for publication in its newspapers, and whether that copyright interest extends to reproduction of those articles in another medium.

Journalist Heather Robertson discovered that several articles she had authored for *The Globe and Mail* were available through online databases that could be searched by title, author, or keyword. The articles were also accessible through a *Globe and Mail* CD-ROM that archived the paper's daily editions by date of publication. Robertson's contract had not addressed these uses of her work. The lawsuit was certified as a class action on behalf of all freelance authors for *The Globe and Mail* since 1944.

The central issue was whether the newspaper could republish those individual articles in electronic databases such as Info Globe Online without further compensation to the freelance authors. The republication in the databases was distinct from the republication of the newspaper as a collective work.

The majority decision of the Supreme Court ruled that the *Copyright Act* did not permit the newspaper to reproduce individual freelance articles as part of an electronic database without the author's consent. The Court found that the electronic databases were not simply conversions of the newspaper from the "print realm to the electronic world"; they were instead a new collective work. The newspaper's copyright is in the newspaper as a compilation of articles, and is thus limited to the right to reproduce the newspaper in its entirety or a substantial part of the newspaper (as long as the "essence" is preserved). Thus, the newspaper could offer users a daily compendium of daily newspaper editions, in the CD-ROM format; that format retained the originality of the original work. The newspaper's copyright, however, does not extend to the republication of freelance articles as part of a different compilation of works. The freelance writers, as owners of their freelance works, hold the exclusive right to reproduce their articles. The Court confirmed that the *Copyright Act* expressly protects the writers' copyright in their articles, even if the article is part of a compiled work, by restating section 2.1(2): "[t]he mere fact that a work is included in a compilation does not increase, decrease or otherwise affect the protection conferred by this *Act* in respect of the copyright in the work."

The dissenting opinion focused on the concept of media neutrality in the copyright of the newspaper. The minority judges were critical of the way that the majority applied the notion of technological neutrality in the context of the case.

Source: *Robertson v. Thomson Corp.*, 2006 SCC 43, [2006] 2 S.C.R. 363.

---

customer to the rights in the work.[8] Another exception is where an engraving, photograph, or portrait is ordered by a customer and there was no agreement concerning ownership. In this case, the first owner of copyright is the person who ordered the engraving, photograph, or portrait. Thus, under current Canadian copyright law, a corporation can be an "author" of a photograph, but not of other traditional works. Proposed reforms to the *Copyright Act* introduced during the summer of 2008 would provide photographers with the same right to be, as authors, the first owner of a work. Corporations can be, and often are, the owners of copyright works. As noted by David Vaver, "worldwide, the vast majority of copyrights of both traditional and non-traditional material are owned by corporations".[9]

---

[8] For industrial designs or integrated circuit topographies (ICTs), by contrast, the person who orders the work to be done, under contract, will be the first owner of the design or the ICT, whether the maker of the design or the ICT is a freelancer or an employee.

[9] David Vaver, *Intellectual Property Law* (Toronto: Irwin Law, 1997) at 73.

What Works Are Protected by Copyright?

The *Copyright Act* (s. 5(1)), provides that copyright subsists in Canada for every "original literary, dramatic, musical and artistic work". A "literary work" includes "tables, computer programs, and compilations of literary works" (s. 2). Copyright law protects the expression of ideas in these works. It does *not* protect the ideas themselves, but only the expression of those ideas. The ideas are public property, and it is the expression of the ideas that belongs to the author. This means that a work must be fixed in material form to attract copyright protection. Copyright does not protect methods or principles of manufacture or construction. The *Copyright Act* (s. 64) will remove copyright protection from design elements of finished "useful" articles, such as boats, kettles, dresses, and so on (but not ornamental sculptures) *if* more than 50 copies of the article are made. Note that photographs, or sketches or patterns for those useful items, are not covered by this stipulation (and thus stay within the *Copyright Act*), since they are merely carriers of artistic or literary matter, rather than useful articles.

Industrial Design Protection Distinct from Copyright

Industrial designs are defined by the Canadian Intellectual Property Office (CIPO) as the features of shape, configuration, pattern, or ornament (or combinations of those) which are applied to finished articles. An article is defined as any thing that is made by hand, tool, or machine. Examples of industrial designs include the shape of a table or ornamentation on a spoon handle. Industrial designs give an article "eye appeal". Legal protection will not cover the following: functional features, the principles of construction, ideas, or colour *per se*.

To obtain protection, a design must be original, which means that it must be either novel in itself (distinct from previously registered designs) or applied to a different article (i.e., new use for an old design) and it must be registered. To register a design under the *Industrial Design Act*, it is necessary to submit an application to the Industrial Design Branch of the CIPO. Industrial design protection provides an absolute right to exclude, not just a right to prevent copying. Protection lasts for 10 years.

Industrial designs can qualify for protection under *both* the *Industrial Design Act* and under the *Copyright Act*, as long as the articles concerned do *not* have a utilitarian function and are *not* mass produced (i.e., less than 50 copies are to be made), as noted just above.

Copyright Works Must Be Original

"Originality" is the defining feature of a copyrighted work. For a work to be original, the work must be an expression of the author's "skill and judgment" and must not be copied. The standard of whether a work is "original" is an oft-litigated issue. The case law has seen two competing doctrines concerning the standard of originality in order for copyright to subsist. One approach requires there to be "creativity", which is the prevailing standard in U.S. case law. The other approach, adopted by the United Kinggdom and Australia, is the "sweat of brow" or "industriousness" standard in which copyright subsists where there is an investment of labour.

Canada adopts a middle-ground approach in requiring an exercise of skill and judgment in the creation of a work. For example, copyright exists where discernment and ability are used in the arrangement of a database and the compilation of data. Hence, under Canadian law, it is necessary for the work to be more than a mere copy of another work, but it need not be creative in the sense of being novel or unique. At minimum, there must be sufficient intellectual effort to go beyond a merely mechanical exercise. For example, changing a font in the publication would be considered a mechanical exercise. However, originality is found in a newspaper in that it is a compilation of articles arising out of the arrangement of content brought about by the exercise of skill, judgment, and labour.

The Supreme Court has emphasized that the adoption of the *skill and judgment* standard of originality serves to balance the public interest in promoting the creation and dissemination of works of arts and intellect and in obtaining a just reward for the creator. Requiring the exercise of skill and judgment encourages innovative enhancements to works already in the public domain and, thus, the creation of new works.

Term of Copyright Protection

The term of copyright protection is the life of the author plus 50 years following the remainder of the calendar year in which the author dies (s. 6). In a case of joint authorship, the term of copyright continues for 50 years following the end of the calendar year of the death of the last author to die (s. 9). In other jurisdictions, such as the United States and the European Union, the term of copyright protection is 70 years plus the life of the author.

Moral Rights

The author of a work has the right to the "integrity of the work" and "to be associated with the work as its author by name or under pseudonym and the right to remain anonymous" (s. 14.1). The "integrity of the work" refers to being protected from acts that "prejudice the honour or reputation of the author". **Moral rights** are infringed if the work is "distorted, mutilated or modified" or "used in association with a product, service, cause or institution" in such a way that it injures the author's reputation. For example, the *Copyright Act* presumes that there is prejudice where a painting, sculpture, or engraving is distorted, mutilated, or modified without the artist's consent. The term of moral rights is the same as the term of copyright. Moral rights may not be assigned, but can be waived in part or in whole. Thus, an author can waive, or decline to exercise, his or her moral rights, but he or she cannot enter into a contract to assign them to another (i.e., they are not "for sale").

A leading Canadian moral rights case involved the prominent artist Michael Snow, whose public art work, *Flight stop*, is a familiar site to visitors of Toronto's Eaton Centre shopping mall. The shopping centre's management decided to bedeck the installation of life-sized Canadian geese in flight with red ribbons as Christmas decorations in 1981. Michael Snow pursued legal action against the Eaton Centre, requesting an injunction to have the ribbons removed, arguing that they distorted, and offended the integrity of, his work. The then-Ontario High Court of Justice granted the injunction, thereby upholding Snow's moral rights.[10]

Neighbouring Rights

Neighbouring rights are generally those rights that are not related to the right of the author who created the work, but are the rights related to the performance or broadcast of a work, or to the making of a sound recording. In 1997, the *Copyright Act* was amended to include three categories of neighbouring rights: (i) rights of performers in performances; (ii) rights of makers of sound recording (producers of phonograms), and (iii) rights of broadcasters in their communication signals (e.g., radio and television programs). These amendments fulfilled Canada's obligations under the *Rome Convention*. Neighbouring rights are rationalized as legal protection designed to benefit those persons who assist intellectual creators to communicate their messages and to disseminate their works to the public at large.

[10] *Snow v. Eaton Centre Ltd.* (1982), 70 C.P.R. (2d) 105. A photo of the sculpture can be found online: <http://www.deathbycopyright.ca/index.php?/archives/56-Michael-Snows-geese-sculpture-at-the-Eaton-Centre.html>.

Copyright Board and Copyright Collectives The administration of copyright and remuneration for copyright holders are set out in Part VII of the *Copyright Act*. In Canada, administration is generally carried out by a cluster of collective societies, and the determination of tariffs and royalties for copyright holders is regulated by the Copyright Board of Canada. A "collective society" is defined in the *Copyright Act* as a society, association, or corporation that carries on the business of collective administration of copyright for the benefit of those who authorize the collective to act to their behalf. The *Copyright Act* recognizes the collective societies under the four regimes: (i) music performing rights and certain neighbouring rights, (ii) general or hybrid regime, (iii) re-transmission regime, and (iv) private copying regime.

The collective applies to the Copyright Board for a tariff to be certified. The tariff is the price for a particular use of a copyrighted work. Examples include the applications for tariffs submitted to the Copyright Board by the Neighbouring Rights Collective of Canada to cover the following:

- Royalties for payments to performers (i.e., recording artists and musicians) and makers (i.e., record labels) for the public performance of their sound recordings in movies played by movie theatres, drive-ins or similar establishments (Tariff No. 7)

- Royalties for performers and makers for the communication of their sound recordings over the Internet by simulcasting and non-interactive webcasting services (Tariff No. 8)

- Royalties for performers and makers for the use of sound recordings in programming provided by commercial television stations, as well as cable and satellite companies (Tariff No. 9)[11]

The Copyright Board of Canada has jurisdiction over copyright collective societies representing film and television producers and broadcasters, authors of works and dramatic works, musicians and performers, owners of re-transmission, broadcasters, screenwriters, and visual artists. The mandates of the Copyright Board, as authorized in the *Copyright Act*, are to establish royalties for the use of copyrighted works that a collective society has been mandated to administer for the benefit of those owners of works, and to supervise agreements between users and licensing bodies. It can also issue licences when copyright owners cannot be located. The Copyright Board is essentially an economic regulatory body created and authorized by the *Copyright Act* to carry out its functions in the form of a quasi-judicial tribunal.

Collectives predominate in Canada, so a large proportion of copyright-enforcement activity relating to tariffs (i.e., royalties) is handled by collectives. Copyright matters not within the jurisdiction of the collective are handled by the right holder.

Fair Dealing Defence Distinct from Fair Use As a matter of public policy, "fair dealing" defences are carved out in section 29 of the *Copyright Act*. The permitted activities are enumerated, and specified. The fair dealing defence permits use of copyrighted works where the work is used: (i) for research or private study, (ii) criticism or review, or (iii) news reporting, without any "motive of gain". In the cases of criticism or review and news reporting, it is not an infringement if the source of the work is given, or if acknowledgment is given of the author, performer, maker of the

---

[11] Neighbouring Rights Collective of Canada, Information Sheets for Tariff No. 7, Tariff No. 8, and Tariff No. 9 <http://www.nrdv.ca/english/docs/Info%20Sheets%20on%20NRCC%202008%20Tariff%20Filings.pdf>

Fair Dealing?

EXHIBIT 33.4

The *CCH* case illustrates the "fair dealing" defence in the case of "research and private study". The case is about the balance between the rights of an author and the rights of access for users. The Law Society is the statutory body that regulates the legal profession in Ontario in the public interest. The legal publisher, CCH Canadian Ltd., sued the Law Society for copyright infringement. The issue was whether the Law Society breaches copyright when it provides a custom photocopy service and self-serve photocopiers for copying summaries of case law produced by CCH. The patrons of the service include lawyers, judges, students, and researchers.

The case has attracted considerable attention due to the judicial language, which emphasizes the need for a "proper balance" between the rights of copyright owners to exploit works, and the rights of the public, often characterized as "users' rights", to access copies for purposes of legal research. To benefit from the fair dealing defence, a user needs to prove: (i) that the purpose of dealing with the work (i.e., copying) was for research or private study, and (ii) that the dealing was fair in the circumstances.

The Supreme Court unanimously held that the Law Society did not infringe copyright by providing single copies of the publisher's works to its members through the custom photocopy service. The Law Society's dealings with the case summaries were for research and thus are considered fair dealing under section 29 of the *Copyright Act*. The Court clarified that "research" must be given a large and liberal interpretation to ensure that user's rights are not unduly constrained. Research is not limited to non-commercial or private contexts. Research for the purpose of advising clients in legal cases, including preparing legal briefs and arguments, is considered research under the *Copyright Act*. The determination of "fair dealing" is a question of degree and impression. Consideration is made of the number and extent of quotations and extracts, the use of the extracts, and the proportion of extracts to commentary.

Source: *CCH Canadian Ltd. v. Law Society of Upper Canada*, 2004 SCC 13, [2004] 1 S.C.R. 339.

---

sound recording, or broadcaster of the communication signal. In the *Law Society of Upper Canada v. CCH Canadian Ltd.* case, the Supreme Court had occasion to elaborate on the substance of the fair dealing defence, in particular as it pertains to research (Exhibit 33.4).

It is important to emphasize that the **fair dealing** defence is different, in important ways, from the **fair use** defence that is provided under the United States *Copyright Act*. Under the U.S. *Copyright Act*, making use of copyrighted work for purposes such as criticism, comment, news reporting, teaching (including multiple copies for classroom use), scholarship, or research, is *not* an infringement of copyright. The fair use provision is considered to be much broader than the fair dealing provision found in Canadian law, and includes uses such as parody, which are not found in the Canadian *Copyright Act*.

Factors for Fair Dealing

The Supreme Court set out the following factors for applying the fair dealing exception in the context of private study or research in the *CCH Canadian Ltd. v. Law Society of Upper Canada* case:

1. **Purpose of the Dealing**
   Elaboration: There must be an allowable purpose, one that is mentioned expressly in the Act. Moreover, within allowable purposes there is variability, such that philanthropic research is more likely to be fair than commercial research.

2. **Character of the Dealing**
   Elaboration: This refers to the way that the allegedly infringed work was dealt with. For example, reproducing a single copy for a single requester is more likely to be considered fair than providing for widespread dissemination. Destroying a copy after use will favour a finding of fairness.

3. **Amount of the Dealing**
   Elaboration: Here, it is important to consider the number and types of activities undertaken. As to what would be unfair, the court suggested this example: one patron requesting copies of multiple reported judicial decisions from the same series or volume over a short period of time. In such a case, the patron would be expected to purchase the works from the publisher.

4. **Alternatives to the Dealing**
   Elaboration: Can the dealing be carried out with equivalent and non-copyright protected material instead? Circumstances to be considered include "whether the material is reasonably available elsewhere, or whether the publishers have an effective monopoly". The more alternatives available, the less fair copying would be, and *vice versa*. Consider whether the source work was available within a reasonable time at an ordinary commercial price.

5. **Nature of the Work**
   Elaboration: If the work has not yet been published, its reproduction could lead to wider dissemination and, thus, could potentially be fair in accordance with the goals of copyright law. If a work was confidential, however, that could tip the scales towards a finding that the dealing was not fair. Some of the jurisprudence suggests that for works which are factual in nature, fair dealing may be more readily found than for works which are creative or imaginative.

6. **Effect of the Dealing on the Work**
   Elaboration: Under this heading, courts consider the degree to which the use may prejudice the sale, or diminish the profits, or supersede the objects, of the original work. If the copying was done in order to be incorporated into a competing work, it is less likely to be considered fair.

Copyright Infringement

In determining whether a substantial part of a work has been reproduced, one has to consider the qualitative nature of the reproduction rather than simply the quantitative amount. Independent creation is allowable under copyright law, whereas independent creation can be an infringement of a patent, an industrial design or a trademark.

COPYRIGHT CONTROVERSIES

Music Downloading and Peer-to-Peer File Sharing

There is a general pattern that new technologies (such as the photocopier and the videocassette recorder) create opportunities for widespread and inexpensive copying of works. The advent of computer programs to facilitate peer-to-peer (P2P) file sharing has led to the mushrooming of unauthorized reproduction of recorded music and, more recently, movies distributed through the Internet. Various economic studies have been done to try to quantify the amounts of revenue the music industry is losing out on owing to the popular-

---

Copyright Infringement over the Internet

EXHIBIT 33.5

The case originated in an attempt by the Canadian Recording Industry Association (CRIA), representing BMG Canada Inc. and other record companies, to discover the identities of 29 Internet users who had downloaded music through the use of peer-to-peer (P2P) file sharing programs (KaZaA), thereby allegedly infringing copyright. The CRIA asked the Federal Court to order five Internet Service Providers (ISPs) — Bell Canada/Sympatico, Rogers Cable, Shaw, Telus, and Videotron Ltée. — to disclose names and contact information of clients (identified by their Internet Protocol or IP addresses), so as to facilitate CRIA suing them. The trial judge, Mr. Justice Von Finckenstein of the Federal Court, refused to order the release of that information, holding that CRIA had not made a strong enough case, and that it was not clear that the acts the 29 users were accused of were actually acts of copyright infringement. Justice Von Finckenstein held that users engaging in P2P music file sharing were not necessarily infringing copyright, nor "distributing" or "authorizing" reproduction of sound recordings contrary to Canadian copyright law. The trial judge set out a multi-part test for identification of "John Does", which included the following particulars:

(i) a *prima facie* case of copyright infringement being made by the applicants against the alleged wrongdoers;

(ii) determination that the ISPs in question were the only practical sources to identify the peer-to-peer users; and

(iii) finding that legitimate privacy concerns evidenced in the case were outweighed by the applicants' interest in an order for disclosure.

The trial judge highlighted the potential for an innocent account holder to be wrongly identified, given the complications of ascertaining the actual identities of alleged infringers in the light of the practices of ISPs. An example was provided by Shaw of the same IP address being assigned to many users in situations involving local area networks and network routers. Not finding the conditions set out just above to have been satisfied, the trial judge declined to issue an order for disclosure.

The trial decision was appealed to the Federal Court of Appeal, which unanimously dismissed the appeal. The FCA held that CRIA needed to adduce additional evidence before proceeding with the 29 actions filed to date. The Court of Appeal did call into question some of the statements made by the trial judge in the lower court, such as the statement that downloading a song for personal use did not amount to infringement under the *Copyright Act*. The Court of Appeal noted that the trial judge had not considered whether all requirements for application of the "personal use" exemption (copy for private use) had been met. Furthermore, the Court of Appeal held that where an Internet user invites other persons with Internet access to have copyright music transferred to them, and then copied, authorization may be established. Moreover, placing a copy on a shared directory linked to a P2P file-sharing program may amount to distribution for the purposes of the *Copyright Act*. Sexton J.A. emphasized that while privacy concerns have to be taken into account, those concerns must yield to public concerns for protecting intellectual property "in situations where infringement threatens to erode those rights". Ultimately, the Federal Court of Appeal did not find in favour of CRIA.

Source: *BMG Canada Inc. v. John Doe (F.C.A.)*, 2005 FCA 193, [2005] 4 F.C.R. 81.

---

ity of the new technologies; the music industry insists that it is in the billions, with significant declines in CD sales as the proof. In the United States, the Recording Industry Association of America (RIAA), a trade group representing the major record labels, has pursued a strategy of aggressive litigation. RIAA took legal action for copyright infringement against the Napster online centralized file-sharing service created by an American university student (Shawn Fanning), leading to it being shut down (it was started up again in a different form by others). Then, the RIAA started taking legal action against consumers who have engaged in unauthorized downloading of

| EXHIBIT 33.6 | Should ISPs Pay for Their Customers' Copyright Infringement? |

The issues in this case concerned the extent to which music communicated through the medium of the Internet is protected under Canadian copyright law and whether caching constitutes infringement. The Society of Composers, Authors and Music Publishers of Canada (SOCAN) made the claim that Canadian Internet providers should pay royalties because some of their customers download copyrighted works. The case also looked at whether or not the creation of "cache" copies of copyrighted works constitutes infringement. (Cache refers to a means of temporarily storing files used to house documents being transferred across the Internet.)

The Supreme Court found that communication occurs between the host and the recipient, and that ISPs merely facilitate that communication (they are the "means of telecommunication"). The Court held that neither Internet Service providers (ISPs) nor host server operators "communicate" or "authorize the communication" of musical works in violation of SOCAN's rights under the *Copyright Act*. Authorization requires that a defendant give approval to, sanction, permit, favour, or encourage infringing conduct.

When ISPs limit their activities to providing the means for others to use their service to communicate by telecommunication, they are in effect shielded from liability. The use of a cache server was included in the rubric of acceptable practices since it was deemed by the Court to be merely a way to deliver faster and more economical service, undertaken only for technical reasons. The Court noted that it would be impracticable to require ISPs to monitor the content posted on their servers in order to determine whether that content is in compliance with copyright and other laws.

Nonetheless, where an ISP acts as a content provider, or is otherwise associated with the provision of content, it may become liable for effecting or authorizing the communication of music, if the circumstances so warrant. If it can be shown that a certain relationship, or degree of control, exists between the ISP and the provider of infringing content, or the ISP's activities cease to be "content neutral", then the ISP could potentially become liable for authorizing infringing communications. An ISP will be especially vulnerable to liability if it neglects to remove material upon being notified of infringing content on its system, in a timely manner. The practice recommended to avoid potential liability is known as "notice and takedown".

The Court commented on the importance of ISPs in the Canadian context as follows: "It is clear that Parliament did not want copyright disputes between creators and users to be visited on the heads of the Internet intermediaries, whose continued expansion and development is considered to be vital to national economic growth".

Source: *Society of Composers, Authors and Music Publishers of Canada v. Canadian Assn. of Internet Providers*, 2004 SCC 45, [2004] 2 S.C.R. 427.

music through a variety of other decentralized file-sharing programs (including kaZaA). Some of the alleged infringers sued have been college students and parents of file-sharing children. News reports have estimated that about 20,000 lawsuits have been initiated; the vast majority of those have ended in settlements.

In Canada, the CRIA (Canadian Recording Industry Association), which is the Canadian equivalent to the RIAA, attempted to sue peer-to-peer file-sharing Internet users in the case of *BMG Canada Inc. v. John Doe*. The plaintiffs were unable to convince the courts (both the Federal Court and the Federal Court of Appeal) to order the release of the identities of the Internet service providers' customers in order to proceed with litigation (Exhibit 33.5). In another case on related issues, *SOCAN v. Canadian Association of Internet Providers*, the collective copyright society SOCAN was unable to convince the Supreme Court that Internet service providers should be required to pay royalties because some of their customers download copyrighted works (Exhibit 33.6).

Digital Copyright Reform

Canada is a signatory to what are known as the World Intellectual Property Organization's Internet treaties. One deals with Copyright (WIPO Copyright Treaty, or WCT) and the other deals with Neighbouring Rights (WIPO Performances and Phonograms Treaty, or WPPT). The previous Liberal government had promised to implement reforms to the *Copyright Act*, in accordance with those treaty obligations, but Bill C-60 died on the order table when the government fell. The minority Conservative government indicated in its Throne Speech that copyright reform was on their agenda, and they have subsequently brought forth Bill C-61. The bill went through first reading in June of 2008, and it is too soon to tell whether the Conservatives will ultimately be successful in getting it passed through Parliament.

The main purposes of the proposed amendments of the *Copyright Act* are to

(a) update the rights and protections of copyright owners to better address the Internet, in line with international standards
(b) clarify the liability of Internet service providers
(c) permit certain uses for educational and research purposes of Internet and other digital technologies to facilitate technology-enhanced learning, inter-library loans, the delivery of educational material and access to publicly available material on the Internet
(d) permit certain uses of copyright material for private purposes, and
(e) amend provisions of the Act relating to photographs to give photographers the same rights as other creators.[12]

The new law is designed to ban peer-to-peer file sharing, and to make it illegal for consumers to get around digital locks, in provisions known as anti-circumvention rules, which echo those found in the *Digital Millennium Copyright Act* (*DMCA*) in the United States. Copyright owners have come to rely increasingly upon technological protection measures (TPMs) and digital rights management (DRM) to block access to digital content, except with the authorization of the owner. CDs and DVDs thus often come with encryption to prevent copying. The new bill would make it contrary to law to circumvent the encryption, as does the *DMCA*, and potentially even to possess devices or software capable of doing so. The daily newspapers and countless information technology-related blog entries evidence the negative consumer reaction those particular features of the legal reforms have provoked. Other aspects of the new law, which should be less contentious, include provisions allowing consumers to legally time shift (i.e., to record a television show for later viewing), format shift (e.g., to convert a purchased VCR tape into a DVD format), and to make private copies of music (e.g., by transferring songs from a purchased CD to an iPod for personal use).

Another, related legal reform has already been implemented. In 2007, the federal government passed an amendment to the *Criminal Code* (s. 432), making it an offence to (i) record a movie in a theatre without the consent of the theatre manager, and/or (ii) to do so for the purpose of selling, renting, or other commercial distribution. The court can now order the forfeiture of any equipment used in the commission of those offences. Although the *Copyright Act* already contained a provision (s. 42) making the camcording of a movie a part of copyright infringement (i.e., making a copy of work for sale or rental), the Canadian Motion Picture Distributors Association (CMPDA) and the Motion Picture Association of America (MPAA) aggressively advocated for the

---

[12] Canada, Bill C-61, *An Act to amend the Copyright Act*, 2nd Sess., 39th Parl., 2007–2008, Summary (first reading, June 12, 2008). Available online: <www.parl.gc.ca>. A series of Fact Sheets are also available on the Industry Canada website: "Copyright Reform Process", <www.ic.gc.ca/epic/site/crp-prda.nsf/en/h_rp01157e.html> (accessed: August 31, 2008).

much stronger criminal sanctions to provide a more effective deterrent. Previously, people were simply ejected but not charged for camcording in a movie theatre (claiming it was for personal use), and they kept their equipment. Now, charges could be laid and recording equipment confiscated.

There are international trade implications to these legal developments. Section 301 of the U.S. *Trade Act* enables the U.S. government to impose trade sanctions on countries that it deems to be lacking adequate protection for American intellectual property. The 2008 report of the Office of the U.S. Trade Representative (USTR) indicated that Canada was singled out for "serious concern", although it was left on a "watch list" (along with 35 other countries meriting bilateral attention) rather than elevated to the "priority watch list" as had been recommended by the International Intellectual Property Alliance (IIPA), a private sector coalition representing U.S. copyright-based industries. The USTR emphasizes Canada's failure to implement the WIPO Internet treaties. Having been "put on notice" by USTR in this way, Canada is expected to address the U.S. industry's concerns, or face the risk of possible trade sanctions in the future.

The federal government has recently announced that it will work with other international trading partners towards a possible Anti-Counterfeiting Trade Agreement (ACTA).

PATENT LAW

What Is a Patent?

A patent is a government-issued document granting an inventor or an owner of a patented invention a monopoly to exclude others from making, using, and selling the invention for a limited period of time. This exclusive right of exploitation is intended to protect business interests. The right to exclude others from using the invention gives the patent owner a head start to commercially exploit the patent. In exchange for this monopoly, the inventor provides disclosure of the invention to the public, so that the public may gain the benefit of the disclosure. Otherwise, the inventor could simply keep the invention secret. This exchange is often referred to as the *quid pro quo* of the patent right, or the bargain theory of patent law. The bargain between the inventor and the public serves the public policy of encouraging research and development, innovation, and economic activity. Hence, fulfilling the requirements of disclosure is crucial.

Whereas copyright protection applies from the moment of creation, patent protection will apply only once a patent has been granted by the Canadian Intellectual Property Office. The person who is "first to file" a patent application is entitled to patent protection in Canada and in most other jurisdictions. Some inventions, such as computer programs, may be eligible for both copyright and patent protection.

Defining "Invention": Criteria for Patentability

The "invention" must meet several conditions in order for a patent to be granted. First, "invention" is defined in the *Patent Act* (s. 2) as "any new and useful art, process, machine, manufacture or composition of matter". Hence, the invention must be patentable "subject matter", meaning that it must fall within one of the categories of "useful art, process, machine, manufacture or composition of matter". The invention must also meet the conditions of being "new", "useful", and "non-obvious". The disclosure in the patent application must meet the requirements for specification of an invention set out in section 27(3) of the *Patent Act*. The specification can include drawings, illustrations, and so on. The disclosure must fully describe the invention and how it operates or is used so that a "person skilled in the art" can make or use the invention. It must set out the steps in a process or the method of making or using a machine, manufacture, or composition of matter in a clear and concise way.

The first condition of patentability is that the invention must fall within one of the classes of patentable *subject matter*, that being "any new and useful art, process, machine, manufacture or composition of matter". The case of *Harvard College v. Canada (Commissioner of Patents)* addresses the issue of whether a transgenic non-human organism can be an invention (Exhibit 33.7).

What Is an Invention?   EXHIBIT 33.7

Dupont licensed the invention of a mouse ("oncomouse") that was bred to be susceptible to cancer for the purpose of biomedical research. The genetically altered gene is incorporated into a plasmid and injected into a fertilized mouse egg, which is then implanted into a host mouse. That implanted egg, when born, becomes a "founder mouse", used to produce offspring containing the oncogene. The commercial value and utility of the invention is in the alteration of the genetic code of the oncomouse.

Harvard College had filed for a patent on the invention in Canada. Harvard's patent application covered three claims: (i) a method for creating the mouse using a modified gene, (ii) the cellular material making up the mouse, and (iii) a transgenic mammal containing the modified gene. The Patent Commissioner rejected the third claim to the end product of the mouse itself, and Harvard appealed that decision. The Commissioner's decision emphasized that the inventors did not have full control over all the characteristics of the founder mouse.

The case went to the Federal Court Trial Division (upholding the Patent Commissioner's decision), and then to the Federal Court of Appeal (overturning the lower court's decision and finding in favour of Harvard), ending up in the Supreme Court of Canada. The issue was whether the oncomouse, as a higher life form produced by genetic engineering and natural gestation, is patentable under section 2 of the *Patent Act*. Several public interest advocacy groups, including the Canadian Council of Churches, the Canadian Environmental Law Association, and Animal Alliance, were granted intervenor status in the case. There was significant media coverage of the case by the time it reached the final stage.

Both the majority and dissenting decisions of the Supreme Court found the fertilized, genetically altered oncomouse *egg* to be patentable. However, the Court differed by a margin of five to four as to whether the mouse produced by natural gestation (but wholly composed of altered cells not found in nature) is as itself an "invention" defined in the *Patent Act*.

The majority decision (authored by Mr. Justice Michel Bastarache) held that a transgenic non-human mammal does not qualify as a "manufacture" or "composition of matter" and hence is not patentable. The body of the genetically altered mouse does not consist of substances or ingredients that have been mixed together by a person. It was the majority opinion that the issue of patenting higher life forms should be left to Parliament to legislate, as it is beyond the institutional competence of the Supreme Court to rule on the related policy issues concerning the research and experimental use, exemption, and value issues concerning the commodification of human life.

The minority opinion (authored by Mr. Justice Ian Binnie) concluded that patenting of higher life forms should be patentable, and insisted that doing so would not involve a radical departure from the traditional patent regime. The mouse should be deemed a "composition of matter", according to the dissenting judges.

The implication of the *Harvard Mouse* case is that patent applications for higher-life-form patents will be denied in Canada. Canada is now the only developed country to disallow higher life forms as patentable subject matter. However, both majority and dissenting decisions found the fertilized genetically altered oncomouse egg to be patentable subject matter, even though the mammal is not patentable. Thus, Harvard was granted patent protection for the method of creating the mouse and the cells that make up the mouse.

Source: *Harvard College v. Canada (Commissioner of Patents)*, 2002 SCC 76, [2002] 4 S.C.R. 45.

The *Patent Act* is not meant to protect mere ideas in the abstract. Mere scientific principle or abstract theorem is set out in the statute (s. 27(8)) as a non-patentable exception. Mathematical formulae and calculations made by a computer are not considered patentable subject matter. The rationale for this exception is that the purpose of the *Patent Act* is to protect ideas that produce tangible results that are reproducible and have practical application.

Devices or drugs for treating illness in humans or animals are patentable. But professional skills or methods of medical treatment such as a method for cleaning teeth (to make them bacteria free) or for using adhesives in post surgical suturing have been held to be excluded from patentability in Canada. In contrast, American patent law does allow for claims relating to methods of medical treatment or invasive surgical methods. For example, a patent claim to "A method of treating rhinitis [inflammation of nasal passages] comprising administering X" would potentially be allowable in the United States but not accepted in Canada.[13] The reasoning for this exclusion in Canadian patent law is that professional skills such as medical treatment fall outside industry, trade, and commerce, which are the fields that the patent system was designed to serve. Secondly, the exercise of discretion and judgment in carrying out the professional skill leads to uncontrollable or irreproducible outcomes. There is also a public policy rationale for the exclusion from patentability of medical or surgical treatments, since otherwise operating surgeons or prescribing physicians could be vulnerable to patent-infringement actions. Some claims pertaining to cosmetic methods and methods of treating animals for economic benefit are allowed in Canadian patent applications.

The other criteria for patentability are **novelty**, **non-obviousness**, and **utility**. An invention is "new" or "novel" if it is not anticipated by "prior art". **"Prior art"** is the body of knowledge existing prior to the date of the filing of the patent. The invention must also be "non-obvious" in the sense that it must not be obvious to a "person skilled in the art" (s. 28(3)), who is a fictitious person deemed to have reached an average level of skill in the field of the invention in a patent application. This notional person is used as a standard by which to judge the novelty and especially the non-obviousness of the invention. An invention must also be "useful" or have "utility" in the sense that it can be applied towards a practical purpose, as opposed to being purely theoretical. Unpatentable inventions include perpetual motion machines, or Mr. X's "death ray".[14] Systems for doing things that do not result in a tangible product have been found to be unpatentable in Canada. Examples include systems for becoming rich, efficient conduct of a business, securing payment of a discount, and for better government.

Term of Patent Protection

For patents based on applications filed on or after October 1, 1989, the term of protection is 20 years from the filing date (as per s. 44 of the *Patent Act*). For patents based on applications filed before October 1, 1989, that had not expired as of July 12, 2001, the term of protection is the later of 17 years from the date on which the patent is issued, or 20 years from the filing date (as per s. 45(2) of the Act). As a point of interest, the provisions of the *Patent Act* relating to the term of protection were amended in 2001 to bring the Act into conformity with TRIPs, after the World Trade Organization ruled in 2000 that Canada's term of protection for certain patents (those filed before October 1, 1989) was inconsistent with TRIPs.

---

[13] Euan Taylor, "Patenting Methods of Medical Treatment", Davis and Company, *Intelligence*, 10 (February 2007).

[14] *X v. Canada (Commissioner of Patents)* (1981), 59 C.P.R. (2d) 134 (F.C.A.).

Infringement of Patent Rights

The test for patent infringement is whether the acts or conduct in question deprive the inventor, in whole or in part, directly or indirectly, of the advantage of the patented invention.

PATENT CONTROVERSIES

There have been several flashpoints for public debates over the desirability of patent protection; one concerns essential medicines and another concerns patents on genes and life forms.

Essential Medicines

Researchers and activists who focus on the global health crisis surrounding HIV/AIDS have targeted patent protection for essential, life-saving medicines, as a crucial barrier to dealing with the problems faced by developing countries. There is currently a global campaign to advocate for legal and policy reforms in both developed and developing countries to try to ameliorate the impact of the high costs of existing medicines to treat HIV/AIDS.[15]

The Government of South Africa was faced with litigation from pharmaceutical companies owning patents on drugs to treat HIV/AIDS during the late 1990s. The government had passed a law which sought to do two things to bring down drug prices: (i) take advantage of a "grey market", or parallel importation (from unlicensed but cheaper sources of the drugs), and (ii) use compulsory licensing, which would enable local manufacturers to be licensed to produce generic versions of patented medicines. The brand-name pharmaceutical companies objected to the undermining of their intellectual property rights and pushed for trade sanctions against South Africa. Forty drug companies joined together and threatened to pursue lengthy and costly litigation against the South African government. After global protests, and considerable pressure from the international non-government organization (NGO) community, the drug companies backed off from the lawsuits.

The World Trade Organization negotiations for the Doha Declaration resulted in a separate declaration on TRIPS (the *Trade-Related Aspects of Intellectual Property Rights*) and public health, which was designed to respond to concerns about the possible implications of the TRIPS Agreement for access to essential, life-saving medicines. That special declaration emphasizes that "[the] TRIPS Agreement does not and should not prevent member governments from acting to protect public health. It affirms governments' right to use the agreement's flexibilities in order to avoid any reticence the governments may feel."[16]

In 2005, Canada passed Bill C-9, known as the *Jean Chretien Pledge to Africa Act*, which amended the *Patent Act* and the *Food and Drugs Act*. The legislation was a response to a 2005 decision of the World Trade Organization (WTO) to waive certain obligations in TRIPs (relating to s. 31(f)). The result of that WTO decision is that developed countries such as Canada are now able to authorize someone other than a patent holder to manufacture and export essential medicines under compulsory licences to countries with no, or insufficient, pharmaceutical manufacturing capacity. The legislation contains

---

[15] Campaign for Access to Essential Medicines, <http://www.accessmed-msf.org/>. In addition to focusing on the high cost of prescription drugs, the campaign emphasizes the need to stimulate research into new medicines for neglected diseases such as tuberculosis, sleeping sickness, and malaria.

[16] World Trade Organization, Doha Declaration Explained: <http://www.wto.org/english/tratop_e/dda_e/dohaexplained_e.htm#trips>.

a list of eligible medicines, and aims to provide greater access to pharmaceutical products for addressing public health problems, especially those arising from HIV/AIDS.

Gene Patents and Lifeform Patents

Considerable public debate and discussion has been devoted to the issues of genetic patents and life-form patents, in Canada and abroad. One debate concerns whether higher life forms should be patentable. In Canada, the Supreme Court was asked to rule on the patentability of a mammalian life form, a genetically altered mouse used in cancer research. The Supreme Court ruled, in *Harvard College v. Canada (Commissioner of Patents)*, that while patents could be granted on lower life forms and genes (including micro-organisms, seeds) and human genes, cells, and DNA sequences, higher lifeforms will not be patentable in Canada (Exhibit 33.7). In another case involving patents on genetically altered plants, *Monsanto Canada v. Schmeiser*, issues concerning patent infringement were the focus. See Exhibit 33.8.

The genetic patent on breast cancer genes (BRCA1 and BRCA2) held by the Utah-based firm Myriad Genetics has stimulated controversy in Ontario and throughout Europe. The provincial government in Ontario performs predictive genetic testing for hereditary breast and ovarian cancers, testing which involves the specific breast cancer genes that are the subject matter of Myriad's patents (obtained during the mid-1990s). The Ontario government has not entered into a licensing arrangement with Myriad Genetics. The company sent a "cease and desist" letter to the Government of Ontario in mid-2001, alleging that the government was violating Myriad's patents.[17]

The company demanded that the provincial government send the samples to Myriad's operations in Utah, where the tests would cost on average about US$3,850 (rather than $1,150).[18]

The Ontario government declined to agree to Myriad's request, citing the problematic legal, ethical, and financial implications of doing so. The government insisted that paying Ontario hospitals to carry out the testing did not constitute infringement of "any valid claim" of Myriad's patents. As a point of interest, a similar request by Myriad for payment sent to European governments resulted in the launch of a public campaign in opposition, and the use of an "opposition challenge", which is an administrative proceeding available under European Union patent law. After that administrative intervention, Myriad lost protection for one breast cancer gene patent entirely and the other patent was significantly narrowed.

TRADEMARK LAW

What Are Trademarks, Trade Names, Certification Marks, and Distinguishing Guise?

A trademark is a mark used to distinguish goods or services from other goods and services. The following, while not an exhaustive list, can each be a trademark: a word, a coined word (such as ESSO, then EXXON), numbers, or a combination of numbers and letters, a design (such as Macdonald's Golden Arches), colour combinations, signs and symbols, and sound marks. In contrast, a trade name signifies the entire business entity under which the business is conducted, whether that name is the corporate name, or the name of the partnership or sole proprietorship. A trade name must be registered under

---

[17] Similar letters were sent to the governments of Alberta, British Columbia, and Quebec. Quebec agreed to Myriad's request, while British Columbia temporarily suspended the testing.

[18] Laura Eggertson, "Ontario Defies US Firm's Genetic Patent, Continues Cancer Screening" (2002) 166:4 *Canadian Medical Association Journal* 494.

Gene Patent Infringer or Innocent Infringer?   EXHIBIT 33.8

Percy Schmeiser was a farmer in Saskatchewan whose farm was found to have very substantial amounts of a genetically modified crop invented by Monsanto called Monsanto's Roundup Ready Canola. Monsanto's patent covers the modified gene which, when inserted into the DNA of canola plants, gives the ensuing plants tolerance to glyphosate, which kills weeds, and is marketed under the trademark "Roundup". Hence, the plants are known as "Roundup Ready" canola. Monsanto claimed patent protection not for the genetically modified plant itself, but rather for the genes that make up the plant.

Mr. Schmeiser did not have a licence for the use of Monsanto's Canola. When the GM plants were discovered on his property, Mr. Schmeiser claimed that contamination had occurred in one or more of the following ways: (i) either wind or insect activities had lead to crossfield breeding; or (ii) seeds were blown from passing trucks or dropped from passing farm equipment; or (iii) plants were blown from neighbours' fields. At the initial trial, expert evidence adduced led to the Federal Court finding that none of the alleged sources could explain the concentration or extent of "Roundup Ready" canola found on Mr. Schmeiser's farm. The trial judge found that Mr. Schmeiser knew or ought to have known that the plants from which he had saved seeds for planting were glyphosate tolerant. The case ultimately ended up in the Supreme Court, after Mr. Schmeiser appealed the finding of liability by the Federal Court of Appeal. Both the appeal courts upheld an injunction against using the plants containing the patented gene.

The issue was whether Schmeiser infringed Monsanto's patent through the use of Monsanto's patented gene by collecting, saving and planting the seeds.

The majority of the Supreme Court found that Mr. Schmeiser infringed Monsanto's patent because he used the patented invention within the context of commercial farming without paying a licence fee and, hence, deprived Monsanto of the full extent of its monopoly right. The Court emphasized that the function of the statutory patent monopoly is to protect business interests.

The test articulated for infringement is whether the defendant's conduct deprives the inventor, in whole or in part, directly or indirectly, of the advantage of the patented invention. Infringement can occur where the patented invention (i.e., in this case, the gene) is part of a broader unpatented structure or process (i.e., a plant) if the patented invention is a significant part of, or important to, the defendant's activities that involve the unpatented structure. Even possession of a patented object or an object incorporating a patented feature may be infringement if the infringer derives a "stand-by" or "insurance" utility from the object.

Several court rulings of the case noted that how an invention comes into possession of an infringer is an issue which has especial salience in the context of gene patents. What if somehow plants containing modified genes end up on a person's property unbeknownst to that person (an innocent infringer)? Could the company which owned the patent still obtain a remedy for infringement? The majority of the Court noted that an alleged defendant may be found not to infringe by proving that its possession is "innocent of any actual use or intention to use" the patented invention.

This case, as did the Harvard Mouse case, generated very significant amounts of publicity; it even has its own website developed and maintained by Mr. Schmeiser (The *Monsanto v Schmeiser* website: <http://www.percyschmeiser.com/>).

Source: *Monsanto Canada Inc. v. Schmeiser*, 2004 SCC 34, [2004] 1 S.C.R. 902.

---

the applicable provincial statute governing business names. A trade name could potentially be registered as a trademark under the *Trade-marks Act*, if it is also used as a trademark. The Canadian Intellectual Property Office gives the following example to distinguish a trademark and a trade name: A company called A.B.C. Ltd. (trade name) sells ice cream under the name A.B.C. in association with that ice cream. In that case, A.B.C. Ltd. could also apply for trademark protection for "A.B.C." However, if A.B.C. Ltd. instead promotes its ice cream in association with the word "Northpole", "A.B.C." would not then be considered a trademark.

Under Canadian law, certification marks and distinguishing guises are trademarks. A certification mark is a mark used to distinguish goods and services that meet a defined standard. That standard can be with respect to character, quality, or working conditions under which the good was produced or the service was performed. The wool symbol on clothing tags and the logo of the Association of Professional Engineers are examples of certification marks.

A distinguishing guise refers to a shape of goods or their containers or a mode of packaging goods such that the appearance of the good distinguishes the good from others. The shape of the Toblerone chocolate bar and of the classic Coca-Cola bottles, and the grill on a Rolls Royce car are all examples of distinguishing guises. The *Trade-marks Act* (s. 13) prohibits the registration of a distinguishing guise where the feature would "limit the development of any art or industry". Utilitarian features are also disclaimed from the registration of distinguishing guises.

Registered Trademarks

A trademark can be registered in the Trade-marks Registry with the Canadian Intellectual Property Office (CIPO), or it can be unregistered, in which case it is called a trademark at common law.

The registration is a lengthy process that begins with filing an application setting out the trademark and a description of the goods and services associated with the mark. Next, an examination of the mark is conducted by a trade-marks examiner at CIPO to determine if the trademark is registrable, taking into account the indicia of non-registrability pursuant to section 12 of the *Trade-marks Act*. If the examiner finds the trademark registrable, the trademark is advertised in the *Trade-marks Journal* for interested persons to oppose the registration within a two-month period. The opposition may be pursuant to one of the grounds in the Act (s. 38(2)). If there is no opposition to the application or the opposition is unsuccessful, the trademark is then registered.

Although use of an unregistered mark is protected by common law rights, there are benefits to registering a trademark. The owner of a registered trademark has the exclusive right to use the mark in association with the goods and services described in the registration throughout Canada. Registration confers a presumption at law that the owner is entitled to exclusive use of the mark. Subject to certain enumerated exceptions, the use of a mark that is confusing with the registered trademark is deemed to be an infringement under the Act (s. 20).

Unregistered Common Law Trademarks

In order for an unregistered mark to acquire rights at common law, it must be used such that it becomes a distinguishing mark pointing to the source of a good or service. The mark should have garnered goodwill for the business using it. Use of the trademark is broadly defined to encompass all forms of advertising and verbal usage. In this sense, the mark acquires "reputation" and "distinctiveness". The reputation of the mark may be local or widespread, spanning the country, the continent, or the world. For an unregistered trademark, the scope of legal protection will be limited to the geographical area in which "distinctiveness" is shown for the mark.

The regulation of trademarks has its roots in the prevention of misrepresentation to the public as to source of a good or service. Unregistered trademarks that have acquired a reputation indicating a source of a product or service attracted rights under the common law. Hence, the common law recognition of unregistered trademarks is concerned with preventing misrepresentation.

| The Difference between Trademark Protection and Patent Protection | EXHIBIT 33.9 |

The patent for the Lego blocks had expired in Canada and in other countries. After expiry of the last Lego patent in Canada, Ritvik, the makers of Mega Bloks, brought to market a line of small blocks identical in size to the Lego blocks and featuring the same Lego design of interlocking bricks using the geometrical pattern of stubs on top with tubes underneath. Ritvik sold the bricks in Canada and in other countries under the name "Micro Mega Bloks". Mega Bloks had become a significant global competitor to Lego. Lego attempted to protect its market share and goodwill against its competitor by bringing a passing-off claim pursuant to section 7(b) of the *Trade-marks Act*. Lego asserted that the geometric pattern of raised studs on the top of the Lego bricks is a distinguishing guise. Lego sought to compel its competitor to sell Mega Bloks with a disclaimer that Mega Bloks are not Lego bricks and are not supplied by Kirkbi. Kirkbi argued that consumers would be confused if such a disclaimer is not made, and that would constitute passing-off.

The Supreme Court of Canada unanimously dismissed Kirkbi's claim, stating that a purely functional design may not be the basis of a trademark, whether registered or unregistered. The law of passing-off cannot be used to perpetuate monopoly rights enjoyed under expired patents.

This case also illustrates the distinction between patents and trademark protection. Patents protect new products and processes and are premised on the concept of a bargain between the inventor and the public. In exchange for the disclosure of the invention, the patent confers a time-limited monopoly to the patent owner, giving the owner the exclusive right to use and market the subject matter of the patent.

Trademark protection is concerned not with the product itself but with the distinctiveness of the product's marketing. Trademarks identify for the consumer the source of a product or service in a distinctive manner so that consumers know what they are buying and from whom. Because the consumer market relies on brand marketing, the identity of a product holds great economic value for the trademark owners.

The Kirkbi case asks whether the distinguishing guise can be the product itself. The resulting Court decision says that despite the connection between the mark and its product, a mark must not be confused with the product itself.

Source: *Kirkbi AG v. Ritvik Holdings Inc.*, 2005 SCC 65, [2005] 3 S.C.R. 302.

Trademarks and Overlap with Other Types of Intellectual Property

Trademark protection can potentially apply to the same subject matter as copyright protection. The cartoon character Mickey Mouse, for instance, is subject to copyright protection, and Mickey Mouse is also a trademark of the Disney company. Other companies are legally restricted from using the Mickey Mouse logo in connection with their goods and products without permission from Disney, because doing so would risk confusing consumers.

If an industrial design is associated by the public with a single source of the product, then an industrial design could attract trademark protection as well. The design could be protected under common law trademark rights, or potentially registered as a "distinguishing guise".

See Exhibit 33.9 for a summary of a case involving the LEGO blocks, in which the Supreme Court of Canada elaborated on the distinctions between patent protection and trademark protection.

Term of Protection

The registration period for a trademark is 15 years and is renewable for successive 15-year periods. It is essential that a trademark be in use in order for the owner to maintain its rights. If, three years after registration, a trademark is not used, an interested party may apply to the Federal Court to have the trademark expunged for non-use. A trademark may also be expunged without

---

EXHIBIT 33.10   **When Trademark Protection Doesn't Apply**

A restaurateur applied to register its trademark "Barbie" and related design in association with restaurant, take-out, catering, and banquet services. Mattel opposed the application on grounds that its own "Barbie" mark used in association with dolls and doll accessories is so famous that the average consumer would be misled into making a trade connection between Barbie, the restaurant, and Mattel's doll. The Trade-marks Opposition Board ("Board") found in favour of the restaurant and allowed the application for reason that the use of "Barbie" for a small chain of restaurants in Montreal would not likely create confusion with Mattel's trademark. The Board's decision was upheld on appeal and by the Supreme Court of Canada.

The issue in this case is whether the owner of a famous trademark can use trademark law to prevent the use of a common name such as "Barbie" in relation to other goods and services that are not related to the goods and services associated with the fame of the famous trademark. The fame of the "Barbie" mark was in association with dolls and did not extend to restaurant services as there was no evidence that Mattel used "Barbie" for restaurant services.

The Court found the fame of the "Barbie" brand is a surrounding circumstance of importance, but it is not the overriding factor that would eclipse the other factors listed in section 6(5) of the *Trade-marks Act*. The Court reasoned that no person should be permitted to "fence in the common of the English or French languages and words of a general nature cannot be appropriated over a wide area" (*Mattel, Inc. v. 3894207 Canada Inc.*, para. 75).

The Supreme Court reiterated the purpose and public benefit of trademark law is to assure consumers of the source and quality of the product and services that they are buying. The Court called trademark law a form of "consumer protection legislation" and regulation to encourage "fair competition". Hence, trademark law seeks to balance the competing interests of consumer protection, fair or open competition between merchants, and protecting the investment of the trademark owner in the mark. In seeking this balance, the Court must not grant exclusivity that exceeds the purpose of trademark law.

Source: *Mattel, Inc. v. 3894207 Canada Inc.*, [2006] 1 S.C.R. 772, 2006 SCC 22.

---

the three-year requirement if an interested party applies on the grounds that the trademark has been abandoned, was not registratable, was not distinctive, or the applicant was not entitled to registration (s. 45 and s. 57 of the Act).

Infringement Actions Trademark owners can take legal action to prevent competitors from using the same, or a "confusingly similar", mark in such a way that there is a reasonable likelihood that the public would think the competitor's products or services are being made by the real trademark holder. The trademark owner needs to show that the use by the competitor has done damage to the goodwill or reputation of the owner's business. With respect to a registered trademark, an infringement action is generally commenced in Federal Court pursuant to sections 7 and 20 of the *Trade-marks Act*.

An action to stop the infringement of an unregistered trademark is recognized as a "passing-off" action in common law and can be commenced in Federal Court pursuant to s. 7(c) and (e) of the *Trade-marks Act*. Or, a common law passing-off action may be commenced in a superior court at the provincial court.

Determining Trademark Confusion The *Trade-marks Act* (s. 6) requires that "all surrounding circumstances" be taken into consideration in the determination of confusion. The Act lists five factors to be taken into account:

- The degree of distinctiveness and the extent of the reputation of the trademark
- The length of time the mark has been in use
- The nature of the goods and services or business
- The nature of trade
- The degree of resemblance between the trademarks in the appearance or sound or in the ideas suggested by them

This list is not exhaustive, and the courts have emphasized that all surrounding circumstances be taken into account and that no one factor trumps another factor.

The question of whether two trademarks are confusing is asked from "the point of view of the average hurried consumer having an imperfect recollection of the opponent's mark who might have encountered the trade mark of the applicant in association with the applicant's wares in the market-place" (*Mattel, Inc. v. 3894207 Canada Inc.*, as discussed in Exhibit 33.10). The law recognizes that the consumer's decision-making process will depend on the type of purchase. A person buying a car or appliance will pay more attention to the brand than when buying a mid-price meal. In some contexts, the purchaser will be bilingual. In determining confusion, the intent of the competitor using the similar trademark is not a relevant factor. What needs to be proved is "likelihood" of confusion and not "actual confusion". Evidence of actual confusion is persuasive, although not necessary.

Passing-Off Tort Action

The passing-off action has a long history in the common law, dating back to the seventeenth century. Originally, its roots are the law of deceit, which was concerned with honesty and fairness in trade and competition. The aims of the passing-off action were to ensure that buyers knew what they were purchasing and from whom. It was also to protect the economic interest that traders held in their reputation and name. The modern doctrine of passing-off that evolved from these principles is now enshrined in the federal *Trade-marks Act* while existing concurrently in common law.

Passing-off of a common law trademark is the use of a mark in such a way that it is a misrepresentation of the source of the product or service. The passing-off can take the form of use of the *same mark* to fraudulently pass off a good or service for the legitimate good or service, or it could be the use of a *confusingly similar mark* for products and services of the same type. Passing-off can arise where the mark is used in one locale, and the same or similar mark is used by another business in another location such that it is confusing to those who see the marks. The owner of the mark in the original locale can assert that its advertising and marketing has a spillover effect into other geographic locations and that it has plans to expand its business in those locations and needs to protect the goodwill it has invested in its trademark. In a 1990 English Court of Appeal decision, a test with three criteria was established to determine whether a product or service is passing-off:

1. The common law trademark has acquired reputation or goodwill through the use of the mark in association with the goods or service.
2. The infringing party has made a misrepresentation that is deceptive or is confusing to those who see the mark.
3. The owner of the trademark has suffered damages from the infringing party's benefit of the mark's goodwill and reputation.[19]

---

[19] *Reckitt & Coleman Products Limited v. Borden Inc. and Ors*, [1990] 1 All E.R. 873.

Famous Trademarks and the Depreciation of Goodwill

Famous marks were recognized in trademarks legislation in 1953 when the "depreciation of goodwill" cause of action was added to the *Trade-marks Act*. Section 22 states that "[n]o person shall use a trademark registered by another person in a manner that is likely to have the effect of depreciating the value of the goodwill attaching thereto." The depreciation of goodwill cause of action is similar the "anti-dilution" remedy in the United States. The U.S. concept of "dilution" is not concerned with confusion but with the diminishment of a mark's uniqueness and distinctiveness in the public's perception caused by the unauthorized use of the mark.

In 2006, the Supreme Court of Canada adjudicated two cases involving famous trademarks known worldwide versus lesser-known but registered trademarks used in Canada. The first case involved the trademark "Barbie" used in association with a doll. The second case involved "Veuve Clicquot", the famous mark for champagne and other luxury goods. In both cases, the Supreme Court recognized the existence of famous marks, and of the importance of protecting the goodwill associated with famous marks. However, despite acknowledging the importance of the fame of the marks, the lower courts and the Supreme Court found in favour of the lesser-known marks in both cases.

What is common between both cases is that the fame of the trademark is an important factor but is only one of several factors in determining whether there is confusion when taking into consideration the surrounding circumstances. The *Veuve Clicquot* case is important in that it also clarifies the test for proving deprecation of goodwill under the *Trade-marks Act*.

TRADE SECRETS AND CONFIDENTIAL INFORMATION

The terms "trade secret" and "confidential information" are applied to information (i) that has commercial value, (ii) that is not commonly known, and (iii) for which efforts have been made to maintain confidentiality. Another term lawyers will use is "proprietary information". Such information is said to give the owner an opportunity to obtain an advantage over competitors who lack it. Trade secrets can include any of the following: code, compound, device, drawing, formula, mechanism, pattern, plan, process, program, recipe, tool, technique, provided that it is not generally known or readily ascertainable by the public. The terms **trade secret** and **confidential information** are normally used interchangeably, but they can be distinguished. Trade secrets are often said to relate to know-how, while confidential information may include proposed trade names or compilations of information such as customer lists, for instance. The most familiar example of a trade secret is the recipe for Coca-Cola.

Trade secrets can be sold, licensed, or otherwise exploited for pecuniary gain. Trade-secrecy protection lasts for as long as the object of protection remains secret, which means there is an indefinite term of protection. If a firm X acquires a trade secret owned by Y through industrial espionage or unauthorized disclosure by an employee, then Y could sue X to prevent use of the secret or to require X to pay Y a licensing fee. But if the information becomes publicly known, by independent discovery or examination of the product, it can no longer be protected as a trade secret. For some assets, such as a computer program or a database, which are protected by copyright or patent law, reverse engineering could potentially lead to copyright or patent infringement. If something is a trade secret, then it cannot be patented, because inventions must be disclosed to the public to get patent protection. Inventors must choose whether to keep the invention a secret or to apply for patent protection.

| A Case of Depreciation of Goodwill | EXHIBIT 33.11 |

Veuve Clicquot brought an action against the defendant, a mid-priced women's clothing boutique for confusion in the marketplace under section 20 and for depreciation of goodwill under section 22 of the *Trade-marks Act*. This case is significant for the Supreme Court analysis of the depreciation of goodwill cause of action.

It was established at trial and affirmed on appeal that Veuve Clicquot is indeed a famous trademark representing the very best champagne and extending to other luxury products. The Court affirmed that fame or strength of a trademark is a very important factor but is only one in a number of other circumstances to be weighted. Despite its fame, Veuve Clicquot was not able to prove that the clothing boutique's use of a similar mark was confusing or that it would depreciate the goodwill of the senior mark.

Veuve Clicquot did not give evidence of actual confusion. Nor did the expert evidence given by Veuve Clicquot establish the likelihood of confusion. The evidence merely provided a conjecture of possible confusion. Hence, the claim for confusion was rejected by the lower courts and upheld on appeal to the Supreme Court.

The next stage of analysis concerned the depreciation of goodwill. Goodwill is not defined in the *Trade-marks Act*. Its ordinary meaning connotes "the positive association that attracts customers towards its owner's wares and services rather than its competitors" (*Veuve Clicquot*, para 50). The depreciation of goodwill does not require proof of confusion, but rather, whether the use of the mark creates an association in minds of the relevant group of consumers such that there is likely depreciation in the value of the goodwill attaching to the mark. A mental association does not automatically result in depreciation of goodwill.

There are four elements to prove depreciation of goodwill:

1. The registered trademark was used by the offending party in connection with goods or services regardless of whether the goods or services are in competition.
2. The registered trademark must have acquired goodwill through being sufficiently well known, although the mark need not be famous.
3. There must be a link between the offending use (although not necessarily confusing use) that would likely have an effect on goodwill.
4. The likely effect of the offending use is the depreciation of the value of goodwill.

The plaintiff was unable to prove that the defendant's use of "Cliquot" in its store would cause a consumer to make a link or connection between the plaintiff's mark and mid-priced women's clothing. And, where there is no such mental association, there can be no depreciation of goodwill.

The standard of proof is "likelihood" that the defendant's use would depreciate the plaintiff's mark. It is not sufficient to prove that depreciation "could" occur. Nor is it necessary to prove that depreciation "did" occur. It is essential that the offending use in question caused damage to the goodwill. It is not necessary that the use be confusing. In determining the existence of goodwill, the relevant factors to consider are recognition of the mark, volume of sales, market share of the products carrying the mark, reach and duration of advertising and marketing using the mark, geographic reach of the mark, inherent and acquired distinctiveness of the mark, whether the mark is confined to a narrow or specialized trade, and whether the mark identifies quality.

Source: *Veuve Clicquot Ponsardin v. Boutiques Cliquot Ltée*, 2006 SCC 23, [2006] 1 S.C.R. 824.

Trade secrets can be revealed to particular persons under specified conditions, for instance, with the signing of a confidentiality agreement that forbids disclosure. A business may wish to disclose a trade secret for reasons of marketing, evaluation, or to obtain financial backing. Some contracts of employment contain a confidentiality agreement binding the employee. A non-competition agreement prevents an employee from using contacts or information gained during the course of employment for the benefit of a competitor, or from setting up a competing establishment once that person leaves the original place of employment. Such agreements typically set out a specific period of time and geographic area for the non-competition obligation to apply. Otherwise, if the terms are too restrictive, the agreements are at risk of being found to be in restraint of trade by a court, if challenged.

Confidentiality agreements are also referred to as "non-disclosure agreements". Although such agreements usually take the form of a written contract, an obligation of confidentiality, or non-disclosure, can be implied or inferred in the context of business relationships. As an example, a business that conducts patent searches for inventors would be expected to keep any information about the invention secret, even if no written agreement had been signed, because of the nature of the business.

Significantly, the Supreme Court of Canada has ruled, in *R. v. Stewart*,[20] that misappropriation of confidential information cannot constitute "theft" as that term appears within the context of the *Criminal Code*. So, although confidential information is protected with intellectual property-like measures, it is not considered a fully fledged property right.

To pursue an action for "breach of confidence", a plaintiff needs to show that the information at issue had the "necessary quality of confidence". Numerous factors can be of assistance for determining whether specific information has the requisite "quality of confidence" in a particular case, including the following: (i) the extent to which the information is publicly available; (ii) the extent to which the information is known within the proprietor's business or known by employees and others involved in the owner's business; (iii) measures taken by the owner to guard the secrecy of the information; (iv) the value of the information to the owner and its competitors; (v) the amount of money or effort expended by the owner in developing the information; and (vi) the ease or difficulty with which the information could be properly acquired or duplicated by others through their own independent endeavours.[21]

Other factors considered by courts include (i) the degree to which the owner regards and treats the information as confidential, and (ii) the degree to which the recipient regards and treats the information as confidential.

A plaintiff also needs to establish that information was disclosed to a recipient in circumstances under which the recipient ought to have known that it was confidential, and that the defendant misused the information. A plaintiff can sue for copyright infringement as well as for breach of confidence, if copyright applies.

In the case of *Cadbury Schweppes Inc. v. FBI Foods Ltd.*,[22] the Supreme Court elaborated on the cause of action referred to as "breach of confidence" and on issues relating to remedies. The plaintiff Cadbury Schweppes' subsidiary, Duffy-Mott, had licensed the formula for making "Clamato" to Caesar Canning, the predecessor of FBI Foods. Clamato consisted of a confection of tomato juice and clam broth. The licence agreement had prohibited the recipient of the formula from manufacturing or distributing products, other than "Clamato", which contained tomato juice and clam broth. Duffy-Mott communicated confidential information to Caesar Canning about the recipe before the licensing relationship was terminated. Subsequently, Caesar Canning began to manufacture and distribute its own tomato juice product, "Caesar Cocktail", consisting of the Clamato recipe without the clam broth. After FBI Foods pur-

---

[20] [1988] 1 S.C.R. 963.
[21] *Pharand Ski Corp. v. The Queen in Right of Alberta* (1991), 37 C.P.R. (3d) 288 (Alta. Q.B.).
[22] [1999] 1 S.C.R. 142.

chased the assets of Caesar Canning, upon the bankruptcy of the latter, it continued to put out the Caesar Cocktail product. Cadbury Schweppes eventually commenced an action for breach of confidence against FBI Foods.

Courts at the trial and appeal levels found that FBI Foods was liable for breach of confidence, by virtue of its use of the Clamato recipe to formulate Caesar Cocktail. FBI Foods was enjoined from using the technical information and advice which had been provided by Cadbury Schweppes under the licence. The Supreme Court set aside the permanent injunction, holding that it was unduly prejudicial to the defendant, particularly in light of the plaintiff's delay in pursuing legal action (five years after termination of the licence). The Supreme Court found that the recipe was "not very special information"; it was not "rocket science", as Mr. Justice Ian Binnie, author of the decision, put it. If FBI Foods had wanted to, it could have produced a sufficiently close "copy-cat" product within about a year of the termination of the licence agreement. Thus, FBI Foods effectively got a "head-start" of a year by continuing to use the Clamato recipe. The Supreme Court found that Cadbury was entitled to lost profits for the year following the termination.

REMEDIES

Plaintiffs who pursue civil litigation, for example, intellectual property owners who sue alleged infringers, normally ask the court to provide them with a remedy. The remedies available to intellectual property rights-holders include damages, injunctions, and accounting of profits. Damages consist of monetary compensation for the harm, injury, or loss suffered by the plaintiff through the unlawful acts of the defendant. An **injunction** is an order or decree by which a party to an action is required to do, or refrain from doing, a particular thing. A mandatory, or positive, injunction requires the party so ordered to do something, whereas a restrictive, or prohibitory injunction prohibits the party so ordered from doing something. A mandatory injunction must define precisely what it is that the defendant is ordered to do. Likewise, a prohibitory injunction needs to specify just what wrongful action the defendant is to refrain from committing or continuing. As regards time, injunctions are either interlocutory (interim or temporary) or perpetual (also known as permanent). Temporary, or interim injunctions, are granted pending the final outcome of the dispute at trial and they cease at the end of the trial. Permanent injunctions are granted at the outcome of a trial. A further remedy available to intellectual property rights-holders is delivery of infringing goods (or offending labels) in the possession of the defendant, an ancillary order that can accompany an injunction against infringement. Normally, such an order will provide infringers with the option of destroying the infringing goods on oath.

Another remedy that plays an important role in intellectual property cases is an **account of profits**. If an infringer profits more by its wrongdoing than the right-holder loses, the court can order an account of profit to prevent unjust enrichment and provide a deterrent to infringement. This remedy can be available even when a right-holder has suffered no actual loss (and thus there is nothing to compensate for by way of damages). The infringing party is required to "lay open" its books (to determine the amount of net after-tax profits), and moreover the claimant can usually recover, compound prejudgment interest at prime rate on the profits. The account of profit is typically awarded as an alternative to damages, except in the case of copyright, where a plaintiff may have both. A qualification in those situations is that double counting on the same unit has to be avoided, so that only the amount of the defendant's profits that were not accounted for in the calculation of the plaintiff's damages can be added in.

CHAPTER SUMMARY

Intellectual property law covers three main types of intellectual property in Canada: copyright, patents, and trademarks, each of which is represented by a federal statute. In addition, there is common law protection available for unregistered trademarks, and for trade secrets and confidential information. The point is emphasized in this chapter that many features of intellectual property protection in the domestic context reflect the globalization of norms through international agreements.

This chapter has provided a definition of intellectual property and a discussion of the public policy rationales for legal protection of inventions and creations. The chapter surveys the crucial aspects of the three main types of intellectual property, defining each and setting out the main criteria for protection, the term of protection, and the basis for infringement. We have highlighted several prominent controversies surrounding copyright law and patent law in the modern age. Significant Canadian intellectual property cases are summarized that deal with music downloading (through peer-to-peer file sharing), gene patents, and famous trademarks. The protection of trade secrets and confidential information, very important in the everyday business context, is also briefly surveyed. The types of remedies available to intellectual property rights-holders are explained and differentiated.

GLOSSARY OF NEW TERMS AND KEY CONCEPTS

account of profits A remedy that can be available to plaintiffs in intellectual property litigation, requiring the infringing defendant to detail the profits made from infringing activities and to pay those monies to the claimant.

assignment Voluntary transfer of the ownership of an intellectual property right. The person transferring is the assignor and the recipient is the assignee.

breach of confidence Legally actionable wrong of disclosing or using commercially valuable, confidential information, which a person received in confidence, or took improperly for a purpose not authorized by the confider.

class action A civil lawsuit in which a representative plaintiff acts on behalf of a defined class of plaintiffs (e.g., all consumers injured by a particular faulty product, or all investors induced to invest in a particular fraudulent business scheme). A class action allows the issues common to a large number of separate potential cases to be heard in one trial.

common law Judge-made law, arising from cases as distinct from statutory law.

compilation A copyrighted work comprising of a selection or arrangement of literary, dramatic, musical, or artistic work, or an arrangement of data such as a directory or database.

confidential information Commercial information that is valuable to a business if it remains secret, and that can be protected through contracts, and also through the "breach of confidence" cause of action at common law.

confusion The misleading inference that goods and services derive from a particular source, when those goods and services actually derive from another source. The likelihood of confusion must be proven in order for trademark infringement to be found.

copyright The legal protection given to original artistic, dramatic, literary, and musical works for the term of the author's life plus 50 years in Canada. The French term is "droit d'auteur".

Copyright Board Tribunal established under the *Copyright Act*, which has authority over rate approvals (tariffs) for cable re-transmission, broadcasting, and blank audio-recording media levies. Appeals of the decisions of the Copyright Board go directly to the Federal Court of Appeal.

copyright collective A society, association, or corporation that carries on the business of collective administration of copyright for the benefit of those who authorize the collective to act on their behalf.

digital rights management Technology used to protect the interests of those who own content (such as copyright owners), and which is intended to prevent illegal distribution of content over the Internet. Typically, authorized recipients or users of copyrighted materials — files, music, movies, etc. — must acquire a licence in order to consume the protected material in accordance with rules set by the content owner.

distinctiveness The quality of a trademark that distinguishes the goods and services from other goods and services. Distinctiveness is acquired through use of the trademark.

distinguishing guise The shape of goods or their containers or a mode of packaging goods such that the appearance of the good distinguishes the good from others.

expungement In trademark law, the striking of a trademark from the registry on the basis of non-use after three years of registration, or on grounds that the trademark has been abandoned, was not registrable, was not distinctive, or that the applicant was not entitled to registration. In patent law, a declaration that a patent is void, and is to be struck or deleted from the registry.

fair dealing In Canadian law, a defence to copyright infringement.

fair use In American law, a defence to copyright infringement.

famous trademark A trademark whose "aura" transcends the goods and services with which it is normally associated.

goodwill The positive association that attracts owners towards its owner's goods and services rather than to those of its competitors.

impeachment Proceedings concerning the invalidation of a patent under Canadian law.

industrial design The features of shape, ornamentation, or pattern that are applied to mass-produced finished articles can be protected under the *Industrial Design Act* in Canada. Limited protection for the first fifty copies of such articles can be obtained under the *Copyright Act*.

infringement Violation or breach of an intellectual property right for which the rights-holder could go to court to recover civil remedies against the infringer. Some specified copyright infringements are also criminal offences.

injunction A court order that can require a positive act (a mandatory injunction) or the cessation of an activity (a negative, or restrictive injunction). Such court orders can be granted pre-trial (interim or interlocutory injunction) or after the completion of a trial (final injunction). Failure to comply with an injunction can lead to proceedings for contempt of court. Injunctions are an important remedy in intellectual property cases.

integrated circuit topography The three-dimensional configurations of the materials that form integrated circuits, which are protected under the *ICT Act* in Canada. The equivalent to what is known in the United States as "semiconductor chip protection".

intellectual property Creations or products of the mind, intangible and incorporeal items that can be created, owned, and exploited exclusively by an owner, or by someone authorized by the owner (as under a licence), for commercial advantage.

licence An intellectual property rights-holder can "licence" others to do what only the right-holder (licensor) is legally entitled to do, thereby giving permission for the licencee to exercise those rights. An exclusive licence gives the exploitation right to a licencee to the exclusion of the right-holder, whereas a sole licence enables the right-holder to continue to exercise the intellectual property right. A non-exclusive licence allows the licensor to contract with several licencees in the same area.

moral rights An author's right in the integrity of the work, the right to be associated with the work as its author by name or under a pseudonym, and the right to remain anonymous. Authors of copyrighted works are entitled to have their work properly attributed and for their work not to be prejudicially modified or associated with other products. Moral rights are legally enforceable. The French phrase is "droits moraux".

national treatment	Principle of non-discrimination in matters of trade. International intellectual property agreements oblige member countries, such as Canada, to extend to all other member countries the same rights that accrue to Canadians.
neighbouring rights	Rights that are related to or "neighbour" on copyright.
non-competition agreement	An agreement under which one party agrees not to compete with the other party for a specified period of time or within a particular area. Non-competition terms are generally included in an employment contract (and intended to continue in force after the cessation of the employment) or a contract for the sale of a business.
non-disclosure agreement	A legally binding contract in which a person or business promises to keep confidential certain information or trade secrets imparted by the owner, and agrees not to disclose the confidential information or trade secret to others without proper authorization by the owner.
non-obviousness	One of the statutory criteria for patentability. An invention needs to be non-obvious to those who are skilled in the relevant field of expertise.
novelty	One of the statutory criteria for patentability which requires the invention to be new and not anticipated by prior art (see *prior art*, below).
originality	The threshold requirement for a work to by protected by copyright law in Canada. In Canada, originality arises when the work is not copied, and when the work is, at a minimum, the expression of the author's skill and judgment. Works that are not original cannot be protected by copyright.
parallel import	Importation of a product legally made abroad into Canada without the authorization of the Canadian intellectual property owner. Also known as "grey marketing".
passing-off	The legally actionable wrong of misrepresenting one's business, goods, or services as another's business, goods, or services, to the detriment of the rights-holder.
patent	Intellectual property protection for inventions that meet the statutory criteria (utility, novelty, and non-obviousness) and are patentable subject matter.
piracy	The term commonly used by intellectual property owners to refer to those who infringe their intellectual property rights.
plant breeders' rights	Rights pertaining to new varieties of plants that are new, distinct, uniform, and stable, and are protected under the *Plant Breeders' Rights Act* in Canada.
prior art	The body of knowledge in the area of the invention that exists prior to the filing date of the patent. The patent examiner surveys the prior art of an invention to determine whether the invention meets the criteria of novelty and non-obviousness.
prosecution	Term used in the context of pursuing an action for intellectual property infringement, as in patent prosecution or trademark prosecution, and distinct from prosecution under criminal law.
registered trademark	A trademark registered with the Canadian Intellectual Property Office. A registered trademark confers the exclusive right to use the mark throughout Canada.
rival/non-rival	Goods for which possession by one person reduces the amount available for consumption by another have the feature of "rivalry". Non-rivalry refers to goods for which consumption by one consumer can occur without preventing simultaneous consumption by others.
royalty	Money which is payable for the authorized use of an intellectual property right.
technological protection measures	Devices, mechanisms, or systems designed to protect against, or restrict, unauthorized use of material stored in digital formats. These can include encryption technologies, access-protection codes, and other software and hardware measures.
trademark	A mark used to distinguish the products, goods, or services of one trader from others.
trade name	The name under which a corporation, firm, or individual carries on a business. Trade names are registrable under the *Trade-marks Act*.

trade secret	Commercially valuable information, such as formulas, recipes, plans, or technical know-how. Protection under common law is available for companies who develop trade secrets and make efforts to maintain their secrecy.
treaty	An international agreement, which can also be referred to as a convention. Upon signing onto a treaty, Canada and other member countries are committed to implementing domestic legislation to give effect to the treaty obligations.
unfair competition	A synonym for misappropriation of business interests to the injury of their owner. A term that covers a range of legally actionable wrongs under common law, including passing-off, injurious falsehood, interference with economic relations.
utility	In patent law, one of the fundamental requirements that must be met for an invention to be patentable. Utility requires the invention to apply towards a practical purpose, as opposed to being purely theoretical. In European law, the phrase "industrial application" is used instead.
waiver	Giving up a right to which one is entitled.
WIPO	World Intellectual Property Organization. An agency of the United Nations, headquartered in Geneva, Switzerland. WIPO administers many crucial intellectual property treaties. Established by the WIPO Convention from 1967 with a mandate to promote the protection of intellectual property across the globe.

REVIEW QUESTIONS

1. What is intellectual property? Compare and contrast the purposes of each of the main types of intellectual property protection (i.e., copyright, patents, and trademarks).

2. What are the sources of intellectual property law? Under which jurisdiction(s) do copyright, patents, and trademarks fall in Canada?

3. Who is an author and who is an owner, under copyright law? What is a work and what kinds of works are protectable?

4. What are neighbouring rights? Name three different kinds. How are they connected to copyright?

5. What are moral rights? What is an example of a Canadian case dealing with moral rights?

6. What is the fair-dealing defence and when does it apply? List and describe the six factors for applying the fair-dealing defence.

7. How have technological advancements posed particular challenges for copyright law? How have copyright owners responded to those challenges?

8. What is a patent? What is an invention?

9. What are the main criteria for patentability? What kinds of subject matter are excluded from patentability, and why?

10. Compare and contrast trademarks, trade names, certification marks, and distinguishing guises. Provide examples of each.

11. Describe the process of registering a trademark. How, by contrast, do trademarks get protection under common law?

12. What are the factors that courts take into consideration in infringement actions based on "confusion" under the *Trade-marks Act*? What are the factors that are considered in "passing off" actions?

13. What is a trade secret? Provide examples. Is there a difference between trade secrets and confidential information?

14. What factors are considered when determining whether a particular piece of information has the necessary "quality of confidence" to merit legal protection?

15. How long does legal protection for a trade secret last? When can the information in a trade secret no longer be protected? Can a trade secret be patented?

16. Compare the term of protection for each of copyright, industrial design, integrated circuit topography, patents, plant breeders' rights, trademarks, and trade secrets.

DISCUSSION QUESTIONS

1. What are the rationales for intellectual property protection? How does intellectual property differ from other types of property? Why do some critics object to the expansion of intellectual property as a "privatization of the commons"?

2. The federal government's proposed new amendments to the *Copyright Act* may make it illegal for a consumer to transfer music from a copy-protected CD to his or her iPod (through circumvention of the encryption). What are some of the main purposes of the proposed amendments, and how might consumers respond to them?

3. What are the copyright issues concerning the role of Internet Service Providers that have arisen in Canada, and what have the courts said about their potential liability? Do you agree with the courts' rulings?

4. What are the connections between patent law and access to essential medicines? How has Canadian law been reformed as a result of a World Trade Organization decision dealing with the issue of access to essential medicines? Do you agree with the reform?

5. Should higher life forms be patentable subject matter? What has the Supreme Court of Canada ruled about the patentability of a genetically modified mammal in the case involving the Harvard Mouse?

6. What are famous marks? Give some examples. What is the rationale for giving them special protection? What did the Supreme Court of Canada say about protecting famous marks under Canadian law in recent cases? Do you agree?

7. John Henry has discovered that his intellectual property rights in a computer program have been infringed, and he would like to pursue litigation. What types of remedies are available to him? Compare and contrast these remedies.

SUGGESTED READING

Henderson, Gordon F. (ed.), *Patent Law of Canada* (Toronto, Ont.: Carswell, 1994).
———, *Trade-marks Law of Canada* (Toronto, Ont.: Carswell, 1994).

Judge, Elizabeth, and Daniel Gervais. *Intellectual Property: The Law in Canada* (Toronto, Ont.: Thomson/Carswell, 2005).

Murray, Laura, and Samuel Trosow. *Canadian Copyright: A Citizen's Guide* (Toronto, Ont.: Between The Lines, 2007).

Vaver, David. *Copyright Law* (Toronto, Ont.: Irwin Law, 2000).

———. *Intellectual Property Law* (Toronto, Ont.: Irwin Law, 1997).

WEBSITES

Canadian Heritage, Copyright Policy Branch: <http://www.canadianheritage.gc.ca/progs/ac-ca/progs/pda-cpb/index_e.cfm>

Canadian Intellectual Property Office: <http://www.cipo.ic.gc.ca/epic/site/cipointernet-internetopic.nsf/en/Home>

CIPO Patents: <http://www.cipo.ic.gc.ca/epic/site/cipointernet-internetopic.nsf/en/h_wr00001e.html>

CIPO Trademarks: <http://www.cipo.ic.gc.ca/epic/site/cipointernet-internetopic.nsf/en/h_wr00002e.html>

CIPO Copyrights: <http://www.cipo.ic.gc.ca/epic/site/cipointernet-internetopic.nsf/en/h_wr00003e.html>

Canadian Internet Policy and Public Interest Clinic: <http://www.cippic.ca/en/>

Copyright Board of Canada: <http://www.cb-cda.gc.ca/new-e.html>

World Intellectual Property Organization: <http://www.wipo.int/portal/index.html.en>

Environmental Law

Allan Greenbaum
YORK UNIVERSITY

Alex Wellington
RYERSON UNIVERSITY

Learning Objectives

After reading this chapter, the reader should be able to:

➢ understand where "environmental law" fits in the Canadian legal system and Constitution

➢ understand how pollution is regulated under environmental statute law

➢ explain the difference between regulatory or "quasi-criminal" offences typical of environmental law and "true crimes", with particular reference to the "due diligence" defence

➢ identify, distinguish, and compare the enforcement options available to environmental officials in dealing with infractions of pollution-control laws and regulations

➢ appreciate the significance of liability of directors and officers for pollution offences

➢ understand the basic elements of the environmental assessment process

➢ appreciate the challenges of regulating toxic substances and recognize the complexities of risk assessment

➢ identify and distinguish the main common law causes of action that can be used in lawsuits over environmental harm

➢ understand the advantages and disadvantages of civil litigation as a way of addressing environmental problems

➢ identify and describe some legal tools available to governments to help protect natural areas and rare species

TABLE OF CONTENTS

INTRODUCTION

What Is Environmental Law?

Environmental law is a remarkably broad category, given that the notion of the environment is so all-encompassing. *Webster's Dictionary* defines "environment" as the "circumstances, objects or conditions by which one is surrounded", and, more usefully for our purposes, as "the complex of physical, chemical, and biotic factors (as climate, soil and living things) that act upon an organism or an ecological community and ultimately determine its form and survival". Specifically, "environmental law" refers to laws concerning the discharge of harmful substances into the air, water, or soil; nature preservation laws; and legal procedures for screening projects and substances that might have a harmful impact on human health or the natural environment.

The following examples could all be considered instances of environmental law:

- A lawsuit taken by a property owner against a vendor upon discovery that a newly purchased piece of land is contaminated from previous uses
- A class action lawsuit, on behalf of residents of a neighbourhood contaminated by cancer-causing chemicals, against the company that released the chemicals
- A certificate of approval allowing a pulp and paper mill to emit effluent into a river subject to terms and condition specifying the maximum amounts of which kinds of pollutants allowed to be present in the effluent
- Regulations requiring cars to have emission-control devices in working order
- Rules requiring that in order to be sold, pesticides must undergo a risk assessment to show that they do not pose an unacceptable risk to human health, if properly used
- Laws against killing members of designated endangered species of plants or animals

Environmental law came to be recognized as a distinct field in the late 1960s and early 1970s, when much of the legislative framework of modern environmental law was created. Environmental issues such as climate change and toxic chemical exposure continue to make headlines, however, and environmental law continues to evolve accordingly.

Types and Sources of Environmental Law

Environmental law includes both private (civil) and public (criminal, regulatory and administrative) law. *Private* environmental law mostly falls under the law of torts. Environmental harm caused by a specific identifiable party that threatens the health or property (or interferes with the property rights) of some other specific party may become the subject of a civil lawsuit should the injured party choose to sue. The main *source* of private environmental law is common law (judge-made law, based on precedent).

Public environmental law includes pollution regulation, nature-protection laws, and assessment and approval processes for projects like dams and highways or for potentially hazardous substances like pesticides. Here the state is understood as acting to protect the environment in the public interest (in contrast to **private law**, in which individuals go to court to protect their private rights). The main *sources* of public environmental law are statutes and regulations. *Statutes* are laws passed by Parliament or by provincial legislatures. Important federal environmental statutes include the *Fisheries Act*, the *Canadian Environmental Protection Act*, and the *Canadian Environmental Assessment Act*. Similar legislation exists at the provincial level; examples in Ontario include the *Environmental Assessment Act*, the *Environmental Protection Act*, and the *Ontario Water Resources Act*. Environmental statutes typically do not contain detailed rules about what is or is not allowed. Those rules are found in regulations. *Regulations* are detailed rules created by officials empowered by statutes to do so. The authority for making environmental regulations is usually delegated to Cabinet, although the actual work of drafting regulations falls to civil servants in the relevant department (for instance, the federal Department or provincial Ministry of the Environment). *Judges* play an important role in making public law because it is their job to *interpret* and apply statutes and to rule on their constitutionality. In addition, judges have been especially important in defining the burden of proof and the defences available in environmental cases.

Another source of law are principles enshrined in international agreements, which may then become incorporated into Canadian law through federal or provincial legislation, or judicial interpretation. A particularly influential example in the environmental context is the **precautionary principle**, which holds that actions should be taken to reduce or eliminate likely environmental hazards even if the causal link between a particular, suspected hazard has not yet been proven or fully understood scientifically. It is thus of especial relevance to environmental risk assessment.

The 1992 *Rio Declaration* defines the precautionary principle as follows:

> In order to protect the environment, the precautionary approach shall be widely applied by States according to their capabilities. Where there are threats of serious or irreversible damage, lack of full scientific certainty shall not be used as a reason for postponing cost-effective measures to prevent environmental degradation. [*Rio Declaration*, Principle 15][1]

That definition has been incorporated into the *Canadian Environmental Protection Act, 1999* [CEPA], S.C. 1999, c. 33. Other Canadian federal laws that have incorporated the precautionary principle include the *Canadian Environmental Assessment Act*, S.C. 1992, c. 37; *Pest Control Products Act*, S.C. 2002, c. 28; and the *Species At Risk Act*, S.C. 2002, c. 29. The Nova Scotia *Endangered Species Act*, S.N.S. 1998, c. 11, and the Ontario *Endangered Species Act*, S.O. 2007, c. 6, are examples of provincial laws. The precautionary principle was also cited by the Supreme Court of Canada in the *Spraytech v. Hudson* decision (discussed in Exhibit 34.2 later).

Constitutional Issues: Which Level of Government Is Responsible for the Environment?

The division of powers between the federal and provincial governments is set out in sections 91 and 92 of the *Constitution Act, 1867*. The "environment" is not a matter listed under either the federal or provincial heads of power. This ambiguity, unfortunately, has led to much litigation and intergovernmental wrangling. Exhibit 34.1 discusses a few significant cases that have concerned jurisdiction over the environment.

Provincial environmental jurisdiction is based on provincial jurisdiction over public lands and forests, natural resources, property and civil rights, local works and undertakings, and "all matters of a merely local" nature. *Federal* environmental jurisdiction is based on federal jurisdiction over fisheries, navigation, and shipping; criminal law; international and interprovincial affairs; and the "peace, order and good government" (POGG) power.

As interpreted by the courts, the peace, order and good government (POGG) clause gives the federal government jurisdiction over matters of "national concern", which cannot, by their nature, be adequately addressed by

---

[1] United Nations Conference on Environment and Development, Rio Declaration on Environment and Development, 1992: <http://www.un.org/documents/ga/conf151/aconf15126-1annex1.htm>

EXHIBIT 34.1   **Jurisdiction and Environmental Assessment**

During the late 1980s and early 1990s, the issue of the scope of federal jurisdiction over the environment was examined by the courts in two cases involving dams. One case involved construction of a dam on the Oldman River in Alberta and the other concerned plans by the Saskatchewan Water Corporation to build dams on the Rafferty and Alameda rivers. Project proponents insisted that the projects required approval only from the relevant provincial government. Opponents of the projects challenged them on the basis that the projects impacted on matters of federal government responsibility (including migratory birds and lands owned or administered by the federal government), and thus provincial environmental impact statements were not sufficient for the projects to proceed. Courts in both cases sided with environmentalists in upholding concurrent federal and provincial jurisdiction over environmental matters, even though both federal and provincial governments wanted to see the exercise of federal environmental responsibilities delegated or "downloaded" to provincial governments. The combined effect of these cases forced the federal government to acknowledge and exercise jurisdiction over the environment in matters concerning environmental assessment. As a result, the federal government passed the *Canadian Environmental Assessment Act* in 1992.

The *Friends of the Oldman River* case is also significant because it contains judicial language about the importance of approaching environmental management in an integrated manner. In it, Justice LaForest specifically states: "I cannot accept that the concept of environmental quality is confined to the biophysical environment alone; such an interpretation is unduly myopic and contrary to the generally held view that the 'environment' is a diffuse subject matter" (*Friends of the Oldman River Society v. Minister of Transport*, at 37). In connection with these issues, the Supreme Court of Canada took the view that so long as the subject matter about which a federal department (or provincial ministry) is deciding falls clearly within the (statutory and constitutional) purview of that department or ministry, it may take into account an indefinite range of relevant social, economic and environmental criteria or considerations in making that decision. Commentators emphasize that the passage in question represents the Court's first reference to the Brundtland Report, *Our Common Future*, produced by the World Commission on Environment and Development (WCED).

Sources: *Friends of the Oldman River Society v. Minister of Transport*, [1992] 1 S.C.R. 3; *Canadian Wildlife Federation v. Canada (Minister of the Environment)*, [1989] 3 F.C. 309 (T.D.), aff'd (1989), 99 N.R. 72 (F.C.A.).

---

provincial governments acting separately. The Supreme Court, in *R. v. Crown Zellerbach*,[2] found that the federal *Ocean Dumping Control Act* met that criterion because its purpose had a "singleness, distinctiveness and indivisibility that clearly distinguishes it from matters of provincial concern". In *R. v. Hydro-Quebec*,[3] however, the Supreme Court declined to use the POGG clause to uphold the constitutionality of provisions of the *Canadian Environmental Protection Act* (*CEPA*), because the latter legislation's broader concern with substances harmful to the environment was more diffuse. Rather, a slim 5 to 4 majority found provisions of *CEPA* regulating toxic substances constitutional under the federal criminal law power.

In practice, federal and provincial governments exercise shared or concurrent jurisdiction over environmental law. This arrangement suits both provincial and federal governments, since it allows governments either to take credit

---

[2] [1981] 1 S.C.R. 401.
[3] [1997] 3 S.C.R. 213.

| **Courts Rule on Municipal Pesticide By-Laws** | **EXHIBIT 34.2** |

The courts (up to and including the Supreme Court of Canada) have upheld the power of municipalities to ban or restrict the "cosmetic" use of pesticides, although the pesticides have been approved for use under federal and provincial law. "Cosmetic use" means using insecticides and herbicides (weed killers) to protect lawns and flowers, etc., rather than crops, dwellings, or human health. These bans are based on the argument that the possible (if unproven) health risks associated with these chemicals outweigh merely cosmetic benefits. The first such ban was enacted in 1991 by Hudson, Quebec, a suburb of Montreal.

When Spraytech, a lawn-care company, was charged with violating the Hudson bylaw, it argued that the bylaw was beyond the authority of the municipality to enact. It made two arguments. First, it argued that according to the Quebec *Cities and Towns Act*, municipalities cannot regulate hazardous substances without provincial government approval. Second, it argued that the federal and provincial governments had approved the products in question, and that these laws trump municipal bylaws in case of conflict.

The Hudson case made its way all the way up to the Supreme Court of Canada. In *114957 Canada Ltée (Spraytech, Société d'arrosage) v. Hudson (Town)*, the Supreme Court upheld the bylaw. It ruled that the bylaw was within the general power conferred on municipalities by the *Cities and Towns Act* to make bylaws to secure public health. It also ruled that there was no conflict between the bylaw and federal and provincial pesticides laws, since the latter *permit* people to use the pesticides, but don't *require* them to do so. Municipalities thus have the power to restrict the purposes for which the pesticides are used.

Since the 2001 Supreme Court decision in the Hudson case, hundreds of other cities and towns across Canada have enacted similar by-laws. Toronto passed a cosmetic pesticide ban similar to Hudson's in 2003. Toronto's bylaw was also challenged in court, this time by Croplife Canada, a pesticide industry group, in the case of *Croplife v. City of Toronto*. Again, the courts upheld the bylaw. In both the Hudson and Toronto cases, many environmental, health, and municipal organizations appeared before the courts as *intervenors* arguing in support of the bylaws.

In June 2008, the Ontario government passed legislation (the *Cosmetic Pesticides Ban Act*) prohibiting the cosmetic use of pesticides across the province, but this legislation also nullified the municipal pesticide bylaws.

Sources: *114957 Canada Ltée (Spraytech, Société d'arrosage) v. Hudson (Town)*, [2001] 2 S.C.R. 241; *Croplife Canada v. Toronto (City)* (2003), 68 O.R. (3d) 520 (Ont. Sup. Ct.) (Motions Court), 2003 CanLII 24713 (ON S.C.); *Croplife Canada v. Toronto (City)* (2005), 75 O.R. (3d) 357 (C.A.), (2005), 2005 CanLII 15709 (ON C.A.), leave to appeal to S.C.C. refused, [2005] S.C.C.A. No. 329.

for action or to avoid blame for inaction by "passing the buck", depending on which course seems most politically expedient. In recent years, the different levels of government have taken steps to co-ordinate their environmental responsibilities and to avoid duplication.

Municipalities are a third level of government. Their environmental responsibilities include local land-use planning (which was originally devised as a way to avert environmental tort litigation), urban form, and other matters related to local health and well-being. Unlike the provincial and federal governments, municipalities have no independent constitutional basis of authority, but have only those legal powers given to them by provincial legislation. Courts used to interpret this legislation narrowly, but have lately moved in a more liberal direction when it comes to interpreting the scope of municipal jurisdiction. This means that municipalities can "try out" at the local level policy initiatives that might then be adopted by senior levels of government. See Exhibit 34.2 for discussion of a much-publicized Supreme Court case dealing with municipal environmental jurisdiction.

POLLUTION-CONTROL LAW: THE REGULATORY SYSTEM ————————————

To remedy the deficiencies of the common law (to be discussed later on in this chapter), Canadian governments have set up a statute-based public law system for the regulation of pollution and other threats to the environment. This regulatory system is the main focus of environmental law.

The Legal Structure of the Regulatory System

Both federal and provincial regulatory systems derive from legislation. A typical environmental statute will define a number of *offences* and delegate rule-making, decision-making, and administrative authority to various *officials*. Roughly speaking, there are three levels of rules in pollution-control laws:

1. *Statutory prohibitions* against emitting harmful pollution. The statute will generally make it an offence to violate the statutory prohibition unless the polluter is in compliance with regulations or the terms of a permit or approval.

2. *Regulations*, which are much more specific, detailed, and technical than are the statutory prohibitions. The statute will also typically make it (at least potentially) an offence to be out of compliance with a regulation or approval.

3. In many cases, statutes require that certain kinds of polluters must have a *permit*, *licence*, or **certificate of approval**. To operate a specified kind of polluting enterprise without the appropriate permit or approval would be an offence, as would violating the terms and conditions of the permit. These terms and conditions are often based on regulations but are also tailored to specific circumstances. *Control orders* or *compliance orders* are also rules at this level.

All three levels of rules refer explicitly or implicitly to *standards*. Standards define what is and is not allowed by the rule, such as what exactly constitutes unlawful pollution in a given situation.

Standards and Standard-Setting

A variety of different kinds of standards are used in environmental law. We will describe a few of the major types of environmental standards and then say a bit about how standards are set — in theory and in practice.

Types of Standards

Ambient standards are standards for acceptable or unacceptable environmental quality. They are typically expressed in terms of concentrations of some pollutant such as coliform bacteria in water or particulate matter in air. Ambient standards usually function as guidelines, objectives, or targets used in setting regulatory standards rather than as standards that play a role in rules directly affecting polluters. An exception would be rules that require certain large emitters to stop operations on days when the air pollution index exceeds a certain threshold (the ambient standard).

Prescriptive standards stipulate processes, technologies, or materials. For example, a prescriptive standard might stipulate that a flue-gas scrubber of a particular design must be installed in a smelter or coal-fired power station. Voluntary industry standards and codes of "best practices" are also often prescriptive in form.

Performance standards stipulate a particular outcome but do not say how that outcome is to be achieved. They provide less guidance to polluters than prescriptive standards do, but more flexibility for innovation. Environmental

---

Types of Quantitative Effluent Standards

EXHIBIT 34.3

TYPE	DESCRIPTION
Absolute	x units of pollutant per unit time (e.g., kg. of pollutant per day)
Concentration	x units of pollutant per unit of effluent (e.g., kg. of pollutant per cubic metre of effluent)
Rate/Intensity	x units of pollutant per unit production (e.g., kg. of pollutant per tonne of product)
Relative	percent reduction relative to baseline-level emissions (e.g., 6 percent below 1990 emissions)

performance standards include effluent standards stipulating maximum allowable pollution emissions, energy efficiency standards, and so on.

Effluent standards (discharge standards) are performance standards related to pollution emissions. There are two kinds. *Impact standards* refer directly to the impact of the effluent, such as the toxicity of the effluent to fish or other aquatic organisms (as evidenced by the **fish toxicity test**). *Quantitative standards* stipulate an allowable quantity of a given pollutant in the effluent. Types of quantitative effluent standards are summarized in Exhibit 34.3.

Standard-setting

Regulatory standard-setting, in practice, takes into account both environmental quality objectives and the cost to business of meeting those objectives. Regulations may require polluters to use "best available technology economically achievable" ("BATEA"), or for effluent standards to be set "as low as reasonably achievable" (the "ALARA" principle). This balancing act is illustrated by the practice of the Ontario Ministry of the Environment in relation to hazardous air pollutants. The basic regulatory standard is set on the basis of health criteria (e.g., pollutant concentration that will cause less than a one-in-a-million increase in the risk of cancer to those exposed). Polluters who have trouble meeting the standard may, however, apply for an altered (relaxed) standard, citing technology and cost constraints. The altered standard must, however, meet the ALARA criterion and may not exceed an upper threshold defined (depending on the pollutant) as 10 or 100 times the basic standard.

Traditionally in Canada, environmental regulatory standard-setting has involved much negotiation between government and business. More recently, federal and provincial legislation (most particularly the Ontario *Environmental Bill of Rights*) has given the public the opportunity to review, to comment on, and in some circumstances to appeal the standard-setting and approval-granting decisions of government officials.

Statutory Prohibitions Environmental statutes typically include prohibitions on pollution and other kinds of environmentally damaging activities phrased in very broad language. For example, section 36(3) of the federal *Fisheries Act* makes it an offence to deposit a "deleterious substance" in water "frequented by fish" and outlines conditions under which this will be permitted. Similarly, section 14(1) of the

Ontario *Environmental Protection Act* prohibits "the discharge of a contaminant into the natural environment, if the discharge causes or may cause an adverse effect". Because of the broad and vague language in such provisions, the actual meaning of the prohibition depends on *statutory interpretation* on the part of officials and, ultimately, judges.

In the case of the *Fisheries Act* provision, "deleterious" has been interpreted in terms of an impact standard, namely the fish toxicity test. It has, moreover, been interpreted as an effluent standard, applied to the "substance" itself. If a substance fails the fish toxicity test, then it is deemed "deleterious", and you are prohibited from putting it where it will get into water inhabited by fish, even if it will enter the water in such small quantities as to be harmless. The Ontario *EPA* provision, in contrast, refers to an "adverse effect" on the environment. In interpreting that provision, courts will also use an impact standard, but they will apply it to the receiving medium (e.g., water or air) rather than to the "contaminant" itself. In our example, you would not be in violation of the Ontario *EPA* prohibition if only harmless quantities of the contaminant could reach the water.

Another feature of statutory prohibitions is that they make exceptions for activities authorized by regulations or permits. The extent of these exceptions again depends on the precise wording of the statute, as interpreted by the courts.

Regulations

Regulations, unlike statutory prohibitions, generally contain explicit and detailed standards, as well as detailed rules about how the regulated party is to monitor and report on emissions. Regulations may incorporate either prescriptive or performance standards, or some combination of both. Ontario's Local Air Quality regulation (O. Reg. 419/2005) is an example of a regulation that incorporates ambient standards. It requires designated air polluters to model (with computers) the dispersion of their effluent in the air to ensure that the concentration of regulated pollutants does not exceed concentration standards at specified "points of impingement".

Regulations that legally impose prescriptive standards are sometimes referred to as "command and control" regulations. The term "command and control" (or "command-penalty") regulation is also used more generally to refer to regulations that impose mandatory standards. Under command and control regulations in this sense, polluters are liable to be punished if they violate the standards written into the regulation. Such regulations are contrasted with "economic instruments" such as financial incentives, pollution taxes, or tradable pollution credits, which allow a given polluter to emit more than the standard if they pay more or buy additional credits from polluters who pollute less than the standard (thus rewarding those who pollute less and costing — but not punishing — those who pollute more). Economic instruments are sometimes criticized as creating a "licence to pollute", but it is important to realize that except in rare instances where pollution is banned altogether, command and control regulations *also* create a *free* licence to pollute so long as the regulatory standards are not violated or exceeded. Command and control regulations (especially those with prescriptive standards) are frequently criticized as being rigid, inefficient, and discouraging innovation. They have often proved effective in reducing pollution, however, and compliance costs usually turn out to be lower than predicted (especially as predicted by affected businesses).

Permits and Approvals

Pollution-control statutes typically require those who wish to undertake an enterprise or activity that will release wastes or contaminants into the environment to get official permission to do so. Depending on the jurisdiction, the permission document legally required is called a "permit", "licence", "consent", or "certificate of approval". The process for obtaining a permit, and some of the required terms and conditions, will be set out in the statute and regulations. Although the terms of permits will usually be based on standards in regulations, regulations may also give officials the discretion to vary those standards — for example, to impose stricter standards than those in the regulation to take into account the sensitivity of the environment into which the pollution is being discharged or the cumulative effects of multiple pollution sources.

Polluters generally have the right to appeal official decisions regarding whether and on what conditions to grant approvals. These appeals are heard by an administrative tribunal. Members of the public may also have standing to appeal environmental permit decisions. In some jurisdictions, only those who can show that they are personally affected will have the right to appeal. In Ontario, the *Environmental Bill of Rights* requires all such permits (called "instruments") to be posted on a website for public review and comment, and gives any member of the public the right to apply for leave (permission) to appeal the permit. To be granted leave, the appellant must show they have some grounds to claim that the decision was unreasonable. Approvals granted under the federal *Canadian Environmental Protection Act 1999* are also posted in an online registry for public review and comment, but are not subject to a public right of appeal.

ENFORCEMENT OF POLLUTION REGULATIONS

The Spectrum of Responses to Non-compliance

What happens if a polluter subject to pollution-control laws is detected violating a statutory prohibition, a regulation, or the terms of a permit or approval? Enforcement officials have a range of options, displayed in Exhibit 34.4. We summarize them briefly here and provide more detail below. A notable feature of environmental enforcement is the role of *negotiation* between polluters and enforcement officials. In Canada, polluters have often had the opportunity both to negotiate what the rules will be, and to negotiate what will happen when they have broken those rules.

Forbearance

The first option, which involves the least use of law, is to exercise **forbearance**. That is, the officials in question may decline to impose legal sanctions. Officials are likely to choose forbearance if they are persuaded that (i) the violation poses no serious risk; (ii) the costs of compliance would be too great for the polluter (or society as a whole); (iii) more time is required for the polluter to come into compliance (and that additional time would be reasonable); and/or (iv) the polluter has already made good faith efforts to comply with the law. In some cases, government enforcement agencies will exercise forbearance simply because they lack the resources — in terms of money and personnel — to go after every polluter who is in violation of the law.

Prosecution

At the other end of the enforcement spectrum is *prosecution* — that is, *charging* the polluter with an *offence*. A successful prosecution results in a finding of *guilt*, i.e., in the *conviction* of the *accused*. In environmental cases, the accused is usually a corporation, but individual officers (executives, managers, or directors) may also be held personally liable.

Most environmental offences are what judges call "public welfare", "regulatory", or "quasi-criminal" offences. The prosecution of these offences, in

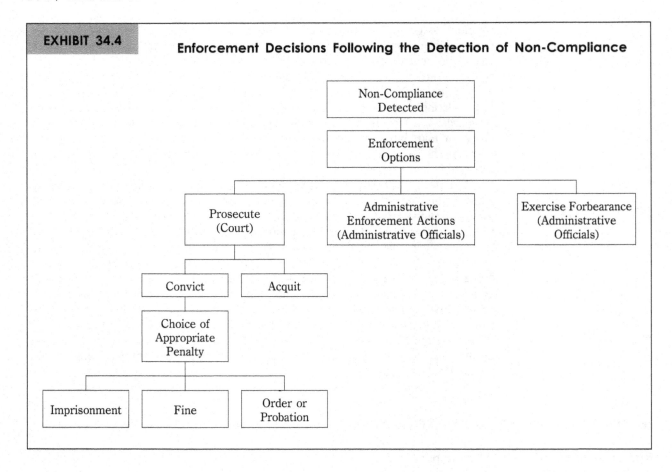

EXHIBIT 34.4

Enforcement Decisions Following the Detection of Non-Compliance

accordance with the *Provincial Offences Act* in Ontario, is procedurally the same as the prosecution of summary conviction criminal offences. The process begins with the laying of an "information". If the accused pleads "not guilty", there is a trial. As in a criminal trial, the prosecutor must prove beyond a reasonable doubt all the relevant facts establishing the *actus reus* (guilty act). For example, in a *Fisheries Act* prosecution, the prosecutor might have to prove — beyond a reasonable doubt and in conformity with the laws of admissible evidence — that effluent emitted from the accused's pulp mill at such and such a place and time in such and such a quantity was toxic to fish (meeting the impact standard used to interpret the statutory prohibition) and that the mill was at that time out of compliance with performance and prescriptive standards found in the relevant regulations and permits. This can be quite a burden for the prosecution to bear.

Strict Liability and the Due Diligence Defence

Where quasi-criminal regulatory offences differ from "true crimes" is with respect to the "mental element". Criminal liability normally requires proof not only of the *actus reus* but of the *mens rea* (guilty mind). That is, the accused must not only have done the illegal act, but to have *intended* it (or at least to have been reckless). Because in most cases it would be almost impossible to *prove* that a company *intended* to violate pollution standards or other "public welfare" rules, courts have been reluctant to hold the prosecution to the "true crime" standard in such cases. At the same time, courts have also been very reluctant to interpret these offences (which can be punishable by heavy fines or imprisonment) as imposing "absolute liability". An **absolute**

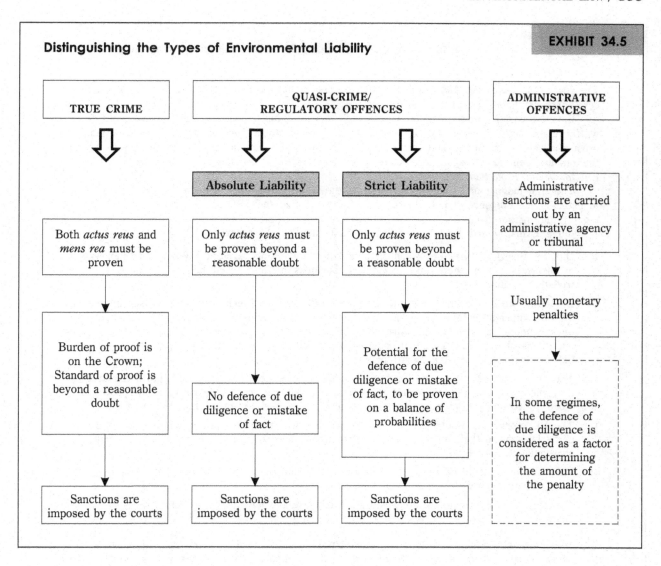

Distinguishing the Types of Environmental Liability

EXHIBIT 34.5

TRUE CRIME	QUASI-CRIME/ REGULATORY OFFENCES		ADMINISTRATIVE OFFENCES
⇩	⇩	⇩	⇩
	Absolute Liability	**Strict Liability**	Administrative sanctions are carried out by an administrative agency or tribunal
Both *actus reus* and *mens rea* must be proven	Only *actus reus* must be proven beyond a reasonable doubt	Only *actus reus* must be proven beyond a reasonable doubt	
			Usually monetary penalties
Burden of proof is on the Crown; Standard of proof is beyond a reasonable doubt	No defence of due diligence or mistake of fact	Potential for the defence of due diligence or mistake of fact, to be proven on a balance of probabilities	In some regimes, the defence of due diligence is considered as a factor for determining the amount of the penalty
Sanctions are imposed by the courts	Sanctions are imposed by the courts	Sanctions are imposed by the courts	

liability offence is one where only *actus reus* need be proven, and there is no potential for a due diligence defence. See Exhibit 34.5 for an illustration of the distinctions between true criminal liability, strict liability, and absolute liability.

The Canadian courts (most notably the Supreme Court in *R. v. Sault Ste. Marie*[4]) have articulated a concept of "strict liability" as appropriate for the vast majority of environmental and other "quasi-criminal" offences. **Strict liability** in this sense is intermediate between true criminal liability (where intent must be proven) and absolute liability (where one may be found guilty for entirely unintended, unavoidable acts). (Strict liability in this context needs to be distinguished from the *tort* of strict liability, discussed below.) For strict liability offences, the prosecution need only prove the *actus reus*; at that point, the onus shifts to the accused to prove (on a balance of probabilities) that they had exercised **due diligence** (reasonable care) to avoid the offence. If the accused persuades the court that the violation had occurred

---

[4] [1978] 2 S.C.R. 1299.

EXHIBIT 34.6   A Case about Pollution, Directors' Liability, and Due Diligence

The *R. v. Bata Industries Ltd.* case illustrates several points about strict liability/due diligence, officers' personal liability, and sentencing options.

Bata Industries Limited operated a shoe factory in Batawa, Ontario. Improperly stored toxic wastes leaked into the soil and contaminated the groundwater. The Ministry of the Environment prosecuted the corporation, and also the corporation's Chief Executive Officer, its President and the on-site General Manager, for violations of the *Ontario Water Resources Act* and the *Ontario Environmental Protection Act*.

The trial judge found that the corporation, the General Manager, and the President had failed to exercise due diligence and convicted them. He found that the CEO had acted reasonably in relying on information from the General Manager and so acquitted him.

Judge Ormston articulated the following influential set of criteria for due diligence:

¤ Did the Board of Directors establish a pollution-prevention "system"? Was there supervision or inspection? Was there improvement in business methods? Did he exhort those he controlled or influenced?

¤ Did each Director ensure that the Corporate officers have been instructed to set up with a system sufficient within the terms and practices of its industry of ensuring compliance with environmental laws, to ensure that the officers report back periodically to the Board of the operations of the system, and to ensure that the officers are instructed to report any substantial non-compliance to the Board in a timely manner?

¤ The Directors are responsible for reviewing the environmental compliance reports provided by the officers of the corporation but are justified in placing reasonable reliance on reports provided to them by corporate officers, consultants, counsel, or other informed parties.

¤ The Directors should substantiate that the officers are promptly addressing environmental concerns brought to their attention by government agencies or other concerned parties, including shareholders.

¤ The Directors should be aware of the standards of their industry and other industries that deal with similar environmental pollutants or risks.

¤ The Directors should immediately and personally react when they have notice the system has failed.

The trial judge also noted: "Within this general profile and dependent upon the nature and structure of the corporate activity, one would hope to find remedial and contingency plans for spills, a system of ongoing environmental audit, training programs, sufficient authority to act and other indices of a proactive environmental policy."

Bata Ltd. was fined $60,000 and ordered to pay that money (subsequently reduced to $30,000 on appeal) into a local toxic waste disposal program. The General Manager and the President were each ordered to pay $12,000 (this was reduced to $6,000 each on appeal). The trial judge found that the CEO had acted reasonably in relying on information from the General Manager and so acquitted him. The probation order required Bata Ltd. to publish information about the conviction and sentences on the front page of its newsletter and prohibited it from indemnifying the President and General Manager for their personal fines (this latter probation condition was struck down on appeal).

Source: *R. v. Bata Industries Ltd.* (1992), 9 O.R. (3d) 329 (Prov. Ct.).

---

despite reasonable precautions to avoid it, then the accused will be acquitted. A well-known statement of due diligence criteria is found in the trial level decision in *R. v. Bata*[5] (see Exhibit 34.6).

---

[5] (1992), 9 O.R. (3d) 329 (Prov. Ct.).

Directors' Liability

When companies pollute, liability might be incurred by both the corporation itself and by the individual flesh-and-blood people who are responsible for the actions of corporations. Thus, there is also the prospect of personal liability for directors, officers, and others for environmental and other offences (see Exhibit 34.6). That liability can be civil or quasi-criminal, or even true criminal liability (as with recent amendments to the *Criminal Code* providing for true criminal liability for some workplace health and safety offences).

Sentencing

Conviction will result in a *sentence*. The commonest sentencing options for environmental offences are *fines* and *probation orders* (which may include publicizing the conviction and taking steps to remedy the environmental harm done and to prevent future infractions). In rare cases, individual officers may be sentenced to prison, usually in cases where they have wilfully and persistently defied court orders or obstructed enforcement efforts. Maximum (and sometimes minimum) sentences (fines and prison terms) are stipulated in the statute under which the accused is charged, but judges have quite a lot of discretion in sentencing. Conviction under federal (but not provincial) statutes may also result in a criminal record.

The stigma of conviction makes prosecution (especially if individual officers as well as companies are charged) a powerful deterrent. For this reason, many environmental advocates and legal scholars would like to see greater use of prosecution. Prosecution is, however, more difficult, costly, and time-consuming for enforcement officials than most other enforcement options.

Private Prosecution

If a polluter is in violation of the law and authorities are declining to enforce the law, a private individual can lay charges. This is called a private prosecution. In a private prosecution, a private party is taking the role usually taken by the Crown. It remains an action to enforce public law, however, and needs to be distinguished from civil litigation to enforce the plaintiff's private rights. The federal *Fisheries Act* provides that private prosecutors receive a share of a fine resulting from a successful prosecution. Even with this provision, private prosecution is difficult and expensive, especially if the prosecutors do not enjoy the active co-operation of government enforcement officials (which they sometimes do).

Administrative Enforcement Measures

Between prosecution and forbearance lie a range of *administrative enforcement measures*. These measures can be divided up in various ways. One way is to distinguish between *administrative compliance measures* (such as orders), which require the violator to do or cease to do something, and **administrative monetary penalties** (AMPs) and tickets, which impose a fine. In Ontario, environmental AMPs are calculated on the basis of a formula that takes into account the type, seriousness, and duration of the offence, the amount of money the polluter saved by polluting, and any mitigating circumstances. Environmental tickets, which are used by both provincial and federal authorities, are like traffic tickets and impose a small fine for minor infractions. Another way to divide up this middle ground between prosecution and forbearance is to draw a distinction between purely administrative actions (such as orders and AMPs), which are imposed by officials or administrative tribunals entirely apart from the court system, and alternative enforcement measures such as tickets and federal "environmental protection alternative measures" (EPAMs), which are technically within the jurisdiction of the courts. With these latter measures, violators have the option of avoiding or suspending prosecution by paying a set fine or agreeing to other terms and conditions.

Administrative measures are an attractive enforcement option because they are usually faster and less expensive than prosecution.

ENVIRONMENTAL IMPACT AND SUBSTANCE RISK ASSESSMENT ─────────

Canadian law prescribes assessment processes for both projects ("environmental assessment") and potentially hazardous substances.

Environmental Assessment

Environmental impact assessment (EIA), or **environmental assessment (EA)**, as it is more often called in Canadian law, is a process by which the environmental effects of a proposed project are examined and a decision made about whether the project should be allowed to go ahead. There are both provincial and federal EA statutes. The cases discussed in Exhibit 34.1 concern environmental assessment and issues of jurisdiction between the two levels of government. EA is mainly required of public sector projects, and (depending on the province) designated categories of private projects (such as waste disposal facilities). Provincial projects are subject to provincial EA. Federal projects, or provincial projects that also require federal approval (such as dams on navigable rivers) or that otherwise impinge on matters of federal jurisdiction, also require federal EA. Federal and provincial EA processes may be combined in a single joint EA, and an EA may also be joined with an approval process required under other legislation.

The project being assessed (e.g., a highway) is called the "undertaking", and the body (usually a public agency, e.g., the Ministry of Transportation) that seeks to carry out the project is called the "proponent" or (in the federal *Canadian Environmental Assessment Act*) the "responsible authority" (RA). It is the responsibility of the proponent to conduct physical, biological, ecological, and social impact studies and to prepare a document describing the impacts of the undertaking as proposed. In cases of major undertakings, there should also be a comparison of expected impacts with the impacts of "alternatives to the undertaking" and with "alternative means of carrying out the undertaking", as well as suggestions for ways of mitigating the expected negative impacts. Since the number of issues and topics that could potentially be addressed in an EA is practically infinite, the proponent will first conduct a preliminary process called "scoping". In that process, the proponent will consult with affected parties (including other government departments and members of the public) to determine which issues and concerns ought to be addressed. Once the EA document is prepared it is again subject to review by other government officials and interested members of the public.

Since the EA document is prepared on behalf of the proponent, it will typically conclude that an undertaking is unlikely to cause undue environmental harm and should be approved. Environmentalists or others concerned about the undertaking may disagree. They may think that the EA report should not be accepted (because it is based on insufficient or faulty research) and/or that, on the basis of information in the report itself, the undertaking should not be approved. In such cases, they may request that the EA be subject to a hearing. At the hearing, the proponent and the opposing parties, often represented by lawyers, will submit evidence, call expert witnesses, and cross-examine other parties' witnesses. Then the EA tribunal will make a decision about whether to accept the report and/or approve the undertaking, and under what conditions.

Because some small undertakings (such as stream crossings) are frequent and routine, they may be assessed as a class (a class EA) rather than on an individual basis. If a particular instance of an undertaking in that class might have significant distinctive impacts not addressed in the class EA, it can be "bumped up" and be subject to its own EA as a separate undertaking.

Substance Assessment and Approval

Potentially hazardous substances, as well as undertakings, may have to go through a **risk assessment** and approval process under Canadian law. For example, under the federal *Pest Control Products Act*, all pesticides must undergo a risk assessment to be approved for use in Canada. Those found to pose an unacceptable risk will not be approved. More generally, all new substances produced in or imported into Canada must be assessed under the *Canadian Environmental Protection Act*. Substances listed as being in use as of 1986 (some 23,000 of them) may continue in use without being assessed but are gradually being assessed on a priority basis by Health Canada and Environment Canada. Substances that are found to be hazardous in some respect are placed on a Toxics List and are subject to a range of regulatory controls, guidelines, and voluntary measures. The definition of "toxic" is very broad and is relative to the quantity being emitted (so, for example, carbon dioxide — which you exhale with every breath and which plants need to survive — is listed because it is being generated in such quantities as to promote dangerous global warming). The nastiest and most persistent of these toxins are placed on the Virtual Elimination List and are effectively banned.

As with EA, the data and analysis upon which the risk assessment is based are provided by the proponents. Whereas EA requirements are openended, new substances regulations are long and complex, and stipulate in precise detail the kinds of data that must be submitted and the kinds of studies and tests that must be conducted to obtain those data. Producers do not, however, have to prove the substance is safe to be allowed to produce it under *CEPA*; rather, they must submit data which the government will use to regulate.

CIVIL LIABILITY FOR ENVIRONMENTAL HARM

If you or your property are harmed or threatened by pollution, noise, vibration, contamination, or changes in water level caused by the actions of another party, you may be able to sue that party. This would be an instance of private (civil) law, specifically tort law. If you (the plaintiff) are successful, the defendant will be found *civilly liable*. If the defendant is found liable, the plaintiff is entitled to a *remedy*. There are two main kinds of remedy: monetary compensation paid by the defendant (*damages*), and a court order requiring the defendant to stop (or not to commence) the harmful activity in question (an *injunction*). A plaintiff can be awarded both types of remedies, if the court so decides.

Although civil litigation is not a major aspect of environmental law, it is one of the best known. A number of high-profile cases (mainly in the United States, but also in Canada) have been based on the alleged contamination of a community by toxic substances from local industry, which is often claimed to result in elevated rates of cancer and other diseases. Such cases are referred to as *toxic torts*. Real-life toxic tort cases were dramatized in the 1998 film *A Civil Action* and the 2000 film *Erin Brockovich*.

In order to succeed, the plaintiff must prove, on a balance of probabilities, that the defendant in fact caused the harm alleged. In environmental cases, this is often no simple matter. For example, if you are claiming that the defendant's pollution caused you to get cancer, it is not enough to show that the defendant has emitted pollutants that have been linked to cancer. You must show that it was the defendant's pollution that probably caused *your* cancer. This usually raises complex technical issues of fact that are fraught with scientific uncertainty. The plaintiff must also show that the defendant's activity falls within a legally recognized **cause of action**.

Common Law Causes of Action

For the most part, civil liability still rests on causes of action derived from common law. Negligence is the most common form of tort liability in general, and it also plays a role in environmental litigation. There are three tort causes of action that arise from the plaintiff's property rights: trespass to land, breach of riparian rights, and private nuisance. Two other causes of action found in environmental tort cases are public nuisance and strict liability.

Negligence

The elements of a **negligence** action are the following:

1. *Duty of care.* The defendant must owe a legal duty to the victim. A duty is a legally enforceable obligation to conform to a particular standard of conduct. Except in malpractice and strict liability cases, the duty is set by what a "reasonable man of ordinary prudence" would have done. There is a general duty to prevent foreseeable injury to a victim.

2. *Breach of the duty.* The defendant breached that duty by failure to conform to the expected standard of care.

3. *Causation.* The breach was the cause of an injury to the victim. The causation does not need to be direct: defendant's act (or failure to act) could begin a continuous sequence of events that ended in plaintiff's injury, a so-called "proximate cause". The breach cannot be too remote a cause of the injury.

4. *Injury.* There must be an injury. In most cases, there must be a physical or financial injury to the victim, but sometimes emotional distress, embarrassment, or dignitary harms are adequate for recovery.

To proceed in a negligence action, a plaintiff does not have to be a landowner. Nor does the defendant have to have caused the environmental hazard in question; the defendant may, for example, have negligently failed to fulfill a duty to inform the plaintiff of the hazard or to remedy the situation. However, the plaintiff must show that the defendant had a duty of care and failed to fulfill that duty.

Trespass to Land

Trespass to land involves the defendant, without authorization, directly and intentionally entering on to the plaintiff's land or placing a foreign object or substance on it. Unlike most other torts, this may result in liability without proof of harm or loss. This means, for example, that you could get an injunction to stop someone from dumping debris on your property even if you could not show that the dumping interfered with your use of the land or diminished its value. This cause of action is of limited use in environmental cases because pollution is seldom introduced directly and intentionally onto the property of those affected. In one New Brunswick case, a company spraying forests with insecticide to control spruce budworm was found liable in trespass for directly and without permission spraying the plaintiffs' property.[6]

---

[6] *Friesen et. al. v. Forest Protection Ltd.* (1978), 22 N.B.R. (2d) 146 (QB).

***McKie v. K.V.P*: A Classic Water Pollution Lawsuit and its Aftermath**	**EXHIBIT 34.7**

In 1946, Kalamazoo Vegetable Parchment (K.V.P.) acquired a pulp and paper mill in Espanola, Ontario, that had closed 15 years earlier in the Depression. The re-opened mill released several tonnes of effluent a day into the Spanish River. The pollution killed fish, destroyed wild rice beds that provided duck habitat, and made the water smell like rotting cabbage — undrinkable by people or farm animals.

In 1948, a group of downstream riparian landowners — including farmers, tourist operators, and a commercial fisher — sued KVP for private nuisance and violation of riparian rights. At the time, the company employed 1,500 people in town and had an agreement with the government that it would put no waste in the river "beyond that reasonably necessary for the operation". The company argued that the agreement gave it permission to pollute the river. It also argued that the pollutants were so diluted by the river as to be harmless, and that the court should take into account the mill's economic importance to the region.

The trial judge, Chief Justice McRuer, found in favour of the plaintiffs. He awarded the plaintiffs $5,600 in damages and an injunction giving the company six months to stop polluting the river. He reasoned that to allow the company to pollute would, in effect, be to expropriate the plaintiffs' riparian rights. This, he ruled, would be unlawful regardless of the economic impact of the injunction and regardless of whether the plaintiffs were actually harmed by the pollution.

K.V.P. appealed the decision and, meanwhile, successfully lobbied the provincial government to amend the *Lakes and Rivers Improvement Act* to include a provision allowing judges to refuse to grant an injunction in riparian rights cases if "having regard for all the circumstances" it is "proper and expedient" not to. By this time the case had reached the Supreme Court, which refused to quash the injunction because the legislation had been passed after the decision was appealed and could not be used retroactively. The Supreme Court also held that in this case damages alone could not provide a "complete and adequate remedy".

Finally, in 1950, the provincial government under Premier Leslie Frost passed special legislation (*An Act respecting the KVP Company Limited*) dissolving the injunction, so as to ensure the economic viability of the mill and the community dependent on it. After retiring from politics, former Premier Frost was appointed to K.V.P.'s board of directors.

Sources: *McKie et. al. v. The K.V.P. Co. Ltd.*, [1948] O.R. 398; *The K.V.P. Co. Ltd. v. Earl McKie et al.*, [1949] S.C.R. 698.

Breach of Riparian Rights

"Riparian" means having to do with a river bank. **Riparian rights** go along with ownership of land that adjoins a watercourse. Riparian owners have a right to use the water flowing through or situated next to their land, so long as they don't unreasonably affect the quantity or quality of water for other riparian owners. This means that if someone pollutes or diverts a stream flowing through or by your property, they have violated your riparian rights and you may sue them. Like trespass to land, breach of riparian rights is a tort in itself even if it does not result in harm or loss to the plaintiff, and the successful plaintiff may obtain an injunction to stop or forestall the pollution. Breach of riparian rights is one of the most important common law causes of action in Canadian environmental law. A famous Canadian riparian rights case is discussed in Exhibit 34.7.

Private Nuisance

Private nuisance arises when the defendant's activities unreasonably interfere with the plaintiff's use and enjoyment of their property. In contrast to the tort of negligence, "unreasonable" here refers to the effect on the plaintiff, not to the carelessness of the defendant. That is, the effect is a nuisance if it is more than what a "reasonable" (i.e., not unusually sensitive) person could be expected to put up with, even if the defendant took reasonable care to avoid causing it. In contrast to trespass to land or breach of riparian rights, the defendant will only be found liable if their activity harms the plaintiff's person or property in some way or substantially interferes with the plaintiff's comfort or convenience.

Any kind of pollution, including noise, vibration, smell, light, or dust, can constitute a nuisance. Many nuisance cases have involved backed-up sewers and flooded basements. One case involved damage to fruit trees in an orchard caused by road salt from a highway.[7] Nuisance is the most important common law cause of action in environmental law.

Public Nuisance

The tort of public nuisance is an odd hybrid of public and private law. **Public nuisance** involves the interference with public, not private, rights. Unfortunately, unless the harm in question *also* infringes the plaintiff's private rights, a private party does not have automatic standing to sue under common law and would require the permission of the Attorney General to be able to bring an action in court. For example, in *Hickey v. Electric Reduction Co.*,[8] commercial fishers of Placentia Bay, Newfoundland, were denied standing to sue a polluter who destroyed the fishery on which their livelihoods depended. The court held that right to fish in the ocean was not exclusive to the plaintiffs but was shared by the general public. In Ontario, the 1994 *Environmental Bill of Rights* eliminated this common law restriction on standing to sue in public nuisance. Public nuisance is still used rarely in Ontario and mainly comes up in conjunction with private nuisance and negligence in the context of class action suits.

Strict Liability (Rylands v. Fletcher Rule)

According to this rule, those who store hazardous substances on their land are liable for damage done should the substances escape, regardless of whether they have taken reasonable care to avoid this mishap. The elements to this cause of action are as follows:

1. The Defendant is in lawful occupation of property.
2. The stored property is a dangerous agent or thing constituting a non-natural use of land.
3. The agent or potential mischief-causing thing escapes from the defendant's property.
4. The escaped agent or potential mischief-causing thing ends up causing damage to the plaintiff.

There may be a fifth element, one which has been added more recently by some British and Canadian courts:

5. Damage should be reasonably foreseeable.

In the original 1868 case, *Rylands v. Fletcher*,[9] the defendant had created a water reservoir on land with improperly sealed abandoned mine shafts. Water drained down the shafts and then made its way into the plaintiff's mine nearby. Recent Canadian cases involving this cause of action include one

---

[7] *Schenk v. Ontario*, [1987] 2 S.C.R. 289.
[8] (1971), 2 Nfld. & P.E.I.R. 246.
[9] (1868), LR 3 HL 330, 339.

where the plaintiff's fishing gear was damaged by a surge of water from the defendant's hydro dam[10] and another where the plaintiff's crops were damaged by herbicides drifting from the defendant's neighbouring farm.[11]

Contract Issues

Common law doctrine concerning contract cases sets out circumstances in which vendors would have a duty to disclose information regarding the contaminated state of a property. *Caveat emptor*, a Latin term, which means "let the buyer beware", articulates "a legal maxim stating that the buyer takes the risk regarding the quality or condition of the property purchased, unless protected by warranty".[12] *Caveat emptor* applies specifically to situations with patent defects, which a prudent and diligent purchaser would be expected to discover upon inspection, exercising ordinary care prior to finalizing a purchase. Yet, for situations where there are latent defects, the purchaser is not expected to make the discovery beforehand.

It is important to note that the doctrine of *caveat emptor* will not apply to situations where there has been fraudulent representations or conduct. If a defect is latent, and if it could pose a risk of danger to life, health or the environment, then failure on the part of a vendor to disclose that information may constitute fraud. The deceived purchaser would then have legal grounds to sue for deceit.

There have been several cases from Ontario addressing these issues and holding that what constitutes a defect must be determined in the context of the intended use of the land. One is a real estate case, *801438 Ont. Inc. v. Badurina*,[13] which exemplifies the *caveat emptor* doctrine. The purchaser's action against the defendant vendor was dismissed because the Ontario Superior Court of Justice found that the vendor had made no representations as to the environmental condition of the land or to its potential for development. The court held that the purchaser could have ascertained for itself what would be the likely impact of adjacent contaminated land upon development potential.

Class Action Suits

A **class action** proceeding is a civil lawsuit in which a representative plaintiff acts on behalf of a defined class of plaintiffs (e.g., all consumers injured by a particular faulty product, or all investors induced to invest in a particular fraudulent business scheme). A class action allows the issues common to a large number of separate potential cases to be heard in one trial. Class actions thus avoid costs and duplication for the court system and the defendants. They also allow justice to be done in cases where one party inflicts a relatively small amount of harm on each of a large number of people for whom an individual lawsuit would not be worth while or would be unaffordable. For this reason they are obviously useful for pollution cases.

It is important to keep in mind that class actions differ from ordinary lawsuits only in respect of procedure, not substance. Class action is not a cause of action. All class action tort suits have to be based on one or more of the causes of action discussed above, just like individual tort actions (for instance, negligence).

---

[10] *Croft v. Nova Scotia Power Inc.* (2003), 125 *All Canada Weekly Summaries* (3d) 740.

[11] *Morassutti v. Lanoue* (2000), 96 *All Canada Weekly Summaries* (3d) 1084.

[12] National Association of Realtors — Real Estate Auction Committee, the National Auctioneers Association and the Auction Marketing Institute, Real Estate Glossary: <http://www.aaauctionservice.com/glossery_files/glossery.htm>.

[13] (2000), 34 RPR (3d) 306 (Ont. S.C.J.).

EXHIBIT 34.8

A Canadian Toxic Tort Class Action

From 1918 to 1984, Inco operated a nickel refinery in Port Colborne, Ontario. Over the years, the Inco refinery had released some 20,000 tonnes of nickel into the environment, mostly in the form of nickel oxide, a potent carcinogen. In 2001, Wilfred Pearson, a homeowner in the most contaminated part of town, launched a class action lawsuit against Inco on behalf of owners of contaminated property. The causes of action are the common law torts of negligence and private nuisance. At the time of writing (spring 2008), the case has yet to come to trial. All the legal decisions discussed here relate to pre-trial motions; they are about whether the case would be allowed to proceed as a class action.

The motions court judge refused to certify the class action. He found the definition of the class (all who resided in a defined area of Port Colborne after 1995) arbitrary and irrational, since it would include some people who had not been harmed and exclude some others who had been. He found that despite a number of valid common issues, so many complex individual issues would remain outstanding that no advantage would be gained by proceeding via a class action. The motions judge also found that Pearson would not make a good representative plaintiff because he lacked the necessary financial resources, his plan of litigation was vague, and, as one of the most seriously affected members of the class, he might have a conflict of interest with those who suffered minor loss and would prefer to settle the case quickly. Pearson was ordered to pay Inco's legal expenses. Pearson appealed the decision to Divisional Court and lost again. He appealed further to the Ontario Court of Appeal.

The Court of Appeal overturned the previous decisions and certified the class. The different outcome was partly due to Pearson having simplified the claim in the meantime, dropping the health issues and focusing on the effect of contamination on property values (which would be similar for all members of the class). It was also due to a shift by the courts to a more liberal interpretation of class action rules. The Court of Appeal recognized that in environmental cases, the definition of the plaintiff class would always have to be somewhat arbitrary, since pollution effects don't have clearly defined boundaries. It also acknowledged that only through class actions could many affected persons unable to afford litigation on their own have a chance seek justice in the courts.

Sources: *Pearson v. Inco et al.,* [2002] O.J. No. 2764, 33 C.P.C. (5th) 264 (Motions Court), *Pearson v. Inco et al.,* 2004 CanLII 34446 [re issues of substance] and 2004 CanLII 4038 [re issue of costs] (ON S.C.D.C.) (Divisional Court), *Pearson v. Inco et al.,* 2006 CanLII 913 (Ont. Court of Appeal).

A class action involves three main stages. First, the representative plaintiff must persuade the court to certify the class — i.e., to allow the case to go ahead as a class action with the plaintiff as its representative. The court will only do so if it is convinced that the members of the class were affected in ways that raise enough common issues of fact and law that it would be advantageous to address those common issues in a single trial. Next there is a trial on the common issues — the class action proper. Finally, there are individual proceedings in which members of the class are awarded damages based on their specific circumstances, in light of the outcome of the common trial.

Class action suits have long been a prominent part of American law. Canadian rules of civil procedure made large class actions impractical until class action legislation was passed, first in Quebec in 1978 and then in Ontario in 1993. Since then, most Canadian provinces have passed class action legislation. Perhaps surprisingly, few recent Canadian class action cases have involved environmental issues, and Canadian courts have been reluctant to certify class actions in environmental cases. Exhibit 34.8 describes an Ontario toxic tort class action currently before the courts.

Shortcomings of Civil Litigation

Civil litigation has major shortcomings as an approach to protecting the environment. It works best in cases where a single pollution source is affecting one or a few people (or, where class actions are available, a clearly definable class of people), and where the causal connection between the pollution and injury to those affected can be clearly demonstrated. Few environmental problems have this character. Imagine if we tried to deal with the problem of pollution from automobile exhaust by having all those affected (i.e., just about everybody) sue those responsible (also just about everybody)! Civil litigation is ill-suited to addressing diffuse environmental harms which affect people indirectly through effects on ecosystems (e.g., the effects of acid precipitation on forests and aquatic life) or on global physical systems (e.g., the effects of greenhouse gases on climate), and it does not take into account harms to nature itself that do not affect humans or their property. Finally, even if all the conditions for a successful environmental lawsuit were met, the economic costs of upholding the plaintiffs' rights might prove politically unacceptable, and the government might undo the ruling of the court through legislation — as happened in the famous case discussed in Exhibit 34.7.

The Walkerton Tragedy

Walkerton is a town of approximately 4,800 people, situated northwest of Toronto. Water for Walkerton's water supply comes from the groundwater of a number of wells, and it is meant to be treated with chlorine before entering the distribution system. Torrential rains falling over several days during the long weekend in May of 2000 washed bacteria from cattle manure into one of the town's water supply wells. The water supply became contaminated with a virulent strain of *Escherichia coli* [*E.coli*] and *Campylobacter jejuni*. As a result, 2,321 people became ill, of whom 65 were hospitalized, 25 were diagnosed with Hemolytic Uremic Syndrome (HUS) a serious and potentially fatal kidney condition, and 7 died.

Mike Harris, the Premier of Ontario at the time, ordered an inquiry into the Walkerton incident. The Walkerton Inquiry, conducted by Mr. Justice Dennis O'Connor,[14] had a broad mandate, including whether budgetary cuts to the Ministry of the Environment and privatization of water testing contributed to the outcome. The provincial government implemented substantial changes to the regulation of drinking water in Ontario, including the passage of the *Nutrient Management Act*, S.O. 2002, c. 4; the *Safe Drinking Water Act*, S.O. 2002, c. 32; and the *Clean Water Act*, S.O. 2006, c. 22. Associated regulations passed pursuant to the new laws provide enforceable prescriptive standards for water treatment and testing.

After the public inquiry and its own extensive criminal investigation, the Ontario Provincial Police charged Stan Koebel, General Manager of the Walkerton Public Utilities Commssion (PUC), and his brother Frank Koebel, the PUC foreman, with public endangerment, fraud, and breach of trust. The brothers subsequently pled guilty to "committing a common nuisance"[15] by failing to discharge a legal duty. Witness testimony and other evidence pro-

---

[14] Dennis R. O'Connor [The Honorable Dennis R. O'Connor], *Part One Report of the Walkerton Inquiry: The Events of May 2000 and Related Issues* and *Part Two Report of the Walkerton Inquiry: A Strategy for Safe Drinking Water* (Toronto, Ont.: Queen's Printer for Ontario, 2002). <http://www.attorneygeneral.jus.gov.on.ca/english/about/pubs/walkerton/>.

[15] The offence is formally called common nuisance, and it is distinct from the common law (civil litigation) cause of action known as nuisance. The *Criminal Code of Canada*, R.S.C. 1985, c. C-46, section 180 provides as follows:

180.(1) Every one who commits a common nuisance and thereby
(a) endangers the lives, safety or health of the public, or
(b) causes physical injury to any person,
    is guilty of an indictable offence and liable to imprisonment for a term not exceeding two years.

vided to the court revealed that the Koebels had failed to properly monitor, sample, test, and treat the water in the water distribution system, and that they had failed to accurately record required information. The court found that "Stan Koebel had put the lives, safety and health of the public at risk in general ... [and crucially] [w]hen the crisis hit, he did not provide complete information ... He contributed at least in part, to the delay in issuing the Boil Water Advisory, which caused some undeterminable number of people to become ill. Finally, he tried to cover up his wrongdoing with an inaccurate document."[16] Frank Koebel had helped his brother try to cover up what was going on when the crisis occurred, but his actions did not contribute to the delay in issuing the Boil Water advisory. Frank's practice of mislabeling samples defeated the purpose of the tests, and then hindered the quest to find the source of the problem.

Stan Koebel (then 51) received a one-year prison sentence. Justice Durno rejected a conditional discharge and probation for Stan as inconsistent with the purposes and principles of sentencing. Frank (then 46) received a conditional sentence, consisting of six months house arrest followed by three months of night curfew. Justice Durno rejected a probation and/or fine as inappropriate for Frank.

Another development arising out of the Walkerton tragedy was a class action lawsuit, *Smith v. Brockton (Municipality)*.[17] The class action was launched on June 14, 2000, in the Ontario Superior Court of Justice by four representative plaintiffs. The original defendants named were the municipality, the local health unit, the Walkerton PUC, and the PUC's general manager, Stan Koebel. On September 14, 2000, the Government of Ontario was added as a named defendant. The cause of action in the lawsuit was negligence (breach of duty of care). The plaintiffs claimed that the defendants were negligent in the design, management, maintenance, and operation of the Water Works system which led to the Class Members being exposed to infection. The lawsuit asked for approximately $300,000,000 in total, with one-third of that amount for general damages, and another third for aggravated and exemplary damages.

Between the launch of the class action and the commencement of the Walkerton Inquiry, the Ontario government set up a Walkerton Compensation plan. That plan was "designed to provide financial support and compensation to individuals and businesses affected by the water contamination in Walkerton Ontario from April to December 2000."[18]

In early 2001, Justice Winkler accepted the certification motion for the class action, and the parties began settlement discussions overseen by Justice Winkler. After an extensive negotiation period, involving 6 law firms and many lawyers, Chief Justice Le Sage accepted the settlement agreement that had been reached by the parties.[19]

---

(2) For the purposes of this section, every one commits a common nuisance who does an unlawful act or fails to discharge a legal duty and thereby
(a) endangers the lives, safety, health, property or comfort of the public; or
(b) obstructs the public in the exercise or enjoyment of any right that is common to all the subjects of Her Majesty in Canada.

[16] Court File No. 04-584 (20041220); 2004 CanLII 48879 (ON S.C.) at 51. [*R. v. Koebel and Koebel*] <http://www.canlii.org/en/on/onsc/doc/2004/2004canlii48879/2004canlii48879.html>

[17] *Smith v. Brockton (Municipality)* (2001), 106 A.C.W.S. (3d) 55.

[18] Website for Walkerton Compensation Plan: <http://www.walkertoncompensationplan.ca/>

[19] Settlement Approval Motion before Chief Justice LeSage at Walkerton, March 19, 2001, Court File 00-CV-192173CP, at p. 1: <http://www.strosbergco.com/walkerton/documents/web-walkerton-justice-lesage-reasons.pdf>. See also Walkerton Class Action Settlement: <http://www.ontla.on.ca/library/repository/mon/1000/10293853.pdf>.

The Aftermath of the Walkerton Tragedy

EXHIBIT 34.9

Notes
[1] *Criminal Code*, s. 180
[2] Stan Koebel — sentenced to one year in jail; and Frank Koebel — sentenced to nine months of house arrest
[3] *Nutrient Management Act* (2002), *Safe Drinking Water Act* (2002), and *Clean Water Act* (2006)

The Walkerton class action settled without a legal judgment being issued. Plaintiffs got the compensation they sought without having to go to trial. In this respect the case was typical, since an estimated 90 to 97 percent of civil cases settle prior to adjudication. The publicity around the Walkerton tragedy and the class action likely moved the provincial government to act decisively in compensating the victims, launching the inquiry, and tightening up the regulations. The Walkerton class action case illustrates how common law litigation can proceed in response to failures of the regulatory system.

Exhibit 34.9 illustrates the intersection of true criminal law, regulatory law, and class action civil litigation in the aftermath of the Walkerton tragedy.

PROTECTION OF SPACES AND SPECIES

In this section we discuss various legal tools for protecting biodiversity and ecological function. These goals overlap, since both require the conservation of green spaces, both as habitat for non-humans and as providers of "ecological services" for humans. Green spaces are also conserved for the sake of their aesthetic, recreational, and amenity values.

Federal and Provincial Parks and Nature Reserves

National Parks

Section 4(1) *Canada National Parks Act* (*CNPA*) sets out the mandate for park management as follows: "The national parks of Canada are hereby dedicated to the people of Canada for their benefit, education and enjoyment, subject to this Act and regulations, and the parks shall be maintained and made use of so as to leave them unimpaired for the enjoyment of future generations." The *CNPA* s. 8(2) further requires *ecological integrity* to be "the first priority ... when considering all aspects" of park management. This somewhat contradictory set of objectives has given rise to litigation by environmentalists claiming that parks managers acted outside their mandate in approving facilities such as new roads or ski resorts in sensitive park areas.

National parks typically do not allow mining, logging, hydroelectric development, or sport hunting (in some cases aboriginal subsistence hunting is allowed). Only a minority of national parks, however, have designated wilderness zones that have only minimal visitor facilities and where no motorized access is permitted. Because resource extraction is excluded from national parks and ecological integrity is a priority consideration in their management, environmentalists and nature preservationists seek the expansion of the parks system as the most reliable way to ensure that a sufficient representation of the country's natural ecosystems and landscapes is protected. By the same token, park expansion is opposed by resource development advocates. Expansion of the system is thus a matter of political controversy.

Provincial Parks

All the Canadian provinces also have parks legislation. Provincial parks and nature reserves have similar objectives to national parks, but provincial parks systems do not necessarily exclude resource extraction activities, though parks may be zoned to exclude such activities from certain areas. For example, logging in Ontario's Algonquin Provincial Park is a perennial topic of controversy.

Municipal Land-Use Planning

Municipal governments (along with regional Conservation Authorities), in their planning and land-use regulation powers, can have tremendous direct and indirect effects (good or bad) on the environment. Municipalities can encourage or discourage urban development on environmentally sensitive lands such as ravines, floodplains, slopes, wetlands, headwaters, prime farmland, wildlife corridors and habitat for species intolerant of urban encroachment. They can encourage sprawling, automobile-dependent urban form or compact form friendly to walking, bicycling, and public transit. Urban planning law is a big topic in itself and beyond the scope of this chapter. In Canada, municipalities have a fair bit of power to restrict what owners can do with their land without having to compensate them, so long as their actions are not discriminatory, in bad faith, or factually baseless.

Endangered Species Legislation

The Committee on the Status of Endangered Wildlife in Canada (COSEWIC) is a body comprised of experts representing federal and provincial governments and agencies and national non-governmental conservation organizations, as well as independent scientists. It designates species of animals and plants as "endangered" (facing imminent extinction or extirpation from Canada) or "threatened" (likely to become endangered if their numbers continue to decline). There are parallel provincial bodies such as the Committee on the Status of Species at Risk in Ontario (COSSARO).

Endangered and threatened species are protected by both federal and provincial legislation. Federal legislation applies to marine species, migratory birds, and species on federal Crown land; provincial legislation applies otherwise. Both federal and provincial legislation prohibits killing, harming, harassing, or trading in members of endangered and threatened species, and contains measures to protect critical habitat. They differ in some respects, however.

Under the federal *Species at Risk Act* (*SARA*), the COSEWIC endangered species list has only an advisory function. *SARA* only actually protects those species on an official list of "species at risk", which Cabinet establishes by regulation, and Cabinet is not required to include all species on the COSEWIC list. Cabinet also takes the economic impact of putting a species or population on the protected list into account. By contrast, Ontario's *Endangered Species Act 2007* requires the province's official species at risk regulation to include all species designated by COSSARO. Once a species is listed, however, both federal and Ontario legislation require that the government prepare a species recovery strategy within a stipulated time frame and that this strategy protect critical habitat. *SARA* requires this strategy to be based on "the best available information", and this provision has been used by environmental groups to challenge recovery strategies in court as being inadequate and protecting insufficient habitat, contrary to the legislation. *SARA* also gives the federal government the power to protect federally protected endangered species on provincial lands if provincial governments fail to do so, but the federal government is reluctant to use this power.

CHAPTER SUMMARY

Environmental law refers to a broad umbrella of mixed, legal tools for protecting ecosystems and human well-being from pollution and other human-caused impacts on the environment. A focus of this chapter has been on pollution control. In some cases, pollution can be the grounds for private tort lawsuits, sometimes in class action proceedings. This chapter has surveyed the most important causes of action for civil litigation over environmental harm. More often, pollution is now addressed through public regulatory law at the federal, provincial, and municipal levels. Environmental statutes enable officials to draft regulations and permits that include legally enforceable standards. Noncompliance with these regulations and permits may result in quasi-criminal prosecution or the imposition of various kinds of administrative sanctions. In the prosecution of quasi-criminal (regulatory or public-welfare) offences, the Crown need not prove criminal intent, but the accused may resort to a defence of due diligence. Environmental law also provides processes for the assessment, approval, and regulation of potentially hazardous substances, and the assessment and approval of projects such as dams, landfills, and highways that may have a negative impact on the environment. Finally, laws relating to parks, nature reserves, and endangered species are used to protect biodiversity and natural heritage.

GLOSSARY OF NEW TERMS AND KEY CONCEPTS

absolute liability   A form of liability for which the prosecution need only show that the *actus reus* was committed (there is no mental element to the offence), and for which the defendant cannot raise the defence of due diligence.

administrative monetary penalty (AMP)   A fine for a regulatory violation imposed by an official or administrative tribunal empowered by legislation to do so.

administrative tribunal   A quasi-judicial body (i.e., something like, but not actually, a court) established by leg-islation to decide in disputes that arise in connection with the administration of legisla-tive schemes. Administrative tribunals are common in areas of regulatory law.

ambient standard   An ambient standard defines an acceptable or allowable level or concentration of pollut-ant in the environment.

cause of action   A legal rule or doctrine that defines a basis for a valid lawsuit; in the case of a partic-ular lawsuit, the set of relevant facts that falls under that rule.

certificate of approval   The term used in Ontario law for a licence or permit to pollute, issued in accordance with the *Ontario Environmental Protection Act* or the *Ontario Water Resources Act*. The terms and conditions in a certificate of approval are binding on the company concerned, and are directly enforceable by prosecution.

class action   A procedure whereby a person may sue on behalf of a large number of other people sharing a common interest in the matter without having to name them all individually as parties to the lawsuit.

due diligence defence   A defence available to persons or companies charged with regulatory offences. A per-son or firm wishing to rely upon this defence must be able to provide evidence that they have undertaken reasonable measures to comply with the requirements of the law and to prevent the prohibited act from occurring.

effluent standard   Defines how much of a given pollutant is allowed to be discharged from a given source over a given period of time, or the maximum concentration of the pollutant allowed in the outflow from that source.

environmental assessment (EA)   EA is an evaluation of the effects of a proposed project on natural and human environ-ments. Its purpose is to predict how a project may damage or harm the environment, and whether unacceptable environmental impacts can be avoided or reduced before sig-nificant environmental changes occur. The term "environmental assessment" is used for both a process and a document resulting from that process.

fish toxicity test   Rainbow trout are placed in a tank containing a solution of a pollutant (e.g., pulp mill effluent) that has been diluted by 35 percent. If after four days more than 20 percent of the trout die, the solution is lethal and an offence has been committed under the *Fisheries Act*. Similar toxicity tests for water pollution use *Daphnia*, a tiny freshwater crustacean.

forbearance   The decision on the part of law enforcement officials to refrain from charging or penal-izing a party who is found to be in violation of the law or in non-compliance with regu-lations.

jurisdiction   The power of a government or level of government to make laws concerning a given matter; the territory over which a government has power; a matter over which a court has power.

negligence   A common cause of action under tort law, in which a defendant can be found liable for breach of a duty of care, which results in injury occurring to a plaintiff. There is also a criminal offence of criminal negligence.

performance standard   Stipulates what must be accomplished (e.g., by how much a pollution source must reduce its emissions), but not how.

precautionary principle   A principle that requires actions to be taken to reduce or eliminate likely environmen-tal hazards even if the causal link between a particular, suspected hazard has not yet been proven or fully understood scientifically.

prescriptive standard   Stipulates the technology, materials, etc. that must be used in order to abate pollution.

private law   Concerned with the rights and responsibilities of private parties in respect of one another (e.g., tort law, contract law, real estate transactions).

private nuisance   The tort of carrying on an activity that interferes with other people's reasonable use and enjoyment of their property (through noise, pollution, flooding, etc.)

public law   Concerned with relationships between individuals and the state, and with the opera-tions of government (e.g., administrative law, constitutional law, criminal law).

public nuisance A tort and a criminal offence covering an activity that harms the general public or interferes with rights common to the public (e.g., that obstructs a public road or damages public property).

riparian rights The common law rights connected with the ownership of land abutting a body of water, specifically the right to undiminished quality and quantity of water in that body of water. Breach of those rights constitutes a tort.

risk assessment The scientific analysis of the degree of risk posed to human and/or environmental health by a particular activity, for example, exposure to a given substance. Risk assessment may be legally required as part of the process of approving the activity or substance.

strict liability In quasi-criminal, or regulatory law: liability for a violation committed without criminal intent, subject to the defence of due diligence. In tort law: liability for damage done by the escape of a dangerous substance stored on one's property, even if the escape was not due to negligence. Also known as the *Rylands v. Fletcher* rule.

REVIEW QUESTIONS

1. What are the differences between private law and public law? Describe and provide examples of each. Where does environmental law fit?

2. What are the three main sources of law? In what ways are they connected or interrelated?

3. Under which constitutional heads of power do federal and provincial governments have power and responsibility to enact environmental legislation?

4. How might municipal governments play a role in environmental protection? Name one other constitutionally relevant jurisdiction in Canada (besides the federal, provincial and municipal levels).

5. What are the differences between a statutory prohibition, a regulation, and a certificate of approval? How are each related to statute law?

6. What are the major kinds of standards that are found in environmental law, and how do they differ from each other?

7. What are the significant distinctions between absolute liability, strict liability, and true criminal liability?

8. What is forbearance and why does it happen?

9. Ministry officials discover that a company is violating pollution-control laws. What options, other than forbearance, do the enforcement officials have to address the issue?

10. What are the main stages in an environmental assessment process?

11. What must you do if you want to use a newly invented chemical in an industrial process?

12. What are the main common law causes of action found in environmental cases? Elaborate on the factors that courts take into consideration with each of those causes of action. Which common law causes of action require the plaintiff to show actual harm or loss in order to sue successfully? Which common law causes of action require that the plaintiff be a landowner?

13. What is a class action lawsuit? What are the three stages of such a lawsuit? What must a would-be representative plaintiff show in order to

certify a class? List some examples of environmental class action law-suits in Canada.

14. How do the federal *Species at Risk Act* and the Ontario *Endangered Species Act, 2007* differ in the ways that they protect endangered species?

DISCUSSION QUESTIONS

1. Why do you think courts have been reluctant to interpret environmental offences as absolute liability offences? Do you agree with this approach? Why or why not?

2. Do you think that individual directors and officers within a company (as opposed to the company as a whole) should be held liable for environmental offences? Why or why not? What are some examples of personal liability for directors and officers, under regulatory law (quasi-criminal) and under true criminal law?

3. Of all the options that enforcement officials have to punish polluters, which do you think is the most effective and when? Why?

4. What are the relative advantages and disadvantages of civil litigation (private law) and the regulation of pollution through statutory law (public law)?

5. What are "toxic torts"? Which popular Hollywood movies have focused on class action litigation concerning toxic torts? How are toxic torts relevant in the Canadian context?

6. Joe (the defendant) has been found to be civilly liable for infringement of Danielle's (the plaintiff's) rights. What are the two main types of remedy that the court may award to Danielle and what are the variations between the two?

7. Should landowners and businesses be compensated for having to avoid disturbing the habitats of rare or endangered species? Why or why not? What problems could arise in either case?

SUGGESTED READINGS

Benidickson, Jamie. *Environmental Law*, 2d ed. (Toronto, Ont.: Irwin Law, 2002).

Boyd, David R. *Unnatural Law: Rethinking Canadian Environmental Law and Policy* (Vancouver, B.C.: UBC Press, 2003).

Greenbaum, Allan, & Alex Wellington. *Environmental Law and Policy in the Canadian Context* (Concord, Ont.: Captus Press, 2008).

Greenbaum, Allan, Alex Wellington, & Ron Pushchak, eds., *Canadian Issues in Environmental Law and Policy* (Concord, Ont.: Captus Press, 2008).

Hughes, Elaine, Alastair Lucas, & William Tilleman. *Environmental Law and Policy*, 3d ed. (Toronto, Ont.: Emond Montgomery, 2003).

WEBSITES

Canadian Environmental Law Association: <http://www.cela.ca/>

Canadian Institute for Environmental Law and Policy: <http://www.cielap.org/>

EcoJustice: <http://www.ecojustice.ca/>

Environmental Commissioner of Ontario: <http://www.eco.on.ca/eng/>

Environmental Defence: <http://www.environmentaldefence.ca/>

Ministry of Environment (MoE), Province of Ontario: <http://www.ene.gov.on.ca/en/index.php>

Immigration and Refugee Law

Sasha Baglay
UNIVERSITY OF ONTARIO INSTITUTE OF TECHNOLOGY

Learning Objectives

After reading this chapter, the reader should be able to:

➢ Become familiar with the legislative and institutional framework of Canadian immigration and refugee system

➢ Know the difference between the statuses of Canadian citizens, permanent residents, and foreign nationals

➢ Understand basic principles of immigrant selection under economic and family class

➢ Understand key concepts of refugee law and stages of the Canadian refugee determination process

➢ Know the basic principles of inadmissibility, immigration detention, and removal

➢ Appreciate the complexity of competing interests involved in immigration and refugee policy- and decision-making

TABLE OF CONTENTS

INTRODUCTION

Immigration and refugee protection are considered an inalienable part of Canada's history and identity. Since 1867, more than 17 million people have immigrated to Canada, including close to one million refugees and other humanitarian cases since World War II.[1] During the past decade, Canada admitted, on average, close to a quarter of a million permanent residents annually.[2]

While Canada is viewed as a nation welcoming immigrants and refugees, it is important to keep in mind that immigration law is inherently selective and exclusionary. It draws a line between citizens and non-citizens; it embodies the country's idea about "desirable" and "undesirable" candidates for admission often to the exclusion of persons with limited financial resources, low skill and education levels or individuals with certain medical conditions that might impose a burden on domestic healthcare or social service systems. This selectivity and differential treatment is based on the long-standing principle that non-citizens do not have an unqualified right to enter or remain in the country[3] and that the state has a sovereign right to control their admission and conditions of stay.

Immigration law applies to non-citizens only. Thus, many of those who have acquired Canadian citizenship at birth will hardly ever face the direct effect of Canadian immigration law (except perhaps for the inevitable border control at Canada's ports of entry). At the same time, those who are most affected by immigration law usually have no voice in the political system and/or are in a too vulnerable or precarious position to speak up. For this reason, the work of human rights lawyers and organizations representing immigrants and refugees plays an important role in advocating for and protecting rights of non-citizens.

Thus, any reading of immigration law should be critical, considering not only who is admitted and how Canada benefits from that admission, but also who remains excluded and what are the gender, social class, and race impacts of such exclusion. Immigration law is not only about immigrant selection. It often engages some of the most fundamental individual rights such as the right to life and liberty, the right to be free from torture and other maltreatment. For example, is it permissible to deport a person to a country where he/she might face a risk of torture or persecution? What if that person represents a security threat to Canada? Is it permissible to detain non-citizens suspected of terrorist links for prolonged periods of time without an opportunity for detention review or release? Can a state refuse entry to persons who are fleeing their home countries in search of refugee protection?

Although the chapter discusses a number of cases that have touched on the above questions, it merely outlines the current state of law leaving it up to the reader to further critically engage with and question legal rules and judicial decisions.

---

[1] Citizenship and Immigration Canada, "Facts and Figures 2009", online: <http://www.cic.gc.ca/english/resources/statistics/facts2009/index.asp> [CIC, "Facts and Figures 2009"]. However, in 2010, Canada admitted 280,636 individuals as permanent residents — the highest number in the past 50 years. Citizenship and Immigration Canada, "Preliminary tables — Permanent and temporary residents, 2010", online: <http://www.cic.gc.ca/english/resources/statistics/facts2010-preliminary/01.asp> [CIC, "Preliminary tables — Permanent and temporary residents, 2010"].

[2] *Ibid.*

[3] *Chiarelli v. Canada (Minister of Citizenship and Immigration)*, [1992] 1 S.C.R. 711 at 733–34.

HISTORY OF IMMIGRATION AND REFUGEE LAW IN CANADA ——————————

During the first decades after Confederation, immigration was viewed as a key element in industrial growth and nation-building. Therefore, it was actively promoted and there were relatively few restrictions on admission. However, by the turn of the 20th century, the arrival of immigrants with different culture, traditions, and religion started to raise concerns about the demographic composition of the country and stimulated introduction of restrictions aimed at preserving Canada as a white, predominantly British society. The policy focus shifted from attracting immigrants to selecting those that were viewed as the most desirable,[4] while also actively deterring unwanted immigration. Over the years, the Chinese head tax;[5] "continuous journey" rule;[6] and multiple exclusions targeting the poor, persons with disabilities, and persons of certain ethnic or racial background were introduced. Several economic downturns during the first decades of the 20th century created additional incentives for limiting immigration. The restrictive admission policies, accompanied by increased deportations and exclusions, were largely maintained until the mid-1940s.[7]

The post-World War II period was marked by gradual liberalization of admissions. Between 1947 and 1962, Canada admitted close to 250,000 displaced persons from Europe.[8] Many of them came under arranged labour schemes to remedy labour shortages in certain industries and agriculture or were selected on the basis of general economic potential, ethnic origin, and other characteristics.[9] However, after a period of time, Canada's labour force demands could no longer be satisfied by traditional sources from Europe, and the country had to re-evaluate and expand its selection criteria.[10] In 1962, Canada became the first major immigrant-receiving country to abolish most of its discriminatory admission policies. In 1967, the government introduced a skills-based points system for the selection of immigrants.

In 1969, Canada acceded to the 1951 *UN Convention Relating to the Status of Refugees* (*Refugee Convention*) and the 1967 *Protocol relating to the Status of Refugees* (*Refugee Protocol*). During the 1960s and 1970s, various groups of refugees were admitted to Canada, including Czechs uprooted by the Soviet invasion, Chileans escaping from the Pinochet regime, and Asians expelled by the Amin regime in Uganda. However, there was little evidence of a consistent long-term approach to assisting people in need. Rather, refugee admissions were carried out on an ad hoc basis in response to particular crises.

In 1973, the government announced a review of immigration policy in order to better reflect the ideas of multiculturalism and provide for a more systematic approach to immigrant and refugee admission. The 1976 *Immigra-*

---

[4] Ninette Kelley and Michael Trebilcock, *The Making of the Mosaic* (Toronto: University of Toronto Press, 1998) at 248.

[5] All Chinese immigrants were required to pay a prescribed tax in order to be allowed into Canada.

[6] This rule prevented admission of immigrants who had not travelled directly from their country of origin to Canada. At the time, travel routes from Asia were structured in a way that entailed a stopover, thereby making immigrants using them inadmissible to Canada. One of the famous cases is that of *Komagata Maru*, which arrived from China with 376 persons aboard. None of the passengers was allowed ashore and the ship had to sail back.

[7] Kelley & Trebilcock, *supra* note 4 at 165, 217, 229, 251.

[8] Valerie Knowles, "Forging Our Legacy: Canadian Citizenship and Immigration, 1900–1977" (2000), online: <www.cic.gc.ca>.

[9] Valerie Knowles, *Strangers at Our Gates: Canadian Immigration and Immigration Policy, 1540–1992* (Toronto: Dundurn Press, 1992) at 127.

[10] Jock Collins & Francis Henry, "Racism, Ethnicity and Immigration" in Howard Adelman et al. (eds.), *Immigration and Refugee Policy: Australia and Canada Compared*, (Toronto: University of Toronto Press, 1994) 515 at 530.

tion Act established many of the principles and procedures of contemporary Canadian immigration law, including classes of immigrants, refugee protection mechanisms, family reunification, and federal–provincial consultations and agreements on immigration.

In 2002, the *Immigration Act* was replaced with the *Immigration and Refugee Protection Act* (*IRPA*). The post-2002 period is characterized by several key trends:

- Increased focus on security and border control
- Optimization of selection of economic immigrants to facilitate their better labour market integration and to increase Canada's competitiveness in a global market for labour force (as demonstrated, for example, by the changes to the skilled worker class described below)
- Increasing admissions of temporary residents (particularly international students and temporary foreign workers) and introduction of the Canadian Experience Class, which allows some of these temporary residents to transition to permanent residence
- Restrictions on refugee protection, which are evident in the changes brought about by the 2010 *Balanced Refugee Reform Act*

LEGAL FRAMEWORK

Constitution Act, 1867: Division of Powers over Immigration

Two provisions — sections 91(25) and 95 — in the *Constitution Act, 1867* are of direct relevance to immigration and citizenship. Section 91(25) confers on the federal Parliament exclusive jurisdiction in the areas of naturalization and aliens. Section 95 establishes concurrent federal–provincial jurisdiction over immigration: the federal government may regulate immigration "into all or any of the Provinces" and each province may regulate immigration "in and for the Province". In case of a conflict between a federal and a provincial law, the former prevails.[11]

The role of the provinces in immigration regulation has fluctuated over time. Prior to Confederation and during the first decades afterwards, the provinces maintained a certain role in admission screening and immigrant recruitment. However, by the early 20th century, their interest in immigration regulation has decreased, and immigration became *de facto* an almost exclusively federal matter. The gradual revival of provincial involvement in immigration took place only in the late 1970s. First, Quebec negotiated progressively more powers over immigrant selection and settlement. From the 1990s onwards, other provinces and territories also started to seek roles in immigrant selection by negotiating Provincial/Territorial Nominee Agreements with the federal government. These agreements allow provinces and territories to select immigrants who have the potential to benefit a given province or territory and nominate them for immigration. Federal programs, however, currently remain the main avenues of admission and will be the main focus of discussion in this chapter.

The *Charter of Rights and Freedoms*

Immigration law traditionally and strictly distinguishes between citizens and non-citizens. However, the *Charter of Rights and Freedoms*, which enshrines a number of rights that are guaranteed to everyone, to a certain extent allows such a rigid distinction to be overcome. Four *Charter* rights have been most frequently invoked in the immigration context: section 7 (right to life, liberty

---

[11] *The British North America Act, 1867* 30 & 31 Victoria, c. 3 [*BNA*] subsequently entitled the *Constitution Act*, 1867 by Item 1 of the Schedule to the *Constitution Act, 1982*, (U.K.) 1982, c. 11, s. 95.

and security of person); section 10 (right to counsel); section 12 (prohibition of cruel and unusual treatment or punishment); section 15 (equality).

The *Charter* litigation has had an impact on the treatment of non-citizens in a number of areas and in some instances has also led to marked institutional changes. Two cases below are illustrative of this impact (see also the *Charkaoui* case in the section on security certificates).

Singh v. Minister of Employment and Immigration[12]

Are refugee claimants (that is, persons who are alleging a risk of persecution in their home countries and who have made a claim for protection in Canada) entitled to an oral hearing to determine whether they should be given protection?

Decisions on refugee protection have a crucial impact on the life and security of refugee claimants: if a person who fears persecution is denied protection, he/she may be returned to a country where his/her life would be at risk. Given the seriousness of the consequences of a negative decision, refugee claimants are entitled to fundamental justice under section 7 of the *Charter*, which at a minimum, requires that a refugee claimant is provided with an adequate opportunity to state his case and to know the case he/she has to meet.[13]

In the 1980s, a refugee determination process consisted of two main stages: first, a claimant was interviewed by an immigration officer; then, the transcript of the interview was sent to the Refugee Status Advisory Committee (RSAC), which decided whether to recommend acceptance of the claim. This procedure did not allow claimants an opportunity to be heard before the RSAC or to know and effectively challenge the information on the basis of which the decision on the claim was made. Thus, the Supreme Court found that the procedure violated principles of procedural fairness under section 7 of the *Charter* and that it could not be saved under section 1. The decision led to an overhaul of the inland refugee determination system with a view to provide for an oral hearing for all refugee claimants. To this end, the Immigration and Refugee Board was established in 1989 and since then has become an integral part of the institutional framework of immigration and refugee decision-making.

Suresh v. Canada (Minister of Citizenship and Immigration)[14]

May Canada deport a suspected terrorist to a country where he might face torture?

Mr. Suresh came to Canada from Sri Lanka in 1990 and was recognized as a **Convention refugee** in 1991. However, in 1995, the Canadian authorities detained him and commenced deportation proceedings on security grounds: the Canadian Security Intelligence Service was of the opinion that Mr. Suresh was a member and fundraiser of the Liberation Tigers of Tamil Eelam (LTTE), an alleged terrorist organization. Mr. Suresh fought the deportation, claiming that he would face torture in Sri Lanka. The Supreme Court emphasized that both Canadian and international law reject deportation to torture. Accordingly, the Court concluded that deportation to face torture is generally unconstitutional and that Canada should generally decline to deport persons to torture.

---

[12] *Singh v. Minister of Employment and Immigration*, [1985] 1 S.C.R. 177 [*Singh*].

[13] *Singh* at paras. 52–61.

[14] *Suresh v. Canada (Minister of Citizenship and Immigration)*, [2002] 1 S.C.R. 3.

However, the Court has failed to endorse an absolute prohibition on removal to torture and left open a possibility that in extraordinary circumstances such removal may be justified.

Legislation

The *Immigration and Refugee Protection Act* (*IRPA*) sets out the objectives of immigration and refugee policies, immigration classes, principles of non-citizens' admission to and stay in Canada, principles of refugee protection, as well as the authorities of the Minister of Citizenship and Immigration and of the Immigration and Refugee Board (IRB).

As framework legislation, the *IRPA* is concise and necessarily presupposes the broad delegation of legislative power to elaborate on the implementation of its core principles through regulations. The *Immigration and Refugee Protection Regulations* outline the details of various immigration categories and requirements, including selection criteria for each immigration class. For example, the *IRPA* stipulates that applicants in the economic class are selected on the basis of their ability to become economically established in Canada,[15] but it is the *Regulations* that spell out how this ability is to be evaluated (for example, they specify that applicants under the skilled worker class must demonstrate at least one year of work experience, availability of settlement funds and detail how the applicant's education, language proficiency, and other relevant credentials are to be assessed under the points system[16]).

Under the current legislative scheme, there are two major sets of conditions that an applicant must satisfy in order to be admitted for permanent residence:

1. Meet criteria of a particular immigration/refugee class. The Canadian immigration program is divided into three broad streams: economic, family, and refugee. The criteria under each stream reflect its underlying rationale: (a) economic stream — to satisfy Canada's objectives of economic, social, and cultural development; (b) family stream — to allow for family reunification; (c) refugee stream — to implement Canada's commitment to humanitarianism and international obligations. The economic class makes approximately 60 percent of the annual immigrant intake, while the family and refugee classes account for approximately 22 percent and 10–12 percent respectively.[17]

2. Not be inadmissible. In contrast to selection criteria, which reflect qualities considered desirable in potential applicants, **inadmissibility** describes individuals who are "undesirable" for admission. As a rule, persons found inadmissible will not be allowed to enter Canada or, if they are already in Canada, will be ordered removed.

INSTITUTIONAL FRAMEWORK

The institutional framework of Canadian immigration and refugee protection system is comprised of three key bodies: Citizenship and Immigration Canada (CIC), Immigration and Refugee Board (IRB) and Canada Border Services Agency (CBSA).

[15] *Immigration and Refugee Protection Act*, 2001, c. 27, s. 12(2) [*IRPA*].
[16] *Immigration and Refugee Protection Regulations*, SOR/2002-227 [*Regulations*], ss. 75–83.
[17] The rest is comprised of "other immigrants" such as those admitted under Humanitarian and Compassionate consideration and for reasons related to the person's need of protection in Canada. CIC, "Facts and Figures 2009", *supra* note 1.

Citizenship and Immigration Canada (CIC)

CIC is the government department with overall responsibility for immigration and refugee matters. It processes applications for permanent residence and for temporary admission of visitors, workers, and students; issues travel documents; decides on citizenship applications; determines eligibility of refugee claims made in Canada (see section on refugee law, below); and administers the resettlement of refugees from abroad.

Immigration and Refugee Board (IRB)

The Immigration and Refugee Board (IRB) is an independent administrative tribunal responsible for making decisions on a number of immigration and refugee matters. According to the *IRPA*, the IRB consists of four divisions:

- The Refugee Protection Division (RPD), which decides on refugee claims made in Canada
- The Immigration Division (ID), which holds admissibility hearings and detention reviews
- The Immigration Appeal Division (IAD), which hears appeals from refused family sponsorship applications and from removal orders
- The Refugee Appeal Division (RAD)

The RAD was intended to hear appeals on RPD decisions, but the provisions on the RAD have never been implemented and it currently does not exist. However, the recently passed *Balanced Refugee Reform Act* provides for the establishment of the RAD within one to one-and-a-half years.

Cases before the IRB are usually decided by one-member panels. Each division usually holds an in-person hearing; a hearing may also be conducted by phone or by videoconference. The person concerned has a right to be represented by counsel. Proceedings are usually conducted in public, except in refugee protection cases or where confidentiality may be required for other reasons. The hearings proceed in a less formal manner than before courts and are not limited by strict rules of evidence. Each division has its own rules of procedure, which outline applicable deadlines, disclosure requirements, and other issues. In addition, the IRB has developed "soft law" instruments (guidelines, jurisprudential guides, policies, instructions) which provide guidance on substantive or procedural issues and seek to ensure consistency of decision-making.

Canada Border Services Agency (CBSA)

The CBSA is responsible for border services related to the admission of persons, goods, animals, and plants into Canada. In the area of immigration, it conducts screening of individuals at ports of entry, carries out enforcement such as immigration detention and removal, and determines the eligibility of refugee claims made at the border.

CATEGORIES OF INDIVIDUALS IN CANADIAN IMMIGRATION LAW

Canada's immigration law distinguishes three types of status: foreign national, permanent resident, and Canadian citizen. Each of them demonstrates a different level of connection to Canada and provides for different scopes of rights for its holders.

Most of the rights under the *Charter* are guaranteed to "everyone" or "anyone" (for example, freedom of conscience and assembly, right to counsel, protection against arbitrary detention). Therefore, these rights will be available equally to Canadian citizens, permanent residents, and foreign nationals. However, the extent of other rights, especially in social and economic areas, often depends on the individual's immigration/citizenship status.

Citizens of Canada

Citizenship gives its holders full-fledged rights in Canada and creates certain expectations about Canada's consular assistance and diplomatic protection while abroad. For example, such *Charter* rights as the right to vote and stand in elections as well as the unconditional right to enter, remain in, and leave Canada are reserved exclusively for citizens. In addition, Canadian citizenship may be required in order to hold certain public offices[18] or perform certain public duties.[19]

Canadian citizenship may be acquired in one of the following ways:

- *Jus soli*: by birth in Canada's territory, except for children of foreign diplomats, consular, or other similarly situated officials

- *Jus sanguinis* (by descent): by birth outside of Canada to a Canadian citizen.

  Previously, Canadian citizens residing overseas were able to pass citizenship down to their children from generation to generation.[20] However, in 2008, the *Citizenship Act* was amended to limit citizenship by descent to the first generation born outside Canada. This means that a child born overseas will obtain Canadian citizenship only if at least one of his/her parents was born in Canada or became a Canadian citizen by naturalization. There are some exceptions to this rule, which apply to Canadian parents working abroad for the Canadian armed forces, the federal public administration or the public service of a province. Children who do not have access to automatic citizenship by *jus sanguinis* may be sponsored by their parents for permanent residence in Canada under the family class and subsequently apply for citizenship.

  > *Example:* Mary is born abroad to Canadian parents. Both of her parents were born in Canada, and Mary is the first generation born overseas. Thus, she will obtain Canadian citizenship by descent. However, if Mary gives birth outside of Canada, her child (second generation born overseas) will not automatically acquire Canadian citizenship by descent.

- By naturalization: this process allows immigrants to obtain Canadian citizenship. A person needs to first become a permanent resident and then, after a period of time, may apply for citizenship. To gain citizenship, a permanent resident must (a) make an application; (b) be at least 18 years of age; (c) demonstrate that he/she has resided as a permanent resident in Canada for at least three years in a four-year period immediately preceding the application; (d) have adequate knowledge of Canada, of citizens' rights and responsibilities, and of one of the official languages; (e) not be under a removal order or the subject of a declaration that he/she is a threat to the security of Canada or is a part of organized crime.

---

[18] For example, ombudsman and provincial court judges in Alberta. *Ombudsman Act*, R.S.A. 2000, c. O-8, s. 3(3); *Provincial Court Act*, R.S.A. 2000, c. P-31, s. 9.1.

[19] For example, to serve as a juror. *Jury Act*, 1998, S.S. 1998, c. J-4.2, s. 5; *Jury Act*, R.S.P.E.I. 1988, c. J-5.1, s. 4; *Juries Act*, R.S.O. 1990, c. J.3, s. 2; *Jury Act*, S.N.B. 1980, c. J-3.1, s. 2; *Jury Act*, R.S.A. 2000, c. J-3, s. 3.

[20] However, in order to retain that citizenship, the child needed to take the following steps by the age of 28: apply for retention of citizenship and either reside in Canada for at least a year before the application or demonstrate a substantial connection to Canada. Failing to do so would result in automatic loss of citizenship.

Permanent Residents In order to become a permanent resident, an individual needs to apply under one of Canada's immigration streams and meet the prescribed requirements. Permanent residents enjoy many of the same rights as citizens: they may freely work and study, access provincial healthcare and various types of programs such as social assistance, Child Tax Benefit, and student loans. However, permanent residents do not have a *Charter*-protected right to vote or run for office. Neither do they have an unqualified right to enter and remain in Canada, but they enjoy the right to inter-provincial mobility.

The central peculiarity of permanent resident status is its conditional nature. A permanent resident may lose his/her status in one of the following circumstances:

1. Failure to comply with the residency obligation. In order to maintain their status, permanent residents must be physically present in Canada for at least 730 days in each five-year period.

2. An individual is determined to be inadmissible and a removal order against him/her comes into force. For example, a permanent resident who has committed certain crimes may become inadmissible and, as a result, be subject to removal. The Supreme Court has confirmed that the deportation of a long-term resident who has committed a serious criminal offence does not infringe the *Charter*.[21]

3. Failure to comply with immigration class requirements. While the two above scenarios are applicable to any permanent resident, certain categories of immigrants may be subject to additional conditions. For example, persons under the entrepreneur class are required to demonstrate within the three-year period following their admission that they have established a qualifying business in Canada, control at least a third of the equity of the business, provide active and ongoing management of the business, and have created at least one full-time job for a Canadian citizen or a permanent resident (other than the entrepreneur's family members).

Foreign Nationals A "foreign national" is a person who is not a Canadian citizen or a permanent resident.[22] Foreign nationals may be admitted to Canada on a temporary basis as students, workers or visitors. They have a limited scope of rights largely determined by the intended purpose of their stay in Canada (see section on temporary residents, below); and they must depart at the end of their authorized stay. Foreign nationals who have applied for refugee protection in Canada as well as those who have been granted protection enjoy more extensive rights than other foreign nationals. This is done in recognition of Canada's international obligations as well as on an understanding that those who have fled violence, persecution, torture, and other risks need additional support and exemptions from certain immigration requirements (see the section on refugee protection for further details).

---

[21] *Chiarelli, supra* note 3.

[22] *IRPA, supra* note 15, s. 2(1).

IMMIGRATION LAW ——————————————————————————————

Economic Immigration

By definition, immigrants in the economic class are selected on the basis of their ability to become economically established in Canada.[23] Thus, the selection criteria focus on characteristics that are considered indicative of this ability, namely education, work or business experience, language proficiency, financial resources, and other factors facilitating successful integration.

The economic class encompasses six categories, each governed by a distinct set of selection criteria:

- Skilled workers
- Canadian Experience Class (CEC)
- Business immigrants (investors, entrepreneurs, self-employed)
- Provincial and territorial nominees
- Quebec-selected immigrants
- Live-in caregivers

By way of illustration, this section will outline requirements under two of the above classes: skilled worker and the Canadian Experience Class. In addition, it will provide a brief overview of provincial/territorial nominee programs.

Skilled Worker Class

The skilled worker class is currently the major source of admissions in the economic stream, amounting to over 40,000 principal applicants and approximately 50,000 to 60,000 accompanying dependents (spouses and children) annually.[24]

In order to be approved for permanent residence under the skilled worker class, applicants must meet the following basic requirements: (a) have at least one year of full-time work experience in a skilled occupation in the past 10 years; (b) have adequate settlement funds;[25] and (c) accumulate at least 67 points on six selection factors.

The points system was designed to predict applicants' prospective employability in Canada. However, it was criticized as poorly linked to actual labour market needs.[26] Furthermore, due to the high volume of applications, applicants often had to wait for a decision for a number of years. In 2008, the CIC had a backlog of over 900,000 applications (two-thirds of them in the federal skilled worker class), and wait times could be as long as six years.[27]

In 2008 and 2010, the Minister of Citizenship and Immigration responded to the above concerns by introducing eligibility requirements, which sought to make the system more efficient. Before 2008, applicants in all skilled occupations could apply: as long as the application was complete and the required fees were paid, it was put into the processing queue to be assessed under the

---

[23] *Ibid.*, s. 12(2)

[24] CIC, "Facts and Figures 2009", *supra* note 1.

[25] The amount of settlement funds is determined according to the applicant's family size. Currently, the requirements are as follows: 1 family member — $11,115; 2 — $13,837; 3 — $17,011; 4 — $20,654; 5 — $23,425; 6 — $26,419; 7 or more — $29,414. Applicants who have arranged employment in Canada do not need to demonstrate availability of such funds. Citizenship and Immigration Canada, "Skilled workers and professionals: Who can apply — Proof of funds", online: <http://www.cic.gc.ca/english/immigrate/skilled/funds.asp>.

[26] L. Hawthorn, *Labour Market Outcomes for Migrant Professionals: Canada and Australia Compared* (2006), online: <http://cic.gc.ca/english/resources/research/2006-canada-australia.asp>; Jeffrey Reitz, "Tapping Immigrants' Skills: New Direction for Canadian Immigration Policy in the Knowledge Economy" (2005) 11 *IRPP Choices* 1.

[27] Citizenship and Immigration Canada, "Action Plan for Faster Immigration: Ministerial Instructions." (2008), online: <http://www.cic.gc.ca/english/DEPARTMENT/media/backgrounders/2008/2008-11-28.asp>.

points system and other requirements. In 2008, the application process under the skilled worker class changed and currently includes two stages:

1. Eligibility — to determine whether an application can be put into processing.
2. Assessment of eligible applications under the points system and other requirements of the skilled worker class.

Currently, eligibility is limited to persons with (a) an offer of employment in Canada or (b) one year of full-time work experience in one of 29 listed occupations[28] (these occupations were identified on the basis of labour market demands and stakeholder consultations). In addition, all applicants must supply results of an official language test confirming their proficiency in English and/ or French. Applications that do not meet these eligibility requirements will not be put into processing. Further, only a total of 20,000 applications will be considered annually under the category of 29 occupations in demand; within the 20,000 cap, only 1,000 applications can be considered per occupation. Thus, eligibility requirements effectively limit the range of applicants who will be considered under the skilled worker class.

Eligible applications are further assessed under the six selection factors of the points system:

- Education (maximum of 25 points)
- Language proficiency (maximum of 20 points)
- Work experience (maximum of 21 points)
- Arranged employment (maximum of 10 points)
- Age (maximum of 10 points)
- Adaptability (maximum of 10 points)

Exhibit 35.1 demonstrates how points are assigned under each factor, and Exhibit 35.2 illustrates how the point system applies on a skill worker application.

Canadian Experience Class

The Canadian Experience Class (CEC) was introduced in 2008 to allow foreign students and skilled temporary foreign workers who are already in Canada to apply for permanent residence. Accordingly, there are two streams within the CEC:

1. Temporary foreign workers — applicants must demonstrate at least two years of full-time skilled work experience in Canada within a three-year period preceding the application

2. Foreign students — applicants must have been enrolled in a full-time program of study of at least two years' duration in Canada; have completed the program and obtained a Canadian educational credential (e.g., degree, diploma, or certificate); and acquired at least one year of full-time skilled work experience in Canada within the two years preceding the application.

Applicants under both streams must demonstrate proficiency in English and/or French by providing results of an official language test. The CEC is a pass/fail system and does not rely on the points assessment. Currently, the CEC is a small program (only close to 4,000 principal applicants and their

---

[28] For the list of occupations, see Citizenship and Immigration Canada: <http://www.cic.gc.ca/english/immigrate/skilled/apply-who-instructions.asp#list>.

EXHIBIT 35.1	Assessment under the Points System

Education	Points
¤ You have a master's degree or PhD and at least 17 years of full-time or full-time equivalent study	25
¤ You have two or more university degrees at the Bachelor's level and at least 15 years of full-time or full-time equivalent study	22
¤ You have a three-year diploma, trade certificate or apprenticeship and at least 15 years of full-time or full-time equivalent study.	22
¤ You have a university degree of two years or more at the Bachelor's level and at least 14 years of full-time or full-time equivalent study.	20
¤ You have a two-year diploma, trade certificate or apprenticeship and at least 14 years of full-time or full-time equivalent study.	20
¤ You have a one-year university degree at the Bachelor's level and at least 13 years of full-time or full-time equivalent study.	15
¤ You have a one-year diploma, trade certificate or apprenticeship and at least 13 years of full-time or full-time equivalent study.	15
¤ You have a one-year diploma, trade certificate or apprenticeship and at least 12 years of full-time or full-time equivalent study.	12
¤ You completed high school.	5

Language Proficiency	Points for Each Ability (write, speak, listen, read)
First official language	
High proficiency	4
Moderate proficiency	2
Basic proficiency	1
Second official language	
High proficiency	2
Moderate proficiency	2
Basic proficiency	1

Work experience	Points
1 year	15
2 years	17
3 years	19
4 or more	21

Arranged Employment in Canada	Points
¤ You currently work in Canada on a temporary work permit and your employer has made an offer to employ you on an indeterminate basis.	10
¤ You currently work in Canada in a job that is exempt from confirmation by Human Resources and Social Development Canada (HRSDC) under an international agreement or a significant benefit category; your employer has made an offer to employ you on an indeterminate basis.	10
¤ You do not currently have a work permit and you do not intend to work in Canada before you have been issued a permanent resident visa; you have a full-time job offer that has been approved by HRSDC; your employer has made an offer to give you a permanent job if your permanent resident visa is issued.	10

Assessment under the Points System

EXHIBIT 35.1 (continued)

Age	Points
21–49 (2 points deducted for each year that the applicant is below 21 or over 49)	10

Adaptability

Your spouse or common-law partner's level of education   3–5

¤ Secondary school (high school) diploma or less   0

¤ A one-year diploma, trade certificate, apprenticeship or
university degree, and at least 12 years of full-time or full-
time equivalent studies   3

¤ A two- or three-year diploma, trade certificate, apprenticeship
or university degree, and at least 14 years of full-time or full-
time equivalent studies   4

¤ A master's degree or PhD and at least 17 years of full-time
or full-time equivalent studies   5

Previous Work in Canada

¤ You or your accompanying spouse or common-law partner have completed
a minimum of one year of full-time work in Canada on a valid work
permit.   5

Previous Study in Canada

¤ You or your accompanying spouse or common-law partner have completed
a program of full-time study of at least two years' duration at a post-
secondary institution in Canada. You must have done this after you were
17 years old and with a valid study permit.   5

Arranged Employment in Canada

¤ You can claim five additional points if you have arranged employment as
described in the Arranged Employment selection factor.   5

Relatives in Canada

¤ You or your accompanying spouse or common-law partner have a relative
(parent, grandparent, child, grandchild, child of a parent, sibling, child of a
grandparent, aunt or uncle, or grandchild of a parent, niece or nephew)
who is residing in Canada and is a Canadian citizen or permanent
resident.   5

Source: Citizenship and Immigration Canada, "Skilled workers and professionals: Who can apply —
Six selection factors and pass mark", online: <http://www.cic.gc.ca/english/immigrate/skilled/apply-fac-
tors.asp>.

EXHIBIT 35.2	The Immigration Points System: A Skilled Worker Example

Eduardo is a citizen of Mexico who wishes to apply for immigration to Canada under the skilled worker class. He is 32 years old, married with no children. Eduardo is a social worker with 2 years of work experience; he has a Bachelor's and a Master's degree in Social Work (and a combined 17 years of full-time study). His high proficiency in English (writing, speaking, reading, and oral comprehension) is confirmed by results of an official language test. His wife, Maria, is also a social worker and has a Master's degree and 17 years of study. Eduardo and Maria have approximately $17,000 saved in their bank account. Is Eduardo likely to be approved for immigration under the skilled worker class?

Eligibility

Social workers are on the list of 29 occupations in demand, and the number of applications received in this category has not yet reached the 1,000 cap (see <http://www.cic.gc.ca/english/immigrate/skilled/complete-applications.asp>). Eduardo also has results of an official language test ready. Thus, Eduardo's application is eligible for processing.

Assessment under the Points System

On the six selection factors, Eduardo is likely to score as follows:

Education	25 points	(a Master's degree and 17 years of study)
Language proficiency	16 points	(4 for each ability)
Work experience	17 points	(2 years of experience in social work)
Arranged employment	0 points	(Eduardo does not have arranged employment in Canada)
Age	10 points	(Eduardo is between 21 and 49)
Adaptability	5 points	(for the educational credentials of Eduardo's wife)
Total	73 points	(above the pass mark of 67)

Given that Eduardo does not have arranged employment, he will have to demonstrate at least $13,837 in settlement funds (for himself and Maria). Eduardo and Maria currently have $17,000 saved and, thus, would meet the requirement. In addition, both Eduardo and Maria must not be inadmissible.

When Eduardo applies for permanent residence, he will include his wife, Maria, in the application. Eduardo will be considered the principal applicant and Maria his accompanying family member. If Eduardo meets all the selection criteria and his application is approved, he and Maria will be issued permanent resident visas. Once admitted to Canada, they will become permanent residents and may subsequently apply for citizenship.

---

dependents admitted for permanent residence in 2010[29]), but it is projected to become a significant source of economic immigrants with a target of 26,000 by 2012.[30]

Provincial/Territorial Nominee Programs (PTNPs)

The skilled worker class and the CEC are federal programs. Their selection criteria are prescribed by the federal legislation; applications are processed by the federal department of CIC, and all applicants must meet the same criteria, regardless of their intended destination in Canada (except for Quebec). For the most part of the 20th century, admission to Canada was carried out overwhelmingly through federal streams. While such centralization of

---

[29] CIC, "Preliminary tables — Permanent and temporary residents, 2010", *supra* note 1.

[30] Auditor General of Canada, "Selecting Foreign Workers Under the Immigration Program" (2009), s. 2.27, online: <http://www.oag-bvg.gc.ca/internet/English/parl_oag_200911_02_e_33203.html#hd4c>.

selection criteria and processing offers many advantages, it may not always be effective in responding to regional diversity and specific provincial labour needs. Neither does it contain mechanisms to address the challenges associated with uneven distribution of newcomers across Canada (during 1999–2009, approximately 80 percent of newcomers settled in British Columbia, Ontario, and Quebec (mostly in Toronto, Montreal, and Vancouver[31])). In part due to these concerns, provinces and territories started to seek greater role in immigration regulation. This has been achieved, among other things, through the development of PTNPs, which allow provinces and territories to select immigrants who have the potential to benefit a given province or territory and nominate them for immigration.

All provinces (except for Quebec) and two territories (Yukon and Northwest Territories) have established nominee programs. Each province/territory is free to develop its own selection streams and criteria that best respond to its particular needs. Given significant regional diversity and distinct provincial/territorial objectives, there are currently over 50 selection streams under different PTNPs. Most provinces merely establish a minimum set of requirements that applicants must meet on a pass/fail basis, but some provinces (e.g., Manitoba) also use a provincially developed points system. All PTNPs have at least two streams: (skilled) worker and business stream. All provinces allow nomination of skilled workers, but some also provide opportunities for low skilled and semi-skilled workers in certain occupations (e.g., trucking, hotel and lodging, food processing, and food services industries in Alberta). In addition, some provinces allow nomination on the basis of family or community support. Thus, some PTNPs may provide a path to permanent residence for individuals who would not qualify under federal programs (e.g., a low-skilled worker who is ineligible under the skilled worker class or the CEC may qualify under Manitoba Provincial Nominee Program (PNP), which allows nomination of workers of all occupation levels).

The immigration process under PTNPs involves two steps:

1. Potential immigrants submit PTNP applications to a given province; those who meet the provincial selection criteria are nominated for immigration.

2. The nominated applicants submit applications for permanent residence to the CIC; security, criminality, and health checks are conducted and the CIC makes a decision on the permanent residence applications.

Thus, under the PTNP stream, both levels of government are involved in immigration processing: provinces are in charge of immigrant selection, while the federal CIC remains responsible for inadmissibility screening and final decision-making.

Over the past decade, PTNPs have grown significantly, from some 500 admissions in 1999 to over 36,000 in 2010.[32] This growth is likely to continue in the future and it is important to be aware of PTNPs as an emerging feature of the Canadian immigration system. Each PTNP has a website with detailed information about the selection and application process;[33] students are encouraged to check these websites and compare provincial/territorial programs to the federal skilled worker class and the CEC.

[31] CIC, "Facts and Figures, 2009", *supra* note 1.
[32] CIC, "Preliminary tables — Permanent and Temporary Residents, 2010", *supra* note 1.
[33] For example, Ontario PNP: <http://www.ontarioimmigration.ca/en/pnp/index.htm>; Manitoba PNP: <http://www2.immigratemanitoba.com/browse/howtoimmigrate/pnp/>; Alberta PNP: <http://www.albertacanada.com/immigration/immigrating/ainp.html>; Nova Scotia PNP: <http://novascotiaimmigration.com/nova-scotia-nominee-program>.

Family Immigration

Family reunification is one of the objectives of Canada's immigration policy.[34] Unlike the economic class, members of the family class are selected not on the basis of their ability to become economically established in Canada, but based on their relationship to a Canadian citizen or a permanent resident. In order to obtain permanent residence under the family class, two basic requirements must be met: (i) existence of an eligible Canadian sponsor and (ii) a qualifying familial relationship between the sponsor and the sponsored. The sponsor and the sponsored must meet a number of criteria and, correspondingly, the application process consists of two parts: (i) approval of a Canadian citizen or permanent resident as a sponsor; (ii) approval of the sponsored individual for permanent residence.

The following individuals may qualify to be sponsored under the family class:

- Sponsor's spouse, common-law partner, or conjugal partner
- Sponsor's dependent children, including adopted children
- Children under 18 years of age whom the sponsor intends to adopt in Canada
- Sponsor's parents
- Sponsor's grandparents
- Sponsor's orphaned brothers, sisters, nieces, nephews, and grandchildren who are under 18 years of age and who are not married and are not in a common-law relationship
- Any sponsor's relative, regardless of age, if the sponsor does not have a family member from the list above or an aunt or an uncle who could be sponsored or who is already a Canadian citizen, Indian, or permanent resident[35]

The above definition of family is notably different from our everyday understanding of family. For example, non-orphaned siblings and cousins are not on the list of persons who can be sponsored. Thus, immigration law not only imposes a certain definition of family but also, by virtue of that definition, controls the ability of Canadians to reunite with their relatives. Further, the *Regulations* outline in detail the meaning of each sponsored category. By way of illustration, we will briefly review the definitions of spouse, common-law partner, conjugal partner, and dependent child. Canada draws some distinctions between the "core" family members, such as a sponsor's spouse, partner, and children, and other family members. "Core" family enjoys more favourable treatment in the form of certain exemptions,[36] as well as expedited processing under the CIC policy.

Spouse

A marriage must be valid under the laws of the jurisdiction where it took place as well as under Canadian law. Following the redefinition of marriage as a "union of two persons",[37] same-sex marriages performed in Canada as

---

[34] *IRPA, supra* note 15, s. 3(1)(d).

[35] *Regulations, supra* note 16, s. 117(1).

[36] For example, spouses, partners and dependent children are exempt from medical inadmissibility on the grounds of excessive demand on health or social services. A Canadian sponsor who is seeking to sponsor his or her spouse, partner or dependent child is exempt from sponsorship ineligibility for lack of minimum income.

[37] *Civil Marriage Act*, S.C. 2005, c. 33, s. 2 (as amended by Bill C-38).

well as marriages performed in some foreign jurisdictions are valid for the purposes of immigration. In addition to requiring formal validity, immigration law takes into consideration the genuineness of a relationship (whether married or unmarried). A marriage, a common-law, or conjugal relationship will not be recognized if it was entered into primarily for immigration purposes or is not genuine. Further, some relationships are excluded from the family class and thus cannot be sponsored:

• Where a sponsor's spouse, common-law, or conjugal partner is under 16

• Where a sponsor or a sponsored individual is already married to someone else

• If the sponsored has lived apart from the sponsor for at least one year and either the sponsor or the sponsored are the common-law or conjugal partner of another person

• Where a sponsored individual was a sponsor's non-accompanying family member, but was not examined at the time when the sponsor applied to immigrate to Canada[38]

• Where a sponsor previously sponsored another spouse, common-law partner, or conjugal partner and a sponsorship undertaking (see explanation below) with respect to that spouse or partner is still in effect

Common-Law and Conjugal Partner

The *Regulations* define a common-law partner as an individual who is cohabiting with the sponsor in a conjugal relationship and who has cohabited with him/her for a period of at least one year.[39] A conjugal partner is "a foreign national residing outside Canada who is in a conjugal relationship with the sponsor and has been in that relationship for a period of at least one year."[40] The notion of conjugal partner was created to encompass couples who are prevented from marrying or living together due to circumstances beyond their control (e.g., immigration barriers; marital status — one of the persons is married to someone else and is living in a country where divorce is not possible; sexual orientation — same-sex relationships are not permitted in the country of person's residence).[41] Similarly to marriage, common-law and conjugal partnerships are defined in gender-neutral terms and therefore include same-sex and heterosexual relationships alike.

Unlike in a marriage, where a couple publicly declares its commitment to shared life at a specific point in time through a marriage ceremony, in a common-law or conjugal relationship there is no single point in time or a legal document (such as, for example, a marriage certificate) that attests to

---

[38] Applicants for immigration are required to list all their family members (spouse, common-law or conjugal partner and dependent children) in an immigration application, whether those family members will or will not accompany them to Canada. Further, all those family members (even if they do not accompany the applicant to Canada) must undergo medical examination and submit police clearances. For example, Eduardo (in Exhibit 35.2) is applying to immigrate to Canada under the economic class. He is married to Maria. Maria does not want to accompany Eduardo to Canada, but Eduardo nevertheless must list her on his application for permanent residence. If he fails to do so and Maria does not undergo the required examination, Eduardo will be precluded from sponsoring her under the family class at a later point. Section 117(9)(d) of the *Immigration and Refugee Protection Regulations* excludes from the family class a non-accompanying family member (in our case, Maria) who had not been examined at the time when the sponsor (Eduardo) applied for immigration to Canada.

[39] *Regulations*, *supra* note 16, s. 1.

[40] Ibid., s. 2.

[41] Citizenship and Immigration Canada, Overseas Processing Manual "Processing Members of the Family Class" at 31, online: <http://www.cic.gc.ca/english/resources/manuals/op/index.asp>

the couple's commitment. Thus, a determination of whether a common-law or a conjugal partnership exists is fact-based and is focused on examining a couple's attachment and interdependence — financial, social, emotional, and physical — over the passage of time. The CIC has identified a number of characteristics that usually have to be present in common-law, conjugal, and marital relationships:

- Mutual commitment to a shared life
- Exclusive — cannot be in more than one conjugal relationship at a time
- Intimate — commitment to sexual exclusivity
- Interdependent — physically, emotionally, financially, socially
- Permanent — long-term, genuine, and continuing relationship
- Present themselves as a couple
- Regarded by others as a couple
- Caring for children (if there are children)[42]

Dependent Child

The definition covers both biological and adopted children, who are in one of the following situations of dependency:

1. The child is under the age of 22 and is not married and not in a common-law relationships.

2. The child is a full-time student and has depended substantially on the parent's financial support since before the age of 22 or before getting married or forming a common-law relationship (if this happened before the age of 22).

3. The child is 22 or older and has depended substantially on the parent's financial support since before the age of 22 and is unable to be financially self-supporting due to a physical or mental condition.[43]

Requirements for Sponsors

In order to be eligible to sponsor relatives under the family class, an individual must meet three basic requirements: (i) be a Canadian citizen or permanent resident; (ii) be at least 18 years of age; and (iii) reside in Canada. Canadian citizens living abroad are eligible to apply for sponsorship of their spouse, common-law partner, conjugal partner or a dependent child as long as they demonstrate that they will return to reside in Canada once the sponsored individual becomes a permanent resident.

Even if the above requirements are met, an individual is ineligible as a sponsor if any of the following situations occurs:

- He/she is subject to a removal order.

- He/she is detained in a correctional institution.

- He/she has been convicted in or outside Canada of (a) an offence of a sexual nature, or an attempt or a threat to commit such an offence; or (b) a family violence offence that results in bodily harm, or an attempt or a threat to commit such an offence. Persons convicted in Canada become eligible for sponsorship five years after the completion of the imposed sentence. Persons convicted outside Canada become eligible for sponsorship if at least five years have elapsed since the completion of

---

[42] *Ibid.* at 19–20.
[43] *Regulations, supra* note 16, s. 2.

the imposed sentence and the person demonstrates that he/she has been rehabilitated.

- He/she is in default of any undertaking or any support payment ordered by a court.

- He/she is in undischarged bankruptcy.

- He/she has lower than the minimum necessary income. This requirement ensures that the sponsor is able to support his/her family and all sponsored persons. The minimum necessary income is based on the Low Income Cut-Off levels (LICO) for urban areas calculated by Statistics Canada. The required amounts of minimum necessary income are updated on a yearly basis and are based on the size of the sponsor's family unit.[44] Individuals sponsoring their spouse, partner or a dependent child are exempt from the requirement of minimum necessary income.

- He/she is in receipt of social assistance for a reason other than disability. The sponsor becomes eligible once he or she discontinues reliance on social assistance.

In addition, prospective sponsors must sign an undertaking to the Minister of Citizenship and Immigration, which ensures that the responsibility for supporting the sponsored individual(s) lies with the sponsor rather than the host society. The sponsor takes an obligation to provide for the basic needs of the sponsored during a prescribed period (see below). If during that period, the sponsored person(s) applies for social assistance, the sponsor undertakes to reimburse the government for the amounts received.

The length of a sponsorship undertaking is as follows:

1. For sponsor's spouse, common-law partner, or conjugal partner: 3 years.

2. For a dependent child who is under 22 when he or she becomes a permanent resident: 10 years or the day when the child reaches the age of 25 — whichever is shorter.

3. For a dependent child who is 22 or older when he or she becomes a permanent resident: 3 years.

4. For any other member of the family class: 10 years.

If family sponsorship is refused, a sponsor may appeal (with some exceptions[45]) to the Immigration Appeal Division of the IRB. If the appeal is allowed, CIC will resume processing the sponsorship application.

Temporary Residents There are three main categories of temporary residents: visitors, students, and temporary workers. During the past three years, Canada has been admitting, on average, over 180,000 foreign workers and over 80,000 foreign students annually.[46] There has been a steady increase in the admission of students and

---

[44] The 2011 LICO are as follows: a 2-person family unit — $27,674; 3 people — $34,022; 4 persons — $41,307; 5 persons — $46,850; 6 persons — $52,838; 7 persons — $58,827; more than 7 persons — for each additional person, add $5,989. Citizenship and Immigration Canada," Sponsorship of parents, grandparents, adopted children and other relatives — The sponsor's guide", online: <http://www.cic.gc.ca/english/information/applications/guides/5196E10.asp>.

[45] An appeal is not allowed for persons found inadmissible on the following grounds: serious criminality punished by a sentence of two years or more of imprisonment; organized criminality; security; violations of human or international rights; misrepresentation (unless the sponsored family member is the sponsor's spouse, common-law partner, or child).

[46] CIC, "Preliminary Tables — Permanent and Temporary Residents, 2010", *supra* note 1.

temporary foreign workers: a growth of over 40 percent between 2005 and 2010.[47] The increase is particularly noticeable in the category of low-skilled workers — largely due to the introduction of the Low-Skilled Project in 2002 in response to employer demands, particularly in the oil, gas, and construction industries. This is a change from the past when the emphasis in temporary admissions was on skilled workers and on two specific lower-skilled sectors (live-in caregivers and agricultural workers).[48]

As a general rule, foreign nationals need to apply for a visa prior to travelling to Canada, but nationals of some countries are exempt from this requirement.[49] In addition, individuals wishing to work or study in Canada usually need to apply for a work or a study permit, respectively. All applicants must satisfy Canadian immigration officers that they will comply with the conditions of stay and will leave Canada by the end of their authorized stay. In addition, there are specific requirements attached to applications for a work or a study permit.

As a rule, an applicant for a work permit needs to have a job offer from a Canadian employer that has been confirmed by Human Resources and Social Development Canada (HRSDC). The system of work permits seeks not only to regulate and track foreign nationals employed in Canada, but more importantly, to protect the Canadian labour market and in particular ensure that the employment of a foreign national is likely to have a neutral or positive effect on it. The latter objective is achieved through the process of HRSDC confirmation. It is usually an employer that seeks a job confirmation by demonstrating that it was not able to find a qualified Canadian citizen or permanent resident to fill the position. In addition, the work permit authorization process seeks to ensure that the foreign worker will be paid the prevailing wage rate in his/her occupation and that the recruitment of a foreign worker does not affect any labour dispute. Some types of jobs are exempt either from a requirement of a work permit or from a requirement of an HRSDC approval.

On April 1, 2011, new rules that seek to strengthen protection of temporary foreign workers from potential abuse and exploitation have come into effect. They include (i) more rigorous scrutiny of the genuineness of the job offer; (ii) a two-year prohibition from hiring temporary foreign workers for employers who fail to meet their commitments to workers with respect to wages and working conditions; and (iii) a limit on the length of time a temporary foreign worker may work in Canada: after working in Canada for four years, many workers will be required to wait for four years before becoming eligible to again temporarily work in Canada.

As a rule, foreign students must possess a study permit. As part of the application process, prospective students must produce an acceptance letter from an educational institution and demonstrate financial ability to pay tuition and subsistence expenses. Although the primary purpose of applicants' stay is study, Canadian immigration law provides for three scenarios in which foreign students are allowed to work:

1. On campus: full-time students with a valid study permit may work on campus without a work permit.

[47] CIC, "Facts and Figures, 2009", supra note 1; CIC, "Preliminary Tables — Permanent and Temporary Residents, 2010', *supra* note 1.
[48] Naomi Alboim, "Adjusting the Balance: Fixing Canada's Economic Immigration Policies" (2009), online: <www.maytree.com>.
[49] For a list of visa-exempt countries, see Citizenship and Immigration Canada at <http://www.cic.gc.ca/english/visit/visas.asp#exemptions>.

2. Off campus: full-time students enrolled at an educational institution that participates in the Off-Campus Work Permit Program may apply for a work permit to work off campus; students need to demonstrate that they have studied at the institution and maintained satisfactory academic standing for at least 6 months in the 12 months preceding the application;

3. After graduation: a post-graduation work permit allows students who have completed their studies to obtain Canadian work experience. They may accept employment in any field and are not required to obtain an HRSDC confirmation of a job offer. In order to be eligible for a post-graduation work permit, a student must have studied full-time at a Canadian institution in Canada, have completed a full-time program lasting at least eight months, and hold a valid study permit at the time of application. The application must be made within 90 days of formal notification that they have met the requirements of the program. A work permit can be up to three years, but not longer than the period of the student's studies.

The value of temporary work or study in Canada has increased with the introduction of the Canadian Experience Class (CEC), which provides foreign students and temporary skilled workers with an opportunity to apply for permanent residence. It is likely that more foreign nationals will consider choosing Canada as a destination for study or temporary work with a view to subsequently transitioning to permanent residence. However, the CEC provides a path to permanent residence to workers in skilled occupations only; it does not create similar opportunities for increasing numbers of low-skilled foreign workers in Canada.

Inadmissibility, Detention, and Removal

Immigration law outlines not only the positive characteristics that are sought in potential immigrants (for example, selection criteria in the economic class), but also features that make an applicant "undesirable." The latter are reflected in the grounds of inadmissibility, which either preclude an applicant's admission to Canada or if he/she is already in Canada may trigger enforcement action such as immigration arrest, detention and, ultimately, removal. The powers of removal, immigration arrest, and detention are quintessential exercises of state power to control admission of non-citizens as well as to contain and expel those who have violated immigration law or are otherwise considered to pose a risk to Canada or Canadians.

Grounds of Inadmissibility
The *IRPA* contains 10 grounds of inadmissibility:

1. **Health.** An individual's health condition is likely to be a danger to public health or safety or might be reasonably expected to cause excessive demand on health or social services; spouses, common-law partners, and dependent children of Canadian sponsors under the family class as well as resettled refugees and protected persons are exempt from inadmissibility on the basis of "excessive demand".

2. **Financial.** An individual is or will be unable or unwilling to support himself/herself or his/her dependents in Canada.

3. **Inadmissible family member.** An individual may be inadmissible if his or her accompanying family member and, in some circumstances, non-accompanying family member is inadmissible (for example, if the

applicant's dependent child is inadmissible on health grounds, the applicant may be inadmissible, too).

4. **Criminality.** This ground covers the following situations:
   (a) Conviction in Canada of an offence under an Act of Parliament punishable by way of indictment, or of two offences under any Act of Parliament not arising out of a single occurrence.
   (b) Conviction outside Canada of an offence that, if committed in Canada, would constitute an indictable offence under an Act of Parliament, or of two offences not arising out of a single occurrence that, if committed in Canada, would constitute offences under an Act of Parliament.
   (c) Committing an act outside Canada that is an offence in the place where it was committed and that, if committed in Canada, would constitute an indictable offence under an Act of Parliament.
   (d) Committing, on entering Canada, an offence under the *Criminal Code*, the *Immigration and Refugee Protection Act*, the *Firearms Act*, the *Customs Act*, or the *Controlled Drugs and Substances Act*.

5. **Serious criminality.** This ground covers the following situations:
   (a) Conviction in Canada of an offence under an Act of Parliament punishable by a maximum term of imprisonment of at least 10 years, or of an offence under an Act of Parliament for which a term of imprisonment of more than six months has been imposed.
   (b) Conviction outside Canada of an offence that, if committed in Canada, would constitute an offence under an Act of Parliament punishable by a maximum term of imprisonment of at least 10 years.
   (c) Committing an act outside Canada that is an offence in the place where it was committed and that, if committed in Canada, would constitute an offence under an Act of Parliament punishable by a maximum term of imprisonment of at least 10 years.

6. **Organized criminality.** An individual may be inadmissible on this ground for being a member of a criminal organization or for engaging, in the context of transnational crime, in activities such as people smuggling, trafficking in persons or money laundering.

7. **Security.** This ground encompasses such situations as engaging in espionage, in subversion of force of any government, in terrorism or in acts of violence that would or might endanger the lives or safety of persons in Canada; being a danger to the security of Canada or being a member of an organization that there are reasonable grounds to believe engages, has engaged or will engage in espionage, terrorism or subversion of any government by force.

8. **International and human rights violations.** An individual may be inadmissible on this ground for committing acts of genocide, war crimes or crimes against humanity outside Canada or for being a senior official in a government that engages or has engaged in terrorism, systematic or gross human rights violations, genocide, war crimes or crimes against humanity; this ground also applies to foreign nationals subject to travel sanctions by an international organization, of which Canada is a member.

9. **Misrepresentation.** This ground captures situations where an individual directly or indirectly misrepresented or withheld material facts that

induce or could induce an error in the administration of the *IRPA*; this ground does not apply to protected persons.

10. **Non-compliance with the *IRPA*** (e.g., failing to leave Canada once a person's authorized stay has expired; working without authorization).

The first four grounds apply only to foreign nationals; the rest apply to both foreign nationals and permanent residents.

Persons seeking to enter Canada, permanently or temporarily, must satisfy immigration officers that they are not inadmissible. For example, for this purpose, applicants for permanent residence are required to undergo a medical examination (to determine health admissibility) and provide police clearances from each country where they have resided for at least six consecutive months since reaching the age of 18 (to determine criminality admissibility). In addition, the CIC conducts background checks on applicants and their family members to find out if they may be inadmissible on other grounds.

If inadmissibility is discovered prior to entry, the person may not be issued a visa to enter Canada. If inadmissibility arises at the point of entry or after entry to Canada, an inadmissibility proceeding is started, which may ultimately lead to removal. First, an immigration officer prepares a report and submits it to the Minister's delegate (a senior official empowered to review inadmissibility reports). In some cases, the Minister's delegate can issue a removal order on the basis of the report. However, in most cases, the case is referred to the Immigration Division of the IRB for a hearing to determine whether the person concerned is inadmissible. If the person is inadmissible, the Division may issue a removal order.

Permanent residents and, in limited circumstances, foreign nationals can appeal a removal order to the Immigration Appeal Division. However, the right to appeal is removed from individuals who are inadmissible on the grounds of security, violating human or international rights, serious criminality, or organized criminality. If the appeal is allowed, a person is permitted to remain in Canada.

Health Inadmissibility: Excessive Demand on Health or Social Services

To illustrate the interpretation and application of inadmissibility grounds, this section discusses medical inadmissibility based on excessive demand on health or social services. Section 1 of the *Regulations* defines "excessive demand" in the following way:

> (*a*) a demand on health services or social services for which the anticipated costs would likely exceed average Canadian per capita health services and social services costs over a period of five consecutive years immediately following the most recent medical examination required by these Regulations, unless there is evidence that significant costs are likely to be incurred beyond that period, in which case the period is no more than 10 consecutive years; or
>
> (*b*) a demand on health services or social services that would add to existing waiting lists and would increase the rate of mortality and morbidity in Canada as a result of an inability to provide timely services to Canadian citizens or permanent residents.

The above definition, however, does not fully answer how excessive demand is to be established. For example, if a person has a health condition that is known to require services and supports that are expensive or in high demand, does this automatically lead to inadmissibility? What if an applicant is willing to attenuate public expenses and pay himself/herself for the necessary services? Is the applicant's financial ability and willingness to cover health or social service expenses relevant to the evaluation of "excessive demand"? Two important cases — Hilewitz[50] and Deol[51] — provided useful clarification of these issues.

The Hilewitz family applied to immigrate to Canada under the investor class (this class required applicants to have at least $800,000 net worth and make a $400,000 investment in Canada[52]) and has met the necessary financial requirements. However, one of the family's children, Gavin, had an intellectual disability, which was deemed to impose excessive demand on Canadian social services (such as special education and vocational training). As a result, he was inadmissible. The family indicated that it was able and willing to send Gavin to a private school and, thus, he would impose no demand on social services. Nevertheless, the family's application for permanent residence was refused. The Hilewitzes challenged the refusal, and their case reached all the way to the Supreme Court of Canada. The Supreme Court held that the family's ability and willingness to pay for social services was a relevant consideration in assessing "excessive demand". The Court emphasized that assessments need to be individualized. It is impossible to realistically determine the nature and extent of demands on services without considering medical as well as non-medical factors, including the applicant's ability and intention to pay for social services. If the need for services is determined only by the classification of a health condition, it becomes generic rather than individual and leads to an automatic exclusion of individuals with particular disabilities. Although Hilewitz was decided in the context of the investor class, as subsequently suggested by the Federal Court of Appeal, the holding applies to other categories of immigrants.[53]

Although ability and willingness to pay are relevant in the context of social services, this is not so in relation to health services. This is explained by the different funding and delivery schemes of health and social services. The social services scheme contemplates the contribution of families to the costs of providing certain services. As noted by the Supreme Court in Hilewitz, even if the intentions of the Hilewitz family regarding Gavin's education and training did not materialize, under the provincial social services scheme, the family would likely be required to contribute a substantial portion, if not the entire, cost of services. In contrast, healthcare is publicly funded and services are available without payment. Thus, it is not possible to enforce a personal undertaking to pay for health services after a person is admitted for permanent residence. Hence, in Deol, the Federal Court of Appeal found that the decision-maker made no error in not giving regard to the financial ability of the applicant to pay for health services.[54]

Immigration Detention

Like other aspects of immigration law, immigration detention applies to non-citizens only. It is considered to be of preventative and not penal nature. This is reflected in the three major grounds for arrest and detention:

---

[50] Hilewitz v. Canada (Minister of Citizenship and Immigration); De Jong v. Canada (Minister of Citizenship and Immigration), [2005] 2 S.C.R. 706.

[51] Deol v. Canada (Minister of Citizenship and Immigration), [2003] 1 F.C. 301 (C.A.).

[52] In 2010, these requirements were changed. Now an investor needs to have at least $1.6 million net worth and make an $800,000 investment in Canada. Regulations, supra note 16, s. 88(1).

[53] Colaco v. Canada (Minister of Citizenship and Immigration), [2007] F.C.J. No. 1172 (C.A.).

[54] Ms. Deol applied to sponsor her father, mother and siblings to immigrate to Canada. The application was refused because the father had degenerative osteoarthritis, which was considered to cause excessive demand on health services in Canada (his condition would likely require knee replacement surgery at a cost of approximately $40,000).

- Inadmissibility and danger to the public (there are reasonable grounds to believe that a person is inadmissible and is a danger to the public)

- Flight risk (there are reasonable grounds to believe that a person is unlikely to appear for a future examination, inadmissibility hearing or removal from Canada)

- Identity (where an officer is not satisfied about a person's identity; for example, an individual has no identity documents or the documents are fraudulent)

Immigration arrest and detention is used to contain individuals, often in order to enable further enforcement action such as removal. Depending on the circumstances, arrest and detention may be carried out with or without a warrant, on entry into Canada or after admission to Canada. A person's right to counsel arises at the moment when he/she is ordered detained.[55]

Neither the *IRPA* nor the *Regulations* prescribe a temporal limit on detention. The *IRPA*, however, provides for regular detention reviews, and the *Regulations* establish safeguards against indefinite detention.[56] Detention reviews are conducted by the Immigration Division of the IRB, which has the power to order continued detention or release. Detention reviews are conducted with the following regularity:

1. First detention review — within 48 hours after the person was taken into detention or "without delay afterwards".
2. Second detention review — at least once during the seven days following the first review.
3. Each subsequent review — at least once during each 30-day period after each review.

Security Certificates

Security certificates are a special procedure that allows for detention and removal of foreign nationals and permanent residents who are inadmissible on grounds of security, violating human or international rights, serious criminality or organized criminality.[57] As seen from the grounds of inadmissibility, the procedure is intended for cases that are considered particularly serious and seeks to ensure containment and speedy removal of the persons concerned.

The procedure works in the following way:

1. The Minister of Citizenship and Immigration and the Minister of Public Safety and Emergency Preparedness sign a certificate stating that a given individual is inadmissible on one of the above-mentioned grounds; the Ministers may also issue a warrant for the arrest and detention of the person named in the certificate.

2. The certificate is referred to the Federal Court, which determines whether the certificate is reasonable.

3. If the certificate is upheld by the Court, it serves as conclusive proof that the person named in the certificate is inadmissible and clears the path for the person's removal from Canada.

---

[55] *Dragosin v. Canada*, [2003] F.C.J. No. 110.
[56] *IRPA*, *supra* note 15, s. 57; *Regulations*, *supra* note 16, s. 248.
[57] *IRPA*, *supra* note 15, s. 77(1).

Between 1991 and 2007, 28 security certificates were issued; 19 of them resulted in deportations.[58] The procedure proved highly problematic, particularly in relation to the five recent cases of Hassan Almrei, Adil Charkaoui, Mohammad Harkat, Mahmoud Jaballah, and Mohammad Mahjoub. All five persons have been subject to certificates for suspected links to terrorist organizations and, as a result, have spent anywhere between 2 and 7.25 years in detention.

Some of the major concerns as highlighted by the five cases were as follows:

1. *Inability to know the case to be met and effectively challenge government evidence.* The security certificate procedure provides for limitations on disclosure of information to the person concerned where such disclosure may be injurious to national security. Thus, the person named in the certificate may not be allowed to see all the evidence on which the government is building its case. The confidential information will be heard by the Federal Court in the absence of the person concerned and his/her counsel; they will be given only a summary of such evidence.

2. *Prolonged detention with limited opportunity for detention review and release.* Under the 2002 provisions of the *IRPA*, permanent residents subject to security certificates could be detained, but they had access to periodic detention reviews from the very start of detention. In contrast, foreign nationals had to be automatically detained, but they did not have similar access to detention review. They could apply for release only after the certificate was determined reasonable and if they had not been removed from Canada within 120 days after the certificate was upheld. Given the complicated process of collecting intelligence in national security cases and the lengthiness of its examination, in some cases, it took years until the decision on the certificate's reasonableness could be made. As a result, at least two of the five named persons have spent anywhere between three and five years in detention without even the possibility of applying for release (for example, a certificate against Mr. Jaballah was issued in August 2001, but it was determined reasonable only in 2006).

3. *Potential removal to face torture, risk to life or other ill-treatment.* All five named persons allege that they would face torture or persecution in the countries of intended destination. Hassan Almrei, Mohammad Harkat, and Mohammad Mahjoub have been granted Convention refugee status in Canada; that is, Canadian authorities have recognized that these three individuals would face persecution in their countries of origin. Adil Charkaoui and Mahmoud Jaballah, while not refugees, allege risk of torture if removed to Morocco and Egypt, respectively. Given that the Supreme Court decision in *Suresh* did not impose an absolute prohibition on removal to torture, it is possible that security certificates may become those "extraordinary circumstances" when removal may be justified.[59] However, given that the Supreme Court did not provide any

---

[58] Special Senate Committee on the *Anti-terrorism Act*, Fundamental Justice in Extraordinary Times: Main Report of the Special Senate Committee on the Anti-Terrorism Act (February 2007), <http://www.parl.gc.ca/39/1/parlbus/commbus/senate/Com-e/anti-e/rep-e/rep02feb07-e.htm#PROCEDURAL_FAIRNESS:_THE_NEED_FOR_A_SPECIAL_ADVOCATE>.

[59] It should be noted that in *Jaballah (Re)*, [2006] F.C.J. No. 1706, the Federal Court determined that the case did not create an exceptional circumstance warranting deportation to torture. The Court, however, also remarked that

indication as to what these extraordinary circumstances might be, it is likely that another Supreme Court decision will be necessary to ultimately resolve the issue.

In February 2007, the Supreme Court found that the security certificate procedure violated sections 7, 9, and 10 of the *Charter* and could not be saved under section 1.[60] Due to the lack of disclosure, the persons concerned were not able to know the case to be met and effectively respond to the allegations made by the government. This, in turn, undermined the ability of a judge to make a decision based on all available facts and the law and violated the right to a fair hearing under section 7. Further, the lack of regular detention reviews for foreign nationals violated the right not to be subject to arbitrary detention and the right to a prompt detention review.

As a result of the *Charkaoui* decision, the *IRPA* was amended to provide for a single regime of regular detention reviews for both permanent residents and foreign nationals as well as to establish a position of special advocate in order to mitigate concerns associated with the lack of disclosure. The function of the special advocate is to protect the interests of a person named in a security certificate during proceedings where confidential information is heard in his/her absence. The special advocate is given access to all information that is not disclosed to the person concerned and his/her counsel. The special advocate can challenge the relevance, reliability, and sufficiency of confidential information; make oral and written submissions; and cross-examine witnesses. Although the special advocate model partially compensates for non-disclosure, it is far from an optimal solution. Most notably, once the special advocate receives confidential information, he/she is prohibited from communicating with the person concerned, unless authorized by a judge. This significantly undermines the ability of special advocates to challenge or counter the information relied upon by the government.

The Minister of Justice established a list of lawyers who may act as special advocates. They are selected by an advisory committee which reviews applications and makes recommendations to the Minister. There are currently 23 lawyers on the list.[61]

In 2009, the Federal Court found that there was not sufficient information to conclude that Mr. Almrei was a member of Al Qaeda or an affiliated organization and quashed a certificate against him.[62] The same year, a certificate against Mr. Charkaoui was determined void as there was not sufficient evidence to justify it.[63] Both men have launched lawsuits seeking damages from the federal government for negligence and false imprisonment. The certificate against Mr. Harkat was upheld in December 2010,[64] but the decision is currently on appeal before the Federal Court of Appeal. The certificates against Mr. Jaballah and Mr. Mahjoub still await examination before the Federal Court.

---

this conclusion did not mean that Mr. Jaballah could not be deported. Rather, the Minister was not to exercise discretion in a manner that would violate the respondent's rights under the *Charter*.

[60] *Charkaoui v. Canada (Citizenship and Immigration)*, [2007] 1 S.C.R. 350.

[61] Justice Canada, online: <http://canada.justice.gc.ca/eng/news-nouv/nr-cp/2007/doc_32198.html>.

[62] *Almrei (Re)*, [2009] F.C.J. No. 1579.

[63] *Charkaoui (Re)*, [2009] F.C.J. No. 1208. The government was ordered to disclose a portion of confidential information on which it relied, but the authorities decided to withdraw that information instead of disclosing it to Charkaoui. As a result, the remaining evidence was not sufficient to justify the certificate.

[64] *Harkat (Re)*, [2010] F.C.J. No. 1428.

Removal Orders

There are three types of removal orders, which produce different consequences for persons subject to them:

- **Exclusion orders:** As a general rule, an exclusion order obliges a foreign national to obtain a written authorization in order to return to Canada during the one-year period after the exclusion order was enforced. A harsher regime applies to foreign nationals who are issued exclusion orders as a result of misrepresentation: they are subject to the requirement of obtaining a written authorization to return to Canada for a period of two years after the exclusion order was enforced.

- **Deportation orders:** A deportation order requires a person concerned to obtain a written authorization in order to return to Canada at any time after the deportation order was enforced.

- **Departure orders:** The departure order regime seeks to encourage speedy voluntary compliance with removal orders. Unlike exclusion or deportation orders, departure orders do not require an individual to obtain a written authorization to return to Canada. In order to benefit from this regime, a person must leave Canada within 30 days after the order became enforceable and verify the departure with immigration authorities. Failure to depart will lead to a departure order automatically becoming a deportation order.

REFUGEE LAW

Unlike immigrants, who are considered to move voluntarily in pursuit of better opportunities, refugees are involuntary migrants who are fleeing for their lives. To account for this reality, admission of refugees is based on principles that are different from immigrant selection. While immigrants are admitted on the basis of their potential contribution to Canada or relationship to a Canadian, the defining consideration in case of refugees is their need for protection.

The *Refugee Convention*

The 1951 *UN Convention Relating to the Status of Refugees (Refugee Convention)* and the 1967 *Protocol* create an international framework for refugee protection. Including Canada, 141 countries are parties to the *Convention* and the *Protocol*[65] and are consequently guided by their provisions in decision-making on refugee claims. At the international level, refugee protection efforts are led and coordinated by a specialized agency — the United Nations High Commissioner for Refugees (UNHCR). The UNHCR performs a variety of tasks, including assistance to refugees and other persons in need of protection, advocacy, response to emergency situations, refugee determination in certain countries, and promotion of durable solutions for the displaced.

According to the UNHCR, there were 43.3 million forcibly displaced people worldwide at the end of 2009.[66] The largest numbers of refugees originated from Afghanistan, Iraq, and Somalia, and the top three refugee-hosting

---

[65] United Nations High Commissioner for Refugees (UNHCR), "States Parties to the Convention and the Protocol", online: <http://www.unhcr.org/pages/49da0e466.html>.

[66] United Nations High Commissioner for Refugees (UNHCR), "2009 Global Trends: Refugees, Asylum-seekers, Returnees, Internally Displaced and Stateless Persons", online: <http://www.unhcr.org/4c11f0be9.html> [UNHCR, "2009 Global Trends"].

countries were Pakistan, Iran, and Syria.[67] Overall, approximately four-fifths of refugees are located in developing countries.[68] Thus, refugee burdens are distributed unequally: countries with fewer resources are also usually the ones bearing a significant refugee burden. These patterns are essential to understanding the global dynamics of refugee protection and the positioning of industrialized countries such as Canada in this context.

The regime of the *Refugee Convention* rests on three core concepts:

1. Definition of a refugee
2. *Non-refoulement* (means "no return")
3. Standards of treatment of refugees

The refugee definition forms the basis for determining whether a person concerned should be granted protection. It is discussed in detail in the section below.

The *non-refoulement* principle (Art. 33 of the *Refugee Convention*) prohibits expulsion of a refugee to a country where he/she may face persecution, unless that refugee constitutes a danger to security or poses a threat to the public of a host state. As a result of this principle, states' ability to remove refugees is more constrained than their ability to remove other categories of migrants.

Refugee protection can be considered meaningful and effective only if it allows for the inclusion of refugees in a host society. To this end, the *Refugee Convention* imposes an obligation on States Parties to ensure certain standards of treatment of refugees in a number of areas, including access to courts, freedom of religion and association, freedom of movement, elementary education, access to employment, housing, and social assistance. In Canada, these obligations have led to refugee claimants and refugees enjoying certain benefits that are not normally available to other foreign nationals. For example, refugee claimants and refugees have access to social assistance and the Interim Federal Health program; they are not required to have an HRSDC approval in order to be issued a work permit.

A refugee claim may be made inside or outside Canada. These two avenues correspond to the two streams of Canada's refugee protection system: inland refugee determination and refugee resettlement. A person who has made a claim for protection from within Canada and who is awaiting a decision on it is called a **refugee claimant** (often also referred to as an "asylum-seeker"). Since 2005, Canada has received between 20,000 and 37,000 refugee claims a year (the lowest was close to 20,000 in 2005 and the highest was approximately 37,000 in 2008).[69] Internationally, it ranked as the fourth largest recipient of asylum applications among industrialized countries in 2009.[70]

Grounds for Protection

In Canada, refugee protection may be granted on one of three grounds: (i) the *Refugee Convention*; (ii) risk of torture; and (iii) risk to life or risk of cruel and unusual treatment or punishment. The refugee determination procedure and the benefits of protection under all three grounds are the same.

---

[67] *Ibid.* at 6–8.

[68] *Ibid.*

[69] United Nations High Commissioner for Refugees (UNHCR), "Asylum Levels and Trends in Industrialized Countries: 2009" at 13, online: <http://www.unhcr.org/4ba7341a9.html> [UNHCR, "Asylum Levels in Industrialized Countries: 2009"].

[70] Close to 800,000 applications for asylum were made in 159 countries around the world in 2009. Out of these, over 222,000 were registered in South Africa — almost as many as were lodged in the 27 member states of the European Union combined. The United States ranked second, with 47,900 applications; France — third, with 42,100 claims, and Canada — fourth, with 34,000 applications. *Ibid.* at 16–17.

Definition of a Refugee

Article 1A(2) of the *Refugee Convention* defines a refugee as a person who

> ... owing to well-founded fear of being persecuted for reasons of race, reli-
> gion, nationality, membership of a particular social group or political opinion,
> is outside the country of his nationality and is unable or, owing to such fear,
> is unwilling to avail himself of the protection of that country; or who, not
> having a nationality and being outside the country of his former habitual resi-
> dence as a result of such events, is unable or, owing to such fear, is
> unwilling to return to it.

The UNHCR and national decision-making bodies have developed extensive jurisprudence and guidelines on the interpretation of key aspects of the
definition:

1. **Persecution.** The *Convention* does not define the term "persecution",
    but it has been understood as serious human rights violations — sys-
    temic and sustained denial of core human rights.[71] The claimant must
    show that there is a "reasonable chance" or a "serious possibility" that
    he/she will be persecuted if returned to his/her **country of origin**.[72]

2. **Well-founded fear of persecution.** In order for fear to be considered
    well-founded, a subjective and objective element must be present: fear
    has to exist not only subjectively in the claimant's mind, but also be
    supported by the situation in the claimant's country of origin.[73] The
    objective element is established on the basis of information about the
    country of origin. To this end, the Canadian IRB has developed national
    documentation packages on individual countries, which contain a selec-
    tion of documents on human rights, security conditions, and other issues
    relevant to refugee determination. The packages usually include such
    sources as reports of human rights organizations (e.g., Amnesty Interna-
    tional, Human Rights Watch), media articles, and information collected
    by the IRB research directorate on specific issues.

3. **State protection.** The refugee definition reflects the surrogate nature
    of refugee protection: only where the claimant is unable or unwilling to
    obtain protection from his/her own state, can he/she turn to another
    state for protection. Such unwillingness or inability may arise in a vari-
    ety of situations. For example, where the claimant's state itself is the
    persecutor (for example, government persecution of members of political
    opposition) protection is generally considered unavailable. Protection
    may also be unavailable where war, internal strife or other grave distur-
    bance has led to the breakdown of the state apparatus. Claimants may
    also be unable or unwilling to obtain state protection where persecution
    is inflicted by private individuals and groups, but is tolerated by the
    authorities or where state authorities refuse to provide protection (for
    instance, a claimant suffers from domestic violence at the hand of her
    husband, but when she repeatedly complains to police, they take no
    action).

---

[71] *Canada (Attorney General) v. Ward*, [1993] 2 S.C.R. 689 at paras. 64–69. See also United Nations High
Commissioner for Refugees (UNHCR), *Handbook on Procedures and Criteria for Determining Refugee Status under the
1951 Convention and the 1967 Protocol relating to the Status of Refugees*, HCR/IP/4/Eng/REV.1, 1979 (re-edited January
1992) at para 51 [UNHCR, Handbook on Determining Refugee Status].

[72] *Adjei v. Canada (Minister of Employment and Immigration)*, [1989] 2 F.C. 680 (C.A.).

[73] *UNHCR, Handbook on Determining Refugee Status*, *supra* note 72 at para. 38.

4. **Protection grounds.** The *Convention* makes protection available only in cases where persecution is inflicted on one or a combination of the five grounds: race, religion, nationality, political opinion, or membership of a particular social group. While the first four grounds are relatively self-explanatory, membership of a particular social group requires some elaboration. Internationally, there developed two major approaches to the definition of a "particular social group": the social perception approach and the protected characteristics approach. The **social perception approach** is focused on the external perception of the group by others, including persecutors. It asks whether a certain group is viewed as a distinct social group by reason of some characteristic, activity or goal that unites them.[74] The **protected characteristics approach** focuses on internal characteristics that unite persons in a group. In Canada, the foundations of this approach were laid by the Supreme Court in *Ward*,[75] which identified the following categories of particular social groups:

> (1) groups defined by an innate, unchangeable characteristic;
> (2) groups whose members voluntarily associate for reasons so fundamental to their human dignity that they should not be forced to forsake the association; and (3) groups associated by a former voluntary status, unalterable due to its historical permanence.

The examples of recognized particular social groups are women suffering from domestic violence, homosexuals, persons subject to forced sterilization, the poor, and trade unionists.

Exclusion from Refugee Protection

The issues of refugee definition go hand in hand with the issue of exclusion, i.e., who is not entitled to protection. The *Convention* envisions two scenarios in which a claimant who meets the refugee definition is nevertheless excluded from protection: (i) an individual is considered undeserving of protection or (ii) an individual is considered not to be in need of protection.

The first group is outlined in Art. 1 F of the *Refugee Convention* and includes situations where there are "serious reasons" to believe that the claimant (a) committed a crime against peace, a war crime, or a crime against humanity; (b) committed a serious non-political crime outside the country of refuge; or (c) is guilty of acts contrary to the purposes and principles of the United Nations.

The second set of grounds is found in Article 1E and applies in situations where a claimant has established residence outside the country where he/she fears persecution and has been granted most of the rights normally enjoyed by citizens in the new country of residence. This usually implies that the person, while not having citizenship, can safely live in the new country of residence and is protected against expulsion.[76] As a result, such a person is considered not to be in need of refugee protection elsewhere. For example, Miriam faces persecution in her **home country**, but then flees to country A where he/she is safe and is granted most of the rights enjoyed by citizens. If subsequently Miriam moves to a country B and makes a refugee claim there, she may be excluded from protection on the basis of Art. 1E.

---

[74] James C. Hathaway & Michelle Foster, "Membership of a Particular Social Group" (2003) 15:3 Int'l J. Ref. L. 477 at 483.

[75] *Ward, supra* note 72.

[76] UNHCR, *Handbook on Determining Refugee Status, supra* note 72 at para. 145.

Cessation of Protection

Cessation of protection refers to situations where refugee protection is no longer necessary. It may occur in the following situations:

- Where a refugee has voluntarily re-availed himself/herself of the protection of the country of his/her nationality
- Where a refugee has voluntarily reacquired his/her previous nationality
- Where a refugee has acquired a new nationality
- Where a refugee has voluntarily re-established himself/herself in the country which he/she left, owing to fear of persecution
- Where the circumstances that led to the individual's recognition as a refugee have ceased to exist[77]

Definition of Person in Need of Protection

The category of **person in need of protection** encompasses two grounds: (i) risk of torture, and (ii) risk to life or risk of cruel and unusual treatment or punishment. These two grounds give effect to Canada's obligations under the *Convention against Torture* (prohibition of torture and of removal to torture) and the *International Covenant on Civil and Political Rights* (ICCPR) (prohibition of torture, cruel, inhuman or degrading treatment or punishment and prohibition on removal to face such maltreatment). Unlike the *Refugee Convention*, neither of the two grounds requires that risk be connected to race, religion, nationality, political opinion or membership of a particular social group. Thus, they expand protection opportunities for persons who do not meet the Convention definition, but are nevertheless at risk.

The first ground is determined in reference to the definition of torture under the *Convention against Torture*:

> ... any act by which severe pain or suffering, whether physical or mental, is intentionally inflicted on a person for such purposes as obtaining from him or a third person information or a confession, punishing him for an act he or a third person has committed or is suspected of having committed, or intimidating or coercing him or a third person, or for any reason based on discrimination of any kind, when such pain or suffering is inflicted by or at the instigation of or with the consent or acquiescence of a public official or other person acting in an official capacity. It does not include pain or suffering arising only from, inherent in or incidental to lawful sanctions.[78]

As seen from the above definition, "torture" has distinct characteristics: (i) it causes severe pain or suffering; (2) it is inflicted for a certain purpose; (iii) it is carried out by or with the acquiescence of the state. Persons claiming protection on this ground must demonstrate that there are substantial grounds to believe that they would be subjected personally to a danger of torture.

The second ground within the notion of "person in need of protection" is risk to life or risk of cruel and unusual treatment or punishment. According to the *IRPA*, a claimant relying on this ground must demonstrate that he/she would face risk in every part of his/her country of origin; that the risk is not faced generally by other individuals in the country and that he/she is unable or unwilling to avail himself/herself of the protection of that country.[79]

Neither the *Convention against Torture* nor the ICCPR define "inhuman or degrading treatment or punishment". The distinction between torture and

---

[77] *Refugee Convention*, Art. 1C.

[78] *Convention against Torture and Other Cruel, Inhuman or Degrading Treatment or Punishment*, Adopted by General Assembly resolution 39/46 of 10 December 1984, Art. 1(1).

[79] *IRPA*, *supra* note 15, s. 97(1)(b).

inhuman or degrading treatment or punishment is often based on the difference in the kind, purpose, and severity of treatment, torture being considered an aggravated form of cruel, inhuman, or degrading treatment or punishment. Section 97(1)(b) of the *IRPA* excludes two types of risk from consideration under the risk to life or the risk of cruel and unusual treatment or punishment:

1. Risk inherent or incidental to lawful sanctions, unless they are imposed in disregard of accepted international standards
2. Risks caused by the inability of the claimant's home country to provide adequate health or medical care

Inland Refugees

Access to Inland Protection

The *Refugee Convention* does not compel States Parties to admit asylum-seekers or refugees. In fact, obligations under the *Convention* arise only once a person finds himself/herself in the territory of a State Party. Access to territory therefore becomes a determinative factor in the ability of asylum-seekers to access refugee protection; at the same time, states are using regulation of access to their territories to manage (often contrary to the spirit of the *Convention*) asylum flows and the extent of their refugee protection obligations. The measures that seek to prevent asylum-seekers or other migrants from arriving in a state territory are commonly known as **interdiction**. Interdiction includes, for example, visa requirements, carrier sanctions, stationing of immigration officers overseas, interception of boats at sea, and safe third country agreements.

Imposition of visa requirements on refugee-producing countries has been frequently utilized to reduce asylum flows. For example, high volumes of refugee claims from Mexico and the Czech Republic have been expressly cited as the reason for Canada's imposition of visa requirements on those countries in 2009.[80]

Carrier sanctions include imposition of fines on transportation companies that bring unauthorized migrants into a country as well as making carriers responsible for costs of removing those unauthorized migrants. Such sanctions create strong incentives for carriers to co-operate with immigration officials in pre-boarding checks and other screening in countries of origin.

The **safe third country** principle is usually used to preclude refugee claimants who have travelled through "safe" countries from being considered for protection in the state of final destination. So far, Canada has designated only one country — the United States — as "safe" and to this end has concluded a *Safe Third Country Agreement*[81] with the United States. According to the *Agreement*, which came into force in 2004, the state in which a refugee claimant arrived first should be responsible for determining his/her claim. This means that, for example, a claimant who travelled to Canada through the United States will not be given access to the Canadian refugee determination system, but instead will be directed to have his/her claim processed in the United States. The application of the *Agreement* is, however, limited in two respects. First, it applies only to claims made at the Canada–U.S. land border;

[80] CIC, News Release, "Canada imposes a visa on Mexico" <http://www.cic.gc.ca/english/department/media/releases/2009/2009-07-13.asp>. During 2008–2009, Mexico ranked as the top country of origin of refugee claimants in Canada; the Czech Republic was among the top ten countries of origin. UNHCR, "Asylum Levels in Industrialized Countries: 2009", *supra* note 70 at 33–34.

[81] *Agreement between the Government of Canada and the Government of the United States of America for Cooperation in the Examination of Refugee Status Claims from Nationals of Third Countries*, 5 December 2002, online: <http://www.cic.gc.ca/english/policy/safe-third.html>

if an individual has managed to enter Canadian territory, he/she will not be precluded from having a claim considered in Canada. Second, there are four main exceptions, which allow a claim to be considered in a state where an asylum-seeker wishes to seek protection and not in the state of first arrival. The following groups benefit from the exceptions:

- Unaccompanied minors
- Claimants who have a family member whose refugee claim was granted or who has lawful status (other than a visitor) in a receiving state
- Claimants who have a family member who is at least 18 years old and has a refugee claim pending in a receiving state
- Claimants who arrived in the receiving state's territory on a valid visa or who do not require a visa

In addition to the four exceptions outlined above, the *Agreement* allows Canada and the United States to make additional exceptions on public interest grounds. Canada has chosen to provide a public interest exception for individuals who have been charged with or convicted of an offence that could subject them to the death penalty in the United States or in any other country.

The *Agreement* has been criticized on a number of grounds, including for exposing many claimants to less favourable treatment in the United States than that accorded to refugee claimants in Canada. For example, the United States is more likely to detain asylum-seekers and to provide less sensitive consideration to gender-based claims. More claimants travel through the United States to Canada than the other way around. Thus, the *Agreement* has a disproportionate impact on the claimant's access to Canada's refugee system. In fact, the number of refugee claims made at the land border decreased by approximately 55 percent in 2005 compared with 2004 — a development that can be largely attributed to the *Agreement*.[82]

In 2005, the Canadian Council for Refugees (CCR), Amnesty International, and the Canadian Council of Churches, along with a Colombian asylum-seeker in the United States, challenged the *Agreement* in the Federal Court. They argued that the designation of the United States as a "safe third country" was invalid because the United States does not respect its obligations under the *Convention against Torture* and the *Refugee Convention* and that by returning refugee claimants to the United States, Canada is violating its international obligations and the claimants' *Charter* rights to life, liberty and security and to equality. The Federal Court upheld those arguments.[83] However, the decision was overturned by the Federal Court of Appeal[84] (leave to appeal to the Supreme Court denied) and, consequently, the Agreement remains in force.

Refugee Determination Process

The *Refugee Convention* sets out the key principles of refugee protection, but leaves it open to the states to decide on the specific design of their refugee determination systems. For this reason, one observes significant variation in refugee determination processes around the globe.

The Canadian refugee determination process consists of the following stages:

---

[82] CIC, "A Partnership for Protection: One-Year Review" (November 2006), online; CIC <http://www.cic.gc.ca/english/policy/partnership/index.html>

[83] *Canadian Council for Refugees v. Canada*, [2007] F.C.J. No. 1583.

[84] *Canadian Council for Refugees v. Canada*, [2008] F.C.J. No. 1002 (C.A.).

1. **Eligibility determination.** The first step after a refugee claim is made is to determine whether it should be referred to the IRB for a hearing. Claims are ineligible for a IRB hearing in the following situations:

   (a) Protection has already been conferred under the *IRPA*.

   (b) A person has been recognized as a *Convention* refugee in another country and may be returned there.

   (c) A claim has been previously rejected by the IRB or declared ineligible, withdrawn or abandoned.

   (d) A person came from a safe third country (currently, the United States).

   (e) A person was determined to be inadmissible on grounds of security, violating human or international rights, serious criminality or organized criminality.

   While the eligibility of claims made at the Canadian border is determined by the CBSA, eligibility of claims made from within Canada's territory is determined by the CIC. A decision that a claim is ineligible does not mean that a person is removed immediately. As a rule, he/she will be streamlined to the PRRA stage described below.

2. **Referral of the claim to the IRB.** Individuals with eligible claims are given a **Personal Information Form (PIF)**, which they must complete and submit to the IRB within 28 days. The PIF asks claimants to provide detailed information about themselves, including their education and employment history, travel route to Canada, and most importantly, their story and reasons for requesting protection. On the basis of the PIF, the IRB determines the most appropriate way to handle the claim (whether it will go through an expedited process or a regular hearing), identifies relevant issues to be considered at a hearing, and collects information on the claimant's country of origin.

3. **Hearing before a Refugee Protection Division** (RPD) of the IRB (see detailed description below).

4. **Claim accepted.** If a claim is accepted, the claimant receives protected status and may apply for permanent residence.

5. **Claim rejected.** If a claim is rejected, the claimant may pursue the following options:

   (a) Judicial review of the RPD decision before the Federal Court.

   (b) Pre-Removal Risk Assessment (**PRRA**). If no application for judicial review is filed or if the application for leave or for judicial review is rejected, a claimant will be getting closer to the removal stage and will usually be invited to submit a PRRA. As a rule, a successful PRRA leads to conferral of refugee protection and enables a person to apply for permanent residence.

6. **Removal.** If the PRRA is unsuccessful, arrangements are made by the CBSA to effectuate the person's removal.

Hearing before the RPD

Depending on the strength and complexity of a claim, it is scheduled for an expedited process or a hearing process.[85] In an expedited process, a

---

[85] Immigration and Refugee Board, "Process for Making a Claim for Refugee Protection", online: <http://www.irb.gc.ca/Eng/brdcom/references/procedures/proc/rpdspr/Pages/rpdp.aspx>.

claimant is interviewed by an IRB employee, a Refugee Protection Officer, who makes a recommendation about the claim. If the recommendation is positive, it may lead to acceptance of a claim without a hearing. However, if a positive determination cannot be made on the basis of the interview, the case is sent for a full hearing.

Most cases are decided through a hearing. The refugee determination process presupposes certain participatory rights for refugee claimants, namely the right to counsel, the right to submit documentary evidence in support of a claim, and the right to an interpreter.

A hearing typically includes the following participants:

- Refugee claimant
- Claimant's counsel
- Interpreter (if required)
- RPD Member
- Refugee Protection Officer (RPO) (not present in fast-tracked hearings if a case is relatively simple and has only one or two issues in question)

An RPD Member is in charge of the overall conduct of the hearing. He/she has the power to inquire into any matter that he/she considers relevant to establishing whether a claim is well-founded. The RPD Member determines whether the claim will be accepted or rejected. Currently, RPD Members are independent decision-makers appointed by the Governor in Council; they are selected through a multi-stage process, including screening and assessment by a Selection Advisory Board, a written test, an interview and a reference/validation check.

An **RPO** is an employee of the Board charged with assisting the Board in the handling of refugee claims. His/her task is to ensure that all relevant information is brought forward before the RPD Member. At a hearing, the RPO will typically question the claimant and make observations regarding the merits of the claim at the end of a hearing. However, unlike counsel for the claimant, the RPO is formally disinterested in the outcome of the claim and is not bound to take a particular side.

A hearing typically involves an RPO, Board Member, and claimant's counsel asking questions of a claimant. IRB Guideline 7 prescribes a particular order of questioning: first by the RPO, then by the Board Member, and finally by the claimant's counsel. This order of questioning may be varied (to allow the claimant's counsel to ask questions first) in cases where vulnerable claimants (such as survivors of torture, minors, elderly) are involved. The purpose of questioning is to obtain clarification on various aspects of the claim that are relevant to establishing the individual's need for protection. For the most part, they centre on the definitions of *Convention* refugee and person in need of protection and usually include such questions as the following: Can a claimant obtain protection from his/her country of origin? What is the nature of the risk feared? Who is persecuting the claimant (e.g., state agents or private groups/individuals)? Is the Board satisfied about the identity of the claimant? In addition, the RPD considers whether the claimant is generally credible. Refugee hearings are supposed to be non-adversarial. However, given that some questions may draw attention to inconsistencies or other issues that potentially undermine the claim, the hearing may become contentious.

A decision on a claim may be announced at the end of the hearing or may be reserved and communicated to the claimant at a later date. A person who receives protection on the basis of the *Refugee Convention* receives the status of a *Convention* refugee; a person who is granted protection on the basis of risk to life or risk of torture receives the status of a person in need of protection.

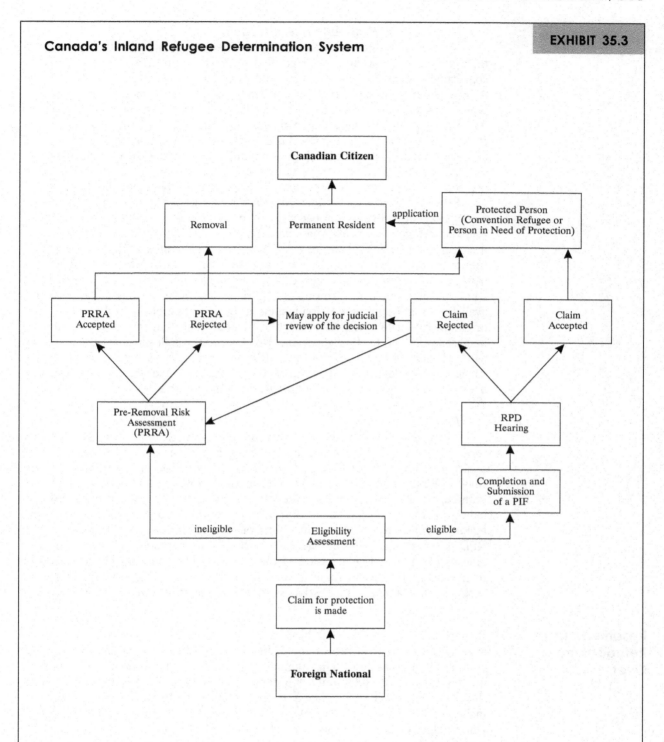

Canada's Inland Refugee Determination System

EXHIBIT 35.3

PIF = Personal Information Form
RPD = Refugee Protection Division
PRRA= Pre-Removal Risk Assessment

Note: This chart is valid until the changes under the *Balanced Refugee Reform Act*, S.C. 2010, c. 8, are implemented.

Pre-Removal Risk Assessment (PRRA)

As a rule, foreign nationals are presumed to be able to safely return to their countries of origin. However, there may be situations where the person concerned alleges that he or she would face risk in the country of destination. A Pre-Removal Risk Assessment (PRRA) is intended specifically for these types of situations to ensure that Canada does not return persons to danger. As a rule, PRRA applications consider the same protection grounds as the RPD, namely the risk of persecution, risk of torture, risk to life or risk of cruel and unusual treatment or punishment.[86] However, PRRA applications are usually decided without a hearing and are instead based on the written submissions of the applicant. In some cases, an interview may be held.

PRRA considers only new circumstances that have developed since the completion of previous proceedings (e.g., a refugee hearing). In cases of rejected refugee claimants, the main rationale behind a PRRA is to examine new risks that might have arisen between the date of a refugee hearing and the date when the claimant became ready for removal. Months often pass between these two events, especially if an application for judicial review of an RPD decision was made. During this period, new evidence might have become available or the applicant's circumstances or the situation in his/her country of origin might have changed to such an extent that they give rise to new or heightened risks to the applicant. However, an applicant may present only new evidence that arose after the IRB rejection, evidence that was not reasonably available, or evidence that the applicant could not reasonably have been expected to have presented at the time of the rejection.[87]

Judicial Review

As a rule, when an applicant for immigration or a refugee claimant receives a negative decision, he/she may apply for judicial review of that decision in the Federal Court. However, there is no automatic right to judicial review. First, an individual must seek leave (permission) to appeal. If leave is granted, then the case will proceed to the actual review. If an application for judicial review is successful, the case is returned to the original decision-making agency for re-determination. For example, if a judicial review of an RPD decision is successful, the case is sent back for another hearing before a different RPD panel. A decision of the Federal Court may be further appealed to the Federal Court of Appeal, but only if the judge of the Federal Court has certified that a serious question of general importance is involved.

Resettlement of Refugees from Overseas

Resettlement is one of the durable solutions, which is used in cases where a refugee can neither return to his/her country of origin nor integrate in the country of first asylum. The numbers of refugees who benefit from resettlement are small: in 2009, only one percent of the world's refugees were resettled.[88] A total of 112,400 refugees were admitted by 19 resettlement countries, including the United States (79,900), Canada (12,500), and Australia (11,100).[89] On average, Canada resettles around 12,000 refugees annually and consistently ranks among the top three countries of resettlement in the world.

---

86 *IRPA, supra* note 15, s. 113(c).
87 *IRPA, supra* note 15, s. 113(a).
88 UNCHR, "2009 Global Trends", *supra* note 67 at 10.
89 *Ibid.* at 12.

Although the resettlement process is governed by the same principles and basic definitions[90] as the inland refugee determination, it has some peculiarities. First, unlike spontaneous arrivals of refugee claimants, resettled refugees are processed overseas and are admitted to Canada only after having been determined to meet the criteria for protection and other applicable requirements. The more controlled nature of resettlement makes it possible to manage admissions and establish annual targets acceptable to the Canadian government. Second, the pre-planned nature of resettlement makes possible (and in fact requires) the presence of a Canadian sponsor who would support a resettled refugee both financially and emotionally upon arrival in Canada. Unlike in the inland process, where claimants may submit their claim directly to the authorities and do not need to have a Canadian sponsor, an application for resettlement usually must be accompanied by an undertaking or a referral. A referral is made by the UNHCR who identifies an individual for resettlement and transmits his/her file to Canadian authorities for consideration. Persons referred by the UNHCR are usually streamlined into government sponsorship. An "undertaking" is used in the context of refugee sponsorship by private groups or organizations; it is a written commitment to the Minister of Citizenship and Immigration that a group of persons or an organization will provide resettlement assistance, lodging, and other basic necessities in Canada for a resettled refugee and his/her family members.

The resettlement process entails two major components:

1. A decision on an individual's application for resettlement
2. An approval of a Canadian sponsor for that individual

Refugee sponsorship can take one of three main forms:

1. By the Canadian or Quebec government
2. By private entities (for example, an incorporated or an unincorporated organization; a group of five Canadian citizens or permanent residents)
3. Joint private–government initiatives

All groups or organizations who wish to sponsor refugees must complete an application and be approved by the CIC. They must meet a set of prescribed criteria, including proof of financial resources and a settlement plan for the refugee's arrival.

As a rule, resettled refugees are provided with assistance (such as income support, housing, settlement services) for up to 12 months after their arrival.[91] Persons with particular vulnerabilities (for example, survivors of torture, persons with disabilities) usually need extended support and may benefit from up to 36 months of assistance. Such cases are usually assigned to a joint government–private sponsorship, with government providing income support and private sponsors ensuring emotional support, guidance, and resettlement services.[92]

---

[90] Canadian legislation allows for resettlement of two categories of individuals: (i) persons who meet the *Convention* refugee definition; and (ii) persons in circumstances similar to those of *Convention* refugees. The latter category encompasses individuals who are at risk, but who do not fully meet the *Convention* refugee definition (for example, persons who have not left their countries of origin). For detailed definition of the second category, see Regulations, *supra* note 16, ss. 146–48.

[91] Citizenship and Immigration Canada, Overseas Processing Manual 5 "Overseas Selection and Processing of Convention Refugees Abroad Class and Members of the Humanitarian-protected Persons Abroad Classes" at 72.

[92] *Ibid.* at 20–21.

BALANCED REFUGEE REFORM ACT, 2010: CHANGES TO THE INLAND REFUGEE DETERMINATION PROCESS ——————

In June 2010, Parliament passed the *Balanced Refugee Reform Act*, which was designed to bring significant changes to the refugee protection system. Given the extent of the changes, the implementation is to occur in several stages over the course of 12 to 18 months. Certain changes have already come into effect, but those requiring alteration of the current refugee determination process and its institutional structure will take several months to be implemented. Exhibit 35.4 summarizes the changes to the refugee determination process brought by this Act.

Some of the other major changes are as follows:

1. The Minister of Citizenship and Immigration will obtain power to designate countries of origin, which are considered normally non-refugee producing. While claims from designated countries will still be considered

---

EXHIBIT 35.4 Changes to the Refugee Determination Process

CURRENT SYSTEM	NEW SYSTEM
1. Eligibility determination.	1. No change.
2. Completion of a Personal Information Form (PIF) within 28 days.	2. The PIF will no longer exist. Instead, information on a claim will be gathered through an interview with an IRB employee; the interview will take place no sooner than 15 days after referral.
3. Hearing before an independent decision-maker (RPD Member) currently within about 19 months.	3. Hearing by a permanent public servant (RPD) within a timeframe to be established in the *Regulations*.
4. No appeal to the Refugee Appeal Division (RAD).	4. The RAD will be established where claimants rejected by the RPD can appeal their cases.
5. Access to multiple recourses for rejected claimants, including judicial review by the Federal Court after each, rejection — estimated 3 years.	5. Following the last negative IRB decision, access only to the Federal Court with a leave decision anticipated within 4 months.
6. Pre-Removal Risk Assessment (PRRA) application may be submitted once an individual is ready for removal, regardless of when the decision on refugee status was made. The PRRA is currently conducted by the CIC.	6. One-year bar on PRRA applications after the last decision at the IRB. The PRRA will be decided by the IRB.
7. Removed approximately three years after the last IRB decision.	7. Removed within one year after the last IRB decision without any access to a PRRA.

Source: Citizenship and Immigration Canada, "Operational Bulletin 222 — September 3, 2010", online: <http://www.cic.gc.ca/english/resources/manuals/bulletins/2010/ob222.asp>.

by the IRB, they will be fast-tracked with shorter timelines than other claims (for example, the RPD hearing will take place within 60 days as opposed to 90 days for other claimants; a RAD decision will be expected within 30 days as opposed to 120 days for the other claimants).

2. The RPD will have the authority to identify "manifestly unfounded claims", that is, claims considered by the decision-maker to be clearly fraudulent. These claims will be treated similarly to those from designated countries of origin and fast-tracked before the RAD.

3. Access to Pre-removal Risk Assessments (PRRA) will be limited. Rejected claimants will be precluded from making a PRRA for one year following the final IRB decision. However, persons who have not been removed within one year will be allowed to make a PRRA application.

4. Imposition of restriction on the factors that may be considered in applications for humanitarian and compassionate consideration (H&C). Currently, rejected claimants may make an H&C application to remain in Canada. In deciding on those applications, immigration officers may consider various factors, including risks that the applicant would face in his/ her country of origin. Under the new amendments, the risk factors will no longer be considered. This amendment has already come into effect.

5. An Assisted Voluntary Returns program will be introduced to encourage rejected claimants to voluntarily depart Canada. Persons eligible to participate in the program will be given a plane ticket home and up to $2,000 in reintegration assistance. The assistance could be used for education, vocational training, job placements, or business pursuits. The money usually will not be given directly to the rejected claimant; instead, program funds would be managed and distributed by an independent service provider on behalf of the Government of Canada.

CHAPTER SUMMARY

The chapter has introduced the reader to the key concepts of immigration and refugee law. In Canada, individuals may be admitted for permanent residence under one of three streams: economic, family or refugee. Each stream has specifically tailored criteria to reflect the underlying rationale for admission. Economic immigrants are selected on the basis of their ability to become established in Canada and to contribute to the country's economic and social growth. With the development of PTNPs, selection of immigrants under the economic stream is exercised through (i) federal programs such as the CEC and skilled worker class and (ii) various provincial/territorial programs. Some applicants, particularly those in skilled occupations, may now have an opportunity of choosing between CEC, skilled worker class or various PTNPs, depending on which program offers faster processing and a higher likelihood of approval.

The family stream reflects the value of family reunification and provides for admission of foreign nationals on the basis of their relationship to a Canadian citizen or permanent resident. However, the opportunity for reunification is to an extent limited by immigration law's particular definition of family as well as sponsor eligibility requirements. Finally, refugee admissions are carried out in recognition of Canada's international obligations and are based on the individuals' need for protection as determined on the basis of the *Convention* refugee definition and the definition of a person in need of protection.

In addition to prescribing characteristics that warrant applicants' admission to Canada, immigration law sets out screening and enforcement mechanisms through inadmissibility, detention, and removal provisions.

GLOSSARY OF NEW TERMS AND KEY CONCEPTS

Convention **refugee**	A person who meets the definition of refugee in the 1951 *UN Convention relating to the Status of Refugees*. In general, it is someone who has left his or her home country and has a well-founded fear of persecution based on race, religion, nationality, political opinion, or membership of a particular social group and is unable or, by reason of his or her fear, unwilling to seek the protection of the home country.
eligibility determination	The first step in the refugee claim process to determine whether a claim is eligible for a hearing before the Immigration and Refugee Board.
home country (or country of origin)	The country of which an individual is a citizen, permanent resident or if an individual is stateless, the country in which he/she has regularly lived.
inadmissibility	A category in law meaning that a person cannot enter or remain in Canada or cannot become a permanent resident.
interdiction	measures designed to prevent non-citizens, including asylum-seekers, from entering state territory.
person in need of protection	A person in Canada whose removal to his/her home country would expose him/her to personal risk of torture or a risk to life or a risk of cruel and unusual treatment or punishment.
PIF	Personal Information Form — a form that contains a series of questions about the claimant's identity, family, work history, military service, and other aspects of his/her life, including citizenship and immigration matters; currently, every claimant must complete a PIF before his/her IRB hearing.
protected characteristics approach	An approach to identification of "particular social groups" for the purposes of the *Refugee Convention* definition; it focuses on internal characteristics that unite persons in a group. In Canada, the following categories of particular social groups have been identified: (i) groups defined by an innate, unchangeable characteristic; (ii) groups whose members voluntarily associate for reasons so fundamental to their human dignity that they should not be forced to forsake the association; and (iii) groups associated by a former voluntary status, unalterable due to its historical permanence.
protected person	A person who has received refugee protection from Canada either as a *Convention* refugee or as a person in need of protection.
PRRA	Pre-Removal Risk Assessment — a procedure conducted before removal to ensure that a person is not removed to face torture, risk to life or persecution in his/her country of origin; if the PRRA is successful, a person will usually receive refugee protection.
refugee claimant (or asylum seeker)	A person who has made a refugee claim in Canada, but whose case has not been decided yet.
refugee protection officer (RPO)	An IRB employee who is present at the refugee hearing and who helps to ensure that all relevant questions and information are put before the decision-maker.
safe third country	A country designated by the *Regulations* as a safe country of transit or residence in which an individual could have found protection as a refugee before arriving in the country where the person is now claiming refugee protection. For the purposes of Canadian refugee determination, the United States is currently the only country considered "safe".
social perception approach	An approach to identification of "particular social groups" for the purposes of the *Refugee Convention* definition; it is focuses on the external perception of the group by others, including persecutors.
Visa	An authorization to enter a country on a temporary or permanent basis.

REVIEW QUESTIONS

1. What is the difference between a citizen and a permanent resident of Canada?
2. Can a permanent resident lose his/her status? If yes, in what circumstances?
3. Are foreign students allowed to work in Canada? If yes, in what circumstances?
4. What is the role of the Immigration and Refugee Board in the Canadian immigration and refugee system?
5. Who is a refugee?
6. What does "non-*refoulement*" mean?
7. What are the stages of the current inland refugee determination process?
8. What is the "points system", and what are its main selection factors?
9. When can a person be subject to immigration detention?
10. What is a security certificate and what are some of the concerns associated with this procedure?
11. Who can be sponsored under the family class?
12. How can Canadian citizenship be acquired?

DISCUSSION QUESTIONS

1. Dan wants to sponsor his nephew to come to Canada under the family class. Dan is a 40-year-old Canadian citizen, but has lived outside Canada for the past three years and is not planning on returning to Canada in the near future. Is Dan likely to be approved as a sponsor? Is his nephew considered a member of the family class under Canadian immigration law?

2. Is it acceptable to deport non-citizens who pose a security risk to Canada to countries where they might face a risk of torture? Discuss in light of the Supreme Court decision in *Suresh* as well as Canada's obligations under the *Convention against Torture* (for the text of the *Convention*, see <http://www2.ohchr.org/english/law/cat.htm>).

3. Discuss the following scenario:

   Alex came to Canada from Zimbabwe in 2003. He asked for refugee protection in Canada as he was afraid to return to his own country. Alex claimed that he was persecuted by the police and ZANU-PF supporters because of his membership in the opposition party Movement for Democratic Change (MDC). He is claiming that if he goes back, he would be arbitrarily detained and possibly killed. Research the human rights situation in Zimbabwe (look for human rights reports, articles that document situation in the country). In your opinion, is Alex likely to obtain refugee protection in Canada?

   (Make sure to refer to the *Refugee Convention* definition.)

4. Ram is a 55-year-old biologist from Singapore. He has a Bachelor's and a Master's degree in biology from the National University of Singapore and a combined 17 years of study. He has 10 years of work experience as a biologist. He has high proficiency in English on all four abilities (speaking, writing, listening, and comprehension). Ram has no relatives in Canada and has never been to Canada. His wife has only secondary

school education and is a homemaker, but she hopes to get a part-time job when she settles in Canada. Ram and his wife have some $100,000 in savings. Is Ram eligible to apply under the skilled worker class? (For the list of in-demand occupations, see Citizenship and Immigration Canada: <http://www.cic.gc.ca/english/immigrate/skilled/apply-who-instructions.asp#list>.) If yes, what are his chances of getting approved for immigration? Is he likely to score above the pass mark on the points system?

SUGGESTED READINGS

Carasco, Emily, et al., *Immigration and Refugee Law: Cases, Materials, and Commentary* (Toronto: Emond Montgomery, 2007).

Castles, Stephen. "The Factors That Make and Unmake Migration Policies" (2004) 38 *International Migration Review* 852.

Kelley, Ninette, & Jean-François Durieux. "UNHCR and Current Challenges in International Refugee Protection" (2004) 1 *Refuge* 22.

WEBSITES

Citizenship and Immigration Canada: <www.cic.gc.ca>

Immigration and Refugee Board: <http://www.cisr-irb.gc.ca/index.htm>

Canada Border Services Agency: <http://www.cbsa-asfc.gc.ca/menu-e.html>

Canadian Council for Refugees: <http://www.ccrweb.ca/eng/engfront/frontpage.htm>

UN High Commissioner for Refugees: <http://www.unhcr.org>

Law and Policy in Theory and Practice

Sasha Baglay
UNIVERSITY OF ONTARIO INSTITUTE OF TECHNOLOGY

Alberto Salazar Valle
YORK UNIVERSITY

Learning Objectives

After reading this chapter, the reader should be able to:

➢ Appreciate the complexity and diversity of factors involved in the law- and policy-making process
➢ Appreciate the impact of the media and interest groups on the law- and policy-making process
➢ Understand with various strategies used by interest groups to influence public policy
➢ Understand the interaction of the legislative and judicial branches in developing regulatory frameworks

TABLE OF CONTENTS

INTRODUCTION

In the eyes of the general public, the law appears to be made on the basis of reason, knowledge, scientific evidence, and in pursuit of the general social good. As a result, it is often assumed that courts and legislators strike a reasonable balance among multiple values and interests involved in the making and enforcement of laws. While the public good is the underlying consideration of legal regulation, there are multiple factors affecting the content and design of laws. The process of law making is not necessarily unbiased and objective; in order to understand why and how a certain law has come about, it is important to be aware of the complexity of the law-making process and the various factors that influence it, directly or indirectly. By way of illustration, this chapter will discuss three such factors: interest groups, the media, and the judicial–legislative dialogue. It will also highlight the importance of critically examining whose interests are represented in or excluded from the law-making process; what perspective a given law reflects; and what is its impact on various groups in society.

INTEREST GROUPS, PUBLIC CHOICE, AND POWER

Definition and Types of Interest Groups

Interest groups can be defined as groups of individuals or organizations that share a common set of goals and have joined together to persuade the legislative, executive, or judicial branch to adopt a policy, law, or decision that will help protect or advance the interest of a given group.[1] These groups seek to influence legislators, government agencies, and courts so that the enactment, interpretation or enforcement of the law reflects their interests. This may result in giving a new content, direction or meaning to the law, which in turn may assign rights and obligations differently than originally intended.[2]

Almost any law or legal policy is likely to attract the attention of an **interest group**. A statute, regulation or court decision normally assigns rights and obligations that permit or prohibit certain behaviours or courses of action, affecting the social, economic or political positions of individuals and groups in society. Some groups may see this as a threat or an advantage to preserving or enhancing their interests. This perception of a threat or an opportunity may ignite individuals or groups with similar interest or those similarly affected by a law to collaborate and collectively communicate their views to legislators, regulators or courts. For example, Canada's Parliament enacted the *Tobacco Act* and the *Tobacco Products Information Regulations*, which permit information and brand-preference advertising, but forbid lifestyle advertising and promotion, advertising appealing to young persons, and false or misleading advertising or promotion. In addition, the size of mandatory and attributed

---

[1] Theodore J. Lowi & Benjamin Ginsberg, *American Government: Freedom and Power* 6th ed. (New York: W.W. Norton, 2000) 307; Anthony Champagne, *Interest Groups and Judicial Elections* (2001) 34 Loy. L.A. L. Rev. 1391 at 1392. Others have defined interest groups as non-political party, non-governmental organizations with members. See Michael T. Heaney, "Brokering Health Policy: Coalitions, Parties, and Interest Group Influence" (2006) 31 J. Health Pol. Pol'y & L. 887 at 930; Robert H. Salisbury, "Interest Representation: The Dominance of Institutions" (1984) 78 American Political Science Review 64–76.

[2] For instance, the regulation of interest-rate ceilings for consumer credit varies among the United Kingdom (no ceilings), France (ceilings), and Japan (lowered ceilings), and the explanation to these differences should be sought in the dynamics of the influence of interest groups and the institutional settings in each country. See Iain Ramsay " 'To heap distress upon distress?': Comparative Reflections on Interest-Rate Ceilings" (Spring 2010) 60:2 UTLJ 707–30. See also Iain Ramsay, "Interest Groups and the Politics of Consumer Bankruptcy Reform in Canada" (2003) 53:4 UTLJ 379–423.

health warnings on packaging was increased from 33 percent to 50 percent of the principal display surfaces. Several big tobacco manufacturers felt that this new legislation harmed their business interests and collectively decided to bring a legal action to challenge it, alleging that some provisions limited their right to freedom of expression under s. 2(*b*) of the *Charter* and that those limits were not justified under s. 1 of the *Charter*. In *Canada (Attorney General) v. JTI-Macdonald Corp.*,[3] the Supreme Court of Canada ruled that the requirement in the *Tobacco Products Information Regulations* that the government's health warnings occupy at least 50 percent of the principal display surfaces of packages infringes s. 2(b) of the *Charter*, but the infringement is justified under s. 1. Thus, the introduced increase in the size of tobacco warnings was deemed to be constitutional.

Multiple interest groups exist across almost any area of the social, economic, legal, political, and cultural life of society. As the law increasingly regulates most areas of life, diverse interest groups will form around multiple areas of law. These groups may range from business groups, minority groups, labour unions to professional associations. Generally, interest groups can be classified as self-interest groups (advance interests of members), public interest (advance the public good), and sectoral groups (represent specific sectors of society).[4] Often, these groups with diverging interests may compete in a single legal conflict. For instance, a legislation requiring the labelling of food products is likely to attract the interest of individual consumers, farmers, producers, retailers, advertisers, food scientists, food corporations, and consumer associations The Canadian Federation of Agriculture, for example, has said that the industry would face huge losses if mandatory labelling of genetically modified food (GM food) were implemented. "The fear is that consumers will see the labels as a warning and avoid these foods, and that food processors will reformulate their products to avoid GM foods rather than place labels."[5] It has also claimed that labels will increase the price of foods produced and processed in Canada. On the other hand, the Canadian public appears to appreciate the value of GM food labelling. According to a 1999 Environics poll, 80 percent of Canadians want GM foods to be labelled. Greenpeace Canada believes that number is closer to 95 per cent. Furthermore, consumer groups have noted that people just want to know what they are putting in their mouths, and any labelling would at least provide them with information so that they are in a better position to make an informed eating decision.[6]

These diverse interest groups often have multiple and conflicting expectations about how a given issue should be regulated. It is not surprising, then, that these groups engage in fierce competition to protect and promote their interests and values before legislators, regulators or courts. In order to penetrate the legal system, these groups are required to translate their interests into legal discourses, and for this purpose employ multiple strategies to influence law making.

Strategies Employed by Interest Groups

Among the strategies most commonly used by interest groups are (i) lobbying law- and policy-makers and (ii) litigation before courts.

---

[3] 2007 SCC 30, [2007] 2 S.C.R. 610.

[4] Eric Mintz, Livianna Tossutti, and Christopher Dunn, *Democracy, Diversity, and Good Government: An Introduction to Politics in Canada* (Toronto: Pearson Canada, 2011).

[5] "Genetically Modified Foods: A Primer" (CBC News Online, May 11, 2004) online: <http://www.cbc.ca/news/background/genetics_modification/>.

[6] *Ibid.*

Lobbying

The first strategy involves such activities as interaction with various political actors, advocacy and action campaigns to mobilize public opinion, letters and submissions to government bodies. As a rule, interest groups focus their efforts on one or more of the three target groups: politicians, government bureaucrats and political parties.[7] Ideally, interest groups would like to be involved at early stages of law- and policy-making, since this allows them to influence the very formulation of issues and policy agendas. Given that most legislation is usually initiated by the government in power, interest groups may target the cabinet and individual ministers in an attempt to attract attention to issues in need of a legislative response, as well as civil servants who are involved in research and drafting of law and policy proposals. However, the initial stages of law and policy formation are often not easily accessible. Instead, there may be more opportunities for providing input once a bill has been introduced in Parliament. One of the most common avenues for interest groups to influence a bill is at the committee stage (which usually happens after the second reading of a bill). As a part of their task of analyzing the bill, parliamentary committees often hear testimony and receive submissions from individuals and groups, which may, in turn, influence the committee's recommendations on the bill. In addition to directly pressuring policy-makers and bureaucrats, interest groups may use indirect strategies such as media and awareness campaigns to create a critical mass of public opinion on a given matter and thereby force politicians to act. For example, in the fall of 2010, the Canadian Council for Refugees (CCR), an umbrella organization committed to advocating on behalf of refugees in Canada, conducted a "take action" campaign against Bill C-49, which proposed measures that would negatively affect persons seeking asylum in Canada (e.g., in some cases provide for mandatory 1-year detention, impose restrictions on their access to permanent residence or permanent protection in Canada). The campaign sought to raise public awareness as well as encourage concerned individuals to write or speak to their members of Parliament to persuade them to vote against the bill. As of December 1, 2010, all opposition parties (Liberal Party, New Democratic Party, and Bloc Québécois) stated that they could not support Bill C-49 — a stance that in part may be attributed to the active advocacy campaign.[8]

Litigation

Unlike political lobbying, which is concentrated on either placing a certain issue on a legislative agenda or on influencing proposed legislation during the statutory enactment process, litigation usually seeks to challenge laws already in force. History demonstrates multiple instances where litigation was used to challenge the status quo, advance individual rights, or expose issues of discrimination and inequality. For example, in *Halpern v. Canada*[9], seven same-sex couples and Metropolitan Community Church of Toronto challenged the definition of marriage as a union between a man and a woman. Because the definition excluded same-sex couples, opposite-sex couples were able to marry, while same-sex couples were not. The Court found that such exclusion violated s. 15 (equality) under the *Charter* and could not be saved under s. 1. Effective immediately, the Court declared the existing definition invalid, and

---

[7] Robert K. Jackson & Doreen Jackson, *Canadian Government in Transition*, 5th ed. (Toronto: Pearson Canada, 2010) at 229.

[8] Canadian Council for Refugees, "C-49 — Anti-smuggling or anti-refugee?", online: <http://ccrweb.ca/en/c49>.

[9] [2003] O.J. No. 2268.

reformulated it as "the voluntary union for life of two persons to the exclusion of all others".

Interest groups can participate in court cases in one of two ways: (i) launch a case by either sponsoring it or filing a lawsuit in their own name; (ii) seek intervenor status in a pending case. As a rule, a legal action has to be brought by an individual or an entity affected by the legislation or government action in question. However, in some cases an interest group may be granted public interest standing to advance a case on behalf of affected individuals.

While launching a case allows an interest group control over the scope and formulation of issues, it is a very expensive, complex, and lengthy undertaking. Not every interest group will have the resources to support ongoing litigation. Furthermore, if the group loses a case, it may be ordered to pay a substantial portion of the costs of the winning side.[10]

Partially due to the financial constraints as well as procedural barriers associated with obtaining standing, some interest groups may choose to seek intervenor status in an already pending action launched by someone else. While intervenors do not have much control over the formulation of issues, they are able to advance legal arguments that reflect the group's position as well as bring to light additional information on the impact of the law in question on the segments of population whose interests the group represents. By introducing these additional perspectives, intervenors help mitigate one of the limitations of the adversarial process — its narrow focus on the positions of the two parties to the case. In fact, interest groups have been parties or intervenors in many of the Supreme Court's landmark cases where the Court was called to decide on important public interest issues such as abortion, aboriginal rights and land claims, equality of voters, euthanasia, capital punishment, gay rights, hate speech, judicial salaries, language rights, pornography, prisoner voting rights, sexual assault, Sunday closing, and tobacco advertising.[11] For example, in *Halpern v. Canada*, discussed above, the public importance of the definition of marriage attracted several interest groups and organizations as intervenors. The Canadian Human Rights Commission, Canadian Coalition of Liberal Rabbis for Same-Sex Marriage, Egale Canada (a national organization committed to advancing equality and justice for lesbian, gay, bisexual and trans-identified people, and their families) supported the position of the same-sex couples who challenged the definition of marriage. Two other intervenors — the Association for Marriage and the Family in Ontario and the Interfaith Coalition on Marriage and Family — made arguments against the redefinition of marriage.

Similarly, the case of Sue Rodriguez[12] on the issue of assisted suicide has had a number of intervenors, representing different points of view. Sue Rodriguez was suffering from amyotrophic lateral sclerosis — an illness due to which she would soon lose the ability to swallow, speak, move or breathe without assistance. She did not wish to die as long as she had the capacity to enjoy life, but, once she lost that capacity, she wanted to be able to terminate her life, at the time of her choosing, with the assistance of a physician. Given that s. 241(b) of the *Criminal Code* prohibits the giving of assistance to commit suicide, Sue Rodriguez brought a challenge to this section arguing that it violated s. 7 (right to life, liberty and security of person), s. 12 (prohibition of

---

[10] Kent Roach, "The Role of Litigation and the Charter in Interest Advocacy" in F. Leslie Seidle (ed.), *Equity and Community: The Charter, Interest Advocacy and Representation* (Montreal, Que.: Institute for Research on Public Policy, 1993) 159 at 173.

[11] Frederick Morton, *Law, Politics, and the Judicial Process in Canada*, 3d ed. (Calgary, AB: University of Calgary Press, 2002) at 302.

[12] *Rodriguez v. British Columbia (A.G.)*, [1993] 3 S.C.R. 519.

cruel and unusual treatment or punishment), and s. 15 (equality) of the *Charter*. The list of intervenors in her case included the British Columbia Coalition of People with Disabilities, Dying with Dignity, the Right to Die Society of Canada, the Coalition of Provincial Organizations of the Handicapped, the Pro-Life Society of British Columbia, the Pacific Physicians for Life Society, the Canadian Conference of Catholic Bishops, the Evangelical Fellowship of Canada, and People in Equal Participation Inc. Organizations such as the Coalition of Provincial Organizations of the Handicapped (COPOH) (a national, not-for-profit, umbrella organization which represents people with disabilities), Dying with Dignity (a national non-profit organization that provides education, information, and confidential support for individuals faced with making end-of-life decisions) and the Right to Die Society of Canada (an organization providing lobbying and education on the right-to-die options) supported Sue Rodriguez's arguments with respect to autonomy and self-determination in making decisions on life and death. COPOH also brought attention to the concerns of people with disabilities. It argued that the criminal prohibition of assisted suicide discriminated against people with disabilities who could not commit suicide without someone else's assistance. In addition, COPOH emphasized the importance of having safeguards in place to ensure that assisted suicides are a result of informed, mentally competent decision-making, free from coercion or undue influence. Five groups — the Conference of Catholic Bishops of Canada, the Evangelical Fellowship of Canada (a national association of Protestant faiths), People for Equal Participation (PEP) (an advocacy organization for disabled persons), Pro-Life Society of British Columbia, and Pacific Physicians for Life Society (a professional association of physicians) — made arguments that opposed Sue Rodriguez's motion. Most of these groups emphasized the value of protecting human life and promoting a life ethics. PEP largely focused on the vulnerability of persons with disabilities and the concerns about assisted suicide exacerbating such vulnerability.

Lobbying vs. Litigation

The relative advantages of lobbying versus litigation depend on a variety of factors, including the nature of the issue and the resources and status of a given interest group. The political disadvantage theory suggests that groups usually choose to litigate if other avenues of law or policy change, such as legislatures, are foreclosed.[13] However, this theory offers only a partial explanation of interest group behaviour. For example, it does not explain why more advantaged groups choose to litigate. Further studies have suggested that advantaged groups may opt to litigate in order to protect the gains achieved through legislatures or previous litigation.[14] It has also been noted that more advantaged groups may litigate more frequently because they have the resources to do so.[15] This is, for example, the case with business interest groups, which may resort to litigation to counter increasing government regulation in areas key to their activity.[16] For instance, tobacco corporations have

---

[13] Christopher Manfredi, "Constitutional Rights and Internet Advocacy: Litigating Educational Reform in Canada and the United States" in F. Leslie Seidle (ed.), *Equity and Community: The Charter, Interest Advocacy and Representation* (Montreal, Que.: Institute for Research on Public Policy, 1993) 91 at 93.
[14] Manfredi, *ibid.* at 94; Kim Lane Scheppele & Jack L. Walker, "The Litigation Strategies of Interest Groups" in Jack L. Walker (ed.), *Mobilizing Interest Groups in America* (Ann Arbor: Michigan University Press, 1991); Lee Epstein, *Conservatives in Court* (Knoxville: University of Tennessee Press, 1985).
[15] Manfredi, *ibid.*
[16] See generally, Gregory Hein, "Interest Group Litigation and Canadian Democracy" in Paul Howe & Peter H. Russell (eds.), *Judicial Power and Canadian Democracy* (Montreal and Kingston: McGill-Queen's University Press, 2001).

EXHIBIT 36.1	Litigation vs Lobbying: Action of Canadian Bar Association on Legal Aid

The Canadian Bar Association (CBA) is a professional association whose primary purpose is to serve its members (legal professionals, judges, law students). However, it is also concerned with issues that have implications for the public at large, such as access to justice, law reform, and a fair justice system. One of the issues on its agenda is legal aid. Due to decades of financial cutbacks, legal aid, which is intended to provide access to legal services to low-income individuals, is inaccessible to many people in need and the scope of services is too limited. This, in turn, results in a cascading negative impact on people's lives.

For a number of years, the CBA has focused on lobbying and political advocacy on the issue. However, failing to achieve a desired result through lobbying, it turned to litigation. In 2005, it launched a court challenge, arguing that the inadequacies in the provision of legal aid amounted to breaches of the *Charter*, written and unwritten provisions of the Constitution, and international human rights instruments. The CBA sought a series of declarations and an order directing the government to maintain an effective and meaningful legal aid system. The lawsuit was dismissed, since the Court determined that the CBA lacked public interest standing and that it failed to meet the threshold requirements for establishing a reasonable cause of action. The CBA was also ordered to pay the defendant's costs (the government was the defendant). Despite the dismissal of the lawsuit, the CBA has not abandoned the idea of litigation and is working on identifying appropriate cases for further court challenges. It also continues lobbying and engaging in national education and awareness campaigns, as well as research, analysis, and policy development for legal aid reform.

This example is illustrative of several issues. First, advocacy on a given issue may require the use of a combination of strategies; it is not merely about choosing between litigation or lobbying. Second, although often viewed as an alternative to reform when lobbying is unsuccessful, litigation does not guarantee success either. Third, lack of success in pursuing traditional avenues of lobbying and litigation may lead to re-evaluation of these strategies as well as new emphasis on other means, such as public education and awareness. Fourth, as a public interest litigant, the CBA did not have a direct interest in the action. If the lawsuit had been successful, it would have improved legal aid to members of the community at large and only indirectly advance the interests of the Association's members by likely providing for an increase in the legal fees paid to lawyers.

Note

As a rule, claims with respect to *Charter* breaches have to be advanced in the context of individual cases (i.e., there has to be a specific situation involving an individual or an organization where a *Charter* breach has occurred). The CBA, however, took the position that its claim was of a systemic nature and did not advance it in the context of a specific case. The Court of Appeal upheld the decision of the lower court and concluded that (i) the statement of claim did not involve the particulars of individuals or their cases, and (ii) the breaches they suffered were too general to allow the courts to adjudicate such a claim. Similar reasoning applied to the CBA's arguments with respect to unwritten constitutional principles.

Sources
1. *Canadian Bar Assn. v. British Columbia*, [2006] B.C.J. No. 2015.
2. *Canadian Bar Assn. v. British Columbia*, [2008] B.C.J. No. 350.
3. Melina Buckley, *Moving Forward on Legal Aid: Research on Needs and Innovative Approaches*. Report for the Canadian Bar Association (July 2010), online: <http://www.cba.org/CBA/Advocacy/legalaid/default.aspx>.
4. CBA Considering Options for Phase II — Litigation Strategy to Improve Civil Legal Aid, <http://www.cba.org/CBA/Advocacy/legalaid/Litigation.aspx>.
5. CBA Position on Legal Aid, <http://www.cba.org/CBA/Advocacy/legalaid/position.aspx>.

sued the government of Canada several times seeking court decisions to strike down tobacco regulations. In 1995, in *RJR-MacDonald Inc. v. Canada (Attorney General)*,[17] the Supreme Court of Canada struck down provisions of the *Tobacco Products Control Act* that broadly prohibited all advertising and promotion of tobacco products, subject to specific exceptions, and required that unattributed warning labels be affixed on tobacco product packaging. In response to the Court's decision, Parliament enacted the *Tobacco Act* and the *Tobacco Products Information Regulations*, which among other things increased the size of warnings. Once again, tobacco manufacturers challenged the new legislation (see *Canada (Attorney General) v. JTI-Macdonald Corp.* discussed above), although in this case, the Supreme Court upheld the *Tobacco Products Information Regulations*.

The Challenge of Governing Interest Groups

While a sound expression of the views of various groups helps lawmakers to acquaint themselves with the values, interests, and social impact at stake, the reality is that interest groups do not necessarily compete on a level playing field and the influence of some interest groups may distort, rather than aid, the process of making and enforcing laws. Some groups may be better organized, greatly informed, more resourceful, more financially and political powerful, and more active than others. Often the difference in influence and power among interest groups reflects the social, political, economic, and legal inequalities in society. For instance, an interest group composed of ordinary citizens is likely to be less influential and powerful than a business group. Groups with greater social, political, economic or legal power will be in a better position to promote their interests and influence the making and enforcement of the law. For example, a study of over 2,500 Supreme Court and Federal Court decisions for the 1988–98 period found that, among the multiple organizations involved as litigants or intervenors coming from across the political spectrum, the most frequent participants were corporate interest groups, representing 56 percent of the total.[18] They brought 468 legal actions, far more than the other interests. Companies engaged in civil litigation against private parties and challenged regulations governing banking, federal elections, international trade, environmental protection, and the pharmaceutical industry.[19] Unlike other groups, corporations and business groups had the financial and organizational resources to bring numerous legal actions and to sustain prolonged and expensive litigation, which enabled them to defend or promote their interests before the courts. Thus, judges, legislators, and regulators may find themselves under significant pressure, particularly from the groups that have greater resources to advance their causes, and will have to make a serious effort to make independent decisions seeking to advance the best interest of society.

Yet, a search for independence and unbiased law making and enforcement involves more than having the determination to decide with impartiality and on the basis of reason, legal knowledge, and socially accepted values while balancing multiple competing interests. It requires that lawmakers are both familiar with the multiple strategies and methods that interest groups use and committed to containing excessive or distortive pressures from some interest groups. If courts, legislators. or regulators are to deal with strategic litigation

---

[17] 1995 CanLII 64 (S.C.C.), [1995] 3 S.C.R. 199.

[18] Gregory Hein, "Interest Group Litigation and Canadian Democracy" (March 2000) 6:2 Choices. Institute for Research on Public Policy, online: <http://www.irpp.org/choices/archive/vol6no2.pdf>.

[19] *Ibid.*

or the threat thereof, lobbying, participation in public consultations, media pressure, social networking, public protest, or public elections, they ought to do so in a manner that is democratic and effective in protecting the integrity of the process of making and enforcing the law.

The challenge for courts, legislators, and regulators is not only to channel and control the over-influence of powerful interest groups, but also to create real and effective opportunities for powerless groups to communicate their interests. It is ideal that lawmakers seek a democratic and fair engagement of all relevant groups so the law does not evolve solely on the basis of the input of influential groups. On the one hand, lawmakers should be receptive and open to the multiple ways of expressing the interests of relevant groups and must also create effective mechanisms to facilitate the communication of such interests. Governments should, for instance, expand the practice of conducting public consultations about proposed legislation as a way of reaching relevant unorganized groups or should provide financial and administrative support to less powerful groups. On the other hand, lawmakers should seek to enhance the transparency of any law-making process so that the general public and all interest groups know the content, procedure, and participants of a legal development, and, as a result, can hold lawmakers accountable. For example, while disclosing the number and names of interest groups that have participated in a law-making process, the government should release detailed information about the extent to which the concerns of multiple groups have been incorporated. This should also include a list of lobbyists and the groups that have been absent from such a process. These measures can help ensure that the law-making process is both reflective of multiple interests and more democratic in nature.

MEDIA, PUBLIC PRESSURE, AND LAW MAKING

The Media and the Legal System

The mass media is another factor that influences the making and enforcement of the law. While the media is often perceived as a provider of general information and evolving independently from the legal system, it may be instrumental in shaping the development of the law in society. The media gathers and disseminates information on new legal developments, communicates the opinions of various stakeholders on those developments, creates a forum for discussion and draws attention to pressing social and legal issues. In particular, this section examines the role of the mass media in improving the social acceptance and public accountability of the legal system.[20]

The gathering and mass communication of new court decisions, legislative changes, or various government policies through media such as radio, TV, or newspapers contribute to the dissemination of legal information and public awareness of the law. The public may be better informed and prepared to understand, accept, and abide by the new laws as the media selects, translates, synthesizes and spreads increasingly abundant and complex legal information. This helps improve social acceptance of the law and aids in creating a facilitative environment for respect and for enforcement of the law. The media may thus help the law gain greater acceptance and legitimacy in society.

---

[20] Jessica Feinstein, "The Hybrid's Handmaiden: Media Coverage of the Special Court for Sierra Leone, 7 Lyuchiilr 131" (Spring/Summer 2010) Loy. U. Chicago Int'l L. Rev. at 134 (discussing two general roles of the media in the context of criminal cases: "1) as facilitator of public awareness and distributor of information; and 2) as 'watchdog,' a critical check on abuse of power." For a discussion of an example, see John King Gamble and Nicole Lee Dirling, "Mass Media Coverage of International Law: (Benign) Neglect?, Distortion?" (2006) 18 Fla. J. Int'l L. 211.

On the other hand, the media may report on the performance of courts, legislatures, and regulators and as such play a role in holding them accountable to the public.[21] The mass media coverage and public reporting of legal developments may ignite public debate and critical awareness and mobilize individuals and interest groups. These groups and individuals will quickly learn about important legal changes, develop an opinion, and may organize to support or oppose a court decision, a legislative change, or a new regulatory policy. While the media often provides only brief versions of legal developments so that interested individuals and groups need to gather more information about the specifics and legal technicalities, the contribution of the media to such public accountability lies in its ability to rapidly and massively disseminate plain legal information among the general public, often exposing wrongs in the legal system.[22] This may trigger public action and public pressure on courts, legislators, regulators, and other actors and force them to eventually respond to it. For example, TV news and newspapers, covering the political and legal battles for the rights of various marginalized groups such as women, Aboriginal peoples and gays and lesbians, have helped people mobilize around such rights movements.[23] The media thus becomes not only a source of legal information and a factor in raising public awareness, but also an instrument for interested individuals and groups to communicate their dissent or support. The role of the media in improving the social acceptance or the public accountability of the legal system is unique in that it elevates a dissent or support to a massive phenomenon, namely a potentially widespread public pressure that lawmakers and other actors may find difficult to ignore.

Limits on the Role of the Media

A number of problems may, however, hinder the ability of the mass media to enhance the social acceptance and public accountability of the legal system and to facilitate legal change. Such a role for the media requires the presence of a significant number of independent, competent, and well-funded journalists and media corporations or organizations. Journalists should ideally be capable and committed to gathering, examining and reporting legal news on issues that are important to society and present the information with accuracy and independence and without fear of affecting the interests of powerful individuals and groups. Yet, journalists may misread laws, and judicial decisions are sometimes misinterpreted, sensationalized, and even lampooned[24] in the media, giving the public an inaccurate impression of the law and thus eroding confidence in the legal system.

Moreover, journalists may not necessarily be committed to such independence or can be under great pressure from those who manage and own media corporations. Media owners and managers may specify a particular role

---

[21] Feinstein, *ibid.* at 136 ("...the media may also play the role of watchdog over the judiciary or court. ...media coverage of court proceedings allows the public to monitor the judiciary's performance of its allotted duties, insuring that it is doing so without economic, jurisdictional, or political mismanagement"); M.A. "Mike" Kautsch, "Press Freedom and Fair Trials in Kansas: How Media and the Courts Have Struggled to Resolve Competing Claims of Constitutional Rights" (2009) 57 U. Kan. L. Rev. 1075 at 1140 (concluding "... Openness leads to public confidence in the judicial system. It enables the media to illuminate how the justice system works and to perform a checking function, holding judges and law enforcement accountable for their exercise of power and authority"); Lieve Gies, *Law and the Media: The Future of Uneasy Relationship* (New York: Routledge-Cavendish, 2008) at 93 (referring to the belief that the media contributes to the monitoring of the three branches of government as the Liberal media doctrine).

[22] Gies, *ibid.* at 91 (noting the self-chosen role of the media in exposing wrongs and problems in the legal system).

[23] Florian Sauvageau, David Schneiderman & David Taras, *The Last Word: Media Coverage of the Supreme Court of Canada* (Vancouver, BC: UBC Press, 2006) at 15.

[24] *Ibid.* at 9.

that a TV or radio program or newspaper should play in relation to the legal system. They may select journalists who are more willing to follow their views and values rather than being committed to independent journalism and the public interest. Managers and owners of media organizations may also set strict instructions as to how their journalists and, more generally, how a newspaper, TV or radio program should cover some legal news, including the desirable position to be adopted. This lack of independence often manifests itself through bias in the selection, gathering, reporting, timing, and examination of legal news as well as the direction of an opinion developed by journalists or editors. For instance, from 1998 to 2000, the *National Post*, owned by Conrad Black, waged a fierce ideological crusade against the activism of Canadian judges, attacking their judgments with relish and questioning the assumptions upon which the authority of the court rests.[25] Thus, the mass media may become an instrument for media owners and managers to set their own agenda or attempt to streamline the opinion of the public and lawmakers in a particular direction. These problems may be more severe when corporate groups or wealthy individuals control a large share of media ownership.[26]

Even if the traditional mass media is fairly independent, not all groups and individuals in society are equally able to use the mass media to communicate their views and thereby attempt to influence the making and enforcement of the law. Due to their financial resources and business and political connections, wealthy and powerful individuals and business or political groups are more likely to have access to the media to, for instance, promote a legal reform, launch a public campaign against a court decision or proposed law, or simply be in a better position to pressure journalists, media owners, and managers to serve a particular interest.[27] In contrast, ordinary citizens, consumers, and small civil society groups may have little or no access to the traditional mass media. While these groups may have their legal agenda and a message to communicate to lawmakers, they hardly have the power, finances, and organizational resources to use the media for such purposes. Not only may they be unable to engage in massive campaigns to promote their views, but they may also be exposed to the influence of biased legal news that is often produced and spread by non-independent journalists and influential individuals and groups. For example, the media coverage of tobacco litigation frequently neglects to discuss the significant resource imbalance between tobacco corporations and individual plaintiffs. Tobacco corporations hire the most powerful law firms and spend millions of dollars on producing documents to substantiate their interests in court. Yet, these factors of radically unequal wealth and disproportionate power among corporate defendants and individual plaintiffs are notably absent from most news coverage.[28] Individual plaintiffs rarely have access to the media to raise concerns about such power disparities, and the general public may ignore the extent to which such imbalances distort the decisions on tobacco litigation cases.

---

[25] *Ibid.* at 16.

[26] Enrique Armijo, "Media Ownership Regulation: A Comparative Perspective" (2009) 37 GAJICL 421 at 423–25 (noting that most Western democracies have adopted some form of restriction on media ownership concentration on the presumption that preventing excessive media ownership by a few powerful individuals or entities is desirable because "if allowed, [it] grants them the ability to shape opinion or exploit the market for personal gain by overrepresenting their own biases, interests, and viewpoints in public debate").

[27] Slavko Splichal, *Principles of Publicity and Press Freedom* 9 (Lanham, MD: Rowman & Littlefield Publishers, 2002) at 194 (noting that the "traditional media often block[s] innovation, particularly when they are heralds of particularistic interests of powerful interest groups behind them").

[28] See William Haltom & Michael J. McCann, *Distorting the Law: Politics, Media, and the Litigation Crisis* (Chicago: University of Chicago Press, 2004) at 287.

Furthermore, the ability of the media to help disseminate legal knowledge and improve the accountability of the legal system is limited by the pressures of consumer society. While the media may provide important legal information and seek to attract the attention of the public to critical social issues, ordinary citizens do not necessarily read or engage with them due to, for example, time constraints or the difficulties in processing overwhelming amounts of information. Moreover, reading and following legal news may be less attractive when compared with sport and business news. If this problem generally exists, it should not be surprising that legal news does not necessarily attract the interest of the general public, particularly when referring to complex legal information. In times of busy lifestyles, limited income, consumerism, and easy entertainment, reading legal news may not be appealing to a large section of the population. So, the so-called advantages of the media for enhancing the legitimacy and accountability of the legal system may only make sense for highly educated, legally minded or affluent citizens, and organized interest groups.

All of the above disparities obviously create unequal opportunities for different groups to use the media. This in turn affects the degree of influence that groups may exert on lawmakers and enforcers. It should thus not be a surprise that powerful and organized individuals and groups more frequently make effective use of the media to shape public knowledge of the law; develop and campaign for potentially leading legal opinions; and seek to alter the views of courts, legislators, regulators, and enforcers in a manner that serves their interests. Whether these individuals and groups succeed depends on the independence of courts, legislatures, and regulators as well as the presence of active, independent journalists and media corporations committed to promoting the public interest.[29]

The Growing Role of Social Media

These limitations on the traditional mass media have, in part, given rise to alternative media organizations and various forms of public activism through the Internet.[30] The public is increasingly posting information outside the traditional mass media and using not only the Internet but also signs, physical postings, and local radios. News, stories, and views otherwise not covered or under-reported by the traditional mass media are beginning to surface and gain public exposure. While it is unclear whether this informal media is having a significant direct impact on the legislature, courts or regulators, it is conceivable that at least it is helping to raise awareness and build public opinion on legal matters that may put some pressure on lawmakers.[31] As this informal media grows in influence and the limits of traditional media worsen, it is becoming hard for courts, legislatures, and regulators to completely ignore it. For example, since 2007, a Facebook group led by University of Ottawa law professor Michael Geist has been raising criticisms of Bill C-61, *An Act to*

---

[29] The ability of the media to influence the legal system is obviously an empirical matter and will also depend on the approach that one may adopt about the relationship between the media and the legal system. See Gies, *supra* note 21 at 92 (claiming that "[i]n common with the Liberal watchdog model, autopoietic theory envisages a strong degree of independence and friction between the media and the legal system but, unlike the liberal narrative, it arrives at the rather different conclusion that media discourse is necessarily and systematically at variance with the truth claims validated by the legal system").

[30] See e.g., L. Bennett, "New Media Power: The Internet and Global Activism" in N. Couldry & J. Curran (eds.), *Contesting Media Power: Alternative Media in a Networked World* (Oxford: Rowman and Littlefield, 2003).

[31] See e.g., Kautsch, *supra* note 21 at 1142 (noting that "judges face an expanding media, ranging from bloggers who seek courtroom seats during high-profile cases, and who may well be packing cell-phone cameras, to citizen-operated websites that are devoted to disseminating public but sensitive court information, such as the identities of undercover agents").

amend the Copyright Act, tabled in the second session of the 39th Parliament.[32] The Facebook group has almost 90,000 members and it is claimed that this online campaign contributed to the government's decision to conduct public consultations on copyright legislation in 2009.[33] It is thus desirable to both welcome the growth of the informal or social media and promote greater independent journalism for a vibrant democratic society and a solid legitimacy and accountability of the legal system.

INTERACTION BETWEEN THE LEGISLATURE AND THE JUDICIARY

The interaction between the legislature and the judiciary is the third and final factor of the law-making process to be discussed in this chapter. While the discussion of interest groups and the media exemplifies external pressures on government actors (e.g., legislators and regulators) forcing them to change the law or introduce a new one, judicial–legislative interaction deals with the relationship between branches of government. Two aspects of this interaction are of importance for a better understanding of the law-making process. First, a judicial decision that declares a certain law unconstitutional may force Parliament to re-examine the issue and amend the law or enact a new one. Thus, judicial decisions may be viewed as one of the factors that forces an issue on a legislative agenda. Second, the notion of the law-making process needs to appreciate that both legislatures and courts are involved in developing the law; knowledge of the roles played by each branch can help observers to better understand how a given law has emerged and whose perspective it reflects. In this respect, a number of questions need to be considered. For example, can each branch have a different perspective on how a given issue should be regulated? If the courts and legislature differ on a given issue, which of the two institutions has the final word on the regulation of that issue? Is it appropriate for courts to decide on issues of public policy or are these matters better suited for the legislature?

Academics are not unanimous in their assessment of the interaction between the two branches. Some emphasize the importance of Parliament's leading role in law making and express concerns about courts making decisions that profoundly affect public policy. Others suggest that the two branches work collaboratively in developing a shared constitutional interpretation.[34] Yet others suggest that the nature of interaction varies, depending on the issue at stake.[35] In some cases, courts and legislature may engage in a constructive "dialogue" where the perspectives of both branches are considered in developing a regulatory regime. In other cases, a dialogue does not occur in a productive way, but rather turns into a strong tension between diverging perspectives of the judiciary and the legislature.

While the legislature has the power to pass laws, courts possess the power of judicial review, whereby they can determine, among other things,

---

[32] Amanda Clarke, "Social Media: 4. Political Uses and Implications for Representative Democracy" Library of Parliament Background Paper (Publication No 2010-10-E, 22 March 2010, Ottawa, Canada, Library of Parliament) at 3, online: <http://dsp-psd.pwgsc.gc.ca/collections/collection_2010/bdp-lop/bp/2010-10-eng.pdf>.

[33] *Ibid.*; Michael Geist, "Critics Misjudged the Power of Digital advocacy" *Toronto Star*, January 18, 2010.

[34] Michael C. Dorf & Barry Friedman, "Shared Constitutional Interpretation" (2000) 2000 Sup. Ct. Rev. 61. See also similar position in Heather MacIvor, *Canadian Politics and Government in the Charter Era* (Toronto: Thomson Nelson Canada, 2006) at 148–49.

[35] See generally Kent Roach, *The Supreme Court on Trial: Judicial Activism or Democratic Dialogue* (Toronto: Irwin Law, 2001).

The Interaction between the Supreme Court and Parliament in Creating a Regulatory Framework: Canada's Abortion Laws

EXHIBIT 36.2

Until 1969, abortions in Canada were effectively prohibited. In 1969, Parliament amended the Criminal Code to allow abortions in certain circumstances, namely when performed in a hospital with the approval of a Therapeutic Abortion Committee (s. 251 of the Criminal Code); in the absence of such approval, obtaining or performing an abortion constituted a criminal offence. In 1983, Dr. Morgentaler, who provided abortions to women who had not obtained an approval from a committee, was charged under s. 251; in 1988, his appeal was heard by the Supreme Court. The majority of the Court concluded that s. 251 of the Criminal Code violated s. 7 of the *Charter* (right to life, liberty and security of person) and, thus, was of no force and effect. Section 251 was deemed to interfere with a woman's physical and bodily integrity; it also denied her the fundamental liberty of making decisions about her life and pregnancy. Although the legislative objective of protecting the fetus was pressing and substantial, the means chosen to achieve it (s. 251) were not reasonable and demonstrably justified under s. 1 of the *Charter*.

This decision demonstrates the different roles and perspectives of Parliament and the Supreme Court in developing abortion laws. Parliament has established a regulatory regime that allowed abortions in limited and controlled circumstances. The Supreme Court, exercising its power of judicial review, questioned the means that Parliament has chosen and the balance that it has struck between respect for women's rights and public interest in protecting the fetus. The effect of the Supreme Court's decision was that abortion was no longer criminalized. Yet, this did not mean that the Court had the last word on the issue. It was open to Parliament to respond to the judicial ruling by passing new legislation. In particular, it could pass a law that would still limit abortion rights, but in a less stringent manner than s. 251. In fact, in 1989, the government introduced a new abortion law — Bill C-43. However, due to the controversial nature of the issue it was never passed. Thus, the Supreme Court's decision effectively remained the last word on abortion practice in Canada, but it is still open to Parliament to revisit the issue in the future.

---

the constitutionality of acts passed by the legislative branch. When legislation or a part of it is struck down, this not only leads to a change in the regulatory regime concerning the matter at hand, but also provides a judicial assessment of the choices that the legislature made in passing the law. For example, a court may find that a legislative objective was not compelling enough to justify limitations on certain rights or that the legislature did not strike a reasonable balance between individual rights and social objectives. Given that such judicial decisions may alter public policy set out by the legislature, much debate has arisen about this so-called **judicial activism** and about whether it is appropriate for courts to engage in policy-making.

Judicial Activism

There is no single definition of judicial activism, but it usually refers to judicial decision-making that has the potential to re-evaluate and change public policy or regulatory regime set out by other branches of government. Roach has identified four components that help determine whether a court is acting in an activist manner:

1. The degree to which judges are free to introduce their own preferences into constitutional interpretation

2. The degree to which judges are eager to make and impose law

3. The degree to which judges are likely to recognize that constitutional rights would trump other rights or social interests

4. The extent to which courts displace decisions of other branches of government.[36]

The indicators of judicial activism include judicial willingness to make law, to dismiss reasons of other branches for restrictions on constitutional rights (a tendency to conclude that constitutional rights trump social interests) and to render decisions that are likely to leave limited options for legislative response or to force significant change to the preferred government policy.[37]

Judicial activism has been subjected to a number of criticisms. It is contended that activist courts engage in law making as opposed to their intended role of discovering and applying pre-existing law. The activist judiciary is seen as hijacking the role of Parliament. As Greene points out, the controversy over the law-making role of judges is rooted in part in a concept of democracy as government by a majority of elected legislators.[38] Then, judicial activism is viewed as undemocratic, since it leads to unelected and unaccountable courts making public policy decisions.[39] It is also feared that interest groups use litigation to bypass the traditional democratic process of elected legislatures and that activist courts may make decisions that unduly favour certain interest groups.[40] Some of these concerns are rooted in the nature of the adversarial process and in a misunderstanding of the capacity of courts to make policy decisions. When a legislature creates a law, it needs to consider the multiple competing interests that are involved and find a compromise that both respects those various interests and permits the achievement of necessary social objectives. To this end, government and legislative committees may conduct public consultations, hearings, and other activities intended to solicit the perspectives of multiple stakeholders. In contrast, courts make decisions based on legal arguments presented by the parties to a case (and intervenors, if present). These legal arguments may not necessarily represent the wider views of multiple groups that are not participating in the court case but may be affected by the decision. Further, litigation is an adversarial process and is not intended to find a compromise solution in the interests of society as a whole. While litigation can and has produced judgments supporting the rights of various groups, it is poorly equipped to address systemic causes of inequalities and, thus, in itself does not necessarily lead to more social justice.[41] In light of these limitations, it is argued that the parliamentary process may provide a better setting for not only considering the multiple perspectives and interests at stake, but also for developing a solution that strikes a better bal-

---

[36] *Ibid.* at 106–10.

[37] *Ibid.*

[38] Ian Greene, *The Courts* (Vancouver. BC: UBC Press, 2006) at 17.

[39] Kim Campbell, "Parliament's Role in Protecting the Rights and Freedoms of Canadians" in Philip Bryden, Steven Davis & John Russell (eds.), *Protecting Rights and Freedoms: Essays on the Charter's Place in Canada's Political, Legal, and Intellectual Life* (Toronto: University of Toronto Press, 1994) 23 at 31.

[40] See e.g., Greene, *supra* note 38 at 146. For example, left-wing critics claim the *Charter* litigation has legitimized neo-conservative policies and exacerbated societal inequalities (Andrew Petter, *The Politics of the Charter: The Illusive Promise of Constitutional Rights* (Toronto: University of Toronto Press, 2010)). In contrast, right-wing critics contend that *Charter* litigation has been used primarily by the so-called "court party" — social-reform-minded, left-leaning interest groups, professionals, and activists (Frederick Lee Morton and Reiner Knopff, *The Charter Revolution and the Court Party* (Toronto: Broadview Press, 2000)).

[41] Harry Arthurs, "More Litigation, More Justice? The Limits of Litigation as a Social Justice Strategy" in Julia Bass, W.A. Bogart & Frederick Zemans (eds.), *Access to Justice for a New Century* (Toronto: Irwin Law, 2005) 249 at 253–54. See also similar ideas by Petter, *ibid.*

ance among those interests.[42] Thus, it is argued that courts need to exercise restraint in adjudicating such matters and not replace the decision of the legislature with their own.

The Canadian Supreme Court: Activist or Not?

In Canada, the debate about judicial–legislative interaction became particularly lively following the adoption of the *Charter*. The *Charter* created preconditions for greater judicial involvement in social policy and expanded opportunities for interest groups to use litigation as a tool for reform.[43] Much of this debate has focused on the Supreme Court, since its decisions are likely to have the greatest policy implications. In fact, some argue that with the adoption of the *Charter*, the Supreme Court was transformed from a primarily adjudicative body to a policy-making body.

Why and how often do courts and particularly the Supreme Court, act in an activist manner? There is no agreement among scholars on several issues, such as whether the Supreme Court has been highly activist or not; what is the proper extent of such activism; and whether judicial activism has had a negative or positive impact on public policy. Some suggest that in certain instances the Supreme Court may be inclined to step in as a response to the failure of the legislative branch to address the matter.[44] Others suggest that the use of litigation by disadvantaged groups has compelled the Court to intervene to correct the disadvantage and at the same time has been used to legitimize the Court's activist role in certain types of cases.[45] For example, s. 15 litigation has been used by groups representing immigrants, sexual minorities, the poor, and ethnic groups to attain equality rights status.[46] Yet, others contend that the Supreme Court's willingness to act in a more or less activist manner depends on its perception of the issue at hand. Where the Court believes that the legislation in question involves issues that are more appropriately left to the legislature, the Court takes a hands-off approach and is more likely to uphold legislation. At the same time, where the Court considers itself to have a degree of first-hand expertise in the matter and where the legislature is not seen as possessing any comparative advantage, the Court is willing to be more activist.[47]

Parliament's Response to a Judicial Ruling: What Options Are Available?

As mentioned above, a judicial decision that strikes down a law or part of a law, may force Parliament to react. In Canada, Parliament can react to a judicial ruling in several ways:

1. It may pass a new law or modify existing law, keeping judicial guidance in mind; a new law may still contain restrictions on certain rights, but Parliament will need to consider the reasoning of the Court and the permissible limits outlined by the Court to ensure that the new law strikes a reasonable balance within the meaning of s. 1 of the *Charter*.

2. Parliament may take no action.

---

[42] Campbell, *supra* note 39 at 26.

[43] Manfredi, *supra* note 13 at 91.

[44] Roach, *supra* note 10 at 178; see also Greene, *supra* note 38 at 150.

[45] Ian Brodie, *Friends of the Court: The Privileging of Interest Group Litigants in Canada* (New York: State University of New York Press, 2002) at xiv.

[46] See useful discussion in Brodie, *ibid.*

[47] Patrick Monahan, "The Charter Then and Now" in Philip Bryden, Steven Davis & John Russell (eds.), *Protecting Rights and Freedoms: Essays on the Charter's Place in Canada's Political, Legal, and Intellectual Life* (Toronto: University of Toronto Press, 1994) 105 at 116.

3. Parliament may choose to pass new legislation that overrides a judicial decision; in its most forceful form, Parliament may use the s. 33 notwithstanding clause in order to immunize the new law from judicial scrutiny.

According to Hogg and Bushell,[48] a judicial–legislative dialogue occurs when Parliament responds to a judicial ruling. However, the nature of this dialogue will greatly depend on the nature of Parliament's response. The first option suggests a respectful and productive collaboration where each institution can learn from the other and appreciate different perspectives.[49] A judicial decision may bring to light interests and rights that have been neglected; at the same time, a legislative response may allow Parliament to educate the public and the Court about compelling objectives that justify reasonable limitations on certain rights.[50] This kind of interaction may lead to a better understanding of the issues and a more nuanced approach to their regulation. However, when Parliament chooses to override a judicial decision, the dialogue is transformed into a confrontation between the two branches. Parliament's response may suggest that the court's decision was unacceptable or that the court wrongly interpreted the law.[51] Such a scenario is well illustrated by Parliament's response to the Supreme Court's *Daviault* decision, described below. Another frequently invoked example of a legislature using the s. 33 notwithstanding clause to override a judicial decision is found in relation to Quebec language laws. Quebec courts and subsequently the Supreme Court have ruled that Bill 101, which required all commercial signs to be in French only, violated freedom of expression and could not be saved under s. 1 of the *Charter*. Within a week of the decision, the Quebec legislature used the notwithstanding clause and enacted a law that overrode the judicial decision (although in respect to outdoor signs only; other languages could be used in indoor advertising).[52]

The nature of judicial–legislative interaction is likely to remain a topic of lively debate for years to come. Regardless of one's position on the issue, it is important to acknowledge that both branches have a role to play in law- and policy-making. A robust democratic system requires a combination of both judicial and legislative activism as well as a constructive dialogue between the two in discovering a reasonable balance among competing interests.[53] While the parliamentary process offers opportunities for hearing views of multiple stakeholders and for developing a solution that is in the interests of society as a whole, in reality, this process may be tarnished by the effects of lobbying, media, and other pressures on legislators. In certain respects, judicial activism

---

[48] Peter W. Hogg & Allison A. Bushell, "The Charter Dialogue between Courts and Legislatures (or Perhaps the Charter of Rights Isn't Such a Bad Thing After All)" (1997) 35 Osgoode Hall L.J. 75; Peter W. Hogg, Allison A. Bushell Thornton & Wade K. Wright, "Charter Dialogue Revisited — Or "Much Ado about Metaphors" (2007) 45 Osgoode Hall L.J. 1. It should be noted that although the idea of dialogue has become rather influential in characterizing the interaction between Parliament and the Supreme Court, it has also been criticized on a number of grounds — see, for example, F.L. Morton, "Dialogue or Monologue?" in Paul Howe & Peter H. Russell (eds.), *Judicial Power and Canadian Democracy* (Montreal and Kingston: McGill-Queen's University Press, 2001) 111; Christopher P. Manfredi & James B. Kelly, "Six Degrees of Dialogue: A Response to Hogg and Bushell" (1999) 37 Osgoode Hall L. J. 153.

[49] Roach, *supra* note 35 at 264.

[50] Roach, *supra* note 35 at 264; also see Janet L Hiebert, *Charter Conflicts: What Is Parliament's role?* (Montreal: McGill-Queen's University Press, 2002).

[51] Roach, *supra* note 35 at 265.

[52] Roach, *supra* note 35 at 190.

[53] Roach, *supra* note 35 at 250–51.

may help to correct a structural defect of democracy, in that decisions made in response to political majorities may ignore or be insensitive to minorities.[54] It is thus important to look at the courts and legislature holistically, as parts of a larger political system and judicial–legislative interaction as one of the dynamics of that system.

The following two case studies illustrate the impact of the three factors — interest groups, the media, and judicial–legislative dialogue — on the development of regulatory regimes in two specific areas: defence of intoxication under criminal law and labelling of genetically modified foods.

Case Study: *R. v. Daviault*, [1994] 3 S.C.R. 63

Should extreme intoxication to the point of automatism or insanity be available as a defence to a charge of a general intent offence such as sexual assault? This question was at the centre of the *Daviault* case, and the Supreme Court's answer to it has produced an unprecedented amount of public and legislative debate. The case is thus a useful illustration of the role of the media, interest groups and judicial–legislative interaction in the crafting of the legal regime pertaining to the **defence of intoxication**.

Facts of the Case

The accused, Mr. Daviault, arrived at the complainant's house bringing her a bottle of brandy at her request. The complainant, a 65-year-old partially paralyzed woman in a wheelchair, drank some brandy and fell asleep. When she awoke during the night, Mr. Daviault grabbed and sexually assaulted her.

Prior to arriving at the complainant's house, Mr. Daviault consumed seven or eight bottles of beer and then some 35 ounces of brandy at her house. He claimed to have no recollection of what happened and denied sexually assaulting the complainant.

At trial, an expert witness estimated that Mr. Daviault's blood-alcohol content on the night in question would have been between 400 and 600 milligrams per 100 millilitres of blood — concentration that would cause death or a coma in an ordinary person. Given that Mr. Daviault was a chronic alcoholic, he was less susceptible to the effect of alcohol and, in his case, such extreme intoxication led to a blackout. The trial judge found that the accused committed the offence as described by the complainant, but nevertheless entered an acquittal as he had a reasonable doubt as to whether Mr. Daviault, due to extreme intoxication, possessed the intent necessary to commit the sexual assault. The Quebec Court of Appeal overturned the decision. Mr. Daviault appealed to the Supreme Court.

Background on the Defence of Intoxication

Prior to discussing the Supreme Court decision, it is worth providing some background on the applicable principles of criminal law and the defence of intoxication. Criminal offences consist of two elements: prohibited conduct (*actus reus*) and a mental element (*mens rea*). In order to obtain a conviction with respect to the so-called "true crimes",[55] the Crown has to prove both *actus reus* and *mens rea* beyond a reasonable doubt. The requirement of a mental element in particular, serves to ensure that morally innocent individuals — those who do not understand or intend the consequences of their acts —

---

[54] Brodie, *supra* note 45 at 123.

[55] Criminal law distinguishes between the so-called true crimes (acts or omissions that are considered inherently wrong and that require proof of both *mens rea* and *actus reus*; sexual assault is considered a true crime); strict liability offences (only *actus reus* needs to be proven, but the accused may raise the defence of due diligence) and absolute liability (only *actus reus* needs to be proven).

are not convicted. In the *Daviault* case, the trial judge has accepted that the *actus reus* of sexual assault had been committed, but he was not satisfied that the accused possessed the necessary *mens rea*; hence, acquittal was entered.

The defence of intoxication has developed as a common law rule (in other words, it was shaped by courts rather than by the legislature). Initially, courts have treated intoxication as an aggravating circumstance, but over time, it has been recognized that alcohol may impair individuals' ability to form the necessary *mens rea*. The key rules of intoxication have been authoritatively summarized in the 1920 UK House of Lords' decision on *Beard*.[56] According to that decision, intoxication could be a defence to a charge of specific intent offence, but never to a charge of general intent offence.[57] It is reasoned that the mental element in general intent offences is so minimal that no amount of alcohol or drugs would prevent one's capacity to form such intent.

Supreme Court Decision in R. v. Daviault

Until 1994, Canadian courts largely followed the *Beard* rules. Indeed, in overturning the trial judge's decision, the Quebec Court of Appeal essentially adhered to the *Beard* rules. However, on further appeal, the majority of the Supreme Court departed from the *Beard* rules by holding that where intoxication was so extreme as to lead to a state akin to automatism[58] or insanity, it could be a complete defence to a charge of a general intent offence[59]. The majority of the Supreme Court reasoned that extreme intoxication akin to automatism could render the accused incapable of either performing a voluntary act or of forming the minimal intent required for a general intent offence. If no defence were allowed in such circumstances, an accused would have to be found guilty even though there was a reasonable doubt regarding the voluntariness of his/her actions — this would go against one of the most fundamental principles of criminal law. The majority concluded that the rule that intoxication could never be a defence to crimes of general intent violated principles of fundamental justice under s. 7[60] and the presumption of innocence under s. 11(d) of the *Charter*.[61]

Reaction to the Supreme Court Decision

Although the extreme intoxication defence was likely to be successful only in rare situations — where an accused established on the balance of probabilities that he/she was in a state of intoxication akin to automatism or insanity — the decision provoked strong public reaction and extensive media coverage. The decision was criticized, *inter alia*, for ignoring the issue of violence against women and victims' rights generally. The decision of the majority of the Supreme Court was heavily focused on the due process rights of the accused, but it failed to consider the victim's perspective, particularly the gendered nature of sexual assaults and the link between intoxication and

---

[56] *Director of Public Prosecutions v. Beard*, [1920] A.C. 479 (H.L.).

[57] A general intent offence is an offence that seeks to achieve a certain immediate objective and requires only a conscious doing of a given prohibited act (e.g., a basic intent to apply force in the offence of assault). In contrast, special intent offences possess a further ulterior intent that goes beyond performance of an immediate act at hand (e.g., murder contains not only a general intent to, for example, fire a gun, but also an ulterior intent to do so in order to cause another person's death).

[58] Automatism refers to a situation where an accused has no control over his or her actions.

[59] *R. v. Daviault*, [1994] 3 S.C.R. 63.

[60] Section 7 reads: "Everyone has the right to life, liberty and security of the person and the right not to be deprived thereof except in accordance with the principles of fundamental justice."

[61] Section 11(d) reads: "Any person charged with an offence has the right ... (d) to be presumed innocent until proven guilty according to law in a fair and public hearing by an independent and impartial tribunal."

increased risk of violence.[62] Concerns have also been raised about the implications of the decision for women's trust in the criminal justice system. It was feared that *Daviault* would have a chilling effect on the willingness of victims to report abuse and press charges.[63]

Media Coverage of R. v. Daviault

The mass media was key in attracting the attention of the public to the decision and in keeping the debate alive for a prolonged period. On the one hand, it provided information on the decision, helped promote public awareness of various concerns associated with the decision, and provided a forum for debate. On the other hand, the style of reporting (in particular, how the gist of the decision was presented and whose commentaries of the decision were more widely cited) shaped public opinion of and reaction to the *Daviault* decision.[64] Given that most people do not have the time or interest to monitor and read Supreme Court decisions, media reports became one of the main sources of information and, consequently, the basis for forming an opinion on the issue.

Much of the media coverage focused on the immediate implication of the decision — that the defence of intoxication could be used with respect to all offences, including sexual assault — but the reasoning of the Court was not explained. The media has depicted the decision as allowing a person to become extremely intoxicated and then to use such extreme intoxication as a shield from criminal responsibility.[65] For example, some headlines read: "A License to Rape?"; "Drinking Ruled a Rape Defence"; "Has the Highest Court Lost Touch with Reality?"[66] As noted by some, public opinion was 'poisoned' by these representations.[67] Absent the explanation of the limits of the intoxication defence and the reasoning of the Court, media messages made it easy for the public to jump to conclusions and dismiss it as not making sense rather than seek to understand the multiple considerations involved in the judicial decision. This highlights not only the tremendous influence that the media may have on public opinion, but also the responsibility that comes with it: it is important that cases are reported in a way that not only presents the ultimate conclusion, but also the reasoning behind it.

While many articles acknowledged that the extreme intoxication defence was likely to succeed only in the rarest cases, this caveat was immediately overshadowed by the reporting on five acquittals based on the *Daviault* principles.[68] In fact, it was suggested that part of the problem was the way in

[62] Kent Roach, *Due Process and Victims' Rights: The New Law and Politics of Criminal Justice* (Toronto: University of Toronto Press, 1999) at 177–78.

[63] Elizabeth Sheeny, "A Brief on Bill C-72" (Ottawa: National Association of Women and the Law, 1995); Randha Jhappan, "The Equality Pit or the Rehabilitation of Justice?" in Randha Jhappan (ed.), *Women's Legal Strategies in Canada* (Toronto: University of Toronto Press, 2002) 175 at 212; Elizabeth Grant — invisibility of victims, gendered nature of sexual assault; Tu Thanh Ha, "Men's Defence of Drunkenness Sparks Plans to Change Law" *The Globe and Mail* (November 2, 1994); Debra Black, "A Licence to Rape? Women Fear That a Supreme Court Ruling Tells Men Sexual Assault Is Okay as Long as They're Drunk" *Toronto Star* (October 27, 1994) E1.

[64] See, for example, Black, *ibid.*; David Vienneau, "Drinking Ruled a Rape defence Feminists Outraged at Supreme Court Decision" *Toronto Star* (October 1, 1994) SA2; David Vienneau, "Drunkenness Ruling Said Based on Error: Intoxication Doesn't Cause 'Automatism,' Researcher Says", *Toronto Star* (April 12, 1995) A2; Sean Fine, "Has the Highest Court Lost Touch with Reality?" *The Globe and Mail* (October 8, 1994) D2; Clyde Farnsworth, "Women in Canada Upset by Court Rulings on Drunkenness" *New York Times* (November 10, 1994) 7; Ha, *ibid.*

[65] Professor Alan Young (Osgoode Hall Law School) quoted in Stephen Bindman, "Licence to Rape Outraged Many" *Southam News* (December 27, 1994).

[66] Black, *supra* note 63; Vienneau, "Drinking Ruled a Rape Defence", *supra* note 64; Fine, *supra* note 64.

[67] David Vienneau, "Judges under Fire for Drunkenness Defence" *Toronto Star* (November 9, 1994).

[68] Roach, *supra* note 62 at 178.

which lower courts have applied the decision.[69] While the reported acquittals have ignited further fears and opposition to *Daviault*, no similar attention was paid to the reversal of two of the acquittals on appeal and six unsuccessful cases that used the *Daviault* defence.[70]

Some sources reported that the *Daviault* decision has put under fire not only the Supreme Court, but also the judiciary generally. In a survey conducted by the *Toronto Star*, lower court justices have almost unanimously supported the Supreme Court decision, but they acknowledged the particular difficulty that the decision created, given the repulsive character of its factual circumstances.[71]

The media's continuing attention to the *Daviault* has likely contributed to the mobilization of public opinion on the issue and created indirect pressure on the government to promptly consider a legislative response. In fact, it was suggested that under this pressure, the Justice Minister's initial "go-slow" response to *Daviault* eventually turned into a promise to table legislation in February 1995 — only some five months after the release of the decision.[72] In the *Daviault* instance, the media acted not as a facilitator helping to promote public acceptance of a judicial decision, but, to the contrary, as a force igniting opposition to it and pushing for change.

Parliament's Response to the Daviault Decision

Several options for responding to the *Daviault* decision were considered, including the creation of a new offence of "criminal intoxication." According to this approach, even if someone was acquitted of assault on the basis of *Daviault* principles, he or she could still be found guilty of an offence of "criminal intoxication." Eventually, the government did not proceed with the criminal intoxication offence. Instead, it introduced s. 33.1 into the *Criminal Code* (Bill C-72), which provided that self-induced intoxication, no matter how extreme, cannot be a defence to a charge of any general intent offence that "includes as an element an assault or any other interference or threat of interference by a person with the bodily integrity of another person." The preamble to the bill provided extensive justification for the amendment that was strongly rooted in concerns about violence in Canadian society and particularly violence against women and children. Politically, the bill was presented as both a response to violence against women and as part of measures to get tougher on crime.[73]

As a result, the defence of intoxication is currently governed by a combination of common law and statutory rules:

1. With respect to general intent offences involving violence or the threat of violence, self-induced intoxication can never be a defence (s. 33.1 of the *Criminal Code*).

2. With respect to general intent offences that do not involve violence or threat of violence (e.g., a property offence), an accused may benefit from the intoxication defence if he/she proves on the balance of probabilities that the intoxication was so extreme as to lead to a state akin to automatism or insanity (as per *Daviault*).

---

[69] Professor Allan Hutchison (Osgoode Hall Law School) quoted in Stephen Bindman, "Licence to Rape Outraged Many", *Southam News* (December 27, 1994).

[70] Roach, *supra* note 62 at 178.

[71] Vienneau, *supra* note 67.

[72] Stephen Bindman, "Drunkenness Ruling Provoked Outrage" *Hamilton Spectator* (December 24, 1994).

[73] Roach, *supra* note 62 at 180.

3. With respect to specific intent offences, intoxication may be a defence where it prevents an accused from forming a specific intent (*Beard* rules).[74]

Judicial–Legislative Dialogue on the Defence of Intoxication and the Role of Interest Groups

The *Daviault* case is a good illustration of the factors involved in the law-making process discussed in the first half of the chapter. First, it demonstrates the role of both courts and the legislature in shaping legal rules: the defence of intoxication is governed by a combination of common law and statutory rules. Second, *Daviault* is a vivid example of judicial–legislative dialogue.[75] Bill C-72 was a direct response to the Supreme Court decision. Both the Supreme Court and Parliament have engaged with the issue of the defence of intoxication. In choosing to exercise its power to effectively override the judicial decision, Parliament not only conveyed its reaction to the *Daviault* decision, but also expressed its opinion on the proper balance that should be struck between protecting the rights of the accused and the interests of the public. Roach has characterized Bill C-72 as Parliament's "in-your-face" response to the Supreme Court, which essentially said that the Court decision's was unacceptable.[76] Notably, the judicial and legislative response represent different perspectives on the issue of criminal responsibility: the Court focused on the rights of the accused whereas Parliament framed Bill C-72 in the context of protecting the victim from violence.

Third, Parliament's response and the very choice of the amending language was shaped by public pressure and the input from various advocacy and interest groups obtained during the examination of Bill C-72 at the committee stage. The House of Commons Standing Committee on Justice and Legal Affairs received submissions and heard testimony from a number of organizations, including the National Association of Women and the Law, the Metro Action Committee on Public Violence Against Women and Children (METRAC), the Canadian Bar Association (CBA), the Canadian Psychiatric Association, and the Addiction Research Foundation.[77] Most of these groups are well known for engaging in advocacy to advance the causes of their members and other affected populations. It is of note that there were no intervenors in the *Daviault* appeal, but active advocacy campaigns have been undertaken by a number of organizations, particularly those concerned with women's rights, following the decision. Most likely, interest groups did not see the need to intervene in the case because it was not anticipated that the Supreme Court would make a new rule affecting women's interests and other public policy issues.[78]

Prior to the committee hearings on Bill C-72, a number of interest groups had been vocal in the media and awareness campaigns raising their concerns about the *Daviault* decision. A group of women's organizations formed a coalition that called for a national Day of Action against the *Daviault*

---

[74] Simon N. Verdun-Jones, *Criminal Law in Canada: Cases, Questions and the Code*, 5th ed. (Toronto: Nelson Education Limited, 2011) at 266–67.

[75] Hogg & Bushell, *supra* note 48 at paras. 49–50.

[76] Roach, *supra* note 35 at 274–77.

[77] House of Commons Standing Committee on Justice and Legal Affairs, Evidence — Meetings 158–163 (June 1995), online: <http://www.parl.gc.ca/35/Archives/committees351/jula/english_committee.html>.

[78] Christopher Manfredi, *Feminist Activism in the Supreme Court: Legal Mobilization and the Women's Legal Education and Action Fund* (Vancouver, BC: UBC Press, 2004) at 32.

decision on February 25, 1995.[79] Bill C-72 was tabled on February 24, the day before the national day of action.

At the committee stage, various interest groups contributed different perspectives on the proposed legislation to help the legislators make a more informed choice about the defence of intoxication. For example, the National Association of Women and the Law and METRAC represented women's organizations and provided critical assessment of the bill in the context of violence against women. In particular, they were concerned that the intoxication defence works to reinforce and excuse male violence against women by attributing the blame to alcohol and minimizing the significance of the violence.[80] The CBA, which represented the interests of lawyers across Canada, concentrated mostly on the clarifications of the bill's language and broader issues of criminal law reform.[81] For example, the testimony of CBA representatives provided some explanation on the distinction between general and specific intent offences, commentary on the usefulness of having a statement of purpose in Bill C-72, alternative ways to address *Daviault* such as introducing an offence of criminal intoxication and other legal issues. While the CBA provided legal analysis of Bill C-72, the Canadian Psychiatric Association and the Addiction Research Foundation supplied insights into the issues of intoxication, automatism, and amnesia from a medical perspective.[82] In particular, the briefs and testimony from the Canadian Psychiatric Association and the Addition Research Foundation pointed out that, in scientific terms, alcohol in and of itself cannot induce a state akin to automatism. They were concerned that the *Daviault* decision seemed to have created the legal defence of alcohol-induced intoxication akin to automatism, which is indefensible in scientific terms.

Case Study: Regulating Labelling of Genetically Modified (GM) Food in Canada

The Debate about GM Food Regulation

For centuries, people have consumed food largely produced from nature. Not any more. In recent decades, most foods we consume are genetically modified. Everything from bread to tomatoes, corn and soya oil are produced from altered food organisms. As people consume more and more genetically modified food (GM food), the controversy grows over the risk to public health and the environment associated with the consumption of GM food. Increasingly, the general public wonders if GM food poses a risk to human health and whether greater public awareness and further scientific research are needed. A central response to these concerns has been the strengthening of the regulation of food safety so that GM foods are scientifically examined before they are approved for human consumption. Nevertheless, GM food science is not sufficiently developed, and the regulatory framework for food safety is not necessarily fully reliable. Thus, concerns over the risk that GM food poses remain on the agendas of consumers, regulators, and the food industry.

---

[79] Testimony of Susan Bazilli (METRAC) before the House of Commons Standing Committee on Justice and Legal Affairs (June 6, 1995), online: <http://www.parl.gc.ca/35/Archives/committees351/jula/evidence/158_95-06-06/jula158_blk101.html>.

[80] Testimony of Liz Sheehy (National Association of Women and the Law) before the House of Commons Standing Committee on Justice and Legal Affairs (June 6, 1995), online: <http://www.parl.gc.ca/35/Archives/committees351/jula/evidence/158_95-06-06/jula158_blk101.html>.

[81] Testimony of Sheldon Pinx, Michelle K. Fuerst, Joan Bercovitch (CBA) before the House of Commons Standing Committee on Justice and Legal Affairs (June 6, 1995), online: <http://www.parl.gc.ca/35/Archives/committees351/jula/evidence/159_95-06-06/jula159_blk101.html>.

[82] Testimony of John Bradford (Canadian Psychiatric Association), Harold Kalant and Perry Kendall (Addiction Research Foundation) before the House of Commons Standing Committee on Justice and Legal Affairs (June 13, 1995), online: <http://www.parl.gc.ca/35/Archives/committees351/jula/evidence/161_95-06-13/jula161_blk101.html>.

An important regulatory solution to the controversy over the risk of consuming GM food has been labelling, which may indicate whether any food product is genetically modified. This information may enable consumers to freely choose or reject GM food and to decide the risk they can tolerate. However, food companies often question the necessity of GM food labelling because it imposes a significant cost on food production and marketing and creates an unnecessary disincentive for GM food consumption, thereby hindering the competitiveness of the agro-sector. Similarly, regulators are not necessarily persuaded of the need for GM food labelling, since they tend to believe that a strict pre-marketing regulation of GM food safety should be sufficient and serve the purpose of balancing consumers' interest in safety, on the one hand, and food companies' concern over the competitiveness of the food industry, on the other. These diverging views about GM food labelling have given rise to an ongoing debate over whether labelling is necessary and, if so, whether it should be voluntary or mandatory.

In the midst of public controversy, the Government of Canada decided to officially adopt voluntary labelling for GM food in 2004. That is to say, companies may voluntarily label GM food, but they are not legally required to indicate that the food is a product of genetic engineering. In order to regulate this regime, a Canadian standard for voluntary labelling of genetically engineered (GE) foods entitled *Voluntary Labelling and Advertising of Foods That Are and Are Not Products of Genetic Engineering* [the Standard] was developed.[83] This Standard addresses "non health and safety labelling (rather, labelling for method of production, for example, whether a food has or has not been produced through genetic engineering".[84] It was adopted by the Standards Council of Canada and seeks "to provide meaningful criteria for labelling, understandable messages for consumers, and a consistent policy to verify the truthfulness of labels."[85]

It is important to note that GM food labelling is concerned with information about the genetic modification of a food product and must be distinguished from the current mandatory labelling that is required for any food that poses a risk due to general health and safety concerns other than genetic modification.[86] For example, if the nutritional value or composition of the food has been changed, or if there is an allergen present in the food, genetically modified or not, the food must be labelled as such.[87] While there are several regulatory solutions, labelling may mitigate such a risk by informing or alerting consumers about the risk. This required labelling applies to all foods, including GM foods.[88]

The Role of Interest Groups and the Media in the Development of GM Food Labelling

The adoption of voluntary labelling of GM food in Canada may be seen by the public as a purely technical legal process of making food laws. The Standard passed after some consultation and was apparently developed on the basis of advice from regulators and scientists. However, in reality, the adoption of voluntary labelling of GM food was the culmination of a long process of public consultation and pressures from multiple interest groups. Biotechnology

[83] Health Canada, <http://www.hc-sc.gc.ca/sr-sr/pubs/biotech/reg_gen_mod-eng.php>.
[84] *Ibid.*
[85] *Ibid.*
[86] *Ibid.*
[87] *Ibid.*
[88] *Ibid.*

companies, the food industry, government agencies, political and business elites, consumer groups, and the media played an important role in the debate over GM food labelling and influenced the ultimate decision to make this labelling voluntary and not mandatory in Canada.

The public debate over GM food regulation has brought to light the diverging views that the government and multiple groups hold, as well as the pressures they have exerted to influence public policies in this area. Although there has not been a wide public debate over GM food in Canada, the government has sought the views of the general public. The government held a multi-stakeholder workshop in 1993 that included industry representatives and consumer, environmental, and health groups.[89] In 1994, the government also organized a workshop devoted to the issue of GM food labelling.[90] In March 1999, a consensus conference on genetically modified foods was held in Calgary, Alberta. The conference was organized by researchers at the University of Calgary, using funding from a federal research grant and the provincial government of Alberta. Many citizens were recruited to participate in this conference. The government eventually created a Canadian Biotechnology Advisory Committee, including a citizen representative from the Calgary conference, thus recognizing that more participatory legitimation for policy might be desirable.[91] The Canadian citizens' report resulting from the 1999 conference nevertheless reached substantially precautionary conclusions in contrast to the optimistic outlook more common among governing elites.[92] For example, raising concerns about biased information and the lack of public participation, the participating citizens noted that "[w]hile food biotechnology offers potential benefits, its long-term effects on the environment are unknown."[93]

The Canadian Biotechnology Advisory Committee (CBAC) attempted to provide Canadians with opportunities to discuss the social and ethical concerns associated with plant biotechnology until May 2007, when the Conservative government disbanded it.[94] In addition to advising the Government of Canada on the multiple aspects of biotechnology policy, the Committee had the mandate of enhancing public awareness of the technology and facilitating an open, transparent national conversation on key issues.[95] These forums for public participation created by the CBAC quickly revealed the tension between the views of the government and the public. In 2001, CBAC launched a public consultation on GM food, but the majority of environmental and public interest non-governmental organizations boycotted it, claiming that the remit of the CBAC was too narrow and lacked independence from the government.[96] In 2003, CBAC issued a "dialogue tool on genetically modified foods and feeds", the premise of which was that the different biotechnology products were acceptable and which reiterated that GM crops and food should be approved

---

[89] Grace Skogstad, *Internationalization and Canadian Agriculture: Policy and Governing Paradigms* (Toronto: University of Toronto Press, 2008) at 215.

[90] *Ibid.*

[91] Alberto R. Salazar V., "NAFTA Chapter 11, Regulatory Expropriation and Domestic Counter-Advertising Law" (2010) 27 Ariz. J. Int'l & Comp. L. 31 at 79–80.

[92] John Dryzek, Robert Goodin, Aviezer Tucker & Bernard Reber, "Promethean Elites Encounter Precautionary Publics: The Case of GM Foods" (2009) 34 Sci. Tech. & Human Values 263 at 274–75.

[93] Canadian Citizens' Conference on Food Biotechnology. Citizens' Final Report presented March 7, 1999, available at <http://www.ucalgary.ca/~pubconf/report.html>.

[94] Skogstad, *supra* note 89 at 224.

[95] *Ibid.*

[96] *Ibid.*

solely on the basis of scientific assessments.[97] This probably heightened the controversy over CBAC's independence and further revealed its discrepancy with the views of non-governmental interest groups.

The media also played a role in raising concerns about the controversial ties between the government and the biotechnology industry and the excessive influence of the food industry on the development of GM food policies in Canada. In an article published in the *Ottawa Citizen*, it was reported that the CBAC office was located in a government department, Industry Canada, and was a paid member of BIOTECanada, an advocacy group for biotechnology companies.[98] Furthermore, the close ties between the government and the biotechnology industry became evident as the media revealed the financial support that the government gives to that industry. Mark Abley, writing in the *Montreal Gazette*, reported that BIOTECanada received annual grants of $1.1 million under Industry Canada's Technology Outreach Program, some of which went directly to changing public perceptions of the biotechnology industry.[99] Angela Rickman, deputy director of the Sierra Club of Canada, a non-governmental organization dedicated to the protection of the environment, complained that "[t]he government is acting as both the protector and the regulator of this industry".[100] The fact that biotechnology companies and the government appear to have been working toward improving the social acceptance of GM food becomes even more controversial in light of the opposite view held by the Canadian public. The polls reported by the media suggested that the Canadian public wants GM food labelled, and the majority are willing to pay more to identify genetically modified products.[101]

Given the prevailing ideas about the acceptability of GM food and the focus on the competitive advantage, productivity, and profitability of the Canadian agro-sector, it is conceivable that biotechnology companies have found GM food mandatory labelling too costly and contrary to their desire to expand GM food consumption and exports. There is some evidence that local business groups have in the past opposed the labelling of genetically modified products in Canada. This happened with the Biosafety Protocol. The United Nations' Protocol on Biosafety, in effect since September 2003, seeks to protect biodiversity by managing the environmental risks of the transboundary movement of living modified organisms (LMOs).[102] Among other things, exporters of commodities are required to label them as "may contain LMOs".[103] Canada has signed but has not yet ratified the Protocol.[104] "Its delay can be attributed to pressure brought by the Canadian farm community and export traders who fear the Protocol will raise their cost of exporting food products by requiring them to implement identity preservation systems".[105] This seems to have been the outcome of the organized efforts of the biotechnology industry. Indeed, as reported by the media, a number of companies and associations banded together in 1998 to form the Biosafety Protocol Consortia, which

[97] *Ibid.*

[98] See James Baxter, "Government paying to Lobby Itself: Industry Canada Is a Member — and a Client — of Group Organized to Influence Biotech Policy", *Ottawa Citizen* (April 10, 2000) A1.

[99] Mark Abley, "Biotech Lobby Got Millions from Ottawa: Public Cash Used to Alter Image", *Montreal Gazette* (February 28, 2000), also available at <http://healthcoalition.ca/archive/Biotech-IC.pdf>.

[100] Quoted in Abley, ibid.

[101] Sarah Staples, "Public Wants GM Food Labelled: Poll Finds Majority Willing to Pay More to Clearly Identify Modified Products" *Ottawa Citizen* (June 12, 2002) A1.

[102] Skogstad, *supra* note 89 at 221.

[103] Ibid.

[104] Skogstad, *supra* note 89 at 222.

[105] Ibid.

included Monsanto, BIOTECanada and CanGene (which, in 1999, received a loan of $700,000 from the Western Economic Diversification program, a government initiative).[106] This group hired Rick Walter (president of Biotech Consulting Group Inc.) to act as a lobbyist in Ottawa.[107]

The influence of the food industry on the regulation of food consumption and particularly genetically modified food should not be surprising. Marion Nestle has documented this problem in the United States,[108] and several pieces of evidence suggest that it may also be a serious problem in Canada. To further add to the above evidence, consider the following. A Canadian dietitian, commenting on Marion Nestle's book *Food Politics*, reveals some of the strategies that food corporations use in Canada to influence food regulations:

> In the [United States] and Canada, food is political for the simple reason that there is a lot of money, and profits, at stake . . . . While the details of the book are all American, in this era of free trade, its fundamental concepts and the issues it raises are also applicable in Canada. Indeed, I was told by a representative of a multinational food corporation at an industry-sponsored dietitians' event that his company loves to sponsor such events, because they know that when it comes time to change government regulations, they will have the support of dietitians.[109]

It should not come as a surprise that non-governmental groups have protested the expansion of GM crops and food and the over-influence of biotechnology companies on the development of GM food policies in Canada, including the lack of GM food labelling. For instance, in 2001, a coalition of farm, consumer, health, environmental, and industry organizations opposed Monsanto's attempts to commercialize genetically modified wheat in Canada. These groups raised serious concerns about market acceptance, environmental risk, and the lack of a democratic and transparent process in biotech regulation and policy.[110] Consumer groups, environmentalists, and social activists have been concerned about the fact that genetically modified food may provide abundant and cheap food at the expense of negatively affecting the environment and human health.[111]

Nevertheless, the attempts to make GM food labelling mandatory in Canada failed. A free vote in Parliament on October 17, 2001, defeated a bill by Liberal MP Charles Caccia. His private member's bill, C-287, would have required mandatory labelling of genetically altered foods. Interestingly, a year later, in August 2002, the Canadian Biotechnology Advisory Committee, often criticized for its close ties to the biotechnology companies, issued a report recommending the adoption of voluntary labelling of GM food, which in fact was officially adopted in 2004:

> We note that the mandatory labelling of GM foods is already required for health and safety reasons. CBAC recommends that the federal government adopt a voluntary system for labelling GM foods for matters other than health and safety. The majority of CBAC members believe that Canada

---

[106] Abley, *supra* note 99.

[107] *Ibid.*

[108] Marion Nestle, *Food Politics: How the Food Industry Influences Nutrition and Health* (Berkeley, CA: 2002); *Safe Food: Bacteria, Biotechnology, and Bioterrorism* (Berkeley, CA: 2003).

[109] Elaine Power, "Resource Review — Food Politics: How the Food Industry Influences Nutrition and Health", *Members Online Newsletter* (Dietitians of Canada, Toronto, Ontario), May 2003, available at <http://web.archive.org/web/20060630034213/http://foodpolitics.com/pdf/resrevfoodpoli.pdf>.

[110] Emily Eaton, "Getting Behind the Grain: The Politics of Genetic Modification on the Canadian Prairies" (2009) 41 Antipode 256.

[111] Skogstad, *supra* note 89 at 210.

should begin with a voluntary labelling system for GM foods to allow time for testing the system's adequacy and efficiency and to develop an accepted international standard; to provide consumers who wish to purchase GM-free products with the ability to identify them; to limit costs; and to avoid trade action where a mandatory labelling scheme would contravene trade agreements. ...

...

We recommend:

...

7.3 That the voluntary system be widely promulgated and promoted. ... [112]

Canada chose a lenient approach to GM food regulation in spite of the fact that the old international consensus that there were no fundamental differences between GM and non-GM products evaporated after 1997.[113] In fact, disparate regulatory frameworks of GM food developed in North America and Europe after 1997,[114] evidencing the existence of regulatory options and lack of consensus over the risks associated with GM food and the importance of consumer choice. Unlike in Canada, for instance, GM food labelling is mandatory in Europe. It should not be surprising, then, that public criticism of Canadian GM policies continues to increase and that the government has been forced to improve the legitimacy and effectiveness of its controversial policies in this area. In sum, "the Canadian institutional framework has been sensitive to the preferences of biotechnology plant developers and users, and less hospitable to critics of the technology and the Canadian regulatory approach".[115] This is despite the growing support of the Canadian public for GM food labelling.[116]

GM food policies, including labelling, have clearly developed in the midst of competing interest groups seeking to advance their discourses about risk and its regulation. On the one hand, the government, political elites, and the food industry have emphasized the focus on science-based food safety and the contribution of GM food and crops to improving the competitiveness and profitability of the Canadian agro-export sector.[117] On the other hand, consumer, environmental, and health groups have often raised concerns about the public health and environmental impact of GM food. Yet, it appears that the views of the biotechnology industry against mandatory GM food labelling have prevailed in the end. The views of the government and the biotechnology companies have been dominant in the decision on whether to require GM labelling despite significant public opposition and have overshadowed the views of consumers and even GM food scientists.

Clearly, there is a democratic deficit in the making of GM food laws, particularly in deciding the voluntary or mandatory nature of GM food labelling in Canada.

A critical factor in improving the democratic governance of GM food may be the role that independent food scientists can play. This is impor-

---

[112] The Canadian Biotechnology Advisory Committee, *Improving the Regulation of Genetically Modified Foods and Other Novel Foods in Canada* (Report to the Government of Canada, Biotechnology Ministerial Coordinating Committee, Ottawa, August 2002), xi and xviii, online: <http://dsp-psd.pwgsc.gc.ca/Collection/C2-589-2001-1E.pdf>.

[113] Skogstad, *supra* note 89 at 210.

[114] *Ibid.*

[115] Skogstad, *supra* note 89 at 211.

[116] Staples, *supra* note 101. See also The Canadian Biotechnology Advisory Committee, *supra* note 112, xi (noting that "[t]he dissenting member, Anne Mitchell, is strongly in favour of proceeding directly to mandatory labelling, and notes that a majority of respondents to our Interim Report urged a mandatory system.")

[117] Skogstad, *supra* note 89.

tant because knowledge of the risks associated with GM crops and food continues to be uncertain, and more solid and independent scientific research is needed.[118] Yet, private corporate interests increasingly dominate the research agenda, challenging the impartiality of food scientists and ultimately compromising the integrity of the regulatory system.[119] There are also concerns about the lack of public funding for independent research, which deprives scientists of a real opportunity to make independent research in this area. While regulation of GM food, particularly GM labelling, requires an advanced and reliable knowledge of the risks involved, that information is not necessarily available and, when progress is made, it is not necessarily widely discussed. Thus, there is a need to promote greater impartial research in this area and to make the views of independent food scientists more prominent in public debate to the extent of influencing regulatory policies and balancing corporate views.

It thus appears desirable to encourage some form of *independent scientist activism*. Independent food scientists, as another important interest group, should conduct intensive research on the risk of GM food for human health and the environment. Their findings should not only inform lawmakers and help review existing risk assessments and regulatory decisions,[120] but also provide key information for consumer education programs funded by the government and carried out independently from biotechnology companies.[121] In this respect, the media may also aid in promoting the independence of food scientists as well as disseminating research findings and greater information about the risks associated with GM food. The ensuing public awareness and the wider public debate based on independent scientific information will likely improve the democratic deliberation on the issue of GM food labelling. Rather than politicians or corporations deciding in boardrooms, the public in dialogue with scientists and other interest groups is to decide the level of risk it may want to tolerate and whether it needs GM food labels to make such a risk decision. Citizens, not business or political elites, should freely decide the degree of risk they wish to bear. This active participation of the public helps to democratize regulatory capitalism, since regulatory power is delegated not only to the government, the food industry, corporate agents, and professional

[118] See, e.g., The Canadian Biotechnology Advisory Committee, *supra* note 112, ix–xii ("...it is prudent to establish programs to determine whether there are any long-term adverse or beneficial effects attributable to these foods that are not revealed in pre-market assessments. ... The current approach to the assessment of environmental risk and ecosystem impacts of GM plants could be improved. ... We conclude that no scientific evidence exists to suggest that GM plants and foods currently in the market pose any greater health or environmental risk than other foods.... There is a need not only to develop methods for long-term surveillance of health and environmental impacts, but also to ensure that regulatory processes are able to deal effectively with the more complex products on the horizon."), online: <http://dsp-psd.pwgsc.gc.ca/Collection/C2-589-2001-1E.pdf>.

[119] Royal Society of Canada, Expert Panel on the Future of Food Biotechnology, *Elements of Precaution: Recommendations for the Regulation of Food Biotechnology in Canada*. Prepared for Health Canada, Canadian Food Inspection Agency, and Environment Canada, Ottawa, 2001, at ix and 212, online: <http://www.rsc.ca/files/publications/expert_panels/foodbiotechnolgoy/GMexsummaryEN.pdf>.

[120] In the past, the Royal Society of Canada's Expert Panel on the Future of Food Biotechnology, among several solutions, proposed an independent panel of experts to review the data and rationales upon which risk assessments and regulatory decisions were based. This recommendation was rejected by the Government of Canada. See Skogstad, *supra* note 89 at 228.

[121] Similar recommendations for greater information disclosure and public involvement in regulating GM food were made by CBAC in the past. See Canadian Biotechnology Advisory Committee, *supra* note 112 at ix, online: <http://dsp-psd.pwgsc.gc.ca/Collection/C2-589-2001-1E.pdf>.

It is important to note, however, that CBAC was criticized for its close ties to biotechnology companies. See Baxter, *supra* note 98. Its recommendations may then be taken with caution.

associations, but also to ordinary consumers and citizens, particularly when their health is at stake.

CHAPTER SUMMARY

Law making is a complex process influenced, directly and indirectly, by a variety of factors. This chapter has examined only three such factors: interest groups, the media, and judicial–legislative interaction. Each of the three has its own peculiar dynamics and is unique in how it may impact the law-making process. Interest groups may attempt to influence the nature and content of legal rules throughout the legislative process (e.g., by lobbying politicians to introduce a certain bill, making submissions at the committee stage) as well as after a law is passed (e.g., by challenging it in the courts). In contrast, the media plays a less direct role in the legal system: while not challenging a certain law or a government decision before the courts, it can subject an issue to the court of public opinion, thereby creating pressure for change. As a disseminator of mass information, it is able to influence public perception of laws, specific judicial decisions, and the legal system as a whole, as well as draw attention to and mobilize public opinion on certain issues. For example, the media scrutiny of the *Daviault* decision can be seen as one of the factors that not only moulded public opinion, but also pressured the government to react more quickly by introducing Bill C-72. Finally, judicial–legislative interaction refers to the dynamics between the two branches of government. The nature of such interaction varies: in some cases, it becomes a struggle between two opposing views on an issue; in others, it has been characterized as a productive dialogue seeking to find a reasonable balance among competing perspectives. The impact of these three factors — interest groups, the media, and judicial–legislative dialogue — should always be kept in mind in order to understand why and how a certain law came about as well as to be able to critically assess its underlying rationales.

GLOSSARY OF NEW TERMS AND KEY CONCEPTS

actus reus   A concept in criminal law denoting an act or omission that forms a part of an offence.

mens rea   A concept in criminal law that denotes the mental element of an offence.

defence of intoxication   A set of criminal law rules that outline in what circumstances intoxication may be a defence to a criminal charge.

interest group   A group of individuals or organizations that share a common set of goals and have joined together to persuade the legislative, executive or judicial branch to adopt a policy, law or decision that will help them protect or advance their interest.

judicial activism   A concept that refers to judicial decision-making that has the potential to re-evaluate and change public policy or a regulatory regime set out by other branches of government.

REVIEW QUESTIONS

1. What is an interest group?
2. What are the two main strategies used by interest groups to influence law and policy?
3. Why are powerful interest groups in a better position to influence law making?

4. How does the mass media influence the law-making process?
5. What are some of the problems that may prevent the mass media from having a positive impact on the legal system?
6. What are the advantages and disadvantages of pursuing litigation as a tool for social reform?
7. What is "judicial–legislative dialogue'?
8. Why can the case of *R. v. Daviault* be viewed as an example of legislative–judicial dialogue?
9. To what extent does the influence of interest groups explain the adoption of voluntary labelling of GM food in Canada?
10. What role did the mass media play in the regulation of GM food labelling?

DISCUSSION QUESTIONS

1. Using the concept of judicial–legislative dialogue, analyze the development of prisoners' right to vote in Canada. For the purpose of your discussion, examine the following sources: *Canada Elections Act*, R.S.C. 1985, c. E-2, s. 51(e) (prior to amendments in 1993), *Sauvé v. Canada (Attorney General)*, [1993] 2 S.C.R. 438; *Canada Elections Act*, R.S.C. 1985, c. E-2, s. 51(e) (as amended in 1993); and *Sauvé v. Canada (Chief Electoral Officer)*, [2002] 3 S.C.R. 519.
2. Research the Internet and find a Canadian-based interest group. Identify whose interests it represents and what techniques it uses to advance its cause.
3. What should be the interrelationship between the judiciary and the legislature in the law-making process? Should the perspective of one or the other prevail?
4. Explore potential solutions to the problem of the distortion of the ideal role of the media in law making by the over-influence of powerful interest groups.
5. Is the social media capable of engaging an increasing number of ordinary citizens so that they actively participate in the process of making and enforcing the law?

SUGGESTED READINGS

David Schneiderman & Kate Sutherland (eds.), *Charting the Consequences: The Impact of the Charter Rights on Canadian Law and Politics* (Toronto: University of Toronto Press, 1997).

Ian Greene, *The Courts* (Vancouver, BC: UBC Press, 2006).

Lori Hausegger et al., *Canadian Courts: Law, Politics, and Process* (Don Mills: Oxford University Press, 2009).

Heather MacIvor, *Canadian Politics and Government in the Charter Era* (Toronto: Thomson Nelson Canada, 2006).

Florian Sauvageau, David Schneiderman & David Taras, *The Last Word: Media Coverage of the Supreme Court of Canada* (Vancouver, BC: UBC Press, 2006).

Enrique Armijo, "Media Ownership Regulation: A Comparative Perspective" (2009) 37 Ga. J. Int'l & Comp. L. 421.

Residential Landlord and Tenant Law

Arlene Blatt
SENECA COLLEGE

Learning Objectives

After reading this chapter, the reader should be able to:

➢ Understand the basic rights and responsibilities of residential landlords and tenants in Ontario

➢ Explain how tenancy agreements are created

➢ Identify the different types of tenancies

➢ Explain the rules regarding rent and rent increases

➢ Describe how landlords and tenants can terminate a tenancy

➢ Understand sublets and assignments

➢ Describe proceedings at the Landlord and Tenant Board

➢ Understand mediation and other settlements between landlords and tenants

➢ Explain how to enforce orders from the Landlord and Tenant Board

TABLE OF CONTENTS

INTRODUCTION

Imagine that you are living in a house or apartment that you rent from the owner, your landlord. One of your main concerns as a tenant is likely about the rent. You want to know, for example, whether your rent will increase and, if so, by how much. You probably assume that your landlord will fix any repair or maintenance problems in your home, but that otherwise he or she will leave you alone and respect your privacy. You may have also have concerns about whether your landlord can ever force you to move out.

Now picture yourself as the owner and landlord of that house or apartment. You want a tenant who will pay the rent, not cause any damage to your property, and not disturb you or any other tenants living there. You certainly want the right to force a tenant to leave, if necessary.

As you can see, the interests of a landlord and tenant are quite different. The nature of the residential landlord–tenant relationship requires that a balance be struck between the interests of the landlord as owner of the rental property on the one hand, and the interests of the tenant as the person living there, on the other hand. The *Residential Tenancies Act, 2006* ("Act"),[1] the law that governs residential landlords and tenants in Ontario, attempts to achieve this balance. The Act defines the rights and responsibilities of both landlords and tenants, and sets out the procedures that must be followed when enforcing these rights and responsibilities. Since the Act governs most residential rental properties in Ontario, landlords and tenants must know what it says so that they can fully understand the extent of their legal rights and responsibilities.

This chapter examines the relationship between residential landlords and tenants in Ontario. It discusses how tenancies begin, how they end, the rights and responsibilities of both landlords and tenants, and rules about rent. This chapter talks about **eviction** and explains when and how a landlord can end a tenancy and evict the tenant. It also talks about how tenants can end their tenancy. Finally, it describes proceedings at the Landlord and Tenant Board (the "Board"), the administrative tribunal that administers the Act and resolves disputes between residential landlords and tenants. This chapter focuses only on the most common type of residential rental property — an apartment, duplex, house, or condominium unit. Other types of residential properties such as care homes, boarding houses, and mobile homes will not be discussed. While this chapter does address many of the main issues concerning residential landlords and tenants in Ontario, it is not a complete discussion of this area of law.

THE *RESIDENTIAL TENANCIES ACT*

The *Residential Tenancies Act* is the law that governs residential landlords and tenants in Ontario. The Act covers most types of rental residential properties and provides full and partial exemptions for some types of housing. For example, the Act does not apply at all to people who are in jail or who live in a hospital, hotel or motel, or an emergency shelter. It also does not apply at all to any type of living accommodation that requires the occupant to share a kitchen or bathroom with the owner, or a close family member of the owner. For certain other types of rental residential properties, the Act may provide only a partial exemption. For example, some of the rules about rent do not

---

[1] S.O. 2006, c. 17.

| EXHIBIT 37.1 | The *Residential Tenancies Act* |

Purposes of the Act — Section 1

The purposes of this Act are to provide protection for residential tenants from unlawful rent increases and unlawful evictions, to establish a framework for the regulation of residential rents, to balance the rights and responsibilities of residential landlords and tenants and to provide for the adjudication of disputes and for other processes to informally resolve disputes.

Definition of "landlord" and "tenant" for the purposes of the Act

"landlord" includes,

(a) the owner of a rental unit or any other person who permits occupancy of a rental unit, other than a tenant who occupies a rental unit in a residential complex and who permits another person to also occupy the unit or any part of the unit,

(b) the heirs, assigns, personal representatives and successors in title of a person referred to in clause (a), and

(c) a person, other than a tenant occupying a rental unit in a residential complex, who is entitled to possession of the residential complex and who attempts to enforce any of the rights of a landlord under a tenancy agreement or this Act, including the right to collect rent.

"tenant" includes a person who pays rent in return for the right to occupy a rental unit and includes the tenant's heirs, assigns and personal representatives, but "tenant" does not include a person who has the right to occupy a rental unit by virtue of being,

(a) a co-owner of the residential complex in which the rental unit is located, or

(b) a shareholder of a corporation that owns the residential complex.

---

apply to people who live in subsidized housing. All of the full and partial exemptions are set out in the Act.

The Act defines the meaning of some of the terms that are used in its provisions. For example, s. 2 defines a "rental unit" as follows:

[A]ny living accommodation used or intended for use as rented residential premises, and "rental unit" includes,
(a) a site for a mobile home or site on which there is a land lease home used or intended for use as rented residential premises, and
(b) a room in a boarding house, rooming house or lodging house and a unit in a care home.

You should refer to this section to see if a term has a defined meaning for the purposes of the Act.

The Act provides that it applies with respect to rental residential units in Ontario despite any agreement or waiver to the contrary. This means that landlords and tenants cannot agree, for example, that some or all of the provisions of the Act will not apply to them. The Act also provides that any provision in a **tenancy agreement** that is inconsistent with the Act is void and will not be enforced by the Board. The practical effect of these provisions is that the tenancy agreement is essentially irrelevant except as it specifies the amount of rent and the date when rent is due, whether utilities, parking and/or other services are included in the rent, and the term of the tenancy agreement. This is because the Act covers all the matters governing the landlord and tenant relationship, including the rights and responsibilities of both landlords and tenants.

THE TENANCY AGREEMENT

A tenancy begins with a written or oral agreement between a landlord and tenant for possession of a rental unit. A tenancy can also start with an implied agreement if, for example, the landlord accepts rent from a person who is living in the rental unit after acquiring it from a former tenant, but without entering into an oral or written tenancy agreement with the landlord. If there is a written tenancy agreement, no particular form of agreement is required. However, as noted above, any terms that are inconsistent with the Act are void and will not be enforced by the Board.

When considering a prospective tenant, a landlord may perform credit checks and can ask for banking information and other information about income, employment history, rental history, and personal and/or credit references. While a landlord may refuse a prospective tenant based on this information, a landlord cannot refuse to rent to someone based on any of the prohibited grounds of discrimination set out in Ontario's *Human Rights Code*.[2] This statute provides that "every person has a right to equal treatment with respect to the occupancy of accommodation, without discrimination because of race, ancestry, place of origin, colour, ethnic origin, citizenship, creed, sex, sexual orientation, age, marital status, family status, disability or the receipt of public assistance".[3] A landlord should not, for example, ask a prospective tenant about his or her ethnic background or whether he or she is gay, married, divorced, or plans on having children.

When a tenancy agreement is entered into, the landlord must provide the tenant with the landlord's legal name and address so that the tenant can contact the landlord if necessary and give the landlord any notices or other documents. If the tenancy agreement is not in writing, the landlord must provide the tenant with the landlord's contact information, in writing, within 21 days after the tenancy starts. If the tenancy agreement is in writing, the landlord must give the tenant a copy of the signed agreement within 21 days after the tenant signs it. The tenant is not required to pay rent until the landlord complies with this obligation. However, as soon as the landlord complies, the tenant must pay any withheld rent. Landlords must also provide all new tenants with information about the rights and responsibilities of landlords and tenants, the role of the Board, and how to contact the Board.[4] The landlord must give this information to the tenant on or before the date the tenancy begins. The Board has an information brochure available on its website that landlords can download and use for this purpose.

A tenancy starts on the day the tenant is entitled to possession of the rental unit, whether or not the tenant actually moves in on that date, regardless of the reason. For example, if a tenancy agreement says the tenant can move in on March 1, then the tenant will be responsible for March's rent, even if the tenant is unable to move in until the following month.

---

[2] R.S.O. 1990, c. H.19.

[3] *Ibid.*, s. 2(1).

[4] General information about the rights and responsibilities of landlords and tenants can be found on the Landlord and Tenant Board website: "Information for New Tenants", <http://www.ltb.gov.on.ca/en/Key_Information/STEL02_111600.html>.

TYPES OF TENANCIES: PERIODIC AND FIXED-TERM TENANCIES

Tenancies are either fixed-term or periodic. A **fixed-term tenancy** has a specified start date and end date, and can be for any length of time. Most new tenancy agreements provide for a fixed term of one year. A tenancy does not end when the fixed term expires. Instead, the tenancy automatically continues as a **periodic tenancy**, with all the same terms and conditions of the original tenancy, unless of course it has been renewed for another fixed term. A tenant does not have to agree to a landlord's request to renew a fixed-term tenancy that is coming to an end.

When a tenancy agreement does not specify an end date, the tenancy is deemed to be a periodic tenancy. The period involved is determined by the frequency with which the tenant pays rent. For example, if the tenant pays rent weekly, it is a weekly periodic tenancy. If the tenant pays rent monthly, it is a monthly periodic tenancy. Most tenants pay their rent monthly and therefore have a monthly periodic tenancy, also known simply as a monthly tenancy.

A periodic tenancy renews automatically at the end of each relevant period and continues this way until the tenancy is terminated by either the landlord or tenant. For example, a monthly periodic tenancy starts on the first day of the month and ends on the last day of that month, and then automatically renews for another month.

RIGHTS AND RESPONSIBILITIES OF RESIDENTIAL LANDLORDS AND TENANTS

Security of Tenure

The Act balances the right of tenants to **exclusive possession** of the rental unit for as long as they want against the right of landlords to evict tenants when the circumstances justify it. Tenants in Ontario have **security of tenure**, which means that they are protected against unjustified and unlawful evictions by their landlords. A landlord can evict a tenant only for the reasons specified in the Act and only after the landlord obtains an order from the Board terminating the tenancy and evicting the tenant. For example, even when a landlord has a reason specified in the Act to evict a tenant, the landlord is not allowed to lock the tenant out of the rental unit or otherwise force the tenant to move out. The only person who is allowed to evict a tenant is the **Sheriff**.

Privacy

The law recognizes that while tenants should have the right to privacy while living in a rental unit, landlords, as owners of the rental property, should have the right to enter a tenant's unit in certain circumstances.

The Act protects these rights by specifying when and how a landlord is allowed to enter a tenant's rental unit. In most cases, a landlord can enter only after giving the tenant 24 hours' prior written notice, and only for one of the permitted reasons set out in the Act. These reasons all deal with situations where a landlord will reasonably need to enter the rental unit, such as to fix something, inspect the unit for maintenance problems, or show the unit to a purchaser, mortgage lender, or insurer. As long as the landlord has a reason permitted under the Act, and gives the tenant the required written notice, the landlord is allowed to enter the rental unit anytime between the hours of 8 a.m. and 8 p.m., even if the tenant is not home.

The only times a landlord can legally enter a tenant's unit at any time of the day or night, and without telling the tenant ahead of time, are either when there is an emergency or when the tenant agrees to let the landlord enter, at the time of entry.

A landlord can also enter a tenant's unit without telling the tenant ahead of time, but only between the hours of 8 a.m. and 8 p.m., if the tenancy agreement requires the landlord to clean the rental unit, or if the tenancy agreement is ending and the landlord is showing the rental unit to a potential new tenant.

It is illegal for a landlord to enter a tenant's unit without complying with the provisions of the Act.

Maintenance and Repairs

Landlords are responsible for providing and maintaining a tenant's rental unit in a good state of repair, and for complying with all health, safety, housing, and maintenance standards set out in applicable bylaws. The rental unit includes whatever comes with it, such as appliances, as well as all the common areas of the **residential complex**, such as the lobby, hallways, elevators, stairwells, and parking areas. Even if a tenant was aware of a problem or maintenance issue before agreeing to rent the unit, the landlord must still take care of it. A landlord cannot, for example, refuse to fix a broken appliance just because the tenant knew it was broken before the tenant moved in. The landlord must provide the tenant with working appliances, not new or improved ones. This means that a landlord can replace a broken appliance that is beyond repair with a used appliance, as long as it works, and the tenant cannot insist on a new or better model.

If a tenant has a repair or maintenance problem in the rental unit, the tenant should notify the landlord of the problem, in writing, and ask the landlord to look after it. If the landlord does not fix the problem within a reasonable amount of time, the tenant may start an application at the Board for an order determining that the landlord has breached his or her repair and maintenance obligations under the Act. There are a number of different remedies the Board can order in this situation, the most common being an **abatement of rent** and/or an order requiring the landlord to repair or replace something in the rental unit by a certain date.

Many tenants who need repairs in their rental unit are tempted to withhold rent until the landlord completes the repairs. Tenants should not do this because the landlord will likely treat it as non-payment of rent and start eviction proceedings.

Tenants are responsible for any damage to the rental unit or the residential complex that is caused by them or their guests, whether intentionally or by accident. If a tenant fails to repair or pay for any such damage, the landlord may start an application at the Board not only for an order requiring the tenant to pay the cost of repairing the damage but also for an order to terminate the tenancy and evict the tenant.

Tenants are also responsible for keeping their rental unit reasonably clean. This does not mean they must be tidy, but rather that their place cannot be so filthy that it poses a health or safety risk to others.

Rent and Rent Control

There is no rent control on an empty rental unit, and a landlord is therefore free to charge a new tenant whatever amount of rent the landlord wants. The only exception to this rule is if the Board has ordered the landlord to complete certain repairs or maintenance in the rental unit. In this case, the landlord must charge a new tenant the same amount of rent as the previous tenant, but may increase the rent once the landlord completes the required work and removes the order.

The tenancy agreement will specify the amount of rent and when rent payments are due. It should also specify whether the rent includes any services, such as parking, electricity, heat, or cable.

Once a tenant moves into the rental unit, rent control takes effect and, in most cases, the landlord can increase the rent only once every 12 months by the rent increase **guideline**, which is set by the Ontario government every year. The guideline is expressed as a percentage and is the maximum percentage by which a landlord can raise the tenant's rent without obtaining approval from the Board. For example, assume the guideline for year 0 is 1.3 percent. During year 0, a landlord can increase a tenant's rent by 1.3 percent, assuming it has been 12 months since the tenant moved in or since the tenant's rent was last increased. For a tenant paying $1,000.00 per month, the increased rent will be $1,013.00. Even though landlords do not need approval for a guideline rent increase, they do have to provide the tenant with written notice of the rent increase at least 90 days before the date on which the increase is to take effect. If a tenant does not receive the required notice from his or her landlord, the tenant does not have to pay the increased rent.

In limited circumstances, the landlord and tenant can agree to increase the rent if, for example, the landlord offers to make major repairs or renovations in the rental unit, buy new equipment for the rental unit, or provide the tenant with a parking space or a new service or item such as satellite television, an air conditioner or a locker.

If the landlord wants to increase the rent above the guideline and cannot do so by agreement with the tenant, the landlord must start an application at the Board for an order approving the increase above the guideline. A landlord can apply for an increase above the guideline if his property taxes or utility costs have significantly increased, if he has completed necessary major repairs or renovations, or if he has incurred costs related to security services carried out by persons who are not employed by him. The landlord cannot increase a tenant's rent above the guideline amount without an order from the Board.

Payment of Rent

Rent is due on the date set out in the tenancy agreement, which is usually the first day of each month. Tenants pay their rent in advance, which means that the September 1st rent payment, for example, represents rent for the month of September, not August. If the tenant does not pay the rent in full, on or before the date it is due, the landlord is entitled to start proceedings to terminate the tenancy and evict the tenant for non-payment of rent. As you will see later, however, the tenant is given an opportunity to pay the rent owing and stop further proceedings.

Residential landlords do not have the right to seize any of the tenant's personal property in the rental unit as security for the payment of **arrears of rent**. This is known as **distraint** and is available only for commercial landlords. Residential landlords also do not have the right to charge the tenant **accelerated rent** under any circumstances.

Tenants usually pay their rent by cheque or cash. Tenants can choose to pay their rent by post-dated cheques or automatic payments (credit card or bank account debits) but landlords cannot insist that tenants pay by either of these methods. Landlords can request it, but tenants are entitled to refuse. If a tenant (or former tenant) asks the landlord for a receipt for any rent payments, the landlord must provide it, free of charge.

Last Month's Rent Deposit

On or before the date the tenancy starts, the tenant must give the landlord the first month's rent as well as a **last month's rent deposit**. The landlord can use the last month's rent deposit only as the rent payment for the last month of the tenancy, and for no other reason. For example, the landlord cannot use a tenant's last month's rent deposit to pay for damage caused by the tenant. When a tenant's rent increases, the landlord can ask the tenant to increase the amount of the last month's rent deposit to bring it up to the same amount as the new rent. Landlords are required to pay tenants interest on the rent deposit once a year. The interest rate is the same as the rent increase guideline. The practical effect of this is that in most cases, the amount owing to a tenant for interest on the last month's rent deposit will be offset by the amount owing to the landlord for increasing the deposit to the same amount as the new rent.

The last month's rent deposit is the only type of **security deposit** the landlord can require from a new tenant. A landlord is not allowed to charge the tenant a damage deposit or any other type of charge or fee as a condition of entering the tenancy agreement. However, the regulations made under the Act permit a landlord to ask a tenant for a key or remote entry card deposit, which cannot be more that it would cost to replace them and which must be refunded when the key or card is returned. The landlord can also charge the tenant the bank charges and an administrative charge not exceeding $20 for any NSF cheque.

Vital Services; Reasonable Enjoyment; Locking System

Landlords are not allowed to withhold or interfere with the reasonable supply of any **vital service** that they are obligated to provide under the tenancy agreement. Vital services include heat (from September 1 to June 15), electricity, gas, and water. Landlords are also not allowed to harass, obstruct, coerce or threaten tenants, or to interfere with the reasonable enjoyment of the rental unit or residential complex by a tenant or members of his or her household. Finally, a landlord is not allowed to change the locks on any doors in the rental unit or residential complex without giving the tenant replacement keys. If the landlord breaches any of these obligations, the tenant can apply to the Board for relief.

ASSIGNMENT AND SUBLETTING

Assignment and subletting are different and are treated differently under the Act. A **sublet** occurs when a tenant moves out of the rental unit temporarily and plans to move back into the unit before the end of the tenancy. The tenant finds someone else, called a **subtenant**, to live in the unit and pay rent during the tenant's absence. An **assignment** occurs when the tenant moves out of the rental unit permanently and transfers the tenancy to someone else, called an **assignee**. For example, assume that Lianisse, a tenant in Toronto with a fixed-term tenancy for one year that expires on March 31, accepts a part-time employment contract in Nova Scotia, commencing July 1. Assuming that Lianisse plans to move back into her rental unit when her contract ends, she will need to sublet her tenancy. If, on the other hand, her contract becomes permanent and she decides not to move back to Toronto at all, she will need to assign her tenancy. A tenant can sublet or assign the rental unit to someone else with the landlord's consent. The law protects the landlord's right to control who lives in his or her rental property and gives the landlord the right to withhold consent to a sublet or assignment of the unit to a potential subtenant or assignee, but only on reasonable grounds.

In an assignment, the landlord is also given the right to refuse consent to any assignment at all, regardless of who the potential assignee is, and the reason doesn't matter. This is because the law recognizes that a landlord can increase the rent charged only for a new tenant, but not for an assignee. Therefore, the provisions dealing with assignment protect the landlord's right to decide, based on **market rent**, whether or not to consent to the assignment, even before the tenant proposes a potential assignee. However, if the landlord refuses to consent to any assignment at all, the tenant is given the right to terminate the tenancy. For example, assume that Lucy is a landlord and one of her tenants, Jose, asks if he can assign his rental unit. If Jose's rent is well below market rent, and Lucy says no, Jose will terminate the tenancy, and Lucy will then be able to enter in to a new tenancy agreement and charge market rent. If, on the other hand, Jose's rent is well above market rent and **vacancy rates** in the area are high, Lucy will want Jose to assign the tenancy agreement to someone else. In this case, even if Lucy agrees to the idea of an assignment, she still has the right to refuse a potential assignee, but only on reasonable grounds.

If a tenant asks the landlord to consent to an assignment of the tenancy and the landlord does not respond within 7 days, the tenant has the right to terminate the tenancy on 30 days' notice to the landlord.

After an assignment, the assignee is responsible to the landlord for any breach of the tenancy agreement from the date of the assignment and may enforce against the landlord any of the landlord's obligations under the tenancy agreement or the Act. The original tenant is released from all future obligations but remains responsible to the landlord for any breaches that occurred before the assignment took place.

After a sublet, the subtenant is responsible to the tenant for the subtenant's obligations under the subletting agreement, and the original tenant continues to be responsible to the landlord for the payment of rent and for the tenant's other obligations under the tenancy agreement or the Act. A tenant cannot charge a subtenant a higher rent, or collect any kind of fee or deposit from the subtenant.

Sometimes a tenant will assign or sublet the tenancy without telling the landlord. The Act provides that any assignment or sublet that takes place without the landlord's consent is an unauthorized sublet or assignment. A landlord who finds out about an unauthorized sublet or assignment may apply to the Board to have the subtenant or assignee evicted. Alternatively, the landlord may negotiate a new tenancy agreement with the subtenant or assignee.

TERMINATING A TENANCY

Termination by the Tenant

Tenants can move out of the rental unit whenever they want but must give proper notice to the landlord, in accordance with the Act. The amount of notice a tenant must give is determined by the type of tenancy the tenant has. If the tenant has a fixed-term tenancy, the tenant must give the landlord at least 60 days' notice to terminate the tenancy effective the last day of the fixed-term tenancy. Even if the tenant gives more than 60 days' notice, the tenant cannot terminate the tenancy earlier than the date the fixed-term tenancy ends.

For example, assume that Carlos is a tenant with a fixed-term tenancy that expires on June 30. If Carlos wants to terminate his tenancy, he must give notice to his landlord by no later than May 1, for the tenancy to terminate effective the last day of his tenancy, or June 30. Even if Carlos gives notice to his landlord well before May 1, for example on January 1, his tenancy will still terminate effective June 30, because it is the last day of his fixed-term tenancy.

If a tenant with a monthly periodic tenancy wants to move out, the tenant must give the landlord at least 60 days' notice to terminate the tenancy effective the last day of the relevant month. In other words, the tenant counts 60 days from the date notice is given, and the earliest day the tenancy can be terminated is the last day of that month. For example, assume that Juanita is a tenant with a monthly periodic tenancy. If she gives her landlord notice on May 14, the earliest date she can terminate her tenancy is July 31. If on the other hand Juanita knows that she wants to terminate her tenancy effective the last day of a particular month, she must count backwards 60 days to determine the latest date by which she must give her landlord notice. For example, if she wants to move out on July 31, she must give her landlord notice by no later than June 1. Because February has only 28 days, the Act provides an exception to the 60-day notice period when the month of February is involved. It basically treats February as if it has 30 days.

If a tenant moves out without giving proper notice, the tenancy ends on the date the landlord rents the unit to a new tenant, or the earliest date the tenant can terminate the tenancy pursuant to the Act, whichever is earlier, and the tenant will be responsible to pay the rent owing up to this date. For instance, assume that Juanita (from the above example) forgot to give her landlord notice on or before June 1 and does not give notice until June 10. Unless Juanita's landlord finds a new tenant who can move in on August 1, Juanita's tenancy will end on August 31, which is the earliest date she can terminate her tenancy if she gives notice June 10. Juanita will be responsible for the rent owing for the month of August, even if she moves out at the end of July. The only way Juanita can avoid responsibility for the additional month's rent is if her landlord agrees to let her out of the tenancy agreement early, which the landlord may be willing to do if the tenant's rent is below market rent.

A tenant who gives notice to terminate the tenancy, or who reaches an agreement with the landlord to terminate the tenancy, cannot change his or her mind and must move out of the rental unit on or before the date the tenancy terminates. If the tenant does not move out of the rental unit on or before the date the tenancy ends by notice or agreement, the landlord can start an application at the Board for an order terminating the tenancy and evicting the tenant.

A tenant may also be able to terminate his or her tenancy by starting an application at the Board for an order ending the tenancy agreement because the landlord breached his/her obligations under the Act. If, for example, a landlord harasses a tenant, fails to maintain the rental property, alters the locking system, enters a tenant's unit illegally, withholds vital services, or interferes with a tenant's reasonable enjoyment of the rental property, one of the possible orders the Board can make is an order terminating the tenancy. The tenant will have to convince the Board that termination is a reasonable remedy in the circumstances.

Termination by the Landlord

Introduction

As discussed earlier, tenants have security of tenure, which means that the landlord can terminate a tenancy only in accordance with the Act. While the law protects tenants against unlawful evictions, it also recognizes that, in certain circumstances, termination of a tenancy by a landlord is necessary or justified. Therefore, the Act provides landlords with the right to terminate tenancies, but only for the reasons specified in the Act. Some of the reasons are based on the behaviour of the tenant, and are referred to as "fault" or "for cause" reasons. These reasons include such behaviour as causing damage or committing an illegal act in the rental property. If a landlord has a "for cause" reason, the landlord is allowed to terminate the tenancy early, in other words, before the end of a fixed term or period of the tenancy agreement.

Other reasons set out in the Act allow the landlord to terminate a tenancy even though the tenant has not done anything wrong. The Act recognizes that termination is justified in some circumstances, not because of the tenant's behaviour, but because of a legitimate need or interest of the landlord, such as if the rental property is going to be demolished or converted to a non-residential use. These reasons are often referred to as "no fault" reasons and allow the landlord to terminate the tenancy but, in this case, not before the end of a fixed term or period of the tenancy agreement. For both "no fault" and "for cause" reasons, the landlord must give the tenant proper notice of termination, in accordance with the Act.

Early Termination by the Landlord

A landlord may terminate a tenancy early (before the end of a fixed term or period of the tenancy agreement) only for a "for cause" reason specified in the Act. The Act permits early termination by the landlord if the tenant

- does not pay the rent in full,
- commits an illegal act in the rental unit or residential complex,
- does something in the rental unit or residential complex that impairs the safety of other tenants or the landlord,
- misrepresents his/her income (applies to subsidized or public housing only),
- causes damage to the rental unit or residential complex,
- substantially interferes with the reasonable enjoyment of other tenants or the landlord, or
- lets too many people live in the rental unit,

Having an animal in the rental unit is not, by itself, a ground for early termination. Tenants are allowed to have pets, even if they signed a tenancy agreement with a no-pet clause. Any clause that prohibits the presence of animals in the rental unit is deemed to be void under the Act.

The Act does, however, recognize that a "for cause" reason for terminating a tenancy early may be grounded on the presence or behaviour of an animal in the residential complex. It deals with applications based on animals in a separate provision, which is very complicated and confusing, but seems to suggest that a tenant can be evicted for owning a pet only if the pet is damaging the rental property, disturbing the landlord or other tenants, or causing the landlord or other tenants to suffer a serious allergic reaction. The provision also suggests that a tenant can be evicted if the breed or species of the tenant's pet is inherently dangerous.

If a landlord has a "for cause" reason to terminate the tenancy early, the landlord cannot attempt to evict the tenant him/herself by, for example, changing the tenant's locks or telling the tenant to move out. Instead, the landlord must start proceedings to terminate the tenancy and evict the tenant, following the specific procedures set out in the Act.

The first thing the landlord must do is to give the tenant a form called the **notice of termination**. There are different notice forms, depending on the reason for terminating the tenancy. For example, when a tenant has not paid rent, the landlord must use the "Notice to End a Tenancy Early for Non-payment of Rent" (also known as the form "N4"). All the notice forms can be downloaded from the Board's website. The notice of termination must set out the reasons why the landlord is terminating the tenancy and must specify the date the tenancy is being terminated. This date is called the termination date. Each "for cause" reason defined in the Act will set out how to determine the earliest possible termination date to insert in the notice of termination. For example, the earliest termination date that can be inserted in the form N4 is

Reasons for Early Termination by the Landlord

EXHIBIT 37.2

REASON FOR EARLY TERMINATION	RELEVANT SECTION OF ACT	EARLIEST TERMINATION DATE TO INSERT IN NOTICE OF TERMINATION*	AVAILABLE REMEDY PERIOD (AFTER RECEIVING NOTICE)
Non-Payment of Rent	59(1)	14th day after notice is given to tenant	14 days
Misrepresentation of Income	60(1)	20th day after notice is given to tenant	None
Illegal Act	61(1)	20th day after notice is given to tenant (10th day if illegal drugs are involved)	None
Damage	62(1)	20th day after notice is given to tenant	7 days
Extreme/ Wilful Damage	63(1)	10th day after notice is given to tenant	None
Substantial Interference with Reasonable Enjoyment	64(1)	20th day after notice is given to tenant	7 days
Substantial Interference with Reasonable Enjoyment (Landlord resides in building AND building contains not more than 3 units.)	65(1)	10th day after notice is given to tenant	None
Impairs Safety	66(1)	10th day after notice is given to tenant	None
Too Many Persons	67(1)	20th day after notice is given to tenant	7 days
Further Contravention (previous notice of termination under s. 62, 64, or 67 became void and within 6 months new ground arises under sections 60, 61, 62, 64, or 67)	68(1)	14th day after notice is given to tenant	None

* Add 5 days if the notice is going to be mailed to the tenant

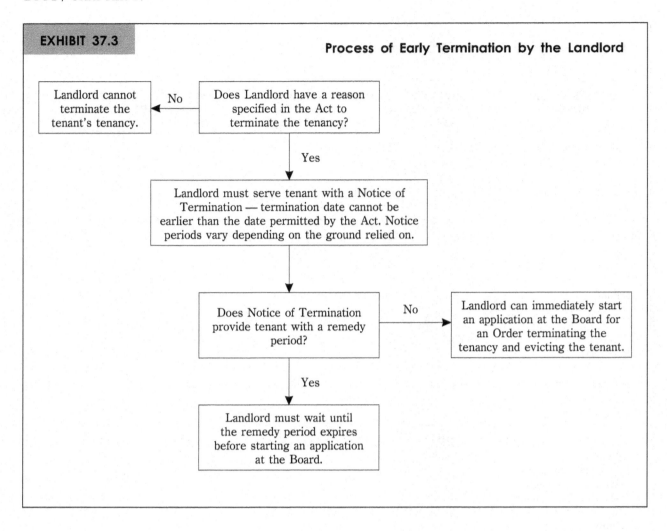

EXHIBIT 37.3

Process of Early Termination by the Landlord

Does Landlord have a reason specified in the Act to terminate the tenancy? → No → Landlord cannot terminate the tenant's tenancy.

Yes ↓

Landlord must serve tenant with a Notice of Termination — termination date cannot be earlier than the date permitted by the Act. Notice periods vary depending on the ground relied on.

↓

Does Notice of Termination provide tenant with a remedy period? → No → Landlord can immediately start an application at the Board for an Order terminating the tenancy and evicting the tenant.

Yes ↓

Landlord must wait until the remedy period expires before starting an application at the Board.

the 14th day after the date notice is given to the tenant (unless it's a daily or weekly tenancy, in which case it's the 7th day). In other words, if the landlord is giving a form N4 to a monthly tenant on September 5, the earliest termination date that the landlord can insert in the form N4 is September 19. (When counting days, do not include the day the notice is given, but do include the termination date. Add 5 days if the notice is going to be mailed to the tenant.)

Some "for cause" reasons allow the tenant to avoid further proceedings by doing something that is set out in the notice by a specific date. For example, the form N4 tells the tenant to either move out of the rental unit, or pay all the rent owing to the landlord, on or before the termination date set out in the notice. For each "for cause" reason that allows a tenant to do something to remedy the problem and stop further proceedings, the Act sets out what the tenant must do, and by when he/she must do it. The notice of termination form given to the tenant also contains this information.

If a tenant does not comply with the notice of termination, the landlord can start an application at the Board for an order terminating the tenancy and evicting the tenant. The application can be started as soon as the deadline for doing what is required to remedy the problem has expired.

If there is nothing the tenant can do to remedy the problem, for instance, if the tenant has committed an illegal act, then the tenant will be unable to avoid further proceedings. In this situation, the landlord can start an applica-

Notice to End a Tenancy Early for Non-Payment of Rent (Form N4): An Example

EXHIBIT 37.4

Louis Lopez is the owner of a duplex located at 123 Majestic Road West, Toronto, ON, M5N 3Z9. Trina Thompson is the tenant in unit #2. Trina's monthly rent is $1,000, due on the first of each month. Trina did not pay the rent due on September 1, year 0. Louis gives Trina the notice of termination on September 5, year 0.

Louis lives in unit #1. His phone number is 416-222-2222 and his e-mail address is <louis.lopez@hotmail.com>.

Notice To End a Tenancy Early For Non-payment of Rent

Form N4

To: (Tenant's name)	**From:** (Landlord's name)
Trina Thompson	Louis Lopez

This is a legal notice that could lead to you being evicted from your home.

Address of the Rental Unit

Street Number: `1` `2` `3` Street Name: `M` `A` `J` `E` `S` `T` `I` `C`

Street Type (e.g. Street, Avenue, Road): `R` `O` `A` `D` Direction (e.g. East): `W` `E` `S` `T` Unit/Apt./Suite: `2`

Municipality (city, town, etc.): `T` `O` `R` `O` `N` `T` `O` Province: `O` `N` Postal Code: `M` `5` `N` `3` `Z` `9`

This information is from your landlord:

I am giving you this notice because I believe you owe me $ `1` `,` `0` `0` `0` `.` `0` `0` **in rent.**

See the table on the next page for the details about how I calculated this amount.

I can apply to the Landlord and Tenant Board to have you evicted if you do not:

- **pay this amount* by** `1` `9` / `0` `9` / `0` `0` `0` `0`   This date is called the **termination date**.

  dd / mm / yyyy

or

- **move out by the termination date**

* If another rent payment comes due on or before the date you make the above payment to your landlord, you must also pay this extra amount.

WHAT YOU NEED TO KNOW

The following information is provided by the Landlord and Tenant Board

The termination date	The date that the landlord gives you in this notice to pay or move out must be at least: • 14 days after the landlord gives you the notice, if you rent by the month or year, or • 7 days after the landlord gives you the notice, if you rent by the day or week.
What if you agree with the notice	If you agree that you owe the amount that the landlord is claiming, you should pay this amount by the termination date in this notice. If you do so, this notice becomes void and the landlord cannot apply to the Board to evict you. If you do not pay the amount owing, and the landlord applies to the Board to evict you, you will likely have to pay the landlord's filing fee of $170.00, plus what you owe. **If you move out** by the date in this notice, your tenancy will end on the termination date. However, you may still owe money to your landlord. Your landlord will not be able to apply to the Board but they may still take you to Court for this money.
What if you disagree with the notice	If you disagree with what the landlord has put in this notice, you do not have to move out. You could talk to your landlord. You may also want to get legal advice. If you cannot work things out, and the landlord applies to the Board, you will be able to go to a hearing and explain why you disagree.

10101

Version. 16/10/2009   This form has been approved by the Landlord and Tenant Board   Page 1 of 2

EXHIBIT 37.4 (continued)

Notice to End a Tenancy Early for Non-Payment of Rent (Form N4): An Example

How you will know if the landlord applies to the Board	The earliest date that the landlord can apply to the Board is the day after the termination date in this notice. If the landlord does apply, the Board will schedule a hearing and send you a letter. The landlord must also give you a copy of the Notice of Hearing and the application.
What you can do if the landlord applies to the Board	• Get legal advice immediately; you may be eligible for legal aid services. • Talk to your landlord about working out a payment plan. • Go to the hearing where you can respond to your landlord's claims; in most cases, before the hearing starts you can also talk to a Board mediator about mediating a payment plan.
How to get more information	For more information about this notice or about your rights, you can contact the Landlord and Tenant Board. You can reach the Board by phone at **416-645-8080** or toll-free at **1-888-332-3234**. You can also visit the Board's website at **www.LTB.gov.on.ca**.

This table is completed by the landlord to show how they calculated the total amount of rent claimed on page 1:

Rent Period From: (dd/mm/yyyy)	To: (dd/mm/yyyy)	Rent Charged $	Rent Paid $	Rent Owing $
01/09/0000	30/09/0000	1,000.00	,0.00	1,000.00
/ /	/ /	,.	,.	,.
/ /	/ /	,.	,.	,.
			Total Rent Owing $	1,000.00

Signature ■ Landlord ☐ Agent

Signature	Date (dd/mm/yyyy)
Louis Lopez	05/09/0000

First Name
| L | O | U | I | S | | | | | | | | | | | | | | | | | | | |

Last Name
| L | O | P | E | Z | | | | | | | | | | | | | | | | | | | |

Company Name (if applicable)

Mailing Address
| 1 | 2 | 3 | | M | A | J | E | S | T | I | C | | R | O | A | D | | W | E | S | T | | | |

Unit/Apt./Suite
| 1 | | | | |

Municipality (city, town, etc.)
| T | O | R | O | N | T | O | | | | | | | | | |

Province
| O | N |

Postal Code
| M | 5 | N | | 3 | Z | 9 |

Phone Number
(4 1 6) 2 2 2 2 2 2 2

Fax Number
( )

E-mail Address
| l | o | u | i | s | . | l | o | p | e | z | @ | h | o | t | m | a | i | l | . | c | o | m |

10101

Page 2 of 2

tion at the Board for an order terminating the tenancy and evicting the tenant immediately after giving the notice of termination to the tenant.

Termination by the Landlord at the End of a Fixed Term or Period

The Act provides additional grounds for a landlord to terminate the tenancy, but for these grounds, termination cannot be effective before the end of a fixed term or period of the tenancy. These grounds deal with situations where the landlord requires possession of the rental unit for reasons that, with one exception, have nothing to do with the tenant's behaviour. They are referred to as "no fault" grounds and include the following reasons:

- The landlord personally requires possession of the property (for him/herself, a member of his/her immediate family, or their caregiver).

- The landlord has agreed to sell the property and the purchaser, a member of his/her immediate family, or their caregiver want to move into the rental unit (this only applies if the residential complex contains three or fewer rental units).

- The landlord plans to demolish, carry out extensive repairs or renovations, or convert the rental property to a non-residential use.

The landlord can also terminate the tenancy at the end of the fixed term or period if the tenant is persistently late in paying the rent. Even though this reason *is* related to the tenant's behaviour, the Act includes it with the other "no fault" reasons for termination. Presumably this is because the rent is being paid, albeit late.

To proceed with termination for any of these reasons, the landlord must follow the specific procedures set out in the Act, which are generally the same as those discussed above for terminating a tenancy early. The "no fault" reasons provide quite lengthy notice periods (the longest being 120 days), and the termination date will always be at the end of a fixed term or period of the tenancy. For example, assume that Luisa is a landlord who wants to terminate a tenant's monthly tenancy because she intends to move into the rental unit. Luisa must give the tenant at least 60 days' notice, and the termination date will be on the last day of the month. If Luisa gives notice to her tenant on September 10, the earliest possible termination date is November 30. For all of the "no fault" reasons, the landlord can start an application at the Board immediately after giving the notice of termination to the tenant. However, the tenancy will not be terminated any earlier than the termination date set out in the notice. For instance, assume that the hearing for Luisa's application is in early October. Even if the Board allows her application, the Board will not order the termination date to be any earlier than November 30.

The End of the Tenancy

Even though the notice of termination tells the tenant that he or she must move out of the rental unit by the termination date, the tenant does not in fact have to move out. However, if the tenant does not move out and has not complied with any available remedy within the prescribed period of time, then the landlord can start an application at the Board for an order terminating the tenancy and evicting the tenant.

A tenant must be in possession of the rental unit at the time the landlord starts the application. If a tenant is no longer living in the rental unit, the Board has no jurisdiction over the matter.

To start an application, a Landlord must file a document, called the **application,** with the Board, together with a copy of the Notice of Termination the landlord previously gave to the tenant. While the Notice of Termination explains to the tenant the reasons for terminating the tenancy, the application explains to the Board what order the landlord is asking the Board to make. There are different types of applications about eviction depending on the reason for eviction, which are all available on the Board's website. When a landlord files an application, the Board schedules a hearing so that the landlord and tenant can present their case to an **adjudicator** who will make a decision about the application. The Landlord must give the tenant a copy of the application together with a **Notice of Hearing**, setting out the time and location of the Board hearing. As mentioned above, if the adjudicator decides to terminate the tenancy and evict the tenant, the tenancy will end on the termination date specified in the notice of termination.

PROCEEDINGS AT THE LANDLORD AND TENANT BOARD

Overview of the Board

The Board is the **administrative tribunal** that administers the Act and resolves disputes between residential landlords and tenants. It has exclusive jurisdiction over all landlord and tenant applications under the Act that come within the Board's monetary jurisdiction, which currently is $25,000. The Board also controls rent increases for most residential tenancies in Ontario. The Board maintains a website (www.ltb.gov.on.ca) that provides a great deal of information for both landlords and tenants about their rights and responsibilities under the Act. The website also provides a link to the Act and regulations, as well as to the Board's **Rules of Practice, Interpretation Guidelines** and selected decisions.

Types of Applications

Most applications that are started at the Board are landlord applications. In the Board's most recent fiscal year, 91 percent of applications filed were by landlords and only 9 percent were by tenants.[5] The majority of landlord applications are for termination of the tenancy and eviction. Of these, close to 80 percent involve arrears of rent.[6] If an application involves arrears of rent, a tenant is allowed to raise issues the tenant could have raised had the tenant started his or her own application, such as maintenance and repair issues, harassment, or illegal entry by the landlord.

The most common types of tenant applications are applications about maintenance, or about tenant rights such as the landlord interfering with the tenant's reasonable enjoyment of the rental unit.

The parties to an application are referred to as the **applicant** and the **respondent**.

The Hearing

Hearings at the Board are resolved by a government-appointed adjudicator, known as a Member of the Board. At the hearing, the Member listens to what each party has to say about the application. The applicant tries to convince the Member that the application should be granted, while the respondent tries to persuade the Member that it should not. This is done by presenting evidence that supports a party's case, such as documents, pictures, or the testimony of a witness. Parties to an application can represent themselves or have an agent act on their behalf. An agent can be a paralegal, lawyer or even a party's friend or relative. After both parties have presented

---

[5] Landlord and Tenant Board Annual Report 2009–2010, p. 16
[6] *Ibid.*, p. 18

their case, the Member will make a final decision about the application. A written copy of the decision, called an order, will be mailed to both the applicant and respondent.

Mediation and Other Settlements

The Board strongly encourages parties to try and resolve their dispute through mediation with a Board Mediator and employs mediators who are readily available to help parties reach an agreement. An important benefit of resolving an application through mediation as opposed to adjudication is that only an agreement mediated with a Board Mediator may override the provisions of the Act. For example, if the parties choose to meet with a Board Mediator, their mediated agreement can provide that the tenant will pay rent by post-dated cheques, or that the tenant will not have a pet in the rental unit. At a hearing, the Board Member cannot make an order containing these terms. The Board Member's decision must be within the limits of the Act.

If the parties resolve the entire application through mediation, the hearing is cancelled.

Otherwise, the hearing goes ahead and the member makes a final decision about the application. The mediation process is confidential meaning that the Board Member cannot be told anything that was said by the parties during their session with the mediator. All the Board Member will know is that the parties attempted mediation but were unable to resolve their dispute.

Parties to an application can also try to resolve their dispute themselves, without the assistance of a Board Mediator. If the parties reach an agreement, they can ask the Board Member to incorporate the terms of their agreement into an order, called a consent order.

If a party breaches any term of a mediated agreement or other settlement, the other party can pursue the remedies available under the Act. In most cases, either party can ask the Board to re-open the application and schedule a new hearing. In addition, landlords usually have the right to bring an **ex-parte application** to terminate the tenancy and evict the tenant when the tenant breaches a term of the mediated agreement or consent order.

Reviews, Amendments, and Appeals

Generally speaking, an order of the Board is final and binding on the parties to an application. However, the Act does allow a party to request an amendment, review or appeal of an order, in limited circumstances. For instance, if a party thinks the order contains a clerical error such as a misspelled name or incorrect calculation, the party can ask the Board to amend the order. The Board Member who prepared the order will correct any errors and replace the order with an amended order, which will be mailed to both parties. If a party thinks the order contains a more serious error, such as an error in how the member interpreted the law, then the party can ask the Board to review the Member's order. The order will be reviewed by a different member and, if he/ she agrees that a serious error may have occurred, a new hearing will be scheduled to allow the parties to participate. Finally, a party can appeal an order of the Board to the Divisional Court (of the Superior Court of Justice) but only on a **question of law**.

Enforcing Board Orders

If a tenant does not move out as ordered by the Board, the landlord must file the Board order with the Sheriff's office. Only the Sheriff can enforce orders for eviction.

A tenant can stop the eviction only by paying all amounts owing to the landlord, including the Sheriff's fees, any time before the Sheriff enforces the

Board order. Once the Sheriff enforces the eviction order by changing the locks, the landlord regains possession of the rental unit.

A landlord must give a tenant who has been evicted the opportunity to collect his or her personal belongings that were left in the rental unit. The tenant has the right to come and pick them up any time between 8 a.m. and 8 p.m. during the 72 hours after the Sheriff has changed the locks.

If the Board order provides for the payment of money, the order is enforced using the enforcement mechanisms of the Small Claims Court, assuming the amount is not more than $25,000. The order is treated as if it were an order of the Small Claims Court. In other words, you do not need to get another order from the Small Claims Court to be able to enforce the Board order.

CHAPTER SUMMARY

This chapter provided an overview of the residential landlord and tenant relationship in Ontario. It examined the rights and responsibilities of both landlords and tenants under the Act, and included a discussion about how those rights and responsibilities are enforced. This chapter looked at how the law protects tenants against illegal evictions and rent increases, and guarantees their rights to privacy and exclusive possession of the rental unit. It also looked at how the law protects a landlord's interest in the rental property and explained under what circumstances landlords can enter a tenant's rental unit during the tenancy. It also explained when landlords can terminate a tenant's tenancy and evict the tenant. This chapter examined how landlords and tenants resolve disputes and familiarized you with Board procedures, including starting an application, mediation and other settlements, and the hearing. Finally, this chapter talked about Board orders and explained how they are enforced.

GLOSSARY OF NEW TERMS AND KEY CONCEPTS

abatement of rent	A reduction in the amount of the tenant's rent.
accelerated rent	The full amount of rent payable for the entire fixed term of a tenancy.
adjudication	At the Board, the dispute resolution process that gives a government-appointed member the power to preside over a hearing and make a final decision or order about an application.
administrative tribunal	A quasi-judicial (almost like a court) independent agency established under federal or provincial legislation.
applicant	The person who starts an application at the Board.
application	The form that starts proceedings at the Board and explains what the applicant is asking the Board for.
arrears of rent	Unpaid rent owing to the landlord.
assignee	The person to whom a tenant transfers the rental unit when the tenant moves out permanently.
assignment	Occurs when a tenant moves out of the rental unit permanently, and transfers the tenancy to someone else.
distraint	A landlord's right to seize the tenant's property in the rental unit, as security for the payment of arrears of rent.
eviction	Lawful removal of a tenant from the rental unit.

exclusive possession	The right to live in the rental unit to the exclusion of everyone else, including the owner.
ex-parte application	An application that is started at the Board without notice to the respondent.
fixed-term tenancy	A tenancy with a specified start date and end date.
guideline	The maximum percentage by which a landlord can annually increase the tenant's rent, without obtaining approval from the Board.
interpretation guidelines	The Board's policy statements that explain how members interpret the Act and deal with issues that arise in applications.
last month's rent deposit	A one-month rental payment, which is to be applied to the last month of the tenancy.
market rent	The amount of rent a landlord can reasonably expect to get for a rental unit.
notice of hearing	The notice that sets out the time and place of a Board hearing.
notice of termination	The form a landlord uses to give notice to the tenant that the landlord intends to end the tenancy for the reasons set out in the notice.
NSF cheque	A cheque that is returned because there are not sufficient funds in the account.
periodic tenancy	A tenancy without a specific end date, which renews automatically on a weekly, monthly or yearly periodic basis.
question of law	A question that is answered by interpreting and applying the relevant law.
residential complex	A building or house in which one or more rental units are located, including all the common areas, services, and facilities.
respondent	The person against whom an application has been started.
Rules of Practice	Procedural rules that must be followed under the Act.
security deposit	Defined in the Act to mean "money, property or a right paid or given by, or on behalf of, a tenant of a rental unit to a landlord or to anyone on the landlord's behalf to be held by or for the account of the landlord as security for the performance of an obligation or the payment of a liability of the tenant or to be returned to the tenant upon the happening of a condition".
security of tenure	Translated means: Security of the right to possess the property; provides tenants with legal protection against unlawful evictions.
sheriff	An officer of the superior court who is in charge of enforcing orders for eviction.
sublet	Occurs when a tenant moves out of the rental unit temporarily and gives someone else the right to live there for a prescribed amount of time.
subtenant	The person to whom a tenant gives the right to occupy the tenant's rental unit for a prescribed amount of time.
tenancy agreement	An oral, written or implied contract between a landlord and tenant for occupancy of a rental unit in exchange for the payment of rent; also known as a "lease agreement" or "lease".
vacancy rates	The percentage of rental units that are not occupied or rented at a given time.
vital service	Water, fuel, electricity, gas and, from September 1 to June 15, heat.

REVIEW QUESTIONS

1. What happens if there is a conflict between the terms of a tenancy agreement and the provisions of the *Residential Tenancies Act*?

2. How are disputes between residential landlords and tenants resolved?

3. A tenant pays $1,000.00 a month. When the tenant moves out, what will the rent be for a new tenant?

4. Can a landlord enter a tenant's rental unit to carry out a repair?

5. Does a tenant have to move out of the rental unit when the tenant's fixed term expires?

6. Does a landlord need a reason to refuse consent to an assignment of the rental unit?

7. What does a landlord have to do if a tenant's oven stops working?

8. Can a landlord change the locks and evict a tenant who is running an illegal drug trafficking operation in the rental unit?

9. What types of deposit can a landlord charge a new tenant?

10. How can a landlord enforce an order for the payment of arrears of rent?

11. In a sublet, who is responsible for the payment of rent to the landlord, the original tenant or the subtenant?

12. Can a landlord ever terminate a tenancy when the tenant has not done anything wrong?

13. Can a mediated agreement contain terms that are inconsistent with the *Residential Tenancies Act*?

14. What should you do if you receive an order from the Board and see that your name has not been spelled correctly?

DISCUSSION QUESTIONS

1. What is the earliest date a tenant can terminate a fixed-term tenancy that expires November 30, Year 0, assuming notice to terminate is given to the landlord on April 15, Year 0?

2. What is the earliest date a tenant can terminate a monthly periodic tenancy, assuming notice to terminate is given to the landlord on April 15, Year 0?

3. Tony Tenant entered into a one-year lease with Lucy Landlord on July 1, 2007. Tony bought a house and wants to terminate his tenancy. His house will be ready to move into at the end of June, so Tony hopes to be able to end his tenancy and move out of the rental unit on June 30. What is the latest date by which Tony must give notice to Lucy?

4. Lucinda is the landlord of an apartment building and is having a problem with three of her tenants. The first tenant has not paid the rent that was due two weeks ago, the second tenant is selling illegal drugs from the rental unit, and the third tenant just got a puppy, even though the tenancy agreement prohibits tenants from having pets. Discuss what Lucinda can do regarding the problem with each of these three tenants.

5. Telusa Tenant lives in an apartment building owned by Lorenzo Landlord. Before Telusa entered into the tenancy agreement, she noticed that the ceiling in the living room was damaged. She showed Lorenzo this damage and assumed it would be repaired by the time she moved in. Lorenzo will not repair the damage because he says Telusa knew it was there when she agreed to rent the unit. Discuss Telusa's rights in this situation, explaining whether or not it matters that the damage existed before she entered into the tenancy agreement.

6. Olivia entered into a tenancy agreement that provided she could move in to the rental unit on September 1. At the end of August, Olivia was in a serious car accident and was hospitalized for almost 8 weeks. She was unable to move into the rental unit until November 1. Who is responsible for the rent for the months of September and October?

7. Mohammed and Lucerne are tenants living in a three-bedroom house owned by Lionice. The rent is $1,000 per month, and they each give Lionice $500 per month. Lionice wants to rent the third bedroom in the house to another tenant so that Lionice can collect more rent. Explain whether or not Lionice can do this.

8. Sanjaya moved into an apartment in Toronto on September 1, Year 0 under a written lease for a fixed term of one year. While vacationing in Cuba at Christmas, Sanjaya met the love of his life and wants to return to Cuba as soon as possible. Discuss what Sanjaya can do if he wants to end his tenancy and move permanently to Cuba.

SUGGESTED READINGS

Butkus, Mavis J. *The 2011 Annotated Ontario Landlord and Tenant Statutes* (Toronto, Ontario: Carswell, 2010).

WEBSITES
Residential Tenancies Act: <http://www.canlii.ca/en/on/laws/stat/so-2006-c-17/latest/so-2006-c-17.html>
Landlord and Tenant Board: <http://www.ltb.gov.on.ca>
Community Legal Education Ontario (CLEO): <http://www.cleo.on.ca/english/index.htm>
Ontario Ministry of Municipal Affairs and Housing: <http://www.mah.gov.on.ca/>
Centre for Equality Rights in Accommodation (CERA): <http://www.equalityrights.org/cera/>
Landlord's Self Help-Centre: <http://www.landlordselfhelp.com/frontpage.asp>
Canada Mortgage and Housing Corporation: <http://www.cmhc.ca/>
Advocacy Centre for Tenants Ontario (ACTO): <http://www.acto.ca>
Federation of Metro Tenants' Associations: <http://www.torontotenants.org/>
Ontario Tenants Rights: <http://www.ontariotenants.ca/>

Index

security certificates *943–945*
    Charkaoui case, amended detention review *945*
    Charter and *945*
    grounds for *942–943*
    legal issues *944–945*
    procedure *943*
    special advocates *945*
security deposit *1003*
security of tenure, meaning *1000*
self-defence *240, 284*
self-interest group *966*
sellers   *see* retailers
sentencing *185–186, 264–267*
    absolute or conditional discharge *265*
    aggravating factors *264*
    conditional sentence of imprisonment *267*
    dangerous offenders *267*
    environmental offences *901*
    fines *266*
    imprisonment *267*
    intermittent sentences *267*
    mitigating factors *264*
    pollution-control law *901*
    pre-sentence report *265*
    principles *264*
    probation *266*
    restitution *266*
    sentencing process *265*
    suspended sentence *266*
    types of sentences *265–267*
    victim impact statement *265*
    victim surcharge *266*
    young offenders *269–270, 764–765*
serious criminality
    immigration and *940*
service *395*
servient tenement *340, 341*
settlement *181–182*
settlements, Landlord and Tenant Board *1013*
severance pay *426*
sexual abuse *759–761, 768*
sexual activity, age of consent *755*
sexual assault and therapy records *745–746*
shareholders *371–373*
shares *371*
    misleading offerings *461*
Sheriff's Office
    eviction and *1013–1014*
    Landlord and Tenant Board order filed with *1013–1014*
show cause hearings *258*
skilled worker class *928–929*
    basic requirements *928*
    current eligibility requirements *929*
    new eligibility requirements *928, 929*
    points systems/assessment *928, 930–931*
slander *283*
Small Claims Court *176*
small claims proceedings *393–394*
sobriety tests *256*
social change *10–11*
social media *975–976*
social perception approach *949*
social services *757*
sole proprietorships
    advantages/disadvantage *362*
    closing *362*
    growing out of *362*
    licensing and registration requirements *361*
    nature of *360, 361*
    taxes *361*

solicitor-client privilege *212*
sound recording, copyright protection *856, 859*
sources of law *43–60*
    conflicts between *31*
    major sources *43–56*
    miscellaneous sources *57–58*
    valid source concept *43*
    valid source determination *43*
special advocate *945*
Special Olympics *668*
specialization of lawyers *202*
    certification *202*
    continuing education *202–208*
    history *197–198*
    peer review *202*
Species at Risk Act 913
specific intent offences *985, 986*
sponsors *934, 934n18, 934–935*
    ineligibility *936–937*
    requirements *936–937*
    undertaking *937*
sponsorship
    resettled refugees *957*
sponsorship undertaking
    signed *937*
sport   *see also* sport system
    Aboriginal sport *see* Aboriginal sport
    athletes with a disability *see* athletes with a disability
    charitable statu *671–672*
    defined *663*
    in Canada *664*
    levels in sport *664*
    non-professional *see* amateur sport
    women in *673–674*
Sport Canada *667*
    Aboriginal objectives *678*
    accountability framework *674*
    athletes with a disability, lack of policy *680*
    doping policy *684*
    Official Languages Act and *682–683*
    policy on women *673*
    visible minorities, lack of policy *679*
sport system *see also* amateur sport; sport
    Aboriginal sport *see* Aboriginal sport
    athletes with a disability *668–669, 679–680*
    dispute resolution *686–687*
    human rights legislation and *680–682*
    international movement *see* international sport movement
    National Sport Organizations *663, 665*
    Official Languages Act and *682–683*
    organization of amateur sport *663–665*
    Provincial Sport Organizations *663, 665*
    regulation of sport in Canada *665–669*
    Sport Canada *see* Sport Canada
    tobacco sponsorship and *670*
    under-represented groups *673–680*
    visible minorities and *679*
    women in *673–674*
Sport Dispute Resolution Centre of Canada *687*
spousal rollovers *788*
spousal support *706*
    guidelines *701*
spouse, and immigration, *934–935*
stakeholders
    public as in food regulation *992*
standards
    definition *458*
    product standards *458–459*
    Safety Standards Certificate *486*